VISUAL BASIC 6

Programming

Blue Book

Fast-Paced Learning

Peter G. Aitken

Publisher

Keith Weiskamp

Acquisitions Editor

Stephanie Wall

Project Editor

Melissa D. Olson

Production Coordinator

Meg E. Turecek

Cover Design

Anthony Stock

Layout Design

April Nielsen

CD-ROM Developer

Robert Clarfield

The Coriolis Group, Inc.
An International Thomson Publishing Company
14455 N. Hayden Road, Suite 220
Scottsdale, Arizona 85260

602/483-0192
FAX 602/483-0193
http://www.coriolis.com

Library of Congress Cataloging-in-Publication Data
Aitken, Peter G.
   Visual Basic 6 Programming Blue Book / by Peter G. Aitken.
     p. cm.
   Includes index.
   ISBN 1-57610-281-5
   1. Microsoft Visual BASIC 2. Microsoft Internet Explorer.
3. Internet Programming. I. Title.
QA76.73.B3A3827 1998
005.7'12768 — dc21   98-34270
                                  CIP

Printed in the United States of America
10 9 8 7 6 5 4 3 2 1

CORIOLIS *an International Thomson Publishing company*

Albany, NY • Belmont, CA • Bonn • Boston • Cincinnati • Detroit • Johannesburg
London • Madrid • Melbourne • Mexico City • New York • Paris • Singapore
Tokyo • Toronto • Washington

Dedicated to my daughter Claire, an extra-special kid!

About The Author

Peter G. Aitken (Chapel Hill, North Carolina) is an experienced and well-known computer book author, with some 25 titles and over 1 million copies in print. His previous books include *Digital Camera Design Guide*, *Web Developer's Guide to JavaScript and VBScript*, *Teach Yourself C In 21 Days*, and *Visual Basic Insider*. Peter is a contributing editor for *Visual Developer Magazine*, for which he writes the popular *Basically Visual* column. You can visit his Web site at **www.pgacon.com**.

Acknowledgments

This book lists only one author, but many people had a hand in bringing it from idea to completion. Melissa Olson, project editor, kept everything on track and made sure I stuck to my schedule. Copyeditors Susan Holly and Bill McManus caught all my awkward sentences and dangling participles. Technical editor Dykki Settle made sure all my code worked as it was supposed to. Meg Turecek, Robert Clarfield, and Anthony Stock also played important roles. Thanks, everyone.

Table Of Contents

Part 2
Sharing Data And Code

Chapter 6
Component Madness 133

Chapter 10
Object Linking And Embedding 227

Part 3
Making Things Happen

Chapter 11
Working With Text **263**

Chapter 12
Graphics **295**

Chapter 13
Working With Files

Chapter 18
Using The Internet Controls 463

Part 5
Database Programming

Chapter 19
Database Basics 491

Chapter 22
Forms And Fields, Fields And Forms 565

Part 6
Final Touches

Introduction

If you have chosen Visual Basic as your programming tool, let me be the first to congratulate you. Visual Basic is by far the most popular programming tool in history, and there are a lot of good reasons for this popularity. When Visual Basic was originally introduced, it was the first development tool that took Windows programming out of the realm of the specialist and brought it to a level where normal, intelligent people could get something useful done. The ideas of drag-and-drop interface design and event-driven programming are almost universal now, but Visual Basic was the first to make them available to the general programmer. There are plenty of Visual Basic imitators now, and some of them are quite good. In my opinion—and I am not alone—Visual Basic is still the leader of the pack when it comes to Windows development tools. You have made a wise choice.

Now in its sixth release, Visual Basic offers unparalleled power and ease of use for today's development needs. In particular, features for database programming, client/server deployment, and Internet development provide the capabilities that programmers demand most. If you have used earlier versions of Visual Basic, I bet you will be thrilled with the new features. If you are a novice programmer, Visual Basic's unparalleled combination of power and ease of use make it the ideal choice.

Welcome to *Visual Basic 6 Programming Blue Book*. This book is aimed at individuals who are just getting started with Visual Basic programming, as well as those who have a bit of experience with Visual Basic and are now ready to learn more. I take a different approach toward teaching programming than you'll find in most other books. Instead of trying to teach with dry, boring theoretical explanations, I actually show you how things are done in working, real-world programs. Once you see how something works, the explanation is a lot easier to understand. Learn by doing, that's my motto.

The first five chapters provide necessary fundamental information about Visual Basic programming, and I suggest that you read these in order. Although the remaining chapters are probably best read in order also, it is not necessary to do so, and you can skip ahead to a topic of particular interest if you so desire. Later chapters, from Chapter 6 onward, sometimes build on information presented in earlier chapters, but I have tried to keep this to a minimum. The exceptions are Chapters 19 through 24, which deal with database programming and should be read as a unit.

You are welcome to contact me at the email address given below. I would love to hear from readers who are enjoying the book, but I also need to hear about errors in either the text or the code. Despite the best efforts of author and editor, mistakes will sometimes slip through into a published book. In addition, Microsoft has been known to make minor changes in software products between the prerelease version (which I used in writing this book) and the final commercial version. If you discover any errors, please email me and let me know. To check for updates and corrections, visit my Web site at the URL below. Also on the Web site, I maintain an up-to-date list of Visual Basic programming-related links.

Peter G. Aitken
Chapel Hill, North Carolina
July 1998

peter@pgacon.com

www.pgacon.com/visualbasic.htm

PART 1

Programming The Visual Basic Way

Chapter 1
RAD, Baby

Visual Basic is the leader of the pack when it comes to rapid application development.

RAD used to stand for *radical*, but in today's "I need it yesterday" world of computer programming, it means *rapid application development*. There's an ever-expanding need for speedy development of applications programs that are sophisticated, reliable, and full-featured. Visual Basic was the first RAD tool for the Windows operating system, and to many people it is still the best. With Visual Basic, you will be surprised at the speed and ease with which you can create real programs. Whether you are programming for yourself, your boss, or a paying client, Visual Basic is the best tool for getting the results you need when you need them.

Getting the most out of Visual Basic requires some knowledge and effort on your part. That's the purpose of this book—to help you along the path to becoming a skilled Visual Basic programmer. The information you need to work effectively can be divided into two areas. First, of course, are the unavoidable details of using the Visual Basic development environment, writing Basic code, and so on. Most of the book is devoted to explaining the details. Equally important as the details, however, is a general overview of how Visual Basic works—how a program is put together, how the various parts of a program talk to each other, and how a program interacts with the user. With a good comprehension of the overall Visual Basic framework, you'll find the details a lot easier to learn and understand. This is true whether you are totally new to programming or have some previous experience.

In the first few chapters, my main goal is to help you develop this overall understanding of how Visual Basic works. We will also start learning some of the details and see how to use the Visual Basic development environment.

Put On Your Thinking Cap

To understand how Visual Basic works, sit back for a moment and think about the various Windows programs you have used. The type of program—word processor, Web browser, home finance organizer—doesn't matter. Then, complete the following sentence:

Windows programs _____.

Did you come up with an answer? What I was looking for is *have a lot in common*. At first, you may think that this is a strange way to complete the sentence. How can I say that your graphics program has a lot in common with the software you use to track your investments? Sure, they are different in many ways, but they also have plenty of similarities. For example, they all have screen windows that can be resized, moved, minimized, and so on. (Why do you think they call the operating system Windows?) They also have a subset of the same fundamental components: pull-down menus, option buttons that can be turned on or off, command buttons that carry out an action when clicked, text boxes for display and entry of text, and so forth. The list goes on and on, but the conclusion is clear: *To a large extent, Windows programs consist of the same components combined in different ways.*

The original release of Visual Basic was the first development tool that recognized this fact and made use of it to make the programmer's life easier. Rather than making you create your own components each and every time your program needs one, Visual Basic provides a toolbox of predefined components that are thoroughly tested and ready to use. Need an option button or a text box? All you need to do is grab one from the toolbox and drop it into your program.

Now let's go a step further and ask what these components do. The specific tasks vary from one program to the next, of course, so consider this question at a more fundamental level. A menu drops down when its title is clicked, a text box permits text entry and editing, an option button switches between on and off when selected. Again, I could go on and on, but the point is made: *Windows components respond to the user.*

Putting these two insights together, we see that a significant part of any Windows program consists of these "responsive components"—that is, the fundamental Windows objects through which information passes from the user to the program and from the program to the user. And *that's* the genius of Visual Basic—providing these responsive components and making it easy for you to put them together to obtain whatever functionality you need in your program.

TIP   Get Familiar With Windows

Before launching our Visual Basic adventure, you should have a decent understanding of Windows applications and of the Windows operating system itself. I'm not talking about programming or being an expert. I'm saying only that you need some experience—if only a couple of hours worth—using Windows programs. Which programs you use doesn't really matter, because the objective is gaining a feel for the commonalities among Windows programs. Knowing what has been done in existing Windows programs is one of the best ways to get an idea of what you can do in your own programs using Visual Basic. The sample programs supplied with Windows are excellent choices—the games and the Paint program, for example. Because you'll be using Visual Basic to create Windows programs, you want to have some idea of what the end product will be like.

Maybe It's Too Easy?

Before we continue, I am going to sound a warning. Believe it or not, some people never reach their full potential as programmers because of the sheer simplicity of creating Windows programs using Visual Basic. I am using the term *simple* in the comparative sense, of course, but as you'll see, knocking out an attractive, functioning program in Visual Basic is surprisingly easy. In fact, achieving this level of ease was one of the goals behind the development of Visual Basic. After all, programming should be accessible to any reasonably intelligent computer user—not just to the trained professional.

Unfortunately, this thinking has created a two-edged sword: Many users obtain only a surface knowledge of Visual Basic, sufficient to create working programs, but not enough to take full advantage of its features and power. This results in wasted time and effort, not to mention programs that don't perform as well as they could. The situation is similar to the guy who fancies himself "Mr. Fix It" and goes around using his screwdriver as a chisel.

We'll have none of that here. My goal is not only to teach you the nuts and bolts of Visual Basic programming, but also to show you its underlying structure, so you can *use* those nuts and bolts to your best advantage. When we're finished, you'll not only have a full set of chisels *and* screwdrivers in your toolkit, but you'll know exactly when and how to use each tool.

Under the Hood

You have probably guessed that a great deal goes on behind the scenes in Visual Basic. You're absolutely correct, but what exactly is going on, and what is it for? The answer to the second question is easy: It's for *you*, the programmer, and the purpose is to make your life easier. But what is this stuff that goes on? Let's take a look "under the hood."

The Skeleton In Your Program

To use some official terminology, we can say that Visual Basic is an *applications framework*. It provides the bones—the skeleton, if you will—for your applications. All the fundamental building blocks of a Windows program are included in Visual Basic, waiting for you to use them. No longer do you have to write dozens of lines of code to display a dialog box or an option button. (Yes, believe it or not, that's the way Windows programs used to be written.) The process is so simple that you are free to spend almost all your time and mental energy working on the important parts of your program—those elements that make it unique in the world of Windows programs.

The idea here—and I know I'm repeating myself, but this is important, so listen up—is that a lot of what goes on in *any* Windows program goes on in *every* Windows program. Each time you put a text box or a menu in a program, a thousand other programmers are doing the same—from London to Sydney, from Bombay to Cherepovets. (Look it up. Hint: It's not in Silicon Valley.) The folks at Microsoft reasoned, "Why should every programmer have to spend time writing the same code for the same program elements? Let's do all that basic stuff for them." Thus was born one of the fundamental ideas behind Visual Basic: the concept of an applications framework. Let the development tool—that is, Visual Basic—do all the boring, repetitive work and free the programmer to work on the creative aspects of the program. Which brings us to an essential rule: *Don't reinvent the wheel.*

Visual Basic's job, then, is to provide a whole bunch of the "wheels" that your Windows programs need. The time you might have spent reinventing these wheels will be better spent creating meaningful, unique program features. I hope you'll forgive the mixing of metaphors—one minute Visual Basic is a framework, the next it's a skeleton, and now it's wheels—but this is a critical point. When you're creating a Visual Basic application that requires a certain feature or capability, the first question to ask is whether Visual Basic provides what you need. Visual Basic doesn't have everything, but you will be surprised to discover just how much it does have. These "wheels" are, of course, the components that I spoke about earlier.

A Framework Is Not Enough

The framework provided by Visual Basic is pretty darned amazing. Visual Basic's framework is so complete, in fact, that you can create an impressive-looking program without writing a single line of code (or very few lines, at most). The program could have multiple windows, each containing an impressive array of option buttons, lists, text boxes, and so on. Menus would display when needed, dialog boxes would come and go, and everything would look terrific. Only one thing would be lacking, but it's a very important thing—the program wouldn't *do* anything (other than look nice). The meaningful parts of the program—the parts that make it into a word processor, a stock market analyzer, or a multimedia presentation—are missing. This is what you, the programmer, must add. To teach you how to do this is the main goal of this book. As you'll see in this and subsequent chapters, the task is divided into two main parts:

- Select those components from the Visual Basic framework that are best suited to your program.

- Write Basic code to tie the framework components together and provide the needed functionality.

In the remainder of this chapter, we'll take a closer look at the different parts of Visual Basic. I know you're probably itching to sit down at your computer and get to work with Visual Basic, and I promise some hands-on work in the next chapter. But please try to stay with me for the next few pages; I think you'll find this theoretical material to be a real help down the road.

Objects Is Objects

The framework that Visual Basic provides comes in the shape of components, or *objects*. Sometimes, you'll see the term *class* used as well. This confusing terminology is unfortunate but there's not much to be done about it. Just remember, when you see *component*, *object*, or *class*, it refers to something that is reusable and independent and can be used in a program to perform some useful function.

Software components have been around for a long time, sometimes under another name. The complexity of Windows programming, however, and the continued development of sophisticated programming tools, such as Visual Basic, have made an increased reliance on software components not only possible, but necessary.

Is Visual Basic Object-Oriented Programming (OOP)?

In a word, sort of. Okay, I know that's two words, but it's the best answer I can offer. With all the talk of objects in Visual Basic, you might well think that Visual Basic lets you do "real" OOP like C++ and Java. While Visual Basic lets you perform some programming tasks in a manner that is similar to OOP, it does not have all the characteristics of a true object-oriented language. For example, it lacks inheritance and polymorphism. The term *object* is used differently in Visual Basic. This does not mean that Visual Basic is inferior in some way; it's just a different approach to programming (and for many purposes, a better one).

A software component is nothing more than a self-contained chunk of software that performs a specific task. The task can be just about anything—from the very simple, such as calculating a cube root, to the very complex, such as providing a spreadsheet-like grid in a window. The *self-contained* part of the definition is important. To reap the maximum benefits from a software component, you should be able to take it off the shelf (so to speak) and drop it directly into your program without any fuss. The more software components you have at your disposal, the easier your programming will be. Instead of writing, testing, debugging, and rewriting the code yourself, all you do is pop the component into your program. Remember the "wheels" I was talking about earlier in the chapter and our rule, "Don't reinvent the wheel"? Software components are those ready-made wheels.

You may be thinking that Visual Basic's objects are software components, and you are 100-percent correct. This is one of the three levels of software components in Visual Basic. By themselves, they are powerful, but there's more.

On a second level, Visual Basic permits you to create your own software components. As you gain more programming experience, you'll probably find yourself doing certain tasks over and over in different programs. This is particularly true if all your programming tends to fall in a specialized category, such as graphics or database. For example, many of your programs may need a dialog box that lets the user select from a palette of background patterns. Whatever the specifics, Visual Basic provides the tools that permit you to wrap the functionality in a self-contained component that you can then easily drop into future programs.

The third level at which Visual Basic uses software components is that of custom controls (also referred to as OCX and ActiveX controls). A custom control is not part of the Visual Basic package, but is provided by Microsoft or another vendor as an enhancement. When you install a custom control, it is available within Visual Basic just like the controls that come with Visual Basic. As you plan or work on a project, you should have some knowledge of the custom controls that are available. Some are free or available for minimal cost as shareware, while others are commercial products at various prices. Finding just the right custom control can often save you days or weeks of tedious programming and is usually well worth any associated cost.

Kinds Of Objects

The universe of Visual Basic objects contains two main categories: *forms*, which are simply screen windows; and *controls*, which are placed on forms to provide functionality. Among the many different kinds of controls are text boxes, option buttons, and command buttons. A Visual Basic program consists of one or more forms; each form usually contains one or more controls. I say "usually" because it is possible (although not common) to do things with a blank form. A form can also contain a menu, just like the menus you find in other Windows programs. Visual Basic has a menu editor that makes menu design easy.

You can see that a large part of creating a Visual Basic program consists of working with objects. You must decide how many forms your program needs, as well as which controls to place on each form. The mechanics of creating the forms and placing controls is quite easy, as you'll learn in the next chapter when you create your first Visual Basic program. The technique of visual interface design—painting your program's screens—is one of the two landmark innovations that Visual Basic brought to programming. We'll meet the other technique later in the chapter.

Many, but not all, Visual Basic objects have a visual interface, which is to say that they display on the screen when the program is running. Some objects do not display, but work behind the scenes to perform some task.

Properties

Each Visual Basic object has properties that determine its behavior and, if the object has a visual interface, appearance. For example, almost all visible objects have **Top** and **Left** properties, which specify the screen position of the upper-left corner of the object. Likewise, the **Height** and **Width** properties specify the size of the object. Each type of object has its own set of properties, often running to a couple dozen or more. While some properties (such as those just mentioned) are common to many or all objects, other more specialized properties are relevant to only one or, at most, a few types of objects.

Object properties play an important part in a Visual Basic program's interactions with the user. For example, if the user has entered text in a Text Box control, the program can access that text via the control's **Text** property. In a similar manner, by reading a Check Box control's **Value** property, the program can determine whether the user has turned the corresponding program option on or off. Note that when I say *the program*, I am referring to the Basic code in the program—code that you write.

You can change object properties during program design (referred to as *design-time*). Properties can also be read and modified at runtime, while the program is executing (*runtime*). The ability to read and modify properties at runtime may sound trivial, but it plays an essential role in Visual Basic's power. This flexibility permits a program to be *self-modifying*—to change its appearance and behavior in response to current conditions and user input. You'll see plenty of examples of this throughout the book.

You'll find that a significant portion of your Visual Basic programming time will be spent dealing with these properties, which is a good indication of their importance. We can think of properties as the edges, or skin, of objects. Our knowledge and control of an object is limited to the properties the object makes available to us. All sorts of complicated stuff may be going on inside an object, but we have no way of knowing about it. More importantly, we don't *want* to know about it. We only need access to the object's properties to make full use of its capabilities.

Methods

Most Visual Basic objects have one or more *methods* associated with them. A method can be thought of as a chunk of code that does something to, or with, the object. Instead of you having to write the code, however, it is an integral part of the object.

The methods that are available differ from object to object. For example, the **Move** method, which moves an object to a different location on screen, is available for most objects. In contrast, the **Print** method, which displays text on an object, is available only for forms and a few other objects where the display of text makes sense.

Events Make It Happen

The second major innovation that Visual Basic introduced is *event-driven programming*. (The first—in case you were dozing for the first part of the chapter—is the use of visual objects.) What are events, and how do they work? The first part of this question is easy. With a few exceptions, events are things the user does with the mouse or the keyboard while the program is running. In other words, *event* means user input. So far so good, and hardly surprising. But I can hear you saying, "Of course a program must respond to user input, so what's the big deal?" The big deal is *how* a Visual Basic program responds to user input, and how *easy* it is for the programmer. The way that Visual Basic deals with user input is intimately tied in with the Windows operating system, so let's start there.

Interacting With Windows

If you've used Windows at all and given just a little thought to how it works, you are probably already aware of the way that Windows handles user input, or events. (If Windows is a foreign entity to you, I'll repeat my suggestion that you become familiar with it before continuing.) With rare exceptions, Windows is *always* responsive to events. Even if the currently active program is not responding, Windows itself is—whether you press Alt+Tab to switch to the next task, click on a button on the taskbar, or whatever, Windows detects the event. Of course, Windows does not respond to every user event; that would lead to chaos. To be completely accurate, I should say that Windows detects every event, but responds only to certain ones. How does this happen?

Hello, Western Union?

At the heart of Windows' event-detection capabilities is its messaging architecture. In fact, messages play a vital role in just about everything Windows does, but we will limit ourselves to a basic look at messages and events.

Whenever Windows is running, Windows is running. Now this may seem like a nonsensical statement, but it serves to emphasize the intimate relationship between the Windows operating system and individual programs that are executing. Many (if not most) of what a program does is actually performed by Windows at the program's request. Among these tasks is complete management of user input via the keyboard and mouse. When any mouse or keyboard event happens, Windows knows about it and dispatches a message identifying the event to Windows' message queue. The message might say, in effect, "The mouse was clicked at screen coordinates such-and-such" or "the F5 key was pressed." All programs that are running at the moment can receive the message. This includes application programs, as well as Windows' own processes. The message is available to all programs, but only the one that is interested in the event will bother to "read" the message and respond. It's sort of like a mother going to the front porch and yelling, "Herman, if you don't get yourself home for dinner this instant, I'll tan your behind!" All the kids in the neighborhood have access to the message, but only Herman will respond (at least if he knows what's good for him).

Figure 1.1 shows a simplified diagram of the Windows messaging system. My account is simplified as well—the actual system is quite complex. You don't need to understand all the details; it's enough for you to grasp the basics of messaging.

Just remember that Windows does all the work of event detection, dispatching messages to identify each event that occurs. All your program needs to do is keep an eye on the message stream and latch on to the messages of interest. How is this accomplished? As you'll see next, it's ridiculously easy.

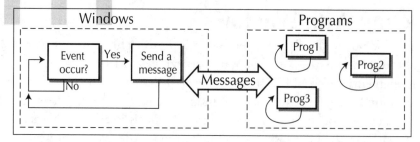

Figure 1.1   *Windows is continually looking for events. When it detects one, it dispatches a message to the running programs, which can respond.*

Event Procedures

Earlier in this chapter, I mentioned that Visual Basic brought two groundbreaking innovations to Windows programming. The first one was visual interface design. Now we'll meet the second one: event detection. Well, not event detection itself; that's nothing new. The real innovation is the ease with which a programmer can make his or her program respond to events, and this is all accomplished with *event procedures.*

An event procedure is a block of Basic code associated with an event. When the event is detected, the code in the procedure is automatically executed. Creating an event procedure in Visual Basic is a simple two-step process:

1. Select the object (Text Box, Command Button, etc.) that will respond to the event.

2. Choose the desired event from a list of events that the selected object can detect.

It's really that simple. Carrying out these steps creates the skeleton of an event procedure that has this general form:

```
Sub ObjName_Event()

End Sub
```

The name of the event procedure identifies both the visual object and the event. **ObjName** is the name of the object (its **Name** property), and **Event** is the name of the event. For example, the event procedure to detect a mouse click on a Command Button named **ExitButton** would be **ExitButton_Click**. This procedure is executed when the program runs and the user clicks on the button. Nothing more is involved in getting the program to respond to events.

Of course, you must still write the code that will be executed within the event procedure. The skeleton procedure above is empty and does nothing when it executes. We'll be spending a lot of time learning Basic code, so you'll soon be able to write event procedures that perform useful tasks. Actually, event procedure code usually does not perform the task itself, but rather calls code that is located elsewhere—outside the event procedure—to do the work. The reasons for this will be explained in a later chapter. In any event (pardon the pun), the result is the same: The program responds to user input. Visual Basic puts the entire range of user events at your fingertips. When creating a program, you need only decide which events the program should respond to, and what the response will be. If you do not create an event procedure for a particular event, the program will ignore that event.

The Software Component Mindset

Sure, software components sound like a good idea, and anyone can see the advantages of using them. But to derive the maximum benefit from components, you will have to develop a specific way of thinking when creating Visual Basic programs. This attitude is something I call the *software component mindset*, and it goes beyond thinking, "Oh yeah, maybe I can use a software component here." Rather, it's the habit of starting at the very beginning, when the structure of your Visual Basic program begins to take shape in your mind, with the goal of using as many software components as possible. In simple terms, invent as few wheels as possible.

Not only do you want to maximize the use of existing components in your program, you also want to remain aware of creating your own components. Almost all of the programs you write will include certain tasks for which you will not be able to use an existing component. You'll have to write them yourself. With a bit of planning, you can create components for these functions, and these components will be available to you in the future. After a while, you'll find yourself with a small library of software components that perform the functions you need most often in your programs.

As for custom controls, you can't use them if you don't know what's available. Dozens of publishers and private programmers are continually devising new custom controls, expanding the already wide variety available. To keep aware of what's out there, you may want to subscribe to a Visual Basic programming magazine, place yourself on some manufacturers' mailing lists, attend Visual Basic trade shows, browse Visual Basic newsgroups on the Internet, and frequent the Visual Basic programming forums on CompuServe, America Online, and other online services. The cost of certain commercial custom controls may seem high at first, but they all turn out to be relatively inexpensive when you figure in the time and aggravation you'll save. This is particularly true if you are writing Visual Basic programs for paying clients, who can be mighty impressed when you deliver a robust, powerful program ahead of schedule.

The Role Of Code

What's the role of Basic code in Visual Basic? Isn't programming supposed to require writing lots of code? So far, I've been talking about everything *except* code—objects, properties, components, and whatnot. Where's the code?

Don't worry, you'll be writing plenty of code for your Visual Basic programs. While some programs require less code than others, some behind-the-scenes code is always needed to tie everything together and perform the real work of the program. If you want to perform mathematical calculations, read data from disk, display on-screen graphics or text, or send data over a modem, you'll have to write the code for it. If you want to display a form, change an object's properties, or respond to an event, you'll have to write code. If you want your program to recover gracefully from errors, you'll have to write code. Code ties all the program's objects together, linking them to each other, to the user, and to the outside world. Code plays a mighty big role in Visual Basic.

What's Next?

If you've managed to slog though this entire chapter, you are probably raring to take Visual Basic for a spin. We'll get to that in the next chapter. If you'll bear with me for another moment, I'd like to finish with a few suggestions and reminders about Visual Basic programming:

- *Plan ahead*—As with all types of programming, creating a Visual Basic program will always go more smoothly if you spend some time planning. Think about what you need to do in the context of Visual Basic's available tools. This sort of planning is more difficult when you're just starting out with Visual Basic, because you are unfamiliar with its capabilities. But as you gain expertise, planning should become a top priority.

- *Think like a user*—Design your program from the user's perspective. Don't base the design on what's easy for you to program. What data will the user want to see? How will he or she want it displayed? What tasks (and in what order) will the user need to perform? Many technically talented programmers have seen their work collect dust on users' shelves because they neglected to follow this advice.

- *Think components*—Once you have some idea of what your program will do, start looking for existing software components that can handle parts of the job. When you're doing it yourself, try to encapsulate your interface and code elements in self-contained components that you can reuse in future projects.

- *Learn by doing*—Programming is like surgery (except for the pay, of course): You can read every book on the market, but you'll never learn how to do it until you actually *do* it. That's the approach I take in this book, and so should you. Yes, you should definitely read the rest of this book, but you should also spend as much time as possible working with Visual Basic. You'll be pleasantly surprised at how quickly your programming skills improve.

- *Learn from other Visual Basic programs*—Take time to examine other Visual Basic programs. You never know when you might trip over an idea or technique that you can use in your own work. Sources for Visual Basic programs include the samples provided with the Visual Basic package, Visual Basic programming forums provided by online services, and books and magazines.

And now, friends, into the fray.

Chapter 2
Visual Basic For Intelligent Folks

Let's get to work and write your first Visual Basic program.

If someone were to ask me to sum up my approach to teaching programming, I would say, "Learn by doing." There is just no substitute for sitting down at your computer and putting together a working program, even if you start out with something small and simple. In the previous chapter, you got an overview of Visual Basic; now it's time to see it in action. I'll show you the fundamentals of using Visual Basic, and then we will work through the creation of a simple program from start to finish. What's more, it will be a real program that actually does something useful.

I assume that Visual Basic is already installed on your system. If not, follow the installation instructions in your Visual Basic package. We'll start by learning how to use some of Visual Basic's tools, then we'll move on to the sample program that I promised you.

Visual Basic Basics

After installing Visual Basic on your system, you start it from the Windows Start menu. The exact details will depend on how you got Visual Basic, which is available both as a standalone product and as part of Microsoft's Visual Studio development platform. In any case, the process will be as follows:

1. Click on the Start button on the Windows taskbar.

2. Click on Programs.

3. On the next menu, click on Microsoft Visual Basic 98 or Microsoft Visual Studio 98.

4. Finally, click on Visual Basic 98.

 Is It Visual Basic 6 Or Visual Basic 98?

As of this writing, Microsoft has not decided whether to refer to the new Visual Basic by its version number, 6, or by its year of release, 98. Be assured that Visual Basic 6 and Visual Basic 98 refer to the same product.

When Visual Basic starts, it displays the New Project dialog box, as shown in Figure 2.1. (Depending on the details of your Visual Basic installation, you may see one or more other dialog boxes as well; you can ignore them for now.) In this dialog box, you specify whether you will be working on an existing project or starting a new one. If you are starting a new project, you select the type from the list of project types that Visual Basic supports. You'll learn more about these options in later chapters. For now, select the Standard EXE icon and click on Open.

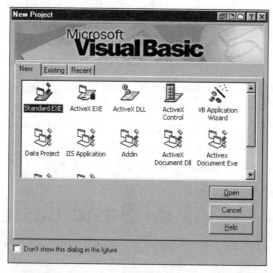

Figure 2.1 *The New Project dialog box is displayed when you start Visual Basic.*

Visual Basic next displays its main window on the screen. As you can see from Figure 2.2, this window contains a lot and can be somewhat intimidating. If your screen does not appear exactly as the figure, don't worry; we'll deal with that in a moment. Don't let the complexity of the screen scare you—you'll be learning all about these elements soon. Remember, our goal now is to create a working Visual Basic program without stopping to explain all the details along the way. Visual Basic is carefully designed to provide an efficient and easy-to-use interface. Once it becomes more familiar to you, I think you'll agree.

The next step is to open the View menu and select Toolbox, which will display the Visual Basic toolbox. If your screen did not initially look like Figure 2.2, it should now. (If your toolbox was already displayed, this command will have no effect.) We are now ready to examine some of the individual elements on the screen.

> **Note:** *I assume that while readers of this book may be new to Visual Basic, you have at least a basic familiarity with Windows. Thus, I expect that you already know how to select commands from menus, use the mouse, and so on.*

Aside from the menu and toolbar, the initial Visual Basic screen has six different elements, or windows (counting the main window itself).

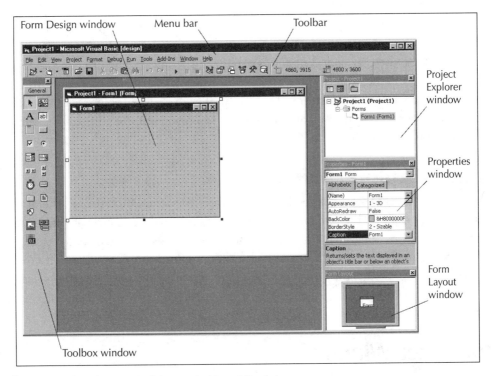

Figure 2.2 *The elements of the main Visual Basic screen.*

Main Window

The main Visual Basic window serves two primary purposes. First, it contains the other windows that the program displays. Second, it displays the menu bar and toolbar along the top of the window. The menu bar contains the titles of Visual Basic's menus, which contain the program's commands. The toolbar displays buttons you can click on to carry out commonly needed commands. Note that if you position the mouse pointer over a toolbar button for a moment (don't click), Visual Basic will display a brief description, called a *tool tip*, of the button's function.

Form Design Window

Near the center of the screen is the Form Design window where you will draw your program's visual interface. You start each new project with one blank form, adding others as you develop the project. Each form in a project corresponds to a window or dialog box in the final program. During program design, a grid of dots aids you in aligning the elements placed on the form. These dots are not displayed in the final program.

Toolbox Window

On the left side of the screen is the toolbox. This window contains icons representing the various visual objects, or controls, that you can place on a Visual Basic form. To place a control, click on the corresponding toolbox button, then point and drag on the form to specify the size and location of the control. The toolbox buttons display tool tips in the same manner as the toolbar buttons. The top left button in the toolbox—the arrow—is not a control, but represents the pointer. Select it when you want to edit controls that you have already placed on the form.

Project Explorer Window

At the top right of the screen is the Project Explorer window, which lists all the modules in the current project. The term *project* simply means a Visual Basic program under development, with all its component objects. A *module* is just a component of a Visual Basic project. For example, each form is a module. When you start a new project, it contains only a single module—a form with the default name *Form1*. Likewise, the project itself has the default name *Project1*. You'll assign more meaningful names to modules and the project as you work.

Properties Window

Below the Project Explorer window is the Properties window. This window lists the properties of the currently selected object, the name of which is displayed in the box at the top of the window. A form is an object, and the controls you place on it are also objects. An object's properties control its appearance and behavior—for example, the color of a form's background is one of its properties. You'll be learning a lot about object properties throughout this book, so I won't go into any further detail right now.

Form Layout Window

In the lower right corner of the Visual Basic screen is the Form Layout window. It shows a miniature representation of a computer screen with a small icon showing the relative size and position of each of your project's forms. You use the Form Layout window to view the relationships among your program's forms. If you point at a form icon and drag it to a new location, you'll change the screen position where the form initially displays during program execution.

Other Windows

Visual Basic has a number of other windows you will use during program development. They are not shown in Figure 2.2 because Visual Basic displays these windows only when you need them. For the most part, we'll deal with these other windows as the need arises. One type of window, however, is so central to Visual Basic programming that I'll take a moment to introduce it now. In a code window, you enter and edit Basic code. It works pretty much like any other Windows text editor: You can type text, delete it, move and copy it from place to place, and so on. If you want to see what a code window looks like, click on the View Code button in the Project Explorer window. An empty code window will open.

> **TIP**
>
> ### Using Visual Basic Windows
>
> Visual Basic's main window is like any other Windows window—you can change its size and position, minimize it to an icon, and so on. Its subwindows are even more clever. As you resize the main window, the subwindows all stretch or shrink to fit. If you point to the border between two subwindows, you can drag it to adjust the window sizes, making one larger and one smaller. Click on the X in the title bar of a subwindow to close it; select the corresponding command from the View menu to display the subwindow again.

A Visual Basic Overview

Now that you've had a look at the most important parts of Visual Basic, you may be wondering how they all fit together. With Visual Basic, more than with other programming tools, understanding how all the parts fit together is essential if you are going to realize its full potential. We went over the most important points in the previous chapter, but let's go over them again briefly before beginning your first Visual Basic project.

- *A Visual Basic program consists of one or more windows, or forms; each form contains a number of controls.* A wide variety of different controls is available, providing just about any functionality your program could need—entering and editing text, selecting options, displaying graphics, and so on. Together, the forms and controls make up a program's *visual interface.*

- *Each object (form or control) in a Visual Basic program has a number of properties associated with it.* An object's properties control the way it behaves and looks. Properties can be modified by the programmer during program design and by Basic code as the program is executing.

- *Visual Basic objects have the ability to detect events, such as mouse clicks and key presses.* This ability is built in and requires no effort on your part. What *happens* when an event is detected, however, is up to the programmer.

- *Basic code written by the programmer defines the functionality of the program—in other words, what the program does.* Whether it's text processing, graphical display, or numerical calculations, the programmer's job is to write the code to perform the desired actions. Basic code also serves to link the program's visual interface to the program's functionality—to control what happens in response to those events that Visual Basic objects can automatically detect.

Your First Visual Basic Program

All right, enough talk. It's time to dive in and get your fingers dirty. We're going to create a real, live Visual Basic program—and not just some silly demonstration program, but a real program capable of doing something useful. We'll write a mortgage calculator that will display the monthly payment on a mortgage or other loan. It won't be the world's fanciest program (not even close), but it is a good start to learning Visual Basic.

You will create this program in four steps. These are the same steps you would use for any Visual Basic project.

Step 1: Planning Ahead

Programming projects always benefit from a bit of planning, and Visual Basic is no different. What will a mortgage calculator require? Put on your thinking cap, and get out your paper and pencil. (Yes, even in this computerized age, paper and pencil are still the ideal tools for some tasks.) A few moments of thought yields the conclusion that the program will need to do three things: Gather input information from the user, perform the calculations, and display the answer.

Let's start with the input. We need three pieces of information to perform the calculations: the amount, or principal, of the loan; the interest rate being charged; and the duration, or term, of the loan. Right away, we know the program will need places for the user to enter these three items. One of Visual Basic's controls, the Text Box, is intended for entering and displaying information of this sort. At the completion of this first planning step, we know the project will need three Text Box controls for input.

As for output, our program will generate only one piece of information—the monthly loan payment. Again, a Text Box control is ideal for this purpose, so we'll add one output Text Box to the three input Text Boxes, for a total of four. Note that these are all the same type of Text Box control; designating them as *input* and *output* reflects only the way the program will use them.

We also need some way to identify the Text Box controls to determine which one is for the interest rate, which is for the loan term, and which is for the amount. The Label control is ideal for this purpose, and we'll need one for each input Text Box.

Finally, we need some way for users to quit the program. Yes, we could let them quit by using the default window controls and clicking the X button in the upper right corner. For a little more elegance, let's provide a Quit button instead. Visual Basic's Command Button control is suited for such a task, and we'll need only one.

Our planning is now complete. Well, almost. We also need to know how to calculate the mortgage payment when given the amount, term, and rate. Fortunately, I happen to have a *Handbook of Financial Formulas* on my shelf. If we define the following:

rate = interest rate per period

amount = loan amount

nper = term of loan in periods

then:

monthly payment = (amount * rate) / (1 - (1 + rate) ^ -nper)

Because the formula is written in Basic, it may not be clear to you. You'll learn all about "Basic-speak" in later chapters. For now, all you need to know is that * means multiply, / means divide, and ^ means "raised to the power of." In this formula, all items must be expressed in the same units. In other words, if you want to calculate monthly payments, you have to enter the monthly interest rate and the loan term in months.

Okay, now the planning is really complete. Of course, your plan is not engraved in stone. The freedom to make changes later is one of the beauties of Visual Basic. But now, it's time to get to work.

Step 2: Designing The Interface

The next step in creating a Visual Basic program is usually the design of the visual interface. This means we are going to start with a blank form and place the needed controls on it. Because we were wise enough to plan ahead, we already know what controls will be on the form. All we need to do now is decide on the visual layout—where the controls are located, what size they are, and so on.

Adding The Label Controls

Working with the blank form and the toolbox, we'll place the four Label controls on the form. First, if you did not follow the procedures earlier in this chapter, you need to start Visual Basic and select Standard EXE from the New Project dialog box. If the toolbox is not displayed, select View | Toolbox. Then follow these steps to place the first label:

1. Point the mouse cursor at the Label button in the toolbox and click. The Label button is in the second row and has a large A on it.

2. Move the mouse pointer to the form, where it will display as a cross. Point at the location where you want the top left corner of the first label to be located. You can always change the control's position and size later, so don't worry about being precise.

3. Click and hold the left mouse button, and move the pointer to the opposite corner of the Label. As you do this, you'll see a rectangular outline follow the pointer, indicating the label size. This technique is called *dragging*. You'll also see a small window open that displays the height and width of the control as you drag. This is useful when you need to make your control a specific size, but for now, we'll just work visually.

4. When the outline size appears as you want it, release the mouse button. Visual Basic will place a Label control with the caption *Label1* on the form, as shown in Figure 2.3. Don't worry if your form size or label location is not exactly like the figure.

Now that the Label control is on the form, let me call your attention to three things:

- *The new control has eight small boxes displayed around its perimeter.* These are called *handles* and are used to change the size and shape of the control. Point at one of the handles, and you'll see the mouse pointer change to a double-headed arrow. Click and hold the mouse button, drag the control outline to the desired size and shape, then release the mouse button. You can also move the control without changing its size by pointing inside the control (not at a handle) and dragging to the new location.

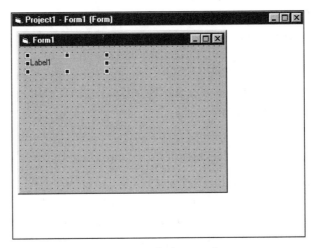

Figure 2.3   *The form after adding the first Label control.*

- *If you try to change the size or position of the Label control, you are constrained by the grid of dots.* In other words, you cannot set a size or position between the dots. This snap-to-grid feature is helpful in designing neat forms with nicely aligned controls. It can be turned off if you need finer control in placing objects, but I suggest that you leave it on for the present.

- *The Properties window displays the new control's properties.* This is shown in Figure 2.4. Make the Properties window active by clicking on its title bar (the bar at the top of the window that says "Properties - Label1"). You can now scroll through the list of properties using the scroll bar at the right of the window. The left column lists the property name, and the right column lists the current value (setting) of each property. As you can see, we have no shortage of properties here. Don't be intimidated—you'll learn about these properties while working through the book.

Figure 2.4   *The Properties window displays the properties of the currently selected object.*

Changing The Label Control's Properties

When you add a control to a form, Visual Basic assigns the default set of properties to the control. For now, we are interested in the **Caption** property, which specifies the text that the label displays on the form. We'll need to change the current value of this property, *Label1*, so the label will identify one of the Text Box controls that we will be placing on the form. Use the following steps:

1. Be sure that the Label control you just placed on the form has handles displayed around it. If not, click on the control to activate the handles.

2. Double-click on the **Caption** property name in the left column of the Properties window. You may need to scroll the properties list to bring the **Caption** property into view. The current caption *Label1* in the right column of the Properties window will be highlighted—that is, it will display as white letters on a dark background.

3. Type the new caption "Annual interest rate:". The old caption will be replaced by what you type. If you make an error, press the Backspace key to erase it.

4. When you finish, press Enter.

You may find that the new caption is too long for the Label control and that the end of the text is cut off. No problem. Simply point at the handle on the right border of the control and click, hold, and drag to stretch it until it's big enough.

Okay, the first Label control is finished. We need three more for this project, which you can create by using the same techniques. Go ahead and add the three additional Label controls to the form, then change their **Caption** properties to read:

```
Loan period (months):
Loan amount:
Monthly payment:
```

Your form will now look similar to that of Figure 2.5. Note that you can change the size of the form itself at any time. First, select the form by clicking on it. A selected form displays eight handles, three of them dark (as shown in the figure). Point at one of these dark handles and drag to change the form's size.

Adding The Text Box Controls

With the Label controls in place, the next step is to add the four Text Box controls that we outlined in our planning stage. The procedure is similar to what you just learned, but I'll walk you through it anyway.

1. Click on the Text Box icon in the toolbox. This icon has a white box with *ab* in it and is usually located just to the right of the Label icon.

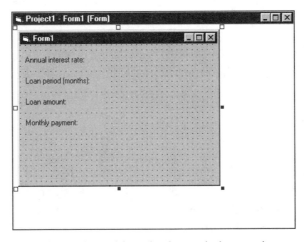

Figure 2.5   *The project's form after adding the four Label controls.*

2. Place the mouse pointer on the form where you want the Text Box located and press and hold the mouse button.

3. Drag to place the Text Box.

4. Release the mouse button.

Repeat these steps to add all four Text Boxes, placing each one to the right of each Label. You'll see that each Text Box is assigned a default caption of *Text1*, *Text2*, and so on. We'll change those next.

Changing Text Box Properties

As with the Label controls, we'll need to modify some properties of the Text Box controls that we just placed on the Mortgage Calculator form. This time, however, two properties need changing for each of the four Text Boxes. One is the **Text** property, which controls the text that is displayed in the Text Box. We want to specify a blank **Text** property, so the Text Box control is empty when the program starts. The other is the **Name** property, which specifies the identifying name associated with the control. We want to assign a meaningful name. Here are the steps to follow for the first Text Box:

1. Click on the Text Box that is next to the *Annual interest rate:* label so that its handles are displayed.

2. Double-click on the **Text** property in the Properties window (you may have to scroll through the Properties window to bring the desired property into view). The current setting, *Text1*, will be highlighted.

3. Press the Del key to erase the text.

4. Press Enter.

5. Double click on the **Name** property in the Properties window (again, scrolling if necessary).

6. Type "txtInterestRate".

7. Press Enter.

The procedure for changing the properties of the other Text Box controls is the same: Click on the Text Box to select it, then change the properties in the Properties window. All of the Text Box controls should be given a blank **Text** property. Table 2.1 shows the proper values for the **Name** properties.

We still have one more property to change. While the first three Text Boxes are designed to accept input from the user, the last one—txtMonthlyPayment—does not need to accept user input. To prevent errors, therefore, we will *lock* it, which means the user cannot change it while the program is running. (The program will still be able to display the answer there, of course.) Click on the Text Box next to the *Monthly payment* label, then click on the **Locked** property in the properties window. The property setting in the right column will display False with a small button displaying a downward-pointing arrow. Click on the button to display a list of possible settings for the property; in this case, there are only two: True and False. Click on True to lock the Text Box.

I want to point out two things about the names we assigned to the Text Box controls. Each name consists of two parts: a prefix to identify the type of control and an identifier that describes the function of the control. This is not necessary as far as Visual Basic is concerned—we could have called them Moe, Larry, and Curly—but when you are writing a larger program with lots of controls and code, you will find it useful to be able to tell from the name of a control what type of control it is and what its function is.

Once all of the Text Box controls are complete, one more step will complete the visual interface.

Table 2.1   Proper values for the Text Box Name properties.

For The Text Box Next To This Label	Assign This Name Property
Loan period (months):	txtLoanPeriod
Loan amount:	txtLoanAmount
Monthly payment:	txtMonthlyPayment

*Note: Why didn't we change the **Name** property of the Label controls? Because the Label controls are not referenced in the program's code, their names are unimportant, and the default names assigned by Visual Basic (Label1, Label2, and so on) are perfectly adequate.*

Adding A Command Button

During the planning stage, we decided that the Mortgage Calculator should have a Quit button allowing the user to exit the program. Visual Basic's Command Button control is what we need, and we place this on the form in the same manner as the other controls. Click on its icon in the toolbox (the icon is a small gray rectangle, normally located just below the Text Box icon), then drag on the form to place the control. You'll need to change the Command Button's **Name** and **Caption** properties, too. You already learned how to do this by using the Properties window; set the **Name** property to **cmdExit** and the caption property to **Exit**.

Adjusting The Form Size

If you find that the form's size is too big or too small for the controls you have placed on it, the problem is easily fixed. All you need do is select the form by clicking on it, then point at one of its dark handles and simply drag the form to the desired size. This might be a good time to fine-tune the position and sizes of the controls as well. Change each control that you want to adjust by dragging it to its new position, or dragging its handles to change its size.

Changing The Form's Caption

While it's not strictly necessary for the program to function, we can do one more thing to improve its appearance: We can have the main program window—the form—display the name of the program while it's running. As you might guess by now, the text displayed in the window's title bar is controlled by a property. In this case, it happens to be a property of the form, and here's how to change it:

1. Click anywhere on the form between the controls. When selected, the Properties window will display "Form1 form" on the first line below its title bar.

2. Double-click on the **Caption** property.

3. Type "Mortgage Calculator".

4. Press Enter.

The visual design stage of this project is now complete, and your Visual Basic design screen should look more or less like Figure 2.6. We can now move to the third stage of development: writing the code. But first, saving the project to disk will safeguard our work against your three-year-old tripping over the computer's power cord or some other unexpected disaster.

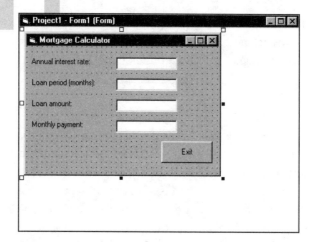

Figure 2.6   *The completed Mortgage Calculator form.*

Saving The Project

As you work on a Visual Basic project, all associated information is stored in your computer's random access memory (RAM). The problem with RAM is that information is lost when the power is turned off. If you want your project to be there tomorrow, you must save it to disk. If you have any experience with other Windows programs, you probably already know how to do this, but I'll run through the procedure just in case. This step has two parts: saving the form and saving the project.

Pull down the File menu by clicking on File in the Menu window or by pressing Alt+F. Next, select the Save Project command from the menu by clicking on it or by pressing *v*. Visual Basic will display the Save File As dialog box, in which you specify a name for the disk file that the form is stored in. In the dialog box's File Name box, Visual Basic suggests a default file name that is the same as the form's **Name** property. Because we have not changed the form's **Name** property from its default value of *Form1*, that's what Visual Basic will suggest as a file name. We can do much better, however. Type "Mortgage" and press Enter.

Next, Visual Basic displays the Save Project As dialog box. Again, we have a File Name box with a default project name, typically *Project1*. Type "Mortgage Calculator" and press Enter. If, during this process, you are asked whether you should add the project to SourceSafe, just click on No.

That's all there is to it. Your project is now saved to disk, and you'll be able to load and continue working on it the next time you use your computer. Now that you have assigned file names to your project and form, pressing Ctrl+S automatically saves them under the existing names. Do this once in a while as you work on a project—and, of course, when you are finished and ready to quit Visual Basic.

Step 3: Writing The Code

The Mortgage Calculator's visual interface is complete. You can run the program now by pressing F5, by clicking on the Start button (the right-pointing arrowhead) on the toolbar, or by selecting Start from the Run menu. You'll see the window you designed with all of its elements in place. You'll even be able to enter text in the three top Text Box controls. The program does not do anything, however, and you'll have to click on the Close button in the title bar (the button with the X on it) to end the program and return to Visual Basic.

Our next step, therefore, is to write the code that does the actual work of the project. In this case, the "work" consists of retrieving the input data that the user has entered in the three input Text Boxes, calculating the corresponding mortgage payment, and displaying the result in the fourth Text Box. Also, we want the program to terminate when the user clicks on the Quit button.

The code required to retrieve the input data and perform the calculation is relatively simple, requiring only a dozen or so lines, as you can see in Listing 2.1. Not all readers will be familiar with Basic code. I will, of course, delve into the details of Basic code later in the book. For now, the object is for you to catch a quick glimpse of a working Visual Basic program. Just trust me on the code and type it as shown in the listing.

Listing 2.1   The Calculate procedure.

```
Public Sub Calculate()

Dim answer As Currency, rate As Single
Dim months As Integer, amount As Single

If Val(txtInterestRate.Text) > 0 Then
    If Val(txtLoanPeriod.Text) > 0 Then
        If Val(txtLoanAmount.Text) > 0 Then
            rate = Val(txtInterestRate.Text) / 12
            months = Val(txtLoanPeriod.Text)
            amount = Val(txtLoanAmount.Text)
            answer = (amount * rate) / (1 - (1 + rate) ^ -months)
            txtMonthlyPayment.Text = Format(answer, "Currency")
        End If
    End If
End If

End Sub
```

The first step in adding the code is to switch Visual Basic from form design mode to code editing mode. You can do this in two ways: by double clicking anywhere on the Mortgage Calculator form, or by clicking on the View Code button in the Project Explorer window (it's the left button at the top of the window). Visual Basic will open a code editing window, as shown in Figure 2.7. (Don't worry about any code that may be displayed in this window; we don't need it.)

Next, display the Tools menu and select Add Procedure. Visual Basic displays the Add Procedure dialog box, which is shown in Figure 2.8.

In the dialog box, type "Calculate" in the Name box, then press Enter. Don't worry about the options in the dialog box. We'll use the default settings. Visual Basic adds the following two code statements to the code editing window:

```
Public Sub Calculate()

End Sub
```

These two statements define the beginning and end of a Basic *procedure*, a discrete section of code that has been assigned a name (in this case, the name is Calculate). In later

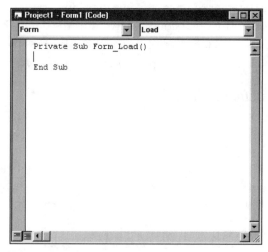

Figure 2.7 *A code editing window.*

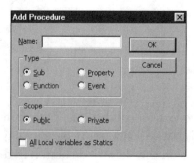

Figure 2.8 *The Add Procedure dialog box.*

chapters, you'll see how Basic procedures are central to Visual Basic programming. For now, we are concentrating on finishing the project—explanations will follow. Type the remaining code from Listing 2.1 into the code editing window. Be careful with spelling and remember not to duplicate the first and last lines of code. The code editing window is used in the same way as a word processor. Here are the basics:

- Text that you type appears at the cursor (the blinking vertical line).

- Use the arrow keys to move the cursor.

- Press Enter to start a new line.

- Use Backspace to delete characters to the left of the cursor.

Once the code has been entered, you should press Ctrl+S to save the additions to the project. The Mortgage Calculator is now ready to take for a spin. You may be thinking, "Hold on, it isn't finished yet!" That's absolutely correct, but running the program now will illustrate an important point about Visual Basic programming.

To run the program, press F5 or select Start from the Run menu. The program will start and display its dialog box. You can move the blinking cursor between Text Boxes by pressing Tab or Shift+Tab or by clicking on the desired box with the mouse. You can also enter numbers in the three input Text Boxes, just like a real Windows program. (Well, of course, it *is* a real Windows program.) Funny thing, though—no answer appears in the Monthly Payment box. Also, nothing happens if you click on the Exit button (you'll have to press Alt+F4 or click on the X button in the title bar to exit the program). What could be wrong?

Nothing is wrong, but something is missing. We've written the code to perform the program's calculations, and we've created the visual interface. The missing link is the *connection* between the interface and the code. This is our next task.

> **Note:** *You'll find yourself switching between viewing objects and viewing code quite often. Visual Basic gives you several ways to do it: (1) click on the View Code or View Object button in the Project Explorer window; (2) press F7 or Shift+F7 to view code or object, respectively; or (3) select Code or Object from the View menu.*

Step 4: Connecting The Code To The Interface

When I describe this step as "connecting the code to the interface," it may sound rather technical. It's not, though; all it means is enabling the program to respond to the user. Think about what happened when you ran the incomplete Mortgage Calculator. The program ran, but didn't respond to your input. Whether you entered numbers in the input boxes or clicked on the Exit button, the program just sat there like a bump on a log. We need the program to respond to *events*—to things the user does. So exactly what events are we interested in? Let's deal with them one at a time.

Exiting The Program

Let's take the Exit button first. The event of interest, of course, is when the user clicks on the button. We want:

- To write code that causes the program to terminate.

- To cause that code to be executed when the user clicks on the button.

We accomplish this by creating an *event handler*, a procedure that executes when the event (the click) occurs. Dealing with user events, such as button clicks, is one of Visual Basic's strong points, as I mentioned in the previous chapter. You'll learn more about this soon, but for now I just want to show you how easy it is.

We need to work with the form. If it is hidden behind the code editing window, click on the View Object button in the Project Explorer window to display it. Now, double click on the Exit Command Button control. Visual Basic displays a code editing window containing the following two lines of code:

```
Private Sub cmdExit_Click()

End Sub
```

Now, add the following single line of code between those two lines:

```
End
```

The **End** statement is the Basic command to terminate a program. The job of this event-handling procedure can be ascertained from its name. The first part of the name, **cmdExit**, is the name of the Command Button control (remember, we assigned this name earlier when we placed the Command Button on the form). The second part, **Click**, is the name of the event that interests us. Thus, we know that the code in this procedure will be executed when the control named cmdExit receives a click event. Note that Visual Basic detects the click automatically. All we need to do is write the code to be executed when the event occurs.

Try running the program (remember, press F5). Now when you click on the Exit button, the program ends, just as it should. The mortgage calculations are still not working, however. We'll tackle that problem next.

Note: Visual Basic gives you two ways to view the code associated with an object. Full-module view displays all of the object's procedures in the code editing window, with a horizontal line separating procedures from each other. Procedure view displays only a single procedure at a time. In procedure view, you can press PgUp and PgDn to scroll other procedures into view. Switch between these two views by clicking on the small buttons at the bottom of the code editing window, just to the left of the horizontal scroll bar.

Performing The Calculations

You may have caught on already that getting the program to perform the mortgage calculation and display the answer will be triggered by some event. But what event? With no Calculate button to click, we can't use the **Click** event. (Actually, we could use this method, but the one I have selected is more elegant.) Think for a moment about what the user will be doing; he or she will be entering or changing information in the three input Text Boxes. Can we use this as the event to trigger the program's calculations? Indeed we can. Text Box controls have a **Change** event that is automatically triggered whenever the data in the box changes.

Our strategy is now clear: We will write an event-handling procedure for each of the three input Text Box controls. Because we have already written the Calculate procedure that does the work of performing the mortgage calculations and displaying the answer, all that the code in the **Change** event procedures will need to do is execute the Calculate procedure.

As before, we begin by double-clicking on the control of interest—in this case, the Annual interest rate Text Box control. Visual Basic displays a code editing window containing these lines of code:

```
Private Sub txtInterestRate_Change()

End Sub
```

You can see from the event procedure name that it will be executed when the control named **txtInterestRate** receives a **Change** event. Add the following line of code between the two existing lines:

```
Call Calculate
```

This line says, in effect, "Execute the code in the procedure named Calculate." After adding the code, you can close the code editing window by clicking on the X button in the top right corner.

We want the program to respond to changes in all three input Text Boxes, so repeat these steps—double clicking on the control and adding the same line of code—on the other two input Text Box controls, txtLoanPeriod and txtLoanAmount. When you've finished, press Ctrl+S to save the project.

Trying It Out

Congratulations! You have just completed your first Visual Basic program. Press F5 to run the program. Enter values in the three input Text Boxes. As soon as something appears in each box, the program will display an answer in the Monthly payment box. As you change your input values, the answer automatically changes to provide the correct answer. Click on the Exit button to quit the program.

Remember that the interest rate values must be entered as decimals—.08 for 8 percent, for example. Also, numbers must be entered as plain numbers—150000 and not $150,000, for example. You can have fun seeing just how much the payments on that $500,000 house would be. Note that the Mortgage Calculator is not limited to mortgages. It can be used for any type of loan with a fixed interest rate and regular payments, such as a car loan. Figure 2.9 shows the Mortgage Calculator in action, displaying the monthly payments for a certain Italian sports car that I can't afford.

What's Next?

Now that you have joined the ranks of Windows programmers, where do you go from here? There's a lot more to learn about Visual Basic, of course. This first program has only scratched the surface. I hope that this quick introduction to the power of Visual Basic has whetted your appetite for more. The next two chapters will show you more details of drawing your program's visual interface and will teach you more about writing Basic code. Then we will tackle a more complicated project to test drive your new Visual Basic skills. If you think that the Mortgage Calculator is cool, wait until you see what else Visual Basic can do.

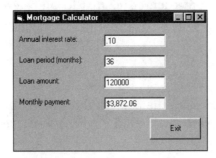

Figure 2.9.   The Mortgage Calculator in action.

Chapter 3

Drawing Your Way To Success

One of the revolutionary innovations that Visual Basic brought to programming was the ability to draw your program's visual interface. In this chapter, I'll show you the techniques of visual interface design.

The first two chapters introduced you to some of the concepts and theory behind Visual Basic and guided you through creating and running your first project. Hopefully, you're excited and eager to dig in, because we've just begun to scratch the surface. Now it's time to learn more about objects and properties.

I cannot overemphasize the close relationship between objects and properties. They really can't be separated—an object *is* its properties, to a very large degree. To derive the most from Visual Basic's objects, you need to develop an intimate knowledge of their properties. And because objects are central to the whole idea of Visual Basic programming...well, you get the idea.

Let's begin with the fundamentals of starting and opening Visual Basic projects, saving files, and other basic tasks. From there, we will explore the tools and techniques that Visual Basic provides for visual interface design. Next, we'll explore properties, and finally, we'll work through a demonstration project to illustrate these concepts.

Working With Projects

Every time you start Visual Basic, you'll do one of two things: begin a new project or open a project that already exists. Either of these tasks can be accomplished in the New Project dialog box. This dialog box is normally displayed when you start Visual Basic. As shown in Figure 3.1, this dialog box has three tabs with the following functions:

- *New*—Use this tab to start a new project based on one of Visual Basic's project types (to be explained in a future chapter). For now, you will be using the default type, Standard EXE.

- *Existing*—Use this tab to locate an existing Visual Basic project on disk and open it.

- *Recent*—This tab lists Visual Basic projects that you have worked on recently, permitting you to select one to open.

Note that the New Project dialog box has a Don't Show This Dialog in the Future checkbox. If you turn this option on, the dialog box will not be displayed when Visual Basic is started. Instead, a new Standard EXE project will be created as a default. If you have selected this option and want to re-enable display of the New Project dialog box when Visual Basic starts, follow these steps:

1. Select Options from the Tools menu to display the Options dialog box.

2. Click the Environment tab.

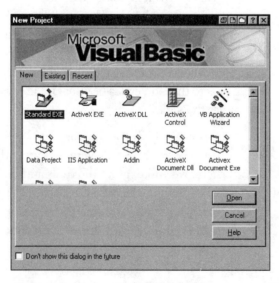

Figure 3.1   *The New Project dialog box is displayed when you start Visual Basic.*

3. In the When Visual Basic Starts section, turn on the Prompt for Project option.

4. Click on OK.

If the New Project dialog box is not displayed when you start Visual Basic, you start a new project by selecting New Project from the File menu. To open a recent project, open the File menu and select from the list displayed near the bottom of the menu. To select a project from disk, select File | Open Project or press Ctrl+O to display the Open dialog box.

Understanding Modules

Every Visual Basic project contains at least one module, and a complex project may contain a dozen or more. Each module in a project is saved to disk in its own file. The file gets a name that you assign and an extension that identifies the type of module. The most important type of module is the *form module*, corresponding to one form or window in your project. With rare specialized exceptions, every Visual Basic project contains at least one form module. Form module files are given the .FRM extension. Another type of module you will frequently use is simply called *module*, although I prefer to use the term *code module*, because it contains only Basic code and no visual elements. Code module files are given the .BAS extension. There are some other types of modules, and we will deal with them as the need arises.

Saving Projects

Each Visual Basic project consists of at least two separate parts that must be saved to disk if you want to preserve them. First are one or more modules, as described in the previous section. You can have multiple form and code modules open at the same time, but only one of them will be current—the one you are working on at the moment (as selected in the Project Explorer window). To save the active module, press Ctrl+S or select Save XXX from the File menu (XXX representing the name of the module).

When you save a module for the first time, Visual Basic suggests a default name for it. In the case of form modules, this is the form's **Name** property, which, if you have not changed it, will be a default name—*Form1*, *Form2*, etc. For code modules, the default name is *Module1*, etc. The first time you save a module, you will be prompted for a file name, with this default name suggested by Visual Basic. If you have assigned your form a meaningful **Name** property that is descriptive of its function (and you should do so), then accepting this name is perfectly fine. You can also assign another name, but be sure to assign a name that actually helps you identify the module.

If you have multiple modules, you need to save each one individually. Fortunately, Visual Basic will help avoid lost data by reminding you to save modules, if they have not already been saved, before quitting the project. Once you assign a name to a module, selecting File | Save or pressing Ctrl+S will save the current version of the module under the original name without prompting. If you want to assign a new file name to a module that has already been saved, select Save XXX As from the File menu (again, XXX is the current name of the module).

Module Name Confusion

It's easy to get a bit confused about Visual Basic module names, because most modules have two names: the **Name** property that you assign to the module in the Properties window, and the file name that you assign when you save the module. These two names can be the same, but do not have to be. Code modules are the one exception, as they do not have a **Name** property and so have only a file name. In the Project Explorer window, form modules are listed with both their **Name** property and, in parentheses, their file name.

The second part of a Visual Basic project that needs to be saved is the project itself. This *project file* does not contain any forms or code, but rather identifies the modules in the project, the current Visual Basic environment settings, and so on. When you load an existing project, you are loading this project file; Visual Basic, in turn, uses the information in the project file to load the component modules. Project files receive the .VBP extension.

To save the current project, select Save Project from the File menu, or click on the Save Project button on the toolbar. You'll be prompted for a project name the first time you save it. Once a project name has been assigned, you will not be prompted further.

The Freedom To Roam

While you can keep all files for each project in a single folder, it isn't necessary. In fact, Visual Basic's strengths in reusing software components means that a project's various modules will often be scattered here and there on your disk.

Drawing Your Way To Success

When Visual Basic first burst onto the scene, the feature that most amazed programmers was the way it allowed them to draw the program's visual interface. No more writing long and complex code statements to display something on screen; just point, click, drag—and that's all there was to it. Now that Visual Basic has been around a while and spawned a whole fleet of copycats, the idea of drawing a program's interface has become accepted as the norm. Even so, I still think it's fun. In this section, I'll describe the tools and techniques Visual Basic provides for interface design.

The controls you can use are represented by buttons in the Visual Basic toolbox. The picture on each button makes an attempt to represent the corresponding control. If you're still not sure, just rest the mouse pointer over the button for a second or two: A *tooltip* will display next to the mouse pointer, describing the button's control.

I should mention that the controls displayed in the toolbox are only a small subset of what is available to you. When you start working, the default set of controls is displayed; these are called the *intrinsic* controls. Other controls are displayed in the toolbox only when you specify. I'll explain how later in the chapter.

Placing Controls On A Form

When you start Visual Basic, a new project and a blank form will display in the Project window. Generally, you will just begin working with this form. If you need another blank form, simply select Add Form from the Project menu. While a Visual Basic program can contain multiple forms, we are going to limit ourselves to single-form projects for now.

Visual Basic has two methods for placing controls on a form. If you double-click on a button in the toolbox, Visual Basic places a default-size control in the center of the form. This method is certainly quick—if you want a default-size control in the middle of your form. Otherwise, you'll have to move and size the control after it has been placed on the form. The alternative, and I believe preferable, method is to click on the desired button and then drag to place the control on the form. As you drag, a small window opens showing the current dimensions of the control, its width and height. The units of measurement are *twips*, Visual Basic's default unit of screen measurement. You'll learn more about twips in a later chapter; for now, it's enough to know that there are 1,440 twips in an inch. The click-and-drag method has the advantage of letting you place the control and set its position and size in one step, but you can use whichever technique you prefer.

If you've placed a control on the form and want to place more controls of the same size and type, you can copy the original. Be sure that the control you want to copy is selected (small *handles* will appear around the edges of a selected control). If not, click on the control to select it. Then follow these steps:

1. Press Ctrl+C (or select Copy from the Edit menu). Visual Basic places a copy of the control on the Windows Clipboard.

2. Press Ctrl+V (or select Paste from the Edit menu). Visual Basic displays a dialog box asking if you want to create a control array.

3. Select No (learning about control arrays comes later). A duplicate control is placed on the form.

4. Repeat Steps 2 and 3 to place additional copies of the control on the form.

Every control that you place on a form is given a default set of properties. As we will cover later in this chapter, modifying the properties of controls is a central part of designing your Visual Basic interface. Most importantly, each control is assigned a default **Name** property in a form that combines the name of the control type and a sequential number. For example, the first Text Box control that you place on a form is assigned the name *Text1*, the second one is *Text2*, and so on.

TIP **Pop-Up Menus**

If you right-click on a control, a form, or just about anything on the Visual Basic screen, a pop-up menu will be displayed. The commands available on this menu are those relevant to the item clicked. You can access the same commands by using the regular menus at the top of the Visual Basic window, but the pop-up menus are often faster. Generally, I will not specifically mention pop-up menu commands, but you should know that they are available.

Manipulating The Form

The size and position of a form during program design is the size and position it will have when the final program runs (unless you modify the size or position in code). You can change the relative screen position that the form will have during program execution by pointing at the form's icon in the form layout window at the lower right corner of the Visual Basic screen. When the mouse pointer changes to a four-headed arrow, drag the form icon to the desired screen position.

To change the form's size, click on it to select it (be sure to click between any controls that are on the form). The form will display eight handles on its corners and edges indicating that it is selected. Three of the handles will be dark; point at any one of them and drag the form to its new size.

As you may have guessed, a form's size and position are properties that can be changed by the program's code when the program executes. Most Visual Basic programmers don't worry about form position during design. If it is necessary to display the window at a specific position when the program runs, it is better done in code. This permits you to take the user's screen resolution into account. Size is a different matter. Forms that contain a lot of controls—like most dialog boxes—will have their "proper" size dictated by their contents. If the form is too small, some of the controls may be hidden, whereas a form that is too large wastes valuable screen space. The usual approach is to adjust the size of the form visually during design, then set the form's **BorderStyle** property to *Fixed Single* or *Fixed Dialog*, so the user will not be able to change its size while the program is running. In other forms where size is not critical, the **BorderStyle** property is usually left at the default setting of *Sizable*, so the user can adjust its size while the program is running.

Table 3.1 lists some other form properties you need to know about. Note that you can view information about any property by selecting it in the Property window and pressing F1.

Moving, Sizing, And Aligning Controls

Once you have placed controls on a form, you will probably need to tweak and fine-tune their sizes and positions. A sloppily constructed form—one with poorly aligned and inconsistently sized controls—will *not* impress your customers.

To work with controls on a form, you must select the control or controls that interest you. To select multiple controls, click on the first one, then press and hold the Shift key while you click on the others. As I mentioned previously, selected controls display handles on their edges. If only one control is selected, its handles are dark. If two or more controls are selected, the handles on each control are white—except for the last one that was selected, which has dark handles.

Easy Deletions

To delete a control, select it and press Del. If you select multiple controls, you can delete them all at once.

When you have one control selected, you can change its size by pointing at one of its handles and dragging the outline to the desired size. As you drag, a small window displays the control's size in twips. You can change the selected control's position by pointing to

Table 3.1   Some important properties of form objects.

Property name	Description
BackColor	The color of the form background, behind any controls.
BorderStyle	Determines whether the form can be sized by the user and the type of border displayed around it.
Caption	The text in the form's title bar.
Font	The typeface used for text displayed on the form. Does not affect text displayed in controls.
ForeColor	The color used for text and graphical objects displayed on the form. Does not affect the color of controls.
MousePointer	Determines the appearance of the mouse pointer when it is over the form.

the control (not a handle) and dragging. As you do so, a small window displays the position of the control within the form. As with control size, position is expressed in twips and gives you the horizontal and vertical distance between the control's top left corner and the top left corner of the form.

With more than one control selected, you can move them as a group, allowing the individual controls to retain their positions relative to each other. You cannot, however, change the size of multiple selected controls.

Aligning Controls

Alignment of controls is an important design issue. The Visual Basic design grid greatly simplifies basic alignment tasks by displaying a grid of dots on the design form. Visual Basic's normal behavior is to "snap" controls to this grid. In other words, when you are moving or sizing a control, its edges always align with the grid—they cannot take intermediate positions. By aligning controls to the grid, it is relatively simple to ensure that a group of controls are all the same size and are also equally spaced.

You can control the design grid using the Options dialog box, which you display by selecting Options from the Tools menu. In the dialog box, click on the General tab and look for the Form Grid Settings section. You have several options to set here:

- *Show Grid* determines whether the grid dots are displayed. Controls will snap to the grid whether or not the grid is displayed.

- *Width* and *Height* set the spacing of grid dots in twips.

- *Align Controls to Grid* specifies whether controls snap to the grid or are free to be positioned at any location.

Changing the width or height of the grid does not affect controls already on the form; only controls added after the grid has been modified will snap to the new settings. The same is true of turning alignment on or off.

A more powerful way to align controls is with the Align command on the Format menu. First, select two or more controls that you want to align by holding the Shift key down while clicking on the controls. Be sure to click last on the control you want the others to align with—it will display dark handles while the others will display white ones. Then select Align from the Format menu and choose the desired alignment. Here are the options: ·

- *Tops, Middles, or Bottoms*—The controls will be moved vertically so that the specified locations all align with the master control. Horizontal position does not change.

- *Lefts, Centers, Rights*—The controls will be moved horizontally so that the specified locations all align with the master control. Vertical position does not change.

- *To Grid*—The controls are all moved to align with the nearest grid location. This command is useful if you have placed controls with Snap to Grid turned off and now want them aligned with the grid.

 Multiples And Masters

After selecting multiple controls, you can change the "master" control (the one with the dark handles) by clicking another control in the group. To deselect the controls, click on any other object on the form (or the form itself).

Modifying Control Size And Spacing

Visual Basic also has a command that simplifies the task of making a group of controls all the same size. Select the controls, again making sure that the master control is the last selection. Then select Make Same Size from the Format menu and choose which dimension(s) to make the same as the master control. To make the size of the selected controls snap to the design grid, select Size to Grid from the Format menu.

Visual Basic also provides commands that simplify the task of setting the spacing between controls. You can work with vertical or horizontal spacing, as required. Start by selecting three or more controls, then select either Vertical Spacing or Horizontal Spacing from the Format menu. Regardless of the spacing you select, your choices are the same:

- *Make Equal*—Spacing between selected controls is made equal; the two controls that are farthest apart remain the same distance apart.

- *Increase*—The distance between controls is increased by a small amount; the leftmost or topmost control does not move.

- *Decrease*—The distance between controls is decreased by a small amount; the leftmost or topmost control does not move.

- *Remove*—Spacing between the controls is removed so their edges touch.

Other Visual Design

You should know a few other visual design tricks:

- *You can overlap controls.* Normally, the one that was placed on the form first will be totally or partially hidden by the one that was placed later.

- *You can modify the relationship of overlapped controls*. Use the Bring to Front and Send to Back commands, both accessed by selecting Order from the Format menu.

Bring to Front makes the selected control the top one in the "pile" of overlapping controls, so it will be visible and hide the other controls. Send to Back has the opposite effect.

- *Finally, you can lock the controls on a form to prevent them from being accidentally modified.* Select the Lock Controls command on the Format menu, and all controls on the form—both existing ones and those you add subsequently—are locked and cannot be moved or resized. They can be deleted, however. Select the command again to unlock the controls. When locked, selected controls display white handles.

 A Toolbar For All Reasons

The Form Editor toolbar displays buttons for common design tasks, such as control alignment and sizing. To display this toolbar (or hide it again), select View|Toolbars|Form Editor.

A Control Gallery

Now that you know how to place and arrange controls on a form, it's time for a brief overview of some of the controls that Visual Basic provides. This is not intended to be a detailed summary of the entire Visual Basic control set. My goal is simply to make you aware of the most fundamental of the controls, those that are used most often. You'll be meeting the other controls later in the book. Figure 3.2 illustrates the more commonly used Visual Basic controls.

Commonly used Visual Basic controls include:

- *Command Button*—Provides a way for the user to tell the program "go" or "start." Its most typical use is to cause the program to take some action when the user clicks on the button or selects it using the keyboard.

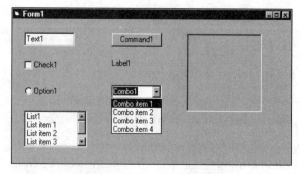

Figure 3.2   *The most commonly used Visual Basic controls.*

- *Text Box*—Used for the display, input, and editing of text. A Text Box can display anything from a single word to a document containing hundreds of lines of text. You'll find that the Text Box is one of Visual Basic's most useful and powerful controls.

- *Check Box*—Lets the user turn an option on or off. A Check Box consists of a small box with an adjacent label. Check Boxes toggle on and off: Clicking on the box or selecting it with the keyboard places (or removes) an X in the box. The program can query the Check Box's **Value** property to see if it is in the on or off state.

- *Option Button*—Similar to the Check Box in that it provides an option that the user can turn on or off. The difference is that Option Buttons are always arranged in groups of two or more, and only one option in the group can be on at any time.

- *Picture Box*—Does just what its name suggests: It displays a picture. You can also create graphics in a Picture Box using Basic statements. The Picture Box control has a lot of hidden power that greatly simplifies the otherwise complex task of handling and displaying graphics and images. In Figure 3.2, the Picture Box displays as a blank rectangle because it has not yet been loaded with a picture.

- *Label*—Perhaps the simplest control, with the main purpose of displaying fixed text on a form. *Fixed* means that the user cannot edit or modify the text, so Labels are generally used to identify other items on a form.

- *List Box*—Displays a scrollable list of text items from which the user can select. With automatic sorting of its contents, a List Box is a common method of present-ing a list of options, such as font names, to the user.

- *Combo Box*—A combination of a Text Box and a List Box. It normally displays as a single-line Text Box, but clicking on its arrow opens a list of items from which the user can choose.

This list includes only eight of Visual Basic's controls, which are an integral part of the Visual Basic development environment and are always displayed in the toolbox. Visual Basic also supports *custom controls*, drop-in components that represent one of the founda-tions of the software component philosophy. Most custom controls are a special category of object called *ActiveX controls*.

You can control which of the available custom controls are displayed in the toolbox by selecting Components from the Project menu and clicking on the Controls tab in the dialog box that is displayed. As shown in Figure 3.3, this tab lists all of the custom controls that you have available. Only those controls and objects with an X in the box next to their name will be displayed as buttons in the toolbox. While you can click on the boxes to turn

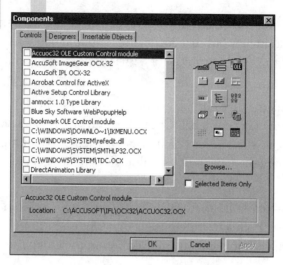

Figure 3.3   *The Controls tab in the Components dialog box.*

the option on or off, you cannot remove a control that is used in your project (i.e., has been placed on a form). My system offers 39 custom controls, and displaying all of them all the time—along with the 20 intrinsic controls—would result in a confusing and unwieldy toolbox. In addition, many of the custom controls are rather specialized, so you can see why Visual Basic lets you determine which controls are displayed in the toolbox.

TIP   Which Controls Are Available?

The controls listed in your Components dialog box will depend on what is installed on your system. Some controls are provided as part of Visual Basic, and which ones you have depends on the edition of Visual Basic you have. Other controls are part of other softw are packages. Don't be concerned if your list of controls does not look like the one in Figure 3.3.

What about the other two tabs in this dialog box? Both insertable objects and designers are like custom controls in two respects: They are software components that you can use in your Visual Basic projects, and they display as icons in the toolbox. How are they different?

A custom control, or an ActiveX control, is a self-contained component that depends only on its OCX file. It has no use except for being dropped in a Visual Basic program (or a program being created with another development tool that supports custom controls).

In contrast, an insertable object represents a data object that is supported by an existing application on your system. An insertable object is available to your Visual Basic programs only if the corresponding application is installed on your system. For example, you can create a chart in Microsoft Excel and then insert the chart into your Visual Basic program. People using your programs, however, will be able to use the inserted object only if they also have the application on their system.

A designer, on the other hand, provides a visual design window within the Visual Basic development environment. The Visual Basic forms designer is included by default in all versions of the development environment. The Professional and Enterprise editions of Visual Basic provide additional designers.

Properties Make The Object

Every Visual Basic object has a set of properties that controls how it looks and behaves. This is true even of insertable objects, although their property sets are relatively small, because so much of their behavior is determined by the parent application and not by Visual Basic. Rather than just talking about properties, let's create a simple Visual Basic project that demonstrates how they work. This program will display text in a Text Box, permitting the user to change the size of the Text Box and the color of the text.

Starting To Design The Interface

This project is designed specifically to illustrate the relationships between objects, properties, and code. It consists of a single dialog box with eight controls. I'll be honest and admit that the program does not do anything useful, but I believe it will be a valuable learning tool. To start, fire up Visual Basic; if it is already running, select New from the File menu. Choose Standard EXE from the New Project dialog box. The first control we'll place on the form is a Text Box. Using the techniques you learned earlier in this chapter, place a Text Box in the upper left corner of the form. The exact size doesn't matter—perhaps two grid units high by eight units wide—you can always adjust it later. There are other controls to be placed, but first let's set the properties for the Text Box that we just added.

Changing The Text Property

Make sure that the Text Box is selected, then take a look at the Properties window. If this window is not displayed, press F4. The Properties window displays the properties of the selected object, with the object's name (that is, its **Name** property) displayed in the title bar. Just below the title bar is a box that displays the object's name and its type. This box is like a Visual Basic Combo Box control—you can click on the arrow at the right end of the box to see a list of all the controls on the current form. Select a control by choosing it from the list, just as if you had clicked on it on the form.

The list in the Properties window lists all of the control's properties, either in alphabetical order (on the Alphabetic tab) or organized by category (on the Categorized tab). The property names are in the left column, and the property values in the right column. You use the scroll bar to display different properties, then select a specific property by clicking on it. The area at the bottom of the Properties window displays a brief description of the highlighted property. Scroll until the **Text** property is visible—on the Categorized tab, it is listed in the Misc section. The default value for this is *Text1*, as shown in Figure 3.4. The **Text** property of a Text Box specifies the text that is displayed in the control.

We need to change the **Text** property of this control. Follow these steps:

1. Scroll the Properties list to bring the **Text** property into view.

2. Double-click on the **Text** property name to highlight the property value in the right column.

3. Type in the new text. I used "Visual Basic", but you are welcome to use any short phrase you like. The text you type will replace the highlighted text.

4. Press Enter, select another property, or click on the form to end editing. If you want to cancel your changes and reset the property to its original value, press Esc.

Notice that the new property is reflected not only in the Properties window, but also in the Text Box control on the form.

Suppose you made a typing error while entering the **Text** property. Do you have to go back and retype the whole thing? Not at all. If you click on the property value in the right column of the Properties window, Visual Basic will display an editing cursor at the end of the text, allowing you to edit the text using the regular editing keys. Here are brief descriptions of each of the keys:

- The left and right arrows move the cursor one character at a time.

- Ctrl+Left arrow and Ctrl+Right arrow move the cursor one word at a time.

Figure 3.4 *Changing the Text Box control's **Text** property.*

- The Home and End keys move the cursor to the start or end of the text.

- The Del key erases selected text or the character to the right of the cursor.

- The Backspace key erases the character to the left of the cursor.

- New text is inserted at the cursor.

- To select text, drag over it with the cursor.

Changing The Font Property

Next, we'll change the Text Box's **Font** property. As you can guess, this property determines the font used for the text in the control. Scroll the Properties list to bring the **Font** property into view and click once on the property name. A small button with three dots displays next to the current font value. Click on the button to display the Font dialog box, which is shown in Figure 3.5. You can also double-click on the **Font** property name to go directly to the dialog box. Select from the Font, Font Style, and Size lists to specify the font you want, then click on OK. I suggest using a font 12 points in size. The new font is reflected immediately in the Text Box on the form. Depending on the size of the font you selected, you may need to increase the size of the Text Box to display all of the text.

Adding The Other Controls

Now that the first control is complete, we'll add all of the remaining controls and then change their properties as needed. We need three Command Buttons, three Option Buttons, and one Frame.

What is the Frame control for? Think back to our discussion of Option Button controls. I mentioned that only one Option Button in a group can be set to on at any time. The

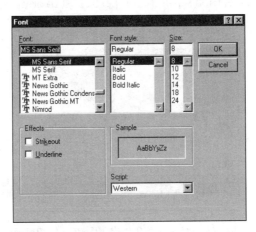

Figure 3.5 *Changing the control's **Font** property.*

obvious question is, "How does one define a group of option buttons?" By placing them in a Frame, that's how. If you want more than one group of Option Buttons on a form, you need one Frame for each group.

Placing Option Buttons in a Frame requires a specific technique. If you add some Option Buttons to a form, add a Frame, and finally drag the Option Buttons onto the Frame, they will certainly appear to be in the Frame, but Visual Basic will not treat them as a group. To have a set of Option Buttons treated as a group, you have to put the Frame on the form first, then draw the Option Buttons within the Frame. Here are the steps required:

1. In the lower left corner of the form, place a Frame large enough to hold three Option Buttons.

2. Click on the Option Button icon in the toolbox.

3. Point at the interior of the Frame and drag to place the Option Button.

4. Repeat Steps 2 and 3 to place the additional Option Buttons.

Next, add the three Command Buttons, placing them in the lower right area of the form. At this point, the form will look more or less like Figure 3.6.

Before changing the properties of these newly added controls, we should save the project. Select Save Project from the File menu. Because the project and form files have not been given names yet, Visual Basic will prompt you for names. I used "Properties Demo" for the project and "Properties" for the form, but you can assign other names if you like.

Setting The Remaining Properties

The last part of creating the project's visual interface is setting the properties of the controls. Start by selecting the Frame, then scroll the Properties list to bring its **Caption** property into

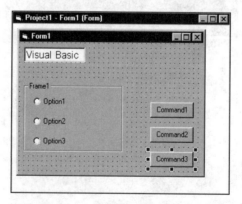

Figure 3.6   *Placement of the Frame, Option Buttons, and Command Buttons.*

view. Double-click on the **Caption** property name, type "Text Colors", and press Enter. (This is the very same method you used to set the **Text** property for the Text Box, remember?) Visual Basic maintains as much consistency as possible in the techniques for dealing with properties, which makes the learning process move as quickly as possible.

Next, select the top Option Button. Set its **Name** property to *optBlack* and its **Caption** property to *Blac&k*. That's not a typo—an ampersand goes before the *k*. What's that for? And what is the **Name** property?

If you place an ampersand in a control's **Caption** property, the ampersand does not display on the form, but it causes the following letter—in this case, the *k*—to be underlined. This defines an *access key* for the control. When the program is running, the user can select the control by pressing Alt+*letter*, and the effect will be the same as clicking on the control. Because some people prefer to use the keyboard rather than the mouse, it's wise to provide keyboard alternatives for as many program tasks as possible. Access keys are one way to do this.

A control's **Name** property is used to refer to the control in Basic code. While all controls are given a default name when you create them, assigning names that reflect both the type of control and its specific function is a good idea. Thus, the name *optBlack* identifies an Option Button that sets the Black option. Note that we did not change the default names of the Text Box or the Frame controls. We will not need to refer to the Frame in code, so its **Name** property is irrelevant. With only one Text Box in the project and no chance of confusion, its default name of Text1 will be okay.

We need to change one more property for this Option Button control. Scroll the Properties list to display the **Value** property, click on it, and then click on the down arrow in the right column. You'll see two possible values for this property—True and False—corresponding to on and off states for the Option Button. The default value is False, but we want to set this one to True.

 Rapid True/False Changes

Numerous properties take True/False values. To toggle the property quickly from one value to the other, double-click on it in the properties list.

Change the properties for the remaining two Option Buttons as follows:

Second Option Button
> Caption: *&Red*
> Name: *optRed*

Third Option Button
Caption: *&Blue*
Name: *optBlue*

We'll leave the **Value** property at False for these two buttons. We really have no choice here, because we've already set the **Value** property of the first Option Button in this group (optBlack) to True, and only one button in a group can be on at a time. If you did set the **Value** property of one of the other buttons to True, the **Value** property of the optBlack button would automatically switch to False.

We also need to change the **ForeColor** property of the second and third Option Buttons. This property sets the color of the control's caption text (the first Option Button will be left at its default **ForeColor** property of black). Scroll down to the **ForeColor** property. You'll see a property value that is a weird-looking combination of letters and numbers, something like this:

&H80000012&

What kind of color is this? Actually, it's a number that represents a color—in this case, black. The leading &H identifies it as a hexadecimal number, and the trailing & indicates that it's a type **Long** number. If you don't know what I'm talking about here, don't fret; you'll learn about these things in Chapter 4. But why does Visual Basic use a number to represent a color? Couldn't it have used something easier to work with, like a color name or a sample of the color?

I agree that the numbers are useless—and fortunately, you don't need to work with them directly. If you select the **ForeColor** property and click on the down arrow in the property value column, Visual Basic displays a small dialog box. Click the Palette tab if necessary to display a palette of the available colors, as shown in Figure 3.7. Select a shade of Blue for the optBlue button and a shade of red for the optRed button.

The final properties you need to set are for the three Command Buttons. I'm sure by now you're well acquainted with the process of setting properties, so I won't repeat the steps. Here are the properties to set:

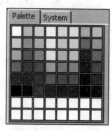

Figure 3.7   *Selecting a color for the **ForeColor** property.*

Upper Command Button
>Caption: *&Bigger*
>Name: *cmdBigger*

Middle Command Button
>Caption: *&Smaller*
>Name: *cmdSmaller*

Lower Command Button
>Caption: *&Quit*
>Name: *cmdQuit*

Our Command Buttons will allow the user to change the size of the Text Box control or quit the program entirely.

The final step in our form design is to set a couple of properties for the form itself. Select the form by clicking on it between the controls, or by selecting Form1 from the objects list in the Properties window. (Form1 is the default name that Visual Basic assigned to the form.) Set its **Caption** property to *Playing With Properties* and its **BorderStyle** property to *3-Fixed Dialog*. The **Caption** property specifies the text that is displayed in the form's title bar; the **BorderStyle** property controls the form's border and whether or not it can be resized by the user.

You have now completed the visual design part of the project. Your form should look more or less like Figure 3.8. Select Save Form1 from the File menu (or press Ctrl+S) to save the changes you've made to the form. You can run your program now if you like. Select Start from the Run menu (you can also click on the Start button on the toolbar or press F5). You'll see the dialog box you just designed pop up on the screen, minus the design grid. But when you click on the various buttons, nothing happens. You have a beautiful interface, but it's brain dead—it doesn't respond to anything. Our next task is to add the code that will respond to user input.

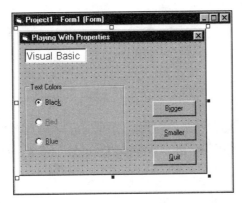

Figure 3.8 *The completed form.*

Adding The Code

What exactly do we want the program to do? Let's make a list:

- When the user selects one of the Option Buttons, change the color of the text in the Text Box accordingly.

- Each time the user selects the Bigger Command Button, enlarge the size of the Text Box by 20 percent.

- Each time the user selects the Smaller Command Button, reduce the size of the Text Box by 20 percent.

- When the user selects the Quit Command Button, end the program.

We'll start with the last item in the list. The Basic statement to end a program is

```
End
```

and we want it executed when the user selects (clicks on) the Quit button. In other words, we want the **End** statement in the Quit button's **Click** event procedure. For a refresher on event procedures in general, take another look at Chapter 1. To create this procedure, double-click on the Quit Command Button to open the code editing window with the skeleton of the event procedure already entered, as shown in Figure 3.9. (Double-clicking on an object automatically brings up its most frequently used event procedure, which happens to be **Click** in the case of a Command Button.)

What do I mean by *skeleton*? It refers to the first and last statements of the event procedure, the statements that actually define the start and the end of the procedure. The last

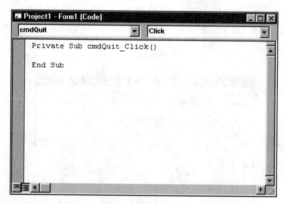

Figure 3.9   *Entering the code for the Command Button's **Click** event.*

statement, **End Sub**, is common to all event procedures, and does nothing more than mark the end of the procedure. Of more interest is the first statement:

```
Private Sub cmdQuit_Click()
```

Don't worry about the **Private** and **Sub** keywords—all event procedures have them, and you'll learn about them later in the book. Look at the actual name of the procedure, **cmdQuit_Click**. The first part is the name of the control, and the second part is the name of the event. Visual Basic names event procedures to identify both the control and the event. If you later change the control's **Name** property, the names of its event procedures are automatically changed, too. You'll be hard pressed to find anything more user-friendly than that.

If you want to work with another event or another object, you can select from the two lists at the top of the code editing window. The one on the left lists the module's objects, and the one on the right lists the events that are supported by the selected object. But for now, it's the **Click** event procedure we want. All you need to do to make this procedure functional is to add the statement **End**, so it reads as follows:

```
Private Sub cmdQuit_Click()

End

End Sub
```

If you run the program now (press F5 or select Start from the Run menu), you'll see the dialog box you designed. Click on the Quit button (or press Alt+Q) to end the program. Cool! Your event procedure really works, but we have a few more event procedures to add before the project is complete.

We'll do the Option Buttons next. We'll start with the optBlack button. Create the **Click** event procedure skeleton for this button by selecting the object from the Object list at the top of the code editing window (or by returning to the form and double-clicking on the control). When this control is selected, we want the color of the text in the Text Box—its **ForeColor** property—set to black. But Visual Basic uses those weird numbers to represent colors. Do we have to figure out the number for black? No. We have a better way.

Remember that we have already set the color of each Option Button to the corresponding color. The number we need is therefore already present in the Option Button's **ForeColor** property. All we need to do is copy that number from the Option Button's **ForeColor** property to the Text Box's **ForeColor** property, and we accomplish our task without having to worry about the exact color number. Here's the event procedure with the single necessary line of code added:

```
Private Sub optBlack_Click()

Text1.ForeColor = optBlack.ForeColor

End Sub
```

> **Note:** *As you create these event procedures, be careful with the spelling and punctuation in the code; the computer is very literal in its interpretation and will catch even the smallest mistake.*

You can see how Visual Basic represents object properties in code: the name of the object (that is, its **Name** property), followed by a period and the property name. The equal sign is Basic's *assignment* operator. In effect, it says, "Make the thing on the left (in this case, the **ForeColor** property of the Text1 object) equal to the thing on the right (the optBlack object's **ForeColor** property)."

We use the same technique for the other two Option Buttons. The code for the optBlue button **Click** event procedure is shown here:

```
Private Sub optBlue_Click()

Text1.ForeColor = optBlue.ForeColor

End Sub
```

And here is the code for the **Click** event procedure of the optRed button:

```
Private Sub optRed_Click()

Text1.ForeColor = optRed.ForeColor

End Sub
```

The last steps in creating this project are writing the event procedures for the other two Command Buttons. Each time the user clicks on the Bigger button, we want to increase the size of the Text Box by 20 percent. The size of a control is determined by its **Width** and **Height** properties. To increase the width by 20 percent, we would perform the following steps:

1. Obtain the current width from the control's **Width** property.

2. Multiply the value by 1.2.

3. Set the **Width** property equal to the new value.

In code, we can accomplish all three steps with a single Basic statement:

```
Text1.Width = Text1.Width * 1.2
```

The asterisk is Basic's multiplication operator, and the equal sign is the assignment opera-tor we discussed earlier. We also want to increase the height, which we can do by using the same formula. Thus, the complete event procedure for the cmdBigger button looks like this:

```
Private Sub cmdBigger_Click()

Text1.Width = Text1.Width * 1.2
Text1.Height = Text1.Height * 1.2

End Sub
```

The final step for our project is to create the event procedure for the Smaller button. We'll use the same approach as for the Bigger button, except this time we need a multipli-cation factor of 0.8 to decrease the control size by 20 percent. Here's the completed event procedure:

```
Private Sub cmdSmaller_Click()

Text1.Width = Text1.Width * 0.8
Text1.Height = Text1.Height * 0.8

End Sub
```

That's it! The project is complete. Let's take it for a spin. Press F5 to execute the project, and you'll see the dialog box shown in Figure 3.10. Click on the Option Buttons to change the color of the text in the Text Box. Click on the Bigger and Smaller Command Buttons to resize the Text Box. You'll see, by the way, that the size of the Text Box is not con-strained by the design grid during program execution. This may not be the most exciting program in the world, but I think it's an effective demonstration of the use of properties in Visual Basic.

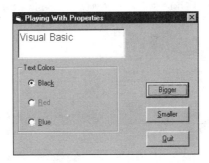

Figure 3.10   *The Properties Demo program in action, after enlarging the Text Box a few steps.*

Note that you can click on the Text Box control and edit the text there. How can this be? We didn't program any editing capabilities. Actually, you are just seeing the built-in capabilities of the Text Box control.

Here's another example of the built-in power of Visual Basic controls: If you click on the Smaller button several times, you will see that the Text Box height reaches a certain size and then does not change (although the width will continue to shrink). A Text Box always maintains at least the minimum height necessary to display text. This height will depend on the size of the font in use, which you set in the **Font** property.

Summing Up

The project in this chapter is fairly simple, but it illustrates some important Visual Basic concepts. You've seen how an object's properties control its appearance and behavior, and how these properties can be manipulated both during program design and by code during program execution. We've touched on only a few object properties—it's obvious from browsing through the Properties list that there are lots more. We'll be visiting many of them in the following chapters, but it's hardly possible to cover them all.

If you highlight a property name in the list and press F1, the Visual Basic Help system will display a page of information about the property. A typical Help screen is shown in Figure 3.11. Click on the underlined keywords, or *links*, to view related information. Among

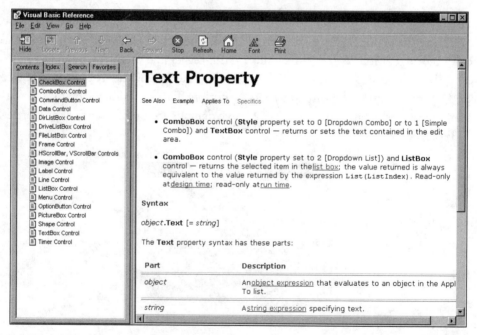

Figure 3.11   *Using Visual Basic's Help system to obtain information about a property.*

the useful features that the Help system provides are examples of how various properties are used (click on the Example link), links to related topics (click on the See Also link), and a list of the objects that this property applies to (click on the Applies To link). Click on a term with a dotted underline to see a definition of the term. The left side of the Help window lets you navigate among all the available Help topics.

Perhaps the best way to explore Visual Basic's properties is to experiment on your own. Whipping up a small project is so easy that experimenting with various property settings should be a regular part of your Visual Basic explorations. Often, seeing something in action is much more effective than simply reading about it. Remember, to learn by doing is our approach.

Chapter 4
The Basics Of Basic

Underneath Visual Basic's fancy objects and events lies a foundation of Basic code doing the grunt work. Let's take a comprehensive look at just what Basic is and what you can do with it.

S omeday, you might be able to create a complete applications program by doing nothing more than combining a few software components, but that day has yet to arrive. By now, I hope you are convinced of the power and flexibility of Visual Basic's objects. Despite all this power, Visual Basic still requires some glue to stick the objects together into a functioning program. As you saw in the example in the previous chapter, that glue is Basic code.

What exactly is Basic? The name is an acronym for Beginner's All-Purpose Symbolic Instruction Code, a language that was originally developed for instructional purposes many moons ago at Dartmouth College. While the original Basic may have been ideal as a teaching aid, for many years it had a reputation among programmers for being slow and inflexible. The reason for this negative connotation was that Basic *was* slow and inflexible. "Greasy kid stuff," snorted the serious programmers as they went off to struggle with C or FORTRAN.

Over the years, however, Basic gradually improved. With Microsoft QuickBasic leading the way, Basic evolved from a language suited only for students and hobbyists to a powerful tool that was up to the task of creating full-fledged business and scientific applications. And this, my fellow programmers, is the Basic that you'll discover inside Visual Basic. It is a powerful, flexible, and efficient language capable of handling just about any programming task you ask of it. The fundamentals of the language are fairly easy to learn; you will do so in this chapter.

We won't be covering the complete Basic language here. That could be—and, in fact, has been—the subject of complete books. If I tried to squeeze any sort of complete coverage of Basic into one chapter, I would end up with a very long and boring chapter. Instead, I'll cover what I feel are the real basics (again, no pun intended) of the language: the tools you will need to get started writing Basic code. Then, as more advanced language topics arise during the remainder of this book, I'll provide you with more detailed information.

Where Did I Put That Data?

Almost every program works with data, or information, of one kind or another. Whether the data is a chunk of text to be edited, a graphic image, or a table of numbers, the program needs a place to keep the data while the program is executing. I'm not talking about disk files here, although that's an important topic in its own right. I'm referring to something else. Permit me to explain.

During execution, a program stores its data in *variables* and, to a lesser degree, *constants*. A variable derives its name from the fact that its stored information can change, or vary, during program execution. In contrast, the information stored in a constant does not change. Visual Basic offers a rich variety of variables and constants to suit all your programming needs.

Visual Basic's variables can be divided into three general categories: *Numeric variables* store numbers; *string variables* store text; and the third category consists of data types that cannot be clearly categorized as either string or numeric. Each of these basic categories is further subdivided. Let's start with the numbers.

Numeric Variables

Working with numbers is something that computers do frequently, so we certainly need a type of variable to store them. Visual Basic actually has several types of numeric variables: **Byte**, **Integer**, **Long**, **Single**, **Double**, and **Currency** (more on these variable types in a moment). Why not just have a single numeric variable that can hold any number? Efficiency. The number 5 can be stored in less memory space and manipulated more quickly than 123,513,465,760.74666. By providing several subtypes of numeric variables, each suited for a certain numerical range and degree of accuracy, program efficiency can be improved.

Numbers can be divided into two types: *integers*, which have no fractional part (digits to the right of the decimal point); and *floating point numbers*, which can, but do not have to, contain a fractional part. The three integer variable types are called **Byte, Integer**, and **Long**; the three floating point types are referred to as **Single, Double**, and **Currency**. These types all differ in the ranges of values—the largest and the smallest—they can hold. The floating point types also differ in their precision, or accuracy, which refers to the number of digits to the right of the decimal point. The sixth type of numeric variable, **Currency**, is specifically designed to work with financial figures. As Table 4.1 shows, Visual Basic numeric variable types provide for just about any imaginable situation.

How do you decide which type of numeric variable to use in a particular situation? The general rule is to use the smallest type that will suffice. For an integer variable, use a type **Integer** in preference to a **Long**, but only if you're sure that the data stored there will never exceed the limits of a type **Integer**. Because of its extremely limited range, type **Byte** can be used only in special situations (but can be very useful indeed). Similarly, use a **Single** in preference to a **Double** whenever possible. **Currency** is usually the best choice when you're working with money amounts.

The next logical questions are: "How do you create variable names?" and "How do you inform Visual Basic of the type of variable you want?" We'll address these questions in our next topic.

Naming And Declaring Variables

Each variable that you use in your program must have a unique name. Several rules apply to creating variable names:

- The maximum length is 255 characters.

- The first character must be a letter.

- The name cannot contain a period, space, or any of the following characters: ! @ # & % $.

Table 4.1   Numeric variables.

Variable Type	Minimum Value	Maximum Value	Precision	Storage Space
Byte	0	255	N/A	1 byte
Integer	-32,768	32,767	N/A	2 bytes
Long	-2,147,483,648	2,147,483,647	N/A	4 bytes
Single	-3.4×10^{38} *	3.4×10^{38} *	6 digits	4 bytes
Double	-1.79×10^{308} *	1.79×10^{308} *	14 digits	8 bytes
Currency	-9.22×10^{11} *	9.22×10^{11} *	4 digits	8 bytes

* An approximate value. See Visual Basic Help for exact figures.

Variable names should follow one other guideline. While it may not be an absolute requirement, it is nonetheless important enough to merit the designation of a rule: *Use descriptive variable names*.

This means simply that the name of a variable should describe the data it holds. For example, if your program deals with the population genetics of bats, and you need a variable to hold the number of bats, you should use a name such as **Bat_Count** or **NumberOfBats**. You could legally name the variable **XY**, **J89**, or **BillClinton**, and Visual Basic wouldn't care. But when working on the program later, you'll find that descriptive variable names make a big difference in the readability of your code. It's a good habit to cultivate right from the get-go.

Some programmers believe that descriptive variable naming should be taken a step further so that the name of each variable identifies not only its contents but its type. This is typically done with a type of prefix called *Hungarian notation*. Using this prefix, the name of an integer variable might be preceded with an *i* for integer. For your bat count, therefore, you would have a variable named **iNumberOfBats**. The idea behind Hungarian notation is the ability to discern the variable type immediately whenever you see a variable name in code.

In my opinion, there is no need for the inconvenience of Hungarian notation in Visual Basic. The Visual Basic code editor already has a feature that makes it a cinch to determine the type of any variable. Simply right-click on any variable name, then select Quick Info from the pop-up menu. Visual Basic will display a small window with the variable type indicated. You can get the same result by placing the editing cursor on the variable and pressing Ctrl+I. With such easy access to variable types, why bother with the awkward and inconvenient variable names created by Hungarian notation?

TIP Standardizing Variable Naming Conventions

Visual Basic does not care one whit about the case of variable names. As far as Basic is concerned, **Count**, **count**, and **COUNT** all reference the same variable. For the sake of code readability, I suggest that you adopt a standard variable naming scheme and stick to it. My method is to use a combination of upper- and lowercase letters for variable names. This approach makes the names easier to read, particularly when a variable name has been constructed by combining two or more words. For example, I think that **MaxDataCount** is much easier to read than **maxdatacount**. As I'll soon explain, I reserve names that are all uppercase for constants.

Visual Basic's code editor makes it easy to be consistent with your use of capitalization. Once you've entered the first instance of a variable name, which is usually in a **Dim** statement, Visual Basic automatically corrects future instances of the name to match the original capitalization.

How is a variable's type assigned? You have two choices. You can explicitly declare the variable in a **Dim** statement, or you can use a type declaration character at the end of the variable name. An explicit declaration takes the following general form:

```
Dim name As type
```

Here's a specific example:

```
Dim X As Integer, Y As Single, Z As Currency
```

Each variable name is listed, followed by the **As** keyword and the type name. You can have one or more variables in a single **Dim** statement, and you can have as many **Dim** statements as you need, each on its own line.

The use of type declaration characters makes **Dim** statements unnecessary. I'll explain in a minute why I think that the use of type declaration characters is a bad idea, but you do need to know about them. To use the type declaration characters, simply place the character corresponding to the desired variable type at the end of the variable name. The characters are shown in Table 4.2.

At this point, because no **Dim** statement is necessary, you simply use the variable in code as needed. For example, if you need a type **Integer** variable to hold the value 100, you would write as follows:

```
Count% = 100
```

In other words, you use the variables only when and where they are needed—you don't have to declare them first. This all sounds quite convenient, but now I'll explain why it's a bad idea.

To Declare Or Not To Declare

The answer to this question—to declare or not—is an easy one. *Always* declare your variables. In fact, you can tell Visual Basic to require variable declaration. Select Options from the Tools menu, click on the Editor tab, and turn on the Require Variable Declaration

Table 4.2   Type declaration characters.

Type	Declaration Character
Integer	%
Long	&
Single	!
Double	#
Currency	@

option. When this option is active, Visual Basic will report a Variable Not Defined error if you try to use a variable that has not been declared in a **Dim** statement.

> **Note:** *When the Require Variable Declaration option is on, Visual Basic inserts the* **Option Explicit** *statement in your code.*

Why am I so adamant about *always* declaring your variables? Why wouldn't the use of type declaration characters be easier? Though it may appear easier at first, it always seems to lead to problems. Here's why. Let's say you've created a variable, but at some point in the code the name is misspelled. Without **Option Explicit** active, Visual Basic will simply create a new variable using the misspelled name (as far as Visual Basic is concerned, you are creating a new variable). New variables are automatically given the value of zero. Because the program is using this new variable instead of the one it should be using, you are almost sure to get program errors that are extremely hard to track down. If **Option Explicit** were active, however, Visual Basic would immediately flag the misspelled variable name as an undeclared variable. The problem would never arise.

But this isn't the *only* reason to declare your variables. Some of Visual Basic's variable types—**Byte**, **Boolean**, and **Date** (I'll get to the last two soon)—do not have a type declaration character associated with them. If you want to create a variable with one of those types, you must use a **Dim** statement. If you are not requiring variable declarations, you'll find yourself in a situation where some of your program's variables are declared in **Dim** statements, while others are not. This is a recipe for confusion, and any seasoned programmer knows potential confusion should be nipped in the bud.

Heed my advice: Turn on the Require Variable Declaration option, and leave it on. In fact, I feel so strongly about this point that I'm going to elevate it to the exalted status of a rule: *Always require variable declarations*.

When you are typing a variable declaration and enter the **As** keyword followed by a space, the Visual Basic editor automatically displays a list of all the data and object types that you could use for the variable. If you start typing a type name, the list scrolls to the corresponding entry. This is shown in Figure 4.1, although the list contains many more types than the ones we've learned about here. As we will cover in a later chapter, Visual Basic variables can refer to objects as well as to data, hence the extra types on this list. You can turn this auto-list feature on and off by selecting Options from the Tools menu, displaying the Editor tab, and clicking on the Auto List Members option.

String Variables

The second major category of variables is *strings*. This is simply computer talk for text, but I am guessing this use of *string* comes from the fact that text is nothing more than a string of characters. A string variable can hold a single character or thousands of characters, or it

Figure 4.1 *Automatic listing of data types.*

can be empty. Depending on the needs of your program, you can choose from Visual Basic's two types of string variables. A *fixed-length string* has a maximum capacity that you set when you declare it. A fixed-length string can hold any number of characters up to this maximum length—but not over it. In contrast, a *variable-length string* is akin to a rubber bag that automatically adjusts its size to hold however many characters you place in it. For both types of string variables, the maximum capacity is some 2 billion characters—that's right, *billion*.

Fixed-length string variables *must* be declared (another argument for using **Option Explicit**). The declaration takes the following form:

```
Dim LastName As String * 5
```

The number in the declaration (in this example, 5) specifies the string length. Remember, this is the maximum number of characters you can store in the string. If you try to put more characters in the variable, they will be lost. For example, if you execute the statement

```
LastName = "Aitken"
```

only the first five characters will be stored; the *n* will be lost. You can, however, put fewer than the maximum number of characters in a fixed-length string.

As for variable-length strings, you can create one by using its type declaration character $, but the **Dim** statement remains the preferred method of declaring it:

```
Dim FirstName As String
```

Now you have a string variable named **FirstName**, into which you can stuff as large a string as you like—at least up to 2 billion characters, which I don't consider too limiting.

Which type of string variable should you use? For the most part, the decision is based on your program's data. True, you can manipulate fixed-length strings a bit more quickly. With today's lightning-fast processors, however, it won't make any noticeable difference unless your program performs an enormous amount of text processing. If you are absolutely sure your string data won't ever exceed a certain length, a fixed-length string is probably best. Otherwise, use a variable-length string.

Other Variable Types

Four more Visual Basic data types are used in special situations: **Boolean**, **Date**, **Variant**, and **Object**. The **Boolean** type holds information that takes the form of yes/no or on/off. In other words, a **Boolean** variable can hold only two possible values, referred to by the Basic keywords **True** and **False**. You'll see that **Boolean** variables are closely related to logical expressions, which I'll cover later in the chapter. A **Boolean** variable requires two bytes of storage, the same as type **Integer**.

The **Date** type holds date and time information. It is a floating point type, with the whole-number portion representing the date and the fractional portion representing the time. The date is encoded as the number of days since December 30, 1899, with negative numbers representing earlier dates. The time is encoded as a fraction of the 24-hour day, with 0.0 representing midnight, 0.25 representing 6:00 a.m., 0.5 representing noon, and so on.

Variant is Visual Basic's catchall data type. It can be assigned any of Visual Basic's data types except fixed-length strings. The main use of **Variant** variables is to simplify dealing with numerical data that sometimes needs to be treated as a string. Later in the book, I'll cover some other specialized uses of type **Variant**.

Finally, the **Object** data type is used to hold a reference to an object. You'll learn more about using this data type in later chapters.

None of these four data types has a type declaration character associated with it. The **Date**, **Boolean,** and **Object** types *must* be declared in a **Dim** statement:

```
Dim Answer As Boolean, OrderDate As Date, MyThing As Object
```

The **Variant** type can also be declared in a **Dim** statement. If you are not requiring variable declarations and you use a variable name without a type declaration character, Visual Basic automatically makes it a type **Variant**. Remember, however, that using variables without explicitly declaring the type is to be avoided.

User-Defined Data Types

One of Basic's handiest features is the ability to create user-defined data types. A user-defined type (also called a *structure*) is a compound data type containing two or more other data types. You can define exactly what goes into a structure, designing it around the exact needs of your program. You use the **Type...End Type** statement to define a structure. Here's how it looks:

```
Type StructureName
    element1 As Type
    element2 As Type
    ...
End Type
```

If you were writing a program to maintain an inventory list, for example, you could define a structure as follows to hold information about each item:

```
Type StockItem
    Name As String * 25
    PartNumber As String * 12
    Cost As Currency
    NumberOnHand As Integer
End Type
```

The individual elements of a structure can be any of Basic's fundamental data types *except* variable-length strings. You can even use one structure type as an element in another structure type. Furthermore, while I haven't introduced *arrays* yet (that comes soon), I will mention that an array can be an element of a structure—and you can also create arrays of structures.

When you define a structure with the **Type...End Type** statement, that's all you are doing—defining it. The **Type...End Type** statement does not create any actual variables of the defined type. You must use the **Dim** statement to create *instances* of the structure—actual variables with names and with memory space allocated to them. Using our previous example, once we have defined the **StockItem** type, we can then create an instance of the type as follows:

```
Dim NewPart As StockItem
```

Now that you have a structure of type **StockItem** named **NewPart** to work with, how do you access its various elements? You use the variable name followed by a period and the element name, as shown here:

```
NewPart.Name = "cam tensioning spring"
NewPart.PartNumber = "L-101-6J"
NewPart.Cost = 99.76
NewPart.NumberOnHand = 8
```

To define a structure that contains another structure as an element, follow the same syntax. The definition of the embedded structure—in this case, **StockItem**—must come first in the code. Then:

```
Type OrderData
    Part As StockItem
    Supplier As String * 30
End Type
```

To access elements of the embedded structure, use the period syntax as follows:

```
Dim LastOrder As OrderData
LastOrder.Part.Name = "cam tensioning spring"
LastOrder.Part.Cost = 99.76
```

You must define structures at the module level. In other words, you cannot include a **Type...End Type** statement inside a procedure. No special rules exist for using the elements of structures in your program; you can use them anywhere you could use a simple variable of the same type. If your project includes a definition of a user-defined type, the auto list of data types that Visual Basic displays while you are typing a **Dim** statement will include the type. You'll learn about using arrays of user-defined types and arrays in user-defined types later in the chapter.

Arrays

An *array* stores a large number of variables under the same name. All the individual variables, or *elements*, of an array must be the same data type. These elements are distinguished from each other by a numerical *array index*. You create an array with the **Dim** statement, as shown here:

```
Dim Data(100) As Integer
```

This statement declares an array containing 101 type **Integer** elements. Why 101 rather than 100? In Visual Basic, array indexes begin with 0, so this array starts at element Data(0) and ends at Data(100), for a total of 101 elements. An array can be any of Visual Basic's data types, including both variable- and fixed-length strings. You can also create an array of user-defined types that you have defined with the **Type...End Type** statement. If the data type is not specified in the **Dim** statement, the array defaults to **Variant**.

You can use the elements of an array anywhere you can use regular variables of the same type. The real power of arrays becomes evident when you use variables as the array index, or subscript. In fact, any numerical expression that evaluates to a value within the array's index range can be used as the subscript. For example, here's a **For...Next** loop that fills all the elements of a 1,000-element array with the values 1 through 1,000:

```
For i = 0 To 999
    Array(i) = i + 1
Next I
```

Visual Basic array indexes start at zero by default, but you can modify this. To set the lower index to 1 for all arrays, include the **Option Base 1** statement at the module level before any array declarations. After executing **Option Base 1**, the declaration

```
Dim Array(100) As Integer
```

creates an array with 100 elements numbered 1 through 100. A more flexible way to modify the lower index is with the **To** keyword. You use **To** in the array declaration statement:

```
Dim Array1(1 To 10)     ' 10 elements 1 through 10
Dim Array2(-5 To 5)     ' 11 elements -5 through 5
```

Arrays can have more than one index; these are called *multidimensional arrays*. To create a multidimensional array, include the size of each dimension in the declaration statement. The statement

```
Dim Array(9, 9)
```

Declares an array with 100 elements, Array(0, 0) … Array(0, 9) … Array(9, 9). You can have as many as 26 dimensions in an array, although it is rare to need more than 3 or 4 even for the most specialized applications.

If you try to reference a nonexistent array element, Visual Basic generates a "Subscript out of range" error. For example, if you declare an array as follows:

```
Dim Array(10)
```

then the statement

```
Array(11) = 5
```

will generate the error, because the array does not have an element 11.

You can create arrays of user-defined structures, and you can also include an array as an element of a structure. To create an array of structures, you must first define the structure with the **Type...End Type** statement, as shown here:

```
Type Person
    FirstName As String * 15
    LastName As String * 20
End Type
```

Then, you use the **Dim** statement to create instances of the structure. For example, the line

```
Dim MyFriends(100) As Person
```

will create an array of 100 type **Person** structures. You access the elements of the structures within the array by using a combination of the structure's period notation (covered earlier in this chapter in the section "User-Defined Data Types") and the array subscript notation. Thus, the code

```
MyFriends(n).FirstName = "Bill"
MyFriends(n).LastName = "Gates"
```

would place data in both the **FirstName** and **LastName** elements of the *n*th structure in the array.

To use an array as an element of a structure, include it in the structure definition as follows:

```
Type Person
    FirstName As String * 15
    LastName As String * 20
    Likes(10) As String * 20
End Type
```

If you create a single instance of the structure, you can access the elements of the array element by using array subscript notation on the right side of the period:

```
Dim MyBestFriend As Person
MyBestFriend.FirstName = "Pat"
MyBestFriend.LastName = "Smith"
MyBestFriend.Likes(1) = "chocolate"
MyBestFriend.Likes(2) = "old movies"
```

Declaring an array of a structure that includes an array as an element complicates matters. For example, consider this code (assuming the definition of type **Person** shown previously):

```
Dim MyFriends(100) As Person
MyFriends(1).FirstName = "Pat"
MyFriends(1).LastName = "Smith"
MyFriends(1).Likes(1) = "chocolate"
MyFriends(1).Likes(2) = "old movies"
```

All you need to remember is that the subscript for an array of structures goes to the left of the period, and the subscript for an array within a structure goes to the right of the period.

Dynamic Arrays

The arrays I have discussed so far are known as *static* arrays. Their size—number of dimensions and number of elements—is set when the array is declared and cannot be changed. Another type of array, called *dynamic*, does not have these limitations. When you first declare a dynamic array, you specify its data type, but that's all. For example, the following statement declares a dynamic array of type **Integer**:

```
Dim MyArray() As Integer
```

Then, when you know the required size of the array, use **ReDim** to specify it. Here are some examples:

```
ReDim MyArray(100)
ReDim MyArray(10,10,20)
ReDim MyArray (1 to 100)
```

Once you have applied **ReDim**, you can use the array like any static array. Even more flexibility is provided by the fact that you can **ReDim** a dynamic array as many times as needed, changing the number of dimensions and/or elements to suit the program's needs. **ReDim** is permitted only in procedure-level code.

Dynamic arrays follow the same scope rules as static arrays. In other words, if you declare the array at the module level with **Dim**, its scope is limited to that module. To make the dynamic array visible outside the module, use the **Public** keyword:

```
Public MyArray() As Integer
```

Of course, if you declare a dynamic array at the procedure level its scope is local to that procedure.

When you use **ReDim** to change the size of a dynamic array, the default is for all data in the array to be lost. This means that all elements in the newly sized array will be initialized to zero (numeric arrays), an empty string (string arrays), the **Empty** value (**Variant** arrays), or **Nothing** (object arrays). If you want to change the array's size while preserving its data, you can do so (with some limitations) by using the **Preserve** keyword. Clearly this is applicable only the second and subsequent times the array's size is changed with **ReDim**, otherwise there will be no data in it to save. Here's how to use **Preserve**:

```
ReDim Preserve MyArray(100)
```

There are some limitations on using **Preserve**:

- If you increase the number of elements in the array, data in the existing elements will be preserved, and the new elements will be initialized by the usual rules.

- With a multidimensional array, you can use **Preserve** only to change the last dimension of the array. Thus, after **ReDim X(5, 5)** you could execute **ReDim Preserve X(5,10)** but not **ReDim Preserve X(10, 5)**.

- You cannot use **Preserve** when you are changing the number of array dimensions.

There's a lot more to arrays, including multidimensional arrays, but at least you know enough to get started using them. I'll deal with the other array topics as we encounter them throughout the book.

Because the size of a dynamic array can change, it is useful to be able to determine its upper and lower bounds—that is, the highest and lowest index values that can be used. The **LBound** and **UBound** functions let you do this. The syntax is as follows:

```
UBound(arrayname[, dimension])
LBound(arrayname[, dimension])
```

The *dimension* argument is used for multidimensional arrays only, and it specifies the dimension whose upper or lower index is to be returned by the function. If the argument is omitted, one is assumed. Here are some examples, using an array that was resized as follows:

```
Redim Data(10, 5 to 20)
UBound(Data) returns 10
LBound(Data, 2) returns 5
LBound(Data, 1) returns 0
```

The **UBound** and **LBound** functions can be used with static arrays as well as dynamic arrays.

Constants

You can use two types of constants in a Visual Basic program: literal and symbolic. A *literal constant* is nothing more than a number or string typed directly into your source code. In the following lines of code,

```
Dim MyString As String, MyNumber As Integer
MyString = "New York"
MyNumber = 123
```

"New York" and **123** are literal constants. You type them in while you are editing your source code, and they (of course) do not change during program execution—they are "constant."

Much more useful is the so-called *symbolic constant*. It has a name and a data type, just like a variable, and generally follows the same rules. Here is the difference: A symbolic constant is assigned a value when it is declared, and this value cannot change during program execution. To create a symbolic constant, use the **Const** keyword in the declaration statement:

```
Const MAXIMUM As Integer = 100
```

This statement creates a constant named **MAXIMUM** with the value 100. You could then use the name **MAXIMUM** anywhere in the program where you could use a literal constant 100, and the result would be the same. Note that the **As** part of the **Const** declaration is optional. If you do not specify a data type, Visual Basic will automatically use the type most appropriate for the specified value. For example, the declaration

```
Const RATIO = 15.12
```

will result in **RATIO** being assigned type **Single**.

What is the purpose of symbolic constants? Why not just type in literal constants wherever they are needed? The major advantage is being able to change the value of a symbolic constant throughout the program simply by editing its declaration statement. Another advantage is that the constant's name can help in making the program easier to read.

You may have noticed that in the previous two examples, I used all uppercase for the constant names. This is *not* required by Visual Basic. In fact, the rules for naming constants are the same as for naming variables. Using all uppercase for constant names, while identifying variable names with a combination of upper- and lowercase makes it easy for me to distinguish constants from variables in my own code—a distinction that would not otherwise be apparent.

This wraps up our introduction to Visual Basic variables and constants. You now have the fundamentals under your belt, although we have some ground yet to cover in regard to Visual Basic data storage. In particular, arrays and the **Type** statement are indispensable tools. As mentioned earlier, I will cover these and other topics later in the book as the need arises.

Commenting Your Code

Using comments liberally in your Basic code is a good idea. Visual Basic ignores comments; their only purpose is to provide anyone reading the code with reminders or explanations of what's going on. Some programmers don't use comments, or they use them sparingly—and they are usually sorry later. Aspects of your code design and program structure that seem perfectly clear during the writing process may appear less than crystalline a month or a year later when you need to modify the code.

To insert a comment, type an apostrophe anywhere in your code, except within a literal string (that is, inside double quotation marks). Anything from the apostrophe to the end of the line is treated as a comment and ignored by the Visual Basic compiler.

Enums

An enumeration, identified by the Visual Basic keyword **Enum**, is used to associate sequential integer values with names. These names then serve as constants within the program, but with certain advantages over regular constants declared with the **Const** keyword. To declare an enumeration, use the **Enum…End Enum** statement:

```
Public Enum OrderStatus
   pgaBackordered
   pgaInProgress
   pgaShipped
End Enum
```

This code creates an enumeration named **OrderStatus** with three members. The **Public** keyword is optional; all enumerations are public by default. You can declare an enumeration as **Private** in which case its members will be visible only in the module where it is declared. Note that enumerations can be declared only in module-level code within a class or code module.

When you do not assign specific values to the members of an enumeration, they are assigned integer values starting at zero. Therefore, **pgaBackordered** = 0, **pgaInProgress** = 1, and so on. To start at a value other than zero, you would assign the desired starting value to the first member:

```
Public Enum OrderStatus
   PgaBackordered = 1
   pgaInProgress
   pgaShipped
End Enum
```

Now, **pgaInProgress** = 2 and **pgaShipped** = 3. You can assign non-sequential values also:

```
Public Enum OrderStatus
   PgaBackordered = -1
   PgaInProgress = 15
   PgaShipped = 123
End Enum
```

Why use an enumeration instead of named constants, as shown here?

```
Const pgaBackordered = 0
Const pgaInProgress = 1
Const pgaShipped = 2
```

In terms of using the constant names, there is no advantage. The advantage to using an enumeration lies in the fact that it becomes a type you can use for variables and for the parameters and return values of procedures. Thus, you could declare a variable as follows:

```
Dim StateOfOrder As OrderStatus
```

Or, declare procedures to take the enumeration type as a parameter:

```
Public Sub SetStatus (X As OrderStatus)
...
End Property
```

Or as the return value of a function:

```
Public Function GetOrderStatus(OrderNumber As Integer) As OrderStatus
...
End Function
```

Enumerations can be viewed in the Visual Basic Object Browser, and the AutoList feature will display a list of enumeration members while you are writing code.

TIP

Naming Enumeration Members

To avoid conflicts with other variable or constant names, it is standard practice to create enumeration member names that all start with the same series of lowercase letters. In the examples, I used my initials *pga,* but it is more convenient to use something that relates the enumeration members to the class they are defined in. Within a module that deals with order processing, for example, you might prefix member names with *ordr.*

I'm The Manipulative Type

Now that you know how to store data in your program, you'd probably like to know what you can do with the data. The answer is, "Lots."

Some of the most important tasks involve Visual Basic's *operators.* An operator is a symbol or word that instructs Visual Basic to manipulate data in a certain way. You've already been introduced to the assignment operator (=), which tells Visual Basic to make the variable or object property on the left of the operator equal to the expression on the right side of the operator.

> ## What's An Expression?
> You'll see the term *expression* used frequently, and you're probably wondering just what exactly it refers to. It is quite simple, actually. An expression is anything that evaluates to a number, a string, or a logical (True/False) value. Thus, the literal constant 5 is an expression, as is 5+2.

Arithmetic Operators

The arithmetic operators perform mathematical manipulations. There are seven of them. The first four, listed in Table 4.3, are the common operations that I'm sure you are familiar with.

The last three arithmetic operators may be more obscure. *Integer division*, represented by the \ symbol, divides two numbers and returns an integer result, discarding any fractional part of the answer. Thus, 7 \ 2 evaluates to 3, as does 6 \ 2. No rounding occurs; any fractional part of the answer is simply discarded. Thus, both 21 \ 10 and 29 \ 10 evaluate to 2.

The *exponentiation* operator raises a number to a power. The symbol for this operation is ^. In Basic, therefore, X ^ Y means the same as the more common notation X^Y. If X is negative, then Y must be an integer; otherwise, both X and Y can be floating point values.

The *modulus* operator, represented by the keyword **Mod**, divides two numbers and returns only the remainder. The expression 7 **Mod** 2 evaluates to 1, 23 **Mod** 4 evaluates to 3, and 25 **Mod** 5 evaluates to 0. Any fractional part of the answer is truncated, so 23.5 **Mod** 4 evaluates to 3, not 3.5.

String Manipulation

The only operator that works with string data is called the *concatenation* operator, represented by the symbol &. Concatenation simply means to tack one string onto the end of another. For example, if **MyString** is a string variable, then executing the statement

```
MyString = "Visual " & "Basic"
```

Table 4.3   Arithmetic operators.

Operation	Symbol	Example	Result
Addition	+	2 + 5	7
Subtraction	-	18 - 10	8
Multiplication	*	2 * 5	10
Division	/	10 / 2	5

results in the string "Visual Basic" being stored in the variable. You can also use the + symbol for string concatenation. It is provided for compatibility with old Basic programs, but it's best to stick with & for new programs.

 Is That All?

Is concatenation all that Visual Basic can do with strings? Not by a long shot. It performs other string manipulations, not with operators, but with the built-in string procedures. These will be covered in Chapter 11.

Operator Precedence

What happens if an expression contains more than one operator? What difference does it make? An example will illustrate. Consider this expression:

```
5 + 3 * 2
```

What does it evaluate to? If we perform the addition first, it evaluates to 16 (5 + 3 = 8, 8 * 2 = 16); but if we perform the multiplication first, the result is 11 (3 * 2 = 6, 5 + 6 = 11). Which is correct? Because of such potentially ambiguous expressions, Visual Basic includes strict rules of operator precedence. This is just a fancy way of determining which operations are performed first. The precedence of Visual Basic's operators is given in Table 4.4. Operators with low precedence numbers are performed first.

Returning to the original example, we can see that the expression 5 + 3 * 2 will evaluate to 11, because multiplication has a higher precedence than addition and thus will be performed first. For operators that have the same precedence level, such as multiplication and division, the order of execution is always left to right.

What if the order of execution specified by the operator precedence rules isn't what you want? Let's say you would like to add variables A and B, then multiply the sum by variable C. Can this be done? Yes. Parentheses come to the rescue. By including parentheses in an

Table 4.4   Operator precedence.

Operator	Precedence
Exponentiation ^	1
Multiplication (*), division (/)	2
Integer division (\)	3
Modulus (MOD)	4
Addition (+), subtraction (-)	5
String concatenation (&)	6

expression, you force operators inside parentheses to be evaluated first regardless of precedence. If you write

```
A + B * C
```

the precedence rules will cause the multiplication to be performed first, and the result will not be what you want. If, however, you write the expression like this

```
(A + B) * C
```

the parentheses force the addition to be performed first, and the expression evaluates properly. You can use as many parentheses in an expression as you need, as long as they always come in pairs; each left parenthesis *must* have a matching right parenthesis. If you create an expression with an unmatched parenthesis, Visual Basic displays an error message when you try to move the editing cursor off the line. When parentheses are nested (one set inside another set), execution starts with the innermost set and proceeds outward.

You can use parentheses in an expression even when they are not needed to modify the order of operator precedence. Particularly with long, complex expressions, parentheses can help make the expression easier to read and understand.

A Need To Control

You've seen that Basic code consists of a series of statements, one to a line. When a chunk of Basic code executes, the normal execution order begins with the first statement and then executes all the statements in order, top-to-bottom. Sometimes, however, this just won't do. One of the most powerful Basic programming tools available to you is the ability to control program execution—to determine which Basic statements execute, when they execute, and how many times they execute. Before I show you how to do this, however, you need to know about logical expressions and Visual Basic's comparison and logical operators.

Logical Expressions

Computer programs often need to deal with yes/no questions. When a question or an expression has only these two possible outcomes, it is called a *logical expression*. In computer programming, the two possible outcomes are referred to as **True** and **False**. As an example, consider the question, "Is the value stored in the variable X larger than the value stored in the variable Y?" Clearly, either it is (answer = **True**) or it is not (answer = **False**). Because computers use numbers for everything, it has become standard practice to use 0 for **False** and -1 for **True**. Now let's take a look at how to construct and manipulate logical expressions.

Visual Basic has a special data type, **Boolean**, designed specifically to hold logical values. Such variables are sometimes referred to as *flags*. For example, if your program needed a way to track whether the current data has been saved to disk, you could declare a flag variable as follows:

```
Dim DataSaved As Boolean
```

When the user saves the data to disk, assign a value like this:

```
DataSaved = True
```

Likewise, when the data has been modified since the last save:

```
DataSaved = False
```

Even though Visual Basic uses numbers internally to represent the Boolean values **True** and **False**, you can (and should) use the predefined identifiers **True** and **False** in your code.

Comparison Operators

Visual Basic provides a number of operators you can use to construct logical expressions by asking questions about the data in your programs. Specifically, these *comparison operators* perform comparisons between expressions, returning a value of **True** or **False**, depending on the result of the comparison. Table 4.5 lists the comparison operators.

We can see that if X is equal to 10 and Y is equal to 5, then the expression X < Y will evaluate as **False** and X <> Y will evaluate as **True**. Assuming both Q and Z have been declared as type **Integer**, we can use the numerical value of a logical expression like this

```
Q = X < Y
Z = X <> Y
```

which would result in the variable Q having the value 0 and Z having the value -1. More often, however, logical expressions are used in program control, as you'll see soon. But

Table 4.5   Comparison operators.

Operator	Comparison	Example	Meaning
=	Equal to	X = Y	Is X equal to Y?
>	Greater than	X > Y	Is X greater than Y?
<	Less than	X < Y	Is X less than Y?
>=	Greater than or equal to	X >= Y	Is X greater than or equal to Y?
<=	Less than or equal to	X <= Y	Is X less than or equal to Y?
<>	Not equal to	X <> Y	Is X not equal to Y?

first, we need to take a look at how to combine two or more logical expressions to arrive at a single **True/False** answer.

Logical Operators

The logical operators work to combine two or more logical expressions into a single **True** or **False** answer. Why would we want to do this? Here's an example from everyday life. You receive a call inviting you to join a group of friends for dinner. If Mary is coming along, you'd like to go, because you're a bit sweet on her; otherwise, you'll pass. This is a single logical condition, and easy to understand. Now, assume for a moment that you also like Helen; if she's coming with the group, you'd also like to go. But if both Mary and Helen are coming, the situation will get a bit too complicated, so you again will pass. In this situation, we have two **True/False** questions ("Is Mary coming?" "Is Helen coming?") that you need to combine in some way before answering the **True/False** question: "Are you going?"

Similar situations arise in computer programming. For example, you need an answer to the question: "Are X and Y both greater than aero?" Here's where the logical operators come in, letting you combine and manipulate logical expressions to get the answer you need. The six logical operators (shown in Table 4.6) are each designated by a keyword. As you review this table, assume that X and Y are both logical expressions.

Now we can cast the earlier question using the comparison operators and the logical operators. The expression

```
(X > 0) And (Y > 0)
```

will evaluate as **True** if, and only if, both X and Y are greater than zero. Likewise, if you need to know whether at least one of these two variables is greater than zero, you would write:

```
(X > 0) Or (Y > 0)
```

Table 4.6 Logical operators.

Operator	Example	Evaluation
And	X And Y	True if both X and Y are True; False otherwise
Or	X Or Y	True if X or Y, or both of them, are True; False only if both X *and* Y are False
Xor (exclusive Or)	X Xor Y	True if X and Y are different (one True and the other False); False if both are True or both are False
Eqv (Equivalence)	X Eqv Y	True if X and Y are the same (both True or both False); False otherwise
Imp (Implication)	X Imp Y	False only if X is True and Y is False; True otherwise
Not	Not X	True if X is False, False if X is True

Of course, you can use the comparison and logical operators to ask questions about object properties, too. Let's say you have two Check Box controls on a form and want to determine if one or both of them are checked. Here's the expression to do so:

```
(Check1.Value = True) Or (Check2.Value = True)
```

I have been talking about comparison and logical operators for a while now, but I haven't really demonstrated how they can be useful. Don't worry; that's our next topic: how to use logical expressions in conjunction with Basic's decision and loop structures to control program execution.

Basic Code Line Wrapping

Some lines of Basic code can be rather long. While the Visual Basic editor is able to handle long lines, it can be a nuisance to have your lines of code running off the right edge of the editor window where you can't see them without scrolling. You can avoid this problem by using the line continuation character to break a long line of code into two or more lines. All you need to do is type a space followed by an underscore, then press Enter. All code on the new line will be treated by Visual Basic as part of the first line. The only restriction is that you cannot place the line continuation character in a literal string within double quotation marks.

Decision Structures

Visual Basic's *decision structures* control program execution based on whether certain logical conditions are met. In other words, program statements are either executed or not executed, based on the evaluation of logical expressions. These logical expressions typically evaluate the state of program data or user input, so the execution of the program can be controlled according to the specific needs of the application.

If...Then...Else

The **If** structure executes a block of one or more statements only if a specified logical expression evaluates as **True**. Optionally, you can include a second block of statements that is executed only if the logical expression is **False**. An **If** structure has the following form (in these examples, X stands for any logical expression):

```
If X Then
    ...
    Statements to be executed if X is TRUE go here.
    ...
Else
    ...
```

```
    Statements to be executed if X is FALSE go here.
    ...
End If
```

The **Else** keyword and the block of statements between it and the **End If** keyword are optional. If no statements are to be executed when X is **False**, you can write as follows:

```
If X Then
    ...
    Statements to be executed if X is TRUE go here.
    ...
End If
```

If your blocks of statements are only single statements, you can use the concise single-line form of the **If** structure:

```
If X then Statement1 Else Statement2
```

For more involved situations, you can include the **ElseIf** keyword to create what are effectively nested **If** structures:

```
If X Then
    ...
    Statements to be executed if X is TRUE go here.
    ...
ElseIf Y Then
    ...
    Statements to be executed if Y is TRUE go here.
    ...
Else
    ...
    Statements to be executed if both X and Y are FALSE go here.
    ...
End If
```

You can have as many **ElseIf** statements as you like. Keep in mind, however, that, at most, one of the blocks of statements in an **If** structure will be executed. In the preceding example, if both X and Y are **True**, only the statements associated with the X condition are executed. The rule is that only the statements associated with the first **True** condition are executed. Note, however, that for situations that would require more than one or two **ElseIf** clauses, you are usually better off using the **Select Case** structure, which I'll cover next.

You might have noticed the indentation style in the previous code samples; within each block, all statements are indented with respect to the statements that mark the beginning and the end of the block. This is not required by Visual Basic, but in my opinion it makes the code more readable.

Select Case

You will find that the **Select Case** structure is more appropriate than the **If** structure when you have more than a couple of conditions to be tested:

```
Select Case TestExpression
   Case Comparison1
      ...
      Block1
      ...
   Case Comparison2
      ...
      Block2
      ...
   Case Else
      ...
      ElseBlock
      ...
End Select
```

TestExpression is any numeric or string expression. **Select Case** goes through the list of **Case** statements, comparing **TestExpression** with each **Comparison** until a match is found. At that point, the statements in the associated block are executed. If no match is found, the statements associated with the optional **Case Else** statement are executed. If there is no **Case Else** and no match, none of the statements is executed. The number of **Case** statements allowed in a **Select Case** structure has no limit.

In the simplest situation, each **Comparison** is a numeric or string expression against which **TestExpression** is compared for equality. You can also use the **To** keyword to check **TestExpression** against a range of values, and the **Is** keyword in conjunction with one of the comparison operators to make a relational comparison. Thus, if you want a match when **TestExpression** is between 1 and 5, you would write

```
Case 1 To 5
```

and if you want a match when **TestExpression** is greater than 10, you would write:

```
Case Is > 10
```

You can use multiple **Comparison** expressions that are associated with one **Case** statement by separating them with commas. For example, here's a **Case** statement that would match **TestExpression** if it is equal to -1 or -2, between 8 and 12, or greater than 100:

```
Case -1, -2, 8 To 12, Is > 100
```

Loop Structures

You've seen that Basic's decision structures determine whether a block of statements is executed. In contrast, Basic's loop structures control how many times a block of statements is executed. You can accomplish "looping" in one of two ways: by executing a block of statements a fixed number of times or by executing the block repeatedly until a specified condition is met.

For...Next

In its most common use, the **For...Next** loop executes a block of statements a fixed number of times:

```
For Counter = Start To Stop
   ...
   statement block
   ...
Next Counter
```

Counter is a numeric variable that can be any type, although you would generally use type **Integer** unless you have a specific reason to use another type. **Start** and **Stop** are the values that specify the start and stop of the loop; they can be any numeric expression. A **For...Next** loop begins by setting **Counter** equal to **Start**. It then follows these steps:

1. **Counter** is compared with **Stop**. If **Counter** is greater than **Stop**, execution passes to the first statement after the **For...Next** loop.

2. The statements in the loop are executed.

3. **Counter** is incremented by 1.

4. Return to Step 1.

Note that if **Stop** is equal to **Start**, the loop executes only once; if **Stop** is less than **Start**, it does not execute at all.

TIP   **Never Change The Counter Variable**

Basic will not prevent you from changing the value of the **Counter** variable inside the loop. This practice should be avoided, however. It can lead to pesky program bugs and code that is difficult to understand.

Here's an example of a **For...Next** loop that will execute the number of times specified by the variable X.

```
For Count = 1 to X
   ...
Next X
```

You are not limited to starting the loop at 1, of course. You can also use the **Step** keyword to specify that the **Counter** variable be incremented by a value other than 1 with each cycle of the loop. Here's a loop that will execute four times, with the **Counter** variable taking the values 4, 7, 10, and 13:

```
For I = 4 To 13 Step 3
   ...
Next I
```

You can use negative **Step** values to count backward, which, of course, requires that the **Stop** value be smaller than **Start**. You can also use fractional values as long as the **Counter** variable is a floating point type. The following loop will count backward from 4 to 1 by increments of 0.25 (4, 3.75, 3.5, ... , 1.25, 1):

```
For I = 4 To 1 Step -0.25
   ...
Next I
```

If you want to terminate a loop early—that is, before the **Counter** variable exceeds **Stop**—you can use the **Exit For** statement. This is an extremely useful statement, because it lets you specify a variety of conditions that will terminate the loop in addition to the loop's own count programming. Here's a loop that will execute 10 times or until the variable X is less than 0:

```
For I = 1 to 10
   ...
   If X < 0 Then Exit For
   ...
Next I
```

Strictly speaking, you do not have to include the name of the **Counter** variable in the **Next** statement. Basic will automatically associate each **Next** statement with the immediately preceding **For** statement. I suggest, however, that you develop the habit of always including the **Counter** variable name with **Next**, to improve readability of the code.

Do...Loop

The **Do...Loop** structure is the most flexible of Basic's loops. It allows the loop to execute until a specified condition is either **True** or **False**, and it allows the condition to be evaluated either at the start or the end of the loop. In its simplest form, a **Do...Loop** executes as long as a condition is **True**:

```
Do While Condition
   ...
   statement block
   ...
Loop
```

Condition is any logical expression. When execution first reaches the **Do** statement, **Condition** is evaluated. If it is **False**, execution passes to the statement following the **Loop** statement. If it is **True**, the block of statements is executed, execution returns to the **Do** statement, and **Condition** is evaluated again. You can also replace the **While** with the **Until** keyword to continue execution for as long as **Condition** is **False**, as shown here:

```
Do Until Condition
   ...
   statement block
   ...
Loop
```

Both of the previous examples perform the comparison at the start of the loop, which means it is possible for the statement block *not* to be executed—even once. For example, if **Condition** is **False** to begin with, a **Do While Condition...Loop** will not execute even once. If you want to be sure the loop executes at least once, you can place the **Condition** at the end of the loop. As before, you can use either the **While** or the **Until** keyword:

```
Do
   ...
   statement block
   ...
Loop While Condition

Do
   ...
   statement block
   ...
Loop Until Condition
```

To terminate the loop early, use **Exit Do**. Here's a loop that will execute until Y is greater than zero or X is less than zero:

```
Do
   ...
   If X < 0 Then Exit Do
   ...
Loop Until Y > 0
```

You may be thinking that we could have obtained the same result by writing the loop like this:

```
Do
    ...
Loop Unt/il Y > 0 Or X < 0
```

You are correct, but a subtle difference exists between these two loops. In the first example, the statements between the **If X < 0** statement and the **Loop** statement are not executed during the last loop iteration, when X becomes less than zero. In the second example, all of the statements in the loop are executed during the last execution.

While...Wend

The **While...Wend** loop executes a block of statements as long as a specified **Condition** is **True**, but it is not nearly as flexible as **Do...Loop**. In fact, anything that **While...Wend** can do, **Do...Loop** can also accomplish. You may find **While...Wend** in older Basic programs, simply because earlier versions of Basic did not support **Do...Loop**.

Here's the way to write a **While...Wend** loop:

```
While Condition
    ...
    statement block
    ...
Wend
```

You can write all of your Basic programs without ever needing a **While...Wend** loop. Take a look at the following variant of **Do...Loop**, which does exactly the same thing as a **While...Wend** loop:

```
Do While Condition
    ...
    statement block
    ...
Loop
```

Because of its added flexibility, I recommend that you use **Do...Loop** rather than the **While...Wend** structure found in older programs.

Nested And Infinite Loops

A *nested loop* is a loop contained within another loop. There is no limit to nesting of loops in Visual Basic, although nesting beyond four or five levels is rarely necessary or even advisable. If your program seems to need such deep nesting, you should probably reexamine its structure to see if you can accomplish the same task more simply. The only restriction on nesting loops is that each inner loop must be enclosed entirely within the outer loop. The following example is illegal, because the **For...Next** loop is not contained entirely within the **Do...Loop** loop:

```
Do While X > 0
   For I = 1 to 10
      . . .
Loop
   Next I
```

The next example, however, is okay:

```
Do While X > 0
   For I = 1 to 10
      . . .
   Next I
Loop
```

An *infinite loop* is one that executes forever (or until you halt the program). Clearly, if a loop's terminating condition is never met, it will loop indefinitely. This situation can arise from faulty program logic or from unexpected user input. Keep a sharp eye out for this sort of problem. If your program seems to "hang" during execution, you might want to examine your loops.

With...End With

The **With...End With** statement provides a convenient shorthand when you want to access more than one property or method of an object. The syntax is:

```
With object
   .Property1 = ...
   .Property2 = ...
   .Method1
End With
```

The preceding code has the same effect as the following:

```
   object.Property1 = ...
   object.Property2 = ...
   object.Method1
```

When used simply as a shorthand, the **With...End With** statement is at best a minor convenience. It is more useful when used in procedures that take an object as a parameter. Here, for example, is a procedure that will change several font-related properties of any object that is passed to it:

```
Public Sub ChangeFont(ob As Object)

With ob
   .Font.Bold = True
```

```
    .Font.Italic = True
    .ForeColor = RGB(255, 0, 0)
End With

End Sub
```

But Wait, There's More

If you've managed to read this entire chapter—and I suggest that you do read it closely—you should have a good introduction to the foundations of the Basic programming language. Yes, of course, Basic continues far beyond this point. Does that mean this chapter is going to stretch on for another 40 pages? Not to worry. I suspect that your patience is wearing thin and you are itching to try some of the things you have learned. The remaining details of Basic will be covered as individual topics arise. In the next chapter, we'll put together a Visual Basic application that demonstrates how Basic code, objects, and properties combine to create an application.

Chapter 5

Visual Design + Basic Code = Visual Basic

By adding a few more fundamentals to what you have learned, you'll be well on your way to becoming captain of the good ship Visual Basic.

W e've covered a lot of ground in the first four chapters, and I hope you're beginning to get your Visual Basic sea legs. If I've been doing my job well, you're starting to develop at least a hazy picture of how the various parts of Visual Basic—objects, properties, and code—work together to form a fully functioning application program. To bring this picture into sharper focus, we're going to tackle a somewhat more ambitious project in this chapter: an on-screen calculator. As you work through this project, you will see how everything I've crammed into your head in the past four chapters comes together. Along the way, I'll present a few more useful Visual Basic tools and techniques.

Planning The Calculator

The first step in planning a calculator is deciding what type of logic it will use. Calculator logic comes in two types: algebraic (the more common) and reverse Polish notation (RPN). With an algebraic calculator, you perform calculations electronically in the same way you would on paper. For example, to add 4 to 7 on paper, you would write:

4 + 7 = 11

Using an algebraic calculator for this task, you would press 4, press +, press 7, and press =, and the answer would be displayed. In contrast, to perform this calculation using an RPN calculator, you would press 4, press Enter, press 7, then press +. If you are not accustomed to RPN calculators, this probably seems weird to you. It makes a lot of sense, however, and is actually quite similar to internal computer logic. Let's take a look at how it works.

RPN And Stacks

RPN is based on the concept of a *stack*, which is a form of data storage using the "last in, first out" method. In other words, when you retrieve a data item from the stack, you'll get the item that was most recently placed on the stack. If you retrieve another item, you'll get the one before that, and so on. The most common analogy to a data stack is the way cafeteria plates are often stacked in a spring-loaded tube. As you retrieve plates, they come out in the reverse order in which they were inserted. Here's what happens, then, when you add 4 and 7 on an RPN calculator:

- *Press 4*—Puts 4 in the display.

- *Press Enter*—Completes entry of the first number.

- *Press 7*—Moves the first entry (4) to the top of the stack and puts 7 in the display.

- *Press +*—Adds the number in the display (7) to the number at the top of the stack (4), displays the result, and removes the top number (4) from the stack.

For short calculations, the RPN method really has no advantage over the algebraic method. It's the longer calculations where it comes into its own. Let's say you want to add 4 to 7, multiply the result by 2.5, then square that result. Table 5.1 shows how you would enter this calculation, and how it would show in the display.

Table 5.1   The steps in an RPN calculation.

Press	Display Reads
4	4
Enter	4
7	7
+	11
2.5	2.5
x	27.5
2	2
Y^x	756.25

On an algebraic calculator, not only would this equation require a lot more keystrokes, but the order of execution would be more difficult to follow. In any case, I'm not here to sell you on the advantages of an RPN calculator, but we will be using RPN logic for our project. If you want a project to try on your own, work on creating an algebraic calculator. You'll quickly see which type of calculator is easier to program.

Before we get started on the calculator, let's take a closer look at Visual Basic's **Variant** data type, as we will be using it in the project.

The Variant Data Type

Most of the data types we examined in the previous chapters have been rather specific—that is, they could hold either string or numeric data, and the numeric types could hold either integer or floating point values. The **Variant** type is a different animal altogether. A type **Variant** variable can hold just about any kind of data—string, integer, or floating point. Even more amazing (at least to experienced programmers who are used to the standard fixed data types), the data in a type **Variant** is automatically treated in the appropriate way.

What does this mean? For the most part, it means that the data is treated as either a string or a number, depending on how you are using the variable. Here's an example. Suppose that **MyVariant** is a type **Variant**, and you assign data to it as follows:

```
MyVariant = 1234
```

If you add this variable to a numeric variable, the data will then be treated as a number. Thus, after the following statements execute (assuming **X** and **Y** are type **Integer**)

```
X = 111
Y = X + MyVariant
```

the variable **Y** will contain the numeric value 1345. Now, if **S** is a type **String** variable, then after executing the statement

```
S = "abc" & X & "def"
```

the variable **S** will contain the string "abc1234def." Throughout the book, you will see that the **Variant** type can be very useful when your program is working with numeric data that must also be treated as a string—formatting data for display in a calculator, for example. A type **Variant** can also be used to hold an object reference, as we will see in Chapter 7, but this is not relevant to the current project.

To create a variable or an array of type **Variant**, you can use the **Variant** keyword in your **Dim** statement, or you can simply omit the **As** part of the **Dim** statement, because **Variant** is Visual Basic's default data type. The following two statements are equivalent:

```
Dim X As Variant
Dim X
```

Special Values In A Variant

In addition to numbers and strings, a type **Variant** variable can hold three special values: **Empty**, **Null**, and **Error**. They are explained briefly here and then in more detail as the need arises.

A type **Variant** contains the value **Empty** after it has been declared, but not yet assigned a value. This is unlike other variable types that are automatically initialized to 0 (numeric variables) or a zero-length string (string variables). Thus, after the code

```
Dim v As Variant, i As Integer
```

the variable **i** is equal to 0, while the variable **v** contains **Empty**. If you display the contents of a **Variant** that contains **Empty**, it displays as a dash. To determine if a **Variant** contains **Empty**, use the **IsEmpty** function (one of Visual Basic's built-in functions):

```
If IsEmpty(v) Then
...
' Code to be executed if v contains Empty goes here.
...
End If
```

The special value **Null** can be assigned to a type **Variant** variable. **Null** is usually used to indicate invalid or missing data and most frequently is seen in database applications. You can use the **Null** keyword both to assign the value to a variable and also to test for the **Null** value:

```
v = Null
...
If v = Null Then
    Print "Data not valid"
Else
    Print v
End If
```

When you display the contents of a variable that contains **Null**, it displays the string "Null".

The third special value that can be stored in the type **Variant** is **Error**. As you might expect, this value is used when writing code that deals with errors in the program. I'll cover it in detail in Chapter 25.

Trying Out Code

You can use Visual Basic's **Debug.Print** method as a quick way to try out your Basic code. Create a new project, double-click on the form to bring up the **Form_Click** event procedure, and place the code you want to test in the procedure. Press Ctrl+G to display Visual Basic's Debug window. (The Debug window is displayed every time you run a program inside the Visual Basic development environment and is hidden when the program ends. To display the Debug window when a program is not running, as instructed here, simply press Ctrl+G.)

To check your code, enter the **Debug.Print** statement and then enter one or more variable names after the statement, separated by commas. Each **Debug.Print** statement displays on a new line. For example, the statements

```
Debug.Print X, Y
Debug.Print Z
```

will display the values of variables **X** and **Y** on one line and the value of variable **Z** on the next line.

Implementing The Stack

Now let's get back to implementing the stack for the RPN calculator. Our stack will have two parts: a **Variant** array where the stack data is kept; and an **Integer** variable to serve as the *stack pointer*, indicating the current top of the stack. Let's see how this works.

Initially, the stack array is empty, and the stack pointer is pointing at element 0. Adding something to the stack requires that we increment the stack pointer so it points at element 1; then we store the data in that element. If we want to store a second item, we again increment the stack pointer by a value of 1, storing the data item in the array element that is now indicated, as shown in Figure 5.1.

Element 0 of the array will never be used in this method, but that's a small price to pay. If you want to be totally stingy about memory usage, you could use element 0 to store the stack pointer—but we won't use that approach in the project.

Retrieving data from the stack follows the opposite procedure. To read the item on the top of the stack without removing it, simply retrieve the array element at which the stack pointer points. To remove an item from the stack, you must decrement the stack pointer by 1. Figure 5.2 illustrates the removal of two data items from a stack.

Data items removed from the stack are not actually erased; they remain in the array. They are not part of the stack, however, because the stack pointer is now pointing "below" them. If new items are added to the stack, the old ones will be overwritten.

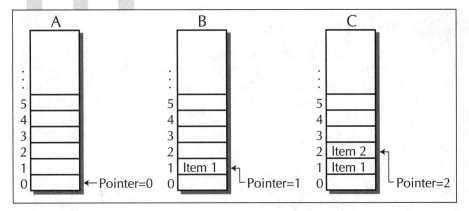

Figure 5.1   *Part A shows an empty stack, Part B shows the stack after adding one item, and Part C shows the stack after adding a second item.*

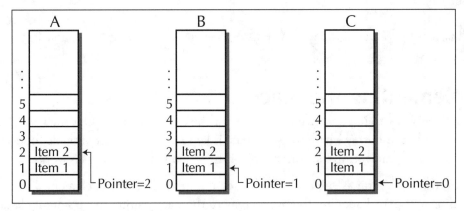

Figure 5.2   *Part A shows a stack containing two data items; Parts B and C show the stack after removing one and then both items, respectively.*

Creating The Calculator

We'll begin by creating a basic calculator that can add, subtract, multiply, and divide. Later in the chapter, we'll add several enhancements, but I think it's a good idea to start simply. In fact, this is a good approach to use for all of your Visual Basic projects. Make sure the basics of your project are working first, and then add features. By working this way, you can deal with problems one at a time as they arise, rather than face a huge mess of difficulties all at once.

Declaring Public Variables And Constants

Create a new Standard EXE project. Double-click on the blank form to open the Code Editing window. At the top of the editing window, open the Object list (the one on the left) and select (General). If necessary, open the Proc list (the one on the right) and select Declarations. We'll start by entering the required public variable and constant declarations into the form. The term *public* means that these data items will be available throughout all parts of the program (the term *global* is sometimes used in place of *public*). I will explain this in detail later in the chapter when I discuss variable scope. For now, enter the code shown in Listing 5.1. **Option Explicit** should appear by default, but if you have changed any of the default settings and **Option Explicit** doesn't appear, make sure to enter this statement at the top of the code window.

Listing 5.1 Variable and constant declarations in the declarations section of the Calculator form.

```
Option Explicit

' The size of the stack.
Const STACKSIZE = 10

' The format strings for formatting
' numbers in the display.
Const DISPLAY_FORMAT1 = "###,###,###,###.0000000000"
Const DISPLAY_FORMAT2 = "#.#######E+000"

' The RPN stack; defaults to type Variant.
Dim Stack(STACKSIZE)

' Keeps track of current stack location.
Dim StackPointer As Integer

' Flag indicating whether we are starting
' a new entry.
Dim NewEntry As Boolean

' Flag indicating whether the display contains
' valid data.
Dim DisplayHasData As Boolean
```

You may be able to figure out what the various statements do just by reading the comments. But in case it isn't evident, I will explain them briefly. The code includes three constants: **STACKSIZE** specifies the number of elements that the stack can hold (I doubt the program will ever need anywhere near 10 elements, but let's play it safe); the two **DISPLAY_FORMAT** constants are used in formatting numbers for display by the calculator. I will discuss them in detail later in the chapter.

The first **Dim** statement declares the array used to hold the stack. Note that the size of the array is specified by the **STACKSIZE** constant that we declared earlier. The other

Dim statements declare a type **Integer** variable to serve as the stack pointer, and a type **Boolean** variable that serves as a flag indicating whether or not we are starting a new number entry on the calculator. The term *flag* is programmer-speak for a **Boolean** variable—one that is either **True** or **False**, just as a flag can be up or down. A second flag variable indicates whether the display contains valid data. We will see how these flags are used soon.

Designing The Form

After the public variables and constants have been entered, we can start designing the form. Click on the View Object button in the Project Explorer window to display the still-blank form. Size the form so that it is about 50 percent wider than it is tall. Set the form properties as follows:

Caption: Calculator

Name: frmCalculator

BorderStyle: 1 — Fixed Single

MinButton: True

The **BorderStyle** property setting creates a calculator form that the user cannot resize, but the **MinButton** property setting allows users to minimize the calculator when it is not in use.

The first control we'll place is a Text Box that will serve as the calculator's display. Stretch it across the width of the form, near the top. Then set its properties as follows:

Name: txtDisplay

Alignment: 1 — Right Justify

Locked: True

MultiLine: True

A right-justified **Alignment** setting causes the text in the Text Box to be aligned at the right edge of the box. Setting the **Locked** property to **True** prevents the user from editing the Text Box while the program is running. The **MultiLine** property has to be set to **True** for the **Alignment** property of Right Justify to work properly. You also need to set the **Font** property of the Text Box, as well as its **ForeColor** and **BackColor** properties. These property settings are a matter of personal preference, so feel free to experiment. I used MS Sans Serif in 30-point size for the font, and I selected a black background with bright green text to simulate the fluorescent display of some hand-held calculators.

Once you have set the font and colors, set the Text Box's **Text** property to a blank string. You'll find it helpful to leave the default text displayed while you are choosing your color schemes—that way, you can see the effect of your various attempts. You may also need to increase the height of the Text Box to accommodate the larger font setting.

Creating The Control Array Of Number Buttons

The next step in creating the calculator's interface is to place the 10 Command Buttons for entering the digits 0 through 9. We will use a new technique called a *control array*. Once you've seen how this works, I think you'll agree that it is a powerful tool.

When you place individual controls on a form, each one has its own name and its own event procedures. In contrast, a control array contains two or more controls of the same type with the same name and the same event procedures. Each control in an array still has its own set of properties, however. In the event procedure, Visual Basic provides an **Index** argument that specifies which of the controls in the array received the event. As a result, you can write a single event procedure that handles events to two or more controls.

This concept will be easier to understand if you try it. Start by placing a Command Button on the form in the position where you want the "0" button (in the lower-left corner, if you're following my design). Change the **Name** property of this button to **cmdNumbers**. With the new Command Button selected, press Ctrl+C to copy the control to the Clipboard, then press Ctrl+V to paste it on the form. The form—and not a control—must be selected for you to use the Paste command. Visual Basic displays a dialog box asking if you want to create a control array. Select Yes. The duplicate Command Button will be inserted in the top-left corner of the form. Drag it to the location where you want the "1" button to appear.

Before adding the remaining buttons, let's briefly look at the properties of the Command Button that was just added. Its name is **cmdNumbers**, the same as the original button that you copied. Its **Index** property, however, is 1. If you select the original Command Button, you'll see that its **Index** property is 0. This is how Visual Basic distinguishes between controls in a control array.

Now you can finish inserting the eight remaining number buttons. For each one, simply press Ctrl+V to paste another copy of the button from the Clipboard, and drag it to the desired location. You should do this in numerical order, beginning with the "2" button. You'll soon see the reason for this.

Once all 10 number buttons have been added to the form, go through and select each one, changing its **Caption** property to the proper number—that is, the same as its **Index** property. When you're finished, your form will look something like Figure 5.3.

Don't forget to save your project. I used the name *Calculator* for both the form and the project.

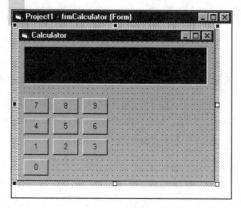

Figure 5.3   *The Calculator form after adding the number buttons and the Text Box for display.*

Creating The Array Of Operator Buttons

The calculator also needs four buttons for the basic arithmetic operations: addition, subtraction, multiplication, and division. We will use a control array for these buttons as well. Place a new Command Button on the form, and change its **Name** property to **cmdOperators**. Then use the copy and paste techniques from the previous section to create a control array of four buttons. Change the buttons' **Caption** properties, as shown in Table 5.2.

Changing The Button Font

Visual Basic's default font is a bit too small for the Command Button captions. Rather than changing the **Font** property of each button individually—a tedious task—you can change a property for multiple controls at one time. First, select all the controls. The controls do not have to be the same type (although, in this case, they will all be Command Buttons). You can either use the Shift+Click method or select the Pointer tool and use the mouse to drag an outline (marquee) around the desired controls. When you release the mouse button, all controls that are completely within the rectangle will be selected. To deselect an individual control while leaving the others selected, press Shift and click on it.

Table 5.2   *Caption property settings for the array of Command Buttons.*

Button Index	Caption
0	+
1	-
2	*
3	/

When you select multiple controls, the Properties window displays only those properties that all of the controls have in common. For example, if you selected a Text Box and a Command Button, you would not see the **Text** property displayed in the Properties window—only the Text Box control has this property. **BackColor** and **Font** (among others) are two properties these two control types have in common, so these properties would display in the Properties window. When you make a change to a common property, the change is reflected in all selected controls.

Now use this technique to change the **Font** property for all the Command Buttons you have placed on the form. Experiment to find a font that looks good to you. I used MS Sans Serif, 18 point.

Adding The Other Calculator Buttons

Any calculator will need a few more buttons: Clear to erase the display, Backspace to delete the last number entered, a Decimal button, and a +/- button to change the sign of the number in the display. Don't forget the Enter button for placing values on the stack. Go ahead and add these five buttons, making the Enter button bigger than all the rest. Note that these are individual buttons, *not* a control array. Set the properties as shown in Table 5.3.

You'll probably want to change the **Font** property for these new buttons also. When you are finished, your form will look more or less like Figure 5.4.

The Number Button Event Procedures

The visual interface is complete—at least for now. We can begin writing the code that will give the calculator its "smarts." A calculator's most basic task is to display numbers as the user clicks on the buttons, so we'll start with that. Double-click on one of the number buttons on the form to display the skeleton of the **Click** event procedure. The first line looks like this:

```
Private Sub cmdNumbers_Click(Index As Integer)
```

Table 5.3   Name property settings for the additional Command Buttons.

Button Caption	Name Property
Enter	cmdEnter
+/-	cmdPlusMinus
Clear	cmdClear
BS	cmdBackspace
.	cmdDecimal

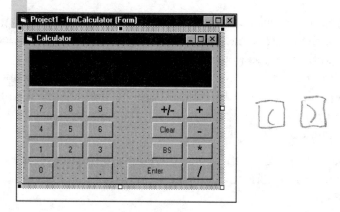

Figure 5.4   *The Calculator form after adding the remaining buttons.*

As the code in the parentheses indicates, when this procedure is called in response to a button click, Visual Basic passes an argument named **Index** to the event procedure. Because the 10 number buttons are all part of a control array, this one **Click** event procedure is called when *any* one of them is clicked on. The value of **Index** (which is the same as the value stored in each button's **Index** property) specifies which of the buttons was selected. Because of the way we created the control array, each button's **Index** property is the same as the number it represents, making programming a bit easier.

What needs to happen when the user clicks on one of the number buttons? Let's begin by taking a look at what's going on. The calculator could be in one of two states. In one state, the user has already entered part of a number, and the just-clicked number needs to be tacked onto the end of what is already in the display. In the other state, the user has completed making the previous entry or calculation, and the just-clicked number represents the start of a new entry. In this latter case, the number in the display should be put on the stack and erased from the display, then the number that was clicked displayed. We will use the Boolean variable **NewEntry**, which we declared in the General section as a flag for the calculator's condition. This flag will be set to **False** if the user is continuing an existing entry; it will be set to **True** if the user is starting a new entry. Therefore, the procedure needs to perform two tasks:

- If **NewEntry** is **True**, erase the display, display the clicked number, and set **NewEntry** to **False**.

- If **NewEntry** is **False**, add the clicked number to the end of the number already in the display.

If **NewEntry** is **True**, do we always want to put the existing number in the display on the stack? Not necessarily. Suppose the user started entering a number then cleared it with the

Clear button (to be programmed soon). In that case, there is no reason to put the 0 in the display on the stack when the new entry is started. The same is true if the calculator has just been started. Thus, we will use the **DisplayHasData** flag to determine whether the existing number in the display should be placed on the stack.

The code for this procedure is shown in Listing 5.2. You can see that it's quite simple. You should also be able to see why I insisted that you match each button's **Index** property with its caption, which results in the **Index** argument to the event procedure holding the button's actual value. In this case, the program needs only to use the concatenation operator to tack **Index** onto the end of the calculator's display.

Listing 5.2   *The Click event procedure for the array of number buttons.*

```
Private Sub cmdNumbers_Click(Index As Integer)

' If we're starting a new entry, clear the text box.
' If current display has valid data put it
' on the stack.

If NewEntry Then
    NewEntry = False
    If DisplayHasData Then
        StackPointer = StackPointer + 1
        Stack(StackPointer) = txtDisplay.Text
    End If
    txtDisplay.Text = ""
End If

' Put the new digit at the end of the text.
txtDisplay.Text = txtDisplay.Text & Index

End Sub
```

You can test the project at this point by pressing F5. The calculator will display, and you can click on the number buttons to enter numbers in the display. Nothing else works yet, however, so clearly we have some more code to write.

Before we continue, notice how I wrote the condition for the **If** statement in this code. We needed to see if the variable **NewEntry** was **True**. Rather than writing

```
If NewEntry = True Then
```

I wrote the following:

```
If NewEntry Then
```

Do you see why these two statements are equivalent? If **NewEntry** is **True**, then the expression **NewEntry = True** evaluates to **True**. Thus, the two expressions are equivalent.

The Display Procedure

Before moving on to the other button event procedures, we are going to create a procedure that will display results in the calculator's display. This will be a *general* procedure, which is different from an *event* procedure. Let's take time out from our calculator project to learn about general procedures, because they are an essential part of Visual Basic programming.

General Basic Procedures

As you have learned, an event procedure is a separate, self-contained chunk of code that is automatically executed whenever the associated event occurs. A general procedure is similar, except that it is not linked to an event. Rather, a general procedure (or simply *procedure*, as I'll refer to it) is executed when code elsewhere in the program calls it. The use of procedures (a technique sometimes referred to as *structured programming*) is a central part of Visual Basic programming as well as all other programming languages. Procedures emphasize breaking a program into a number of partially independent tasks, with the code for each task being placed in its own procedure. Each time the program needs the task performed, it calls the procedure. This approach offers a number of significant advantages:

- The program is easier to write, because the entire project is broken down into a number of smaller, more easily managed tasks.

- The program is easier to debug, because you can localize a problem to a specific section of code.

- The program is easier to maintain, because modifications made in one part of the program are less likely to have unwanted side effects in other parts of the program.

Code that is inside a procedure (including event procedures) is called *procedure level code*. Code that is outside a procedure is called *module level code*. With a few exceptions, you can put any Basic statement in a procedure; the major exception is that you cannot define one procedure within another. There's no limit to the amount of code you can put in a procedure, but it is good programming practice to keep procedures to a small or moderate size by splitting complex tasks into several smaller tasks. What's a moderate size? There's no strict definition, but in my experience it's rare to find a procedure beyond 25 or 30 lines of code that could not be profitably broken into two or more smaller procedures.

There are two types of procedures: A *function* returns a value to the calling program, whereas a *sub procedure* does not. Otherwise, the two types are identical. An important feature of procedures is the ability to define *procedure arguments*, which can be thought of as specialized variables for passing information to the procedure when it is called. We will see how to create and use a sub procedure here. Functions, which I'll cover later, aren't much different.

Creating A Procedure

Visual Basic automates much of the work of creating a procedure. Let's walk through the steps of creating the **DisplayResult** procedure for the Calculator project.

1. Load the Calculator project, then open the Code Editing window (click on the View Code button in the Project Explorer window).

2. Select Add Procedure from the Tools menu. Visual Basic displays the Add Procedure dialog box, shown in Figure 5.5.

3. Enter "DisplayResult" in the Name box. Procedure names follow the same rules as variable names—of course, the name should describe what the procedure does.

4. Be sure that the Sub option is selected in the Type section of the dialog box.

5. Click on OK.

Visual Basic opens a new editing window with the skeleton of the procedure entered in it, as shown here.

```
Public Sub DisplayResult( )

End Sub
```

Public Vs. Private

There are two possibilities when declaring a procedure. The **Public** and **Private** keywords determine whether a procedure can be called only by code in its own module (**Private**) or can be called from other modules in the application (**Public**). Procedures are **Public** by default, but Visual Basic sticks the keyword on them anyway. Use of these keywords is related to the concept of *scope*, which is discussed later in this chapter.

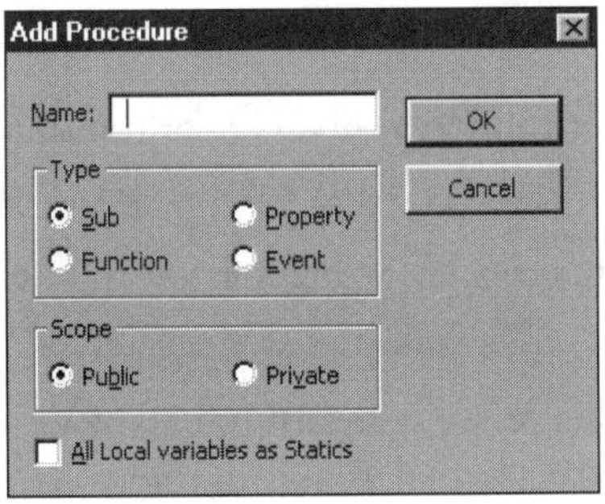

Figure 5.5   *The Add Procedure dialog box.*

The next step is to specify the procedure arguments. An *argument* is the way a program passes information to a procedure. A procedure can have no arguments, or as many arguments as are needed. Arguments can be any Basic data type. We will need only one for this procedure: a numeric argument that passes the number to be displayed by the calculator. Each procedure argument has a name and a type, similar to a **Dim** statement. Edit the first line of the procedure as follows:

```
Public Sub DisplayResult(X As Double)
```

We are specifying that the procedure **DisplayResult** takes one type **Double** argument named **X**. If we needed to specify additional arguments, they would be separated by commas.

The procedure's main job is to display a numeric value with proper formatting. How do we want the number to be displayed? On most hand-held calculators, during entry the number is displayed exactly as it is entered. We've seen how this is done in the event procedure for the number buttons. Once the Enter key is pressed, however, the number is displayed with full accuracy. For example, if you press 2.5 (but not Enter), the display reads "2.5". Once you press Enter, it reads "2.500000000". This enables the user to tell whether he or she is in the middle of an entry or whether the display is showing a calculated or entered number.

We also have to deal with very large and very small numbers. Our calculator display will show approximately 16 digits, with the exact capacity depending on the size of the display Text Box and the font. For very large and very small numbers, however, the use of scientific notation greatly improves readability. This method expresses numbers as a value between 1 and 10, multiplied by 10 raised to a specified power. For example, a small number, such as 120, would be expressed as 1.2 multiplied by 10^2 (or, in computer notation, 1.2E + 002). A large number, such as 1,234,756,000,000,000,000,000, would be expressed as 1.234756E + 021.

What we'll do, then, is test the number that is to be displayed, formatting it according to its value:

- If it's 0, simply display 0.00.

- If it's not too big (greater than 999,999,999) or too small (less than 0.000000001), we will display 10 decimal places, with commas separating the thousands.

- If it's outside these boundaries, we will display it in scientific notation, using six decimal places.

To implement this display scheme, we will turn to two of Visual Basic's built-in functions. These functions are identical to user-defined functions, except they are part of Visual

Basic rather than being written by the programmer. Well over 100 built-in functions are available to perform a variety of commonly needed tasks, such as text handling, trigonometric calculations, date and time manipulation, user input, and error handling. I can't cover all of these functions, but I will explain quite a few as we encounter them. You can view a complete function listing in Visual Basic's online Help: Select Contents from the Help menu, then select Visual Basic Documentation | Reference | Functions to view an alphabetical listing.

The first function we will use is **Abs**, which returns the absolute value of its argument. This means that negative numbers are converted to positive, and positive numbers are not changed. Thus, **Abs(8)** returns 8, and **Abs(-10)** returns 10.

The other function we'll be using is **Format**, which takes two arguments: a number and a format specifier. The *format specifier* is a string containing special characters that indicate how the number is to be formatted for display. The return value is a string containing the formatted number. For full details on how to construct format specifiers, refer to Visual Basic's Help system. For our purposes, we simply need to know the following:

- A # character specifies a digit position that will be used if needed and omitted if not needed.

- A 0 character specifies a digit position that will be displayed whether needed or not, being filled with a 0 as required.

- The E+ characters specify scientific notation.

Now you can see the purpose of the two constants that we declared in the declarations section of the form module. The first one

```
Const DISPLAY_FORMAT1 = "###,###,###,###.0000000000"
```

will format a number with up to 12 digits to the left of the decimal point, with thousands separators, and 10 digits to the right of the decimal point padded with 0s if needed. For example, the number 4098.998 would be formatted as 4,098.9980000000. We will use this format specifier for numbers that are not too big or too small, falling within the range we specified earlier. The second format specifier

```
Const DISPLAY_FORMAT2 = "#.######E+000"
```

will format a number in scientific notation, with up to six decimal places and a three-digit exponent.

Now we have the tools needed to create the **DisplayResult** procedure. Finish editing the procedure, as shown in Listing 5.3.

Listing 5.3 The DisplayResult procedure.

```
Public Sub DisplayResult(X As Double)

' Display the value properly formatted.

If X = 0 Then
    txtDisplay.Text = "0.00"
ElseIf (Abs(X) < 999999999 And Abs(X) > 0.000000001) Then
    txtDisplay.Text = Format(X, DISPLAY_FORMAT1)
Else
    txtDisplay.Text = Format(X, DISPLAY_FORMAT2)
End If

NewEntry = True

End Sub
```

Visual Basic Helps You Out

I'm sure you have noticed that Visual Basic is keeping an eye on you as you enter code. Whenever you complete a line of code and move the cursor away, Visual Basic reviews the line for certain syntax errors. For example, if the line contains an unmatched parenthesis, Visual Basic will catch it. When an error is detected, Visual Basic pops up a dialog box with a description of the error, highlights the line of code, and positions the cursor where it thinks the error might be. You can either close the dialog box and fix the error or wait until you run the program. Certain kinds of syntax errors are caught only when the program runs (in the Visual Basic development environment—not as a standalone). Again, Visual Basic highlights the line with the error and displays a dialog box. After fixing the error, press F5 to restart the program.

Some programmers find the automatic syntax checking to be annoying. To turn it off, select Options from the Tools menu to display the Options dialog box. Click on the Editor tab, and turn off the Auto Syntax Check option. This way, errors will be caught only when the program runs.

Programming The Enter Button

Our next task is to write the event procedure for the Enter button. You'll see that it is relatively simple, because we already put much of the needed functionality in the **DisplayResult** procedure. All that's required is to set the **NewEntry** and **DisplayHasData** flags to **True** and then call **DisplayResult**. Double-click on the Enter button to display its **Click** event procedure, then add the code shown in Listing 5.4.

*Listing 5.4   **The Enter button's Click event procedure.***

```
Private Sub cmdEnter_Click()

' Set NewEntry to True as we are finished
' with this entry.
'
' Set DisplayHasData to True.
'
' Call DisplayResults to put the number
' in the display in proper format.

NewEntry = True
DisplayHasData = True
DisplayResult (txtDisplay.Text)

End Sub
```

Programming The +/-, Clear, Decimal, And Backspace Buttons

The remaining buttons are also fairly easy to program. Remember, double-click on the button to display its **Click** event procedure. You can also select the control and the event from the lists that are displayed at the top of the Code Editing window.

The +/- button changes the sign of the displayed number from negative to positive, or from positive to negative. First, we use the **Left** function to check if the number already begins with a minus sign. To do this, pass this function a string and a number (*n*), and it returns the leftmost *n* characters of the string. In this case, we obtain the first character of the displayed text. If it is not "-", then we know the number is positive and can make it negative by adding a leading "-". If the number is negative, we can use the **Len** and **Right** functions to remove the leading "-" and make the number positive. **Len** is passed a string and returns its length (the number of characters). **Right** works just like **Left**, but returns the rightmost *n* characters of the string. Thus, the expression

```
Right(txtDisplay.Text, Len(txtDisplay.Text) - 1)
```

has the effect of trimming the first character off the display. The full code for this function is presented in Listing 5.5.

*Listing 5.5   **The +/- button Click event procedure.***

```
Private Sub cmdPlusMinus_Click()

' Change the sign of the displayed value.

If (Left(txtDisplay, 1) <> "-") Then
```

```
        txtDisplay.Text = "-" & txtDisplay
    Else
        txtDisplay.Text = Right(txtDisplay.Text, _
            Len(txtDisplay.Text) - 1)
    End If

End Sub
```

The Clear button is an easy one. All we need to do is set the **Text** property of the **txtDisplay** Text Box to an empty string, set the **NewEntry** flag, and clear the **DisplayHasData** flag. The procedure code is given in Listing 5.6.

Listing 5.6   *The Clear button Click event procedure.*

```
Private Sub cmdClear_Click()

' Clear the display to 0, clear valid data
' flag, and set new entry flag.

txtDisplay.Text = "0.00"
NewEntry = True
DisplayHasData = False

End Sub
```

The Backspace button has the task of removing the rightmost character from the display. If the **NewEntry** flag is set, we do nothing—we don't want to erase part of an entered or calculated number. Otherwise, we check to see that the display is not empty. If it isn't, we use the **Left** and **Len** functions to remove the last character from the display. The full event procedure is presented in Listing 5.7.

Listing 5.7   *The Backspace button Click event procedure.*

```
Private Sub cmdBackspace_Click()

' If we're in the process of making an
' entry, remove the rightmost character
' from the display.

If NewEntry Then Exit Sub

If txtDisplay.Text <> "" Then
    txtDisplay.Text = Left(txtDisplay.Text, _
        Len(txtDisplay.Text) - 1)
End If

End Sub
```

The event procedure for the Decimal button is a bit more complicated. As with the number keys, if a new entry is being started, the event procedure clears the Text Box and clears the **NewEntry** flag, then checks the entry for the following two conditions:

- If the display is empty (length = 0), the decimal is added as the first character.

- If the display is not empty, we see if a decimal point already has been entered. If not, the decimal is added at the end of the displayed string.

To determine if one string is present in another string, use the **Instr** function. It takes two arguments: the string to be searched and the string you are looking for. If the string is found, the function returns the position where it was found (with the first character in position 1). If the string is not found, the function returns 0. Here are some examples:

- **Instr("Visual", "V")** evaluates to 1

- **Instr("Basic", "q")** evaluates to 0

- **Instr("Programming", "gr")** evaluates to 4

Now that we know how **Instr** works, we can complete the event procedure. Complete code for this event procedure is shown in Listing 5.8.

Listing 5.8   *The Decimal button Click event procedure.*

```
Private Sub cmdDecimal_Click()

' If we're starting a new entry, clear the text box.
If NewEntry Then
    txtDisplay.Text = ""
    NewEntry = False
End If

' If the display is empty add the decimal
' point as the first character. If the display
' is not empty add the decimal point at the
' end of existing text only if there is not
' already a decimal point entered.

If Len(txtDisplay.Text) = 0 Then
    txtDisplay.Text = "."
Else
    If InStr(txtDisplay.Text, ".") = 0 Then
        txtDisplay.Text = txtDisplay.Text & "."
    End If
End If

End Sub
```

Go ahead and run the project. You'll be able to enter numbers, clear the display, backspace, and so on. Of course, the calculator won't calculate yet. Our next task is programming the operator buttons.

Watching The Stack

By adding a few lines of code to the program, you'll be able to keep track of the calculator's stack—a good way to increase your understanding of how the stack works. Use the techniques you learned in the section "Creating a Procedure" to create a new sub procedure called **ShowStack**, and then add the following code:

```
Public Sub ShowStack()

' If the calculator is running in the VB
' environment, displays the top 5 values
' on the stack with an arrow to the top
' value.

Dim i As Integer

If StackPointer < 1 Then Exit Sub

For i = 5 To 1 Step -1
    If i = StackPointer Then
        Debug.Print i & ": " & Stack(i) & " <<"
    Else
        Debug.Print i & ": " & Stack(i)
    End If
Next i

Debug.Print "=========="

End Sub
```

To call the procedure each time **DisplayResults** is called, insert the line

```
Call ShowStack
```

just before the **End Sub** statement in the **DisplayResults** procedure. In the Debug window, **ShowStack** displays the first five stack positions with an arrow pointing to the top value (the one pointed to by **StackPointer**).

Programming The Operator Buttons

Our last task in creating a functioning calculator is to write the event procedure for the operator buttons. Because we added these buttons to the form as a control array, we will need only a single procedure for all four buttons. As before, with the number buttons, we can tell which button was clicked by looking at the **Index** argument that is passed to the procedure.

The code is actually rather simple. First, we declare a type **Double** variable named **Result** to hold the result of the calculation. We must also ensure that the stack has at least one value on it. Then we perform the requested operation between the value on the top of the stack and the value in the display. For addition and multiplication, the order doesn't matter. For division, it is the stack value divided by the display value; for subtraction, it is the display value subtracted from the stack value.

One more thing is required. Because dividing by 0 is a definite no-no, we must be sure that the display value is not 0 before performing the division (otherwise, Visual Basic would report an error). If the display value is 0, we call the **MsgBox** function to inform the user, then exit the procedure without performing the calculation. The **MsgBox** function displays a small dialog box containing your message and an OK button. We'll be using this function regularly, and you can refer to Visual Basic Help for more information on how to use it and its various options.

Once the calculation has been performed, all we need to do is pass the result to the **DisplayResult** procedure, and, *voilà*, the answer appears in the display. The full event procedure for the operator buttons is shown in Listing 5.9. Make sure that the **Index** property of each operator button matches the proper **Case** statement in the function.

Listing 5.9   *The Operator button Click event procedure.*

```
Private Sub cmdOperators_Click(Index As Integer)

Dim Result As Double

' See if there is at least 1 value on the stack.
' We cannot perform an operation otherwise.

If StackPointer < 1 Then Exit Sub

Select Case Index
    Case 0  ' plus
        Result = Stack(StackPointer) + Val(txtDisplay.Text)
    Case 1  ' minus
        Result = Stack(StackPointer) - Val(txtDisplay.Text)
    Case 2  ' multiply
        Result = Stack(StackPointer) * Val(txtDisplay.Text)
```

```
Case 3  ' divide
    If (Val(txtDisplay.Text) <> 0) Then
        Result = Stack(StackPointer) / Val(txtDisplay.Text)
    Else
        MsgBox "Cannot divide by 0!"
        Exit Sub
    End If
End Select

StackPointer = StackPointer - 1
NewEntry = True
DisplayHasData = True
DisplayResult (Result)

End Sub
```

The calculator is now complete. (Well, at least it's working, as shown in Figure 5.6.) Take it for a spin, and see how it works. We will be adding some enhancements later in the chapter. But, first, let's sit back and think about the miles we've covered.

Is That Cool Or What?

Well, I certainly think so. Just look at what Visual Basic has allowed us to accomplish. While it may have taken you—a Visual Basic programming newcomer—an hour or two to complete this calculator project, even a moderately experienced Visual Basic programmer would have knocked it off in 15 to 30 minutes. So you can see that for a *very* modest expenditure of time, we have a fully functional (albeit basic) calculator with a slick visual interface.

Just thinking about how long this would have taken with the old ways of programming makes me sweat. If you are new to programming, you can't really appreciate the incredible gains. Just imagine the world of difference between a horse and buggy and a 400-horse-

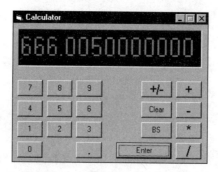

Figure 5.6   *The calculator in action.*

power Jaguar with a wet bar and mink seats—that should give you some idea. For those who are unfamiliar with any other way of programming, the speed and power of Visual Basic are simply the way programming ought to be. I agree completely—I just wish it had been around 10 years ago.

But enough complaining. Let's take a moment to review what we have accomplished so far. The calculator project helps to reinforce some of the Visual Basic tools and concepts you learned in previous chapters: drawing controls on a form, setting control properties, and writing event procedures. You've also been introduced to several powerful new techniques. Let's summarize:

- Data arrays are a useful way of storing large quantities of data in an indexed fashion. Combining arrays with loops is a powerful technique that you'll see frequently in all kinds of Visual Basic programs.

- A control array lets you group two or more controls under the same name. By sharing a name and event procedures, control arrays greatly reduce the coding required for certain tasks.

- General procedures are used to isolate individual program tasks, reducing coding and debugging effort and producing simpler and more robust programs.

- Visual Basic's built-in functions perform a variety of commonly needed tasks.

- The Debug window and the **Debug.Print** method provide a useful way for peeking at what's going on inside your program.

At this point, I think you're ready to start experimenting with Visual Basic on your own. Don't give up reading this book, of course, but by combining further readings with experimentation, you'll learn more quickly than by doing just one or the other. I recommend that you spend some time browsing through Visual Basic's function library; it contains a great deal of useful stuff. If you're feeling ambitious, a good project to try is a calculator that uses algebraic logic. (Hint: It's more difficult than an RPN calculator.)

While our new calculator is quite nice, a few more features would make it even better. We'll spend the remainder of this chapter polishing our project.

Enhancing The Calculator

The enhancements that I have in mind will add more functionality to the calculator. We would like the ability to calculate the trigonometric functions Sin, Cos, and Tan, as well as the inverse (1/X). The capability of raising a number to a power would also be a valuable addition to the calculator. Another useful capability would be copying a number in the calculator's display to the Windows Clipboard for use in other Windows applications. This would permit the user to perform calculations and then paste the answer directly into any application, such as a letter you are writing with Word or WordPerfect. Finally, having a Last X button that displays the top value from the stack would be useful for certain calculations.

For the trig calculations, we will use Visual Basic's built-in **Sin**, **Cos**, and **Tan** functions. As you may already have guessed, we'll use a control array of Command Buttons for these three calculations. Using the techniques you learned earlier, create this array of three buttons on the Calculator form. You may need to enlarge the form and rearrange the other buttons to accommodate new buttons, unless you planned ahead better than I did.

Assign the array of buttons the **Name** property **cmdTrig** and set the **Caption** properties to **Sin**, **Cos**, and **Tan**. The code for the event procedure is shown in Listing 5.10. Again, you must be sure that the **Index** property of each button matches the corresponding **Case** statement in the procedure. After calculating the correct value, all that is required is setting the two flags and calling the **DisplayResult** function. (I told you we would get a lot of mileage out of this function.)

Listing 5.10 *The Trigonometric Command Button Click event procedure.*

```
Private Sub cmdTrig_Click(Index As Integer)

' Trigonometric calculations.

Dim Result As Double

Select Case Index
    Case 0  ' Sin
        Result = Sin(txtDisplay.Text)
    Case 1  ' Cos
        Result = Cos(txtDisplay.Text)
    Case 2  ' Tan
        Result = Tan(txtDisplay.Text)
End Select

DisplayResult (Result)
NewEntry = True
DisplayHasData = True

End Sub
```

The remaining buttons we will put on the calculator are all single buttons and not part of a control array. Add four more Command Buttons, assigning the **Name** and **Caption** properties shown here:

- **Command Button 1**

  Caption: 1/X

  Name: cmdInverse

- **Command Button 2**

  Caption: Y^X

  Name: cmdPower

- **Command Button 3**

  Caption: Last X

  Name: cmdLastX

- **Command Button 4**

  Caption: Copy

  Name: cmdCopy

When you have finished adding the buttons, your form will look similar to Figure 5.7. Although I have rearranged some of the buttons, the final layout is up to you. If you find the default font too small, just change the **Font** property of the new buttons.

The event procedure for the Last X button is shown in Listing 5.11. After verifying that the stack has at least one value on it, the value on the top of the stack is displayed and the flagsare set.

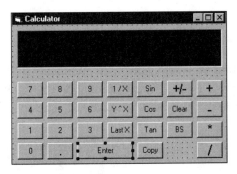

Figure 5.7   *The completed Calculator form.*

Listing 5.11 The Last X button Click event procedure.

```
Private Sub cmdLastX_Click()

' Display the value at the top of the stack.

If StackPointer > 0 Then
    DisplayValue (Stack(StackPointer))
End If

NewEntry = True
DisplayHasData = True

End Sub
```

The code to calculate the inverse of a number (1/X) is simple. The only possible catch would be if the user tries to invert 0, so we'll test for that condition and display a message box if it occurs. Otherwise, all that's necessary is to divide 1 by the value in the display, calling **DisplayResult** to display it. As usual, the **NewEntry** and **DisplayHasData** flags need to be set as well. The code for this event procedure is shown in Listing 5.12.

Listing 5.12 The 1/X button Click event procedure.

```
Private Sub cmdInverse_Click()

' Displays the inverse of the
' number in the display.

If txtDisplay.Text = 0 Then
    MsgBox "Cannot take inverse of 0!"
    Exit Sub
Else
    DisplayResult (1 / txtDisplay.Text)
    NewEntry = True
    DisplayHasData = True
End If

End Sub
```

Raising a number to a power (the Y^X button) is an equally simple calculation, requiring only Visual Basic's ^ operator. Note that the number on the stack is raised to the power of the number in the display—not the other way around. The code for this event procedure is shown in Listing 5.13.

Listing 5.13   The Y^X button Click event procedure.

```
Private Sub cmdPower_Click()

' Raises the number on the stack to the power
' of the number in the display.

Dim Result As Double

If StackPointer < 1 Then Exit Sub

Result = Stack(StackPointer) ^ txtDisplay.Text
DisplayResult (Result)
NewEntry = True
DisplayHasData = True

End Sub
```

Finally, we come to the Copy button's **Click** event procedure. Now, how the devil do you copy something to the Windows Clipboard? You may think it's complicated, but it's actually very simple. In a Visual Basic program, you have direct access to the Windows Clipboard object, which is named (guess) Clipboard. Several methods are available for working with the Clipboard object. One method is **SetText**, which places the specified text on the Clipboard, where any Windows program can retrieve it with a Paste command. You can see from Listing 5.14 how simple the code is, requiring only a single line. We'll be using some of the other Clipboard methods in other parts of the book. Take a look at the Visual Basic Help system for more information.

Listing 5.14   The Copy button Click event procedure.

```
Private Sub cmdCopy_Click()

' Put the display text on the Windows clipboard

Clipboard.SetText txtDisplay.Text

End Sub
```

Believe it or not, the calculator is finished. Take it for a spin. Figure 5.8 shows the calculator in action.

Creating the calculator has been a fairly involved project, but only because you are new to Visual Basic. In comparison with what is possible with Visual Basic, the calculator is really

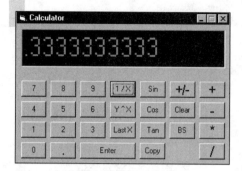

Figure 5.8   *The completed calculator executing.*

quite simple. By this point, you already have many of the most important Visual Basic fundamentals under your belt. I encourage you to start experimenting with Visual Basic, designing and creating small projects on your own. If you want to become proficient at programming, there's no substitute for practice.

Creating An Executable

As you develop a Visual Basic program, you run it within the Visual Basic development environment. This gives you access to several development tools the environment provides, such as the Immediate window and debugging tools (debugging tools are covered in Chapter 26). What happens, though, when the program is complete? You can't just assume that all of your customers will have Visual Basic; will they be able to run the program without it?

Yes, indeed. Once you have put the finishing touches on a program, the next step is to create an *executable file*. A program in this form can be executed independently from the Visual Basic development environment. You can distribute the executable program without restriction.

To create an executable file from your Visual Basic project, select Make *Progname*.exe from the File menu (*Progname* being the name that you have assigned to the project). Visual Basic will display the Make Project dialog box, shown in Figure 5.9. The large box will display the names of any other executable files in the current folder, and the assigned project name will be automatically entered in the File Name box. You can change to a different folder, if desired. You can also change the name of the executable file. Select OK, and Visual Basic will start creating the executable. The amount of time this takes will depend on the size and complexity of your project and the speed of your computer. When the process is complete, the executable file will be in the specified folder. You can use the usual Windows 95 techniques to create a shortcut to the program.

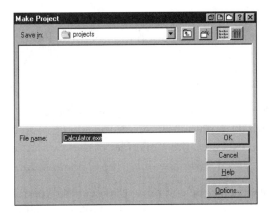

Figure 5.9   *The Make Project dialog box.*

Choosing A Project Icon

Visual Basic will assign a default icon to your project, but you can do better. As you probably know, this icon is displayed for the program's shortcuts and also when it is minimized. Select the project's main form and use its **Icon** property to select an icon (kept on disk in files with the .ICO extension). Visual Basic comes with an extensive icon library. Where these files are located depends on the version of Visual Basic you installed. Look for a Graphics\Icons folder.

While an executable Visual Basic program is independent of the Visual Basic development environment, it is not totally standalone. All Visual Basic executable programs depend on one or more other files to execute. Because you have Visual Basic installed on your system, these files are present, and you can run any Visual Basic executable without a problem. If you give a Visual Basic executable to a friend, he or she may not have these files on his or her system and will not be able to run your program. Determining which files need to be distributed with your programs is not an easy matter. The easiest way to distribute Visual Basic applications is through the Visual Basic Application Setup Wizard, a topic covered in Chapter 26.

Compilation Options

The process of creating an executable file is called *compilation*. During compilation, Visual Basic translates the English-like statements of your source code and the visual specifications of your interface design into the binary code that can be understood by the computer's CPU. When you compile a Visual Basic project, several options are available to you. Some of the compilation options are advanced and rarely, if ever, need to be changed. A few are worth noting, however.

To access the options, select Make XXX.exe to display the Make Project dialog box, as you learned above. Click on the Options button to display the Project Properties dialog box, and if necessary, click on the Compile tab, as shown in Figure 5.10.

The two main options are as follows:

- *Compile to P-code*—The *P* stands for *pseudo*, meaning that the compilation process will perform a partial translation of the project source code into pseudocode. When the program executes, the remainder of the translation process is performed. Until version 5 of Visual Basic, the only type of compilation available was P-code.

- *Compile to Native Code*—The compilation process will perform a complete translation of your source code. No further translation is required when the program executes.

What's the difference between these two compilation modes? Because of the extra translation step required, P-code runs more slowly than native code. In fact, this was a major complaint with earlier versions of Visual Basic: Its programs were always a bit slower than equivalent programs written in C++, Delphi, or other languages that use native code. P-code programs tend to have smaller executable file sizes, but with today's gargantuan hard disks, this is rarely a concern. From my perspective, there's no reason for ever choosing P-code over native code.

When you select the Native Code option, you have several more options available. The ones you need to know about are listed here:

- *Optimize for Fast Code*—Compiles so that program execution speed is maximized, possibly at the expense of EXE file size.

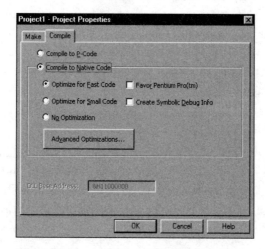

Figure 5.10   *The Compile tab in the Project Properties dialog box.*

- *Optimize for Small Code*—Compiles so that EXE file size is minimized, possibly at the expense of program execution speed.

- *Favor Pentium Pro*—Creates an executable that is optimized for best performance when run on a Pentium Pro system but may run slower on other systems.

If you are unsure of which compilation options to choose, I suggest that you select the Compile to Native Code and the Optimize for Fast Code options.

Variable Scope

Before ending this chapter, we need to explore the concept of variable scope. The *scope* of a variable refers to the parts of the program where it is visible. When a variable is not visible, or is *out of scope*, it may as well not exist. True, it still exists, but somewhere out of your reach. You won't be able to access it again until it comes back in scope. The concept of scope applies to procedures also.

What do I mean by "parts" of a program? In a Visual Basic module, some code is contained in procedures (both general and event procedures) and is called *procedure level code*. Most of the code in the Calculator project is procedure level code. Other code (such as Calculator's **Const** declarations) exists outside any procedure and is called *module level code*. Because some Visual Basic programs contain more than one module, identifying which one the module code is within is also important.

The location of a variable's declaration (its **Dim** statement) is one factor that determines the scope of a variable. If you declare a variable inside a procedure, its scope is limited to that one procedure. Module level code cannot access it, nor can code in other procedures. Such variables are called *local* variables, because their scope is local to the procedure where they are declared. In fact, different procedures can have local variables of the same name. They exist as totally independent variables because their scopes do not overlap. For example, we used a variable named **Result** in more than one procedure in the Calculator project.

If you declare a variable in module level code, its scope is determined by the keyword used to declare it. If you use the **Dim** statement or use the **Private** keyword, the scope of the variable will be limited to that single module. Thus, the following two statements in module level code have the same effect: declaring a variable whose scope is limited to that one module:

```
Dim X As Integer
Private Y As Double
```

If you use the **Public** keyword in a module level declaration, the variable's scope will be the entire project (all modules). You can also use the **Global** keyword with the same effect:

```
Public X As Integer
Global Y As Double
```

You cannot use the **Public** or **Global** keywords within a procedure.

You may wonder why programmers don't simply make all their programs' variables public—why worry about scope? Bad idea! Don't look at scope as a restriction, but as a tool that helps you create bug-free programs. The ability to hide variables in procedures from the rest of the program is a major component of the power of structured programming. With local variables, a procedure can be completely independent from the rest of the program. It receives information via its arguments, and returns information (if it is a function) via its return value. No other part of the program can screw up what goes on in the procedure. Likewise, what goes on in the procedure cannot screw up the rest of the program. The rule to follow is to use local variables as much as possible. Public variables should be reserved for situations where they are really needed.

The Visual Basic Application Wizard

If you have used Microsoft software products, you may have encountered *wizards*. A wizard is a tool that helps you perform some task. Typically, a wizard walks you through a series of steps, asking you questions and offering choices related to the task at hand. Then, it carries out the specified actions, performing a lot of work that you would otherwise have to perform yourself.

One of Visual Basic's neatest features is the Application Wizard. It takes you through the steps of creating a Visual Basic application; then, based on your responses, it creates the skeleton of the program. You must still write the code and design the forms that provide the application's unique functionality, but a lot of the busy work—such as menus and toolbars—will be done for you (at least in their basic form).

Using the Application Wizard—or any wizard—is a fairly simple matter. I will not attempt to explain all the choices that the wizard offers you, for two reasons. First, the wizard dialog boxes are usually quite clear, with explanatory notes for the various choices. You'll probably be able to figure out most, if not all, of the options on your own. Secondly, some of the project choices offered by the wizard—such as menus and multiple versus single document interfaces—have not been covered yet. Therefore, I will explain the basics of using the Application Wizard without going into the details. As you read further in the book, you can experiment on your own to explore its full capabilities.

To start the Application Wizard, display the New Project dialog box by selecting New Project from the File menu. Select the Visual Basic Application Wizard icon and click on OK. The wizard will display the first of its dialog boxes (an example is shown in Figure 5.11).

While the details of each wizard dialog box differ, they all have the following buttons:

- *Next*—Proceeds to the next wizard step. If you are at the last step, this button is not available.

- *Back*—Returns to the previous wizard step, enabling you to change entries you made. If you are at the first step, this button is not available.

- *Cancel*—Terminates the wizard without creating the application.

- *Finish*—Closes the wizard and creates the application. If you click on Finish before going through all of the wizard steps, the wizard will create the application using the default settings for those dialog boxes that you did not visit.

- *Help*—Displays online help information related to the current wizard dialog box and its choices.

Once the wizard has completed its work, you will have the basis for your Visual Basic application with all of the selected elements in place. A wizard-created application is the same as one that you created yourself—just a lot easier. One nice touch is that the wizard can insert "to do" comments in the code, reminding you of the code that needs to be added for various functions.

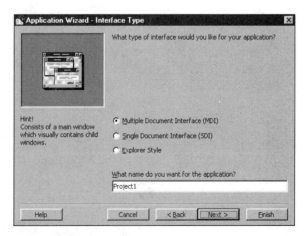

Figure 5.11   *One of the Application Wizard dialog boxes.*

What Now?

With the completion of this chapter, you have finished the first part of the book. You've come a long way and learned a lot. The material we have covered so far has enabled you to do a great deal with Visual Basic, but we haven't even touched on a lot of important stuff: menus, common dialogs, class modules, and much more. From here on, however, the approach will be much less general. Each chapter will delve into a specific area where you might want to apply Visual Basic—text processing and multimedia are two examples. We'll deal with the remaining Visual Basic tools as we go along.

PART 2

Sharing Data And Code

Chapter 6
Component Madness

Visual Basic makes use of components of all shapes, sizes, and types.

Components are at the heart of Visual Basic programming. Not only do you use components in just about anything you do with Visual Basic, but you can also create your own components for use by you and others. This is the first of several chapters devoted to components. For you to be a good Visual Basic programmer, you must have a good understanding of what components are available to use in your projects, as well as the various types of components you can create using Visual Basic. First, however, we need to take a look at the different kinds of projects that Visual Basic can create.

Visual Basic's Project Types

By now, you've probably noticed the various Visual Basic project types available in Visual Basic's New Project dialog box. Up until now, we have used only the Standard EXE type; in fact, for most Visual Basic programmers, this is the type used most often. But what are these other project types? How do they differ, and what are they used for?

The following list gives a brief description of the project types offered in the New Project dialog box. You will not have all of these types available to you unless you are running the Enterprise Edition of Visual Basic. If a project type is covered in this book, the relevant chapter is referenced at the end of the description. No, I don't cover all of the project types. Some of them are simply beyond the scope and space limitations of this book.

- *Standard EXE*—A "regular" Windows application. A Standard EXE program can use ActiveX components but does not expose any components of its own. A Standard EXE can define objects for its own internal use (Chapters 2, 5).

- *ActiveX EXE*—A "regular" Windows application that also exposes one or more ActiveX objects for use by other programs. Microsoft Word is an example of an ActiveX EXE (although it was not created with Visual Basic). It is an executable program that defines ActiveX objects that are used internally and also exposed for use by other programs (Chapter 8).

- *ActiveX DLL*—A dynamic link library that exposes ActiveX objects for use by other programs but has no functionality of its own (Chapter 8).

- *ActiveX Control*—An ActiveX object with a visual interface that can be "plugged" into other programs. Some of Visual Basic's controls are ActiveX controls (Chapter 17).

- *ActiveX Document EXE*—A method of packaging a Visual Basic program so that the program's forms and code can be accessed from within a "container" application, such as Microsoft Internet Explorer. It's most often used in Web publishing.

- *ActiveX Document DLL*—A dynamic link library containing code that supports an ActiveX Document EXE.

- *Application Wizard*—Not a project type *per se*, but rather a "helper" that assists you in putting together the framework of a Standard EXE project (Chapter 5).

- *Addin*—A component that is tied into the Visual Basic development environment to enhance its functionality. Use this project type to create your own add-in.

- *DHTML Application*—A group of related Hypertext Markup Language (HTML) pages that work together, with help from Visual Basic code, to fulfill a task. DHTML applications are "executed" in a Web browser, such as Microsoft Internet Explorer.

- *Data Project*—A database project that is created to contain two specialized designers for database related programming tasks.

- *IIS Application*—An application that runs on a Web server to accept, process, and respond to information requests.

- *Enterprise Edition Controls*—A project that automatically loads all the special Enterprise Edition controls into the Toolbox (as if you had selected them individually in the Components dialog box).

I don't expect you to understand all of these project types yet, but it's a good idea for you to have this introduction now.

Making Components Available In Visual Basic

A typical Windows system will have dozens, if not hundreds, of software components available on it. You may be wondering where all these components came from, but it is no mystery—it's just the way Windows and Windows programs work. Most application programs use components themselves; often, these components are *exposed*, or made available, to other programs. For example, if you have the Microsoft Excel spreadsheet installed on your system, it exposes the Chart, Equation, and Worksheet objects. Likewise, the Adobe Photoshop program exposes the Image object. This is in addition to all of the objects, including controls, that come as a part of Visual Basic. All of these objects are potentially available for you to use in your Visual Basic project.

Why do I say *potentially*? If all of these objects were immediately available to you—in the Toolbox, for example—the Visual Basic development environment would get awfully confusing. Instead, only the intrinsic controls are always available, and you must specifically select other objects to be available in Visual Basic. The available objects fall into two general categories: components and references.

Objects And The Registry

How does Visual Basic (or any other program, for that matter) know which objects are available? The answer lies in the Windows registry. When a new component or a program that exposes objects is installed on a system, information about the objects is put in the registry. Other programs, such as Visual Basic, can retrieve this information to determine which objects are available.

Components

The term *component* may be difficult to define precisely, but for the present discussion, we can say simply that a component is anything you access via Visual Basic's **Components** command. To see what I mean, select Components from the Project menu and press Ctrl+T to display the Components dialog box (Figure 6.1).

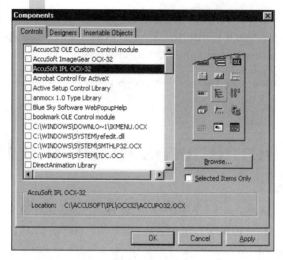

Figure 6.1 *The Components dialog box has three tabs.*

Note that this dialog box has three tabs, corresponding to the following three types of components:

- *Control*—A discrete unit that you can place on a form in your project. You have already worked with some of Visual Basic's intrinsic controls; by selecting other controls on the Controls tab of the Components dialog box, you can display other controls in your Toolbox, making them available for use in your project. Most controls exist as OCX files on your disk, although some are contained in DLL files. For the most part, controls available in Visual Basic are ActiveX, a special type of component that we will cover in more detail later in the book. Available controls display as icons in the Visual Basic Toolbox.

- *Designer*—A component that you use within Visual Basic to assist in developing your program. A designer does not show up in your final program, unlike a control, but the results of using a designer will be evident in the program. You have already used one designer—the Forms Designer. To make other designers available, select them on the Designers tab in the Components dialog box. You access designers by selecting Add ActiveX Designer from the Project menu. The designers you choose in the Components dialog box are listed here (except the Forms Designer, which is always available). What can designers do? They can help you design Web pages or create forms for database programming, for example. We will work with a couple of the designers in other parts of the book.

- *Insertable Object*—A software component made available by another application. The items available in this list will depend on what application programs you have installed on your system. On my system, for example, I have the Adobe Photoshop graphics program installed, so my Insertable Objects list includes "Adobe Photoshop Image". Likewise, I have the Netscape Navigator Web browser installed, so "Netscape Hypertext Document" is available to me in Visual Basic. These insertable objects rely on a process called *OLE automation*, which permits one Windows program to make use of capabilities in another program. We'll learn more about OLE automation in Chapter 10. Note that a Visual Basic program that uses an insertable object is dependent on the parent application. This means that you cannot create a Visual Basic application that uses an Adobe Photoshop image object and distribute it to end users who do not have the Photoshop application installed on their systems, because the object will not function. This is different from controls, whose functioning does not depend on anything being installed on the end user's system. An insertable object that you have made available displays as an icon in the Visual Basic Toolbox.

TIP Browsing For Controls

On the Controls tab of the Components dialog box, you'll see a Browse button. Use this button to locate controls that are installed on your system, but do not show up in the dialog box because they are not properly registered. Browse to find the control's OCX file and select it. It will be registered and appear in the Controls list. Selecting the OCX file of a control that is already registered has no effect but does no harm.

References

The other way to make software components available in Visual Basic is with the **References** command on the Project menu. When you select this command, the References dialog box is displayed (Figure 6.2). Selected references, marked with a check, are grouped at the top of the list. Other available references are listed alphabetically below.

What exactly is a reference? To answer that question, I need to explain the concept of a *Type Library*. When an object is exposed for use by other applications, it is usually necessary to know the details of the object—its methods, properties, and so on—to make use of it. A Type Library contains this information in a standard format. By selecting a reference in the References dialog box, you are, in effect, telling Visual Basic, "Take note of the object information in this Type Library."

You would select a reference in this dialog box for two primary reasons: to make the object information available in Visual Basic's Object Browser, and to enable early binding for object references in your programs. Both of these topics will be covered in more detail in Chapter 10.

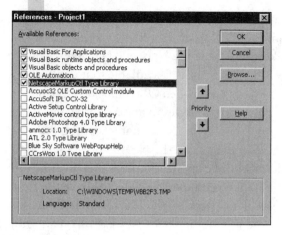

Figure 6.2   *The References dialog box.*

Three of the entries in the References list are always selected, and you are not permitted to unselect them: Visual Basic for Applications, Visual Basic Runtime Objects and Procedures, and Visual Basic Objects and Procedures. These three sets of references are the foundation of Visual Basic itself, so they must always be available. Visual Basic will usually not let you unselect any references that are used in the current project. I say "usually," because in some cases, an object is referenced in a project in a way that Visual Basic does not know about it until the program is executed or compiled. In these situations you are not prevented from unselecting the associated reference in the References list, but you will receive an error message when you try to run or compile the program.

You can, however, have references selected that are not used in the current project. This should be avoided, because when Visual Basic resolves a reference, it looks through all of the available (checked) Type Libraries. Having unneeded references selected will slow down the program compilation process.

Note the Priority buttons in the References dialog box. You use these buttons to move the highlighted reference up or down in the list. When Visual Basic comes across a reference to an object in code, it searches the available Type Libraries in the order they are listed in the References list. In the unlikely event that two or more objects have the same name, Visual Basic will use the one it finds first.

Creating And Using Classes

One of the ways that Visual Basic lets you implement software components is by means of classes. A *class* provides both data storage and code self-contained in a reusable module.

When properly designed, a class isolates you, the programmer, from all of its inner workings. You can simply use it without worrying about what is going on inside. Once you have created a class, you can reuse it in any and all of your Visual Basic projects. You implement a class in Visual Basic by means of a *class module*. The type of class we're talking about now cannot present a visual interface to the user—it is code and data only. Other types of Visual Basic classes do provide a visual interface, and we will get to them in subsequent chapters.

TIP Classes And Objects

What is the relationship between a class and an object? A class can be thought of as a blueprint—the plans for something. An object, on the other hand, is something built, based on those blueprints. You can't actually use a class, just like you can't drive a blueprint for a car. Once you have the blueprint, however, you can build as many objects as you like. In Visual Basic, an object is said to be an *instance* of the class it is based upon.

Designing The Class

To illustrate the basic concepts of classes, and to demonstrate how to use Visual Basic's Class Builder utility, we will work through the process of creating a class, along with a demonstration project to show you how it works. We'll start off with something simple, so the details do not get in the way of learning the underlying concepts. We will create a class that stores string data and improves on Visual Basic's own string data type by providing the ability to determine the length of the string and also to insert characters at a specified location within the string. Let's call the class **SuperString**.

We'll start with the class demo project. Create a new Standard EXE project. Pull down the Add-Ins menu and select Class Builder Utility (if this choice is not available on the Add-Ins menu, use the Add-Ins Manager to make it available). The Class Builder dialog box will be displayed, as shown in Figure 6.3.

The left side of the Class Builder dialog box lists the current project, which is called Project1 at present, because it hasn't been assigned a name. If the project contained any class modules, they would be listed below the project name. The tabs on the right list the properties, methods, and events of the class you are working on. Take the following steps:

1. Click on the Add New Class button on the Class Builder toolbar, or select New from the File menu, then select Class. The Class Module Builder dialog box will be displayed, as shown in Figure 6.4. Type "SuperString" in the Name box, then click on OK. The new class will be listed under the project name on the left side of the Class Builder utility.

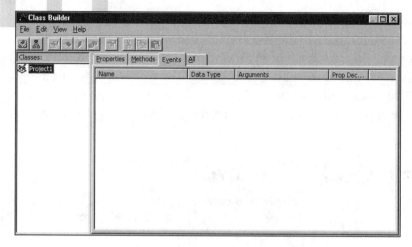

Figure 6.3 *The Class Builder utility.*

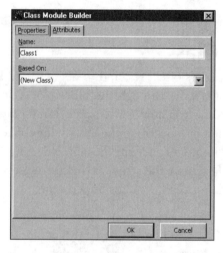

Figure 6.4 *Specifying the name of the new class.*

2. Click on the Add New Property button or select File | New | Property. The Property Builder dialog box will be displayed, as shown in Figure 6.5.

3. Enter "Value" in the Name box and select String in the Data Type box. Click on the Default Property box to place a checkmark there, and leave the Public Property option set. Click on OK when finished.

4. Repeat Steps 2 and 3 to add another property with the name "Length" and the data type Long. For this property, do not check the Default Property option.

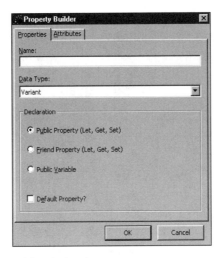

Figure 6.5   *The Property Builder dialog box.*

5. Click on the Add New Method button or select File | New | Method. The Method Builder dialog box will be displayed, as shown in Figure 6.6.

6. In the Name box, enter "Insert."

7. Click on the button with the + on it, to the right of the Arguments box. The Add Argument dialog box will be displayed, as shown in Figure 6.7.

8. Enter "Txt" in the Name box and select **String** as the data type; then click on OK.

Figure 6.6   *The Method Builder dialog box.*

Figure 6.7   *The Add Argument dialog box.*

9. Repeat Steps 7 and 8 to add another argument with the name "Position" and the data type **Long**.

10. Back in the Method Builder dialog box, click on OK to close the dialog box and return to the Class Builder utility.

In the Class Builder window, you can use the Methods and Properties tabs to view the elements you just added. We don't need to do this now, however, so select Update Project from the File menu or press Ctrl+S to save the newly created class to disk and add it to the project. Finally, Select Exit from the File menu to close the Class Builder utility.

When you return to Visual Basic, look at the Project Explorer window. You'll see that the new class has been added to the project in a section called Class Modules. You'll also see that the **SuperString** class module has code associated with it. This is the code that was generated by the Class Builder utility in response to the information we entered. We'll take a look at this code in a moment, but first, save your project. I used the name **ClassDemo** for both the form and the project.

Now let's look at the code that was generated by the Class Builder utility, shown in Listing 6.1. We'll need to modify this code, but the Class Builder has saved us some of the grunt work. You'll have a better understanding of the details of how the code works after completing this chapter and the class project in Chapter 8. For now, the following explanation will be sufficient.

- The variables **mvarValue** and **mvarLength** are used to store the values of the class's two properties. Note that these are declared as **Private**, so that they are accessible only by code within the class module itself.

- A procedure named **Insert** takes one type **String** argument and one type **Long** argument, as we specified when using the Class Builder utility. **Insert** is empty at present, and we will have to write the code to provide its functionality. This procedure represents a method of the **SuperString** class. Note that it has been declared **Public**, so it can be called from outside the class.

- Two procedures named **Value** are specified as **Property** procedures—one is a **Get** and one is a **Let** procedure. A **Property Let** procedure is used by code outside the class to set the value of a property, and a **Property Get** procedure is used by code outside the class to retrieve the value of a property. The name of the procedures— in this case, **Value**—specifies the name of the property.

- **Property Get** and **Property Let** procedures provide access to the **Length** property.

How do property procedures work? When code outside an object wants to set a property, it will reference that property on the left side of an assignment statement. This causes the corresponding **Property Let** procedure to be called, with the value on the right side of the assignment statement passed as the argument to the procedure. For example, suppose we had created an instance of the **SuperString** class called **buf**. We would then set its value as follows:

```
buf.value = "Visual Basic"
```

When this line of code is executed, the **Property Let** procedure for the value property is executed, with the value "Visual Basic" passed as the procedure argument. In this case, code in the **Property Let** procedure simply assigns the value passed to the procedure to the private internal variable **mvarValue**, which is used to store the property. The sequence of events is similar for a **Property Get** procedure. When code wants to retrieve the value of the object property, it will reference the property on the right side of the assignment statement. For example:

```
Text1.Text = buf.value
```

When this line of code is executed, the corresponding **Property Get** procedure is executed. **Property Get** procedures are actually functions, returning a value. In this case, code in the procedure simply returns the value stored in the internal private variable where the value property is stored.

What is the point of using **Property Get** and **Property Let** procedures in a class? Why not simply declare one public variable for each property, so code outside the class could access that variable directly? The reason for doing things in what may seem to be an unnecessarily complicated manner is a principal called *encapsulation*. This principal states that the internal data and workings of a class should be as isolated as possible from the outside world. By requiring that access to a class's properties be done via property procedures,

Visual Basic gives the programmer the opportunity to provide whatever degree of encapsulation is required. We'll see this principal in action as we continue to work on our **SuperString** class.

Listing 6.1   *Code created by the Class Builder utility for the SuperString class.*

```
Option Explicit

'local variable(s) to hold property value(s)
Private mvarValue As String 'local copy
Private mvarLength As Long 'local copy

Public Sub Insert(Txt As String, Position As Long)
End Sub

Public Property Let Length(ByVal vData As Long)
'used when assigning a value to the property, on the left side of an assign-
ment.
'Syntax: X.Length = 5
    mvarLength = vData
End Property

Public Property Get Length() As Long
'used when retrieving value of a property, on the right side of an assign-
ment.
'Syntax: Debug.Print X.Length
    Length = mvarLength
End Property

Public Property Let Value(ByVal vData As String)
'used when assigning a value to the property, on the left side of an assign-
ment.
'Syntax: X.Value = 5
    mvarValue = vData
End Property

Public Property Get Value() As String
'used when retrieving value of a property, on the right side of an assign-
ment.
'Syntax: Debug.Print X.Value
    Value = mvarValue
End Property
```

What modifications will we need to make to this code? Consider these three points:

- *First is the **Value** property, which stores the string.* We want the user of the class to be able to get and to set this value. There are no restrictions on what can be stored, so there is no need to modify the code that was generated by the Class Builder utility.

- *Next is the **Length** property, which stores the length of the string.* The user should not be able to set this property, as it will depend entirely on the string stored in the **Value** property. By deleting the corresponding **Property Let** procedure, we will make **Length** a read-only property that can be read, but not set, by the user. We also need to add code that will calculate the length of the string in the **Value** property and store it in the **Length** property.

- *Finally, we have the **Insert** method.* We need to write code to perform the string insertion.

Okay, let's get to work, dealing with the property procedures first. Select the **SuperString** class in the Project Explorer window and display its code for editing. Then, follow these steps:

1. Delete the entire **Property Let Length** procedure.

2. Add the following line of code at the beginning of the **Property Get Length** procedure (**Len()** is a built-in Basic function that returns the length of a string):

```
mvarLength = Len(mvarValue)
```

3. Add the same line of code as the last statement in the **Property Let Value** procedure.

Step 1, as I've already mentioned, serves the purpose of making the **Length** property read-only. Steps 2 and 3 add code that calculates the length of the string stored in the **Value** property and stores the result in the **Length** property. Why do we need to perform this calculation in two different places? The reason for putting this line of code in the **Property Get Length** procedure is obvious—to ensure that the **Length** property contains an accurate value when it is retrieved by the user. But why do we also need this code in the **Property Let Value** procedure? By doing so, the **Length** property will be updated each time the user changes the **Value** property, and therefore, will contain an accurate value even if the user has not specifically retrieved the **Length** property. The need for doing this will be obvious when we discuss the code for the **Insert** method.

Now we need to turn our attention to the **Insert** method. The task of this method is to insert a new string at a specified position within the string currently stored. For example, if the SuperString object currently has "Visual Basic" stored in it, then calling **Insert** with the arguments "XXX" and 3 will result in the object having "ViXXXsual Basic" stored in it. Let's be specific about what the code in the method needs to do, paying particular attention to special cases:

- If the **Position** argument is equal to or less than 1, the new string is added at the beginning of the old string.

- If **Position** is equal to or greater than the length of the old string, then the new string is added at the end of the old string.

- If the old string is blank, then the new string simply replaces it.

- If the new string is blank, nothing happens.

- Otherwise, insert the new string at the specified position in the old string.

The code for the **Insert** method is shown in Listing 6.2. You should be able to figure out how it works from the comments in the listing and from what you have learned already about Basic code. I will point out one thing: The code in this procedure needs to know the length of the original string stored in **mvarValue**, and it gets this information from the object's **Length** property—in other words, the value stored in **mvarLength**. This is why we updated this value not only in the **Property Get Length** procedure, but also in the **Property Let Value** procedure. Otherwise, the **Length** property could be inaccurate.

Listing 6.2   Code for the Insert method.

```
Public Sub Insert(txt As String, position As Long)

' Inserts txt at position in mvarValue.

Dim s1 As String, s2 As String

' If the new string is blank, exit.
If txt = "" Then Exit Sub

' If the existing string is blank, replace it.
If mvarValue = "" Then
    mvarValue = txt
    Exit Sub
End If

' If Position is <= 1, tack new string on the beginning.
If position <= 1 Then
    mvarValue = txt & mvarValue
    Exit Sub
End If

' If Position equal or greater than the length
' of the existing string, tack the new string
' on at the end.

If position >= mvarLength Then
    mvarValue = mvarValue & txt
    Exit Sub
End If
```

```
' Otherwise stick it in the middle at the
' specified position.
' First get the left part of the old string up to but
' not including the character at position.
s1 = Left(mvarValue, position - 1)
' Now get the right part of the old string from position
' to the end.
s2 = Right(mvarValue, mvarLength - position + 1)
' Now put the pieces back together.
mvarValue = s1 & txt & s2

End Sub
```

We are almost done creating our **SuperString** class, but there's one more thing to do—add initialization code. This code is placed in the class's **Initialize** event procedure. This procedure is called when an instance of the object is first created, and you place code here to set the initial values of properties and perform other needed tasks. For the **SuperString** class, we will initialize the **Value** property to an empty string and the **Length** property to 0. Strictly speaking, these initialization steps are not needed, because Visual Basic automatically initializes string variables to an empty string and numeric variables to 0 when they are declared. Paying attention to class initialization steps is good programming practice, however, and you might as well start developing good habits early.

To add this code, display the **SuperString** class code in the Code Editing window. Then, at the top of the Code Editing window, select Class from the Object list and Initialize from the Procedure list. Enter the code shown in Listing 6.3.

Listing 6.3   *The Class_Initialize event procedure for the SuperString class.*

```
Private Sub Class_Initialize()

' Initialize the properties.

mvarValue = ""
mvarLength = 0

End Sub
```

Using The SuperString Class

A class by itself is not terribly useful. You need to create instances of the class—objects—to do anything. Let's take a look at how this is done; then we'll create a simple demonstration program to show off the **SuperString** class.

Creating Objects

To create an instance of an object, you use the **Dim** statement. The general syntax is as follows:

```
Dim varname As [New] classname
```

Here, **varname** is the name you will use to refer to the object; it follows regular Visual Basic naming rules. **Classname** is the name of the class you want to instantiate. I'll explain the optional **New** keyword in a moment. Here's an example of using **Dim** to create an instance of a class:

```
Dim SS1 As SuperString
```

To be precise, this statement does not actually create an instance of the **SuperString** class, but only creates a variable that can refer to an instance. To create the object, you must execute the following:

```
Set SS1 = New SuperString
```

If, however, you use the optional **New** keyword in the **Dim** statement, then using the **Set** statement is unnecessary. In other words, the following code

```
Dim SS1 As New SuperString
```

has the same effect as these two statements:

```
Dim SS1 As SuperString
Set SS1 = New SuperString
```

Why, then, would we ever need the **Set** statement? There are two cases.

One is when, instead of declaring the object variable as a specific type, called *early binding*, you use the **Object** keyword and *late binding*. Late binding involves declaring the object variable as the generic **Object** type rather than as a specific class type, then referencing a specific class with the **Set** keyword:

```
Dim MyObject as Object
Set MyObject = New SuperString
```

The second case is when you want to change the object reference of a variable. Suppose you had executed the following code:

```
Dim SS1 As New SuperString
Dim SS2 As SuperString
Set SS2 = SS1
```

You would then have two variables, SS1 and SS2, that refer to the same object. This technique can be useful for some programming tasks.

Late binding slows things down somewhat, but provides the added flexibility of being able to use the same object variable for different types of objects. For example:

```
Dim MyObject as Object
Set MyObject = New SuperString
' Do stuff here.
Set MyObject = New SomeOtherClass
```

As you can see, working with object references is a lot like working with ordinary Visual Basic variables, except for the use of the **Set** and **New** keywords.

The Demonstration Program

Now that you have seen how to create objects, we can return to the demonstration program that will use the **SuperString** class we created earlier in the chapter. We will use the same project that the **SuperString** class was created in—it already has a blank form. Start by designing the form, adding five Label controls, five Text Box controls, and one control array of three Command buttons. The captions for the Label controls should be set as shown in Figure 6.8. Assign the following names to the Text Box controls:

```
txtInsert
txtLength
txtOriginal
txtResult
txtPosition
```

Set the **Text** property of all the Text Boxes to a blank string, and position each Text Box next to the corresponding Label control. Assign captions to the three Command buttons as follows:

```
Index 0: Process
Index 1: Quit
Index 2: Clear
```

The final form is shown in Figure 6.8.

Now let's turn to the code. Place the following statement in the General Declarations section of the form's code:

```
Dim SS1 As SuperString
```

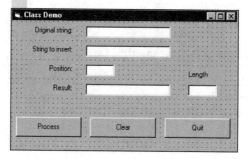

Figure 6.8   *The form for the Class Demo program.*

Next, place this code in the **Form_Load** event procedure:

```
Private Sub Form_Load()
    ' Create the SuperString object.
    Set SS1 = New SuperString
End Sub
```

Finally, here is the code that goes in the **Click** event procedure for the Command buttons:

```
Private Sub Command1_Click(Index As Integer)

Dim C As Control

Select Case Index
    Case 0:     ' Process
        SS1 = txtOriginal.Text
        SS1.Insert txtInsert.Text, txtPosition.Text
        txtResult.Text = SS1
        txtLength.Text = SS1.Length
    Case 1:     ' Quit
        End
    Case 2:     'Clear
        For Each C In Form1.Controls
            If TypeOf C Is TextBox Then C.Text = ""
        Next C
End Select

End Sub
```

That's all there is to the program. Go ahead and run it. Enter some text in the Original String and String to Insert boxes, and enter a position in the Position box. Then click on the Process button. You'll see the resulting string and its length displayed, courtesy of the capabilities that we built into the **SuperString** class. Click on Clear to blank all boxes, and, of course, click on Quit to terminate.

Let's take a closer look at what the code does. When the user clicks on the Process button, here's what happens:

1. The text in the Original box is assigned to the SuperString object SS1 and is stored in its **Txt** property.

2. The object's **Insert** method is called, passing the new text and the position value as arguments.

3. The value of the object's **Txt** property is retrieved and placed in the Result Text Box.

4. The value of the object's **Length** property is retrieved and placed in the Length Text Box.

Using an object that you designed is just as easy as using the objects that are provided with Visual Basic. But what about the code that is executed when the Clear button is clicked? Here, I am using one of Visual Basic's built-in collections, a topic that we will cover in detail in Chapter 7. I'll explain only briefly here: Visual Basic automatically maintains a list of all the controls on each form in a project. Using the **For...Each** statement, you can loop through all of the controls on the list; using the **TypeOf** keyword, you can determine if each control is a Text Box. If it is, set its **Text** property to a blank string. This is the easiest and fastest way to clear all of the Text Boxes on a form.

Chapter 7

Objects And Classes— Beyond The Basics

Objects are such an important part of programming in Visual Basic that it is difficult to think of anything you can do without using them in one way or another. It goes without saying (although I am going to say it anyway) that the more you know about what objects are available in Visual Basic, and how to use them, the better you will be as a programmer. This chapter will show you how to work with some of the more useful objects that Visual Basic offers.

You can do a lot more with classes in Visual Basic.

The Collection Class

One of the most useful classes provided in Visual Basic is the **Collection** class. Not only does Visual Basic use collections in many of the other classes it provides (for example, the **ListView** class will be covered later in this chapter), but it lets you use this class to keep track of almost anything you want. Finally, there are some built-in collection classes that make many Visual Basic operations much easier. In this section, I'll show you how to use the generic **Collection** class. Later in the chapter, we'll look into Visual Basic's built-in classes.

What exactly is a Collection? Let me quote from the Visual Basic Help system: "A collection object is an ordered set of items that can be referred to as a unit." Think of a collection as an expandable set of numbered cubbyholes. You can put just about anything you like in the cubbyholes, and the collection helps you keep track of them and access them. The power of collections is further enhanced in that the items in a collection do not all have to be the same data type (although they often will be). You can do five basic functions with a collection:

- Determine how many items are in the collection with the **Count** property.

- Add a new item with the **Add** method.

- Remove an existing item with the **Remove** method.

- Retrieve an item with the **Item** method.

- Loop through all items in the collection with the **For Each...Next** statement.

Creating a Collection object is no different from creating any other object in Visual Basic. You can use **Dim** with **New**, or use **Dim** without **New**, followed by a **Set** statement. Thus, either

```
Dim C As New Collection
```

or

```
Dim C As Collection
...
Set C = New Collection
```

will create a Collection object named **C**. Once you have a collection, determining how many items it contains is trivial. For example:

```
Debug.Print "Collection C contains "; C.Count; ;" items."
```

You use the **Add** method to add items to a collection. The syntax is as follows (in this and other examples, assume the Collection object is named **C**):

```
C.Add item, key, before, after
```

The arguments for this method are:

- *Item*—An expression that specifies the member to add to the collection.

- *Key*—An optional string expression that uniquely identifies the member.

- *Before*—An optional argument specifying the existing collection member that the new member will be placed before.

- *After*—An optional argument specifying the existing collection member that the new member will be placed after.

You can specify the *before* and *after* arguments either as a number in the range **1-C.Count** or as a *key* expression. You can specify one or the other of these arguments in the **Add** method, but not both. If you omit both, the new member is placed at the end of the collection.

What can you put in a collection? Just about anything. Internally, a Collection object uses type **Variant** to store members, so there are very few limitations. Variables, user-defined objects, forms, user-defined types, arrays—just about anything can go in a collection. You can even put one collection in another, a technique that is potentially very powerful.

What Is "In" A Collection?

It is important to understand that a collection does not contain the actual items, but only references to them. Saying that we "put something in a collection" is not really accurate. When you put, say, an array in a collection, the array continues to exist independently of the collection. The collection contains only a reference to the array; this reference lets you access the array using the Collection object's tools. If you then delete the collection, the array itself is not affected.

Here is sample code showing some of the ways you can use collections. For the first example, assume the project has a form named **Form1**. The code adds the form to a collection, then uses the collection to reference the form and change its caption:

```
Dim C As New Collection
Dim F As Form
Set F = Form1
C.Add F, "my form"
C.Item("my form").Caption = "The Mad Programmer"
```

The following code adds an array to a collection and then uses the collection to access data in the array, adding the contents of elements 1 and 2 together:

```
Dim A(100) As Long, Total As Long
Dim C As New Collection
C.Add A, "array"
Total = C("array")(1) + C("array")(2)
```

In this last example, I made use of the fact that **Item** is the default property of a Collection object. When you refer to an object by name alone, you automatically get the default property. Thus

```
C("array")(2)
```

is the same as:

```
C.Item("array")(2)
```

Finally, here is code to create two collections, **C** and **D**, add **D** as a member of **C**, then use a reference to **C** to add a form to collection **D**:

```
Dim C As New Collection
Dim D As New Collection
Dim F As Form

Set F = Form1
C.Add D, "collection D"
C("collection D").Add F, "form1"
```

The final way you can use a Collection object is to loop through all of its members, using the **For Each...Next** statement. It works like this (assume **C** is your collection):

```
Dim obj As Variant
For Each obj in C
    ' Do something with obj here
Next
```

Here is a more concrete example. Suppose your collection **C** contains a bunch of Text Box objects. The following code will display the contents of all the Text Box objects in the immediate window:

```
Dim obj As Variant
For Each obj in C
   Debug.Print obj.Text
Next
```

The **For Each...Next** statement is not so useful when your collection contains objects of different types. This is because you cannot be sure that the object methods or properties called in the loop are supported by all of the collection members. In the previous code, for example, if **C** contained one Label object along with the Text Box objects, an error would occur, because a Label object does not have a **Text** property.

Now that you know how to create and use your own Collection objects, let's take a look at the collections that are built into Visual Basic.

Visual Basic's Built-In Collections

Working behind the scenes, Visual Basic and the Windows operating system maintain a number of collections that can be extremely useful to programmers. The built-in collections are similar in some ways to the **Collection** class that we just looked at. They differ in that they have no methods and only one property, **Count**. This makes sense, if you think about it. Because the collections are maintained by Visual Basic, the programmer does not need to add or remove members—and in fact, doing so would cause lots of trouble. They differ also in that they are 0-based, with the members having indexes ranging from 0 to Count-1. What exactly are these collections?

- Each Visual Basic project has a **Forms** collection that contains all the loaded forms in your project.

- Each form in your project has a **Controls** collection that contains all of the controls on the form.

- Windows maintains a **Printers** collection that contains a list of all the printers installed on the current system. I'll cover the **Printers** collection in Chapter 12.

You will most often use the **Forms** and **Controls** collections with the **For Each...Next** statement to access each and every form in your project or control on a form. The following code will populate a List Box control with the captions of all the project's forms:

```
Dim f As Form
For Each f In Forms
    List1.AddItem f.Caption
Next
```

Remember that the **Forms** collection contains only those forms that have been loaded. A program's main form is loaded when the program starts. Other forms are loaded either explicitly with the **Load** statement or when referenced in code. Here's another example that moves all of a program's forms up and to the left by a small amount:

```
Dim f As Form
For Each f In Forms
    f.Top = f.Top * 0.8
    f.Left = f.Left * 0.8
Next
```

You can also loop through the **Forms** collection using the indexes of the members, as shown here:

```
Dim i As Integer
For i = 0 to Forms.Count - 1
    Forms(i).Top = Forms(i).Top * 0.8
    Forms(i).Left = Forms(i).Left * 0.8
Next i
```

This approach, however, has no advantage over the **For Each** statement, and in fact, the syntax is a bit messier. Because the order of the forms within the collection is maintained by Visual Basic, you should not write code that depends on the forms being in any specific order in the **Forms** collection.

You can loop through the **Controls** collection in a similar manner. You must specify which form's **Controls** collection you are referring to; otherwise, Visual Basic assumes it is the current form (the one containing the code). Here is code that will switch all the controls on the current form from visible to invisible, then back again, when executed another time:

```
Dim c As Control
For Each c In Controls
    c.Visible = Not c.Visible
Next
```

You can combine looping through the **Controls** collection with looping through the **Forms** collection to access all of the controls in your project:

```
Dim f As Form
Dim c As Control

For Each f In Forms
    For Each c In f.Controls
        'Do something with c here.
    Next
Next
```

Looping though the controls can be more useful when you use the **TypeOf** keyword. This keyword lets you determine the type of a control—Text Box, Command Button, and so on. Then, you can apply code only to certain controls. For example, the following code clears all Text Box controls on a form:

```
Dim c As Control
For Each c in Controls
    If TypeOf c Is TextBox Then c.Text = ""
Next
```

Likewise, this code disables all Command Buttons on all forms:

```
Dim f As Form
Dim c As Control

For Each f In Forms
    For Each c In f.Controls
        If TypeOf c Is CommandButton Then c.Enabled = False
    Next
Next
```

You can refer to the Visual Basic Help system for details on the **TypeOf** names associated with different objects.

The Windows Common Controls

Among the most useful controls available to you as a Visual Basic programmer are the Windows Common Controls. As their name suggests, these controls are not part of Visual Basic *per se* but rather are a part of the Windows operating system. Because they are ActiveX controls, however, they are available for use by any application running under Windows. In fact, you have probably already seen some of these controls in use. Windows Explorer, for example, uses at least three of them.

Surprisingly, even some experienced Visual Basic programmers are unaware that they can use the Windows Common Controls in their projects. Perhaps this is because these controls are not part of the intrinsic controls, so they do not show up in the toolbox unless you put them there. Once you know about these controls, I think you'll use them frequently. One possible pitfall, however, is that some of the Common Controls are rather complex, and figuring out how to use them is not nearly as easy to figure out as, say, a Text Box or Option Button control. I have seen programmers turn away from these controls in frustration. That's too bad, because the effort they will save you in the long run is well worth the effort required to master them.

To help you get started with the Windows Common Controls, I have devoted the remainder of this chapter to the fundamentals of using them. Space limitations make it impossible to cover them all, or even to cover some of them in complete detail. I have, therefore, taken the following approach:

1. I will start by explaining the ImageList control, as it is used by several of the other controls.

2. I will explain the TreeView control in considerable detail. It is the most complex of all the common controls. Once you are familiar with it, learning the other controls will be an easier task.

3. I will explain the TabStrip and ListView controls in less detail, because some of what you learn about the TreeView control will apply here as well.

What about the other Common Controls? I will deal with the Toolbar control in a later chapter, when we use it in the database project. The remaining Windows Common Controls—Slider, Progress Bar, ImageCombo, and Status Bar—are not too complex, so you should be able to figure them out on your own. Remember, to make these controls available in your project, you must display the Components dialog box (Ctrl+T) and put a checkmark next to Microsoft Windows Common Controls. Once you do this, the nine controls will be displayed in your toolbox.

ImageList Control

The ImageList control is designed to let you create and manage a group of images. This control always works "behind the scenes"; you never actually see it when your program is running. It does not display images, but rather it is used to make a set of images available to other controls that use them, such as the TabStrip control discussed later in this chapter. An ImageList control can also perform certain types of manipulations on the images it contains, such as overlaying one image on another. While there is no restriction on the size of images placed in an ImageList control, it is generally used for small images, such as icons.

An ImageList control contains a collection called **ListImages** containing one or more ListImage objects. As with all collections, each object is identified by a 1-based **Index** property, giving its position in the collection, as well as by an optional **Key** property. You can add images to an ImageList control at design time or runtime. At design time, display the control's property pages and select the Images tab. Browse your disk for the image file, and optionally specify a **Key** property for the image. Repeat until you have added all the required images.

At runtime, you use the **Add** method to add images to the ImageList control. The syntax is similar to the **Add** method for other collections. Because we are dealing with loading a picture from a disk file, however, you must use the **LoadPicture** function. The following example adds the image APPLE.BMP to the ImageList and assigns it a **Key** property of "**apple**".

```
ImageList1.ListImages.Add , "apple", LoadPicture("apple.bmp")
```

While all the images loaded into an ImageList control do not have to be the same size, the control constrains them all to the same size once they are in the control. This makes sense, because for most uses, you would want all the images to appear as the same size when they are displayed—for example, on the tabs of a TabStrip control. What determines this size? At design time, you can specify the image size on the general page in the ImageList's property pages. This is permitted only if the control contains no images at the time. Otherwise, the native size of the first image loaded into the control will be used for all other images.

The ImageList control's **Overlay** method permits you to overlay one image on another. Because all images are the same size, overlaying them does not make much sense unless part of the top image is transparent, so that the bottom image can show through. This is achieved with the ImageList control's **MaskColor** property. The color you specify in this property will become transparent in the top image, permitting the second image to show through. Suppose you have an image consisting of a yellow lightning bolt on a green background, and you want to overlay the lightning bolt over another image. First, set the **MaskColor** property as follows:

```
ImageList1.MaskColor = vbGreen
```

Note that **vbGreen** is one of Visual Basic's intrinsic constants. You can find more details on intrinsic constants by searching the Help system. Once the mask color is set, call the **Overlay** method to perform the action. The following code overlays the image with **Index 2** over the picture with **Index 1** and displays the result in a Picture Box:

```
Pbox1.Picture = ImageList1.Overlay 1, 2
```

You could also create the overlay image and add it as a new image in the same ImageList control:

```
ImageList1.ListImages.Add , "overlaid image", _
    ImageList1.Overlay 1, 2
```

You could also specify the images to be overlaid by their **Key** properties, instead of using the **Index** property.

TreeView Control

The TreeView control lets you display and manipulate items in a hierarchical view. An example that most of us see every day is Windows Explorer, which uses a TreeView control to display folders and file names. You can select single or multiple items, open and close branches on the tree, and control the way items are displayed. Each item in a TreeView can have an icon associated with it, such as the file folder and page icons used in Windows Explorer. You're not limited to disk-related items, though—a TreeView control can be used for any information that is arranged hierarchically.

To be honest, the TreeView control is not all that easy to understand and use. It is a complicated control, and it doesn't provide the almost-instant gratification that we Visual Basic programmers have perhaps become too accustomed to. You'll have to exercise your noggin a bit before you can get a TreeView control doing just what you want it to.

The main reason for the TreeView control's complexity is its structure. It is not, as are most Visual Basic controls, just a single object with a set of properties and methods. Oh no, that would make life too easy. Let me explain:

- Each item on a TreeView—each twig on the tree—is a Node object. Each of these Node objects has its own set of properties and methods.

- All of the Node objects belonging to a particular TreeView are organized in the **Nodes** collection, which is itself an object with methods and properties. One of the **Nodes** collection's methods is **Item**, which is used to access the individual Node objects in the collection.

- The TreeView control itself is an object with methods and properties. One of its properties is **Nodes**, which refers to its **Nodes** collection.

- The TreeView object is (optionally) associated with an ImageList object that holds the images to be displayed at the tree nodes.

You can probably see where the confusion comes from. When you want to do something with a TreeView object, it's not always clear whether you use the methods and properties of the TreeView object itself, or whether you must manipulate its associated **Nodes** collection or, perhaps, work directly with a Node object.

While the TreeView control by itself can be useful, it really comes into its own when you associate each node in the tree with something else. When TreeView is used for a folder/file display, the association is automatic. What about other associations? I'll be showing you how to associate a Text Box with each node in a tree, and you can use the same or similar techniques to associate other objects with TreeView nodes. I can't show all the details of using the TreeView control, but I can get you started so you can explore further on your own. I'll include a sample application that illustrates the techniques I cover.

Adding Nodes To A Tree

A TreeView object starts its life with no nodes. In form design, you'll see a few sample nodes displayed on the control, but these are present only so you can view the effect of changing properties that determine how the nodes are displayed. They are not present when you run the program. Nodes exist at various levels. The topmost level is the *root*. Two nodes at the same level are *siblings*. A node that is subsidiary to another is the *child*, while the other is the *parent*. While a program is executing, the user can open a node, displaying all of its children (if any), or close it, hiding any child nodes. You can also open and close nodes in code, so with a single command, you can perform such useful tasks as opening or closing all branches on a given tree.

Nodes must be added programmatically using the **Add** method of the **Nodes** collection. Here's the syntax:

```
NewNode = TV.Nodes.Add(relative, relationship, key, text, image,
selectedImage)
```

TV is the name of the TreeView control. All of the method arguments except one are optional, although it's pretty rare to use this method without using at least some of the optional arguments. Let's take a look at them:

- *Relative*—Required when you want to insert the new node in a relationship to an existing node. You specify the relative node by either its **Index** property or **Key** property (explained in a moment).

- *Relationship*—Used only when you specify *relative*. It determines the relationship that the new node has to the existing node. Your choices are:

  - **tvwLast**—The new node becomes a sibling of the node named in **relative** and is placed after all other siblings.

  - **tvwNext**—The new node becomes a sibling of the node named in **relative** and is placed immediately after it.

  - **tvwPrevious**—The new node becomes a sibling of the node named in relative and is placed immediately before it.

  - **tvwChild**—The node becomes a child node of the node named in relative (this is the default).

- *Key*—A unique string that identifies the node. If you specify this argument, you can later refer to specific nodes by using the **Item** method with the *key* value.

- *Text*—The node label displayed in the TreeView control. This is the only required argument for the **Add** method.

- *Image*—The **Key** or **Index** property of the image in the associated ImageList control that will be displayed as part of the node.

- *SelectedImage*—Specifies the image that will be displayed when the node is selected. If this argument is omitted, the image specified by *image* will be displayed, whether the node is selected or not.

Each node added to a tree is automatically assigned a unique **Index** property. These are nothing more than sequential integers that uniquely identify each node. Each node in a tree, therefore, can always be uniquely identified by its **Index** property, as well as by its **Key** property, if you assigned one. As we will see, the **Index** property provides a method of linking each node to some other object. Note also that each Node object has the **Tag** property, which can provide another way of both identifying and linking nodes.

Displaying Images At Nodes

To display images along with the text in TreeView nodes, you must associate an ImageList control with the TreeView object. This is one of the relatively simple aspects of working with a TreeView control. You need only to place an ImageList control on your form, then include code to load it with the needed images, assigning each one a unique **Key** property. (You learned about the ImageList control earlier in this chapter.) Then, associate the ImageList control with TreeView by setting the appropriate property. You can do this at design time, using the TreeView control's Custom Properties dialog box, or at runtime, as follows:

```
TreeView1.ImageList = ImageList1
```

Finally, each time you add a node to the tree, specify which image is to be displayed with the node, using the image's **Key** property to refer to it. You can also specify a different image to be used when the node is open and displaying its child nodes, just as Windows Explorer displays open or closed file folder images as appropriate. This is done by setting the **SelectedImage** property to the desired image when the node is open.

Where do you get the images? You can create your own, or you can use those supplied by Visual Basic, designed specifically for use with the TreeView control. They are installed in a subfolder off the main Visual Basic folder. Installation of these and other graphics is optional when Visual Basic is installed, so if you cannot find these images, you may need to repeat the Visual Basic installation. Here are the available images:

- OPEN.BMP—An open file folder

- CLOSED.BMP—A closed file folder

- LEAF.BMP—A document page

- PLUS.BMP—A plus sign

- MINUS.BMP—A minus sign

Working With Nodes

At any given moment, a TreeView object has at least one selected node (assuming, of course, that you have added one or more nodes to it). The selected node can be specified in code, and it can be automatically set when the user clicks on a node. You might expect the highlight to move to the selected node, but this is not the case. Being selected and being highlighted are two separate functions as far as a node on a TreeView control is concerned. In many applications, however, you want them to coincide. You must do this in code, using the **DropHighlight** property as follows:

```
Set TV.DropHighlight = Nothing
Set TV.DropHighlight = node
```

The first line removes any existing highlight, and the second line highlights the node referenced by *node*. This code goes in an event procedure, but not in the TreeView control's **Click** procedure. This procedure is called whenever the control is clicked, regardless of whether the click happened on a node or elsewhere on the control. Rather, you use the **NodeClick** event procedure, which is called only when a node is clicked:

```
Private Sub TreeView1_NodeClick(ByVal Node As Node)
```

Keeping track of nodes—which one is selected, which one is highlighted, and so on—can indeed be a bit tricky. Often, you must use an independent program variable to hold the **Index** property of the currently selected node, as I have done in the demonstration program. Then, when the user clicks on another node to select it, you can determine the identity of the previously selected node in case you need to manipulate it in some way, such as removing its highlight.

Associating Data With Nodes

As I mentioned earlier, the TreeView control becomes a lot more useful when you have the capability of associating data with each node. At the simplest level, you can use each Node object's **Tag** property to hold a chunk of text. While this is suitable for some applications, it is too limited to take you very far.

> ### Playing Tag
>
> The **Tag** property is potentially very useful, but is often ignored. Almost every Visual Basic control has this property, but its use is a mystery to most programmers. Actually, Visual Basic does not use the **Tag** property at all—it is provided purely for the convenience of the programmer. You can store anything you want in a control's **Tag** property and use that information in any way you like.

A better idea is to take advantage of the unique **Index** property that each Node object is automatically assigned when it is created. You can use this number as a link between each node and a specific item in any of Visual Basic's data-storage methods that uses indexed retrieval. For example, each node's **Index** could point to a record in a random access file or to an element in an array. Either of these methods would be pretty easy to work out.

Potentially more interesting, I believe, is to combine a TreeView control with a control array. This is the method I have used in the demonstration program. Recall that a control array consists of two or more controls of the same type and name, distinguished from each other by their **Index** property. Thus, you could have 10 Text Box controls named MyText: MyText(0), MyText(1), and so on up to MyText(9). You can create a control array at design time, but you have more flexibility if you do it in code. You must place the first element of the array on a form during design and be sure to set its **Index** property to 0. Then, use the **Load** statement to create new control array elements. If the control you inserted at design time is named MyText, the code to add a new Text Box to the control array would be

```
Load MyText(Index)
```

where **Index** is the index of the new control. The value of **Index** must be unique for each control in the array, of course, but the values do not have to be sequential. Thus, we can add a new node to a TreeView control, inserting it as a child of the currently selected node, and create a new Text Box to go with it as follows:

```
Dim newNode as node
Set newNode = TV.Nodes.Add(TV.SelectedItem.Index, _
      tvwChild, , newNodeName, pictureKey)
Load MyText(newNode.Index)
```

There's Lots More

I wish I had the time and space to tell you more about the TreeView control, but the best I can do is point you in the right direction and let you explore on your own. The TreeView object has a variety of properties that control its appearance, letting you change, for example, the amount of indentation child nodes have with respect to their parent, how lines between nodes are drawn, and the like. You can also specify that all nodes at each level be sorted alphabetically.

The **Nodes** collection has only a few properties and methods. You can add and remove nodes, clear all nodes at once, and determine the number of nodes present.

Each individual Node object has a set of properties and methods that provide a great deal of flexibility to the programmer. You can, for example, determine the parent, children, root, and siblings of any node, as well as refer to the next and previous node in the **Nodes** collection. Using these properties, you can make modifications, such as deleting the current node and all its children, or using the drag-and-drop function to move nodes around in the tree.

A Demonstration

I could go on and on explaining various details of how the TreeView control works, but I think the best way to explain it is to show you. We will create a simple program that demonstrates the most important features of the TreeView control. Start a Standard EXE project. Place the following controls on the form, leaving all properties at their default values except for the ones listed:

- *TreeView*

  Name: TV1

- *ImageList*

- *Command Button*

  Name: cmdAddNode

  Caption: Add a Node

- *Text Box*

  Index: 0

  Multiline: True

Note that you must set the **Index** property of the Text Box control to 0 to designate it as a control array. Even though the array has only this one member at design time, you can add array members at runtime. This would not be possible if the **Index** property were left at its default blank value.

Arrange the controls as shown in Figure 7.1.

Next, use the Add Form command on the Project menu to add a new form to the project. Assign this form the **Name** property of **frmAddNode** and the **Caption** property **Add a Node**. Put the following controls on the form:

- *Text Box*

  Name: txtNodeName

- *Label*

  Caption: Node name:

- *Frame*

  Name: Frame1

  Caption: Node level

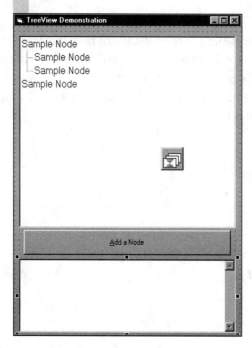

Figure 7.1 *Creating the main form for the TreeView demonstration program.*

- *Frame:*

  Name: Frame2

  Caption: Node type:

- *Command Button* (array of 2)

  Index 0 Caption: OK

  Index 1 Caption: Cancel

Next, you need to draw two Option Buttons on each of the Frame controls. Remember, you must draw each Option Button within the borders of the Frame control, so they can be treated as a group. On the Frame labeled Node level, put these two Option Buttons:

- *First button:*

  Caption: &Sibling

  Name: optSibling

  Value: True

- *Second button:*

  Caption: &Child

  Name: optChild

  Value: False

Then, on the Frame labeled Node type, put these two Option Buttons:

- *First button:*

  Caption: &Folder

  Name: optFolder

  Value: True

- *Second button:*

  Caption: &Document

  Name: optDocument

  Value: False

Your finished form will look like Figure 7.2. Before we turn our attention to the code, let's save the project. I used the names *TreeView1.frm* and *frmAddNode.frm* for the form files, and *Treeview* for the project file.

The code for this project is presented in Listings 7.1 (code in TreeView1.frm) and 7.2 (code in frmAddNode.frm). I am not going to hold your hand through all the details of adding code, as I am sure you know the required procedures by now. Furthermore, you should be able to figure out how the code works by looking at the comment lines.

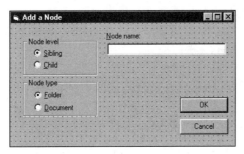

Figure 7.2   *The completed Add a Node form.*

Listing 7.1 Code in TreeView1.frm, the main form in the TreeView demonstration program.

```
Option Explicit

' Global variable to hold the Index
' property of the currently selected node.
Dim CurrentNode As Integer

Private Sub cmdAddNode_Click()

Dim newNode As Node
Dim nodeType As Integer
Dim relation As Integer
Dim picture As String

' Display the "add a node" form.
frmAddNode.Show 1

' If user selected Cancel,
' don't do anything.
If frmAddNode.txtNodeName.Text = "" Then Exit Sub

' Set picture type for document or folder.
If frmAddNode.optDocument = True Then
    picture = "leaf"
Else
    picture = "closed"
End If

' Specify child node or sibling node.
If frmAddNode.optSibling.Value = True Then
    relation = tvwNext
Else
    relation = tvwChild
End If

' Be sure the current node is expanded.
TV1.SelectedItem.Expanded = True

' Create the new node.
Set newNode = TV1.Nodes.Add( _
            TV1.SelectedItem.Index, _
            relation, , _
            frmAddNode.txtNodeName.Text, _
            picture)

' Deselect the current node and
' select the new node.
```

```
TV1.SelectedItem.Selected = False
TV1.Nodes(newNode.Index).Selected = True
CurrentNode = newNode.Index

If (TV1.Nodes.Item(CurrentNode).Tag = "doc") Then
    Text1(CurrentNode).Visible = False
End If

' Unhighlight the highlighted node (if any)
' and highlight the new node.
Set TV1.DropHighlight = Nothing
Set TV1.DropHighlight = newNode

' If the new node is a document node, create its
' Text Box and make it visible.
If frmAddNode.optDocument = True Then
    newNode.Tag = "doc"
    Load Text1(newNode.Index)
    Text1(newNode.Index).Text = Str$(newNode.Index)
    Text1(newNode.Index).Visible = True
Else
    newNode.Tag = "folder"
End If

End Sub

Private Sub Form_Load()

Dim img As ListImage
Dim s As String
Dim newNode As Node

' Initialize current node pointer.
CurrentNode = -1

' Load the ImageList control with bitmaps. Change the
' path to the bitmap files if necessary. This code assumes
' they are in the same folder as the application.

Set img = ImageList1.ListImages.Add _
    (, "open", LoadPicture _
    (App.Path & "\open.bmp"))
Set img = ImageList1.ListImages.Add _
    (, "closed", LoadPicture _
    (App.Path & "\closed.bmp"))
Set img = ImageList1.ListImages.Add _
    (, "leaf", LoadPicture _
    (App.Path & "\leaf.bmp"))
```

```
' Clear the TreeView control.
TV1.Nodes.Clear

' Set Treeview control properties.
TV1.ImageList = ImageList1
TV1.Style = tvwTreelinesPlusMinusPictureText
TV1.LineStyle = tvwTreeLines

' Get top node name.
s = InputBox("Name for top-level node?")
If s = "" Then End

' Create Node object.
' Add the first node.
Set newNode = TV1.Nodes.Add(, , , s, "closed")
newNode.Selected = True
CurrentNode = newNode.Index
Set TV1.DropHighlight = newNode
newNode.Tag = "folder"

End Sub

Private Sub TV1_NodeClick(ByVal Node As Node)

' Called when the user clicks a node.

' If the previous node was a document,
' hide its Text Box.
If TV1.Nodes.Item(CurrentNode).Tag = "doc" Then
    Text1(CurrentNode).Visible = False
End If

CurrentNode = Node.Index

' If the newly selected node is a document,
' show its Text Box.
If Node.Tag = "doc" Then
    Text1(Node.Index).Visible = True
End If

' Highlight the newly selected node.
Set TV1.DropHighlight = Nothing
Set TV1.DropHighlight = Node

End Sub
```

Listing 7.2   Code in frmAddNode.frm, the second form in the TreeView demonstration program.

```
Private Sub Command1_Click(Index As Integer)

Select Case Index
    Case 0: ' OK button
        If txtNodeName.Text = "" Then
            MsgBox ("You must enter a node name!")
            txtNodeName.SetFocus
            Exit Sub
        Else
            Hide
        End If
    Case 1: ' Cancel button
        txtNodeName.Text = ""
        Hide
End Select

End Sub
```

When you start the program, it asks you for the name of the tree's first node. Then you can click on the Add a Node button to add a new node as either a child or a sibling to the current (highlighted) node, which you select by clicking. New nodes can also be designated as Documents, in which case a Text Box is created and associated with it, or as a Folder, which gets no Text Box. You can enter text in the Text Boxes, and when you click on a different **Document** node, its text is displayed. Figure 7.3 shows the program executing.

This is most definitely a demonstration program, because it lacks many of the features that a real-world program would require, such as the ability to save data to disk or to delete existing nodes. The techniques that it uses could, however, form the nucleus of a useful program that permits the user to organize sections of text in a hierarchical manner. Without much thought, I can already imagine many useful enhancements, such as the ability to combine the text from a selected range of nodes into a single document, or to drag and drop nodes to change the tree's organization. There are plenty of possibilities here for you to explore.

TabStrip Control

The TabStrip control is, in my opinion, one of the most useful of the Windows Common Controls. I am sure you have seen it in action many times—for example, in the Visual Basic Options dialog box. It lets you create multipage dialog boxes with each page represented by a tab at the top of the box. You just click on the associated tab to bring its page into view. With a TabStrip control, you can put a lot of functionality in a single dialog box without making it too large or confusing.

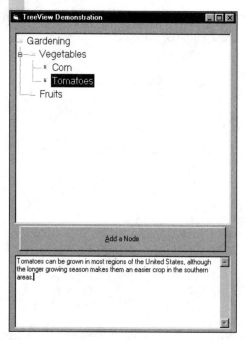

Figure 7.3 *The TreeView demonstration program.*

The TabStrip control contains a collection of one or more Tab objects, with the collection itself called **Tabs**. Each Tab object represents one page in the control. Most of the properties associated with a TabStrip control affect the entire control—for example, you can specify the font used for the captions on the tabs and whether the tabs are displayed at the top or the bottom of the dialog box. A few properties apply to individual Tab objects—for example, specifying the caption displayed on the tab or the Tool Tip Text displayed when the user hovers the mouse pointer over the tab. To work with TabStrip properties, you will need to use its property pages, as some properties are not displayed in the normal Visual Basic Properties window. To access a control's property pages, right-click on the control and select Properties from the pop-up menu.

You can add tabs to or remove them from the control at design time or runtime. At design time, display the control's property pages and display the Tabs tab. Use the Insert Tab and Delete Tab buttons to add and remove Tabs. Each tab in a TabStrip control is identified by an index number, starting at 1. A tab can also be identified by its **Key** property. You can assign any unique string to the **Key** property and then use that value to access the tab at runtime, without worrying about the tab's **Index** property, which might have changed if additional tabs were added to the TabStrip control. I find it most useful to make a tab's **Key** property the same as its **Caption** property.

You can access a specific tab by means of either its **Index** or **Key** property. Here are two ways to set the **Caption** property of the Tab object with **Index** 2 and **Key** "graphics." Assume the TabStrip control is named TabStrip1:

```
TabStrip1.Tabs.Item(2).Caption = "Options"
TabStrip1.Tabs.Item("graphics").Caption = "Options"
```

Note that because the **Item** property is the default property of Collection objects, the following two lines of code are exactly equivalent to the previous two lines:

```
TabStrip1.Tabs(2).Caption = "Options"
TabStrip1.Tabs("graphics").Caption = "Options"
```

To add a tab at runtime, use the **Tabs** collection's **Add** method. The syntax is as follows:

```
TabStrip1.Tabs.Add IndexNumber, Key, Caption
```

If you omit the *IndexNumber* argument, the new tab will be placed at the end of the collection. If you specify an *IndexNumber* argument that is already in use, existing tabs will be bumped up to make room for the new tab. You cannot specify an *IndexNumber* that is more than one higher than the highest index already in use. To determine this value, which also gives the number of tabs in the TabStrip, query the **Tabs** collection's **Count** property. For example, assume your project has a TabStrip control named tabOptions; the following code will add two new tabs:

```
tabOptions.Tabs.Add , "printing", "Printing"
tabOptions.Tabs.Add , "display", "Display"
```

Each tab can display a small image instead of, or along with, its caption. To display images, you must first load the images into an ImageList control and then associate that control with the TabStrip control (further details on the ImageList control will be presented later in this chapter). The ImageList control must be on the same form as the TabStrip. You create the association between the two controls either by using the TabStrip's property pages (on the general page) or in code:

```
TabStrip1.ImageList = ImageList1
```

You then assign a specific image from the ImageList to a specific tab using the Tabs page in the TabStrip control's property pages or in code. The following code assigns the image whose **Index** property in the ImageList control is **2** to the tab with **Index 1** in the TabStrip control:

```
TabStrip1.Tabs(1).Image = 2
```

Visual Basic has other properties that control various aspects of the TabStrip's appearance, but you can explore these on your own. With some experimentation and the assistance of the Visual Basic Help system, I am sure you'll figure them out. More important is that you understand how other controls are displayed on the pages of a TabStrip control and how you manipulate the control to meet the requirements of your program.

You might think that each tab in a TabStrip control provides a separate container in which you can place the other controls—Text Boxes, Labels, etc.; then, when the user clicks on a tab, the associated controls are automatically displayed. This approach makes sense, but it's not the way Microsoft did things. You must provide your own container for the controls to be displayed on each tab, then hide and display the appropriate containers when the user clicks on one of the tabs on the TabStrip control. You can use either Frame or Picture Box controls as containers, but the lower overhead of the Frame control makes it the preferred choice. Here's what you need to do.

At design time:

1. Create a control array of Frame objects with one member for each tab on the TabStrip control. Each Frame will be associated with a tab, based on its **Index** properties. Because control arrays start at an **Index** of 0 and the **Tabs** collection starts at an **Index** of 1, you should associate **Frame(*n*)** with **Tab(*n+1*)**.

2. On each Frame, place the various controls that you want displayed when the user clicks on the corresponding tab.

3. Create a module-level variable that will keep track of which tab is currently displayed.

Then, at runtime:

4. In the **Form_Load** event, specify the tab and Frame that will be displayed initially. Also, use the **Move** method to position each Frame to completely cover the tab's client area.

5. In the TabStrip's **Clicked** event procedure, read the **SelectedItem.Index** property to determine which tab was clicked. If it is the same as the currently displayed tab, do nothing and exit the Sub.

6. If a different tab was clicked, set the **Visible** property of the currently displayed Frame to False and the **Visible** property of the Frame corresponding to the just-clicked tab to True.

7. Set the global variable to reflect the newly displayed tab.

Here is some example code both to set up the TabStrip when the form loads and to respond to clicks. Assume that the TabStrip is named TabStrip1, the array of Frame controls is called Frame1, and the global variable for keeping track of the current Tab is called **CurrentTab**:

```
Private Sub Form_Load()

    Dim i As Integer

    ' Move all frames to fill client area. Set
    ' Visible to False and BorderStyle to
    ' None for all.
    For i = 0 To Frame1.Count - 1
    With Frame1(i)
        .Move TabStrip1.ClientLeft, _
            TabStrip1.ClientTop, _
            TabStrip1.ClientWidth, _
            TabStrip1.ClientHeight
        .Visible = False
        .BorderStyle = 0
    End With
    Next i

    ' Make Tab 1 active and its Frame visible.
    CurrentTab = 1
    Set TabStrip1.SelectedItem = TabStrip1.Tabs(CurrentTab)
    Frame1(CurrentTab - 1).Visible = True

End Sub

Private Sub TabStrip1_Click()

    If TabStrip1.SelectedItem.Index = CurrentTab _
        Then Exit Sub

    Frame1(TabStrip1.SelectedItem.Index - 1).Visible _
        = True
    Frame1(CurrentTab - 1).Visible = False
    CurrentTab = TabStrip1.SelectedItem.Index

End Sub
```

At runtime, you should have the Frame controls display without a border or caption. This can be done by setting the **BorderStyle** property to None. At design time, however, seeing the Frame and its caption is useful, so you might want to consider leaving the **BorderStyle** property at Fixed Single during program design and then setting it to None in code at runtime, as was done in the previous sample code. During design, how do you work with a stack of Frame controls that are by necessity overlapping each other? The trick is to use the Order command on the Format menu. Use Bring to Front to put a Frame on "top" of the stack, so you can add controls to it and arrange them. Use Send to Back to move the current Frame to the "bottom" of the stack, so you can work on another Frame.

ListView Control

The ListView control permits you to display lists of items. I'll bet you are already familiar with this control. Just look at Windows Explorer; the right panel in the Explorer window is a ListView control (this is, after all, why they are called Windows Common Controls—they are used in many different Windows applications). Four types of views are available in a ListView control:

- *Icon*—Descriptive text with a large icon
- *SmallIcon*—Descriptive text with a small icon
- *List*—A sorted list of items
- *Report*—Similar to List view, but permits display of subitems

You can get a feel for what these views are like by opening Windows Explorer and using the commands on its View menu to try out the different views. When a ListView control is in Icon view, you can use the mouse to drag items around, rearranging them within the control as desired. Drag-and-drop is also operative, if it is enabled. SmallIcon view offers similar rearranging capabilities, but the items are displayed in list format with small icons rather than as large icons. List view appears similar to SmallIcon view, except that you cannot rearrange items, and the list is, by default, sorted. Report view offers the option of two or more columns in the list, permitting you to display additional details about each item. For example, in Windows Explorer, Report view (called Details) displays not only the file name but also its size, creation date, and so on.

As is the case with the other controls we have been discussing, the ListView control uses collections. Each item displayed in the control is a ListItem object; all of these objects are within the control's **ListItems** collection. This control uses one other collection, as we will soon see.

Each ListView control can have two ImageList controls associated with it. The ImageList controls are used to store the icons that will be used in Icon and SmallIcon views. You can specify the ImageList controls at design time using the ListView control's property pages, or you can set them at runtime:

```
ListView1.Icons = ImageList1
ListView1.SmallIcons = ImageList2
```

Adding items to the ListView control is done with (of course) the **ListItems** collection's **Add** method. Here's the syntax:

```
ListView1.ListItems.Add index, key, text, icon, smallIcon
```

index and *key* are the same as for all the other collections we have seen—the numerical position of the new item in the collection and a unique identifying string. *Text* is the data to be displayed. The final two arguments—*icon* and *smallIcon*—identify the icons to be displayed with the item in Icon and SmallIcon views, respectively. These images are taken from the ImageList control or controls that were associated with the ListView control, as described earlier. You can specify an image using either its **Index** property or its **Key** property in the ImageList control. Here is how you would add a new item to a ListView control, at the next available **Index** position, specifying an icon by **Index** and a smallIcon by **Key**:

```
ListView1.ListItems.Add , "apricot", "Apricot", 2, "fruit"
```

You can have the ListView control automatically sort the items it displays. The control has three properties that determine how the sorting is done:

- Set **Sorted** to True or False to determine whether the list is sorted or not.

- Set **SortOrder** to **lvwAscending** (value = 0, the default) or to **lvwDescending** (value = 1) for an ascending or descending sort order.

- Set **SortKey** to 0 (the default) to sort based on the values in the ListItem objects' **Text** property. Set **SortKey** to a value of 1 or greater to sort on the subitem with the specified **Index**.

The second collection that the ListView control uses is **ColumnHeaders**. As you can probably guess by now, this collection contains ColumnHeader objects. Each item in this collection corresponds to a column of data displayed in the ListView control and, of course, is relevant only when the control is in Report view. You can add to this collection at design time, using the control's property pages, or at runtime with the **Add** method. The syntax is quite similar to the **Add** method for the other collections we have dealt with:

```
ListView1.ColumnHeaders.Add index, key, text, width, alignment
```

The *index* argument specifies the position of the new ColumnHeader in the collection. If this argument is omitted, the new entry is placed at the end of the collection. Because the columns are displayed across the top of the ListView control in numerical order (left to right), you can use the *index* argument to determine display order.

The *key* argument is a unique string that is used to refer to the object in code, and the *text* argument is the text that is displayed in the column heading. *Width* specifies the width of the column using the scale units of the container that the ListView control is placed in. You can omit the *width* argument, in which case the default value of 1,440 twips (1 inch) is used.

Alignment specifies how both the column header text and the data in the column are aligned. Possible values are **lvwColumnLeft** (value 0, the default), **lvwColumnRight** (value 1), and **lvwColumnCenter** (value 2). I am sure that you can figure out the meanings of these constants. Be aware that the first column must be left-aligned, and if you try to set a different alignment, an error occurs.

The following code will add three column headers to a ListView control, each with a width of 1,000 twips:

```
ListView1.ColumnHeaders.Add 1, , "Last Name", 1000
ListView1.ColumnHeaders.Add 2, , "First Name", 1000
ListView1.ColumnHeaders.Add 3, , "Middle Initial", 1000
```

Once you have set up your columns, how do you add the details that will be displayed there? Each ListItem object in the ListView control has a **SubItems** property that consists of an array of strings. This array holds the detail data that is displayed when the ListView control is in Report view mode. This is a 1-based array; the first element holds the detail item to be displayed in the first extra column (the first, or left-most column displays the text stored in the **ListItem's Text** property). Note that the **ColumnHeader** with **index 2** refers to the column containing the detail data in **SubItems(1)**. The detail information must be added at runtime, as shown here:

```
Dim lvi As ListItem
Set lvi = ListView1.ListItems.Add(, "Aitken", "Aitken")
lvi.SubItems(1) = "Peter"
lvi.SubItems(2) = "G."

ListView1.ListItems.Add , "Clinton", "Clinton"
Set lvi = ListView1.ListItems("Clinton")
lvi.SubItems(1) = "William"
lvi.SubItems(2) = "J."

ListView1.ListItems.Add , "Edison", "Edison"
ListView1.ListItems("Edison").SubItems(1) = "Thomas"
ListView1.ListItems("Edison").SubItems(2) = "A."
```

You can see that I used three different methods of achieving the same thing—adding a **ListItem** and setting two of its **SubItems**. All of these approaches are exactly alike and demonstrate the flexibility of the Visual Basic collections model. After executing the two code fragments, the ListView control will appear as in Figure 7.4. Of course, the control mus have its **View**property set to 3-lvwReport for this code to work.

User access to items displayed in a ListView control is provided by means of the **SelectedItem** property. This property returns a reference to the ListItem object that is currently selected—

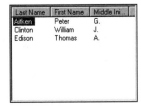

Figure 7.4   *The ListView control after adding three items to it.*

that is, highlighted. For example, place the following code in a ListView control's **Click** event procedure to display a message box identifying the list item clicked on by the user:

```
Private Sub ListView1_Click()

Dim item As ListItem

Set item = ListView1.SelectedItem
MsgBox (item.Text)

End Sub
```

You can also use the **SelectedItem** property to specify programmatically which item in the list will be highlighted. The following code will highlight the second item in the list:

```
Set ListView1.SelectedItem = ListView1.ListItems(2)
```

Chapter 8
ActiveX Components

ActiveX is hot, and Visual Basic lets you join the party.

One of Visual Basic's strong points is its ability to use existing software components that provide sophisticated functionality for your project, freeing you from writing the code or designing the interface. Although controls represent an example of a software component, they are not the only type. Since the introduction of Visual Basic, this notion of software components has continued to expand. In fact, many of the industry's movers and shakers now consider it central to their vision of the future of desktop computing. If you are programming for the Windows operating system, the most important software component technology you need to master is ActiveX. In this chapter, we will see exactly what ActiveX technology is, and we will work through a project in which you create your own ActiveX software component.

What's In A Name?

A number of years ago, programmers realized that the functionality of software would be greatly enhanced if capabilities could be shared among programs. Let me illustrate with an example. Suppose you were creating a report using a word processor and needed to include a table of figures and calculations in your document. Your spreadsheet program is perfectly suited to creating such a table, but how could you access the spreadsheet program from within your word processor? The answer: *Object Linking and Embedding*, or OLE. With OLE, you can insert a spreadsheet object within a word processor document—in other words, create a compound document. While working in the word processor, you can activate the spreadsheet object, which starts the spreadsheet program and allows you to work on the table just as if it were a regular spreadsheet (which, in many ways, it is). When you exit the spreadsheet program, the table, with all of the changes you made, would display in the word processor document.

OLE is based on a broader technology called the *Component Object Model*, or COM. As this technology spread well beyond the creation of compound documents, the name OLE came to be applied to anything that used the COM paradigm—including, but not limited to, compound document capabilities.

Not too long ago, a new term entered the scene: *ActiveX*. Initially, ActiveX referred to technologies that used the COM paradigm for Internet and World Wide Web-related tasks. Before long, however, ActiveX came to subsume more and more of the entire COM world—regardless of whether a specific item was related to the Internet. The term *OLE* has gone back to its original, more limited meaning involving the creation of compound documents. This is where we stand today—although nothing is quite as sure as change, especially in the world of computers.

Whenever you hear the term *ActiveX*, realize that it refers to a wide range of COM-based techniques by which one piece of software makes its capabilities available to another piece of software. It doesn't matter whether the two pieces are on the same computer, are connected via a local network, or are located on different continents and connected by the Internet.

This chapter not only introduces you to Visual Basic's ActiveX capabilities, but it also shows you how to create an ActiveX server (the software that provides the service) and an ActiveX client (the software that uses the service). We'll explore Visual Basic's OLE capabilities in Chapter 10, and we'll take a peek at using ActiveX on the Web in Chapter 17.

Visual Basic's Class Module

At the heart of Visual Basic's ActiveX object creation abilities is its class module. Each class module in a project defines a class, which then can serve as the blueprint for the creation of objects—instances of the class. In Chapter 6, you learned how to use a class module to define a class within a Standard EXE Visual Basic project and how to use that class within the project. The class is limited to use within that project, however, and is not exposed for use by other programs. If you want to create a class that will be available for use by other programs, you must enclose the class within an ActiveX wrapper.

How is this done? Don't worry, it's not at all complicated. All you need to do is create the class within an ActiveX project, one of the project types that Visual Basic makes available to you in the New Project dialog box. Only within an ActiveX project will an object be exposed for use by other applications. An object is exposed by means of its *interface*. This does not refer to a visual interface, but rather to the properties and methods that the object makes available to other applications. An ActiveX object's properties are defined by the **Property Let** and **Property Get** procedures in the class module, and its methods are the public procedures you place in the class module. You had an introduction to this in Chapter 6, and we'll go into more detail in this chapter.

ActiveX terminology can be a bit confusing. An *ActiveX class*, which you define in a Visual Basic class module, is best thought of as a blueprint, or plan. An *ActiveX object* is created from this blueprint when requested by an application. A parallel exists with Basic variables. A variable that you declare is an instance (object) of a certain data type (class). An *ActiveX server* is a program that exposes one or more classes for use by other applications, called *ActiveX clients*. Visual Basic can create programs that are ActiveX clients, ActiveX servers, or a combination of both.

Creating An ActiveX Server

Experience is undoubtedly the best teacher; the whole concept of ActiveX objects became much clearer to me after creating and testing my first one. I'll walk you through the creation of a simple server and then show you how to test it. We'll tackle something simple: a class to calculate square and cube roots. You would probably never create an ActiveX object for such a simple task, but it's a good starting point.

Our demonstration will be an ActiveX DLL. Why a DLL and not an ActiveX EXE? We want only to define a class and expose it for use by other programs. The project will have no functionality beyond this, so a DLL is ideal. I will explain how we could put this class in an ActiveX EXE later in the chapter.

For this project, we will not use Visual Basic's Class Builder utility. We saw in Chapter 6 how this add-in can help with some of the grunt work of creating a new class. By doing all these tasks yourself, however, you will learn more about the details of what is involved in creating a class.

Start Visual Basic and create a new ActiveX DLL project. A new ActiveX project automatically starts with a new class module; with other project types, you must select Add

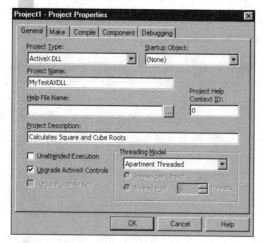

Figure 8.1 *Setting the ActiveX DLL project properties.*

Class Module from the Project menu to create a class module. The first task is to set some project properties, as shown in Figure 8.1.

Select Project1 Properties from the Project menu. Click on the General tab in the dialog box if necessary, then follow these steps:

1. *For StartUp Object, select (None).* You could also select Sub Main here, which would cause the code in a sub procedure named **Main** to be executed when the ActiveX component starts executing. You would have to create this sub yourself, placing in it any initialization code required by the ActiveX server. Our project does not require any such code, however.

2. *Enter "MyTestAXDLL" in the Project Name box.* This will identify the server in the Windows Registry.

3. *In the Project Description box, enter "Calculates Square and Cube Roots".* This is the name that will identify the server in other applications' References lists.

Click on the OK button to close the Project Properties dialog box. Next, use the Properties window to set the class properties. Only two of the properties concern us for this project; the settings and an explanation of each follow:

- **Instancing MultiUse**—This setting permits other clients (outside the project) to create instances of the class, with multiple instances (if requested) supplied by a single running copy of the server. The other possible settings of this property set different restrictions on the class, but these do not concern us at present.

- *Name AXDEMO*—You can use any descriptive name here. This property is used to identify the class. It is displayed in other applications' Object Browser dialog boxes and is used in code (as we'll see later) to create an instance of the class.

Once the class module's properties are set, we can add the declarations of the variables that will be the class's properties. You accomplish this in the General Declarations section of the class module. Here's the code:

```
Option Explicit
Private pObjName As Variant
Private pDateCreated As Date
Private pNumber As Double
Private pSquareRoot As Double
Private pCubeRoot As Double
```

The **Option Explicit** statement should already be present, placed there automatically by Visual Basic. If not, you need to select Options from the Tools menu; on the Editor tab, turn on the Require Variable Declarations option. Lacking the **Option Explicit** statement in a module, Visual Basic does not require variables to be declared—a definite invitation to errors.

If you examine these variable declarations, you'll see that all of them are **Private**, meaning they are not accessible outside the ActiveX server. They can be used for purely internal uses by the class, or they can be exposed to clients as properties (for reading, writing, or both) by means of property procedures. When you expose a variable with a property procedure, it becomes one of the object's properties that can be accessed by clients.

We need to take a short detour from the demonstration project to explore property procedures. First, however, save the project. I used the default names suggested by Visual Basic: **MyTestAXDLL** for the project and **AXDEMO** for the class module (class modules are automatically given the .CLS extension).

Property Procedures

You had an introduction to property procedures in Chapter 6; now the time has come to learn more. Property procedures are a central part of ActiveX server programming. While you may be able to create very simple servers without using property procedures, you'll find them essential for most of your projects. You can use a property procedure to create standard read/write properties that can be both read and set by clients. These procedures also permit you to create read-only properties, perform some action when the property is read or set, or assign a Help topic to the property.

Property procedures come in three varieties. **Property Get** and **Property Let** are usually used in tandem, permitting the client to read and set, respectively, the value of a property in the ActiveX object. **Property Set** is used in place of **Property Let** when the property in question contains a reference to an object. Because the demonstration server does not use object reference properties, I'll limit the discussion to **Property Get** and **Property Let**.

Let's assume we want the object to have a property named **Total**. We would define a **Property Get** procedure as follows:

```
Property Get Total() As Double
    Total = pTotal
End Property
```

The private variable **pTotal** is declared elsewhere in the module to hold the property value. Note the use of the p prefix, a convention I use to identify a variable as being a property. This is not necessary, but it can help make your code easier to read.

We would also need a **Property Let** procedure:

```
Property Let Total(ByVal NewTotal As Double)
    pTotal = NewTotal
End Property
```

The data type of the **Property Let** procedure's argument must be the same as the type of the **Property Get** procedure's return value. The private variable used to hold the data should usually be the same type as well. In this example, therefore, **pTotal** would have to be a type **Double**.

How does the client access the **Total** property? Assume that the ActiveX client has created an instance of the class named **Ob**. To set the property, you would write the following code in the client application:

```
Ob.Total = SomeValue
```

To retrieve the value of the property, you would write this code in the client application:

```
AnotherValue = Ob.Total
```

When a property name (qualified by the object name, as always) is used on the left side of an assignment statement, the corresponding **Property Let** procedure in the server is called, and the value on the right side of the assignment statement is passed as the procedure's argument. Likewise, when a property name is used on the right side of an assignment statement, the corresponding **Property Get** procedure is called, and the return value is the value assigned in the procedure code (by the usual method of assigning a value to the procedure name).

Continuing The ActiveX Server Demonstration

There's more to property procedures, but you've learned enough to proceed with our sample server. To add a property procedure to a class module, select Add Procedure from the Tools menu, then select Property as the procedure type. Be sure the Scope remains at its default setting of **Public**. The procedure name is the name you want to use for referring to the property in the client applications. Adding a property procedure will create skeletons for both the **Get** and **Let** procedures. For a read-only property, leave the **Let** procedure empty. For a property that can be set, but does not need to be read, leave the **Get** procedure empty.

We have five property procedures to create. Three properties will need only **Get** procedures: the calculated square root (stored in the variable **pSquareRoot**), the calculated cube root (stored in **pCubeRoot**), and the object's creation time and date (stored in **pDateCreated**). The **Number** property (the value whose root we are calculating) will need only a **Let** procedure. The **Name** property, on the other hand, requires only a **Get** procedure—we want to be able both to retrieve and set it, but we will use a method to set it. We'll soon see how these values are placed in the variables. Listing 8.1 shows the code in the **Get** procedures. You should add these to your project using the techniques explained in the previous paragraph.

Listing 8.1   The Property Get procedures in the AXDLL_TEST ActiveX server.

```
Public Property Get SquareRoot() As Double
    SquareRoot = pSquareRoot
End Property

Public Property Get CubeRoot() As Double
    CubeRoot = pCubeRoot
End Property

Public Property Get Created() As Date
    Created = pDateCreated
End Property

Public Property Get Name() As Variant
    Name = pObjName
End Property
```

Note that we do not need a **Property Get** procedure for the **Number** property, because we will never need to retrieve its value (which is stored in the private variable **pNumber**). We will, however, need to set the value of **Number**. We can also use the **Let** procedure for the **Number** property to perform the necessary calculations. For this, we'll create a **Property Let** procedure named **Number**, as shown in Listing 8.2. Remember to leave the parallel **Property Get** procedure empty.

Listing 8.2 *The Let procedure for the Number property.*

```
Public Property Let Number(vNewValue As Double)
    pNumber = vNewValue
    pCubeRoot = pNumber ^ (1/3)
    pSquareRoot = pNumber ^ (0.5)
End Property
```

Two actions occur when this procedure is called—which happens, as I mentioned earlier, whenever a client references the **Number** property on the left side of an assignment statement. First, the value assigned to **Number** by the client is passed in the argument **vNewValue** and assigned to the private variable **pNumber**. Next, the cube root and square root of this value are calculated and assigned to the corresponding variables.

Initialization And Termination Procedures

Each class module has **Class_Initialize** and **Class_Terminate** procedures. These are executed when a client application creates an instance of the class and when the object is destroyed. You don't have to place any code in them. If your class requires any initialization or cleanup chores, however, this is where the code would go. If you want to see when your class is instantiated (when an object is created from it) and destroyed, you can place **MsgBox** calls in these procedures. Generally, however, code in these procedures should not interact with the user at all.

In our project, we need no cleanup, and during initialization our only task is to store the date and time in the private variable **pDateCreated**. Open the **Class_Initialize** procedure and add the single line of code shown in Listing 8.3.

Listing 8.3 *The ActiveX server's Class_Initialize procedure.*

```
Private Sub Class_Initialize()
    pDateCreated = Now
End Sub
```

Now is a Visual Basic function that returns the current date and time. The next and final step in creating our ActiveX object is to define its one method.

Defining A Method

ActiveX classes can contain *methods*. These are essentially the same as the methods that are part of Visual Basic objects. A method is like a procedure: It is a chunk of code that performs some action. The action depends on the needs of the object. It can be just about anything that you can do in Visual Basic, from manipulating disk files to displaying information on the screen. In any case, the way you define a method is the same—by creating a **Public** procedure.

The single method this class needs is code to set the **Name** property, which could easily have been done using a **Property Let** procedure. By using a method instead, you will learn how to add methods to ActiveX objects. Use the Add Procedure command on the Tools menu to add a sub procedure named **ChangeName** (be sure you select Sub, not Property, as the type in the Add Procedure dialog box). Make sure that the **Public** option is selected. The code for this method is shown in Listing 8.4.

Listing 8.4   The ChangeName method.

```
Public Sub ChangeName(newName As Variant)
    pObjName = newName
End Sub
```

The code is simple. The value passed as the method argument is assigned to the **pObjName** variable, which is associated with the **Name** property. By making this procedure public, we make it available as a method to clients. You can also define private procedures within an ActiveX object, but they can be called only from within the object itself.

That's it—you can now compile and run your ActiveX server. First, select Make MyTestAXDLL from the File menu to create the DLL file on disk. Then select the Start With Full Compile command from the Run menu. You should always use this command (instead of Start) to run an ActiveX server from within the Visual Basic environment, because this improves your chances of catching errors during compilation rather than later when the server is called by a client. This command will first display the Debugging tab in the Project Properties dialog box, as shown in Figure 8.2. Be sure that the Wait For Components To Be Created option is selected, then click on OK.

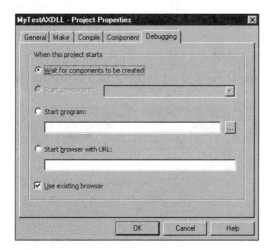

Figure 8.2   *Setting the DLL's debugging properties.*

When it runs, the server won't do anything visible, but it will register your newly created class with Windows, making it available to the test program we are about to create. You should next terminate execution by selecting End from the Run menu, then minimize Visual Basic. Once the class has been registered, Windows knows that the class definition is located in the DLL file that you created. Next, I'll show you how to test the server.

Testing The ActiveX Server

To test our nice new ActiveX object, we'll need an ActiveX client. We'll use Visual Basic to create this as well. Because Visual Basic is minimized with the DLL project loaded, how can we use it to create the ActiveX client? The trick is to start a second copy of Visual Basic and use the second instance to develop and test the client.

The DLL project does not need to be running in Visual Basic for this project to work, so why not just close the DLL project and start a new project for the client program? You could do this, but keeping a copy of Visual Basic in memory with the DLL project loaded will make it a lot easier to switch back and modify the DLL code if required.

When you start the second copy of Visual Basic, create a Standard EXE project. On the project's form, place a control array of four Command Buttons, plus two Text Boxes and two Labels. Figure 8.3 shows this form. Change the Label control's **Caption** properties to **Value** and **Answer**, as shown in the figure.

Assign a **Name** property of **txtInput** to the Text Box that is next to the **Value** label, and a **Name** property of **txtOutput** to the other Text Box. Make the **Text** property of both Text Boxes blank. Set the **Caption** properties of the Command Buttons as shown in Table 8.1.

Remember to save the project. I used the name **TestAX** for both the form and the project.

To use the class we just created, we must add a reference to the project, as with any object. Select References from the Project menu and scroll through the list until you find

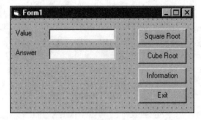

Figure 8.3   The client program's form.

Table 8.1   Caption property settings for the array of Command Buttons.

Index	Caption
0	Square Root
1	Cube Root
2	Information
3	Exit

Calculates Square and Cube Roots, as shown in Figure 8.4. This is the Project Description we assigned for the ActiveX server project's Application Description project option. Click on the box next to this reference so that an X appears, then close the dialog box. Now, the ActiveX class that we created is available within the Visual Basic project.

How did the description of our class come to be included in the References list? When you ran the DLL project in the first instance of Visual Basic, it *registered* itself with Windows. If the server is missing from the References list, you most likely forgot to run it from the other copy of Visual Basic. Note that selecting a reference in this list does not actually add the ActiveX object to the project, but merely makes it available to the project.

While it's not a necessary step for your project to run, pressing F2 to open Visual Basic's Object Browser will be instructive. The browser, shown in Figure 8.5, lets you view all of the classes that are registered and obtain information on their properties and methods. Scroll through the Classes list until you see **AXDEMO**, which is the name we assigned to our class. Highlight the name by clicking on it, and you'll see the class's properties and methods displayed in the Members list. The Object Browser is a useful tool for investigating the properties and methods of the many classes that are registered on most Windows systems.

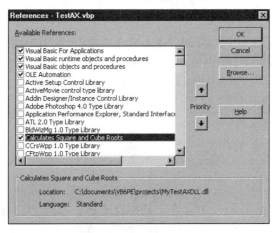

Figure 8.4   Adding a reference to the ActiveX class.

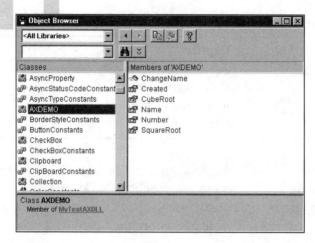

Figure 8.5 *The Visual Basic Object Browser displaying the AXDEMO class's properties.*

But now, let's get back to the client program. In the form's General declarations section, we create a reference to the ActiveX class by declaring a variable of that type, as shown here:

```
Private Ob1 As New AXDEMO
```

Note the use of the **New** keyword, which is necessary, because we want to create a new instance of **AXDEMO** to which the variable **Ob1** will refer. Without **New**, we could make **Ob1** refer to only an existing **AXDEMO** object, using the **Set** statement. Of course, that existing instance of **AXDEMO** would need to be created earlier with **New**. Note also that the **AXDEMO** class is available in the Auto list that Visual Basic displays after you type the **As** keyword. This is an excellent demonstration of how Visual Basic is well integrated to make your life as a programmer as easy as possible.

Declaring a variable of type **AXDEMO** does not actually create an instance of the class. This occurs the first time a property or method of the class is referenced. We'll do this in the client app's **Form_Load** procedure by using the **ChangeName** method to assign a name to the server's **Name** property:

```
Private Sub Form_Load()
    Ob1.ChangeName("MyObject")
End Sub
```

The one line of code in this procedure calls the **ChangeName** method in **Ob1**. As we saw earlier, **Ob1** refers to an instance of **AXDEMO**. Code in the **ChangeName** procedure assigns the argument (in this case **MyObject**) to the private variable **objName**.

Having the object perform the calculations is a simple matter. Clicking on either the Cube Root or Square Root button assigns the number in the first Text Box to the object's **Number** property. Because the code that performs the calculations is located in the **Number** property's **Let** procedure, it is performed automatically each time this property is changed. We can then immediately read back the answer from the appropriate object property—either **CubeRoot** or **SquareRoot**.

To obtain information about the object, we access its **Name** and **Created** properties, placing them together in a string that is displayed with the **MsgBox** procedure. To terminate the program, we destroy the AXDEMO object by setting **Ob1** to the special keyword **Nothing**, then call **End** to terminate. Listing 8.5 shows the code for the **Click** event procedure for the array of Command Buttons.

Listing 8.5   The Click event procedure for the demo program's Command Buttons.

```
Private Sub Command1_Click(Index As Integer)

Dim Msg As String

Select Case Index
    Case 0  ' Square root
        Ob1.Number = txtInput.Text
        txtOutput.Text = Ob1.SquareRoot
    Case 1  ' Cube root
        Ob1.Number = txtInput.Text
        txtOutput.Text = Ob1.CubeRoot
    Case 2  ' Information
        Msg = "Object " & Ob1.Name & " was created " _
            & Ob1.Created
        MsgBox (Msg)
    Case 3  ' Quit
        Set Ob1 = Nothing
        End
End Select

End Sub
```

That's all there is to the client app. Run it, enter a value in the first Text Box, and click on one of the calculation buttons. Because the program has no error checking, be sure to enter a positive value—no negative numbers, please. Click on the Information button to see the object's name and creation time/date.

What if you need to make changes in the DLL code? Switch to the first copy of Visual Basic and make the changes. Be sure to execute the DLL within Visual Basic (to register any changes) and to use the Make command on the File menu to create the DLL file on disk. Then you can switch to the second copy of Visual Basic and run the client program again to see the effects of your changes.

TIP

Overcoming The DLL-To-Disk Hurdle

After testing your client program and switching back to modify the DLL, you may find that you are unable to write the modified DLL to disk. This problem may be solved by the time you read this, but you can get around it by closing the second copy of Visual Basic (the one you are using to develop the client program) before trying to make the DLL. Then restart the second copy of Visual Basic to continue with your testing.

Registering Components

As you have seen, for an ActiveX component to be available to other programs, it must be registered with Windows. If you run an ActiveX server from within the Visual Basic environment, it is automatically—but temporarily—added to the Windows registry. When you terminate execution, the registry entry vanishes. If you "make" the project, creating an EXE or DLL file, the server and its classes are permanently added to the registry. But what about end users who are not running Visual Basic? For them, the class is registered when it is installed by using the Setup tool kit, or when it is executed as a regular EXE file. It can also be registered using the Windows REGSVR32.EXE utility.

Creating An ActiveX EXE

We have seen how to create an ActiveX component contained within a DLL file. You could include more than one ActiveX class in a single DLL simply by adding additional class modules to the project. But what about an ActiveX EXE? As I mentioned earlier in the chapter, an ActiveX EXE combines one or more ActiveX components with a functional program. In almost all cases, the functional part of the ActiveX EXE makes use of its own ActiveX components as well as exposing them for use by other programs. How do you do this?

It's really quite simple. I won't walk you though a complete example, but I will describe the process using our earlier demonstration programs for examples. Suppose you want to combine our ActiveX server with the client demonstration to create an ActiveX EXE that does the following:

- Defines a class to calculate square and cube roots
- Exposes this class for use by other programs

- Provides a visual interface permitting the user to enter data and read the result of the calculations

You can easily accomplish these tasks by creating an ActiveX EXE project. The project will have two modules: a class module containing the same code as the class module in our DLL example, and a regular Visual Basic form module with the same controls and code as the client example. In this case, the class and its client are part of the same Visual Basic project, and the class is also available (once it has been registered) for use by other Windows programs.

Chapter 9

Dynamic Data Exchange

Dynamic Data Exchange allows your Visual Basic programs to exchange data with other Windows programs, as well as send them commands.

Dynamic Data Exchange (DDE) is a feature of Windows that permits programs to send data back and forth. Within certain limitations, it also allows them to send commands to each other. It can be an extraordinarily useful technique, and in many situations is preferable to the other Windows method for interaction between programs: Object Linking and Embedding. (I introduced OLE in Chapter 8 and will cover it more fully in Chapter 10.)

What exactly can DDE do? Once again, an example is the best way to explain. A while ago, I wrote a custom program in Visual Basic for the laboratory where I work; the program was designed to take measurements from digitized data that was collected from our experiments. The final destination for this data was an Excel spreadsheet that handles data manipulation and graphing. My first impulse was to have the Visual Basic program save the results in a text file, which could then be imported into Excel. After a few moments of thought about the capabilities of DDE, however, I came up with a much better way. The final program uses DDE to accomplish the following steps:

1. Start Excel and open a new worksheet.

2. Insert labels into specific cells in the worksheet to provide the date, data labels, and other experiment identifiers.

3. Poke analysis results numbers into specific worksheet cells as the analysis proceeds.

4. Place formulas in other worksheet cells to perform the needed calculations.

5. Save the worksheet file under a user-selected name.

When running an analysis, all I need do is hit Alt+Tab or use the Windows taskbar to switch from the Visual Basic measurement program to Excel, where my data is ready for analysis and graphing. This is a real timesaver, and it represents the way that Windows programs are supposed to work together.

DDE Basics

Perhaps the most common way to copy data from one Windows application to another is to use the Clipboard. As handy as the Clipboard can be, however, it does not provide for automatic updating of the data. In other words, each time the data in the original changes, the copied data must be updated manually. DDE remedies this situation by providing the capability of automatically updating transferred data.

Let's look at a specific example. Suppose we are using a word processor to write a report, and we want to include some numbers from an Excel worksheet. We would start Excel, open the worksheet, select the numbers, and copy them to the Clipboard. Next, we would switch back to the word processor and paste the table into our document. Convenient—as long as we know the numbers will never change.

In practice, this is often not the case. Sales figures change, forecasts are modified. How can we be sure that our report is up to date? With standard Clipboard copy-and-paste, we have to repeat the entire process of copying the numbers from the worksheet to the document. Worse yet, we may not even know when the numbers have changed if we are on a network where other people can modify the worksheet.

DDE to the rescue! DDE allows us to establish a *link* between the worksheet and the document. This link gives us the ability to copy data *and* information about its source. We don't see this information—it is stored internally—but it enables the program to update the copied information automatically when the source changes. We can establish any number of links between multiple applications. Furthermore, the linked data can be just about anything—numbers, text, or a graphical image, for example. With DDE, we need to enter data only once, and the DDE links automatically transfer it to any other place it is needed. The same is true of changes to existing data; manual updates are no longer necessary. The end result? We save time and decrease the potential for errors.

Will OLE And ActiveX Replace DDE?

You've probably heard about Object Linking and Embedding (OLE), which provides sophisticated methods for Windows applications to cooperate in creating compound documents. You've also heard about ActiveX, the hot new software component technology (covered in Chapter 8). Because OLE and ActiveX provide ways for programs to share data, you might wonder if they will eventually replace DDE. Should you ignore DDE and use OLE or ActiveX when your Visual Basic programs need to exchange data? I can't predict the future, of course, but my bet is that the answer will be "no." Why do I feel this way?

OLE and ActiveX are certainly more powerful than DDE (you'll see what I mean in later chapters). Unavoidable consequences of this power include a need for greater system resources, more difficulty in programming, and generally slower speed. OLE and ActiveX are always around when we need them; but when DDE will fill the bill, we're better off using it. Why use a half-ton pickup truck to bring home a bag of groceries when your old Volkswagen can do the job, is easier to drive, and uses less gas? Considering Microsoft's emphasis on backward compatibility, DDE support will probably never be removed from Windows.

DDE Terminology

When you use DDE to link two applications, one application is called the *source* and the other is the *destination*. As you can guess, the data to be exchanged originates in the source application and is transferred to one or more destination applications. The link is sometimes referred to as a *conversation*. It is always the destination application that initiates a DDE conversation.

To initiate a conversation, the destination application must specify the name of the source application. Each Windows application that can act as a DDE source has a unique name for this purpose. Usually, this is the executable file name without the .EXE extension. The destination application must also specify the *topic* of the conversation. The topic identifies the unit of data being linked—a designated unit of information that is meaningful to the source. It often is the name of a data file. While the available DDE topics vary from application to application, one that is almost universally supported is the System topic. Using the System topic, a DDE destination can obtain the other topics that the source supports, as well as other information about the application, including the supported data formats.

The actual data being transferred in the DDE conversation is termed the *item*. The item must be identified in a way that the source application can understand. Thus, a spreadsheet program, such as Lotus 1-2-3 or Microsoft Excel, understands the row and column addresses of spreadsheet cells, and a word processor, such as Microsoft Word, recognizes bookmark names. Here's an example: For a destination application to establish a link to the contents of cell C12 in the Excel worksheet D:\REPORTS\MAY1998.XLS, the conversation will specify EXCEL as the application, D:\REPORTS\MAY1998.XLS as the topic, and R12C3 (row 12, column 3) as the item.

Both the application and the topic remain constant throughout a DDE conversation. The conversation will terminate if either the source or the destination attempts to change the application or topic. In contrast, the item of a DDE conversation can change as many times as desired. For example, the same DDE conversation could refer to different spreadsheet cells at different times, as long as they are in the same file (a technique we'll use later).

Data is normally transferred from the source to the destination. As we'll see later, however, data can travel in the other direction—from destination to source. At first glance, moving the data from destination to source may seem contradictory, but remember that the destination application is the one that initiates the DDE conversation, and it is usually—but not always—the destination that receives the transferred data.

Updating DDE Links

In addition to specifying the application, topic, and item, a DDE link specifies how the link is updated. Three methods are possible:

- *Automatic link*—The destination is updated whenever the source data changes.

- *Manual link*—The destination must specifically request each update from the source.

- *Notify link*—The destination is automatically notified by the source whenever the data changes, but the data is updated only when the destination requests it.

The type of link you will use depends, of course, on the specific situation.

DDE And Visual Basic Objects

The only Visual Basic objects that can serve as the destination in a DDE conversation are the Text Box, Picture Box, and Label controls. Each of these controls has three properties that determine the details of the conversation:

- **LinkTopic** specifies the application and topic of the conversation.

- **LinkItem** specifies the data item.

- **LinkMode** specifies one of the three link modes (automatic, manual, or notify).

Any Visual Basic form (including Multiple Document Interface [MDI] forms) can be the source in a DDE conversation. A form's **LinkTopic** property specifies the topic name that the destination application will use to refer to the form in a DDE conversation. The item in a conversation can be a Text Box, Picture Box, or Label control on the form. In the DDE conversation, the destination application specifies the control's **Name** property as the item.

To have a Text Box, Picture Box, or Label act as a DDE destination, use the control's **LinkTopic** property to specify both the source application and the source topic. The property must list the application, followed by a vertical pipe character, **CHR$(124)**, and the topic name. To link a Text Box to data in the Excel worksheet REPORT.XLS, we would write:

```
Text1.LinkTopic = "EXCEL|REPORT.XLS"
```

or

```
Text1.LinkTopic = "EXCEL" & CHR$(124) & " REPORT.XLS"
```

The control's **LinkItem** property specifies the data item to be linked. The precise content and format of the **LinkItem** property varies from one source application to another (refer to the source application's documentation for details). For spreadsheet programs, such as Excel and 1-2-3, row and column coordinates are usually meaningful. For word processors, such as Microsoft Word, the same is true for bookmark names.

The destination control's **LinkMode** property determines the way in which the link will be updated. The default setting is **0-None**, which specifies no DDE conversation. When you want the control to be an active DDE destination, three settings are possible: **1-Automatic**, **2-Manual**, and **3-Notify**. (I explained the way these three update modes work earlier in this chapter.)

One more destination control property is important to the picture. The **LinkTimeout** property specifies how long a Visual Basic DDE destination control will wait for the source application to respond to a DDE message before generating an error. The wait time is specified in tenths of seconds, and the default setting is 50, or 5 seconds. To obtain the longest possible wait, 65535 tenths of a second (approximately 1 hour and 49 minutes), set **LinkTimeout** to -1.

Using Visual Basic controls as the source in a DDE conversation also involves properties. Because all DDE conversations are initiated by the destination application, in order to act as a DDE source, a Visual Basic application simply responds to the DDE messages that are sent by the destination. To initiate a DDE link, the message sent by the destination must specify three pieces of information: application, topic, and item. How does this information identify a Visual Basic control? Here are the details:

- *Application*—The name of the Visual Basic source application. If the application is running in the Visual Basic development environment, it is the project name without the .VBP extension. If the application is running as a standalone executable, it is the Visual Basic application name without the .EXE extension. In code, we can use the App object's **EXEName** property to obtain the application name.

- *Topic*—The **LinkTopic** property of the Visual Basic form that contains the control with the data to be linked. This property's default setting is in the format Form1, Form2, and so on. If a form will serve as a DDE topic, change its **LinkTopic** property to an appropriate name.

- *Item*—The **Name** property of the control (Text Box, Picture Box, or Label) that contains the data to be linked.

The form's **LinkMode** property controls whether a destination application is permitted to initiate a DDE conversation with one or more controls on the form. If **LinkMode** is set to **0-None** (the default), DDE conversations are not permitted with any control on the form. If **LinkMode** is set to **1-Source**, any Label, Picture Box, or Text Box on the form can serve as the source in a DDE link with any destination application that requests it. Once a DDE link exists, Visual Basic automatically notifies the destination application whenever a change occurs in the contents of a linked control. If you set **LinkMode** to **1-Source** at design time, you can change it to **0-None** and back again in code at runtime. If you set **LinkMode** to **0-None** at design time, you cannot change it to **1-Source** at runtime.

Let's look at a concrete example: Suppose we have a Visual Basic project named SALES.VBP, with a resulting EXE file named SALES.EXE that contains a form with its **LinkTopic** property set to **SalesFigures** and its **LinkMode** property set to **1-Source**. Suppose also that this form contains a Text Box with its **Name** property set to **Total**. A destination application could establish a DDE link with that Text Box by specifying SALES as the application, **SalesFigures** as the topic, and **Total** as the item.

DDE Events

As you might expect, a number of events are associated with DDE conversations. The specific events and the way you use them differ slightly, depending on whether the Visual Basic object is the source or the destination in the DDE conversation.

The **LinkOpen** event occurs when a Visual Basic control acting as a destination successfully initiates a DDE conversation. The event procedure looks like this:

```
Sub CtlName_LinkOpen ([Index as Integer], Cancel as Integer)
. . .
End Sub
```

The **Index** argument identifies the control if it is part of a control array. The **Cancel** argument is not used for **LinkOpen** events when the control is the destination. You use the destination control's **LinkOpen** event procedure to perform those tasks, such as opening files, that are required when a DDE link is established. You can also use this event to assist with program debugging.

The **LinkOpen** event also occurs when an external destination application initiates a DDE conversation with a Visual Basic source form. Under these circumstances, the **LinkOpen** event procedure has the following structure:

```
Sub FormName_LinkOpen (Cancel as Integer)
. . .
End Sub
```

If the **Cancel** argument is left at its initial value of False, the link is established. To prevent the link from being established, code in the event procedure can set **Cancel** to any non-zero value, and Visual Basic will not permit the link to be created. You can use the source **LinkOpen** event procedure to keep track of the number of DDE links sourced by the Visual Basic program, refusing to establish new links once the total number becomes too large for satisfactory performance.

A **LinkClose** event will occur if the DDE conversation is terminated for either a destination control or a source form. The event procedure receives no information about why the conversation was terminated.

A **LinkError** event will occur for either a destination control or a source form under certain error conditions. Visual Basic's standard error-handling procedures are invoked if a DDE error occurs while Basic code is executing, enabling you to trap and handle the error in the usual fashion (as was explained in Chapter 7). The **LinkError** event is triggered only if an error occurs when no Basic code is executing. Occurrences that can cause errors include transfer of data in a format that the destination cannot handle and operating-system resource shortages. I will cover more about handling DDE errors later in this chapter.

A **LinkNotify** event will occur for destination controls where the **LinkMode** property has been set to **3-Notify**. This event is triggered when the source data changes. Code in the **LinkNotify** event procedure can use the **LinkRequest** method to update the destination immediately with the modified data. When the new data is not needed immediately, a flag can be set indicating that an update must be performed later.

A **LinkExecute** event occurs when a source form receives a command string from the destination in the DDE conversation. The **LinkExecute** event procedure format is:

```
Sub Form_Execute (Cmd As String, Cancel As Integer)
. . .
End Sub
```

The **Cmd** argument contains the command string that was sent by the DDE destination. No defined DDE command language is shared among applications, and the specific commands and syntax that a particular DDE source understands differ from program to program. To enable your Visual Basic program to respond to such commands, you have to write the code.

The **Cancel** argument passed to the **Execute** event procedure determines the response sent back to the DDE destination application—the one that sent the command string. If **Cancel** is set to 0, the Visual Basic program sends a positive acknowledgment, usually meaning that the command string was received and acted upon. If **Cancel** is set to any nonzero value, a negative acknowledgment occurs. A negative acknowledgment is automatically sent when the program has no **LinkExecute** event procedure.

Pasting Links Into A Visual Basic Program

One way to create a link in a Visual Basic program is to paste it using the Clipboard. If you have worked with Windows applications, such as a word processor, you have probably seen the Paste Link command—usually found on the Edit menu. Using this command creates a DDE link with any other DDE-aware Windows application. The general procedure for establishing links using the Clipboard is shown here:

1. Make the source application active and select the data to be linked (for example, a column of cells in a spreadsheet).

2. Still in the source application, select Copy (this command is almost always found on the Edit menu). The Copy command places the data and associated link information on the Clipboard.

3. Make the destination application active.

4. Move to the location where you want to place the linked data.

5. Select Paste Link. An automatic link is established between the two applications.

In this section, I'll include a Paste Link command in the sample Visual Basic programs. This type of DDE support can greatly increase a program's usefulness by permitting users to cut and paste DDE links quickly and easily.

DDE And The Clipboard

To use the Copy...Paste Link command sequence to create a DDE link, the Windows Clipboard is used as the intermediate storage location where the link information is kept. A Visual Basic program accesses the Windows Clipboard by means of the Clipboard object.

The Clipboard is not simply a storage buffer that can hold and later return whatever data it receives. No, the Clipboard is actually pretty clever: It has the ability to hold data in several different formats. In fact, the Clipboard can hold more than one data item if they are in different formats. Furthermore, the Clipboard can tell you whether it currently contains a data item of a specified format. The data formats that the Clipboard can work with are:

- Text

- Bitmap (BMP files)

- Metafile (WMF files)

- Device-independent bitmap (DIB files)

- Color palette

- DDE link information

The meaning of the first four items should be clear: Text is, well, text, and the next three are different formats used to hold graphics images. A color palette is a set of color values that is used for the pixels in a specific graphic. But what is meant by *DDE link information*? This is the information required to establish a DDE link to the data on the Clipboard. Let's see how this works.

When you use the Copy command, Windows applications that support active DDE links not only place a copy of the selected data (text, a bitmap, or whatever) on the Clipboard, they also place the information—the application, topic, and item information—that is needed to establish a DDE link to the original data. If you switch to another application and execute the Paste command (not the Paste Link command), only the data will be copied from the Clipboard into the destination, and no link will be established. By executing the Paste Link command, however, you will obtain both the data and the DDE link information from the Clipboard, and an active DDE link will be created.

How can a Visual Basic application determine if data in a particular format is available on the Clipboard? The Clipboard object's **GetFormat** method is designed for just this task. The method's syntax is:

```
result = Clipboard.Getformat(type)
```

The *type* argument specifies the data format, and you can specify type with the Windows global constants, shown in Table 9.1.

The **GetFormat** method returns True if the specified type of data is present on the Clipboard, False if not. For example, you could test for the presence of text data as follows:

```
If Clipboard.GetFormat(vbCFText) Then
    . . .
    ' Text data present on clipboard.
Else
    . . .
    ' Text data not present.
End If
```

The ability to determine whether a specific data format is present on the Clipboard can be useful in a variety of situations. A graphics program, for example, could enable a Paste Picture command only if data in one of the three graphics formats is present on the Clipboard. For DDE, however, it's the DDE link information that is important. You need this information for the Paste Link command to work properly. Let's see how to obtain it.

To retrieve the DDE link information, use the Clipboard object's **GetText** method. You can use this method to retrieve text data from the Clipboard; but if you pass the argument **vbCFLink** (value = &HBF00), **GetText** returns DDE link information (or an empty string if no link information is on the Clipboard):

```
LinkInfo = Clipboard.GetText(vbCFLink)
```

The DDE link information is returned in a specific format. The application name comes first, followed by a vertical pipe character (**CHR$(124)**), then the topic. The topic is followed by an exclamation point; the item is at the end:

```
application|topic!item
```

Table 9.1 Windows global constants related to DDE.

Constant	Value	Format
vbCFLink	HBF00	DDE conversation information
vbCFText	1	Text
vbCFBitmap	2	Bitmap
vbCFMetafile	3	Metafile
vbCFDIB	8	Device-independent bitmap
vbCFPalette	9	Color palette

Some DDE links do not include an item. In this case, only the application and topic are returned, separated by a vertical pipe character.

Once you have the DDE link information, you can use Visual Basic's string manipulation functions to extract individual strings for the application, topic, and item (if present). Next, follow this procedure to establish the link:

1. Set the destination control's **LinkMode** property to **0-None**.

2. Set the **LinkTopic** property to the application and topic retrieved from the Clipboard.

3. If necessary, set the **LinkItem** property using the item obtained from the Clipboard.

4. Set the destination control's **LinkMode** property to **1-Automatic**.

You can see that the steps required to establish a DDE link with your Visual Basic application as the destination are relatively simple using the Clipboard. It's essential, however, that your program verifies that the operation is valid before attempting to establish the link. Screening out invalid links before they have been established can save headaches later.

Two conditions must be satisfied for a Paste Link operation to be valid. First, DDE link information must be available on the Clipboard. Second, the data available on the Clipboard must be in a format that is appropriate for the intended destination control. For example, you can link text data—but not a graphic—to a Text Box control. Similarly, you can link a graphic—but not text—to a Picture Box control. The program needs to verify that both of these conditions are met before attempting a Paste Link. One way to accomplish this is to enable or disable the Paste Link menu command, depending on whether these conditions are met.

Making Paste Link Work For You

Now you're ready to apply some of what you have been learning. In this section, you'll develop a simple program that can act as the destination for a Paste Link command. To make things more interesting, the program will provide two possible destination controls—a Text Box and a Picture Box—so you can link both text and graphics. You'll also see how to enable or disable the Paste Link command, depending on whether appropriate data is on the Clipboard.

The program's single form is quite simple, containing only three controls: a Picture Box on the left side of the form, a Text Box on the right side, and a Command Button at the bottom. All of the control properties can be left at their default values except for the Text Box's **MultiLine** property (which should be changed to True), and the Command Button's **Caption** property (which should be changed to **Exit**).

Next, press Ctrl+E to bring up the Menu Editor. Using the techniques you learned in Chapter 3, create an Edit menu, named mnuEdit, and add to that menu a single item with the caption Paste Link and the name mnuPasteLink. The form is now complete.

Now let's work on the code. The **Click** event procedure for the Command Button is trivial, containing only the **End** statement. You also need to define a couple of constants in the general declarations section of the form, as shown here:

```
Const NONE = 0, AUTOMATIC = 1
```

The program's main functionality resides in event procedures for the menu commands. When the menu is displayed, you want to enable the Paste Link command only if the Clipboard contains both DDE link information and data in a format that is appropriate for the control that currently has the focus (text data for the Text Box, a graphic for the Picture Box). You accomplish this in the **Click** event procedure for the mnuEdit menu command.

Code in this procedure first disables the menu command; it is enabled only if the required conditions are met. Begin by using the Clipboard object's **GetFormat** method with the **vbCFLink** argument to determine whether the Clipboard contains DDE link information. If not, exit the sub, leaving the Paste Link command disabled (remember that the Clipboard can contain data without link information). If the link information is present, determine whether the type of data matches the current control. Because the Clipboard can hold three types of graphics, you have to check for all three. This check is accomplished by these lines of code:

```
X = Clipboard.GetFormat(vbCFBitmap)
X = X Or Clipboard.GetFormat(vbCFMetafile)
X = X Or Clipboard.GetFormat(vbCFDIB)
```

The first line sets X to True if the Clipboard contains a bitmap graphic. Then X is **Or**ed in turn with the result of the questions: "Does the Clipboard contain a metafile graphic?" and "Does the Clipboard contain a device-independent bitmap graphic?" The result is that X is True if the Clipboard contains any one of the three graphics formats, and False otherwise.

But how do you determine which of the form's controls currently has the focus? First, you need to determine the identity of the control with the focus. You do so with the **ActiveControl** property, which returns the control that has the focus. The **ActiveControl** property applies to the Screen object as well as to Form and MDIForm objects. This is a useful property, permitting you to access and manipulate the active control, no matter which control it is. You will use the Screen object's **ActiveControl** property, which returns the control that has the focus on the active form. Note, however, that you can use the Form or MDIForm object's **ActiveControl** property to access the control that has the focus on a form—even when the form is not active.

Once you have retrieved the control that has the focus, how do you determine which type of control it is? You use the **TypeOf...Is** statement, which has the following syntax:

```
TypeOf objectName Is objectType
```

In this syntax, *objectName* is any Visual Basic object. It can be a form or control name, but more often the control returned by the **ActiveControl** property is used here. The *objectType* is the identifier for any Visual Basic control object—that is, any control. For a list of the identifiers associated with each Visual Basic control, search for "Object Type" in the Visual Basic Help system.

Now you can put things together. The **If** statement that follows will execute only if the active control on the screen is a Picture Box:

```
If TypeOf Screen.ActiveControl Is PictureBox Then
...
End If
```

You can do the same for a Text Box, ending up with the following code:

```
X = Clipboard.GetFormat(vbCFBitmap)
X = X Or Clipboard.GetFormat(vbCFMetafile)
X = X Or Clipboard.GetFormat(vbCFDIB)

If X And (TypeOf Screen.ActiveControl Is PictureBox) Then
    mnuEditPasteLink.Enabled = True
    Exit Sub
End If
```

The effect of this code is: "If the Clipboard contains a graphic image and the control with the focus is a Picture Box, then enable the Paste Link command and exit the sub." You must also do the same for the Text Box: Check that the Clipboard contains text data and that the active control is a Text Box. Now the Paste Link command will be available to the user only under the appropriate circumstances, lessening confusion and the chance for errors. Listing 9.1 shows the complete code for this procedure.

Listing 9.1   *The Click event procedure for the Edit Menu command.*

```
Private Sub mnuEdit_Click()

Dim X As Boolean

' This sub enables the Paste Link command only if the Clipboard
' contains link information and also contains data in a format
' that is valid for the currently active control.

mnuEditPasteLink.Enabled = False
```

```
' If the clipboard does not contain valid DDE
' link information, leave the menu command disabled.

X = Clipboard.GetFormat(vbCFLink)
If X = False Then Exit Sub

' Does the clipboard contain a graphic?

X = Clipboard.GetFormat(vbCFBitmap)
X = X Or Clipboard.GetFormat(vbCFMetafile)
X = X Or Clipboard.GetFormat(vbCFDIB)

' If clipboard contains a graphic and the active control
' is the Picture Box, enable the Paste Link command.

If X And (TypeOf Screen.ActiveControl Is PictureBox) Then
    mnuEditPasteLink.Enabled = True
    Exit Sub
End If

' If the clipboard contains text and the active control
' is a Text Box, enable the Paste Link command.

X = Clipboard.GetFormat(vbCFText)
If X And (TypeOf Screen.ActiveControl Is TextBox) Then
    mnuEditPasteLink.Enabled = True
End If

End Sub
```

The only other procedure the program needs is for the Paste Link command—the code that actually establishes the DDE link. You will use the procedures explained earlier: Retrieve the link information from the Clipboard and place it in the destination control's properties. Because you are setting the **LinkMode** to **Automatic**, the data itself is retrieved and displayed automatically. The code for this procedure is shown in Listing 9.2. The only wrinkle here is taking into account that some link information does not include an item specification. Comments in the code explain how this is accomplished.

Listing 9.2 *The Click event procedure for the Paste Link menu command.*

```
Private Sub mnuEditPasteLink_Click()

Dim LinkInfo As String, X As Long

' Get link information from the clipboard.
LinkInfo = Clipboard.GetText(vbCFLink)

' Locate the "!".
X = InStr(LinkInfo, "!")
```

```
' There is a link item only if LinkInfo contains "!".
If X <> 0 Then
    Screen.ActiveControl.LinkMode = NONE
    Screen.ActiveControl.LinkTopic = Left(LinkInfo, X - 1)
    Screen.ActiveControl.LinkItem = Mid(LinkInfo, X + 1)
    Screen.ActiveControl.LinkMode = AUTOMATIC

' If Link does not contain "!" there is no link item.
ElseIf InStr(LinkInfo, "|") Then
    Screen.ActiveControl.LinkMode = NONE
    Screen.ActiveControl.LinkTopic = LinkInfo
    Screen.ActiveControl.LinkItem = ""
    Screen.ActiveControl.LinkMode = AUTOMATIC
End If

End Sub
```

The program is ready to run. Once it is executing, start another Windows program—preferably one that works with both text and graphics, such as Microsoft Excel. In Excel (or another program), select some text or graphics and copy it to the Clipboard. This usually requires the Edit Copy command. Switch back to the Visual Basic program, and click or tab to move the focus to the Picture Box or the Text Box. When you select Edit, you see that the Paste Link command is enabled only if the data on the Clipboard matches the active control. When you select Paste Link, the data appears in the active control. Move back to the source program and modify the data; when you return to the Visual Basic program, you see the changes have appeared there, too. Figure 9.1 shows the program with a linked Excel graph.

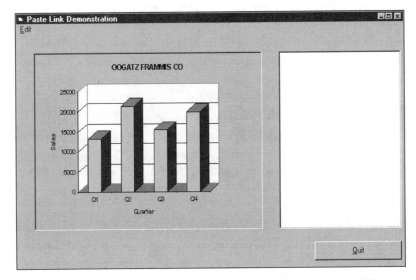

Figure 9.1   *Linking an Excel graph into a Visual Basic application.*

Pasting Links From A Visual Basic Program

Most Windows programs have a Copy command that copies selected data to the Clipboard. To support DDE links, the Copy command must copy not only the selected data to the Clipboard but also the link information that other applications require to establish a link with the data. This information consists of three parts: the application name, the topic, and—in most cases—the item. Another application can then retrieve the data only without a link (usually with the Paste command) or retrieve the data along with the DDE link information and use it to establish a link (usually with the Paste Link command). If you want your Visual Basic program to be able to act as the source in an active link, it must copy DDE link information, along with the data, to the Windows Clipboard when the user selects the Copy command.

Of course, not every occurrence of the Copy command needs to place link information on the Clipboard. Some data may not be appropriate for linking, in which case you would copy only the data to the Clipboard.

The first step before copying to the Clipboard is assembling the link information. Once again, link information consists of three parts: application, topic, and item. The application is the name of the Visual Basic program, the topic is the **LinkTopic** property of the form containing the control, and the item is the name of the control whose data you want to link. Remember, only Text Box and Picture Box controls can act as the source in a DDE link.

If you are running a program from within the Visual Basic development environment, the application name is the project name (without the extension). If you are running a standalone program, the application name is the name of the executable file (minus the .EXE extension). In either case, you can obtain the name from the **EXEName** property of the App object:

```
application = App.EXEName
```

It's All In The Name

You can use the App object's **EXEName** property only if the name of the program's EXE file has not been changed. A DDE link requires the program's original name—the name assigned in the Make EXE dialog box. The **APP.EXEName** property, however, returns the application's current EXE file name.

Once you have the application name, the next piece of information required is the **LinkTopic** property of the form. This can be set at design time or at runtime in code, using just about any name desired. Of course, for purposes of clarity, it should be something that describes the form to which it applies.

A control's **Name** property is not available at runtime. The solution to this problem is to store the control's **Name** in its **Tag** property during program design. The **Tag** property is not used by Visual Basic in any way: It serves as a storage location for any related data the program may need—in this case, the control's **Name** property. Note that if the source control is part of a control array, the name stored in the **Tag** property must include the control name followed by its array index in parentheses.

These pieces of information must be combined in a single string with a specific format that you have seen before: the application name followed by a vertical pipe character (**CHR$(124)**), then the **LinkTopic** followed by an exclamation point and the control name. An example is shown here:

```
LinkInfo = App.EXEName & "|" & LinkTopic & "!" & Screen.ActiveControl.Tag
```

Once you have assembled the string containing the link information, you can place it on the Clipboard.

Copying The DDE Link Information And Data To The Clipboard

When the program user issues the Copy command, the program must copy both the DDE link information and the data itself to the Clipboard. To put the DDE link string on the Clipboard, use the **SetText** method with the argument **vbCFLink**. The **vbCFLink** constant tells the Clipboard to interpret the data passed as DDE link information rather than as regular text. If the link string is stored in the variable **LinkInfo**, the following code will copy it to the Clipboard:

```
Clipboard.SetText LinkInfo, vbCFLink
```

The next step is to copy the data itself to the Clipboard. Remember, only two controls can act as DDE sources: Text Boxes and Picture Boxes. For a Text Box, use the Clipboard object's **SetText** method to copy its text to the Clipboard. The following example assumes that the Text Box is the active control—an assumption the program must verify before executing the **SetText** method:

```
Clipboard.SetText SCREEN.ActiveControl.Text
```

If the source control is a Picture Box, use the **SetData** method to copy the Picture Box contents to the Clipboard. Again, the program must verify that the active control is indeed a Picture Box:

```
Clipboard.SetData SCREEN.ActiveControl.Picture
```

Of course, the program's Copy command should support copying of data from all types of controls, not just Picture Boxes and Text Boxes, which are special only in regard to DDE links. When the Copy command is executed while another type of control is active, the code can copy the control's data—but not its DDE information—to the Clipboard.

Demonstrating Copy Link

Thanks to the inner workings of Windows, copying link information to the Clipboard where other programs can retrieve it is a relatively simple matter. The program COPYLINK.VBP demonstrates how this is accomplished. This program, shown in Figure 9.2, contains only a Picture Box and a Text Box, along with two Command Buttons. Both controls are loaded with some data at design time. For the Picture Box, I used a bitmap image that was on my disk from a previous project. You can use any bitmap you like, including the ones provided with Visual Basic. Remember, set the Picture Box's **Picture** property to specify its image.

You need to set a few other properties during program design. The **Tag** property of the Picture Box and the Text Box must be set to the control's **Name** property. Because these

Figure 9.2   *The COPYLINK demonstration program with Microsoft Word in the background showing text linked from the demo.*

are left at their default values, we have **Picture1.Tag** = "Picture1" and **Text1.Tag** = "Text1". Also, the form's **LinkMode** property must be set to **Source**, or it will not permit other programs to establish a link with any of its controls. Note that a **LinkMode** property setting of **None** does not prevent the link information from being placed on the Clipboard. The problem arises when the destination application attempts to establish the link.

The program also needs an Edit menu with a single command on it: Copy. Assign the name mnuEditCopy to that one command. Set Ctrl+C as the shortcut key; this is standard in Windows programs for the Copy command.

Listing 9.3 shows the program's code. The two Command Button event procedures should be self-explanatory. To clear the Picture Box, I use the **LoadPicture** function with no argument. In the **Click** event procedure for the Edit menu, I use a technique similar to the one shown earlier—enabling the menu command only under appropriate circumstances. In this case, the proper circumstances exist if the active control is a Picture Box or a Text Box. If the focus is on one of the Command Buttons, nothing is available for copying to the Clipboard.

The real action takes place in the **Click** event procedure for the Copy command. Depending on whether the active control is a Picture Box or a Text Box, the code copies the appropriate link information and data to the Clipboard. The procedure for doing this is almost identical for both types of controls, differing only in the method used (**SetText** for a Text Box, **SetData** for a Picture Box) to copy the data to the Clipboard.

To see how the program works, execute it, then select either the Text Box or the Picture Box by clicking on it. Next, select Edit | Copy or press Ctrl+C to copy the data and link information to the Clipboard. Switch to another Windows application that supports DDE links, such as a word processor. If you prefer, use the PASTELNK program that we developed earlier in the chapter. Select the destination program's Paste Link command (or the equivalent) to paste the data and link from the Clipboard. Next, switch back to COPYLINK and modify the linked data by clearing the picture or editing the text. Switch back to the destination application, where you will see the changes automatically reflected.

Listing 9.3   Code in COPYLINK.FRM.

```
Option Explicit

Private Sub Command1_Click()

' Clear the Picture Box.
Picture1.picture = LoadPicture()

End Sub
```

```
Private Sub Command2_Click()

' Quit the program.
End

End Sub


Private Sub mnuEdit_Click()

' Enable the Copy command only if the Picture Box
' or the Text Box is active.

If TypeOf Screen.ActiveControl Is TextBox Or TypeOf Screen.ActiveControl _
    Is PictureBox Then
    mnuEditCopy.Enabled = True
Else
    mnuEditCopy.Enabled = False
End If

End Sub


Private Sub mnuEditCopy_Click()

Dim LinkInfo As String

' Clear the Clipboard.
Clipboard.Clear

' If the active control is the Text Box copy its text and
' DDE information to the Clipboard.
If TypeOf Screen.ActiveControl Is TextBox Then
    LinkInfo = App.EXEName & "|" & LinkTopic
    LinkInfo = LinkInfo & "!" & Screen.ActiveControl.Tag
    Clipboard.SetText LinkInfo, vbCFLink
    Clipboard.SetText Screen.ActiveControl.TEXT
End If

' If the active control is a Picture Box copy its picture and
' DDE information to the Clipboard.
If TypeOf Screen.ActiveControl Is PictureBox Then
    LinkInfo = App.EXEName & "|" & LinkTopic
    LinkInfo = LinkInfo & "!" & Screen.ActiveControl.Tag
    Clipboard.SetText LinkInfo, vbCFLink
    Clipboard.SetData Screen.ActiveControl.picture
End If

End Sub
```

More DDE Magic

DDE offers a great deal more capability than is possible to cover here. However, I would like to finish this chapter with one more use for DDE—something I find very helpful. Using the power of DDE, we can employ Visual Basic to create extensions to existing programs, circumventing omissions or shortcomings in their design and capabilities.

For example, we may like to use the Microsoft Excel spreadsheet program for manipulation and graphing of numerical data. And why not? Excel has a wide range of powerful features, and trying to duplicate even a few of them in a Visual Basic program would be a major programming challenge. In my opinion, however, Excel falls short in one area: data entry. Typing large amounts of data into the spreadsheet's row-and-column structure can be an exercise in frustration and error. As you know, however, Visual Basic makes it easy to create attractive, easy-to-use forms for data entry and other purposes, and also to include data validation code to prevent entry of incorrect data. By using DDE, we can create a Visual Basic data-entry program that sends the data to an Excel spreadsheet. We get the best of both worlds: the convenience of a Visual Basic data-entry form and the analytical capabilities of Excel.

Using DDE in this way is quite different from the uses we covered earlier in the chapter. DDE is used to transfer data, but no link is established. Once a piece of data is "sent" to Excel, we have no link back to the Visual Basic program—the end result is exactly the same as if the data had been typed directly into Excel. In addition to sending data to other programs, DDE can be used to send commands, instructing programs to perform various actions. You'll see that several actions are required for this sort of application.

The first action we will need is the ability to start a program, if it is not already running. To start another Windows application from within a Visual Basic program, you use the **Shell** function. The syntax is shown here:

```
result = Shell(CommandString [, WindowStyle])
```

The **CommandString** argument specifies the name of the program to execute, including any required arguments or command-line switches. If the program name in **CommandString** doesn't include a .COM, .EXE, .BAT, or .PIF file extension, .EXE is assumed. The **WindowStyle** argument specifies the style of the application window when the program starts, such as maximized or minimized. We can omit this argument, and the program is opened, minimized with focus. Table 9.2 shows the possible values for **WindowStyle** and the defined constants.

If the application is successfully initiated, the **Shell** function returns the application's task identification, a unique number that identifies the running application. If the **Shell** function is unable to start the named application, an error occurs.

Table 9.2   Constants for the WindowStyle argument.

Constant	Value	Description
vbHide	0	Window is hidden and focus is passed to the hidden window.
vbNormalFocus	1	Window has focus and is restored to its original size and position.
vbMinimizedFocus	2	Window is displayed as an icon with focus.
vbMaximizedFocus	3	Window is maximized with focus.
vbNormalNoFocus	4	Window is restored to its most recent size and position. The currently active window remains active.
vbMinimizedNoFocus	6	Window is displayed as an icon. The currently active window remains active.

When using the **Shell** function, remember that it runs other applications asynchronously—the Visual Basic program does not wait for the **Shell** command to complete. This means that we can't be sure that a program started with **Shell** will have completed its start-up procedures before the code following the **Shell** function in our Visual Basic application is executed.

Sending Commands To Another Program

Once you have established a DDE link, you can use the link for more than transferring data. You can also use it to send commands to the other application using the **LinkExecute** method. This method is applied to the control that is maintaining the link—the active destination control. That's just a syntax requirement, however, as the control has nothing to do with the command we are sending. The syntax for the **LinkExecute** method is shown here:

```
ControlName.LinkExecute Command
```

ControlName is the name of a control that is the destination in an active DDE link. The *Command* argument is a string that contains the commands to be sent to the DDE source application. The legal commands depend on the specific application. In other words, no universal "DDE command set" exists that contains commands for use with all applications. You'll need to refer to the documentation for each source application for information on the commands it accepts. Excel, for example, accepts any of its macro commands enclosed in brackets.

Sending Data To Another Program

Once an active DDE link is established, you can send data from the destination program to the source program. Note that this is the reverse of the more typical data flow in a DDE conversation, which is from source to destination. To send data from the destination to the source, use the **LinkPoke** method. The procedure is as follows:

1. Put the data to be transferred in a Text Box or Picture Box control.

2. Set the control's **LinkMode** property to **0-None**.

3. Set the control's **LinkTopic** and **LinkItem** properties to identify the location where you want to poke the data.

4. Set the **LinkMode** property to **2-Manual**.

5. Execute the **LinkPoke** method.

For example, the following code will poke the text "Testing LinkPoke" to cell B2 in the Excel spreadsheet TESTDATA.XLS:

```
Text1.Text = "Testing LinkPoke"
Text1.LinkMode = 0
Text1.LinkTopic = "EXCEL|TESTDATA"
Text1.LinkItem = "R2C2"
Text1.LinkMode = 2
Text1.LinkPoke
```

Note the use of "R2C2" to refer to the second row in the second column of the Excel spreadsheet. For DDE commands, Excel uses numbers for both rows and columns rather than using letters for columns, as is the case when you are working directly in Excel.

A Front-End Demonstration

We now have the tools we need to create a Visual Basic front end. We know how to start another Windows program and send it commands and data. The demonstration program developed here is fundamental, but you'll be surprised at how easily you can create even a full-featured front end. This program is designed for use with Excel, but the same techniques will apply to other applications as well. FRONTEND's data-entry form is shown in Figure 9.3.

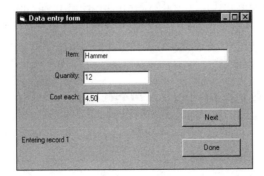

Figure 9.3 *A Visual Basic program for data entry into an Excel spreadsheet.*

Here are the tasks we want it to perform:

- Start Excel.

- Display three Text Box controls for data entry.

- Poke data in the three Text Boxes to columns A, B, and C in the Excel spreadsheet, starting in the first row.

- Poke subsequent entries into the same columns in row 2, row 3, and so on.

- Display an updating label on the form that informs the user of the current record number.

- On exit, prompt for a file-name entry and send commands to Excel to save the spreadsheet under that name; then terminate both itself and Excel.

The program's single form contains three Text Boxes, four Labels, and two Command Buttons. The Text Boxes and Command Buttons are control arrays. Starting with this project, I will be using a new method to describe a form's properties and controls. Rather than describe the steps to you, I will present a list of forms, controls, and properties in the form shown in Listing 9.3. This is, in fact, the same format that Visual Basic uses in a FRM file; you can use WordPad or any other text editor to open a FRM file to see what I mean. The format used is hierarchical, as follows:

```
Begin VB_Form FormName
    [form properties here in alphabetical order]
    Begin VB_CommandButton CommandButtonName
        [CommandButton properties here in alphabetical order]
    End
    Begin VB_TextBox TextBoxName
        [TextBox properties here in alphabetical order]
    End
End
```

An actual FRM file lists all of the properties, but I will include only those you need to explicitly change. For the FRONTEND demonstration program's form, the objects and properties are shown in Listing 9.4. For convenient data entry, ensure that the tab order has the three Text Box controls in the 1, 2, and 3 positions, and the Next button in the 4 position.

Listing 9.4   Objects and properties in FRONTEND.FRM.

```
Begin VB.Form Form1
    Caption         =   "Data entry form"
    LinkTopic       =   "Form1"
    Begin VB.CommandButton Command1
        Caption         =   "Done"
```

```
      Index              =    1
      TabIndex           =    8
   End
   Begin VB.CommandButton Command1
      Caption            =    "Next"
      Index              =    0
      TabIndex           =    7
   End
   Begin VB.TextBox Text1
      Index              =    2
      TabIndex           =    6
   End
   Begin VB.TextBox Text1
      Index              =    1
      TabIndex           =    5
   End
   Begin VB.TextBox Text1
      Index              =    0
      TabIndex           =    4
   End
   Begin VB.Label Label4
      Alignment          =    1  'Right Justify
      Caption            =    "Cost each:"
   End
   Begin VB.Label Label3
      Alignment          =    1  'Right Justify
      Caption            =    "Quantity:"
   End
   Begin VB.Label Label2
      Alignment          =    1  'Right Justify
      Caption            =    "Item:"
   End
   Begin VB.Label Label1
   End
End
```

The program's code is presented in Listing 9.5, and you can see that it is rather short. A flag named **ExcelRunning** is maintained: True if Excel has been started, and False otherwise. This flag is used to prevent the program from trying to send commands to Excel if a DDE link has not been established (which occurs when the user "saves" the first record). This would cause an error. The remainder of the code is straightforward and should be clearly understandable from the comments.

Listing 9.5   Code in FRONTEND.FRM.

```
Option Explicit

Const NONE = 0, MANUAL = 2
Dim ExcelRunning As Boolean
```

```
Private Sub Command1_Click(Index As Integer)

Dim Cmd As String
Dim Filename As String
Dim Prompt As String
Dim X As Long
Dim Item As String
Static Row As Integer

On Local Error GoTo Errorhandler

Select Case Index
    Case 0          ' Next
        If Not ExcelRunning Then
            ' Start Excel minimized without focus. Be sure to put
            ' the path to your copy of Excel here.
            X = Shell("D:\MSOFFICE97\OFFICE\EXCEL.EXE", vbMinimizedNoFocus)
            ExcelRunning = True
        End If

        ' Poke the data to the Excel spreadsheet. Loop once
        ' for each Text Box in the control array. Excel always
        ' starts with the default spreadsheet name SHEET1.
        Row = Row + 1

        For X = 0 To 2
            Text1(X).LinkMode = NONE
            Text1(X).LinkTopic = "EXCEL|SHEET1"
            Item = "R" & Right$(Str$(Row), Len(Str$(Row)) - 1)
            Item = Item & "C" & Right$(Str$(X + 1), Len(Str$(X + 1)) - 1)
            Text1(X).LinkItem = Item
            Text1(X).LinkMode = MANUAL
            Text1(X).LinkPoke
        Next X

        ' Clear the Text Boxes.
        For X = 0 To 2
            Text1(X).TEXT = ""
        Next X

        ' Set focus to the first Text Box.
        Text1(0).SetFocus

        ' Update the counter label.
        Label1.Caption = "Entering record" & Str$(Row + 1)

    Case 1          ' Done
```

```
    ' If Excel is running, save workbook and close.
    If ExcelRunning Then
        ' Get the name for the Excel file.
        Prompt = "Name for Excel file (no extension)"
        Filename = InputBox(Prompt, "File name", "")
        Filename = Filename & ".XLS"

        ' Save the spreadsheet. CHR$(34) is the double quote character.
        Cmd = "[SAVE.AS(" & Chr$(34) & Filename & Chr$(34) & ")]"
        Text1(2).LinkExecute Cmd

        ' Close Excel.
        Text1(2).LinkExecute "[Quit()]"
    End If
    End
End Select

Exit Sub

Errorhandler:
    Resume Next

End Sub

Private Sub Form_Load()

' Display record number.
Label1.Caption = "Entering record 1"

ExcelRunning = False

End Sub
```

Note that I have used the **On Local Error** statement: When an error is detected, an error-handling routine is executed that contains simply a **Resume Next** statement. This tells Visual Basic to ignore errors without reporting them (you will learn details of Visual Basic error handling in Chapter 25). This step was necessary because the program would sometimes report a "DDE time out" error, meaning that Excel had not responded to the DDE request within the allotted time limit. In fact, Excel was responding and everything was working fine—just a bit slowly. You can prevent this type of error by increasing the destination control's **LinkTimeOut** property.

This demonstration program omits most of the error handling and other "idiot proofing" code that a program designed for distribution should include. Even so, it's a good illustration of how Visual Basic and DDE can be teamed up with commercial applications to provide the best solution to a customer's needs.

Chapter 10

Object Linking And Embedding

Object Linking and Embedding makes the software component approach available to the end user as well as the programmer.

You've probably heard a lot about the promise of software components—at the very least, you've read about it in this book. If you've been paying attention for the past nine chapters, you should be aware that the ability to combine prewritten functional software modules into a final application is a powerful approach to programming, indeed. But what about nonprogrammers—a category that includes most end users? Can the software component paradigm be extended to them as well? That's the goal of Object Linking and Embedding, or OLE.

OLE Basics

The meaning of the term OLE has undergone several changes. Not too long ago, it referred to the broad area of software components—the various technologies by which the capabilities of chunks of software were made available to other programs. Under this scheme, Visual Basic controls were called *OLE controls*. Now a shift has occurred, where the new term *ActiveX* refers to Microsoft's overall technology for software components. OLE has come to have a more restricted meaning related to the creation of compound documents—in other words, documents whose contents are created and manipulated by more than one program. With OLE, the Visual Basic programmer has access to the capabilities of a variety of other programs and can combine them to create the most efficient solution to his or her data processing needs.

TIP

OLE Vs. DDE

OLE is similar to DDE (Dynamic Data Exchange) in some respects, but they have more differences than similarities. The two standards should not be viewed as competing methods for achieving the same goal, but rather as two different tools that are appropriate for different tasks. In almost all cases, the nature of the task will determine whether you use OLE or DDE.

What Does OLE Do?

At this point, you may be thinking, "Sounds great, but I still don't know exactly what OLE does." Rather than describe it in the abstract, let's look at a concrete example. Suppose that you are using Microsoft Word to write a document, and you want to include a technical diagram created with the CorelDraw illustration program. Before OLE, you would have to create the diagram in CorelDraw, save it to disk in a format Word could import, then switch to Word and import the figure into your document. If you needed to modify the diagram later, you had to make the changes in CorelDraw, save the file again, and reimport it into Word.

With OLE, the process is a lot simpler—centered more on the document and less on the individual applications used to create it. You use the Insert Object command to insert a CorelDraw diagram in your document. A blank, sizable window appears in the document at the selected location, displaying an empty CorelDraw diagram. You are still in Word, but Word's menus and toolbars have been replaced by CorelDraw's menus and toolbars. Now you have all of CorelDraw's tools and commands available to work on the diagram *even though you have never left Word*. After you create the diagram, click on the document outside the diagram window, and Word's own menus and toolbars reappear, permitting you to continue working on the text part of the document. To modify the diagram, double-click on it, and CorelDraw's menus and toolbars display again.

OLE In Visual Basic

As you might imagine, OLE is terribly complex under the hood. Fortunately, Visual Basic programmers don't have to look under the hood. The OLE Container control makes OLE ridiculously easy, because the complex workings of OLE are hidden within the control. All you have to do to have OLE at your fingertips is drop the control into your Visual Basic program. Okay, it's not quite that easy, but the benefits are worth the effort.

OLE really has three parts: the linking and embedding parts described earlier, and another component called OLE automation. In the first part of this chapter, we'll cover the fundamental concepts and terms of the linking and embedding parts of OLE. Later in the chapter, we'll deal with OLE automation.

OLE Terminology

OLE has a terminology all its own. This section will present these terms and explain some of the details of how OLE works.

Containers, Servers, And Objects

OLE interactions involve two Windows applications known as the *container* and the *server*. In the example presented earlier, Word was the container, and CorelDraw was the server. The unit of data that can be manipulated using OLE is called an *object*. In the earlier example, the CorelDraw diagram was the object. Data objects are provided, or *exposed*, by various applications, such as word processors and drawing programs. A server is an application that can expose OLE objects.

(Earlier versions of OLE had a slightly different terminology—if you happen to be familiar with it, you may become confused. The container application used to be called the *client* or the *destination*, and the server application was the *source*.)

In OLE, *object* is simply a fancy way of saying *data*. More precisely, an OLE object is any item of data that can be displayed by an OLE container application. An object can be almost anything—an entire graphic diagram, a section of a word-processing document, or a single spreadsheet cell. The characteristics of a data object are defined by the server application where the data object originates.

Every OLE object has a *class* that specifies the name of the server application that exposes the data object. In addition to the server application name, the class specifies the object's data type and the server's version number. For example, a chart object exposed by Microsoft Excel version 6 has the class "Excel.Chart.6". When you install applications under Windows, they provide Windows with information about any OLE objects they can expose. This information, which is kept in the Windows registry, is used by container applications to determine the type of OLE objects available on the current system.

You can see a list of the classes that are registered on your system by placing an OLE control on a Visual Basic form and selecting its **Class** property in the Properties window. You'll see the same list if you run a container application, such as a word processor, and issue the command to insert an OLE object (in Microsoft Word, the command is Insert Object). Figure 10.1 shows the Object dialog box in Microsoft Word, listing the OLE objects available on my system.

It's Really Linking *Or* Embedding

OLE should really be called "object linking *or* embedding," because linking and embedding are two different ways of sharing data. You do not link *and* embed an object—you either link it or you embed it. The difference between linking and embedding has to do with where the data is stored and whether other applications have access to it.

Both linked and embedded objects are displayed in the container application and can be edited using the server application. The container application has a placeholder for a linked object, but it does not contain the data itself. The data is stored elsewhere—in a file associated with the server application. When an object is embedded, the container application actually contains the data, and the data is stored as part of the container application's data file.

Let's look at this distinction in terms of the earlier example. If you had linked the CorelDraw diagram to the Word document, the diagram would exist as a separate file in CorelDraw's standard data file format. The Word document would exist as a separate file in Word format, containing a placeholder for the CorelDraw diagram. If you had embedded the diagram, you would not have a separate CorelDraw file containing the diagram. Rather, the diagram data would be part of the Word data file; it would be saved in the same file with the document text.

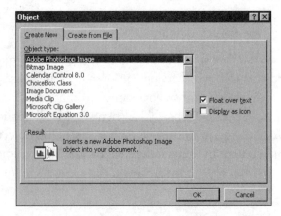

Figure 10.1   *The Object dialog box in Microsoft Word lists the objects that are registered on the system.*

Linked and embedded objects also differ in terms of the accessibility of the data object. A linked data object, because it exists in its own independent data file, can be accessed and modified by multiple container applications. For example, an Excel spreadsheet object could be linked to a Visual Basic container application and a Microsoft Word container document at the same time. Either of these container applications (Visual Basic or Word) could access and modify the spreadsheet, and the changes would appear in the linked object in the other container the next time it was used. You could also open and modify the spreadsheet using Excel as a standalone application; these changes, too, would appear in both the Visual Basic and the Word containers.

An embedded object's accessibility is much more restricted. It is accessible only to the container application in which it is embedded. Other applications cannot access or modify the object's data.

Both embedded objects and linked objects originate in the server application that exposed it. Consider a Microsoft Excel spreadsheet object. Whether linked or embedded, the object becomes a part of the container application, but in different ways:

- *If you link the spreadsheet object, the container document contains links to the spreadsheet file, as well as a visual image of it for display purposes.* The spreadsheet data itself is stored in the original Excel spreadsheet file, just as any other spreadsheet. If that spreadsheet file is modified, the container document will display the changes. The container application saves the link information and an image of the data object, but does not save the actual data.

- *If you embed the spreadsheet object, the data is included as part of the container document.* If the embedded data originated in an existing spreadsheet file, it becomes totally separate and independent from the original file. If the original file is modified, the container does not reflect the changes. The container can, however, use the server application to modify its own copy of the object. It is the container application's responsibility to store the data on disk.

Obviously, whether you use linking or embedding depends upon the specific situation. Linking permits data from a single source to be automatically updated in one or more container applications that depend on it. This sounds similar to DDE, but OLE has an advantage over DDE: An OLE container has quick and direct access to the server application for modification of the linked data. Embedding is not useful for automatic updating of data, because only one application (the container) has access to the data. You use embedding when you want to provide a single application (the container) with access to the data manipulation and presentation abilities of a variety of server applications.

At the risk of generalizing, DDE is most suitable when program code needs access to the data; OLE is preferable when you need only to display the data and edit it using the original application. Like all generalizations, exceptions surely exist, but this generalization serves as a pretty good guide.

In-Place Activation

The new OLE standard supports in-place activation, which permits you to edit an OLE object within the container application, as described earlier. With previous versions of OLE, activating an object caused the server application to start in its own window with the activated object displayed for editing. After completing the necessary editing tasks, you closed the server and were returned to the container application with the modified object displayed.

OLE Containers In Visual Basic

One of the delights of Visual Basic programming is that previously complex tasks are rendered easy or even trivial. Implementing an OLE container is no exception. You let a control—in this case, the OLE Container control—do the work for you. This control has many properties that you have already used with other controls, such as those controlling its size and visibility. Several specialized properties also relate specifically to OLE, which we will cover in this section.

Visual Basic Programs As OLE Servers

A Visual Basic program can be a server, too—but it's not called OLE. Using ActiveX technology, as described in Chapter 8, a Visual Basic program can expose objects for use by other programs.

The Windows Registry

For a Visual Basic program—or any program, for that matter—to act as an OLE container, it must know which OLE server applications are available. A container application cannot assume that a particular server application is available. Information about OLE servers is kept in the Windows *registry*. This information is maintained automatically. When an OLE server is installed, part of the installation process consists of registering the server by placing certain information in the registry. This information includes the server command line, the OLE protocols it supports, the class names of the objects it supports, and so on. This, of course, is exactly the information required by any program trying to establish itself as an OLE container. By obtaining this information from the registry, a container application can be sure that it will attempt to establish an OLE relationship only with servers that are available. A Visual Basic program uses the OLE control to access the registry.

> ## The Deleted Servers Problem
>
> Problems can arise if an OLE server is deleted by simply erasing its program files. Its registration information will still be present in the registry, so container applications may still try to establish an OLE relationship with it. The result, of course, is an error. Whenever possible, use an application's setup program to uninstall it. You can also use the Windows Add/Remove Programs utility. Properly designed uninstall programs remove not only the program files, but also the registry entry, preventing future OLE errors.

Inserting An OLE Object

The OLE control permits an OLE object to be inserted during program design (by the programmer) or while the program is running (by the user). Of course, the program must include the code for the latter action. At runtime, the OLE process can be controlled by the user working with dialog boxes or by program code setting properties of the OLE control. Depending on the circumstances, one of these methods will be more appropriate.

Inserting an object into an OLE container can be accomplished three ways. These three methods apply to both linking and embedding:

- *Paste the object into the container using the Paste Special command (or equivalent).* This is possible only if a valid OLE object is on the Windows Clipboard. This object must have been copied to the Clipboard by the server application—for example, a range of cells in an Excel worksheet. The Paste Special command lets us embed the object with the Paste option or link the object with the Paste Link option. For certain types of objects, only the Paste option is available.

- *Create a new object, a blank "whatever-it-is" you're embedding (linking is not possible with this method).* Specify the server application, which will start (in-place, if supported). Then use the server's tools and commands to create the object and switch back to the container application.

- *Insert the object from an existing file, a data file belonging to the server application.* Specify both the file name and whether the object is to be linked or embedded.

You can use these three methods of inserting OLE objects at both design time and runtime.

Inserting An Object At Design Time

If you insert an OLE object at design time, the link is fixed to the specified object and cannot be switched to another object while the program is running. For example, if you want a specific Excel workbook linked to or embedded in your Visual Basic application each and every time it runs, you would use this approach.

To insert an object during program design, place an OLE control on the form. When you do so, Visual Basic will display the Insert Object dialog box, as shown in Figure 10.2. If you want to create a new, blank object, select the type of object from the list, then click on the OK button (remember, new objects can only be embedded, not linked). The server application associated with the selected object will start, and a blank object will display in the OLE control—or in its own window if you selected the Display As Icon option. Use the application's tools and commands to create and edit the data, or leave the object blank. The server application's menu is displayed—without the File menu. Because the data object is embedded and will be stored within the OLE container, you have no need for the File menu commands.

The exact details depend on the specific server. If you insert an Excel spreadsheet, for example, a grid of cells displays in the OLE control and the Excel menu appears at the top of the Visual Basic form. In any case, you can click on the form outside the OLE control to return to Visual Basic program design.

If you want to insert an object from an existing file, select the Create from File option in the Insert Object dialog box. The dialog box will change, as shown in Figure 10.3. Enter the name of the desired file in the File box, or click on the Browse button to select the file. Click on the Link option to link the object; otherwise, the object will be embedded. Click on the OK button, and the selected object will be displayed in the OLE control. If you select an invalid file—one that is not associated with a registered OLE server—an error message will be displayed.

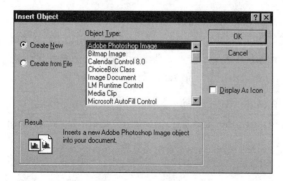

Figure 10.2   *The Insert Object dialog box is displayed when you place an OLE Container control on a form.*

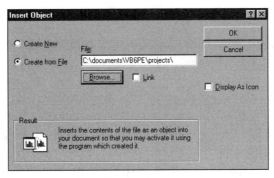

Figure 10.3 *The Insert Object dialog box also permits you to create an object from an existing file.*

To have the object display an icon, rather than the data, in your application, select the Display As Icon option in the Insert Object dialog box. You'll still be able to activate the object for editing by double-clicking on the icon, but you won't be able to view the data in the Visual Basic application. If you don't need to view the data, this choice can speed up screen display.

If you don't want to insert an object now, click on the Cancel button in the Insert Object dialog box, and Visual Basic will place an empty OLE control on your form. You can still insert an object later during program design. To do so, right-click on the OLE control and select Insert Object from the menu that is displayed. The Insert Object dialog box will be displayed, and you can proceed as described earlier.

> ### Restricting OLE Type
>
> An OLE control can hold either a linked or an embedded object. If you want to restrict it to one type or the other, set the **OleTypeAllowed** property to **Linked** or **Embedded** (the default setting is **Either**). The setting of this property affects object insertion during program design and at runtime.

Using Paste Special During Program Design

Another option during program design is to place an object in an OLE control using the Paste Special command. This method is necessary when the object you want to link does not correspond to an entire data file. For example, you can create an object from a single paragraph of a word-processing document or a block of cells in a spreadsheet. Start by placing the OLE control on your Visual Basic form and leaving it empty by selecting Cancel when the Insert Object dialog box is displayed. Then follow these steps:

1. Start the server application and select the data that you want to link or embed.

2. In the server application, select Copy from the Edit menu.

3. Switch to Visual Basic.

4. Right-click on the OLE control and select Paste Special from the pop-up menu. The Paste Special dialog box is displayed, as shown in Figure 10.4. If the Paste Special command on the pop-up menu is disabled, the data you copied to the Clipboard is not a valid OLE object.

5. In the Paste Special dialog box, the As list displays the server applications that are associated with the data object on the Clipboard. In most cases, this list will contain only one application. If it displays more than one, it means that two or more servers are registered on your system for the type of data on the Clipboard. Select the one that you want associated with the data object.

6. Select the Paste option to embed the object. Select the Paste Link option to link the object. For certain types of objects, only one of these options will be available.

7. Select the Display As Icon option if desired (this option was explained earlier in the chapter).

8. Select OK.

Inserting An Object At Runtime

If you don't want the OLE objects in your Visual Basic application to be fixed, they must be inserted while the program is executing. The OLE control is left empty during program design; when the program runs, either the program code or the user will place the desired data object in it.

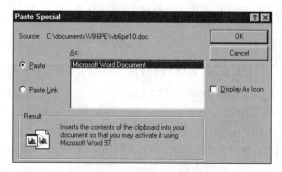

Figure 10.4   *Use the Paste Special command to load an OLE Container control with an object from the Clipboard.*

The CreateEmbed And CreateLink Methods

To create an embedded object, use the OLE control's **CreateEmbed** method. This method allows you to create a new embedded object or one that is based on an existing file. The syntax of **CreateEmbed** is as follows:

```
object.CreateEmbed sourcedoc [class]
```

The identifier *object* specifies the name of the OLE control. If you want to embed an object based on an existing file, *sourcedoc* specifies the file, and *class* can be omitted (or, if not omitted, it is ignored). If you want to create a blank object of a certain class, the *class* argument specifies the class of the object, and the *sourcedoc* argument must be a blank string. Here's an example: If you have an OLE control named **OLE1**, the command

```
OLE1.CreateEmbed "c:\data\report1996.xls"
```

creates an embedded object based on the spreadsheet file REPORT1996.XLS in the folder C:\DATA. In contrast, the command

```
OLE1.CreateEmbed "", "Excel.Sheet.6"
```

creates a new, blank object based on an Excel version 6 workbook.

You can use the **CreateEmbed** method only if the OLE control's **OLETypeAllowed** property is set to **Embedded** or **Both**. Executing this method will erase any object currently in the OLE container without warning. As you'll soon see, it is your program's responsibility to save the existing object.

The **CreateLink** method is used to create a linked object. The syntax is as follows:

```
object.CreateLink sourcedoc [, sourceitem]
```

The required argument *sourcedoc* specifies the data file to which the object is to be linked. The optional argument *sourceitem* identifies the link data item within the file. Let's look at a couple of examples. The statement

```
OLE1.CreateLink "Evaluation.Doc"
```

creates a link to the entire Microsoft Word document Evaluation.Doc. The command

```
OLE1.CreateLink "Evaluation.Doc", "Bookmark6"
```

creates a link to the text in the same document that is identified by the bookmark named **Bookmark6**. The **CreateLink** method can be used only if the OLE control's **OLETypeAllowed** property is set to **Linked** or **Both**.

Successful use of both of these methods requires that the specified data file is present and (when required) that the specified link item is present in the file. If not, an error occurs. Also, the class specified for the **CreateEmbed** method must be a valid class that is present in the system registry.

Using A Dialog Box To Insert An Object At Runtime

I explained earlier in the chapter how to use the Insert Object dialog box during program design to insert an object in an OLE control. You can display the same dialog box during program execution by executing the OLE object's **InsertObjDlg** method. This dialog box permits the user to embed or link a new object of a specified class or an object based on an existing file. If the OLE control's **OLETypeAllowed** property is set to **Linked** or **Embedded** (rather than to **Both**), however, only the specified action will be available in the Insert Object dialog box.

Using Paste Special At Runtime

You can also implement a Paste Special command in your Visual Basic program, permitting the user to paste OLE objects into an OLE control at runtime. Of course, a valid OLE object must be on the Clipboard for this method to work. Then you have two approaches. One is to use the OLE control's **Paste** method, which is usually executed in response to a Paste command on the application's Edit menu. The required steps are as follows:

1. Set the OLE control's **OLETypeAllowed** property to either **Linked** or **Embedded**, depending on whether you want the object to be linked or embedded.

2. Verify that the control's **PasteOK** property is True. If not, it means that the Clipboard does not contain an object that is appropriate for the control's **OLETypeAllowed** setting.

3. Execute the control's **Paste** method.

The second and perhaps easier approach is to execute the OLE control's **PasteSpecialDlg** method. Executing this method displays the Paste Special dialog box—the same one that is displayed when you select Paste Special from the OLE control's pop-up menu during program design. In this dialog box, the user selects from the As list (necessary only if more than one server is listed), chooses between the Paste and Paste Link options (to embed or link, respectively), then selects OK. If the OLE control's **OLETypeAllowed** property is set to **Linked** or **Embedded**, or if the object on the Clipboard permits only linking or embedding, only one of these options will be available.

Inserting An Object With Drag-And-Drop

You can implement a user-friendly interface that permits an object to be inserted in an OLE control with drag-and-drop. The OLE control's **OLEDropAllowed** property must be set to True. The user selects data in the server application, drags it to the Visual Basic application, and drops it on the OLE control. The result is the same as if the user had copied the object to the Clipboard and then executed the OLE control's **Paste** method. If the user is dragging an appropriate object, the mouse pointer displays a special drop icon when it is over the OLE control. Not all objects are appropriate for drag-and-drop, however.

Saving And Retrieving OLE Objects

It is the responsibility of the Visual Basic program to save the data in its OLE controls. Neither embedded nor linked OLE objects automatically save themselves. If the user closes a form containing an OLE control, the OLE object's data is lost. This refers to the actual data with an embedded object; with a linked object, the information defining the link to the file that contains the data. For an OLE object to be available the next time the program is run, the data must be explicitly saved and then reloaded into the OLE control when the program is again executed. Capabilities that are built into the OLE control simplify this task.

Saving OLE Objects To Disk

The data associated with each OLE object is saved in its own file. This is a standard Basic file, opened in binary mode using the file commands that will be covered in Chapter 13. Once the file is open, call the OLE control's **SaveToFile** method, passing the number of the open file as an argument. For example, for an OLE control named Ole1, the following code will save its data in a file named MYOLEFILE.DAT:

```
FileNum = FreeFile
Open "MyOleFile.Dat" For Binary as #FileNum
Ole1.SaveToFile FileNum
Close #FileNum
```

The procedure for saving an OLE object is the same for both linked and embedded OLE objects; but as mentioned previously, the nature of the saved data differs. For a linked OLE object, an image or picture of the data is saved to the file, along with the link information identifying the source data file. The object's actual data, you'll remember, is maintained by the server application in a file of the application's usual format. For an embedded OLE object, the actual data is saved in the Basic file.

Be aware that the OLE control does not keep track of whether or not its data is saved. If you load a new object into the control, any existing data will be overwritten without warning. It is the responsibility of the program to keep track of an OLE object's data status—either saving it automatically or prompting the user to save when necessary.

Retrieving OLE Objects From Disk

Retrieving an OLE object from disk is essentially the reverse of the procedure used to save it. Open the data file in binary mode, then call the OLE control's **ReadFromFile** method, passing the file number as an argument. Here's an example:

```
FileNum = FreeFile
Open "MyOleFile.Dat" For Binary as #FileNum
Ole1.ReadFromFile FileNum
Close #FileNum
```

If you are unsure about using these file commands, I suggest that you read Chapter 13.

Other OLE Control Properties, Methods, And Events

For an OLE container that contains a linked object, the possibility always exists that the data in the linked file has been modified by another program (it could be the server application or another OLE container application that is linked to the file). To be sure that the OLE control displays the current version of the data, execute the OLE control's **Update** method. This may not be necessary, however, depending on the OLE control's **UpdateOptions** property setting. This property has three possible settings:

- **0-Automatic** (*the default*)—The OLE control is updated whenever the linked data changes.

- **1-Frozen**—The OLE control is updated whenever the user saves the linked document from within the server application.

- **2-Manual**—The OLE Client control is updated only when the **Update** method is invoked.

If the setting is **Automatic**, the **Update** method will never be necessary. Of course, the **UpdateOptions** property applies only to linked OLE objects. Because embedded objects store their own data, they never need updating.

You can use the OLE control's **Updated** event to detect when an OLE object has been updated by the server application. This event is triggered each time the server application updates an OLE object. The syntax for this event procedure is:

```
Sub OLE_Updated (Code As Integer)
```

The **Code** argument indicates how the OLE object was updated. Its possible values are as follows (the constant names in parentheses are predefined Windows constants that you can use in your code):

- **0** (**vbOLEChanged**)—The file to which the object is linked has been modified.

- **1** (**vbOLESaved**)—The file to which the object is linked has been saved by the server application.

- **2** (**vbOLEClosed**)—The file to which the object is linked has been closed by the server application.

- **3** (**vbOLERenamed**)—The file to which the object is linked has been renamed by the server application.

This event procedure is frequently used to inform the program that the data in a linked OLE control has been changed since it was last saved. Code in the **Updated** event procedure can set a global "data changed" flag. The program can test this flag—for example, on exit—to determine if the data needs to be saved. You must declare and update this flag yourself, in code.

Activating OLE Objects

Activating an OLE object means starting its server application to manipulate the object. For an OLE control, the default method of activation is to double-click on it or to move the focus to the OLE control and press Enter. Other activation methods are possible, depending on the details of the server application and on the setting of the OLE control's **AutoActivate** property. Table 10.1 shows the possible settings of this property.

Table 10.1   AutoActivate property settings.

Constant	Value	Description
vbOLEActivateManual	0	Manual. The object cannot be automatically activated. You must activate the object in code using the OLE control's **DoVerb** method.
vbOLEActivateGetFocus	1	Focus. If the OLE control contains an object that supports single-click activation, the server application is activated when the OLE control receives the focus.
vbOLEActivateDoubleclick	2	(Default) Double Click. If the OLE control contains an object, the server application is activated when the user double-clicks on the OLE Container control or presses Enter when the control has the focus.
vbOLEActivateAuto	3	Automatic. If the OLE control contains an object, the server application is activated according to the object's normal method of activation, either when the control receives the focus or when the user double-clicks on the control.

Putting OLE To Work

This book is called the *Visual Basic Programming Blue Book*, but so far, all you've been doing in this chapter is sitting around looking at maps. Unavoidable—but hardly exciting. I could present plenty more OLE details, but you've already learned the important stuff—more than enough to put OLE to work in a real-world Visual Basic application.

So let's get to work and take OLE out for a spin. After all, the best way to learn is by rolling up your sleeves and trying it out. In this section, I'll develop a basic OLE container application that demonstrates how some of the techniques presented earlier are applied in a real program. You'll see how to create a new embedded object, how to edit an existing object, and how to save and retrieve objects on disk.

OLE_DEMO.VBP consists of a single form containing only an OLE control and a menu. Other than changing the form's **Caption** property to **OLE Demonstration**, you can leave all object properties at their default values. The two menus consist of a File menu with Save and Exit commands and an Object menu with Insert and Delete commands. Listing 10.1 presents the form's objects and properties.

> *Note: All of the demonstration programs in this chapter were developed using the OLE servers in Microsoft Word 97 and Microsoft Excel 97.*

Listing 10.1   Objects and properties in OLE_DEMO.FRM.

```
Begin VB.Form frmOleDemo
    Caption        =    "OLE Demonstration "
    Begin VB.OLE OLE1
    End
    Begin VB.Menu mnuFile
        Caption        =    "&File"
        Begin VB.Menu mnuFileSave
            Caption        =    "&Save"
        End
        Begin VB.Menu mnuFileSep
            Caption        =    "-"
        End
        Begin VB.Menu mnuFileExit
            Caption        =    "&Exit"
        End
    End
    Begin VB.Menu mnuObject
        Caption        =    "&Object"
        Begin VB.Menu mnuInsert
            Caption        =    "&Insert"
        End
        Begin VB.Menu mnuObjectDelete
            Caption        =    "&Delete"
```

```
        End
    End
End
```

The program code is shown in Listing 10.2. It starts by declaring a few constants and global variables in the form's General Declarations section. For simplicity's sake, I have defined a constant for the name of the OLE data file, OLE_DEMO.DAT. Here's how the program works. When it's running, the user can select the Insert Object command to display the Insert Object dialog box, and then use this dialog box (as described earlier in the chapter) to insert either a new object or one based on an existing file. The inserted object can be activated and edited using the server application; pressing Esc ends in-place activation and returns to the program's own menu. For example, Figure 10.5 shows an inserted Excel spreadsheet activated for editing. Note how the Visual Basic program displays Excel's menu while the object is activated. After editing the object, press Esc to "deactivate" the object and redisplay the Visual Basic program's menus.

Once an object has been inserted, you can use the File Save command to save it to disk under the predefined file name. The Object Delete command deletes the object from the OLE control. The program keeps track of whether the inserted object has been saved to disk. Use Object Insert to insert a different object, if desired.

When the program begins, it checks to see if the data file exists on disk. If it does, you are offered the option of loading it into the OLE control. I assume that the file name OLE_DEMO.DAT will not conflict with an existing file on your disk; if it does, change the constant definition in the program to use another name.

This program is a good demonstration of how the capabilities of the OLE control make it easy to program OLE support into our Visual Basic programs. OLE opens a whole new

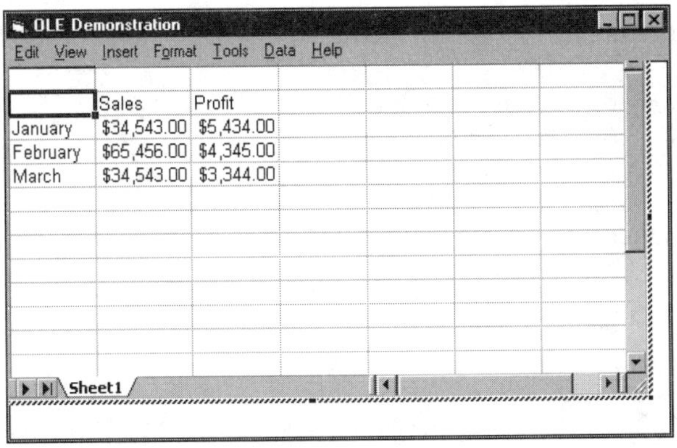

Figure 10.5 *The OLE_DEMO program with an embedded Excel worksheet activated for in-place editing.*

world of possibilities. The power of our programs is no longer limited to the code we have the time and skill to write, or to the custom controls that you can afford to buy.

Listing 10.2   Code in OLE_DEMO.FRM.

```
Option Explicit

Option Explicit

' Constant for OLE object type.
Const OLE_EMBEDDED = 1

' Constant for the OLE data file name.
Const FILE_NAME = "OLE_DEMO.DAT"

' Global variables and flags.
Dim DataSaved As Boolean
Dim ObjectPresent As Boolean


Private Sub Form_Load()

Dim FileNum As Long, Reply As Integer

ObjectPresent = False
DataSaved = True

' See if the OLE data file exists. If it does, offer
' the option of loading it.

If Dir$(FILE_NAME) <> "" Then
    Reply = MsgBox("Load OLE data from disk?", vbYesNo + vbQuestion, _
        "Load Object")
    If Reply = vbYes Then
        Screen.MousePointer = 11
        FileNum = FreeFile
        Open FILE_NAME For Binary As #FileNum
        OLE1.ReadFromFile FileNum
        ObjectPresent = True
        Close #FileNum
        Screen.MousePointer = 0
    End If
End If

End Sub


Private Sub Form_Resize()
```

```
' Size the OLE control to fill the form.
OLE1.Move 0, 0, frmOleDemo.ScaleWidth, frmOleDemo.ScaleHeight

End Sub


Private Sub mnuFile_Click()

' Enable Save menu command only if an object exists.

If ObjectPresent Then
    mnuFileSave.Enabled = True
Else
    mnuFileSave.Enabled = False
End If

End Sub


Private Sub mnuFileExit_Click()

Dim Reply As Integer

' If the object has not been saved, offer the option.

If Not DataSaved Then
    Reply = MsgBox("Save OLE object before quitting?", _
        vbYesNoCancel + vbQuestion, "Delete Object")
    If Reply = vbYes Then
        Call SaveObject
    ElseIf Reply = vbCancel Then
        Exit Sub
    End If

End If

End

End Sub


Private Sub mnuFileSave_Click()

Call SaveObject

End Sub


Private Sub mnuInsert_Click()
```

```
Dim Reply As Integer

' If an object is already present in the OLE control, ask the user if it
' should be deleted. If the reply is no exit sub.

If ObjectPresent Then
    Reply = MsgBox("Delete current object?", vbYesNo + vbQuestion, _
        "Insert Object")
    If Reply = vbYes Then
        Call mnuObjectDelete_Click
    Else
        Exit Sub
    End If
End If

' Permit only embedded objects.

    OLE1.OLETypeAllowed = OLE_EMBEDDED

' Display the OLE Insert Object Dialog.

    frmOleDemo.OLE1.InsertObjDlg

    ObjectPresent = True
    DataSaved = False
    Screen.MousePointer = 0

End Sub


Private Sub mnuObject_Click()

' Enable the Delete menu command
' only if an object is present.

If ObjectPresent Then
    mnuObjectDelete.Enabled = True
Else
    mnuObjectDelete.Enabled = False
End If

End Sub


Private Sub mnuObjectDelete_Click()

Dim Reply As Integer
```

```
' If the object has not been saved, offer the
' user the option of saving it.

If Not DataSaved Then
    Reply = MsgBox("Save the object before deleting it?", vbYesNoCancel _
        + vbQuestion, "Delete Object")

    If Reply = vbYes Then
        Call SaveObject
    ElseIf Reply = vbCancel Then
        Exit Sub
    End If

End If

' Delete the object.

OLE1.DELETE
ObjectPresent = False
DataSaved = True

End Sub


Private Sub OLE1_DblClick()

' The OLE object is automatically activated for editing because its
' AutoActivate property has been left at the default value of 2. Otherwise
' we would have to execute the DoVerb method to activate it.

DataSaved = False

End Sub


Private Sub OLE1_Updated(Code As Integer)

' If the data is changed by the server, clear the Saved flag.


DataSaved = False

End Sub

Private Sub SaveObject()

Dim FileNum As Integer

' Save the OLE object.

FileNum = FreeFile
```

```
Open FILE_NAME For Binary As #FileNum

OLE1.FileNumber = FileNum
OLE1.SaveToFile FileNum
DataSaved = True

Close #FileNum

End Sub
```

OLE Automation

The first part of this chapter presented two sides of the OLE triangle: linking data objects and embedding data objects. These are powerful tools—but triangles have three sides, so something must be missing. There is, indeed: *OLE automation*—the newest component of OLE, and in some ways, the most powerful. In the remainder of this chapter, we'll take a look at the basics of OLE automation in Visual Basic.

How Does It Work?

At the heart of OLE automation is a special kind of data object called a *programmable* data object. Like nonprogrammable objects, programmable data objects can be embedded or linked in a container application. What makes them special is the ability to accept messages from other applications. These messages can contain commands instructing the data object to perform actions on its data. The messages can also pass data to and from the programmable object.

Here's a simple example. Suppose you need to add up a column of numbers in your Visual Basic program. Rather that writing the code yourself, you could use OLE automation to send the numbers to an Excel spreadsheet object, instruct it to add them up, then return the result to the program. You wouldn't use OLE automation for such a simple task, of course, but it gives you an idea of what OLE automation is all about. Server applications that expose programmable objects can be considered custom controls whose capabilities are available to other applications.

Let's look at an example for which you might actually use OLE automation. Imagine you are writing an application for a stock market analyst who needs to download market data from an online service, perform calculations on the data to come up with various economic predictions, then email the resulting report to a list of clients. Using Visual Basic alone, this presents a formidable programming job. With OLE automation, however, the job becomes much easier:

1. Send commands to a communications object, instructing it to download the required data.

2. Send the data to a spreadsheet object.

3. Send commands to the spreadsheet object, instructing it to perform the modeling calculations.

4. Retrieve the results from the spreadsheet object and send them to an email object.

5. Send commands to the email object, instructing it to mail the data to a specified list of recipients.

You can use OLE automation by itself or in conjunction with linking or embedding. If you link or embed a programmable object, you have the option of sending it commands using OLE automation or in-place activation (or both). The method you select will depend on the needs of the project. As a Visual Basic programmer, you can think of programs that support OLE automation as being a kind of custom control. The functionality that these programs expose through the OLE interface are control methods, and the program variables and settings that control its operation are its properties.

Creating An OLE Automation Object

As with embedded OLE objects, you can create a new OLE automation object or open an existing one based on a disk file. In a Visual Basic program, an OLE automation object is identified by a variable of type **Object**. The first step in creating an object, therefore, is to declare a variable of this type:

```
Dim MyObject As Object
```

Next, create a new, empty OLE automation object by using the **Set** statement with the **CreateObject** function. This function has only one argument, specifying the application name and the class name of the object to be created. For example, the statement

```
Set MyObject = CreateObject ("Word.Basic")
```

creates an object based on the Microsoft Word application and the Basic class. You must provide both the application name and class name, because some applications expose more than one class of object.

To create an OLE automation object based on an existing file, use **Set** with the **GetObject** function, as shown here:

```
Set MyObject = GetObject("c:\data\finance.doc")
```

GetObject can accept a second, optional argument specifying the object class name. This argument is required only if the specified file contains two or more object types. An Excel spreadsheet file, for example, can contain both **Sheet** and **Chart** objects. To specify the **Sheet** object in an Excel file, you would write

```
Set MyObject = GetObject("C:\WORKSHEETS\ANNUAL.XLS", "Excel.sheet")
```

where Excel is the server application name and **Sheet** is the object type.

Not all Windows applications expose OLE automation objects. You can be confident that applications from Microsoft do, but other software publishers differ in their degree of support for this technology. I expect that the list of objects will grow rapidly as other software publishers adopt the OLE automation standard. An application's documentation or online help should provide information about the objects it exposes and the methods and properties associated with them.

Just like different Visual Basic controls, objects exposed for OLE automation differ in their capabilities. A **Word.Basic** object, for example, does not permit access to the contents of a document using OLE automation, unless the object is also embedded in an OLE Container control. An **Excel.Sheet** object is different, because it does not need to be embedded for us to use OLE automation for accessing its contents.

Obtaining Object Information

Visual Basic provides two tools for finding information about the objects available on your system. These tools are extremely useful, because a big problem when working with OLE automation is determining the details of the available objects, their methods and properties, and how to use them. For a separate application program, the best source of information is usually the program's own documentation or help system. For online information within Visual Basic, you can use the References list and the Object Browser.

You can display the References list by selecting References from the Visual Basic Project menu. This dialog box was discussed in Chapter 6 and is shown again in Figure 10.6. The list displays all of the object sources, or libraries, that are registered on the system. The ones with a checkmark in the adjacent box are available in the current Visual Basic project. You can add or remove a library from the project by clicking on its box. Because a typical system has many available object sources, loading them all into every Visual Basic project would not be efficient. By selecting only the ones you need, you minimize memory use and maximize speed. If you try to remove a library that is in use, Visual Basic displays a warning message.

An object library that is selected in the References list does not necessarily mean that the library is used by the project—only that it is available. When Visual Basic encounters a

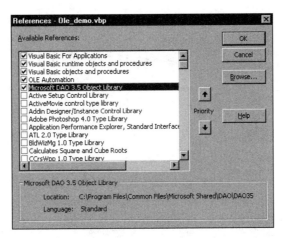

Figure 10.6   *The References dialog box lists the object libraries available on your system.*

reference to an object in our code, it searches the object libraries selected in the References list in top-to-bottom order for a matching object. If two or more applications or libraries expose objects with the same name, Visual Basic uses the first one it finds. Deselecting unused object libraries in the References list will speed up Visual Basic's search process, because it has fewer libraries to search. You can also use the Priority buttons in the References dialog box to move frequently used libraries to the top of the list for additional speed improvement.

Visual Basic will not permit you to deselect a library that is used in the current project. This includes libraries providing objects that are referenced explicitly, as well as libraries used by all custom controls that are installed using the Custom Controls command on the Tools menu. You can never delete the Visual Basic for Applications and Visual Basic Objects and Procedures references; these are necessary for running Visual Basic.

The References list shows which object libraries are available, but it tells you nothing about the objects in those libraries. For this, you need the Object Browser, displayed by pressing F2 or selecting View Object Browser. This dialog box is shown in Figure 10.7.

The dialog box is described here:

- The top Text Box is the Libraries/Projects list, which displays all of the object libraries checked in the References list. It also displays the name of the current Visual Basic project. Select the library whose contents you want to browse, or select <All Libraries> to view the contents of all available object libraries.

- The lower Text Box permits you to search the object database for specific items. Enter in this Text Box the text you want to find and click on the search button (the binoculars icon).

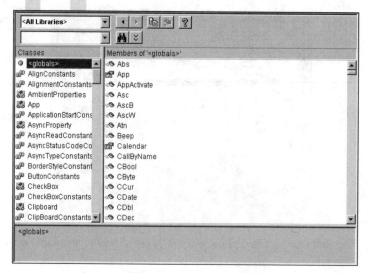

Figure 10.7 *The Object Browser.*

- The Classes list displays the classes and other elements that are available in the selected library or project.

- The Members box lists the methods and properties for the item selected in the Classes/Modules list.

Note the use of different icons in the Class Browser to identify different types of items. In the Classes list, Classes, Enums, and Modules each has its own icon. Likewise, in the Members list, Properties and Methods have unique icons. When you click on an item in the Classes or Members list, the panel at the bottom of the Object Browser displays information about the item.

You may have noticed that many of the items listed in the Object Browser and the References list seem to be related to the various custom controls that are part of Visual Basic. This reflects the fact that Visual Basic controls are implemented using OLE/ActiveX technology. Unfortunately, the Object Browser's usefulness for OLE automation programming is limited, because it shows all of the system's objects—not just those that are OLE automation-capable. You cannot readily use the Browser, therefore, to locate OLE automation objects.

Enums And Modules?

As I mentioned in Chapter 4, an *Enum* is a list of one or more constants in a class module, defined within an **Enum...End Enum** statement. Recall that this is the only way a class can make public constants available. A *Module* is a software component that contains only functions.

If you already know the server and class that you'll be using, however, you can use the Browser to obtain details on the object's methods and properties. Two buttons in the Object Browser dialog box are available to help:

- Click on the Paste button to copy the item selected in the Members list onto the Clipboard. From there, you can paste it into your Visual Basic code.

- Click on the ? button to view the help information related to the selected item.

Properties And Methods Of OLE Automation Objects

Like other Visual Basic objects, OLE automation objects are manipulated by means of their properties and methods. Of course, what you can do with an object depends on the object itself, but the fundamental procedure is similar to working with Visual Basic controls. Each object has its own set of methods and properties. For example, if you created a word-processing document object called **MyObj**, you could manipulate it as follows:

```
MyObj.Insert "Dear Mr. Gates:"        ' Insert some text.
MyObj.Italics = True                  ' Make it italics.
MyObj.SaveAs  "LETTER_TO_BILL.DOC"    ' Save to disk.
```

This code uses the object's **Insert** and **SaveAs** methods and its **Italics** property. The same general principles hold for all objects. If you're used to working with Visual Basic controls, you'll find little difference with OLE automation objects.

Using OLE Automation

I mentioned earlier that you can use OLE automation with objects that are embedded, as well as with objects that aren't. In this section, I will demonstrate both types of OLE automation. These are simple demonstrations, not the sort of tasks that OLE automation would be required to perform. Again, my purpose is to demonstrate the basics—and for that purpose, these programs serve perfectly well.

OLE Automation With A Nonembedded Object

For the nonembedded object, I will use an Excel **Sheet** object. To run this program, you must have Microsoft Excel installed on your system, although other Windows spreadsheet programs may support OLE automation. If you have another spreadsheet program, look through its documentation to see if it supports OLE automation and identify the corresponding methods and properties.

This project, called OLEAUTO1.VBP, is shown executing in Figure 10.8. It has one form that contains two Text Boxes, two Labels, and one Command Button. Enter new **Caption** properties for the Form, the Labels, and the Command Button, as shown in the figure,

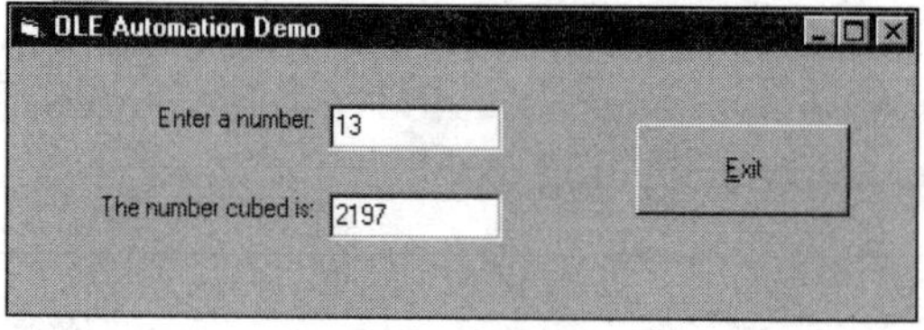

Figure 10.8 *OLEAUTO1 uses an Excel Sheet object to calculate the cube of a number.*

deleting the **Text** property values of the two Text Boxes. Otherwise, the object properties can be left at their default values. Be sure to put the "Enter a number" label next to the Text Box named Text1.

First, the program declares a type **Object** variable in the form's General Declarations section. The **Form_Load** event procedure performs the two required initialization steps: creating the **Excel Sheet** object, and outputting the calculation formula in cell A1 of the spreadsheet object. The two lines of code are shown here:

```
Set XLObj = CreateObject("Excel.Sheet")
XLObj.Worksheets("Sheet1").Range("A2").Formula = "=A1^3"
```

The spreadsheet is now set up to perform the desired calculation. Because the formula you entered in the spreadsheet refers to cell A1, you must place the input value there. You want the calculation to be performed when the user enters or changes a number in the "Enter a number" Text Box. Place the needed code in the Text Box's **Change** event procedure. Once you send the input value to cell A1 of the spreadsheet, the **Sheet** object immediately performs the calculation, and the answer is waiting to be retrieved from cell A2. Place that value in the second Text Box, and the code is complete:

```
' Clear the results text box.
Text2.TEXT = ""

' Put the input value in cell A1 of the spreadsheet.
XLObj.Worksheets("Sheet1").Range("A1").Value = Val(Text1.Text)

' Retrieve the answer from cell B1.
Text2.Text = XLObj.Worksheets("Sheet1").Range("A2").Value
```

To save the spreadsheet to disk, you would execute the object's **SaveAs** method:

```
XLObj.SaveAs "test.xls"
```

You don't want to save the file, however, so all you need to do before quitting the program is to destroy the object:

```
Set XLObj = Nothing
```

Listing 10.3 gives the complete code for OLEAUTO1.FRM.

Listing 10.3   Code in OLEAUTO1.FRM.

```
Option Explicit

Dim XLObj As Object

Private Sub Command1_Click()

' If we wanted to save the object, here's how.
' XLObj.SaveAs "filename.xls".

' Destroy the object.
Set XLObj = Nothing

' Exit the program.
End

End Sub

Private Sub Form_Load()

' Create the Excel sheet object.
Set XLObj = CreateObject("Excel.Sheet")

' Put the cube formula in cell B1.
XLObj.Worksheets("Sheet1").Range("A2").Formula = "=A1^3"

End Sub


Private Sub Text1_Change()

' Clear the results text box.
Text2.Text = ""

' Put the input value in cell A1 of the spreadsheet.
XLObj.Worksheets("Sheet1").Range("A1").Value = Val(Text1.Text)

' Get the answer from cell B1.
Text2.Text = XLObj.Worksheets("Sheet1").Range("A2").Value

End Sub
```

OLE Automation With An Embedded Object

To demonstrate OLE automation with an embedded object, I will use a Microsoft Word document object. The technique of combining OLE embedding with OLE automation is both powerful and flexible. This simple demonstration gives you a taste of what is possible. The program does the following:

- Creates a blank Word document embedded in the Visual Basic program's OLE control.

- When the user clicks on a Command Button, starts the letter by entering the date, return address, and greeting.

- Activates the document for in-place editing, permitting the user to add the body of the letter and format it with Word's tools and commands.

- When the user clicks on another Command Button, finishes the letter by adding the closing.

- When the user clicks on the Done button, asks whether the letter should be printed and saved. If the user requests either one, uses OLE automation commands to instruct Word to print or save the document.

Figure 10.9 shows this demonstration program, displaying the document activated for editing. Notice that the activated document displays Word's menu and provides access to Word's formatting and editing commands.

The program's objects and properties are presented in Listing 10.4, and the code is in Listing 10.5. Rather than walk you though the code a line at a time, I suggest you try to figure out what's going on by yourself. The code is actually fairly simple, so you shouldn't have any problems.

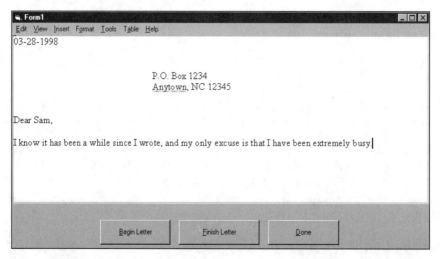

Figure 10.9   *OLEAUTO2 showing the Word document activated for editing.*

Listing 10.4   Objects and properties in OLEAUTO2.FRM.

```
Begin VB.Form Form1
    Caption         =    "Form1"
    LinkTopic       =    "Form1"
    Begin VB.CommandButton Command1
        Caption         =    "&Done"
    End
    Begin VB.CommandButton Command1
        Caption         =    "&Finish Letter"
        Index           =    1
    End
    Begin VB.CommandButton Command1
        Caption         =    "&Begin Letter"
        Index           =    0
    End
    Begin VB.OLE OLE1
    End
End
```

Listing 10.5   Code in OLEAUTO2.FRM.

```
Option Explicit

' The Object variable.
Dim WordDoc As Object

Const vbOLEPrimary = 0

Private Sub Command1_Click(Index As Integer)

Dim Reply As Integer
Dim s1 As String, s2 As String

' Five tabs.
s1 = Chr$(9) & Chr$(9) & Chr$(9) & Chr$(9) & Chr$(9)

Select Case Index
    Case 0       ' Begin Letter.
        ' Insert the date into the document.
        WordDoc.Insert Date$
        WordDoc.InsertPara
        ' Insert two blank lines.
        WordDoc.InsertPara
        WordDoc.InsertPara
        ' Insert the return address preceded by tabs.
        s2 = s1 & "P.O. Box 1234"
        WordDoc.Insert s2
        WordDoc.InsertPara
        s2 = s1 & "Anytown, NC 12345"
```

```
        WordDoc.Insert s2
        WordDoc.InsertPara
        ' Insert two blank lines and the greeting.
        WordDoc.InsertPara
        WordDoc.InsertPara
        WordDoc.Insert "Dear "

        ' Activate for in-place editing.
        OLE1.DoVerb (vbOLEPrimary)

    Case 1      ' Finish Letter.
        ' Add the salutation at the end of the letter.
        WordDoc.InsertPara
        s2 = s1 & "Yours truly,"
        WordDoc.Insert s2
        WordDoc.InsertPara
        WordDoc.InsertPara
        WordDoc.InsertPara
        WordDoc.InsertPara
        s2 = s1 & "Peter G. Aitken"
        WordDoc.Insert s2
        WordDoc.InsertPara

        ' Activate for in-place editing.
        OLE1.DoVerb (vbOLEPrimary)

    Case 2      ' Done
        ' Does the user want to print? If so, instruct
        ' Word to print with the default settings.
        Reply = MsgBox("Print letter?", vbYesNo + vbQuestion)
        If Reply = vbYes Then WordDoc.FilePrintDefault

        ' Does the user want to save? If so, instruct
        ' Word to display the Save As dialog box.
        Reply = MsgBox("Save letter?", vbYesNo + vbQuestion)
        If Reply = vbYes Then
            WordDoc.FileSave
        End If

        ' Destroy the object.
        Set WordDoc = Nothing
        End
End Select

End Sub

Private Sub Form_Load()
```

```
' Position the OLE control to fill the width of the form
' and 3/4 of the height.
OLE1.Top = 0
OLE1.Left = 0
OLE1.Width = ScaleWidth
OLE1.Height = ScaleHeight * 0.75

'Create a new embedded Word document.
OLE1.CreateEmbed "", "Word.Document.6"

' Activate the object(required for OLE automation).
OLE1.DoVerb (vbOLEPrimary)

' Create the OLE automation object.
Set WordDoc = OLE1.object.Application.WordBasic

End Sub
```

PART 3
Making Things Happen

11

Chapter 11

Working With Text

Many programs that are created with Visual Basic deal with text in one way or another.
In this chapter, we'll explore Visual Basic's text processing capabilities by creating a handy text editor.

Have you ever seen a program that doesn't deal with text in one form or another? They're pretty rare, that's for sure. Some programs, such as word processors, are designed specifically to work with text. Others, such as databases, use text as a means for displaying and organizing data. Regardless of the type of Visual Basic project you end up tackling, you'll undoubtedly be dealing with text on a regular basis.

Fortunately for us, Visual Basic has a variety of powerful, text-related tools. In this chapter's project, we'll use these tools to create a fully functional text editor. In addition, I'll show you some other important capabilities, including:

- Storing text data in disk files
- Adding a menu to a Visual Basic program
- Using the Common Dialog control
- Creating a project that uses multiple forms

When we're finished, you'll know a lot more about Visual Basic, *and* you'll have a pretty nice text editor. You can use the editor as a standalone program or as a software component you can add to your other Visual Basic projects that require text-editing capabilities.

Planning The Editor

As always, it pays to take a little time to plan the project before setting fingers to keyboard. We are designing a text editor, which is quite different from a word processor. Word processors, such as Microsoft Word and WordPerfect, include an assortment of complex features for creating professionally formatted documents—styles, footnotes, graphics, and so on. Our project is much less ambitious. A text editor does nothing more than edit text files—that is, add, delete, and rearrange the text in the file. It offers no formatting or automatic word wrap (you must press Enter to start a new line)—no fancy stuff.

> **TIP**
>
> ## Understanding Text Files
>
> What exactly is a text file? A text file contains only the so-called standard characters: letters, numbers, punctuation marks, and so on. Text files are sometimes called ASCII files; the American Standard Code for Information Interchange (ASCII) specifies which numbers are used to represent characters. (Remember, computers use numbers internally for data storage.) For example, the letter *a* is represented by the number 97, and the percent symbol is represented by the number 37. You can find a table of ASCII codes in the Visual Basic Help system.
>
> How do you tell a text file from a non-text file (such as a program file or a word processor document)? Sometimes, the file-name extension can help. The .TXT extension is (or at least should be) reserved for text files. DOS batch files (BAT), Windows INI files (INI), and all Visual Basic program files (VBP, FRM, and BAS) are text files, too. The ultimate test, however, is to view the file's contents, either by using a text editor or the **Type** command from the DOS prompt. If the file displays nothing but recognizable characters, it's a text file.

The editor we will create is what I call a *Baby Editor*—one that provides only the most basic editing functions. It will be quick, simple to use, and easy to customize, should the need arise. What features should it have? Here are the bare essentials I would want in any editor:

- Basic editing: inserting and deleting text, moving the cursor, etc.

- Text selection capabilities

- Cut, copy, and paste operations

- Capability to open any user-specified file

- Capability to save a file under its original name or a new name

- Never losing unsaved changes without warning the user

As you might suspect, we will include all these features in our sample program. I have also added the ability to select the font in which the text is displayed. You may have a different list of "must have" features. That's one of the beauties of the Baby Editor: You can easily customize it.

Programming The Editor

Let's start with the editor's basic text-handling chores: entering and editing text. If you think this sounds like it involves some pretty serious programming, you are in for a pleasant surprise. All you have to do is drop a Text Box control on a form, and most of the work is finished. That's right, many of the text-handling capabilities we need are already built into the Text Box control, including cursor movement, selecting text, and inserting and deleting characters. We only have to add the ability to cut, copy, and paste text (using the Clipboard) to complete the editing part of the project.

Starting The Project

In Visual Basic, start a new Standard EXE project. Resize the form to the size you would like it to be when the program runs (the user can always change it) and set its properties as follows:

Name   **frmBabyEditor**

Caption   Text Editor - untitled

Next, place a Text Box control on the form. Don't worry about the size and position right now. When we execute the program, the Text Box will be adjusted in code to fill the entire form. Set the Text Box properties as shown here:

Multiline   True

Scrollbars   Both

Text   (nothing)

These property settings give us a Text Box that can hold multiple lines of text (as opposed to the default, a single line) and has scrollbars that permit the user to scroll the text both vertically and horizontally using the mouse (the default is no scrollbars). Leave the other properties at their default settings. (Throughout the book, if I do not specifically say to change a property, assume that the default setting is correct or that we will change the setting in code.)

Next, add a Common Dialog control to the form. This control provides several of Windows' standard dialog boxes; we'll see how it works later in the chapter. If the Common Dialog icon is not present in your toolbox, select Components from the Project menu, click on the Controls tab, and click on the box next to the Microsoft Common Dialog Control entry, so a check mark appears in it. Then, close the dialog box.

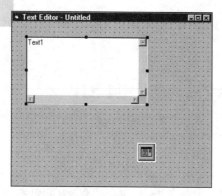

Figure 11.1 *The Baby Editor with the Text Box and Common Dialog controls added.*

Your form should look something like the one shown in Figure 11.1. The Common Dialog control displays as a small icon on the form during program design.

Now is a good time to save your project. I suggest that you use the name BabyEditor for both the form and the project.

Adding Menus To Your Visual Basic Apps

One of the many features that most Windows applications have in common is a menu system. Visual Basic's Menu Editor makes adding menus to your programs a snap—and these menus are every bit as functional as the ones you see in any Windows program. You can add menus to any Visual Basic form; in a multiple-form program, each form can have its own menus. A menu is just another control, and like other controls, it has properties and responds to events. Because of the special requirements of menus, however, you must design a menu and set its properties with the Menu Editor.

To start the Menu Editor (shown in Figure 11.2), display a form and press Ctrl+E or select Menu Editor from the Tools menu. You can also click on the Menu Editor button on the toolbar. Rather than bore you with a long-winded description of how the editor works, I'll walk you through the creation of the menus for our Baby Editor. Once we have completed that, you'll know most of what there is to know about the Menu Editor and menu design. The rest I can fill in quickly and easily.

Creating The Text Editor's Menu

What will our editor need in the way of menu commands? To keep the project simple, we'll create only two menus: a File menu and an Edit menu. The File menu will contain

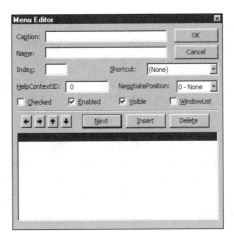

Figure 11.2 *The Visual Basic Menu Editor.*

the New, Open, Save, Save As, and Exit commands. The Edit menu will contain the Copy, Cut, Paste, and Font commands. Let's get to work.

Display the project's form, then press Ctrl+E or select Tools | Menu Editor to display the Menu Editor. Because this form does not yet have a menu, the editor is blank. We will start by adding the first menu command to display on the menu bar. Because we're following Windows conventions, this will be the File menu. In the Caption box, enter "&File" and you'll see the menu caption appear in the large box at the bottom of the dialog box. Next, tab to the Name box and enter "mnuFile", then click on the Next button. The highlight will move down a line in the menu outline, and the Text Boxes will be cleared, ready for you to enter the next menu item.

First, let me point out two things:

- *Menu items can have access keys.* In the menu displayed in the program, an access key is designated by the underlined letter in the menu command. The user can quickly access the menu command by pressing that key when the menu is displayed. As with other control captions, you specify the access key by preceding it with &.

- *In addition, each menu item has a* **Name** *property.* As with other types of controls, the **Name** property is used in the event procedures associated with the item. I have developed the habit of beginning all menu item names with *mnu*, then completing the name with the menu caption(s). Thus, the File menu is named mnuFile, and the Open command on the File menu will be named mnuFileOpen. This naming convention removes any possibility of confusion when dealing with menus.

Now, on to the next menu item. Enter "&New" in the Caption box and "mnuFileNew" in the Name box. Before clicking on the Next button, however, click on the right arrow button. You'll see the New caption—now displayed with an ellipsis in front of it—move over in the outline box. Essentially, we've made the New command subsidiary to the File command. In other words, New will appear as an item on the File menu, not as a separate menu item on the menu bar.

Now click on Next. The new menu item (which is currently blank) is inserted at the same level as the item immediately preceding it (in this case, the New command). Enter "&Open" as the caption and "mnuFileOpen" as the name for this menu item. Open the Shortcut Key list and scroll down, selecting Ctrl+O to specify that the Ctrl+O key combination will be the shortcut for the File | Open command. Notice that Ctrl+O is displayed in the menu outline next to the Open caption.

Add the remaining two commands to the File menu:

- &Save, with the name mnuFileSave and the Ctrl+S shortcut key

- Save File &As, with the name mnuFileSaveFileAs and no shortcut key

At this point, your Menu Editor should look like Figure 11.3.

The next item we need to add to the File menu is not a menu command at all, but rather a *separator*—a horizontal line separating one section of the menu from another. To add a separator, create a menu item with a caption consisting of just a single dash, or hyphen. Because all menu items must be named, we'll assign the name mnuFileSeparator to this item. After clicking on Next, add the last item on the File menu, using the caption E&xit and the name mnuFileExit.

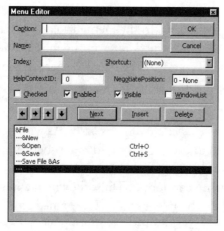

Figure 11.3   *The Menu Editor after partially completing the File menu.*

After entering the Exit command and clicking on Next, you are ready to start with the Edit menu. At this point, any entry you make will be subsidiary to the File menu. Because we want Edit to be a top-level menu, you need to click on the left arrow button to move up one level on the outline. Assign the caption &Edit and the name mnuEdit to this menu item, then click on Next. Click on the right arrow to move down one level on the outline, and add the commands shown in Table 11.1 to the Edit menu.

Don't Stray From The Norm

If you have even a little experience using Windows programs, you have probably noticed that the menus for most programs follow certain conventions. For example, if the program deals with files (and most programs do), the file-related commands are on the File menu, which is the first item on the menu bar. Likewise, the first three entries on the File menu are usually New, Open, and Close. Ctrl+O is the standard shortcut key for the Open command.

Do yourself—and your users—a favor: Follow these standards when organizing menus in your Visual Basic programs. Sure, your unique menu design may be just fine from a functional point of view, but it's guaranteed to confuse your users.

That's it—the menu is finished. Your Menu Editor will look like the one shown in Figure 11.4. Click on OK to close the Menu Editor and return to the form. You will see the menus on the form during design and when the program runs. You can open the menus and select commands—although nothing happens, because we haven't written event code for the menu commands yet. We will be creating the event procedures later.

Before we continue creating the project, let's go over the other Menu Editor commands. Even though you don't need them for this project, you will someday.

Table 11.1   Edit menu commands.

Caption	Name	Shortcut Key
&Copy	mnuEditCopy	Ctrl+C
Cu&t	mnuEditCut	Ctrl+X
&Paste	mnuEditPaste	Ctrl+V
-	mnuEditSeparator	
&Font	mnuEditFont	Ctrl+F

Figure 11.4.   *The completed menu displayed in the Menu Editor.*

Other Menu Editor Options

The Menu Editor contains checkboxes for setting several menu item properties. These properties control how the menu item is displayed when the program is running and the user pulls down the menu:

- **Checked**—Displays a check mark next to the menu item when the menu is displayed.

- **Enabled**—Indicates that a menu item is available. If a menu item is disabled, it is grayed out, indicating it is unavailable to the user.

- **Visible**—Toggles the display of a menu item. You can hide a menu command by setting its **Visible** property to False.

You can also edit the structure of a menu as follows:

- Click on the up or down arrow to move the current menu item (the one high-lighted in the hierarchical list) without changing its left-right position.

- Click on the left or right arrow to change a menu item's position in the hierarchy. You can have as many as four levels in a menu system.

- Click on the Insert button to add a new, blank menu item above the current item.

- Click on the Delete button to delete the current menu item.

A few items in the Menu Editor remain to be covered. I'll let you explore them on your own.

Programming The Editor, Part 2

With the two controls placed and the menus designed, we have completed the visual design part of the Baby Editor project. Now we are ready to turn our attention to the code. Let's start with the general declarations section, which is where we place the declarations of global variables and constants—those variables and constants that must be available in all of the module's procedures. We require two type **Boolean** flags, plus two type **String** variables. The general declarations code is shown in Listing 11.1.

In case you don't remember how to display a specific part of a project's code, let me refresh your memory. If the Code Editing window is not open, click on the View Code button in the Project window. At the top of the window, use the Object list to select the object whose code you want to view (in this case, select General) and use the Proc list to select the specific procedure (in this case, Declarations).

Listing 11.1   General declarations in BABYEDITOR.FRM.

```
Option Explicit

' True if the text being edited has changed.
Dim TextChanged As Boolean

' True if a file has just been loaded.
Dim JustLoaded As Boolean

Dim FileName As String, OldName As String
```

Next, we will write the form's **Form_Load** event procedure, which is triggered when the form is first loaded. With a single-form program such as this one, the form is loaded when the program begins execution. That makes this procedure the ideal place for program initialization code—code that does things like initializing variables and object properties. We have two tasks for **Form_Load**: setting the two flag variables to False and setting the Common Dialog control's **Filter** property. I don't want to explain the details of this property setting here, because I'll be devoting a good deal of attention to the Common Dialog control later in the chapter. For now, try to restrain your curiosity. The code for the **Form_Load** procedure is presented in Listing 11.2.

Listing 11.2   The Form_Load event procedure.

```
Private Sub Form_Load()

Dim Filter As String

' Clear flags.
```

```
TextChanged = False
JustLoaded = True

' Load filters into the common dialog box.
Filter = "Text files (*.txt) | *.txt"
Filter = Filter & "|Batch files (*.bat) | *.bat"
Filter = Filter & "|INI files (*.ini) | *.ini"
Filter = Filter & "|All files (*.*) | *.*"
CommonDialog1.Filter = Filter

End Sub
```

The next procedure, **Form_Resize**, has the job of setting the size and position of the Text Box control to fill the form. The **Form_Resize** event procedure is triggered every time the form's size is changed, as well as when it is first displayed. The code for this procedure is shown in Listing 11.3. By setting the Text Box's **Top** and **Left** properties to zero, it positions the Text Box against the top and left edges of the form. By setting the Text Box's **Width** and **Height** properties to the values of the form's **ScaleWidth** and **ScaleHeight** properties, the Text Box's size is made equal to the form's internal display area.

Listing 11.3   The Form_Resize event procedure.

```
Private Sub Form_Resize()

' Size the Text Box to fill the form.

Text1.Top = 0
Text1.Left = 0
Text1.Width = ScaleWidth
Text1.Height = ScaleHeight

End Sub
```

Note that a form object also has **Width** and **Height** properties, but these differ from **ScaleWidth** and **ScaleHeight**. The former two properties give the outer dimensions of an object; in the case of a form object, these dimensions include its border, title bar, etc. The **ScaleHeight** and **ScaleWidth** properties refer specifically to the form's display area—the area where you can place other objects.

You're probably wondering why we didn't specify an object for the **ScaleWidth** and **ScaleHeight** properties. Why didn't I write the code like this:

```
Text1.Width = frmBabyEditor.ScaleWidth
Text1.Height = frmBabyEditor.ScaleHeight
```

In truth, I could have written it this way. The code would have worked fine; it just wasn't necessary. In an object's own event procedures, any reference to a property without an object name automatically refers to the object's own properties.

If you run the project now, you'll see that you can enter text into the Text Box. You can also select text using the standard methods: dragging with the mouse or holding Shift while using the cursor movement keys.

 Getting "With" It

The **With** statement can save you typing when you are working with several of an object's properties. The general syntax is as follows:

```
With object
    .Property1 = value1
    .Property2 = value2
    ...
End With
```

Thus, to change several properties of a Text Box object named **Text1**, you could write:

```
With Text1
    .Text = "Hello"
    .Visible = True
    .Height = 1500
    .Width = 4000
End With
```

Implementing Cut, Copy, And Paste

The first requirement for the Cut, Copy, and Paste operations is taken care of for us by the Text Box's built-in capabilities. As we'll soon see, so are most of the other parts.

During program execution, the user can select text in the Text Box using the standard Windows techniques. The Text Box control has a property named **SelLength** that gives us the length (in characters) of the selected text in the Text Box, and another property named **SelText** that returns the selected text itself. It's a trivial matter to see if any text is selected (simply verify that **SelLength** is greater than zero) and, if so, to retrieve it.

As for the Copy operation, we'll use the Windows Clipboard, of course, which is represented in Visual Basic by the Clipboard object. This object is automatically available to all Visual Basic programs; explicitly adding it to the project is not necessary. The Clipboard object has several methods, two of which we will use:

- **Clipboard.SetText** places a specified block of text on the Clipboard, replacing any text that might already be there.

- **Clipboard.GetText** returns the text from the Clipboard.

With these tools, implementing the Copy command is easy. The code is placed in the Edit | Copy menu command's **Click** event procedure. You can display this procedure either by selecting it from the lists at the top of the Code Editing window or by selecting the command from the menus when the form is displayed. Listing 11.4 shows the code for this procedure. It verifies only that text is selected in the Text Box, which it then copies to the Clipboard.

Listing 11.4   The Edit|Copy command event procedure.

```
Private Sub mnuEditCopy_Click()

' If any text is selected copy it to the Clipboard.

If Text1.SelLength = 0 Then
    Beep
    Exit Sub
End If

Clipboard.SetText Text1.SelText

End Sub
```

Implementing the Cut command is similar. In fact, the only difference is that the selected text is deleted from the Text Box after being copied to the Clipboard. This is accomplished by setting the Text Box's **SelText** property to an empty string. The code for the Edit | Cut command's **Click** event procedure is shown in Listing 11.5.

Listing 11.5   The Edit|Cut command event procedure.

```
Private Sub mnuEditCut_Click()

' If any text is selected, copy it to the Clipboard,
' then delete it.

If Text1.SelLength = 0 Then
    Beep
    Exit Sub
End If

Clipboard.SetText Text1.SelText
Text1.SelText = ""

End Sub
```

Implementing the Edit | Paste command is the simplest of all, requiring only a single line of code. Set the Text Box's **SelText** property equal to the text returned by the Clipboard's **GetText** method—that's it. Note that if text is selected in the Text Box when the Paste command is executed, the selected text is replaced by the pasted text, which is the standard Windows way. If no text is selected, then the pasted text is inserted at the insertion point. The code for this event procedure is shown in Listing 11.6.

Listing 11.6   *The Edit|Paste command event procedure.*

```
Private Sub mnuEditPaste_Click()

' Paste Clipboard text.

Text1.SelText = Clipboard.GetText()

End Sub
```

You can run the Baby Editor now; you'll be able to enter text and then cut and copy it to other locations (either within the editor's own text or into another Windows application). True, we still have plenty to add, such as file support and font selection, but I think you'll agree that we have a good deal of functionality with very little coding involved.

Enabling And Disabling Menu Items

The editor, as it stands, has one fairly minor problem. If you open the Edit menu, you'll see that both the Cut and Copy commands are enabled, even when no text is selected in the editor. Clearly, these commands are applicable only when text is selected. True, code in both the Edit | Cut and Edit | Copy command event procedures prevents anything from happening should either command be issued with no text selected, but our Baby Editor will appear more professional if the commands are enabled only when appropriate. Likewise, the Paste command should be enabled only when the Clipboard contains text to be pasted. How can we accomplish this?

The enabling/disabling of the menu commands is easy, requiring only that we set the command's **Enabled** property to True or False. Determining whether to enable or disable these commands is equally as easy. We can look at the value of the **SelLength** property to determine if text is selected in the Text Box, and we can use the Clipboard object's **GetText** method to see if the Clipboard holds any text.

Where will we carry out these actions? In other words, what event can we use? Obviously, we don't care whether these menu items are enabled or disabled when the menu is not displayed. What always happens before the menu is displayed? You click on the top-level menu item (in this case, Edit). Therefore, the **Click** event procedure for the top-level menu item is the right place for this code. Listing 11.7 shows the code for the **mnuEdit_Click** event procedure.

Listing 11.7   The mnuEdit_Click event procedure.

```
Private Sub mnuEdit_Click()

' Enable Paste command only if there is text in
' the Clipboard.

Dim x As String

x = Clipboard.GetText()

If x = "" Then
    mnuEditPaste.Enabled = False
Else
    mnuEditPaste.Enabled = True
End If

' Enable Cut and Copy commands only if
' there is text selected.

If Text1.SelLength <> 0 Then
    mnuEditCopy.Enabled = True
    mnuEditCut.Enabled = True
Else
    mnuEditCopy.Enabled = False
    mnuEditCut.Enabled = False
End If

End Sub
```

When you run the project after adding this event procedure, you'll see that the Copy, Cut, and Paste commands are enabled only when appropriate. Remember that the Paste command will be enabled if there's *anything* in the Clipboard, whether or not it was placed there by this program.

Preventing Data Loss

One critical aspect of program design is preventing data loss. This means that the user should not be able to inadvertently exit the editor program, load another file, or start a new file if the current file contains changes that have not been saved to disk. The program should prompt the user to save the current file. Of course, the user can choose to exit without saving; the point here is to prevent accidents.

We'll implement data loss insurance by maintaining a flag named **TextChanged** that is True if the contents of the editor's Text Box have changed since they were loaded or last saved. The obvious place to set this flag is in the Text Box control's **Change** event procedure, which is executed whenever the contents of the Text Box change. The flag will then be cleared when the file is saved. Whenever the user tries to load a file, start a new file, or quit when this flag is True, a warning message will be displayed (we'll see how this is done later).

There's a fly in this ointment, however. When a file is read from disk and loaded into the Text Box, the **Change** event procedure will be triggered and the **TextChanged** flag set, even though the text has not actually been changed. This will trigger false warnings if the user loads a file and then tries to exit without changing the file. The solution is to keep a second flag named **JustLoaded** that is True only when a file has just been loaded, but has not yet been modified. Then the **Text1_Change** event procedure is modified to set the **TextChanged** flag only if the **JustLoaded** flag is False. The code for this procedure, shown in Listing 11.8, executes whenever the contents of the Text Box change.

Listing 11.8   *The Text1_Change event procedure.*

```
Private Sub Text1_Change()

' If the Text Box's contents change, set global
' variable TextChanged to True unless we have
' just loaded a file.

If JustLoaded = True Then
    JustLoaded = False
Else
    TextChanged = True
End If

End Sub
```

The Common Dialog Control

Before continuing with the project, we need to take a look at the Common Dialog control, one of the custom controls provided with Visual Basic. You added a Common Dialog control to the Baby Editor form earlier. What exactly is this control? It's very cool and will save you scads of work.

The Common Dialog control provides your Visual Basic applications with several of the frequently needed Windows dialog boxes: Open, Save As, Font, Color, Help, and Printer. You specify which dialog box you want by the method used to display it. If a particular dialog box offers options—a Color choice in the Font dialog box, for example—you can control their display by setting certain control properties before displaying the dialog box. Similarly, selections the user makes in the dialog box are returned to the calling program in properties.

The Common Dialog control is a terrific timesaver. While you could certainly construct these dialog boxes yourself using Visual Basic controls, why bother? Remember our most basic rule: Don't reinvent the wheel. As you'll see, using the Common Dialog control is quite easy. It also gives you the advantage of having your program's dialog boxes look identical to those used by many other Windows programs that also use the Common Dialogs (which are actually a part of Windows, not Visual Basic). The first task we will use the Common Dialog box for is letting the user select a file to open.

Opening A File

Opening a file means reading the data from a text file on disk and displaying it in the program's Text Box. This process consists of two main parts:

- Using the Common Dialog control to let the user select the file

- Using Visual Basic's file access commands to open, read, and close the file

We'll deal with these issues in turn.

First, which files should we make available to the user? Rather than simply listing all of the files in the selected folder, the better course is to restrict the file listing to those files the user is likely to be interested in—in other words, text files. We already took care of this task in the **Form_Load** event procedure (Listing 11.2) when we initialized the Common Dialog control's **Filter** property as follows:

```
Filter = "Text files (*.txt) | *.txt"
Filter = Filter & "|Batch files (*.bat) | *.bat"
Filter = Filter & "|INI files (*.ini) | *.ini"
Filter = Filter & "|All files (*.*) | *.*"
CommonDialog1.Filter = Filter
```

With this code, we have actually loaded four different filters into the dialog box: one that will display only text files (***.TXT**), one for batch files (***.BAT**), and so on. When the dialog box is displayed, the user will be able to select the desired filter in the List Files of Type list. Note that one of the filters will list all files—a good idea, because we cannot be sure which extensions will be associated with text files on the user's system.

Once the filter has been specified, displaying the Open dialog box requires only two lines of code:

```
CommonDialog1.FilterIndex = 1
CommonDialog1.ShowOpen
```

The first line specifies the filter that will be in effect initially. The second line displays the Common Dialog with the **ShowOpen** method, specifying that the control is to act as an Open dialog box. Execution pauses until the user closes the dialog box, at which time the selected file name can be retrieved from the Common Dialog's **FileName** property. If the user canceled the dialog box without selecting a file, this property will contain a blank string.

Once we have the name of the file to open, we must open it, read the data, and close the file. To open a file, you must supply the file name and a number that will be associated with the file. Because a particular number can be associated with only one open file at one time, and because you have no way of knowing which numbers are in use (Windows can have multiple processes going on simultaneously, so processes other than your program can have numbers associated with open files), use the **FreeFile** function to be sure you select an unused number for your file. The two lines of code required to open a file (whose name is stored in the variable **FileName**) are as follows:

```
FileNum = FreeFile
Open FileName For Input As FileNum
```

Note the syntax of the **Open** statement. It specifies the file name that is being opened for input (because we are just reading the file, not writing anything to it) and the number of the file. Once the file is open, use this number to refer to it in subsequent program statements.

Once the file is open, we will read the text one line at a time. The Basic statement designed for this task is **Line Input**, which reads a single line of text from the file. A "line" is defined as a sequence of characters that ends with either a carriage return (CR) character by itself or combined with a line feed (LF) character. If we repeatedly execute **Line Input** until we reach the end of the file, we will read all lines of text in the file. Each line is placed in a buffer, which is simply a string variable used for temporary storage of data. This buffer is then added to the end of another buffer, using the concatenation operator &. This second buffer then accumulates the entire contents of the file. Finally, the second buffer is copied to the Text Box's **Text** property.

There's one minor complication. Windows text files are stored with a single CR character at the end of each line. While the CR character is sufficient for the **Line Input** statement to detect the end of the line, the Text Box requires the CRLF combination to break a line. If we simply copied the text file's contents directly to the Text Box, we would end up with one very long line of text. To break the text into separate lines, we must add the CRLF combination to the end of each line before putting it in the buffer. We obtain these characters with Visual Basic's built-in **Chr$** function, which returns the character corresponding to a specific numerical ASCII code. The ASCII codes for CR and LF are 13 and 10, respectively, so we can create a string variable holding the CRLF combination as follows:

```
CRLF = Chr$(13) + Chr$(10)
```

Now we can just concatenate this variable onto the end of the buffer after each line is read from the file. An even easier method is to use the built-in constant **vbCRLF** to obtain a CRLF combination.

We also need some way of telling when we have reached the end of the file. The **EOF** function serves this purpose. If you pass a file number as its argument, this function returns True if the end of the file has been reached, False otherwise. We can set up a loop as follows (expressed in pseudocode):

```
Do While Not end of file
    Get next line
    Add to buffer
Loop
```

The final steps include using the **Close** statement to close the file, copying the text to the Text Box, and changing the form's caption to display the name of the file—and we're finished.

The code for the File | Open command's **Click** event procedure is shown in Listing 11.9. Note that this procedure first calls the **SaveChanges** function, which ensures that no editing changes are lost. We'll look at its code later. For now, it's enough to know that the function returns True if there are no unsaved changes. If unsaved changes exist, the user is given the option either to save or discard them. **SaveChanges** returns False if the user decides to cancel, in which case execution exits the **mnuFileOpen_Click** procedure, leaving the original contents of the editor unchanged.

Listing 11.9   The File|Open command event procedure.
```
Private Sub mnuFileOpen_Click()

Dim Buffer1 As String, Buffer2 As String, CRLF As String
Dim Reply As Integer, Flags As Integer, FileNum As Integer

' Verify that changes are saved, if user desires.

Reply = SaveChanges()
If Reply = False Then Exit Sub

' Get a filename from the user.
```

```
CommonDialog1.FilterIndex = 1
CommonDialog1.ShowOpen

' If user canceled.
If CommonDialog1.FileName = "" Then Exit Sub
FileName = CommonDialog1.FileName

' Open the file and read in text.
FileNum = FreeFile
Open FileName For Input As FileNum

Do While Not EOF(FileNum)
    Line Input #FileNum, Buffer1
    Buffer2 = Buffer2 & Buffer1 & vbCRLF
Loop

Close FileNum

' Put the text in the Text Box.
Text1.TEXT = Buffer2

' Display the filename in the form's caption.
frmBabyEditor.Caption = "Text Editor - " & FileName

' Set flag.
JustLoaded = True

End Sub
```

Starting A New File

The File | New command erases the existing contents of the editor (if any), leaving the user with a blank, unnamed document. Again, we use the **SaveChanges** function to guard against losing unsaved data. The operation of this function is quite straightforward. Listing 11.10 shows the File | New command event procedure.

Listing 11.10   *The File|New command event procedure.*

```
Private Sub mnuFileNew_Click()

Dim Reply As Integer

' Verify that changes are saved, if user desires.
Reply = SaveChanges()
If Reply = False Then Exit Sub

' Erase the editor text and the filename.
Text1.TEXT = ""
FileName = ""
```

```
' Change the form caption and clear the TextChanged flag.
frmBabyEditor.Caption = "Text Editor - Untitled"
TextChanged = False

End Sub
```

Saving A File

Saving a file and ensuring against data loss is a bit more complicated, although proper planning simplifies the task. The two menu commands related to saving a file are File | Save and File | Save As. The first of these commands saves the file under its current name; if no name has been assigned yet, the user is prompted to enter one. The second command prompts the user for a file name regardless of whether it already has one. Remember, the global variable **FileName** holds the file name; this will be blank if the user has started the editor and entered some text without saving it, or if the user has selected the File | New command.

We will design the code that does the actual job of saving the file (which we will call **SaveFile**) to prompt the user for a file name only if the **FileName** variable is blank. Otherwise, the file will be saved under its existing name. We can then write the event procedures for the Save and Save As commands, as shown in Listings 11.11 and 11.12. Both event procedures call **SaveFile**. The difference is that the **mnuFileSaveFileAs_Click** procedure first sets **FileName** to a blank (saving its original value in the variable **OldName**).

Listing 11.11   The File|Save command event procedure.
```
Private Sub mnuFileSave_Click()

Call SaveFile

End Sub
```

Listing 11.12   The File|Save As command event procedure.
```
Private Sub mnuFileSaveFileAs_Click()

OldName = FileName
FileName = ""
Call SaveFile

End Sub
```

As you know, the procedure that does the actual saving is **SaveFile**, shown in Listing 11.13. Most of the code deals with the situation when **FileName** is blank. As we discussed a moment ago, this occurs only when the user is saving a new file or has selected the Save As command. We again call on the Common Dialog control, using the **ShowSave** method to display the Save dialog box. In this dialog box, the user can enter the desired file name, changing to a different folder if desired. The name is returned in the Common Dialog's **FileName** property, which will be blank if the user canceled the dialog box. If the user entered a name, the file is saved under that name, and the form's caption is changed accordingly. If the user canceled, **FileName** is set back to its old value (which was saved in **OldName**), and execution exits the procedure.

The actual task of saving the file is, in many respects, identical to the procedure for reading a file. We use **FreeFile** to obtain an unused file number, and we open the file with the **Open** command—this time using the **For Output** qualifier, because we will be outputting data to the file. Unlike reading the file, however, we don't have to output it one line at a time. We can save the entire buffer in one step with the **Print** command. Closing the file and clearing the **TextChanged** flag complete the necessary steps. The code is shown in Listing 11.13.

Listing 11.13   The SaveFile procedure.

```
Private Sub SaveFile()

' Saves current text under original filename.
' If no filename, prompts for one.

Dim FileNum As Integer, Buffer As String

Buffer = Text1.TEXT

' FileName will be blank only if we are saving a
' file for the first time or if user selected
' Save As.
If FileName = "" Then
    CommonDialog1.ShowSave
    FileName = CommonDialog1.FileName

    If FileName = "" Then
        FileName = OldName
        Exit Sub
    Else
        frmBabyEditor.Caption = "Text Editor - " + FileName
    End If
End If


FileNum = FreeFile

Open FileName For Output As FileNum
Print #FileNum, Buffer
Close FileNum
```

```
TextChanged = False

End Sub
```

We finally arrive at the last file-related procedure, **SaveChanges**. This procedure's job is to ensure that the user cannot lose unsaved changes to a file without warning. This procedure is called by both the File | Open and File | New event procedures. This is the first time you have seen a *function*, a type of procedure that returns a value to the calling program. You will also meet Visual Basic's handy **MsgBox** function. Let's cover these two new topics before diving into the function itself.

Function Procedures

In most respects, a function procedure is identical to the sub procedures we covered earlier. You create functions the same way as sub procedures, using the Insert Procedure command from the Visual Basic menu. Simply select the Function option in the Insert Procedure dialog box, and Visual Basic will create the function skeleton. You pass arguments to a function in the same way as you do for a sub procedure. If there are no arguments, leave the parentheses empty.

When creating a function, you need to be concerned with two things that are not relevant to sub procedures. One is the data type of the value returned to the calling program, called the *return type*. A function can return any of Visual Basic's data types, except a fixed-length string or an array. You declare the return type by placing an **As** clause after the function definition. For example, for a function named **MyFunc** that returns a type **Long**, the function skeleton would be:

```
Function MyFunc() As Long

End Function
```

If you omit the **As** clause, the return type defaults to **Variant**.

The second concern is specifying the actual value to be returned. You accomplish this by assigning a value to the function name in code inside the function. For example, this code segment

```
Function MyFunc() As Long

...
MyFunc = x / y

End Function
```

causes the function to return the result of dividing x by y. Note that assigning a return value does not terminate the function. Function execution continues until it reaches the terminating **End Function** statement or encounters an **Exit Function** statement in the body of the function. If you exit a function without assigning a return value, the function will return 0 or a blank string, depending on its type.

The MsgBox Function

The **MsgBox** function is one of Visual Basic's most useful tools. You use it to display brief messages to the user and get a response. In its simplest form, **MsgBox** displays your message in a small dialog box containing an OK button. The title of the dialog box is the same as the project name. For example, the statement

```
MsgBox("This is the message")
```

displays the box shown in Figure 11.5. Program execution pauses while the box is displayed and continues once the user has selected OK.

The **MsgBox** function is a great deal more flexible than this, however. You can specify your own title as well as the display of different combinations of buttons (Yes and No buttons, for example). When more than one button is displayed, the return value of the **MsgBox** function indicates which button the user selected. You can also have a graphical icon, such as a question mark, displayed in the message box. Here is the full syntax of the **MsgBox** function:

```
return = MsgBox(message, flags, title)
```

Let's take a brief tour of the arguments:

- *message*—The string literal or variable specifying the message to be displayed
- *title*—The string literal or variable specifying the message box title
- *flags*—An integer value that controls the display of buttons and icons

Figure 11.5   *A basic message box.*

Table 11.2   Predefined constants for the MsgBox function's flags argument.

Constant	Value	Description
vbOKCancel	1	Display OK and Cancel buttons
vbAbortRetryIgnore	2	Display Abort, Retry, and Ignore buttons
vbYesNoCancel	3	Display Yes, No, and Cancel buttons
vbYesNo	4	Display Yes and No buttons
vbRetryCancel	5	Display Retry and Cancel buttons
vbCritical	16	Display Critical Message icon
vbQuestion	32	Display Warning Query icon
vbExclamation	48	Display Warning Message icon
vbInformation	64	Display Information Message icon
vbDefaultButton2	256	Second button is default
vbDefaultButton3	512	Third button is default

For the **flags** argument, you can use the predefined constants listed in Table 11.2. The last two constants determine which button is the default—that is, which one will be selected if the user simply presses Enter. The normal default is the first button. To combine constants—to specify buttons and an icon, for example—use the **Or** operator. The following call would display the Abort, Retry, and Ignore buttons, an exclamation icon, and make the Retry button the default:

```
x = MsgBox("Message Here", vbAbortRetryIgnore Or vbExclamation Or _
        vbDefaultButton2, "Title Here")
```

The possible return values are also defined by constants, which are listed in Table 11.3.

Table 11.3   Predefined constants for return values of the flags argument.

Constant	Value	Button Chosen
vbOK	1	OK
vbCancel	2	Cancel
vbAbort	3	Abort
vbRetry	4	Retry
vbIgnore	5	Ignore
vbYes	6	Yes
vbNo	7	No

Creating The SaveChanges Function

Go ahead now and create the **SaveChanges** function, assigning it a return type of **Boolean**. The function code is shown in Listing 11.14. Note that the code does not explicitly test for a return from the message box of **vbNo**. If the user selects No (the only possibility besides Yes and Cancel), execution falls through the **If** block, and the function terminates with a return value of True.

Listing 11.14   The SaveChanges function.

```
Private Function SaveChanges() As Boolean

' Determines if the text being edited has changed since the
' last File|Save command. If so, the function offers the user the option
' of saving the file.
' Function returns True if there have been no changes or if
' the user saves the changes; returns False if the user
' selects Cancel.

Dim Title As String, Msg As String
Dim Reply As Integer, Flags As Integer

If TextChanged = True Then
    Title = "Text has changed"
    Msg = "Save changes to text?"
    Flags = vbYESNOCANCEL + vbQUESTION
    Reply = MsgBox(Msg, Flags, Title)

    If Reply = vbYES Then
        Call SaveFile
    ElseIf Reply = vbCANCEL Then
        SaveChanges = False
        Exit Function
    End If
End If

SaveChanges = True

End Function
```

Selecting Fonts

Selecting fonts is the third place where our Baby Editor program will use the Common Dialog control. When used as a Font dialog box, the Common Dialog control has a **Flags** property you set to determine what is displayed in the dialog box. You must specify one of the following flags:

- **cdlCFPrinterFonts**—Displays only printer fonts
- **cdlCFScreenFonts**—Displays only screen fonts
- **cdlCFBOTH**—Displays both screen and printer fonts

You can combine one of these flags with **cdlCFEffects**, which specifies that the Font dialog box should display underline, strikethrough, and color choices as well.

Before displaying the Font dialog box, you should load it with the current font settings—that is, the settings currently in effect in the Text Box control. You can accomplish this task easily by copying the relevant properties from one control to the other, before using the **ShowFont** method to display the font version of the Common Dialog control. When the user closes the dialog box, the program checks the **FontName** property of the Common Dialog. If this is a blank string, the user has canceled the dialog box, so we exit the procedure without making any changes to the Text Box's **Font** property. Otherwise, we reverse the property-copying operation, making the Text Box's font-related properties equal to the corresponding settings in the Font dialog box.

The code for the Edit | Font command's **Click** event procedure is shown in Listing 11.15. The font selected applies immediately to all of the text in the editor. The font setting affects only the display, because font information is not saved in the file along with the text.

Listing 11.15   The Edit|Font command event procedure.

```
Private Sub mnuEditFont_Click()

' Set flags.
CommonDialog1.Flags = cdlCFBoth Or cdlCFEffects

' Set initial values for the dialog box.
CommonDialog1.FontName = Text1.FontName
CommonDialog1.FontSize = Text1.FontSize
CommonDialog1.FontBold = Text1.FontBold
CommonDialog1.FontItalic = Text1.FontItalic
CommonDialog1.FontUnderline = Text1.FontUnderline
CommonDialog1.FontStrikethru = Text1.FontStrikethru
CommonDialog1.Color = Text1.ForeColor

' Display Choose Font dialog box.
CommonDialog1.ShowFont

' If canceled, exit.
If CommonDialog1.FontName = "" Then Exit Sub

' Change the text font according to options selected.
Text1.FontName = CommonDialog1.FontName
```

```
Text1.FontSize = CommonDialog1.FontSize
Text1.FontBold = CommonDialog1.FontBold
Text1.FontItalic = CommonDialog1.FontItalic
Text1.FontUnderline = CommonDialog1.FontUnderline
Text1.FontStrikethru = CommonDialog1.FontStrikethru
Text1.ForeColor = CommonDialog1.Color

End Sub
```

Exiting The Program

To exit the program, we need only the **End** statement, placing it in the event procedure for the File | Exit command. To ensure that unsaved data is not lost, we call the **SaveChanges** function. After that, we either exit the sub procedure or end the program, depending on the return value of the function. The code for **mnuFileExit_Click** is shown in Listing 11.16.

Listing 11.16 The File|Exit command event procedure.

```
Private Sub mnuFileExit_Click()

' Verify that changes are saved, if user desires.

Dim Reply As Integer

Reply = SaveChanges()
If Reply = False Then Exit Sub

End

End Sub
```

That's it for the Baby Editor—it's all finished. Along the way, we have learned a lot about text processing, as well as about other aspects of Visual Basic, such as menus, functions, and file operations. I want to show you one more thing before closing this chapter.

Using Multiple Forms

As I have mentioned several times previously, one of Visual Basic's strong points is its ability to create and use software components. It's time to take a look at one way this is handled. Believe it or not, you have just created a software component—your Baby Editor. The Calculator we built in a previous chapter is another component. A Visual Basic form, in other words, is one type of software component. How do you incorporate multiple forms in a project? It's really quite easy.

A project can have as many forms as needed. To add a form to an existing project, select Add Form from the Project menu. Then do either of the following:

- *To add a new, blank form*—Click on the New tab in the dialog box, click on the Form icon, then select Open.

- *To add a form that already exists as part of another project*—Click on the Existing tab and browse to locate the form file on disk.

When a project contains multiple forms, they will be listed in the Project Explorer window. To select one of these forms, click on its name, then click on either the View Object or View Code button (depending on whether you want to work on the form's controls or its code).

No matter how many forms a project might have, only one can be shown first, when the program begins executing. This *startup form* is normally the first form created during project development. You can change the startup form by selecting Properties from the Project menu and clicking on the General tab in the dialog box that is displayed (Figure 11.6). Pull down the Startup Object list, and you'll see a list of your project's forms. Select the one that is to be the startup form.

How do you switch from one form to another? In other words, how do you control which of your project's forms are visible and which are not? Each Form object has a **Show** method that causes it to be displayed. The syntax is

`FormName.Show style`

where **FormName** is the form's **Name** property and *style* is an integer specifying the type of form—modal (*style* = 1) or modeless (*style* = 0 or *style* omitted). When a modal form is

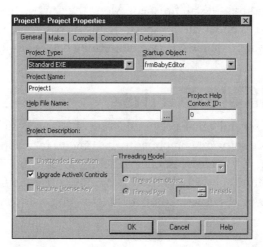

Figure 11.6   *The General tab of the Project Properties dialog box.*

displayed, no keyboard or mouse input can occur for the application except to the modal form. This means the modal form must be hidden (usually in response to user action) before the user can activate or use any other form belonging to the same application. A modal form does not, however, prevent the user from activating or using another application. In contrast, a modeless form does not place these restrictions on the user. Display of a modeless form does not prevent the user from activating another of the program's forms. Thus, if a Visual Basic program has several forms displayed and one of them is modal, only the modal form will accept user input, even though the others are visible. If none of the forms is modal, the user can freely switch among them. Generally, you will use modeless forms unless you have a specific reason to use a modal form.

To hide a form, use its **Hide** method. Note that using the **Show** and **Hide** methods has the same effect as setting the form's **Visible** property to True or False.

 ## What About Me?

You can use the **Me** keyword to refer to the current form. In other words, **Me** always refers to the form containing the code.

As an example of a multiple form project, we will use two of the software components we have already developed: the Calculator and the Baby Editor. Start Visual Basic and create a new Standard EXE project. Add a control array of three Command Buttons to the form, and assign **Caption** properties as follows:

Button Index	Caption
0	Editor
1	Calculator
2	Exit

Next, select the Add Form command on the Project menu. In the dialog box, click on the Existing tab and locate the Calculator form we created earlier, adding it to the project. Repeat to add the Baby Editor form as well. Add the code in Listing 11.17 to the Command Button's **Click** event procedure. Save the project, using the name MultiForm for both the form and the project.

When you run the program, you will first see a form with the three Command Buttons. Click on the Editor button and the Baby Editor appears; click on the Calculator button and the calculator appears. Click on either button again and the corresponding form disappears. When all three forms are displayed (as shown in Figure 11.7), you can switch among forms, move them around the screen, minimize them, and so on. Click on Quit to close all.

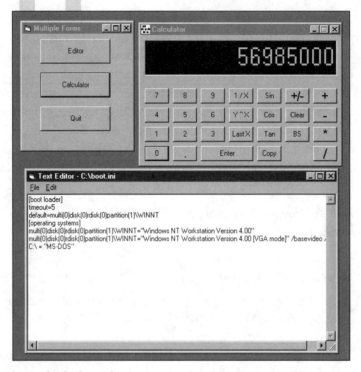

Figure 11.7 *The multiple form demonstration program.*

Listing 11.17 *The Command Button's Click event procedure.*

```
Private Sub Command1_Click(Index As Integer)

Select Case Index
    Case 0:
        If frmBabyEditor.Visible = False Then
            frmBabyEditor.Show
        Else
            frmBabyEditor.Hide
        End If
    Case 1:
        If frmCalculator.Visible = False Then
            frmCalculator.Show
        Else
            frmCalculator.Hide
        End If
    Case 2:
        End
End Select

End Sub
```

Figuring out how the code works is easy. For each form, the code first checks its **Visible** property to see if the form is already displayed. If **Visible** is False, the **Show** method is used to display the form. If **Visible** is True, **Hide** is used to close the form.

In this project, the startup form remains visible when another form is displayed. This is not always desirable, of course, and you can use the **Hide** method to close the first form at the same time you are using **Show** to display the second form. Note also that the three forms in the project are independent of each other—no "master" form contains the others, as is the case with many Windows applications. This effect is obtained with a so-called *multiple document interface* project, which we will explore in Chapter 22.

Additional Text Processing

We have learned a lot about working with text in this chapter, but Visual Basic offers even more. In particular, Visual Basic's collection of built-in functions provides a wide range of useful text handling operations. You can, for example, locate one string within another, change capitalization, extract parts of strings, and apply specific formatting. Table 11.4 includes a brief listing of what's available; I leave it to you to locate the details in the Visual Basic Help system.

Table 11.4   Visual Basic's string processing functions.

Action	Keyword
Compare two strings	StrComp
Convert a string to lowercase or uppercase	LCase, UCase
Create a string of a repeating character	Space, String
Find the length of a string	Len
Format a string	Format
Justify a string	LSet, Rset
Find one string in another	InStr, InstrRev
Extract part of a string	Mid function, Left, Right
Insert one string within another	Mid statement
Replace parts of strings	Replace
Trim leading and/or trailing spaces	LTrim, RTrim, Trim
Set string comparison rules	Option Compare
Work with ASCII and ANSI values	Asc, Chr
Convert strings	StrConv
Process arrays of strings	Filter, Join, Split

Chapter 12
Graphics

Visual Basic is a graphics programmer's paradise. Many difficult graphics tasks are made easy with Visual Basic's controls and methods.

Working with graphics in Visual Basic involves only a few objects: the Picture Box, Image, PictureClip, Shape, and Line controls, and the Picture, Printer, and Form objects. This may seem like a small cast of characters, but you'll soon see they provide a rich and powerful set of graphics capabilities.

Twiddling Your Twips—The Visual Basic Coordinate System

Before we get to the meat and potatoes of this chapter, you need to understand Visual Basic's coordinate system. *Coordinates* are used to define the position of any object displayed on the screen. For some objects, the coordinate system is also used to define the object's size (its height and width). An object's position is always expressed as the distance of its top-left corner from the top-left corner of its container object.

A form's container is always the Screen object, which I'll get to in a moment. The one exception to this rule is MDI (Multiple Document Interface) child forms, whose container is the MDI parent form. A control's container is always the form it is on, unless the control is placed in a Picture Box or Frame, in which case the Picture Box or Frame is the container. The only other possible container is the Printer object, which is used for (you guessed it) printing. I'll deal with the Printer object later in the chapter.

Visual Basic's coordinate system works like the Cartesian coordinate graphing system you learned in school. Any point is represented by two numbers. One of these numbers (traditionally called X) indicates the point's horizontal position, while the other number (Y) indicates the point's vertical position. Of course, a coordinate system must have a zero point, or *origin*—the point where both X and Y are 0. It also must have a *scale* that relates the coordinate units to real measurement units. Does an X value of two mean two inches, two yards, or two furlongs?

In all Visual Basic coordinate systems, the default origin is located at the top-left corner of the container. Positive X values move to the right, and positive Y values move down. Negative coordinates are possible, representing positions above or to the left of the default origin. Note that I said default origin, implying that the origin can be positioned elsewhere. This is indeed true—at least for some container objects—but let's not worry about that for now.

You can use several different scales in Visual Basic coordinates. While many Visual Basic programs are written using only the default scale, you need to know the available options—particularly if you will be doing a lot of graphics programming. The available scale settings are shown in Table 12.1.

Are you wondering what logical means? A logical unit will print at the proper size. For example, a line that is one logical inch long will measure one inch when printed. You set a container object's scale by using the ScaleMode property; however, the only objects that have a ScaleMode property are Form, Picture Box, and Printer. The other objects that can be containers—the Screen object and the Frame control—always use twips for measurement.

Table 12.1   Visual Basic scale settings.

ScaleMode Value	Scale Units
0	Custom
1	Twip (default); there are 1,440 twips per logical inch and 567 twips per logical centimeter
2	Point; there are 72 points per logical inch
3	Pixel; this is the smallest unit of monitor or printer resolution
4	Character; one character unit equals 120 twips horizontally and 240 twips vertically
5	Inch
6	Millimeter
7	Centimeter

Before we look at the various object properties that are related to the coordinate system, let's look at the Big Daddy (or Big Mommy, if you prefer) of all containers, the Screen object.

The Screen Object

The Screen object is Visual Basic's logical representation of the entire display screen. Screen coordinates are always measured in twips, and the top-left corner is always located at (0, 0). The physical size of the screen varies from system to system; knowing the screen size will help you make the best use of available screen real estate. You wouldn't want your program's forms to extend off the edge of the screen. You can query two of the Screen object's properties, **Width** and **Height**, to obtain the screen size:

```
ScreenWidthInTwips = Screen.Width
ScreenHeightInTwips = Screen.Height
```

Although you can't change these properties, knowing their values—and hence, the screen size—will help you determine the appropriate position and size for your forms. The Screen object has some other properties you need to know about.

The **TwipsPerPixelX** and **TwipsPerPixelY** properties return the number of twips per screen pixel. A *pixel* is the smallest dot of light that can be displayed on the screen, and the physical resolution of a particular display is expressed in terms of horizontal and vertical pixels. When a program is running, the number of twips per pixel will depend on the system's hardware configuration, as well as the settings of the Windows display driver. You can use these properties to match your program's graphics to the screen characteristics. For example, to draw the thinnest possible horizontal line, you would set the line thickness equal to **Screen.TwipsPerPixelY** twips. The result is a line that is precisely one pixel thick. You can also calculate the current screen resolution—the number of pixels horizontally and vertically:

```
Xres = Screen.Width / Screen.TwipsPerPixelX
Yres = Screen.Height / Screen.TwipsPerPixelY
```

The **MousePointer** property specifies the appearance of the mouse pointer while it is over a Visual Basic screen element. With the default setting of 0, the pointer is controlled by the **MousePointer** property of the individual objects in the program (form, control, etc.)—that is, whichever object the mouse happens to be over at the moment. Other possible settings for the Screen object's **MousePointer** property are given in Table 12.2.

A **MousePointer** property setting of 99 lets you define your own cursor using the MouseIcon property. In the statement

```
Screen.MouseIcon = picture
```

Table 12.2 MousePointer property settings.

Setting	Description
0	Shape determined by the object (default)
1	Arrow
2	Cross (cross-hair pointer)
3	I-Beam
4	Icon (small square within a square)
5	Size (four-pointed arrow pointing north, south, east, and west)
6	Size NE SW (double arrow pointing northeast and southwest)
7	Size N S (double arrow pointing north and south)
8	Size NW SE (double arrow pointing northwest and southeast)
9	Size W E (double arrow pointing west and east)
10	Up arrow
11	Hourglass (wait)
12	No drop
13	Arrow and hourglass
14	Arrow and question mark
15	Size all (can be customized under Microsoft Windows NT 3.51 and 4.0)
99	Custom icon specified by the **MouseIcon** property

picture specifies the name and path of the icon or cursor file that should be used as the mouse cursor when the **MousePointer** property is set to 99.

The **ActiveForm** property returns the form that is currently active. You will find this property useful in a multiple-form program when you want to write one section of code that will always reference the active form. For example, the line

```
Screen.ActiveForm.MousePointer = 4
```

will change the **MousePointer** property of whatever form happens to be active at the time the code is executed.

A few other **Screen** properties are available, but I will leave those until we need them.

Position And Size Properties

Any Visual Basic object displayed on the screen has properties that determine its position and size. The **Top** and **Left** properties specify the position of the object's top-left corner within its container, and the **Height** and **Width** properties specify its size. All four of these properties use the coordinate units specified by the container's **ScaleMode** property. If you change a container's **ScaleMode** property, during either program design or execution, the properties of any objects in the container automatically change to the new units.

Two other properties, **ScaleHeight** and **ScaleWidth**, apply only to the Form, Picture Box, and Printer objects. These properties provide the dimensions of the object's interior—that is, the area available for graphics operations. These specifications are different from those provided by **Height** and **Width** properties, which indicate the object's overall size, including borders, title bar, and other object components. The most common use for the **ScaleHeight** and **ScaleWidth** properties is at runtime: The program reads them to determine the container object's interior size and then uses the values to position objects or perform drawing operations within the container. You will see how to accomplish this in the first demonstration program, presented later in this chapter.

Take a moment to look at Figure 12.1, which shows the relationships between objects and their containers. Note the three levels of "containerness" in this diagram: A Command Button has been placed in a Frame; the Frame is on a Form; and the Form is on the Screen.

All Visual Basic controls have a **Container** property, which returns the identity of the control's container object. You can also set this property, which would have the effect of moving a control from one container to another. Although I've never seen this technique used in a program, I suppose it might be of value somewhere.

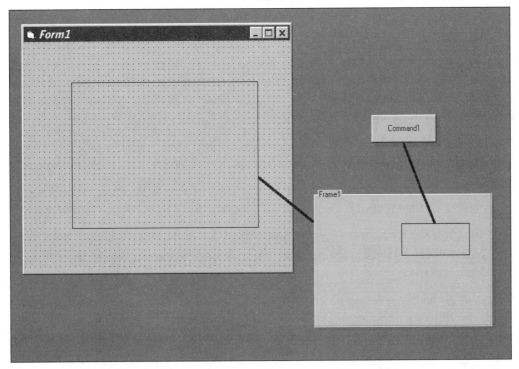

Figure 12.1   *Every Visual Basic object is contained within another object, with the Screen object being the top-level container.*

Using Controls As Containers

Two controls—the Picture Box and the Frame—can serve as containers for other controls. Why would you want to use this feature? For Option Buttons, it's a necessity. Two or more Option Buttons placed in a Frame are treated as a group, and you can select only one of the options at a time. For other control types, however, it remains a matter of design convenience. Because controls that are drawn on a Frame or Picture Box move as their container is moved, you can move them together once you create a group of related controls on a Frame or Picture Box.

To place controls on a Frame or Picture Box, first draw the container control on the form and then draw the controls on the container. If you use another method—such as dragging an existing control onto a Frame—it will *look* like it is on the Frame, but it will neither move with the Frame, nor be positioned with respect to the Frame's origin.

Now let's look at a program that demonstrates some techniques you can use to improve your program's screen display. We want the program to do two things:

- Display the form at a specified size and position when the program starts

- Maintain the relative sizes and positions of the form's controls when the user resizes the form

At startup, this program's form always displays in the center of the screen with a size equal to half the screen size. For this, we use the form's **Load** event procedure. The **Load** event occurs just before a form is displayed, and this is when the program starts for a single-form program. The **Load** event procedure is the ideal place to perform various initialization steps, such as setting a form's size and position. Here's what we'll do:

- To set the form size to half the screen size, we will set the Form object's **Width** and **Height** properties equal to half of the Screen object's **Width** and **Height** properties.

- To center the form left-to-right, we subtract the Form object's **Width** from the Screen object's **Width**, divide the result by 2, and place the result in the Form's **Left** property.

- To center the form top-to-bottom, we subtract the Form object's **Height** from the Screen object's **Height**, divide the result by 2, and place the result in the Form's **Top** property.

Begin this project by creating a new Standard EXE project, placing a Picture Box and a Command Button on the form. Don't worry about their exact position or size; we'll take care of these specifications in code. Leave all the control properties at their default values except for the Command Button's **Caption** property, which should be set to E&xit. Place the single statement **End** in the Command Button's **Click** procedure. Save the project and the form (I used the name CENTER for both). Next, display the **Form_Load** event procedure and add the code shown in Listing 12.1.

Listing 12.1   The Form_Load event procedure.

```
Private Sub Form_Load()

' Make the form width and height equal to
' half the screen dimensions.
Form1.Width = Screen.Width / 2
Form1.Height = Screen.Height / 2

' Center the form on the screen.
Form1.Left = (Screen.Width - Form1.Width) / 2
Form1.TOP = (Screen.Height - Form1.Height) / 2

End Sub
```

When you start the program, the form displays centered on the screen with width and height equal to half the screen dimensions. The controls, however, remain in the positions they were given during program design. Setting the control positions is the next task.

To set the size and positions of the controls, I use an approach like the one used for the form: Specify each control's size and position in terms of its container's size. Where should we place this code? We want the controls to be positioned whenever the form size changes, as well as when the form is first displayed. The ideal place for this code is the **Form_Resize** event procedure, which is called when the form first displays and any time its size is changed (either by the user or in code). I won't bother explaining the code in this procedure (shown in Listing 12.2); I'm sure you'll be able to understand how it works from the comments. Don't forget to save the project as you work on it.

Listing 12.2   The Form_Resize event procedure.

```
Private Sub Form_Resize()

' Make the Picture Box size equal to 90% of the form
' width and 70% of its height.
Picture1.Width = Form1.ScaleWidth * 0.9
Picture1.Height = Form1.ScaleHeight * 0.7

' Center the Picture Box left-to-right.
Picture1.Left = (Form1.ScaleWidth - Picture1.Width) / 2

' Make the distance between the top of the Picture Box and
' the form the same as the distance at the sides.
Picture1.TOP = Picture1.Left

' Make the Command Button width 20% of the form width.
Command1.Width = Form1.ScaleWidth * 0.2

' Make the Command Button height one third of the distance between the
' bottom of the Picture Box and the edge of the form.
```

```
Command1.Height = (Form1.ScaleHeight - Picture1.ScaleHeight) / 3

' Center the Command Button left-to-right.
Command1.Left = (Form1.ScaleWidth - Command1.Width) / 2

' Center the Command Button vertically in the space between the
' Picture Box and the edge of the form.
Command1.TOP = Form1.ScaleHeight - 0.66 * _
    (Form1.ScaleHeight - (Picture1.TOP + Picture1.Height))

End Sub
```

Once the **Form_Resize** procedure is complete, run the program again. You'll see that the Picture Box and Command Button are precisely positioned in the form, as shown in Figure 12.2. If you change the window size by dragging a border, you'll see that the controls maintain their relative sizes and positions.

Using Fixed-Sized Controls

Not all windows need to be resizable. In fact, dialog boxes that contain an array of Text Boxes, Option Buttons, and other controls are best left at a fixed size. You can accomplish this by setting the form's **BorderStyle** property to: **1 - Fixed Single**, **3 - Fixed Dialog**, or **4 -Fixed Toolwindow**. Then you can design the form, placing the various controls in precise positions for the results you want, without worrying about the user messing things up by resizing the dialog box. You could also use the techniques presented here to adapt each control's size and position when the dialog box is resized. In my experience, that's a lot more work than it's worth.

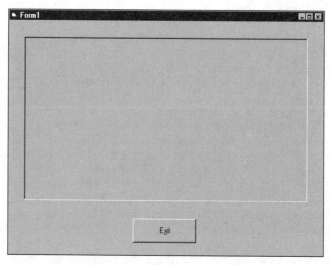

Figure 12.2   *Automatically setting the size and position of controls.*

Who's On First?

Before continuing our discussion of Visual Basic's coordinate system, I think it's wise to take a brief detour to explain the events that occur when a form is being loaded and displayed. This is an area that confuses many programmers, so if you get it straight now, you won't have to worry about it later.

Each form in a Visual Basic project exists in its own disk file. Showing a form on screen requires two steps:

1. Loading the form from disk into memory
2. Displaying the form

In a single-form project, the form is loaded and displayed when the program starts. For a multiple-form project, the designated *startup* form is loaded and displayed when the program starts. Other forms are loaded and displayed under program control.

You can use the **Load** statement to load a form without displaying it:

```
Load formname
```

A form will also be loaded if the program refers to any of its properties. Loading a form and displaying it are two different things, however. The **Show** method, shown here

```
formname.Show
```

is used to display a form. If the form has not already been loaded, **Show** loads it automatically. Rarely will you need to use the **Load** statement. I have found two instances, however, in which **Load** is useful:

- If you want the form's **Load** event procedure to execute without the form being displayed, use the **Load** statement.
- If the form is complex (that is, if it has many controls and/or performs complex processing in its **Load** event procedure), use the **Load** statement to load the form before you need to display it. Complex forms display more quickly if they've been loaded ahead of time.

You can unload a form you no longer need if you want to free memory or to reset all of the form's properties to their original values. To unload a form, use the Unload statement:

```
Unload formname
```

If you want to remove a form from the screen without unloading it, use the **Hide** method:

```
formname.Hide
```

Forms also have a **Paint** event whose occurrence is related to a need to redraw some or all of the form. Figure 12.3 summarizes the relationships among the various methods, statements, and user actions that act on forms and the events that are triggered as a result. You'll see how the **Paint** event is used later in this chapter.

 Understanding The Paint Event And The AutoRedraw Property

The **Paint** event is related to the **AutoRedraw** property. Both Form and Picture Box objects have an **AutoRedraw** property. If **AutoRedraw** is set to Off (the default), graphics and text are written only to the screen, and the **Paint** event is triggered, as indicated in Figure 12.3. The graphics and text are not *persistent*—they must be redrawn using the **Paint** event procedure if the object is uncovered (after being covered by another screen element) or restored (after being minimized). If **AutoRedraw** is set to On, the graphics and text are saved in memory, as well as being written to the screen, and the display is persistent—automatically refreshed from this memory image if the object is restored or uncovered. In this case, the **Paint** event does not occur. **AutoRedraw** applies only to graphics and text created with the **Line**, **Circle**, **Pset**, and **Text** methods; bitmaps and metafiles are persistent regardless of the **AutoRedraw** setting.

Setting **AutoRedraw** to On slows down screen display of graphics and consumes extra memory. Both of these effects are particularly noticeable with large objects.

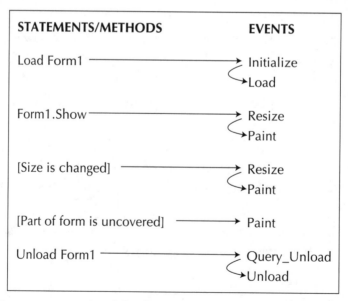

Figure 12.3   *Events associated with loading, showing, sizing, and unloading forms.*

Defining Custom Coordinates

If Visual Basic's assortment of coordinate units doesn't suit you, define your own. A custom coordinate system can include moving the origin to another location, a useful technique for certain applications. For example, a program that draws maps could set the graphical coordinate units to a meaningful value, such as miles or latitude and longitude. You can also "flip" the Y axis so positive values move upward, making it easier to use the Cartesian coordinates commonly used in graphs. A custom coordinate system affects not only graphics operations, but also the placement of controls in a container.

To define a custom coordinate system—which is possible only for Form, Picture Box, and Printer objects—use the **Scale** method. The syntax is

```
objectname.Scale (left, top)-(right, bottom)
```

where (*left, top*) are the new coordinates of the left and top of the object, and (*right, bottom*) are the new coordinates for the right and bottom of the object. For example

```
Form1.Scale (0, 0)-(100, 100)
```

sets a coordinate system where the top-left corner of the object has coordinates (0, 0) and the lower-right corner has coordinates (100, 100). This example does not move the origin, but only changes the measurement unit to be 1/100 of the object dimension. In contrast, the statement

```
Form1.Scale (0, 100)-(100, 0)
```

sets the same measurement units, then moves the origin to the lower-left corner of the object and inverts the Y axis so positive values move upward. When you use **Scale** to set custom coordinates, Visual Basic automatically changes the object's **ScaleMode** property to 0. As you saw in Table 12.1, this indicates that a custom coordinate system is in effect.

Applying the **Scale** method changes the object's **ScaleWidth**, **ScaleHeight**, **ScaleLeft**, and **ScaleTop** properties to reflect the new coordinates. For instance, after executing the previous **Scale** method, the object's **ScaleWidth** property would be 100 and its **ScaleHeight** property would be 100. You can set these properties individually if you want to modify only part of the object's coordinate system. Thus, the statement

```
object.ScaleWidth = 100
```

results in the object's horizontal measurement unit being set to 1/100 of its width, while the location of the origin and the vertical measurement unit remain unchanged. Executing the **Scale** method with no arguments, like this

```
object.Scale
```

will reset the coordinate system to the default (twips with the 0, 0 point at the top left).

You must be aware that the **Scale** method defines its units based on the object's size at the time the method is executed. Subsequent changes to the object's size are not automatically taken into account. We'll see how this works in the custom coordinate demonstration program.

This program uses the **Circle** method in a **For...Next** loop to draw a series of circles on a form. You'll learn the details of the **Circle** method later in the chapter—you needn't worry about it now. The program consists of a form without controls. Leave all of the form's properties at their default values and save your work, calling both the form and the project SCALE. Next, place the code shown in Listing 12.3 in the form's **Paint** event procedure.

Listing 12.3   The Paint event procedure.

```
Private Sub Form_Paint()

Dim i As Integer

Cls

For i = 1 To 5
    Circle (150 * i, 100 * i), 50 * i
Next i

End Sub
```

The **Circle** method draws a circle with its center at the specified coordinates (the values in the parentheses) and with the specified radius. When you execute the program, it will look more or less like Figure 12.4. I say more or less, because the appearance may vary

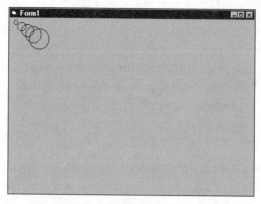

Figure 12.4   *The circles drawn with the form's default coordinate system.*

slightly if you made your form a different size than I did or if your display hardware is different from mine.

After running the program and seeing what the display looks like, add the following statement to the form's **Load** event procedure:

```
Scale (0, 1000)-(1000, 0)
```

Run the program again, and you'll see a quite different display, as shown in Figure 12.5.

Automatic Object References

Why is it that we can sometimes refer to properties and methods without specifying an object? For example, you can write simply **Scale (0, 1000)-(1000, 0)** rather than **Form1.Scale (0, 1000)-(1000, 0)**. In an event procedure, a reference to a property or method automatically refers to the object that received the event, unless another object is specified.

Looking at the new display, you'll see that not only are the circles larger (because the coordinate unit we specified is much larger than a twip), but the circles climb from the bottom of the form rather than descending from the top (because we inverted the Y axis). If you change the size of the form while the program is running, the circles stay the same size—they do not grow or shrink along with the form.

Now let's try one more thing. Copy the **Scale (0, 1000)-(1000, 0)** statement and paste it in the **Paint** event procedure, just after the **Cls** statement. When you run the program and increase the size of the form by dragging its border, the circles are redrawn to keep the same size relative to the form. By resetting the form's coordinate system each time it is painted, we ensure that the coordinate system units are always defined relative to the form's current size—not according to its original size.

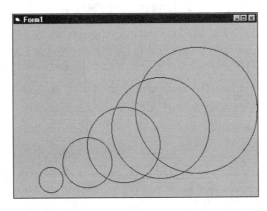

Figure 12.5   *The circle display after changing the form's coordinate system.*

Try decreasing the form size; you'll notice the circles are not redrawn. Why is this? The **Paint** event is triggered when an object's size is increased or when it is uncovered; it is *not* triggered when an object's size decreases.

The Picture Box Control

Now let's look at Visual Basic's most versatile graphics control: the Picture Box. The capabilities of this control fall into three areas:

- Displaying pictures that were created elsewhere and exist in disk files, such as scanned photographs or drawings created with a paint program

- Displaying graphics that are created with program statements, such as the **Circle** method

- Serving as a container for grouping other controls

The third category doesn't relate to graphics, so we won't discuss it further. The other two, while easy to describe, provide a wealth of graphical capabilities limited only by your imagination. Note that most of the graphics actions that apply to the Picture Box control can also be used with the Form object, which we'll cover later in the chapter. Let's see how the Picture Box works.

> ### Image Controls Vs. Picture Box Controls
>
> For displaying existing images, you may prefer to use an Image control rather than a Picture Box. Image controls have only a subset of the capabilities of Picture Box controls, and as a result, they are faster and consume fewer system resources. You'll learn about the Image control later in the chapter.

Loading A Picture During Program Design

You can load a picture into a Picture Box during program design, with the effect of embedding the picture into the project's executable file. (Pictures are often stored as FRX files.) This method is appropriate if a Picture Box will always display the same picture or if you don't want the separate picture file to be distributed with the program. Loading a picture during program design does not prevent you from loading another image into the Picture Box while the program is running. You can load into a Picture Box the image formats shown in Table 12.3.

To load a picture at design time, select the Picture Box's **Picture** property in the Properties window. Visual Basic displays an Open dialog box, which allows you to select the picture file. The picture you select is displayed in the control during design, as well as when the program runs.

Table 12.3 ***Image formats for a Picture Box.***

Format	File Extension	Description
Bitmap	.BMP or .DIB	Windows bitmap. Defines an image as a grid of dots (pixels).
Icon	.ICO	A special kind of bitmap, typically 32 by 32 or 16 by 16 pixels in size.
Cursor	.CUR	Similar to an icon, but also contains a defined *hotspot* that precisely tracks the cursor location. Use for the mouse pointer.
Metafile	.WMF or .EMF	Windows metafile. Defines an image in terms of lines and shapes.
JPEG	.JPG or .JPEG	Joint Photographic Expert Group format. A compressed image format that supports 8- and 24-bit color. Commonly used on the Internet.
GIF	.GIF	Graphical Interchange Format. A compressed format that supports only 8-bit color. Also popular on the Internet.

A picture is loaded into a Picture Box control with the top-left corner of the picture positioned in the top-left corner of the Picture Box. If the image is smaller than the Picture Box, the area outside the image displays the color specified by the Picture Box's **BackColor** property. If the image is bigger than the control, the portion outside the Picture Box is clipped if the **AutoSize** property is set to False (the default). You can set the Picture Box's **AutoSize** property to True, which causes the Picture Box to automatically grow or shrink to fit the image exactly.

You can also load a picture into a Picture Box from the Windows Clipboard. Open the image in the application in which you created or edited it, then copy the image to the Clipboard using the Edit | Copy command. Switch back to Visual Basic, select the Picture Box control, and select Edit | Paste.

Loading A Picture During Program Execution

Several methods are available for displaying a picture in a Picture Box at runtime. One method is to set the control's **Picture** property. You cannot do it directly, as you might expect:

```
Pbox.Picture = filename        ' Does not work!
```

Rather, you must use the **LoadPicture** function

```
Pbox.Picture = LoadPicture(filename)
```

in which *filename* is the name of a file in one of the supported image formats, including the full path, if necessary. The position of the picture and the effect of the control's **AutoSize** property are the same as when you load a picture at design time. You can erase a Picture Box by using **LoadPicture** with no argument:

```
Pbox.Picture = LoadPicture()
```

You can also copy a picture from one Picture Box to another by accessing the source control's **Picture** property:

```
Pbox1.Picture = Pbox2.Picture
```

Loading an image into a Picture Box with these methods is fine for most situations, but it does have a few limitations:

- The image is always placed in the upper-left corner of the Picture Box.

- The image size cannot be changed—that is, the image is always displayed with its original size.

- Only one image at a time can be displayed in a given control.

Fear not, you do have alternatives. The **PaintPicture** method, which we'll discuss next, is one of them.

The PaintPicture Method

The **PaintPicture** method allows you to circumvent the limitations of the previous methods used to load a picture during program execution. Think of **PaintPicture** as a sophisticated cut-and-paste tool. You must start with a source picture, which can be an image in either a Picture Box control or on a form. Then you can take all or part of that picture—any rectangular region, in fact—and place it anywhere you desire on another Picture Box or form, or on the source Picture Box or form. You have numerous options as to how the copied image is combined with any image that already exists in the destination. In addition, you can stretch or shrink the "copied" picture.

Yes, I know that this sounds complicated. Let's take a look at the syntax of the **PaintPicture** method

```
object.PaintPicture source, x1, y1, w1, h1, x2, y2, w2, h2, opcode
```

where the arguments are as follows:

- *object*—The name of the Picture Box, Form, or Printer object where the picture is to be placed. This argument is optional. If it's omitted, the form with the focus is assumed.

- *source*—The source of the graphic. Must be the **Picture** property of a Form, Picture, or Picture Box object.

- *x1*, *y1*—Single-precision values indicating the destination coordinates—in other words, the location on the destination object where the top-left corner of the image is to be drawn. The **ScaleMode** property of the object determines the unit of measure used.

- *w1*, *h1*—Single-precision values indicating the destination width and height of the picture, using units specified by the **ScaleMode** property of the destination object. If the destination width and/or height is larger or smaller than the source width (*w2*) or height (*h2*), the picture is stretched or compressed to fit. These arguments are optional; if they're omitted, the source width (*w1*) and height (*h1*) are used with no stretching or compression.

- *x2*, *y2*—Single-precision values indicating the source coordinates of the region in the source object that is to be copied (in units specified by the source object's **ScaleMode** property). These arguments are optional; if they're omitted, 0 is assumed (indicating the top-left corner of the source image).

- *w2*, *h2*—Single-precision values indicating the width and height of the region within the source that is to be copied (in units specified by the source object's **ScaleMode** property). These arguments are optional; if they're omitted, the entire source width and height are used.

- *opcode*—A type **Long** value that defines the bitwise operation performed between the pixels of the source picture and the pixels of any existing image on the destination (explained shortly). This argument, which is optional, is useful only with bitmaps. If the argument is omitted, the source is copied onto the destination, replacing anything that is there.

Think of the source picture as being printed on a rubber sheet. You can cut out any rectangular part of the picture you want, stretch it vertically and/or horizontally, and stick it down anywhere on the destination picture. Sound useful? You bet it is. The operation of **PaintPicture** is illustrated in Figure 12.6.

The *opcode* argument can be a bit confusing—with good reason. How many ways can you copy a picture from one location to another? Well, you would be surprised—dozens, at least. Here's how it works: In the destination object, where the copied picture is going to be placed, an image already exists. A bitmap picture may be displayed there already, but even if the destination is blank, something is there—perhaps just white pixels. Over the extent of the copied region, therefore, each pixel in the copied image has a corresponding pixel at the same location in the destination. How will these pixels be combined? This is what the opcode argument determines.

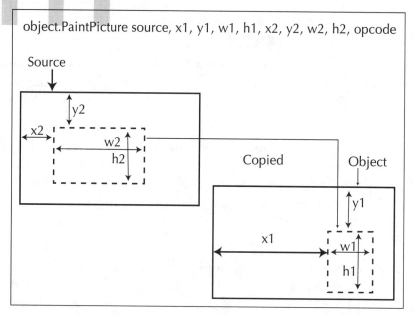

Figure 12.6 *The **PaintPicture** method's arguments.*

The simplest—and perhaps most common—operation is to have each new pixel replace the original pixel. The opcode argument for this is the predefined constant **vbSrcCopy**. Two other useful opcode arguments are **vbBlackness** and **vbWhiteness**, which turn the destination rectangle all black or all white. This really isn't a copy of the source picture, of course; you still have to specify a source in the **PaintPicture** statement. Other opcode arguments perform a variety of logical combinations of the source picture with the destination picture. You can use them to create certain types of visual effects, but I won't go into them here. You can explore the topic further in the Visual Basic Help system.

Hiding The Picture Box

Don't forget that you can set a Picture Box's **Visible** property to False, so it does not display on screen. Even while hidden, it is still a valid source for the **PaintPicture** method, and you can still load pictures into it by setting its **Picture** property or by using the **LoadPicture** statement.

The best way to get a feel for how **PaintPicture** works is to see it in action. The example program PAINTPIC demonstrates three common uses for this statement: enlarging a picture, shrinking a picture, and painting areas with black or white. To start the project, place two Picture Box controls on a form. For the first one (Picture1), set the **AutoSize** property to True, then load the picture GUARD.JPG (provided on the companion CD-ROM) into its **Picture** property. All of the properties for Picture2 should be left at their default values. Change the form's **Caption** property to **Picture Magnifier**.

The program requires three constants, placed in the general declarations section of the form's code. Two of the constants specify the vertical and horizontal magnification, expressed as the portion of the original picture that will be blown up. I used 0.3 for both the vertical and horizontal values; you can experiment with other values if you like. The third constant is the opcode **vbWhiteness**. Unfortunately, this is not predefined by Visual Basic—we have do it ourselves. The declarations code is shown here:

```
Option Explicit
Const vbWhiteness = &HFF0062
Const WIDE = 0.3
Const HIGH = 0.3
```

Adjusting the form and control sizes is accomplished in the **Form_Load** event procedure. Picture1 will already be the size of the loaded picture, because we set its **AutoSize** property to True. The following code makes the form size a bit taller than and a bit more than twice as wide as this Picture Box. Then it makes Picture2 the same size as Picture1 and positions them both on the form. The code is shown in Listing 12.4.

Listing 12.4   *The Picture Magnifier's Form_Load procedure.*

```
Private Sub Form_Load()

Form1.Width = 2.1 * Picture1.Width
Form1.Height = 1.1 * Picture1.Height

Picture1.Left = 0
Picture1.Top = 0

Picture2.Width = Picture1.Width
Picture2.Height = Picture1.Height

Picture2.Top = 0
Picture2.Left = Form1.ScaleWidth - Picture2.Width

End Sub
```

The real action will be triggered by the user clicking on the source picture. A left-button click will trigger the display (in the second Picture Box) of a magnified portion of the picture centered on the location where the mouse was clicked. A right-button click will display nine small copies of the entire picture, each surrounded by a black and white border.

Let's deal with detecting the click first. While the **Click** event procedure might seem like the way to go, a quick examination reveals that it provides no way to tell which button was clicked or where the mouse pointer was located. Clearly, we need something else. Scanning through the list of events that the Picture Box control supports, you will notice **MouseDown** and **MouseUp** events. The **MouseUp** event procedure declaration looks like this:

```
Sub Picture1_MouseUp(Button As Integer, Shift As Integer, X As Single, Y As
Single)
```

The **MouseDown** event procedure has the same details. Let's go over the arguments:

- *Button*—Indicates which button was pressed: left button = 1, right button = 2, center button = 4.

- *Shift*—Indicates the state of the keyboard when the event occurred, whether the Shift, Ctrl, and/or Alt keys were pressed: Shift = 1, Ctrl = 2, Alt = 4. If more than one of these keys is pressed, the values are summed. For example, if Ctrl+Shift is pressed, then **Shift** is equal to 3.

- *X and Y*—Indicates the position where the mouse pointer was located in the object's coordinate system when the event occurred.

When testing for buttons and/or Shift keys, you can use the predefined constants shown in Table 12.4.

As you can see, the **MouseUp** and **MouseDown** event procedures have everything we need. We can determine not only which button was clicked, but at which location.

TIP Mouse-Related Events

Visual Basic has four events related to clicking the mouse. If you're not clear about how they relate to each other, you may end up with some subtle and hard-to-find bugs in your programs.

The **MouseDown** event occurs when the user presses a mouse button. The object that the mouse pointer is over then *captures* the mouse. This means that the object will receive all mouse events up to and including the **MouseUp** event when the mouse button is released—even if the mouse has been moved off the object while the button was down. The **Click** event, however, is generated only if both the **MouseDown** and **MouseUp** events occur on the object. If the mouse is moved off the object before releasing the button, the object receives a **MouseDown** and a **MouseUp** event, but no **Click** event. If the button is released on the object, then the events occur in the order **MouseDown, MouseUp, Click.** If you double-click on an object, the event order is **MouseDown, MouseUp, DblClick, MouseUp.**

Now we can get to the code that does the actual work. If we detect a left-button click, we'll want to perform the following steps:

1. Calculate the coordinates of a rectangle centered on the click location using the magnification constants defined in the declarations section of the program.

2. Check that the rectangle does not extend past the edges of the source picture. If it does, adjust it.

Table 12.4   Constants used to test for buttons and shift keys.

Constant	Value	Description
vbLeftButton	1	Left button is pressed
vbRightButton	2	Right button is pressed
vbMiddleButton	4	Middle button is pressed
vbShiftMask	1	Shift key is pressed
vbCtrlMask	2	Ctrl key is pressed
vbAltMask	4	Alt key is pressed

3. Call **PaintPicture** to copy the contents of this rectangle to the entire Picture2 Picture Box, thus magnifying it.

If it's a right-button click, we'll follow these steps instead:

1. Use **PaintPicture** with the **vbBlackness** opcode to paint the entire destination Picture Box black.

2. Set up a nested loop. The outer loop will loop once for each of three rows, and the inner loop once for each of three columns.

3. In the inner loop, use **PaintPicture** with the **vbWhiteness** opcode to create nine white rectangles over the destination Picture Box, so that each one is slightly smaller than one-third of the Picture Box dimension.

4. Still in the inner loop, use **PaintPicture** with the **vbSrcCopy** opcode to put a small copy of the source picture on each of the white rectangles.

The code for these actions is in the **MouseUp** event procedure, which is shown in Listing 12.5, along with the rest of the form's code. Figure 12.7 shows the program after the user left-clicks on the source image, and Figure 12.8 shows the effects of a right-click.

When you run the program, you may notice one thing: If you cover the program window with another window, then redisplay it, the picture in the right Picture Box does not reappear. This is because the control's **AutoRedraw** property is at the default value of False. As a result, the graphic in the Picture Box is not persistent, as was discussed earlier in this chapter. If you set **AutoRedraw** to True, you'll see the graphic is now persistent. Another way to achieve the same result without setting **AutoRedraw** to True is to put the statements that do the actual drawing (the calls to **PaintPicture**) in the Picture Box's **Paint** event procedure, where they will be executed every time the image needs to be refreshed.

Figure 12.7 *Using the **PaintPicture** method to magnify part of a picture.*

Figure 12.8 *Using the **PaintPicture** method to create nine framed duplicates of a picture.*

Listing 12.5   PAINTPIC.FRM.

```
Option Explicit

' This constant should be predefined by VB, like vbBlackness
' and vbSrcCopy, but it is not, so we must do it ourselves.
Const vbWhiteness = &HFF0062

' Use smaller values for greater magnification.
Const WIDE = 0.3
Const HIGH = 0.3

Private Sub Form_Load()

' Make the form the same height and a bit more
' than twice the width of the Picture Box.
Form1.Width = 2.1 * Picture1.Width
Form1.Height = 1.1 * Picture1.Height

' Put the first Picture Box on the left side of the form.
Picture1.Left = 0
Picture1.Top = 0
```

```
' Make the second Picture Box the same size
' as the first one (which is the size of the loaded picture
' because its AutoSize property is True).
Picture2.Width = Picture1.Width
Picture2.Height = Picture1.Height

' Put the second Picture Box on the right side of the form.
Picture2.Top = 0
Picture2.Left = Form1.ScaleWidth - Picture2.Width

End Sub


Private Sub Picture1_MouseUp(Button As Integer, Shift As Integer, _
    X As Single, Y As Single)

Dim XSrc As Single, YSrc As Single
Dim X1 As Single, Y1 As Single, W1 As Single, H1 As Single
Dim row As Integer, col As Integer

If Button = vbLeftButton Then        ' Left button

    ' Calculate the source rectangle X coordinate. Be sure the
    ' resulting rectangle does not extend past the Picture Box
    ' edge on either the left or the right.
    XSrc = X - ((Picture1.Width * WIDE) / 2)
    If XSrc < 0 Then XSrc = 0
    If (XSrc + (WIDE * Picture1.Width)) > Picture1.Width Then
        XSrc = Picture1.Width * (1 - WIDE)
    End If

    ' Do the same for the Y coordinate.
    YSrc = Y - ((Picture1.Height * HIGH) / 2)
    If YSrc < 0 Then YSrc = 0
    If (YSrc + (HIGH * Picture1.Height) > Picture1.Height) Then
        YSrc = Picture1.Height * (1 - HIGH)
    End If

    ' Paint the contents of the rectangle to the destination Picture Box.
    Picture2.PaintPicture Picture1.picture, 0, 0, Picture2.WIDTH, _
        Picture2.HEIGHT, XSrc, YSrc, Picture1.Width * WIDE, _
        Picture1.Height * HIGH, vbSrcCopy
End If

If Button = vbRightButton Then       ' Right button.
    W1 = Picture2.Width / 3
    H1 = Picture2.Height / 3
    ' The black background.
    Picture2.PaintPicture Picture1.Picture, 0, 0, Picture2.Width, _
```

```
        Picture2.Height, 0, 0, , , vbBlackness
            For row = 1 To 3
                For col = 1 To 3
                X1 = (row - 0.95) * W1
                Y1 = (col - 0.95) * H1
                    ' The white border.
                    Picture2.PaintPicture Picture1.Picture, (row - 0.95) * W1, _
                        (col - 0.95) * H1, W1 * 0.9, H1 * 0.9, , , , , vbWhiteness
                    ' The picture.
                    Picture2.PaintPicture Picture1.Picture, (row - 0.9) * W1, _
                        (col - 0.9) * H1, W1 * 0.8, H1 * 0.8, 0, 0, _
                        Picture1.Width, Picture1.Height, vbSrcCopy
                Next col
            Next row
        End If

        End Sub
```

Using The Image Control

The Image control is another way to display images on your forms. When displaying bitmaps and metafiles, the Image control behaves very much like a Picture Box control. It has only some of the Picture Box's capabilities, which means that an Image control is faster and takes up less of your precious system resources. Image controls are your best bet for displaying pictures; use a Picture Box only when you need its extra features.

Table 12.5 will give you an idea of the differences between the two controls. The Image control is specialized for displaying pictures, and that's about it. Note, however, that the Image control has one capability that the Picture Box lacks: the ability to stretch or shrink an image to fit the Image control's dimensions, without resorting to the **PaintPicture** method. This is controlled by the Image control's **Stretch** property, which can be set to True or False.

The Picture Object

The best way to think of the Picture object is as a temporary storage location for images. That's about all it can do; it does not display or manipulate images in any way. You can load a Picture object with the same image formats that are supported by the Picture Box control. Then, as needed, you can transfer the images to a Picture Box control for display. Because a Picture object uses much less memory and resources, this approach is preferred to the technique of using invisible Picture Box controls as a staging location for images.

To demonstrate, I'll show you how to use the Picture object to create a simple animation. To start, I use a graphics program to create a series of simple images; the first one is shown in Figure 12.9. The other three images are essentially identical, but have the black bar pointing at different angles. I saved these images as SPIN1.BMP through SPIN4.BMP.

Table 12.5 *The Picture Box control vs. the Image control.*

Feature	Picture Box	Image
Load pictures at design- or runtime by setting **Picture** property	Yes	Yes
Load pictures with **LoadPicture** statement	Yes	Yes
Use as source/destination of **PaintPicture** method	Yes	No
Display graphics output created with **Line**, **Circle**, and **Pset** methods	Yes	No
Display text created with the **Print** method	Yes	No
Use to group other controls	Yes	No
Can optionally adjust control size to fit loaded image	Yes	No
Can optionally adjust image size to fit control size	No	Yes
AutoRedraw available	Yes	No

The project's form contains one Picture Box, one Timer, and one control array of three Command Buttons. The objects and properties are summarized in Listing 12.6. I called both the project and the form PICTUREDEMO.

Listing 12.6 Objects and properties in PICTUREDEMO.FRM.

```
Begin VB.Form Form1
   Caption        =    "Picture Object Demo"
   Begin VB.CommandButton Command1
      Caption       =    "Exit"
      Index         =    2
   End
   Begin VB.CommandButton Command1
      Caption       =    "Stop"
      Index         =    1
   End
   Begin VB.CommandButton Command1
      Caption       =    "Start"
      Index         =    0
```

Figure 12.9 *The first animation image.*

```
        End
        Begin VB.Timer Timer1
        End
        Begin VB.PictureBox Picture1
        End
End
```

The form's code is presented in Listing 12.7. The comments should be sufficient for you to understand how it works. Basically, the four images are loaded into an array of Picture objects. Then, a Timer control is set to fire once every 0.25 second. With each cycle, the next image is loaded into the Picture Box, looping back to the first image as needed. The result is a crude animation of a spinning wheel. With more images (and a more skillful artist) the effect would be a lot more pleasing.

The Timer Control

The Timer control lets you execute code at regular intervals. You do not see the Timer on a form, as it works behind the scenes. Set the **Interval** property to the desired number of milliseconds (1/1000 of a second) between events, then put the code to be executed in the **Timer** event procedure. Set the control's **Enabled** property to True or False to start or stop it.

Listing 12.7   Code in PICTUREDEMO.FRM.

```
Option Explicit

' Number of pictures.
Const NUMPIX = 4

' Array of Picture objects.
Dim pics(NUMPIX - 1) As Picture

' Global variable to hold the current pic number.
Dim CurrentPic As Integer

Private Sub Command1_Click(Index As Integer)

Select Case Index
    Case 0  ' Start
        Timer1.Enabled = True
    Case 1  ' Stop
        Timer1.Enabled = False
    Case 2: ' Quit
        End
End Select

End Sub
```

```
Private Sub Form_Load()

'Load the array of Picture objects
Set pics(0) = LoadPicture("spin1.bmp")
Set pics(1) = LoadPicture("spin2.bmp")
Set pics(2) = LoadPicture("spin3.bmp")
Set pics(3) = LoadPicture("spin4.bmp")

' Set up the timer for 250 mSec.
Timer1.Interval = 250
Timer1.Enabled = False

' Set the Picture Box to Autosize.
Picture1.AutoSize = True

'Display the first image.
CurrentPic = 0
Picture1.Picture = pics(CurrentPic)

End Sub

Private Sub Form_Resize()

' Center the Picture Box left to right.
Picture1.Top = 200
Picture1.Left = (Form1.ScaleWidth - Picture1.Width) / 2

End Sub

Private Sub Timer1_Timer()

'Increment the picture number, looping
' back to 0 as needed.
CurrentPic = CurrentPic + 1
If CurrentPic = NUMPIX Then CurrentPic = 0
Picture1.Picture = pics(CurrentPic)

End Sub
```

The PictureClip Control

The PictureClip control is another method for storing images, somewhat like the Picture object. It is specialized to permit storage of composite images, permitting you to retrieve and display only a portion of the image. It is typically used for small images, such as icons, cursors, or animation frames. You can combine, say, 20 icons into one master image, store the image in a PictureClip control, then retrieve individual icons as needed. This is faster and less resource-intensive than keeping the icon files in 20 different Picture objects.

Usually, the individual images that go into the composite image are the same size, and the composite image is a grid of equally spaced smaller images. For example, you could combine 12 icons, each 32-by-32 pixels, into a master image 128 pixels wide (4 icons) and 96 pixels high (3 icons). Then, set the PictureClip control's **Rows** and **Cols** properties to specify that the image has three rows and four columns. You can then retrieve individual images using the indexed **GraphicCell** method. In this example, the master image contains 12 subimages, numbered from 0 at the top left to 11 at the bottom right. This statement would load into a Picture Box the icon in the second row, second column:

```
PictureBox1.Picture = PictureClip.GraphicCell(5)
```

You can also retrieve arbitrary areas of the master image using these properties of the PictureClip control:

- **ClipX**, **ClipY**—Specify the pixel coordinates of the top left corner of the area to be retrieved.

- **ClipHeight**, **ClipWidth**—Specify the pixel dimensions of the area to be retrieved.

Once these four properties have been set, use the **Clip** property to retrieve the specified region of the image in the PictureClip control:

```
Picture1.Picture = PictureClip1.Clip
```

To demonstrate, I have modified the demonstration program I used for the Picture object to use a PictureClip control instead. First, I combined the four individual animation frames into a single image, representing a two-by-two grid of the four images. This is shown in Figure 12.10.

The code is shown in Listing 12.8. I called this project PICTURECLIP. You can see that relatively few modifications have to be made to the code in the PICTUREDEMO project. The only difference in the form is the addition of one PictureClip control, with all of its properties left at the default values. The program looks exactly the same when running.

Figure 12.10   *The image to be loaded into the PictureClip control.*

Listing 12.8   Code in PICTURECLIP.FRM.

```
Option Explicit

Const NUMPIX = 4
Dim CurrentPic As Integer


Private Sub Command1_Click(Index As Integer)

Select Case Index
    Case 0  ' Start
        Timer1.Enabled = True
    Case 1  ' Stop
        Timer1.Enabled = False
    Case 2: ' Quit
        End
End Select

End Sub

Private Sub Form_Load()

' Load the PictureClip control
PictureClip1.Picture = LoadPicture("pic_clip.bmp")

' Set for 2 rows and 2 columns
PictureClip1.Rows = 2
PictureClip1.Cols = 2

' Set the Picture Box to Autosize.
Picture1.AutoSize = True

' Set up the Timer
Timer1.Interval = 250
Timer1.Enabled = False

'Display the first image.
CurrentPic = 0
Picture1.Picture = PictureClip1.GraphicCell(CurrentPic)

End Sub

Private Sub Form_Resize()

' Center the Picture Box left to right.
Picture1.Top = 200
Picture1.Left = (Form1.ScaleWidth - Picture1.Width) / 2

End Sub
```

```
Private Sub Timer1_Timer()

'Increment the picture number, looping
' back to 0 as needed.
CurrentPic = CurrentPic + 1
If CurrentPic = NUMPIX Then CurrentPic = 0
Picture1.Picture = PictureClip1.GraphicCell(CurrentPic)

End Sub
```

Putting Pictures On Forms

You can display bitmap and metafile pictures directly on a form without using a control. A picture on a form is always located "behind" the controls on the form, so you can use the picture as a background. You can display a picture on a form in two ways:

- Set its **Picture** property at design time or runtime; you must use the **LoadPicture** function at runtime, as you do with a Picture Box control.

- Make it the destination of the **PaintPicture** method (it can also serve as the source).

These techniques work in the same way as they do for a Picture Box control.

Drawing In Picture Boxes And On Forms

So far, we have seen how to display and manipulate existing images in Picture Boxes and on forms. What if you want to create an image from scratch? Visual Basic has several statements that let you draw just about anything imaginable. When you draw in a Picture Box or on a form, a *current position* always marks the location where the most recent drawing operation finished. The current position is defined by the object's **CurrentX** and **CurrentY** properties. With no draw operations—or if the object's graphics have been erased with the **Cls** method—these properties both default to zero.

The Line Method

When you want to draw lines and rectangles on Form, Picture Box, and Printer objects, use the **Line** method

object.Line (*X1, Y1*)-(*X2, Y2*), *color, mode*

The arguments are as follows:

- *X1, Y1*—The coordinates of the start of the line. If they're omitted, the object's current position (**CurrentX** and **CurrentY** properties) is used.

- *X2, Y2*—The coordinates of the end of the line.

- *color*—This optional argument specifies the line color. If it's omitted, the object's **ForeColor** property is used.

- *mode*—If set to B, this optional argument specifies that a rectangle is drawn with diagonally opposite corners at the given coordinates. The rectangle is filled with a color and pattern as specified by the object's **FillColor** and **FillStyle** properties. If the mode is set to BF, the rectangle is filled with the same color used to draw the border, and the object's **FillColor** and **FillStyle** properties are ignored.

You can specify color in two ways. The **RGB** function lets you specify a color in terms of the relative intensities of the red, green, and blue components. Here's the syntax:

```
RGB(red, green, blue)
```

Each of the three arguments is a number in the range 0 through 255, specifying the relative intensity of the color. For example, the statement

```
Form1.Line (0,0)-(500,500), RGB(0,0,255), BF
```

will draw a rectangle that is completely blue—both its border and interior. You can also specify color with the **QBColor** function. Its syntax is:

```
QBColor(color)
```

Here, the **color** argument is a number in the range 0 through 15, which corresponds to one of the colors in Table 12.6. The **QBColor** function gives you easy access to the 16 colors available in the old Quick Basic programming language.

Red And Green Make...Yellow?

Some readers may wonder why the **RGB** function uses red, green, and blue. Aren't the primary colors red, blue, and yellow? Yes, but those are the *subtractive* primaries, applicable when the color in question is the result of one color absorbing another, as in mixing paints. For example, red paint looks red because it absorbs, or *subtracts*, the blue and yellow colors. With a computer screen, we are dealing with *additive* colors that are created by adding different color lights together. If you've ever been in a school play, you've probably noticed that the stage lights are composed of red, green, and blue bulbs. For example, adding red light to green light makes yellow—hardly what you would expect, but try it for yourself with the color mixing demonstration program that follows.

Table 12.6   *QBColor color arguments.*

Number	Color	Number	Color
0	Black	8	Gray
1	Blue	9	Light Blue
2	Green	10	Light Green
3	Cyan	11	Light Cyan
4	Red	12	Light Red
5	Magenta	13	Light Magenta
6	Yellow	14	Light Yellow
7	White	15	Bright White

Color Mixing Demonstration

The main purpose of this demonstration program is to show you how the **Line** method and the **RGB** function work, but you'll also gain some experience in using control arrays and Scroll Bar controls. The program's single form contains a Scroll Bar and Text Box for each of the three primary colors. The Text Boxes display numerical values—from 0 to 255— that you change by using the Scroll Bar. The values, of course, represent the color intensity. A rectangle displaying the selected color is drawn on the form whenever the user changes one of the Scroll Bar values. The final program is shown in Figure 12.11.

To create the program, start a new project and place a control array of three VScrollBar controls and another array of three Text Box controls on the form. Add three Label controls with the **Caption** properties set to *Red*, *Green*, and *Blue*, respectively. Position the controls on the form, as shown in Figure 12.11. Be sure that the Scroll Bar and Text Box with Index 0 are under the Red label, that the Scroll Bar and Text Box with Index 1 are under the Green label, and that the Scroll Bar and Text Box with Index 2 are under the

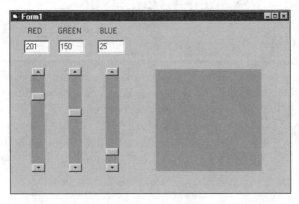

Figure 12.11   *Using the COLORS project to explore the **RGB** function.*

Blue label. Change the form's **Caption** property to **Color Tester** and save both the project and the form with the name COLORS.

Now we can turn to the code, shown in Listing 12.9. Initialization steps are performed in the **Form_Load** event procedure, as usual. This consists mainly of setting the Scroll Bar properties. Because the three Scroll Bars are all part of a control array, we can use a **For...Next** loop to loop through them (another advantage of control arrays). The Scroll Bar's **Value** property returns its current setting. You can set several properties to customize each Scroll Bar to suit your current needs:

- *Max* and *Min*—Values corresponding to the Scroll Bar's maximum and minimum positions.

- *SmallChange*—Amount the Scroll Bar changes when the user clicks on one of the scroll arrows.

- *LargeChange*—Amount the Scroll Bar changes when the user clicks between the thumb (the small, movable box) and one of the scroll arrows.

Because the input arguments to the **RGB** function fall in the range 0 through 255, that's how we'll set the Scroll Bars' **Min** and **Max** properties. We will also set **SmallChange** to 1 and **LargeChange** to 25. The final initialization step is to display each Scroll Bar's value in the corresponding Text Box. Visual Basic's vertical Scroll Bars have their maximum value when the thumb is at the bottom of the bar (which is somewhat counter-intuitive), so we will effectively "flip" the Scroll Bar by subtracting its **Value** property from 255, which gives us the maximum value when the thumb is at the top.

We will place the actual drawing code in its own sub procedure. Use the **Insert Procedure** command to create a sub procedure called **DrawRect**, then add the code shown for this procedure in Listing 12.9. This procedure has only two lines of code. The first one generates a color value by plugging the values of the three Scroll Bars into the **RGB** function. The second statement uses the **Line** method to draw a filled rectangle on the form using this color. You may need to adjust the rectangle's coordinates to position it properly.

As I mentioned earlier, the rectangle is drawn whenever the user changes one of the Scroll Bars. If you haven't guessed, we'll be using Scroll Bar's **Change** event procedure to signal the change in value. Open this procedure and add the code shown for this procedure in Listing 12.9. Using the procedure's **Index** argument (identifying the control in the array that was changed), we update the corresponding Text Box with the new color value and call the **DrawRect** sub procedure to redraw the rectangle. Note another advantage of using control arrays: Think of how much more code would be required if the three Scroll Bars were not in an array, but rather were independent controls.

Finally, we want the rectangle drawn when the form is first displayed, as well as if it is hidden on screen and then uncovered. Because this is the job of the **Paint** event procedure, we place a call to **DrawRect** in that section of code.

The program is complete. Start it up and experiment with color mixing. Try a setting of Red = 255, Green = 255, and Blue = 0. (See, I told you that red plus green make yellow.)

Listing 12.9   Code in COLORS.FRM.

```
Option Explicit

Private Sub Form_Load()

Dim i As Integer

' Set the Scroll Bars for a 0-255 range, with a small
' step of 1 and a large step of 25.
For i = 0 To 2
    VScroll1(i).MIN = 0
    VScroll1(i).MAX = 255
    VScroll1(i).SmallChange = 1
    VScroll1(i).LargeChange = 25
    VScroll1(i).VALUE = 255
    ' Initialize the Text Boxes.
    Text1(i).TEXT = 255 - VScroll1(i).VALUE
Next i

End Sub


Private Sub Form_Paint()

' Draw the rectangle.
DrawRect

End Sub


Private Sub VScroll1_Change(Index As Integer)

' When a Scroll Bar changes, put the new value in
' the Text Box and call the drawing procedure.
Text1(Index).TEXT = 255 - VScroll1(Index).VALUE
DrawRect

End Sub


Public Sub DrawRect()
```

```
Dim color As Long

' Generate the color from the Scroll Bar settings.
color = RGB(255 - VScroll1(0).VALUE, 255 - VScroll1(1).VALUE, _
    255 - VScroll1(2).VALUE)

' Draw the rectangle.
Form1.Line (3500, 1100)-(6000, 3400), color, BF

End Sub
```

> ### Dithering Colors
>
> You may find that some of the colors generated by the program COLORS are not smooth, but instead display a pattern that (if you have good eyesight) appears to be made up of different colors. No, your hardware is not broken. This effect, called *dithering*, is used when your hardware/display driver combination cannot create the exact color called for. Visual Basic then combines two or more colors in a dithered pattern to approximate the color. You will notice this if your Windows display settings are 16 or 256 colors.

The Circle Method

You use the **Circle** method to draw circles, ellipses, and arcs. The syntax for this method is

```
object.Circle (x, y), radius, color, start, end, aspect
```

where the arguments are as follows:

- *object*—The object on which the circle is to be drawn. If the object is omitted, the current form is used.

- *(x, y)*—Single-precision values specifying the coordinates of the center point of the circle, ellipse, or arc. The object's current coordinate system is used.

- *radius*—Single-precision value specifying the radius of the circle, ellipse, or arc.

- *color*—**Long** integer value indicating the color of the circle's outline. If the color is omitted, the value of the object's **ForeColor** property is used. Use the **RGB** or **QBColor** function to specify the color.

- *start, end*—Single-precision values used only when drawing an arc (partial circle or ellipse). These arguments specify (in radians) the beginning and end positions of the arc. The range for both is -2 pi radians to 2 pi radians. The default value for start is 0 radians; the default for end is 2 * pi radians, giving a complete circle or ellipse.

- *aspect*—Single-precision value indicating the aspect ratio of the circle (the ratio of its horizontal diameter to its vertical diameter). Use values greater than or less than 1.0 to draw ellipses. The default value of 1.0 will draw a perfect circle.

To get a feel for using the **Circle** method, create a new project and place the code from Listing 12.10 in the **Form_Paint** event procedure, putting this one line

```
Call Form_Paint
```

in the **Form_Resize** event procedure. Run the program and try moving the window around the screen and changing its size. I called both the form and the project for this demonstration CIRCLES. You can see it running in Figure 12.12.

Listing 12.10   The Form_Paint event procedure in CIRCLES.FRM.

```
Private Sub Form_Paint()

Dim color As Integer, i As Integer
Dim aspect As Single

' Create custom coordinates on the form with (0, 0)
' in the center with width and height both 1000 units.
ScaleLeft = -500
ScaleWidth = 1000
ScaleTop = -500
ScaleHeight = 1000
color = 0

' Make the aspect ratio the same as the form's proportions.
aspect = Height / Width

Cls

For i = 1 To 500 Step 2
    color = color + 1
    If color = 16 Then color = 0
    Circle (0, 0), i, QBColor(color), , , aspect
Next i

End Sub
```

The Pset Method

You can use the **Pset** method to draw individual points on an object. The syntax for this method is

```
object.PSet (x, y), color
```

Figure 12.12 *The display created by the CIRCLES program.*

where the arguments are as follows:

- *object*—The object where the point is to be drawn. If omitted, the current form is used.

- *(x, y)*—Single-precision values indicating the coordinates of the point to set, expressed in the object's coordinate system.

- *color*—**Long** integer value specifying the color of the point. If the color is omitted, the object's current **ForeColor** property setting is used. Use the **RGB** or **QBColor** function to specify the color.

The size of the point is controlled by the object's **DrawWidth** property. If **DrawWidth** is 1, then the point is a single pixel. For larger values of **DrawWidth**, the point is centered on the specified coordinates. To "erase" a single pixel with the **Pset** method, draw a point using the object's **BackColor** property setting as the color argument.

You can use **Pset** to implement a simple drawing program with only a few lines of code, as shown in Listing 12.11. We declare a type **Boolean** variable that will serve as the drawing flag. This flag is set to True when the user presses the mouse button, and cleared (that is, set equal to False) when the user releases the mouse button. Then, in the **MouseMove** event procedure, we test this flag; if it is True, use **Pset** to draw a single point at the mouse location. The program is extremely basic, and if you try it, you'll see that the drawing cannot keep up with rapid mouse movements.

Listing 12.11 Code in DRAWING.FRM.

```
Option Explicit

Dim Drawing as Boolean

Private Sub Form_MouseDown(Button As Integer, Shift As Integer, _
    X As Single, Y As Single)

Drawing = True

End Sub


Private Sub Form_MouseMove(Button As Integer, Shift As Integer, _
    X As Single, Y As Single)

If Drawing Then PSet (X, Y)

End Sub


Private Sub Form_MouseUp(Button As Integer, Shift As Integer, _
    X As Single, Y As Single)

Drawing = False

End Sub
```

Other Drawing Considerations

In this section, I will explain some additional properties and keywords that are relevant when drawing graphics objects.

Using Relative Coordinates

I mentioned earlier that all objects on which graphics can be drawn have a *current position* defined by its **CurrentX** and **CurrentY** properties. All drawing methods (including the **Print** method, covered in the next section) update the current position—that is, after the method is executed, the current position points to the location where the drawing ended. In my explanations of the drawing methods, I provided the syntax that uses *absolute* coordinates—those that do not reference the current position—to specify where the drawing is to take place. You can also specify drawing coordinates that are based on the current position. For the **Line** method, you simply omit the first set of coordinates. For example, the statement

```
object.Line -(X,Y)
```

draws a line from the current position to coordinates X,Y. You can also use the **Step** key-word with either or both of the starting and ending coordinates to specify that the current position be treated as the origin. Here are two examples:

```
object.Line Step(10, 10)-Step(100, 100)
object.Line Step(50, 50)-(100, 100)
```

The first statement draws a line that begins 10 units below and 10 units to the right of the current position, ending 100 points below and 100 points to the right of the current position. The second statement draws a line that begins 50 units below and 50 units to the right of the current position, ending 100 points below and 100 points to the right of the object's origin.

To use relative coordinates with the **Circle** method, include the **Step** keyword before the coordinates. The statement

```
object.Circle Step (0,0), 250
```

draws a circle centered on the current position. **Step** can be used with **Pset** also. The following loop will print a row of 10 dots, starting at the current position, with each dot 10 units below the previous dot:

```
For I = 1 to 10
    Form1.Pset Step (0, 10)
Next I
```

Without the **Step** keyword, this loop would print all 10 dots at the same location—10 units below the form's origin.

Remember that an object's current position is defined by its **CurrentX** and **CurrentY** properties. You can set these properties directly to change the current position. The current position can be outside the visible area of the object, and graphical objects can be drawn there, but of course, they won't be visible.

The DrawStyle And DrawMode Properties

The **DrawStyle** property affects objects drawn with the **Line** and **Circle** methods. It con-trols whether the line drawn (as a line, border of a rectangle, or edge of a circle) is solid or a combination of dots and dashes. The default is a solid line.

All drawing operations on an object (including the Print method) are affected by the object's **DrawMode** property. **DrawMode** governs the interaction between the drawn ob-ject and the background of the object. Of the 16 different **DrawMode** settings, most are dedicated to specialized graphics effects. The default setting, Copy Pen (value = 13), does not produce any special effects, but simply draws the graphical object over the background in the specified color. The other 15 settings create various kinds of logical combinations between the background color and the drawing color. I will explain only the most useful one, Invert. You can explore the remaining settings in the Visual Basic Help system.

Setting **DrawMode** to Invert (value = 6) causes the background color to be inverted where the graphical object is drawn. The specified color of the drawn object is ignored. The value of the Invert setting is twofold. First, the drawn object is guaranteed to be visible no matter what the background, because the existing colors are inverted. Secondly, you can erase an object drawn in Invert mode simply by drawing it again at the same location: The pixels are "re-inverted" to their original values, so the object, in effect, disappears.

TIP — Upside-Down Colors?

How do you invert a color? Colors are expressed in terms of their red, green, and blue (RGB) values, each ranging from 0 to 255. An inverted color is created by making each value equal to 255 minus the old value:

NewR = 255 - OldR

NewG = 255 - OldG

NewB = 255 - OldB

Thus, pure red (255, 0, 0) inverts to cyan, a light blue (0, 255, 255); lavender (153, 153, 240) inverts to olive green (102, 102, 15); and of course black (0, 0, 0) inverts to white (255, 255, 255).

Displaying Text

To display text on a Form, Picture Box, or Printer object, you need to use the **Print** method. The output is created using the font specified by the object's **Font** property. The output is placed at the location specified by the object's current graphics location (**CurrentX** and **CurrentY** properties). You can also use the **Print** method with the Debug object to display text in Visual Basic's Debug window while a program is executing in the Visual Basic development environment (font and current position are meaningless for the Debug object). The **Print** method's syntax is

```
object.Print outputlist
```

where the arguments are as follows:

- *object*—The object to print on. If the object is omitted, the current form is used.

- *outputlist*—A list of one or more expressions to print. If the list is omitted, a blank line is printed.

The *outputlist* argument can contain the following parts, all of which are optional:

- *expression*—Any numeric or string expression.
- *Spc(n)*—Inserts n space characters in the output.
- *Tab(n)*—Positions the insertion point at absolute column number n. If n is omitted, Tab positions the insertion point at the beginning of the next print zone.

If **outputlist** has more than one item, the items can be separated either with a space or a semicolon. After the **Print** method is executed, the default ensures that the output of the next **Print** method is placed on the next line. You can modify the default by placing one of the following arguments at the end of *outputlist*:

- *;* *(semicolon)*—Subsequent output follows immediately on the same line.
- *Tab(n)*—Subsequent output follows at the specified column number on the same line.
- *Tab()*—Subsequent output follows at the next print zone on the same line.

Most of the fonts you will use in Visual Basic have proportionally spaced characters in which a wide letter (such as a W) occupies more horizontal space than a narrow letter (such as an *i*). Therefore, no correlation exists between the number of characters printed and the amount of horizontal space used. You can avoid this problem by using a fixed-pitch font, such as Courier, in which all characters occupy the same amount of horizontal space. Proportional fonts are nicer looking, however, so you'll usually want to use them. When using proportional fonts, how do you know when the output of the **Print** method is going to reach the right edge of the object being printed on, making it necessary to start a new line?

Remember that the **Print** method outputs text at the object's current position. If we know the width of the next chunk of text to be printed, we can do the following (as expressed in pseudocode):

```
If ((current X position) + (Width of text)) > (width of object) then
    it won't fit; advance to beginning of next line
else
    it will fit; output on current line
end if
```

You can obtain the width of a unit of text using the **TextWidth** method. All objects to which the **Print** method applies support this method. If you pass a string as the argument, **TextWidth** returns the width that the text would occupy if printed or displayed, expressed in the object's current horizontal coordinate units. The value takes into account the object's current **Font** property setting.

How do you advance a line? The best way is to manipulate the object's **CurrentY** property directly. First, obtain the height of a line of text using the **TextHeight** method. **TextHeight** works just as **TextWidth,** returning the height (in object units) of the specified text in the current font. The value returned by **TextHeight** includes the *leading,* or space between lines of text. Assume that the variable **S$** contains the next unit of text to be printed on Form1. Assume also that the variables **LMargin** and **RMargin** contain the desired left and right margins, respectively. The following code will wrap to the next line if needed:

```
If ((Form1.CurrentX + Form1.TextWidth(S$)) > (Form1.ScaleWidth - RMargin)
Then
    Form1.CurrentX = LMargin
    Form1.CurrentY = Form1.CurrentY + Form1.TextHeight(S$)
End If

Form1.Print S$;
```

The Line And Shape Controls

If you need to draw permanent lines and shapes on a form, the Line and Shape controls are your best bet. By *permanent,* I mean that you do not need to modify the drawn objects during program execution. What you draw during program design is exactly what will be displayed during program execution. For this reason, they are most often used for decorative purposes, such as providing interesting borders for controls or dividing a form into sections. Neither of these controls has any associated events. Figure 12.13 shows a Picture Box with a border created with several Shape controls, each slightly larger than the next.

To use the Line or Shape control, simply place it on your form as you would any other control. You can choose from the following properties to change the Line control's appearance:

Figure 12.13   *Using the Shape control to create borders.*

- *BorderColor*—The line color.

- *BorderWidth*—The width of the line, in arbitrary units from 1 to 8,192.

- *BorderStyle*—The style of the line (solid, dotted, dashed, etc.).

- *DrawMode*—The appearance of the line. The default setting gives a line in the color specified by the **BorderColor** property. Other settings are explained in Visual Basic Help.

The Shape control has the previous four properties, plus some additional ones:

- *Shape*—The type of shape. Choices are rectangle, square, rounded rectangle, rounded square, circle, and oval.

- *BackStyle*—Indicates whether the interior of the shape is transparent or opaque.

- *BackColor*—The color of the shape's interior. This is ignored if **BackStyle** is set to its default value, **Transparent**.

- *FillColor and FillStyle*—These properties do the same job as **BackColor** and **BackStyle**. If both **BackStyle** and **FillStyle** are set to **Opaque**, the setting of **FillColor** takes precedence over the setting of **BackColor**. You can, therefore, switch a shape's interior color between two values by toggling **FillStyle** between **Transparent** and **Opaque**.

TIP

Exploring Visual Basic Help

Don't forget to make regular visits to Visual Basic's online Help system. It's loaded with all the little details that I can't include in the book. Browsing the Help system and looking at the sample code that is provided will provide you with a lot of useful information.

Printing With The Printer Object

So far, we have limited ourselves to displaying graphics and text on screen. Often, you'll need to send graphics and text to the printer as well. Visual Basic makes this easy with the Printer object. The Printer object has the same properties and methods as the Form and Picture Box objects (those properties and methods related to graphics, at least). Therefore, if you want to print text to the printer, write:

```
Printer.Print message
```

The same goes for the **Line**, **Circle**, and **Pset** methods. Just like the Form or Picture Box objects, the Printer object has a current position defined by the **CurrentX** and **CurrentY** properties, the ability to report the width and height of text with the **TextHeight** and **TextWidth** methods, the ability to act as the destination (but not the source) for the **PrintPicture** method, and so on. For the most part, you can do the same things with the Printer object or a Form object, depending on whether you want the output displayed on the screen or sent to the printer.

A few things are unique to the Printer object. Table 12.7 lists some Printer object-specific methods.

You should be aware that your printer will not support the same fonts as your screen display. Some fonts will be common to both, of course, including the Windows TrueType fonts; but you cannot be sure that a font available for the screen will also be available for the Printer object. To determine which fonts your Printer object has available, use the **FontCount** property to determine the number of fonts, then extract their names from the **Fonts** property. The following code, placed in a form's **Click** event procedure, will load a List Box control with the names of all the Printer object's fonts:

```
Private Sub Form_Click()

Dim i As Integer

For i = 0 To Printer.FontCount -1      ' Determine number of fonts.
    List1.AddItem Printer.Fonts(i)     ' Put each font into List Box.
Next I

End Sub
```

You can use this technique to provide a way for the user to select a font. Remember that the Screen object also has **FontCount** and **Fonts** properties, which you can use to get a list of the screen fonts. One technique I often use is to obtain lists of both the Screen and Printer object fonts, then compare them and generate a list containing only the fonts common to both. This way the user never runs into the problem of using a font on screen that cannot be printed.

Given that you can use the same methods and properties for displaying graphics and text on the screen and the printer, does this mean that you must write two complete sets of

Table 12.7   Printer object methods.

Method	Description
Printer.NewPage	Ejects the current page and starts a new one
Printer.EndDoc	Aborts printing of a long document; however, the portion already sent to the Windows Print Manager will still be printed
Printer.KillDoc	Terminates a print job immediately

program statements—one directing output to the Printer object and the other to a Form? Not necessarily. Visual Basic procedures have the ability to take an argument of type **Object**. In other words, you pass an object to the procedure. This enables you to write a procedure that performs the graphics and text output, and then pass it the Form or the Printer object, depending on where you want the output to go. For example, here's an output procedure that will display a message on either a form or printer:

```
Public Sub Output(Dest As Object, Msg as String)

Dest.Print Msg

End Sub
```

To display the message "Hello" on the form named Form1, use this statement:

```
Call Output(Form1, "Hello")
```

To print the same message on the printer, use this statement:

```
Call Output(Printer, "Hello")
```

This technique is demonstrated in the program PRINT1. The program's form contains a control array of three Command Buttons. The button with Index 0 has the caption *&Display*, Index 1 has the caption *&Print*, and Index 2 has the caption *E&xit*. When you click on the Display button, the form displays the text and graphics shown in Figure 12.14. If you click on the Print button, the same output is produced on your printer. The program's code is presented in Listing 12.12.

Listing 12.12   Code in PRINT1.FRM.

```
Option Explicit

Public Sub Output(Dest As Object)

' Set the font name and size.
Dest.FontName = "Times Roman"
Dest.FontSize = 36

' Display a message.
Dest.Print "Hello world!"

' Print a rectangle to fill the page.
Dest.Line (10, 10)-(Dest.ScaleWidth - 10, Dest.ScaleHeight - 10), , B

' Put an X in the rectangle.
Dest.Line (10, 10)-(Dest.ScaleWidth - 10, Dest.ScaleHeight - 10)
Dest.Line (10, Dest.ScaleHeight - 10)-(Dest.ScaleWidth - 10, 10)
```

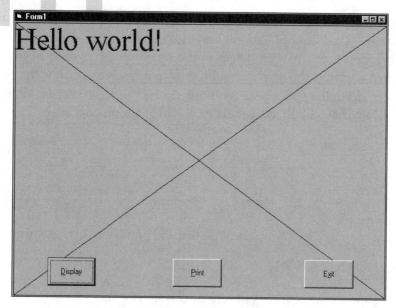

Figure 12.14   *The form displayed by the project PRINT1.*

```
End Sub

Private Sub Command1_Click(Index As Integer)

Select Case Index
    Case 0
        Call Output(Form1)
    Case 1
        Call Output(Printer)
    Case 2
        End
End Select

End Sub
```

The PrintForm Method

The **PrintForm** method—applicable only to Form objects—sends a copy of the Form to the current printer. Everything on the Form—controls, graphics, text, and bitmaps—will be printed (although **AutoRedraw** must be On for graphics created with **Line**, **Circle**, and **Pset** to print). The border and title bar of the form are included in the printout. For the most part, this method is intended as a programmer's aid, permitting you to create hard-copy records of your program's appearance. For end-user printing, you are almost always better off using the Printer object described previously.

The Printers Collection

One of the collections maintained by Windows is the Printers collection, which includes all the printers installed on the system, with each printer represented by a Printer object. In this context, *installed* does not necessarily mean physically present, but only that the printer driver has been installed. If you display the Windows Printers box (select Settings from the Start menu, then select Printers), you'll see the printers installed on your system.

Using **For Each...Next**, you can loop through all the installed printers. For example, this code snippet displays the device names of all installed printers:

```
Dim p As Printer

For Each p In Printers
    List1.AddItem p.DeviceName
Next
```

You can use the Printers collection's **Count** property to verify that at least one printer is installed:

```
If Printers.Count < 1 Then
    MsgBox("No installed printers - you cannot print")
End If
```

While the Printers collection lets you access the installed printers, using the Printers part of the Common Dialog control is a lot easier. You display it as follows (assuming CD1 is the name of your Common Dialog control):

```
Cd1.ShowPrinter
```

With the dialog box, shown in Figure 12.15, users can select from the available printers, set printing options, and so on. This is a lot easier than trying to do it yourself in code.

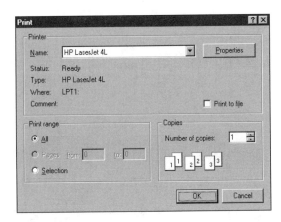

Figure 12.15   *The Printers Common Dialog box.*

Chapter 13

Working With Files

Reading and writing disk files is an essential part of most programs. Visual Basic has a full set of file access tools.

F iles here, files there, files everywhere. The only thing that's been growing faster than hard-disk sizes, it seems, is the number of files you have to store on them. Almost every program you write will need to deal with files, and the way your program handles this challenge has a big impact on its overall quality. Poor design and implementation of file access and management can have a variety of deleterious effects on your program—ranging from slow performance to that ultimate no-no, loss of data.

Note that I draw a distinction between file *access* and file *management*. File access encompasses all the procedures for reading data from and writing data to files, while file management refers to such tasks as creating folders, moving and deleting files, and so on. We'll look at file access in this chapter and file management in the next, covering not only Visual Basic statements but also the controls and objects designed for file-related tasks.

Visual Basic file access can be done in two ways: the traditional methods, which use statements that have been part of the Basic language since the beginning; or the object-oriented method (new with the current version of Visual Basic), which treats the file system as a file system object

(FSO) that has properties and methods. At present, the FSO approach is not as complete as the traditional methods and is applicable mainly to file management tasks (as covered in Chapter 14). As for file access, the FSO model can be used only to read and write text files, as I'll explain later in this chapter. Note that you can mix traditional and FSO methods in the same program.

Reading And Writing Files

If you want to save data until the next time you use your computer, you have to store it in a disk file. If you want to transfer data to another computer using a diskette, you must store it in a disk file. If you want to use data created by another program, you must read it from a disk file. Sure, these rules have a few exceptions, but the general message is clear: Knowing how to use disk files is essential. The Basic language offers a variety of statements and functions that provide complete flexibility in file access. While these program statements and functions are part of the Basic language, they are not directly related to the Visual Basic user interface or to its objects and events. The file manipulation statements will be located in general procedures, or very rarely, in event procedures.

Visual Basic file access consists of three steps:

1. Open the file.

2. Read data from or write data to the file.

3. Close the file.

Sounds relatively simple, but within these three steps hides a multitude of options and pitfalls. Let's start by looking at the three different kinds of file access offered by Visual Basic.

Types Of File Access

All file data, no matter what the source or contents, is stored as a sequence of bytes in the file. Depending on the type of data and the needs of the program, you will choose from one of three ways of accessing those bytes. The type of file access your program uses ultimately determines the methods it can use to read and write data, as well as the way the data is interpreted. Each of the three access methods is appropriate for certain types of data. This section describes each type briefly, with full details given later in the chapter.

Sequential Access Files

A sequential access file stores data as a series of variable-length records. The term *record* simply means a unit of data. For example, if you store the value of a type **Integer** variable in a file, that's one record. Likewise, the contents of a **String** variable would be another record. The records are *variable length*, because each record's length is determined by its contents—not by some overall property of the file. In other words, a sequential access file contains records of different lengths.

The data in a sequential file is assumed to be text, meaning that each byte in the file represents a character. The term *sequential* indicates that this type of file must always be read from the beginning. To read data in the middle of the file, you must first read all the preceding data in sequence. There is no easy way to jump directly to the data in the middle of the file. In a sequential file, numeric data is stored as its corresponding characters, and string data is stored in quotation marks. For example, the value 123 is stored as the string "123"—not as a binary representation of the value 123.

In a sequential file, each record is a line of text terminated with a carriage return-line feed (CR-LF) character. Each record can contain zero or more characters, and the records in a given file can be of different lengths. You treat each record as a single line of text, which is appropriate for manipulating plain text files. You can also treat sequential file records as groups of one or more fields separated from each other by delimiters. This approach is useful for working with data that is divided into units that differ in length.

Random Access Files

A random access file stores data as a series of fixed-size records, with each record the same size as all the others in the file. The records in a random access file are numbered sequentially starting at one. Random access files allow a program to directly access each record by its number, without having to access previous records first. In a 2,000-record file, for example, you could access record 1,199 without first having to read records 1 through 1,198. You can store both text and numbers in a random access file. Text is stored as characters, whereas numbers are stored in a special binary format.

Each record in a random access file consists of a fixed number of bytes, or characters. Each record contains one or more fields, each of which also has a fixed length. It follows that the record size is equal to the sum of the field sizes. The sizes of a file's records and fields are defined by the program when the file is created. Unlike sequential files, random files do not use delimiters to separate fields and records. The fixed lengths of the fields and records are used to determine where each field and record begins and ends. It is this fixed record size that permits random access to data in the file. For example, if the record size is 100 bytes, you know that the 55th record in the file begins at byte position 5,401.

Binary Access Files

Binary access files store data as an unformatted sequence of bytes. No record lengths or delimiter characters are used to provide structure to the file data. Binary access allows us to manipulate the individual bytes of a file without any assumptions about what the bytes represent. Unlike random access and sequential access files, binary access files are not limited to ASCII text or Basic variables. Binary access can be used to read and modify any kind of disk file, as well as to store program data. Because a binary file has no records or other structures, however, the program is completely responsible for keeping track of what is stored where.

Opening Files

A program must open a disk file before it can read or write file data. Files are opened with the **Open** statement, which has the syntax

```
Open filename [For mode] [Access access] [lock] As [#]filenum [LEN=reclen]
```

with these arguments:

- *filename*—A string expression specifying the name of the file to be opened. If *filename* does not include a drive and path specifier, the file is opened in the current folder.

- *mode*—A keyword that specifies the file access mode, as shown in Table 13.1.

- *access*—An optional keyword that specifies the operations permitted on the open file, as shown in Table 13.2.

- *lock*—An optional keyword that controls access to a file by other processes. Valid values for *lock* are shown in Table 13.3.

- *filenum*—An integer expression with a value between 1 and 511. See the next section for more information on file numbers.

- *reclen*—An integer expression that specifies the record length (in bytes) for random access files, and the buffer size for sequential access files (maximum = 32,767; default = 128 for both). The buffer is an internal memory area used by Visual Basic programs to store data temporarily before it is written to disk. A larger buffer size can sometimes speed disk operations, but it also decreases memory available for other purposes. Note that *reclen* is not applicable to binary mode files.

File Numbers

Each file opened by a Visual Basic program has a unique file number associated with it. This number is specified by the *filenum* argument that you pass to the **Open** statement. After the file is open, the program uses the file number to refer to the file when reading and writing the file and when closing it. The file number must be within the range 1 through 511, and only one open file can be associated with a given number at a time. When the file is later closed, the file number is free to be used with another file.

Table 13.1   Mode types.

Mode	File Access
APPEND	Sequential access; if *filename* already exists, new data is added at the end of existing data in the file. If *filename* does not exist, it is created.
BINARY	Binary access; reading and writing. If *filename* does not exist, it is created.
INPUT	Sequential access; the file is opened for reading. If *filename* does not exist, an error occurs.
OUTPUT	Sequential access; the file is opened for writing. If *filename* exists, it is deleted and a new file created. If *filename* does not exist, it is created.
RANDOM	Random access; the file is opened for reading and writing. If *filename* does not exist, it is created. This is the default if the *mode* argument is omitted.

Table 13.2   Access types.

Access	Result
READ	File opened for reading only.
WRITE	File opened for writing only.
READ WRITE	File opened for reading and writing. This mode is valid only for random mode files, binary mode files, and sequential mode files opened for APPEND.

Table 13.3   Lock types.

Lock	Effect
SHARED	Any process may read or write the file.
LOCK READ	No other process may read the file. A program can open a file in LOCK READ mode only if no other process has READ access to the file.
LOCK WRITE	No other process may write to the file. A program can open a file in LOCK WRITE mode only if no other process has WRITE access to the file.
LOCK READ WRITE	No other process may read or write the file. A program can open a file in LOCK READ WRITE mode only if no other process has READ or WRITE access to the file and a LOCK READ or LOCK WRITE is not already in place.

In a multitasking environment, such as Windows, other programs may have opened files that have used some of the available file numbers. Before opening a file, therefore, use the **FreeFile** function to obtain the lowest unused file number. Here's how to use **FreeFile**:

```
Dim filenum As Integer
...
filenum = FreeFile
OPEN "c:\documents\sales.lst" FOR RANDOM AS filenum
```

When called with no argument or an argument of 0, **FreeFile** returns an unused file number within the range 1 through 255. An argument of 1 results in a number within the range 256 through 511:

```
filenum = FreeFile       ' 1-255
filenum = FreeFile(0)      ' 1-255
filenum = FreeFile(1)      ' 256-511
```

Closing Files

A file should be closed when the program is finished using it. Closing a file flushes the file's buffer (a temporary storage area in memory), ensuring that all data has been physically written to disk. Closing a file also frees up the file number that was associated with the file, allowing it to be used for another file and freeing the memory that was assigned to the file's buffer. To close a specific file or files, execute the **Close** statement with the file numbers as arguments. To close all open files, execute **Close** with no arguments:

```
Close #filenum
Close #f1, #f2, #f3
Close
```

All open files are automatically closed when a Visual Basic program terminates. Even so, develop the habit of closing individual files as soon as the program is finished with the file. This technique avoids the possibility of data loss in the event of a system crash or power failure.

Using Sequential Files

As I explained earlier, a sequential file stores data in a series of records where each record is a line of text with a carriage return-line feed (CR-LF) combination at the end. You can use a sequential file to store data in two ways: Each record is a single line of text; or each record is a group of fields separated by delimiters. This section covers both methods. Remember that a sequential file can be opened for only one type of operation at a time: to read data from the file (mode = INPUT), to write data to a new file (mode = OUTPUT), or to write data to the end of an existing file (mode = APPEND). To switch from one operation to another—from writing to reading, for example—you must close the file and reopen it in the new mode.

Fields In Sequential Files

You can use fields in a sequential file when the information to be stored consists of discrete units that all have the same structure. For instance, imagine you are writing a program to keep a catalog of your books. For each book, you want to store the author's name, the title, and an index number that specifies the book's location on your shelf. If you create a sequential file for this data, it will have the following structure:

- The file will contain one record for each book.

- Each record will contain three fields: one for author, one for title, and one for index number.

Let's say that the first entry in the file is *The Aspern Papers* by Henry James, index number 12. The record for that entry will be stored in the file, as shown here:

"Henry James","The Aspern Papers",12

If the second entry is for Dostoyevsky's *Crime and Punishment*, index number 123, it will be stored as follows:

"Dostoyevsky","Crime and Punishment",123

Each record will be stored on its own line. If you opened the file in a text editor, such as the Visual Basic editor or the Windows Notepad, you would see the records just as they are shown here. From these examples, you can see that a sequential file uses commas and double quotation marks to delimit the fields. Fields are separated by commas, and text data is enclosed in quotation marks.

Use the **Write #** statement to write a single record of field-delimited data to a sequential file. Its syntax is

```
Write #filenum [, list]
```

with these arguments:

- *filenum*—The number associated with the file when it was opened in OUTPUT or APPEND mode.

- *list*—A list of one or more Basic expressions to be written to the file. If list contains more than one item, separate them by commas. If list is omitted from the **Write #** statement, an empty record (a blank line) is written to the file.

Here are some examples. The following line of code would write one record to the sequential file of book information:

```
Write #filenum, "Henry James","The Aspern Papers",12
```

Of course, in a real program, you would use variables in the **Write #** statement:

```
book.name = "Henry James"
book.title = "The Aspern Papers"
book.index = 12
Write #filenum, book.name, book.title, book.index
```

Each **Write #** statement writes one record to the file, automatically inserting any necessary comma and quotation mark delimiters. Double quotation marks cannot be included in data written with the **Write #** statement.

To read field-delimited data from a sequential file, use the **Input #** statement. **Input #** reads one or more fields from the input file and assigns them to program variables. Its syntax is

```
Input #filenum, list
```

with the arguments:

- *filenum*—The number associated with the file when it was opened (in INPUT mode).

- *list*—A list of one or more program variables to be assigned data that will be read from the file. If list contains more than one variable name, separate them by commas.

Input # reads one field from the file for each variable in its argument list, assigning the fields to the variables in order. Remember that sequential files must be read sequentially, starting with the first field in the first record and proceeding from that point. Here's a brief example:

```
FileNum = FreeFile
Open "BOOKLIST.DAT" For Output As #FileNum
Write #FileNum, "Henry James","The Aspern Papers",12
Write #FileNum, "Dostoyevsky","Crime and Punishment",123
Close #FileNum
```

Then, in another part of the program:

```
Dim A As String, B As String, C As String, D As String
Dim x As Integer, y As Integer
```

```
FileNum = FreeFile
Open "BOOKLIST.DAT" For INPUT As #FileNum
Input #FileNum, A, B, x
Input #FileNum, C, D, y
Close #FileNum
```

After this code executes, A = "Henry James", B = "The Aspern Papers", x = 12, C = "Dostoyevsky", D = "Crime and Punishment", and y = 123.

The **Input #** statement reads data from the file on a field-by-field basis, assigning fields read from the file in the order in which variables appear in the **Input #** statement's argument list. If you replaced the two **Input #** statements in the previous example with the single statement

```
Input #FileNum, A, B, x, C, D, y
```

or with the multiple statements

```
Input #FileNum, A, B
Input #FileNum, x, C
Input #FileNum, D, y
```

the results would be exactly the same. The way that **Input #** breaks file data into fields depends on the type of variable in the **Input #** statement's argument list. If **Input #** is reading data into a string variable, the end of a field is marked by one of the following:

- A double quotation mark if the field begins with a double quotation mark

- A comma if the field does not begin with a double quotation mark

- A carriage return-line feed (CR-LF)

If **Input #** is reading data into a numeric variable, the end of the field is marked by:

- A comma

- One or more spaces

- CR-LF

When you are using a sequential file to store data, the program is responsible for keeping **Write #** and **Input #** statements synchronized in terms of the type, order, and number of fields in each record. In other words, data items must be read from the file in the same order they were written to it. If this synchronicity is disrupted, two kinds of problems can result:

- *The program might use **Input #** to read a field from a file into a variable of a different type (for example, reading string data into a numeric variable).* No error happens when this occurs, but it will likely produce unexpected results. When a numeric field is read into a string variable, the variable is assigned the string representation of the number. When a string field is read into a numeric variable, the result depends on the string. If the string starts with a non-numeric character, the variable is assigned the value of zero. If the string starts with one or more numeric characters, the variable is assigned the numeric value of those characters.

- *If the number of fields is wrong, the program may lose track of its location within the file.* Remember that the **Input #** statement counts fields—not records—when it reads data from the file. After one **Input #** statement executes, the next **Input #** statement starts with the next field in the file, which may not be the beginning of the next record.

One common use for sequential access files is to store an array of variable-length strings. This code fragment demonstrates how to write the array data to a disk file:

```
Dim notes(100) As String, count As Integer, FileNum As Integer
...
' Code here puts data into the notes array.
...
FileNum = FreeFile
Open "NOTES.TXT" For OUTPUT As #FileNum

For count = 0 TO 100
    WRITE #FileNum, notes(count)
Next count

Close #FileNum
```

The following code retrieves the data from the disk file and places it in a string array:

```
Open "NOTES.TXT" For INPUT As #FileNum

For count = 0 To 100
    Input #FileNum, notes(count)
Next count

Close #FileNum
```

You can also use a sequential file to store arrays of numbers, but as you'll see later in the chapter, another file access mode is actually better suited for this task.

Detecting The End Of The File

When your program is reading data from a sequential file, the **EOF** function enables you to detect when the program has reached the end of the file. The syntax is

```
EOF(filenum)
```

where **filenum** is the number associated with an open file. **EOF** returns True if the last record in the file has been read and False if it has not yet been read. Trying to read past the end of a sequential file will generate an error. The following code shows how to use **EOF** in a loop to read an entire sequential file—one line at a time—into an array:

```
Dim info(1000) As String
Dim count As Integer
...
Open "MYFILE.DAT" For Input As #filenum

count = 0

While Not EOF(filenum)
    Line Input #filenum, info(count)
    count = count + 1
Wend
```

Text In Sequential Files

One common use for sequential files is to store text—such as a document or READ.ME file—that is not divided into fields. Each line, or record, in the file is simply treated as a line of text with no delimiters or other special characters. You can read and write text files using either traditional or FSO methods.

Traditional Text File Access

To write lines of text to a sequential file, use the **Print #** statement. **Print #** does not delimit fields with commas or enclose strings in double quotes. Rather, it writes data to the file with the exact same format as if the data had been displayed on the screen with the **Print** method. You saw **Print #** used in Chapter 11 in the Baby Editor project. The syntax for this statement is

```
Print #filenum [, list] [,|;]
```

with these arguments:

- *filenum*—The number associated with the file when it was opened (in OUTPUT or APPEND mode).

- *list*—One or more string expressions to be written to the file. Multiple expressions in list should be separated by a comma or semicolon. If list is omitted, **Print #** writes a blank line to the file.

The optional comma or semicolon at the end of the **Print #** statement determines the location of subsequent output to the file (that is, the output of the next **Print #** statement):

- *No comma or semicolon*—Subsequent output is placed on a new line.

- *Semicolon*—Subsequent output is placed on the same line immediately following the previous output.

- *Comma*—Subsequent output is placed on the same line at the next print zone.

Looking back to Chapter 9, you will see that the program outputs multiple lines to a file with a single **Print #** statement—a useful feature. If the text that is being output (in Chapter 11, for example, the **Text** property of a Text Box control) contains CR-LF characters, they serve to break the output into multiple lines in the sequential file. It has the same effect as writing each line of the text to the file with a separate **Print #** statement. You can see that **Print #** is quite flexible: It has the ability to output part of a line of text (if terminated with a semicolon or comma) or multiple lines of text (if the text contains its own CR-LF characters). If neither of these conditions is met, **Print #** outputs one entire line of text to the file.

Let's look at some other examples. The following illustrates what happens when a comma or semicolon appears at the end of the **Print #** statement:

- *Without a comma or semicolon*

  Statements:

  Print #1, "Visual"

  Print #1, "Basic"

  Written to file:

  Visual

  Basic

- *With a semicolon*

  Statements:

  Print #1, "Visual";

  Print #1, "Basic"

  Written to file:

  VisualBasic

- *With a comma*

  Statements:

  Print #1, "Visual",

  Print #1, "Basic"

  Written to file:

  Visual Basic

Next, let's take a look at the difference between using a comma or a semicolon as a separator between expressions:

- *With a semicolon*

  Statements:

  Print #1, "Visual";"Basic"

  Written to file:

  VisualBasic

- *With a comma*

  Statements:

  Print #1, "Visual","Basic"

  Written to file:

  Visual Basic

To read lines of text one at a time from a sequential file, use the **Line Input #** statement. **Line Input #** reads an entire line of text from the file without regard to field delimiters, assigning it to a string variable. The syntax is

```
Line Input [#]filenum, var
```

where the arguments are:

- *filenum*—The number assigned to the file when it was opened (for INPUT).
- *var*—The type **String** variable to receive the line of text.

FSO Text File Access

The FSO approach to file access is based upon something called a **FileSystemObject**. The first required step is to create an instance of this class:

```
Dim fs
Set fs = CreateObject("Scripting.FileSystemObject")
```

You can also use the following syntax:

```
Dim fs As New Scripting.FileSystemObject
```

Note the required use of the **Scripting** qualifier, which identifies the library that the **FileSystemObject** class is defined in. You do not need to select this library, called the Microsoft Scripting Runtime, in the Visual Basic References dialog box to use the class, but doing so will give you access to the classes, methods, and properties in the Object Browser. The browser can be a useful source of information when you are programming. Remember, press F2, then select the desired library at the top left. Figure 13.1 shows information about the **Scripting** library displayed in the Object Browser.

Once you have created an instance of the **FileSystemObject** class, the next step is to create a TextStream object, which is nothing more than a regular text file enclosed in an FSO wrapper. **FileSystemObject** has two methods for creating TextStream objects:

- *CreateTextFile*—Creates a new text file. If a file of the same name already exists, it is overwritten.

- *OpenTextFile*—Opens a text file for reading and/or writing. If the file already exists, new data is appended to existing data.

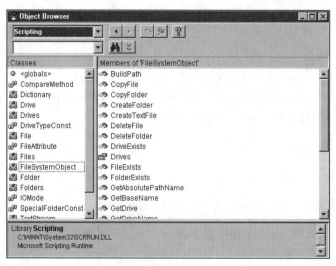

Figure 13.1   *Use the Object Browser to view library information.*

The syntax for these methods is similar. In these examples, assume that **fs** is a **FileSystemObject** and that **ts** has been declared as a type **Variant** or **Object**:

```
Set ts = fs.CreateTextFile(filename[, overwrite[, unicode]])

Set ts = fs.OpenTextFile(filename[, iomode[, create[, format]]])
```

The arguments for these statements are as follows:

- *filename*—A string expression specifying the name, including path information, of the file.

- *overwrite*—True or False indicating whether an existing file will be overwritten. If this argument is omitted, the default is False. If *overwrite* is False and *filename* already exists, an error occurs. You can trap this error to permit the user to verify file overwrites.

- *Unicode*—True to create a Unicode file, False (the default) for an ASCII file.

- *iomode*—Set to the constants **ForReading** or **ForAppending** to read the file or write data to the end of the file. You cannot write to a file opened in **ForReading** mode.

- *create*—True or False specifying whether a new file will be created if filename does not exist. The default is False.

- *format*—A tristate argument (one that can have three values) that determines the format of the file. **TriStateTrue** opens the file as Unicode, **TriStateFalse** (the default) opens the file as ASCII, and **TriStateUseDefault** uses the system default format setting.

What Is Unicode?

When dealing with text, computers use numbers to represent characters, punctuation marks, and so on. The two systems for this are ACSII (or ANSI) and Unicode. ASCII uses one byte per character, permitting only 256 different symbols to be represented. This is adequate for English, but cannot support many other languages. Unicode uses two bytes per character, permitting more than 65,000 different symbols. Which format you use depends on the specific requirements of your project.

Another way to obtain a TextStream object is to create a File object, then use its **OpenAsTextStream** method. Creating a File object is done like this, assuming that **fs** is a **FileSystemObject**:

```
Dim f
Set f = fs.GetFile(filename)
```

For this method to work, the file specified by *filename* must exist (you'll learn more about creating File objects in the next chapter). To create a new file, you would use **CreateTextFile** and then create the File object:

```
fs.CreateTextFile filename
Set f = fs.GetFile(filename)
```

Once you have the File object, you can invoke the **OpenAsTextStream** method. The syntax is:

```
f.OpenAsTextStream([iomode, [format]])
```

The *iomode* and *format* arguments are the same as described earlier for the **CreateTextFile** and **OpenTextFile** methods. Here's the code necessary to create a TextStream object associated with an existing file DEMO.TXT for reading using the **OpenAsTextStream** method:

```
Dim fs, f, ts
Set fs = CreateObject("Scripting.FileSystemObject")
Set f = fs.GetFile("demo.txt")
Set ts = f.OpenAsTextStream(ForWriting, TristateUseDefault)
```

So far, we have seen how to create a TextStream object. Once you have done this, what next? The TextStream object has properties and methods that you use to write and read text. The properties are described in Table 13.4. In reading this table, be aware that TextStream object always has a *current character position*, also called the *file pointer*, that indicates where the next read or write operation will take place. Note that all of these properties are read-only.

You use the TextStream object's methods to read and write data. These methods are described in Table 13.5.

Table 13.4   Properties of the TextStream object.

Property	Description
AtEndOfLine	True, if the file pointer is at the end of a line; False otherwise. This property applies only to TextStream files that are open for reading; otherwise, an error occurs.
AtEndOfStream	True, if the file pointer is at the end of the file; False otherwise. This property applies only to TextStream files that are open for reading; otherwise, an error occurs.
Column	Returns the column number of the file pointer. The first character on a line is at column 1.
Line	Returns the current line number.

Table 13.5   Methods of the TextStream object.

Method	Description
Close	Closes the file associated with the TextStream object. You should always execute the **Close** method when you are done reading/writing the file.
Read(*n*)	Reads the next *n* characters from the file and returns the resulting string.
ReadAll	Reads the entire file and returns the resulting string.
ReadLine	Reads an entire line (up to, but not including, the newline character) from a TextStream file and returns the resulting string.
Skip(*n*)	Skips ahead (moves the file pointer) by *n* characters.
SkipLine	Skips to the beginning of the next line.
Write(*s*)	Writes the string *s* to the file. No extra or newline characters are added.
WriteBlankLines(*n*)	Writes *n* blank lines to the file.
WriteLine(*s*)	Writes the string *s* to the file, followed by a newline character.

Be aware that some of these methods are applicable only when the file has been opened for reading or writing. If you try to use a method that is inappropriate for the file's mode, an error will occur.

An FSO Text File Demonstration

The program given here is a simple demonstration of using FSO to read and write a text file. The program's form, shown in Figure 13.2, contains one Text Box and a control array of three Command Buttons. Other than setting captions, the only property you need to change is to set the Text Box's **Multiline** property to True.

The project's code is presented in Listing 13.1. You can see that the name for the file is defined as a program constant; you could easily modify the program so it would prompt

Figure 13.2   The FSO demonstration program.

the user for a file name. In the **LoadTextFromFile** procedure, I have used error handling to deal with the possibility that the user will try to load the file before saving it. This would result in an error when the **OpenTextFile** method fails to find the file. By trapping the error, the program presents an informative message to the user rather than simply crashing.

Listing 13.1   The code in FSODEMO.FRM.

```
Option Explicit

Const FILENAME = "FSODEMO.TXT"

Private Sub Command1_Click(Index As Integer)

Select Case Index
    Case 0 ' Save
        Call SaveTextToFile
    Case 1 ' Load
        Call LoadTextFromFile
    Case 2 ' Quit
        End
End Select

End Sub

Public Sub LoadTextFromFile()

On Error GoTo ErrorHandler

Dim fs, f, msg
Set fs = CreateObject("Scripting.FileSystemObject")
Set f = fs.OpenTextFile(FILENAME, ForReading)
Text1.Text = f.ReadAll
f.Close
Exit Sub

ErrorHandler:

If Err = 53 Then
    msg = "File Not Found"
Else
    msg = "Error opening " & FILENAME
End If
MsgBox (msg)

End Sub

Public Sub SaveTextToFile()
```

```
Dim fs As New Scripting.FileSystemObject
Dim f

Set f = fs.CreateTextFile(FILENAME, True)
f.write Text1.Text
f.Close

End Sub
```

Using Random Access Files

A random access file is similar to a sequential access file in that both consist of records. Random file records must all be the same size, however, and the program differentiates one record from the next by its position in the file. No special character is used to separate records. For example, if a file's records are each 100 bytes long, bytes 1 through 100 contain the first record (byte positions in a file always start at position 1), and record 4 is at positions 301 through 400. Random file records are numbered sequentially starting at 1, with a maximum of 2,147,483,647. (Not big enough for you? Too bad.) Each record is divided into one or more fields. The fields, too, are defined by their length. Each record in a random file contains the same field structure—the same number of fields and the same field sizes. Before you can create or use a random file, you must define its record structure.

Defining Random File Record Structure

The structure of a random file's records is defined in the same manner as the user-defined data type created with the **Type...End Type** statements covered in Chapter 4. The first step is to create a user-defined data type that has the structure you want to use for the random file. This method works well, because almost all programs that use random files require the same user-defined data type to manipulate the data in the program. Continuing our earlier example of a filing system for books, you could write:

```
TYPE Book_Data
    Author As String * 20
    Title As String * 25
    Index As Integer
END TYPE

DIM Books(100) As Book_Data
```

Now you have a user-defined type that will manipulate the book data in the program, as well as define the record structure for the random access file. When opening a file for random access, one of the required parameters is the length of the file's records (you saw this earlier in the chapter in the discussion of the **Open** statement). This task is easily accomplished using the **Len** function, which returns the length, in bytes, of a data type. The **Open** statement would read:

```
filenum = FreeFile
Open "BOOKFILE.DAT" FOR RANDOM AS #filenum Len = Len(Books(1))
```

Note that you passed the **Len** function one array element, not the entire array. This statement opens the random file with a record length equal to the size of the user-defined data structure.

Reading And Writing Random Files

To write data to a random file, use the **Put** statement. The syntax is

```
Put [#]filenum,[recnum],usertype
```

with the arguments as follows:

- *filenum*—The number associated with the random file when it was opened.

- *recnum*—The record number in the file where the data is to be placed. If *recnum* is omitted, the next record (the one following the position of the last **Get** or **Put**) is used. If no **Get** or **Put** has been executed since the file was opened, record 1 is used.

- *usertype*—A structure of the user-defined type that contains the data to be written.

Continuing with the book-filing example, to write data to the first record in the file, you would write:

```
Books(1).Author = "Henry James"
Books(1).Title = "The Aspern Papers"
Books(1).Index = 12
Put #FileNum, 1, Books(1)
```

When first creating a random access file, you can start writing data at record 1, increasing the record number by 1 for each successive **Put** statement. You could also omit the *recnum* argument in the **Put** statement, and let Visual Basic automatically keep track of record numbers. If you are adding records to an existing file, however, you must control *recnum* to ensure that the data is placed where you want it. If you write new data to a record number that is already in use in the file, the new data will replace the old data. If you don't want to overwrite existing data, you must add new records at the end of the file. In other words, for a file that already has *n* records, start adding new records at record *n + 1*.

How do you determine the number of records in a file? You use the **Lof** function, which returns the file length, or size, in bytes. Its syntax is

```
Lof(filenum)
```

where *filenum* is the number associated with the open file whose length you want to know. What is the benefit of knowing the file's total size? You already know that the **Len** function returns the size of each record in bytes. It follows that the total bytes in a file divided by the bytes per record will give us the number of records in the file.

Therefore, you would write:

```
nextrec = (Lof(1) \ Len(usertype)) + 1
Put #FileNum, nextrec, usertype
```

To obtain the number of the next record to be read or written, use the **Seek** function. Similarly, the **Loc** function returns the number of the last record read or written.

To read data from a random access file, use the **Get** statement. Data is read from a specified record in the file and placed in a user-defined structure of the type used to create the file. The syntax of the **Get** statement is

```
Get [#]filenum,[recnum],usertype
```

with the arguments:

- *filenum*—The number associated with the random file when it was opened.
- *recnum*—The number of the record to be read. If *recnum* is omitted, data is read from the next record (the one after the last **Get** or **Put**). If no **Get** or **Put** has been executed since the file was opened, record 1 is read.
- *usertype*—A variable of the user-defined type where the data is to be placed.

Again using the book-filing example, to read the first record of a random file, you would write:

```
GET #FileNum, 1, Books(1)
```

To read all records from a random file, use a loop that starts with the first record and reads sequential records until the end of the file is reached, placing them in the elements of an array of the appropriate user-defined type. To detect the end of file, use the **EOF** function, as shown earlier in this chapter for sequential files. You can also calculate the number of the last record in the file by dividing the file length by the record length, as shown previously.

Visual Basic maintains a file pointer for each open random access file. This pointer specifies the record number that will be read or written by the **Get** or **Put** statement if the recnum argument is omitted. When a random access file is first opened—whether it's a new file or an existing file—the file pointer initially points at record 1. As you read and write random file data, the file pointer is maintained as follows:

- A call to **Get** or **Put** without a *recnum* argument increments the file pointer by 1.

- A call to **Get** or **Put** with a *recnum* argument sets the file pointer to (*recnum* + 1).

To determine the current file pointer position, you can use the **Seek** and **Loc** functions. **Seek** returns the position of the file pointer (the next record to be read or written). **Loc** returns the position of the last record that was read or written. The syntax is

```
Seek(filenum)
Loc(filenum)
```

where *filenum* is the number associated with an open random access file. The value returned by **Loc** is one less than the value returned by **Seek**. When a file has just been opened, **Loc** returns zero and **Seek** returns one.

Using Binary Files

A binary file stores data as an unformatted sequence of bytes. No record/field structure exists in the file (unless you impose one in code). Binary files provide a great deal of flexibility in storing data, but their unstructured nature forces the programmer to keep track of what is stored in the file. That necessitates keeping track of where you are in the file.

File Position

Every open binary file has its own *file pointer*. The file pointer is a numeric value that points at the position in the file where read and write operations will occur. Each position in a binary file corresponds to one byte of data. Therefore, a file that contains *n* bytes has positions numbered from *1* through *n*. To change the file pointer and determine its value, use the **Seek** statement and the **Seek** and **Loc** functions—the same statements you use when working with random access files. With random access files, the file pointer points at records, not bytes. Visual Basic knows the ACCESS mode in which a given file was opened, and interprets **Seek** or **Loc** correctly when you use them—as bytes for a binary file and records for a random file. The syntax of the **Seek** and **Loc** statements is

```
Seek [#]filenum, newpos
[pos =] Seek(filenum)
[pos =] Loc(filenum)
```

where *filenum* is the number associated with the file when it was opened in binary mode. The **Seek** statement sets the file pointer to *newpos*. The **Seek** function returns the current position of the file pointer (the next byte to be read or written). The **Loc** function returns the position of the last byte that was read or written. Unless you explicitly move the pointer, **Loc** is one less than **Seek**.

Reading And Writing Binary File Data

To read data from a binary file, use the **Get** statement. To write data to a binary file, use the **Put** statement. These are the same statements used for random files; they are interpreted differently, depending on the mode of the file being read or written. The syntax is

```
GET [#]filenum, [pos] , var
PUT [#]filenum, [pos] , var
```

with the following arguments:

- *filenum*—The number associated with the file when it was opened in binary mode.

- *pos*—Specifies the byte position where the read or write operation is to take place. If *pos* is omitted, the current file pointer position is used.

- *var*—Any Basic variable. **Get** reads data from the file into **var**; **Put** writes data from *var* to the file. The statements automatically read or write the number of bytes contained in *var*. If *var* is a variable-length string, the number of bytes transferred is equal to the number of characters currently in **var**.

When a binary mode file is first opened, the file pointer is at position one. Any **Get** or **Put** operation automatically increments the file pointer by the number of bytes transferred.

To determine the length of a binary file, use the **Lof** function

```
[length =] Lof(filenum)
```

where **filenum** is the number associated with the file when it was opened in binary mode. The value returned by **Lof** is equal to the file-pointer position of the file's last byte. A program can quickly read an entire binary file, using **Lof** and a loop. The following code shows how to use binary file access to make a copy of a file. It is assumed that ORIGINAL.DAT is an existing file, and that COPY.DAT does not exist. By using a one-character fixed-length string, the program reads and writes one byte at a time. While this code would certainly work, it is inefficient because of the byte-at-a-time approach:

```
Dim ch As String * 1, count As Integer, f1 As Integer, F2 As Integer
f1 = freefile
Open "ORIGINAL.DAT" For BINARY AS #f1
f2 = freefile
Open "COPY.DAT" For BINARY AS #f2

For count = 1 TO Lof(1)
    Get #f1, , ch
    Put #f2, , ch
Next count

Close #f1, #f2
```

The **EOF** function—described earlier in the chapter—can be used to detect the end of a binary file. For example, the loop in the previous code could also have been written as follows:

```
While Not Eof(f1)
    Get #f1, , ch
    Put #f2, , ch
Wend
```

The flexibility of binary files makes them an excellent choice for storing program data, particularly when the data format does not lend itself to a random access or sequential access file. Remember that the unstructured nature of binary files makes it necessary for our program to keep track of the data-storage format. For example, a program that uses an array of 1,000 double-precision values could store the entire array in a binary file as follows:

```
Dim data(999) As Double, count As Integer

Open "ARRAY.DAT" For BINARY As #f1

For count = 0 To 999
    Put #f1, , data(count)
Next count

Close #1
```

The data could later be retrieved from the disk file back into the array, as follows:

```
Open "ARRAY.DAT" For BINARY As #f1

For count = 0 To 999
    Get #f1, , data(count)
Next count

Close #1
```

Although nothing prevents us from retrieving the data into an array of type **Integer** or any other Basic data type, the results would be meaningless.

Here are a few hints for working with binary files:

- To add new data at the end of an existing file, move the file pointer to the end of the file by executing **Seek** *filenum*, **Lof**(*filenum*)**+1**.

- If you **Put** data in an existing file at a position before the end of the file, the new data will overwrite existing data.

- If you **Put** data at a file-pointer position past the end of a file (for example, at position **Lof**(*filenum*)**+10**), the file will be extended as needed. The intervening byte positions, however, will contain garbage (that is, undefined values).

- If you **Get** data at a file-pointer position beyond the end of a file, no error occurs, but the returned data will be garbage.

Which File Type Should You Use?

If you are a bit confused by Visual Basic's different file-access modes, you are not alone. It's not always clear which type of file is best for a particular application. The following guidelines are designed to help you choose:

- For data that consists of lines of text—whether generated by a Visual Basic program or another application—use sequential access mode. You can use either the traditional or FSO programming techniques for sequential text files.

- To manipulate nontext files generated by other applications, use binary mode.

- To store numerical arrays, use either sequential mode or binary mode. Binary mode is preferred, because it is faster and results in significantly smaller data file sizes.

- To store arrays of variable-length strings, use sequential mode. To store arrays of fixed-length strings, use either sequential or binary mode. Binary mode has a size and speed advantage, although not as significant as with numerical arrays.

- To store data that is organized in a record and field format, use either sequential or random mode. The final choice depends on the specific needs of the program.

- Random access mode provides faster access to individual records in the disk file. It wastes space for string data, because string fields are padded with spaces to fill the allocated field size.

- Sequential mode is slower at accessing specific records in the file. It uses space more efficiently, because strings are not padded with spaces.

These are just guidelines, not meant to be interpreted as hard-and-fast rules. It's important to understand that a file's access mode does not affect the physical file on disk, but only the way a program reads and writes the file data. In other words, any file—regardless of which mode was used to create it—is simply a sequence of bytes stored on the disk. For example, you could create a file using random access mode, then later open and read it in binary access mode. As your programming skills develop, you will sometimes find that mixing file access modes is the preferred approach to your data-storage needs. Until you are quite familiar with all three file access modes, however, I suggest you follow the previous guidelines and limit yourself to one access mode per file.

Chapter 14
File Management

The term *file management* refers to everything you do with files and folders other than actually writing to and reading from them. Deleting files, creating folders, copying files from one drive to another, and looking up the amount of free space on a drive are all examples of file management. Not every program will need these capabilities, but it is comforting to know that Visual Basic has a full set of tools for file management when and if you need them.

Visual Basic's file management tools can be divided into three categories. First, we have what I call the traditional techniques, using Basic statements that have been part of the language from the beginning. Next, and new with the current version of Visual Basic, are the object-oriented file management techniques. For the most part, the traditional and object-oriented techniques have the same capabilities, differing only in the syntax used. Finally, Visual Basic has several controls designed specifically for file management tasks.

Visual Basic provides all the capabilities you need for managing files and folders on your disks.

File Management—The Traditional Way

This section demonstrates how to use Visual Basic's traditional file management statements.

Deleting Files

To delete a file, use the **Kill** statement

```
Kill filename
```

where *filename* is a string expression specifying the file or files to delete. It can contain a drive and path name, as well as the so-called *wildcard* characters * and ?. Deleting a file that does not exist, a file that's open, or a file for which you do not have the needed access privileges will generate an error. As you may know, you can use the wildcard characters to specify groups of files. The * character stands for any sequence of zero or more characters, while ? stands for any single character. Table 14.1 shows some examples.

Deleting And Creating Folders

To delete a folder (also called a subdirectory), use the **RmDir** statement

```
RmDir path
```

Table 14.1   Wildcard characters.

File Specification	Matches	Does Not Match
DATA*.*	DATA.DAT	MYDATA.DAT
	DATASEPT.DAT	DATES.TXT
	DATASUMMARY.TXT	
DATA?.A*	DATA1.ASC	DATA.ASC
	DATA2.A	DATASEPT.ASC
	DATAX.ARG	DATAX.DAT
.	All files	-

where *path* is a string expression that specifies the folder to delete and can include a drive specification. If you try to delete a folder that does not exist or is not empty (contains one or more files or folders), an error is generated.

To create a new folder, use the **MkDir** statement

```
MkDir path
```

where *path* specifies the name of the folder to create and can include a full path and drive specification. If only a name is specified, the new folder is created in the current folder on the current drive.

Changing To Another Folder Or Drive

To make another folder current, use the **ChDir** statement

```
ChDir path
```

where *path* specifies the new folder and can include a drive specification. If no drive is specified, **ChDir** changes the current folder on the current drive. **ChDir** does not change the current drive. If the current drive is C: and you execute

```
ChDir "D:\DATA"
```

the current directory on drive D: is changed to \Data. However, C: remains the current drive and the current directory on drive C: remains unchanged.

To make another drive current, use the **ChDrive** statement

```
ChDrive drive
```

where *drive* specifies the new drive to make current. Only the first character of drive is significant. Attempting to make an invalid drive current will generate an error.

Getting Path And Folder Information

To determine the current path on a specified drive, use the **CurDir** function

```
[path =] CurDir[(drive)]
```

where *drive* specifies the drive of interest. Only the first character of *drive* is significant; unless it refers to a valid drive, an error will be generated. If the *drive* argument is omitted, **CurDir** returns the current path on the current drive.

You can obtain the path of the current Visual Basic application by reading the **App** object's **Path** property:

```
CurrentPath = App.Path
```

This property returns the path where the project file (VBP) is located when the application is running in the Visual Basic environment, and the path where the executable file (EXE) is located when running the program as an executable file. This property is extremely useful when you want to be sure that a program's data or configuration files are stored in the same folder as the EXE file. Be aware that the value returned by this property does not include a trailing backslash, so you must add it when creating a fully qualified file name. The following code opens a file named CONFIG.DAT in the program's EXE directory:

```
Filename = App.Path
Filename = Filename & "\CONFIG.DAT"
Open Filename For Input as #1
```

Current Path Vs. Application's Path

What's the difference between the current path on a drive and an application's path? An application's path is simply the path to the folder containing the program's executable file. It has no special status, except that each application may want to keep certain files in this folder. A drive's current path points to the current default folder on that drive. Each drive in our system can have only one default path at a time, and this information is maintained by the operating system (although it can be changed by programs). The default path is the location where file operations will take place if a particular path is not specified. For example, the statement

```
Open "C:DATA.TXT" For Output As #1
```

will open a file in the folder pointed to by drive C:'s current path. A drive letter followed by only a colon always refers to the drive's current path. The operating system also keeps track of the default drive, which is the disk where file operations will occur if a specific disk is not requested. Thus

```
Open "DATA.TXT" For Output As #1
```

would open the file on the default drive, in the folder indicated by that drive's default path. Likewise

```
Open "\SALES\DATA.TXT" For Output As #1
```

would open the file in the \SALES folder on the default drive.

Finding Files

To obtain the name of the first file that matches a template, use the **Dir** function:

```
[filename = ] Dir[(template)]
```

The *template* argument is the file template you want to match. It can contain a drive specifier, path, and wildcard characters (as explained earlier in the chapter). The first time a program calls **Dir**, it must pass a *template* argument. **Dir** returns the name of the first file in the specified or current folder that matches *template*. If no match occurs, an empty string is returned. If **Dir** is called again one or more times with the *template* argument omitted, it returns the next file that matches the original *template*, or a null string if no other match exists.

The **Dir** function is typically used to see if a particular file exists. This is accomplished by calling **Dir** with the file name as the argument, then seeing if a null string is returned:

```
If Dir "MYFILE.TXT" = "" Then
    ' File does not exist.
Else
    'File exists.
End If
```

You can also use **Dir** to get a list of all files matching a template that includes wildcards. For example, the following code would load List Box List1 with the names of all files that have the .DAT extension and are located in the specified directory:

```
Dim s As String
s = Dir "C:\DATA\*.DAT"
Do While s <> ""
    List1.AddItem s
    s = Dir
Loop
```

To change the name of a file or folder, or to move a file to a different folder on the same drive, use the **Name** statement:

```
Name oldfilespec As newfilespec
```

The *oldfilespec* argument gives the name of the existing file or folder and can include a drive and path; *newfilespec* gives the new file or folder name and must refer to the same drive as *oldfilespec*. You cannot use **Name** with an open file.

To obtain the handle or mode of an open file, use the **FileAttr** function:

```
[result =] FileAttr(filenum, flag)
```

The *filenum* argument is the number associated with the file when it was opened; *flag* specifies the type of information returned by the function. If *flag* = 1, then **FileAttr** returns a code indicating the mode in which the file was opened:

Return Value	File Mode
1	INPUT
2	OUTPUT
4	RANDOM
8	APPEND
32	BINARY

If *flag* = 2, **FileAttr** returns the file's operating-system handle.

Object-Oriented File Management

The FSO approach to file access is based upon the **FileSystemObject** class. This approach is new with the current version of Visual Basic and provides capabilities for both file access and file management. FSO file access was covered in Chapter 13; here, we will examine FSO file management.

The first step is to create an instance of the FSO class. You can do it like this:

```
Dim fs
Set fs = CreateObject("Scripting.FileSystemObject")
```

Or like this:

```
Dim fs As New Scripting.FileSystemObject
```

Note the required use of the **Scripting** qualifier, which identifies the library that the **FileSystemObject** class is defined in. Once you have created an instance of the **FileSystemObject** class, you can use its properties and methods to perform various file manipulation tasks.

The **FileSystemObject** is the "top" object in the FSO hierarchy, providing access to all of the drives (both local and network), folders, and files on the system. The hierarchy has several other objects, which correspond to the way in which disk drives are organized:

- *Drive*—Corresponds to a single disk drive on the system.
- *Folder*—Corresponds to a single folder (subdirectory) on a drive.
- *File*—Corresponds to a single file in a folder.

Here is a brief outline of how the FSO system works:

- The **FileSystemObject** has a **Drives** collection that contains a Drive object for each local and network drive on the system. You can query a Drive object's properties to obtain information about the drive, such as its type and free space.

- Each Drive object contains a Folder object representing the top-level folder on the drive.

- Each Folder object contains a **Folders** collection and a **Files** collection. The **Folders** collection contains a Folder object for each subfolder, and the **Files** collection contains a File object for each file in the folder.

Now let's get to the details.

The Drives Collection And Drive Objects

The one and only property of the **FileSystemObject** is the **Drives** collection, which contains all the Drive objects available on the system (including local drives and shared network drives). The **Drives** collection is like any other Visual Basic collection and is used the same way as you have learned in previous chapters.

Each Drive object has a set of properties that provides information about the physical drive. These properties are listed in Table 14.2. Except as noted, these properties are read-only.

Table 14.2 Drive object properties.

Property	Description
AvailableSpace	The amount of space available to a user on the specified drive or network share. Generally the same as the **FreeSpace** property, but may differ on systems that support quotas.
DriveLetter	The drive letter associated with the drive. Returns a zero-length string for network drives that have not been mapped to a drive letter.
DriveType	A value indicating the type of drive. Possible values are 0 (unknown), 1 (removable), 2 (fixed), 3 (network), 4 (CD-ROM), and 5 (RAM disk).
FileSystem	The type of file system. Available return types include FAT, NTFS, and CDFS.
FreeSpace	The amount of space available to a user on the specified drive or network share. Generally the same as the **AvailableSpace** property, but may differ on systems that support quotas.

(continued)

Table 14.2 Drive object properties (continued).

Property	Description
IsReady	Returns True if the drive is ready, False if not. Used with removable media and CD-ROM drives, returning False if the media (diskette) has not been inserted.
Path	The path of the drive. This consists of the drive letter followed by a colon.
RootFolder	Returns a Folder object representing the drive's root path.
SerialNumber	The unique serial number identifying a disk. Use this property to verify that a removable media drive contains the proper media.
ShareName	The share name assigned to a network drive. For non-network drives, a zero-length string.
TotalSize	The total capacity of the drive.
VolumeName	The volume name of the drive. You can write to this property to change a drive's volume name.

We can write a simple program to demonstrate how you can use the **Drives** collection to obtain information about the drives on the system. Create a Standard EXE project and place a Text Box on the form. Set the Text Box's **Multiline** and **Locked** properties to True and set its size to nearly fill the form. Put the code from Listing 14.1 in the Text Box's **Click** event procedure. When you run the program, click on the Text Box. After a brief pause it will display a list of the system's drives and their total and free space. This is shown in Figure 14.1. I named this program DRIVESDEMO.

Listing 14.1 Demonstrating the Drives collection.

```
Private Sub Text1_Click()

Dim fs, d, dc
Dim msg As String

Set fs = CreateObject("Scripting.FileSystemObject")
Set dc = fs.Drives
For Each d In dc
    msg = msg & "Drive " & d.Path
    If Not d.IsReady Then
        msg = msg & " is not ready." & vbCrLf
    Else
        msg = msg & vbCrLf & Space(5)
        msg = msg & "Total space: " & FormatNumber(d.TotalSize)
        msg = msg & vbCrLf & Space(5)
        msg = msg & "Free space: " & FormatNumber(d.FreeSpace)
        msg = msg & vbCrLf
    End If
Next
```

```
Text1.Text = msg

End Sub
```

The Folder Object

A Folder object represents a single folder, or subdirectory, on a drive. You use the object's methods to copy, move, or delete the folder (as explained later) and the object's properties to obtain information about the folder. Perhaps most important, a Folder object contains two collections, **Files** and **SubFolders**, that provide access to the files and subfolders within the folder. Table 14.3 explains the properties of the Folder object.

Because each Folder object contains information about its parent folder and its subfolders, you can easily traverse the entire folder structure on a drive. This is a powerful tool, as will be demonstrated later. First, however, we need to look at the Folder object's methods.

The **Copy** method copies the folder and its contents to a new location. The syntax is (assuming *f* to be a Folder object)

```
f.Copy destination[, overwrite]
```

where *destination* specifies the destination where the folder is to be copied. Set *overwrite* to True (the default) to overwrite existing files or folders, or to False otherwise. Note that you can also copy a folder using the **FileSystemObject**'s **CopyFolder** method.

The **Move** method moves the folder and its contents from one location to another. The syntax is

```
f.Move destination
```

where *destination* specifies the destination where the folder is to be moved. You can also move folders with the **FileSystemObject**'s **MoveFolder** method.

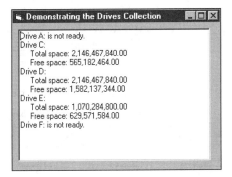

Figure 14.1 *Using the **Drives** collection to obtain information about the system's drives.*

Table 14.3   Properties of the Folder object.

Property	Description
DateCreated	Date and time the folder was created.
DateLastAccessed	Date and time the folder was last accessed.
DateLastModified	Date and time the folder was last modified.
Drive	Drive letter of the drive where the folder resides.
Files	A **Files** collection containing all the files in the folder.
IsRootFolder	True if the folder is the root, False otherwise.
Name	Sets or returns the name of the folder.
ParentFolder	Returns a Folder object representing the folder's parent folder.
Path	The path of the folder, including the drive letter.
ShortName	The short name used by programs that require the old 8.3 style naming convention.
ShortPath	The short path used by programs that require the old 8.3 style naming convention.
Size	The size, in bytes, of all files and subfolders contained in the folder.
SubFolders	A **Folders** collection containing one Folder object for each subfolder.

The **Delete** method deletes a folder and its contents. The syntax is:

```
f.Delete [force]
```

The optional *force* argument specifies whether files or folders with the read-only attribute are to be deleted (*force* = True) or not (*force* = False, the default). You can also delete folders with the **FileSystemObject**'s **DeleteFolder** method.

A Folder Demonstration

To demonstrate the power of the Folder object, I have created a small utility that counts the total number of files and folders on your C: drive. This might seem like a difficult task, but as you'll see, it requires relatively little code. Figure 14.2 shows the program in operation.

The ease with which we can write this program is a result of two things: the design of the Folder object and the use of a recursive algorithm. Here's an outline of how it works:

1. Get the drive's root Folder object.

2. Use the root folder's **Folders** collection to access each of its subfolders.

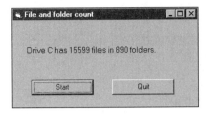

Figure 14.2 *The FOLDERDEMO program.*

3. Determine the number of files and subfolders in each subfolder and add these values to the totals.

4. Use the subfolder's **Folders** collection to access each of its subfolders.

5. Continue until all subfolders have been processed.

I will have more to say about recursive algorithms later in the chapter when I demonstrate the file-related controls. Now let's get started on the demo. Create a standard EXE project with a single form. Place one Label control and a control array of two Command Buttons on the form. Set the Label's **Caption** property to a blank string, and the Command Buttons' **Caption** properties to "Start" and "Quit". Place the following global variable declarations in the General section of the form's code:

```
Dim NumFolders As Long, NumFiles As Long
```

These variables will hold the counts of files and folders. Generally speaking, using global variables, such as these, is not good programming practice; for such a simple program, however, it makes our job easier and will not cause any problems. Next, place the code shown in Listing 14.2 in the Command Button's **Click** event procedure. When the user clicks on Start, this code does the following:

1. Initializes the counter variables to zero.

2. Disables the Command Buttons so they cannot be clicked while the counting process is in progress.

3. Displays "Working ..." in the Label control.

4. Calls the procedure **CountFilesAndFolders** (yet to be written) to perform the count.

5. When execution returns from the procedure, re-enables the Command Buttons.

Listing 14.2   The Command Button's Click event procedure.
```
Private Sub Command1_Click(Index As Integer)

Select Case Index
    Case 0 'Start
```

```
        NumFolders = 0
        NumFiles = 0
        Command1(0).Enabled = False
        Command1(1).Enabled = False
        Label1 = "Working ..."
        DoEvents
        Call CountFilesAndFolders
        Command1(0).Enabled = True
        Command1(1).Enabled = True
    Case 1 ' Quit
        End
End Select
End Sub
```

The process of counting the files and folders is performed by the procedure **CountFilesAndFolders**. To be more accurate, the counting process is started by this procedure. The code is shown in Listing 14.3. Use the Tools | Add Procedure to create this procedure, then type in the code as shown. Here's what the code does:

1. Creates a **FileSystemObject**.

2. Loops through the **Drives** collection until drive C: is found.

3. Passes the drive's **RootFolder**, which you'll remember is a Folder object, to the procedure **DoCount**.

So far so good, but you may have noticed that no counting has yet been done. That is accomplished in the **DoCount** procedure, which is our next task.

Listing 14.3   The CountFilesAndFolders procedure.

```
Public Sub CountFilesAndFolders()

Dim fs, d

Set fs = CreateObject("Scripting.FileSystemObject")

' Get drive C.
For Each d In fs.Drives
    If d.DriveLetter = "C" Then Exit For
Next

Call DoCount(d.RootFolder)

Label1 = "Drive C has " & NumFiles _
    & " files in " & NumFolders _
    & " folders."

End Sub
```

The real work of the program is done by the **DoCount** procedure, shown in Listing 14.4. Given how much work it does, it is deceptively short. It is here that the power of the recursive algorithm comes into play. **DoCount** is passed a Folder object as its argument. Then, here's what it does:

1. Gets the number of subfolders in the folder and adds it to the folders count.

2. Gets the number of files in the folder and adds it to the files count.

3. Calls **DoCount** for each subfolder in the **Folders** collection.

Here is where the recursion occurs—when the **DoCount** procedure calls itself. As this program illustrates, recursion can be a powerful technique for certain tasks. If you don't believe me, try to write a program that counts the files and folders on a drive without using recursion. We will make good use of recursion again later in the chapter.

Listing 14.4   The DoCount procedure.

```
Public Sub DoCount(f As Folder)

Dim f1 As Folder

NumFolders = NumFolders + f.SubFolders.Count
NumFiles = NumFiles + f.Files.Count
For Each f1 In f.SubFolders
    Call DoCount(f1)
Next

End Sub
```

The File Object

In the FSO model, each file on a disk is represented by a File object. This object has methods and properties that you use to get information about the file and manipulate it. First, however, you need to create a File object associated with a specific disk file.

Creating A File Object

There are two ways to create a File object. If you know the name and path of the file, you can use the **FileSystemObject**'s **GetFile** method. The code is as follows, assuming that **fs** is an instance of the **FileSystemObject** class:

```
Dim f
Set f = fs.GetFile(filespec)
```

The *filespec* argument is the relative or absolute path to the file. An error occurs if *filespec* does not exist. Note that executing **GetFile** does not open the file or do anything else to it, but simply returns a File object linked to the file.

TIP Relative Vs. Absolute Paths

An absolute path specifies complete information about the name and location of a file, including drive letter. For example, c:\data\sales\march1998.dat is an absolute path. A relative path specifies a file location relative to the current default path. Sales\ march1998.dat is a relative path, specifying that the file MARCH1998.DAT in the subfolder Sales is the current default folder. If, and only if, the default path is c:\data will the absolute and relative paths given here be equivalent.

Another way to obtain a File object is from a Folder object's **Files** collection. As you learned earlier in this chapter, you can create a Folder object for any subfolder on a disk, and the Folder object contains a **Files** collection containing one File object for each file in the folder. You can write code to iterate through the collection, looking for one or more files that meet a specified criterion. For example, the following code creates an array of File objects containing all the DLL files in the application's current path:

```
Dim fs, f, f1, filelist()
Dim i As Integer, j As Integer
i = 0
ReDim filelist(0)
Set fs = CreateObject("Scripting.FileSystemObject")
Set f = fs.GetFolder(App.Path)
For Each f1 In f.Files
    If LCase(Right(f1.Name, 3)) = "dll" Then
        i = i + 1
        ReDim Preserve filelist(i)
        Set filelist(i) = f1
    End If
Next

If i > 0 Then
    For j = 1 To i
        Debug.Print filelist(j).Name
    Next
End If
```

Working With File Objects

Once you create a File object, you have access to all the properties of the file. You can also use the object's methods for certain types of file manipulation. Let's look at the methods first, listed in Table 14.4. The File object's properties are listed in Table 14.5. Finally, the **Attributes** property provides information about the file's attributes, such as whether it is read-only or a system file. The single value returned by the **Attributes** property is a composite of the individual attribute values, as shown in Table 14.6. This table also indicates which of the individual attributes are read/write and which are read-only.

Table 14.4   The File object's methods.

Method	Description
Copy *dest [, overwrite]*	Copies the file to *dest*. An existing file is overwritten only if *overwrite* is True (the default).
Move *dest*	Moves the file to *dest*.
Delete [*force*]	Deletes the files. Read-only files are deleted only if *force* is True. The default is False.
OpenAsTextStream	Opens the file and returns a TextStream object. See Chapter 13 for details.

Table 14.5   The File object's properties.

Property	Description
Attributes	Returns a value summarizing the file's attributes, as explained in detail later.
DateCreated	Date and time the file was created.
DateLastAccessed	Date and time the file was last accessed.
DateLastModified	Date and time the file was last modified.
Drive	Drive letter of the drive where the file resides.
Name	Sets or returns the name of the file.
ParentFolder	Returns a Folder object representing the file's parent folder.
Path	The path of the file, including drive letter.
ShortName	The short file name used by programs that require the old 8.3 style naming convention.
ShortPath	The short path used by programs that require the old 8.3 style naming convention.
Size	The size, in bytes, of the file.
Type	Returns information about the type of the file (explained in more detail later).

Table 14.6   Values of the Attribute property.

Attribute	Value	Description
Normal	0	Normal file. No attributes are set.
ReadOnly	1	Read-only file. Read/write.
Hidden	2	Hidden file. Read/write.
System	4	System file. Read/write.
Volume	8	Disk drive volume label. Read-only.
Directory	16	Folder or directory. Read-only.
Archive	32	File has changed since last backup. Read/write.
Alias	64	Link or shortcut. Read-only.
Compressed	128	Compressed file. Read-only.

You use Visual Basic's logical operators to convert between individual file attributes and the value of the **Attributes** property. Use **And** to determine if a specific attribute is set. If *f* is a File object, then we can write the following code to determine if the file's **Archive** attribute is set:

```
If f.Attributes And 32 Then
        ' Archive attribute is set.
Else
' Archive attribute is not set.
End If
```

Likewise, the following code checks to see if the file's **ReadOnly** attribute is set and, if it is, clears it:

```
If f.Attributes And 1 Then
        f.Attributes = f.Attributes - 1
End If
```

To perform the reverse—setting the **ReadOnly** attribute if it is not already set—we would write the following:

```
If Not f.Attributes And 1 Then
        f.Attributes = f.Attributes + 1
End If
```

The File-Related Controls

Most of what you will do with files in Visual Basic will use the Basic statements, functions, and objects presented so far. Other types of file access—such as loading a picture into a Picture Box control—are handled more or less automatically by the associated control. Three Visual Basic controls, however, have been designed specifically to work with files: FileListBox, DirListBox, and DriveListBox. These controls are the topic of this section.

The file-related controls are designed to help you navigate your system's disk drives. Think of how things are arranged on the disk. Each disk, or drive, is identified by a letter followed by a colon. On each drive are one or more folders, or subdirectories, arranged in a hierarchical structure. In each folder are one or more files, each with its own name. A folder can also contain other folders, or it can be empty. Thus, locating any file is a three-tiered process: drive, folder, file name. One control is designed to deal with each of these three levels.

FileListBox

The FileListBox control displays a list of all files/folders or selected files/folders in a specified folder, and the user can select from the list. The folder whose files are listed is determined by the control's **Path** property. Thus, to list the files in the folder \DATA on drive C:, you would write (assuming that File1 is the **Name** property of a FileListBox control):

```
File1.Path = "c:\data"
```

Often, the **Path** property for a FileListBox is obtained from a Directory List Box control, as you'll see later. The FileListBox control has several other properties you should know.

The **Pattern** property specifies the template for file names to be displayed. The default **Pattern** is "*.*", which displays all files. Other **Pattern**s let you limit the display to subsets of files. For example, to display only files with the .DAT extension, you would write:

```
File1.Pattern = "*.DAT"
```

You can use multiple templates separated by semicolons. Thus, the code

```
File1.Pattern = "*.DAT;*.TXT;*.BAT"
```

would display only those files with the .DAT, .TXT, and .BAT extensions.

The **Filename** property returns the name of the file currently selected in the list. If no file is selected, this property returns a zero-length string. If you are using FileListBox to permit the user to select a file, you would retrieve the name of the selected file from the **Filename** property. You obtain the path of the selected file separately from the control's **Path** property. For example, if File1 is the name of a FileListBox control, the following code would open the file selected by the user:

```
Dim MyFile As String
...
MyFile = File1.Path & "\" & File1.Filename
If File1.Filename <> "" Then Open MyFile For Output As #1
...
```

You can set the **Filename** property in code, which results in the specified file becoming selected (highlighted) in the control on screen.

A number of events are associated with the FileListBox control. Several of them are the standard events supported by most Visual Basic controls, such as **Click**. A couple of them, however, are special for this control. The **PathChange** event is triggered if the control's **Path** or **Filename** properties are changed in code. The **PatternChange** property is triggered if the **Pattern** property is changed. These events are used to synchronize the operation of a FileListBox with other parts of the program.

DirListBox

The Directory List Box—or DirListBox—displays a list of folders. The user can navigate the folder structure of a drive with this list. Selecting a folder in a DirListBox control actually changes the current active path. By synchronizing a DirListBox with a FileListBox, you can easily provide a display of files in a folder selected by the user.

The **Path** property sets and returns a DirListBox's current path. The control will display the name of the current folder, with an open folder icon next to it. Above will be a hierarchical display of parent folders (if any), up to and including the root folder on the current drive. Below will be a list of any subfolders located in the current folder. This hierarchy is illustrated in Figure 14.3. In this figure, the current folder is SAMPLES. Its parent folder is MSVC20, which is located in the root folder on drive D:, indicated by the backslash. Within the SAMPLES folder are five subfolders: MFC, OLE2, and so on. To make any visible folder current, the user must double-click on it.

The DirListBox's **Change** event is executed when the control's **Path** property changes, either by the user double-clicking on a folder in the list or by programming it in the code. You can use this event to synchronize a FileListBox with the DirListBox. The code shown here will result in the FileListBox's display updating to show files in any new folder selected in the DirListBox:

```
Private Sub Dir1_Change()
    File1.Path = Dir1.Path
End Sub
```

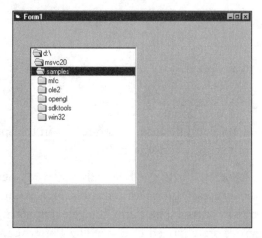

Figure 14.3   A Directory List Box.

DriveListBox

The Drive List Box control (DriveListBox) displays a list of available drives at runtime. It takes the form of a drop-down list. When closed, the list displays the letter of the current drive. The user can pull down the list and select another drive; doing so not only changes the display in the control, but actually changes the system's current drive. The control's **Drive** property returns or sets the current drive. By assigning a DriveListBox's **Drive** property to a DirListBox's **Path** property, you can synchronize the two controls, so that the DirListBox will display folders on the drive selected in the DriveListBox. This step is done in the DriveListBox's **Change** event procedure, which is triggered any time the **Drive** property changes (in code or by the user). Here's the code:

```
Private Sub Drive1_Change()
    Dir1.Path = Drive1.Drive
End Sub
```

If the DirListBox is synchronized with a FileListBox, as described earlier, the three controls can be combined to provide a dialog box where the user can select a drive, select a folder, and then select a file. This combination is at the heart of implementing a File Open dialog.

Demonstrating The File-Related Controls

To demonstrate using the file-related controls, I first considered showing you how to create your own File Open or File Save dialog box. The Common Dialog control provides us with perfectly good Open and Save dialogs, however, and I wanted to come up with something that might actually be useful. A file-finding utility seemed like a good choice. I often have use for this program, so other people are also likely to need it.

A file-finding utility is simple in concept. The user specifies a drive, a starting folder, and a file template. The program searches the specified folder and all of its subfolders for files that match the template, displaying them in a list. But how do you implement this in code? On the surface, it sounds rather complicated. If you approached the problem from a brute-force perspective, your solution might well end up being complicated. Some inside knowledge of how the DirListBox (Directory List Box) control works can greatly simplify the solution. This is an excellent example of how an intimate knowledge of Visual Basic and all its parts is essential to solving programming problems with maximum efficiency.

Finding The Right Tool For The Job

Let's review the problem. You already know how to search a specific folder for files that match a template—just use the **Dir** function that was covered earlier in the chapter. The problem lies in extending the search to the subfolders of the starting folder, to their subfolders, and onward until the entire tree has been searched. If you closely examine the characteristics of the DirListBox control, you'll find the solution.

At runtime, a DirListBox displays the drive's hierarchical folder structure. Above the current folder are listed the parent folder, its parent, and so on—back to the drive's root directory. Below the current folder are listed its subfolders. Each item in this list has an index number, as follows:

- The current folder's index is -1.

- Folders above the current folder have negative indexes.

- The number of subfolders in the current folder is indicated by the control's **ListCount** property. These subfolders have indexes starting at 0 and running to **ListCount** -1.

This last characteristic of the DirListBox is the one we'll use. It enables us to obtain the names of the current folder's subfolders. Apply a recursive algorithm as follows:

1. Start in the directory specified by the user.

2. Use the **Dir** function to search the current directory for files that match the template. If any files are found, add them to the list of matching files.

3. Check for any subfolders in this folder. If none exists, you are finished with this folder and are ready to move up one level to the parent folder. If you have returned to the starting folder, you are finished. If you have subfolders, use the **List** and **ListCount** properties to obtain the subfolder names and create a list of them.

4. Make the first folder in this list current.

5. Return to Step 2.

This general type of algorithm is called *recursion*. The same procedures are applied over and over to the data until no more data remains to process. In this case, the data consists of folder names. As you'll see in the demonstration program, the code required to implement the file search is actually quite simple. As is often the case in computer programming, having the proper algorithm is an important step in designing code.

Creating The Form

One important Visual Basic technique illustrated by this project is the use of hidden controls. Just because a control is hidden (**Visible** property = False) does not mean it is nonfunctional. Of course, the user cannot interact with it, but it can be used by code. In this project, you will use a hidden DirListBox control to implement the file-search algorithm.

Start a new Standard EXE project. Add a DriveListBox and two DirListBox controls, setting the **Visible** property of one of the DirListBoxes to False. Add a Check Box, a List Box,
and a control array of three Command Buttons. Finally, add one Text Box and three labels
to identify the Text Box, the visible DirListBox, and the DriveList Box. The form should
look more or less like Figure 14.4. The DirListBox superimposed on the ListBox is the one
that will be hidden. Set control and form properties as shown in Listing 14.5.

Please note the new format in Listing 14.5. This is the format used by Visual Basic within
a form file to record the form's controls and their properties. If you open a FRM file in a
text editor, you'll see the controls and properties listed at the top of the file and the Basic
code listed at the end. Starting with this project, I will sometimes be presenting controls
and properties in this more efficient format rather than detailing them individually in the
text. While the original FRM file lists all of the properties for each control, I will include
only those that you need to change from their default values. By looking through a con-
trol/property listing, such as Listing 14.5, you can determine the various property settings
you need to make.

Listing 14.5   *Objects and properties in FINDFILE.FRM.*

```
Begin VB.Form Form1
    Appearance      =    0   '3D
    BorderStyle     =    1   'Fixed Single
    Caption         =    "File Finding Utility"
    Begin VB.ListBox lstFiles
        BeginProperty Font
            name    =    "Courier New"
            size    =    9.75
        EndProperty
    End
    Begin VB.CheckBox chkFileInfo
        Caption     =    "Include file information in list"
    End
    Begin VB.DirListBox dirHidden
    Visible         =    False
    End
    Begin VB.DirListBox dirStart
    End
    Begin VB.DriveListBox Drive1
        Appearance  =    1   '3D
    End
    Begin VB.CommandButton Command1
        Caption     =    "&Quit"
        Index       =    2
    End
    Begin VB.CommandButton Command1
        Appearance  =    0   'Flat
        Caption     =    "Sto&p"
```

```
        Index        =    1
   End
   Begin VB.CommandButton Command1
        Appearance   =    0   'Flat
        Caption      =    "&Start"
        Index        =    0
   End
   Begin VB.TextBox txtPattern
        Text         =    "Text1"
   End
   Begin VB.Label Label3
        Alignment    =    1   'Right Justify
        Caption      =    "File template:"
   End
   Begin VB.Label Label2
        Alignment    =    1   'Right Justify
        Caption      =    "Starting directory:"
   End
   Begin VB.Label Label1
        Alignment    =    1   'Right Justify
        Caption      =    "Drive:"
   End
End
```

Writing The Code

The program requires two global variables. The first is a type **Boolean** flag that signals whether the user has canceled the search; the other is a type **Integer** that keeps track of the depth of the search—in other words, how many folders "deep" execution is. These

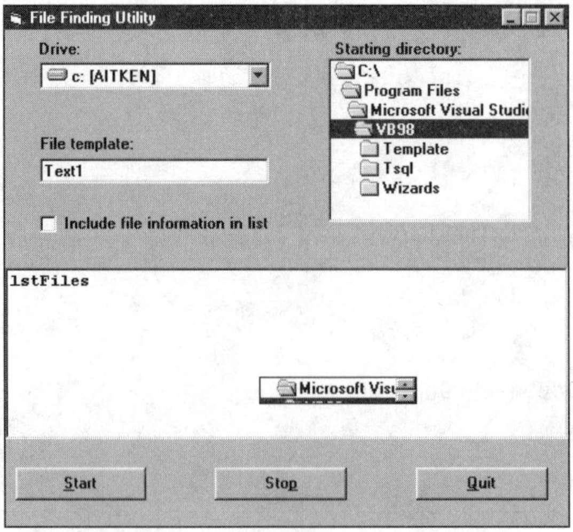

Figure 14.4 *The File Finding utility's form.*

variables should be declared in the general declarations section of code, shown in Listing 14.6.

Listing 14.6 *General declarations in FINDFILE.FRM.*

```
Option Explicit

' Global flag to abort search.

Dim Halt As Boolean
Dim Depth As Integer
```

The program actions are triggered by the **Click** event procedure for the Command Button control array. It's quite simple, as you can see in Listing 14.7. To start the search, it calls the procedure **StartSearch**. To terminate an ongoing search, it sets the flag variable **Halt** to True. To exit the program, it executes the **End** statement.

Listing 14.7 *The Command Button Click event procedure.*

```
Private Sub Command1_Click(Index As Integer)

Select Case Index
    Case 0 'Start button
        Call StartSearch
    Case 1 'Stop button
        Halt = True
    Case 2       ' Exit button
        End
End Select

End Sub
```

The **StartSearch** procedure is where the action begins. This is a general procedure that you add to the module with the **Insert Procedure** command. Its code is shown in Listing 14.8. First, code in this procedure clears the List Box where the search results will be displayed and sets the **Halt** flag to False. It then disables all of the controls that should not be available during a search.

Next, turn your attention to the hidden DirListBox control. It is this control's **Change** event procedure that triggers the actual search action. You need to set this control's **Path** property to the folder that the user specified as the start folder for the search, obtained from the **Path** property of the visible DirListBox. This property change will normally trigger the control's **Change** event. But what if the hidden DirListBox control's **Path** property is already pointing to the desired start directory? Because no **Change** event will be generated, we'll have to generate one ourselves (remember that event procedures can be called in code just like nonevent procedures). Here is the code:

```
If dirHidden.Path = dirStart.Path Then
    dirHidden_Change
Else
    dirHidden.Path = dirStart.Path
End If
```

Note that the program displays the hourglass mouse pointer while the search is in progress. Once that **Change** event is triggered for the hidden DirListBox control, execution recurses within event procedures until the search is completed. Then it returns to the same location in the **StartSearch** procedure. The final lines of code in this procedure reenable the form's controls that were disabled when the search began, returning the normal mouse pointer.

Listing 14.8 The StartSearch procedure.

```
Private Sub StartSearch()

' We come here to start a search.

' Empty the List Box.
lstFiles.Clear

' Clear the Halt flag.
Halt = False

' Disable all controls except the Stop button.
Command1(0).Enabled = False
Command1(1).Enabled = True
Command1(2).Enabled = False
Drive1.Enabled = False
dirStart.Enabled = False
txtPattern.Enabled = False

' If the invisible Dir list is already pointing to
' the same directory as the visible Dir list, we must
' trigger a Change event. If not, change its Path property,
' which will automatically trigger a Change event.

' It is the dirHidden.Change event that triggers the search process.

' Display the hourglass mouse pointer.
Screen.MousePointer = 11

If dirHidden.Path = dirStart.Path Then
    dirHidden_Change
Else
    dirHidden.Path = dirStart.Path
End If
```

```
' We reach here after the search is complete.
' Re-enable all controls except the Stop button.
Screen.MousePointer = 0
Command1(0).Enabled = True
Command1(1).Enabled = False
Command1(2).Enabled = True
Drive1.Enabled = True
dirStart.Enabled = True
txtPattern.Enabled = True

End Sub
```

As noted earlier, the search begins when the hidden DirListBox's **Change** event procedure is triggered. Listing 14.9 shows the code in that procedure. The code here is really simpler than it looks. The first step is to search the current folder (the one you just changed to) for files that match the search template entered by the user. The path is placed in the List Box, then a loop obtains the names of all matching files by calling the **Dir** function repeatedly. These names are also added to the List Box, along with file information if the FileInfo option is selected. Note the Visual Basic functions called **FileDateTime** and **FileLen**; these are available for obtaining the desired information about the file.

Once all of the files in the current folder have been processed, the attention turns to any subfolders. Remember, the DirListBox's **ListCount** property will tell us the number of subfolders. By using that value—plus the control's **List** indexed property—you can loop through the list of subfolders and place them in an array.

When this array is loaded with the names of any subfolders in the current folder, the rest is easy. Set up a loop that goes through the array, assigning each subfolder name (which includes the full path) to the hidden DirListBox's **Path** property. Guess what? Each time you do this, you trigger another **Change** event procedure, repeating the entire process I have just described.

Listing 14.9   The hidden DirListBox's Change event procedure.

```
Private Sub dirHidden_Change()

' Triggered when the hidden directory list changes. It is here
' that the actual search is performed.

Dim Path As String, FileName As String
Dim FileName1 As String, Path1 As String, Entry As String
Dim NumDirs As Integer, X As Integer, Y As Integer
Dim DirAdded As Boolean, Spaces As Integer

Depth = Depth + 1
```

```
' For testing as described in text, uncomment the next line.
debug.Print "Depth = ", Depth

' Get the current path and add a backslash if necessary.
Path = dirHidden.Path
If Right(Path, 1) <> "\" Then
    Path = Path & "\"
End If

' Create the full search pattern by combining the current path
' with the file pattern from the txtPattern Text Box.
Path1 = Path & txtPattern.TEXT

' The Dir function returns an empty string if
' a matching file is not found, and the file name if
' a matching file is found.
FileName = Dir(Path1)
DirAdded = False

' Loop as long as a matching file is found.
Do Until FileName = ""

    ' If the directory name has not already been added to the
    ' List Box, add it now.
    If (DirAdded = False) Then
        lstFiles.AddItem "[ " & dirHidden.Path & " ]"
        DirAdded = True
    End If

    ' Start building the next List Box entry.
    Entry = "    " & FileName

    ' If the FileInfo check box is checked, add the
    ' file's date, time, and length to the entry.
    If chkFileInfo.VALUE Then
        FileName1 = Path & FileName
        Spaces = 16,,Len(FileName)
        Entry = Entry & Space(Spaces) & FileDateTime(FileName1)
        Spaces = 20,,Len(FileDateTime(FileName1))
        Entry = Entry & Space(Spaces) & FileLen(FileName1)
    End If

    ' Add the entry to the List Box.
    lstFiles.AddItem Entry

    ' Look for the next matching file.
    FileName = Dir
Loop
```

```
' How many subdirectories are in the current directory?
NumDirs = dirHidden.ListCount

' Put the subdirectory names in an array.
ReDim DirList(NumDirs) As String

For X = 0 To NumDirs-1
    DirList(X) = dirHidden.List(X)
Next X

' For each subfolder, repeat the search process. Call DoEvents
' to enable user to abort the search by clicking the Stop
' Command button.
For X = 0 To NumDirs-1
    dirHidden.Path = DirList(X)
    Y = DoEvents()
    If Halt Then
        Exit Sub
    End If
Next X

Depth = Depth-1

End Sub
```

Exploring The Recursive Algorithm

When considering how recursion works, you must understand that when a function calls itself—which is what the **Change** event procedure does by changing the control's **Path** property—each call results in a completely new and separate copy of the procedure being executed. Each of these copies has its own independent array of subfolder names, as well as its own set of other local variables. Each copy of the **Change** event procedure sits waiting until the "lower" copies of the procedure have completed (by running out of subfolders to process). Then execution returns to the specific copy of the procedure and continues there until its array of subfolders is exhausted, at which time execution passes "up" one more level. Only when each and every subfolder below the starting subfolder has been processed does execution return to the **StartSearch** procedure.

To get a feel for what's happening, use the **debug.Print** statement to display the value of the **Depth** variable by uncommenting the line of code near the start of the **Change** event procedure. You'll see a sequence of values displayed in the Debug window similar to this:

```
1
2
3
3
```

```
2
3
3
4
4
3
2
```

At each iteration, the value displayed gives us a feeling for how many "layers" of **Change** event procedures exist—each with its own array of subfolders. Once you understand the basic principle behind iterative algorithms, you'll probably find other programming challenges to which they can be applied.

This project requires a bit more code, shown in Listing 14.10. Nothing here is too complicated. You should be able to figure out how it works from the comments in the listing. Before focusing on Listing 14.10, take a look at Figure 14.5, which shows the File Finding utility in operation.

I have found the File Finding utility to be very handy. Actually, I don't often use it as a standalone program, but I have incorporated its algorithm and code into other projects. For example, you can use the three file-related controls plus the file-finding techniques presented here to create a File Open dialog box that permits the user to locate files anywhere on the disk.

This project is an excellent example of using creative thinking to find a use for a Visual Basic control that its creators probably never envisioned. Many other possibilities are waiting in the Visual Basic toolbox, but remember, a working knowledge of the tools is a prerequisite for getting the most out of them.

Listing 14.10   The remaining code in FINDFILE.FRM.

```
Private Sub Drive1_Change()

' If the user changes drives, pass the new path
' to the Dir list control.

dirStart.Path = Drive1.Drive

End Sub


Private Sub Form_Load()

Halt = False
txtPattern.TEXT = "*.EXE"
lstFiles.Clear
depth = 0
```

```
End Sub


Private Sub Text1_GotFocus()

' Highlight entire contents of Text Box.

txtPattern.SelStart = 0
txtPattern.SelLength = Len(txtPattern.TEXT)

End Sub


Private Sub txtPattern_GotFocus()

' Highlight Text Box contents when it gets the focus.

txtPattern.SelStart = 0
txtPattern.SelLength = Len(txtPattern.TEXT)

End Sub
```

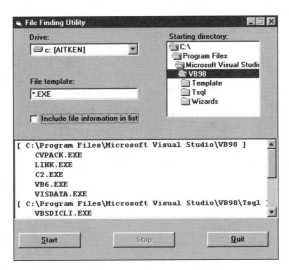

Figure 14.5   *The File Finding utility in operation.*

Chapter 15
Serial Communication

The Visual Basic Comm control makes it easy for your Visual Basic programs to communicate over serial connections.

I t's a rare computer that operates in total isolation these days. Even computers that are not a part of a local area network frequently communicate with other computers to exchange data files, programs, and electronic mail. Most people who access CompuServe, America Online, or the Internet do so with serial communication (via a modem). If you need to transfer that 15MB data file from one computer to another, you'll find that setting up a serial link is much easier than shuffling floppy diskettes for an hour.

Serial communication has many uses that most of us never even consider. Some high-end pen plotters—the kind used to create architectural drawings—require a serial link to the controlling computer. Many laboratory instruments and industrial components are controlled via a serial link. All in all, it's a topic you should know something about—if only the basics.

Serial Communication Fundamentals

Serial communication is called *serial*, because the individual bits of data follow each other over the same electrical connection. It contrasts with parallel communication, where multiple connections enable the link to carry more than one bit at a time (for example, your printer port). Serial communication is bi-directional, meaning that data flows in both directions: from computer A to computer B, and from B to A.

Serial communication is carried out by means of a *serial port* on your computer. Serial ports have many names, including COM ports, RS-232 ports, and asynchronous communication ports. Whatever the moniker, it refers to the same piece of hardware. In theory, a serial link requires only three wires: one wire for the data going out, one for the data coming in, and a ground wire. If you look at the serial ports on the back of your computer, however, you'll find that the physical connection is either a 9-pin D shell on newer models or a 25-pin D shell on older systems. Why all the extra connections? Many of the pins remain unused in the 25-pin serial connection. On the other hand, many more than three lines are employed in most serial connections. These "extra" lines do not carry data; they are used for *handshaking* signals. The computers on the two ends of the serial link use handshaking signals to coordinate their actions.

Of course, you can use serial communication for much more than linking one computer to another. It can also link a computer to a modem, mouse, plotter, and printer, to mention just a few. No matter which two devices are involved in a serial link, however, certain things remain constant. Serial communication standards ensure that all serial ports follow the same rules. Within this set of rules, however, is some room for flexibility. You can control how fast data is sent over the serial link, and you can control certain aspects of the data format. These settings are called *communication parameters*. For serial communication to operate properly, the devices at both ends of the link must use the same parameters.

Making The Serial Connection

If you want to connect two computers by means of their serial ports, you must use a *null modem*. This is a serial cable in which the send and receive lines are crossed, so that one computer's send line is connected to the other computer's receive line.

Serial Communication Parameters

Perhaps the most important parameter is the *baud rate*, which determines the speed at which data is transmitted. The baud rate is approximately equal to the number of bits transmitted per second. Serial port hardware supports a variety of standard baud rates, ranging from the totally obsolete and horridly slow 110 baud to more than 100,000 baud. Note that the baud rates supported by your serial port may differ from those supported by your modem.

Another parameter is the *word length*, which specifies the number of bits that make up each unit of data transmitted. While serial hardware can support word lengths of five to eight bits, PCs always work with word lengths of seven or eight bits.

The *parity* parameter determines whether a parity bit is added to each word. A parity bit enables the serial port hardware to detect certain kinds of errors in transmission. You can set parity to None, Odd, or Even. A setting of None does not add a parity bit. For Odd parity, the parity bit is set to zero or one, so that the total number of bits set to one in the data-word/parity-bit combination is odd. Even parity works the same way, but the total number of set bits is even. At the receiving end, the hardware looks at each data-word/parity-bit set to see if the proper number (even or odd) of bits is set. If a single bit has flipped because of a transmission error, the receiving hardware will detect the error and request that the word be re-sent.

The *stop bit* parameter specifies how many stop bits are used. In serial communication, start and stop bits delineate the beginning and end of each data word. One start bit is always used, and one or two stop bits can be used. Most PC communications use one stop bit.

Serial Ports And Modems

One of the most common uses for serial ports is to connect a modem (even if your modem is internal, it is still logically connected to one of the system's serial ports). Do you need to worry about that alphabet soup of modem protocols when programming a serial port? In a word, no. The various protocols that adorn modem advertisements (such as V.32bis and MNP5) have to do with transmission speeds, error correction protocols, and data compression standards. When you use a modem attached to a serial port (as we'll do later in the chapter), you may send it commands specifying which of these protocols to use. The serial port is still just a serial port, however, and is treated the same, regardless of whether a modem, printer, or plotter is on the other end.

Using The Comm Control

While serial communication is simple in principle, in practice you'll quickly understand what people mean when they say, "The devil is in the details." Serial communication is filled with details, including the various handshake lines that may or may not be used in a specific situation, the importance of setting the serial parameters properly, and so on. Fortunately, Microsoft has extended the concept of software components to this problem, providing us with the Communication, or Comm, control (sometimes called the MSComm control), which greatly simplifies the job of supporting serial communication in your Visual Basic programs.

The Comm control is not visible during program execution, because its sole job is to act as an intermediary between your program and a serial port. You can have two or more Comm controls in a program—each linked to a different serial port. Data to be transmitted is placed in one of the control's properties; data received by the serial port is retrieved from another of the control's properties. Additional properties are used to set and read serial port parameters. Before we look at these properties in detail, we need to understand the two basic methods of using the Comm control.

Polling Vs. Event-Driven Communication

One of the more difficult aspects of serial port programming is dealing with incoming data. To be more precise, the problem lies in knowing when data has been received by the port and is available to be read by the program. The Comm control offers two approaches to this problem:

- *Polling*—The traditional method by which Basic programs handled serial communication before the advent of the Comm control. It is still supported by the Comm control and is perfectly suitable for some applications. This method requires the program code to check the status of the serial port on a regular basis to see if data has been received, if an error has occurred, or if a change has occurred in the status of the handshaking lines.

- *Event-driven communication*—A more powerful technique in which the Comm control generates an event whenever data is received. Your program does not have to sit idly waiting for data. It can busy itself with other tasks and still respond immediately whenever the serial port has data to be read. The same event is also triggered if a communication error occurs, or if one of the handshaking lines changes status.

Polling may be perfectly suitable for relatively simple applications, such as a phone dialer, where the program only has to keep an eye on the serial port. For more demanding applications, however, you will find that the event-driven approach is superior.

Comm Control Properties

The Comm control has a long list of properties, many of which are unique to this control. Some of these properties are related to the various handshaking protocols and signal lines that serial ports support. We won't discuss these advanced properties here, because they are rarely involved in basic serial communication. Rather, we will concentrate on the more fundamental properties always associated with the Comm control.

Setting Serial Port Parameters

You set serial port parameters by means of the **CommPort** and **Settings** properties. **CommPort** specifies the serial port to which the control is linked. It can be set to any value between 1 (the default) and 99, but an error will occur if you specify a port that does not actually exist on the system in use. You must set the **CommPort** property before the port can be opened.

Communication parameters, such as baud rate and parity, are designated by using the **Settings** property. You place a string with the following format in the **Settings** property:

```
BBBB,P,D,S
```

In this **Settings** string, *BBBB* is the baud rate, *P* is the parity, *D* is the number of data bits, and *S* is the number of stop bits. If you do not explicitly change a Comm control's parameters, the default settings are 9,600 baud, no parity, 8-bit data word, and 1 stop bit. The valid baud rates are 110, 300, 600, 1,200, 2,400, 9,600, 14,400, 19,200, 38,400, 56,000, 128,000, and 256,000.

Table 15.1 shows the valid parity values.

The valid data-bit values are 4, 5, 6, 7, and 8, which is the default. Valid stop-bit values are 1 (the default), 1.5, and 2.

For example, the following code would set the Comm control named Comm1 to link with serial port 1, using 9,600 baud, no parity, an 8-bit data word, and 1 stop bit:

```
Comm1.CommPort = 1
Comm1.Settings = "9600,N,8,1"
```

Sending And Receiving Data

Before reviewing the details of how the Comm control sends and receives data, you need to understand the concept of a *buffer*. A buffer is a temporary storage location where data is held before processing. The Comm control has two buffers: input and output. Proper use of these buffers simplifies serial port programming and results in more reliable communications.

Table 15.1   *Parity settings.*

Setting	Description
E	Even
M	Mark
N	None (default)
O	Odd
S	Space

When your program sends data to the Comm control for transmission, the data is placed in the output buffer. The Comm control reads data from the buffer and transmits it. Likewise, when the Comm control receives data, the data is placed in the input buffer, where your program can read it. Reading the **Input** property removes the data from the buffer, so there is no danger of reading the same data twice.

These buffers allow your program to operate without being perfectly synchronized with the serial port. If your program sends data to the Comm control faster than the serial port can transmit it, no problem. The extra data will remain in the output buffer until it can be transmitted. Similarly, if your program is reading data from the Comm control more slowly than the serial port is receiving it, the input buffer will hold the data until the program catches up. Without these buffers, your program would have to use the various handshaking signals to ensure that its activities are synchronized with the serial port—a difficult programming task, to be sure.

The output buffer's default size is 512 bytes. To set a different buffer size or determine the current size, use the **OutBufferSize** property. The default setting is usually sufficient, but you will need to increase it if an overflow error occurs (error handling is covered later in the chapter). Setting the output buffer size too large will not improve performance; it will only reduce the amount of memory available to the application.

To determine how many characters are currently in the output buffer, read the **OutBufferCount** property. To clear the buffer and erase its current contents without transmitting them, set the **OutBufferCount** property to zero.

The size of the input buffer is set with the **InBufferSize** property, whose default value is 1,024. As with the output buffer, too small a value can result in overflow errors, while too large a value simply wastes memory. The **InBufferCount** property specifies the number of characters currently in the input buffer. Setting this property to zero clears the input buffer.

To transmit data over the serial line—or more precisely, to place the data in the output buffer—put the data in the Comm control's **Output** property. To read data received by the serial port, use the **Input** property. By default, reading the **Input** property obtains all the characters currently in the input buffer. To read a specified number of characters, set the **InputLen** property to the desired number of characters before reading the **Input** property. If the input buffer contains fewer characters than specified by **InputLen**, **Input** returns a null string. You can use the **InBufferCount** property to be sure that the buffer contains enough characters before reading it. Reset **InputLen** to its default value of zero to return to reading all characters from the input buffer.

Here is an output example. The following code sends each character typed on a form to the Comm control:

```
Private Sub Form_KeyPress (KeyAscii As Integer)
    MSComm1.Output = Chr$(KeyAscii)
End Sub
```

As an input example, this code checks to see that input data is available, and if so, it uses the Print method to display it on the form:

```
If MSComm1.InBufferCount Then
    Form1.Print MSComm1.Input
End If
```

Determining Port Status

How can you determine the status of the serial port? The **CommEvent** property returns a code that represents the most recent change in port status. These changes include error conditions, as well as communication events. Values between 1,001 and 1,010 represent error codes; you can refer to the Visual Basic Help system for details on what the codes represent and on the defined constants available for your programs. Values between one and seven represent communication events—that is, normal occurrences during error-free serial communication. It's important to realize that the value of the **CommEvent** property reflects the most recent event or change in the Comm control. If the most recent occurrence was reception of data, the property value would be two. If the most recent occurrence was an error, the property value would be the code for that error. How do we know when something of importance has happened? The answer to this question is our next topic.

The OnComm Event

Central to most uses of the Comm control is the **OnComm** event. This event is triggered by a change in the status of the Comm control (with some limitations, as explained later). Expressed another way, this event is triggered any time the **CommEvent** property changes. We now have the answer to the previous question, "How can we know when the Comm control's status has changed?" The answer is simple: by using the **OnComm** event procedure. In this event procedure, we place code that tests the value of the **CommEvent** property, which branches accordingly. The most important use for this event procedure is to read data from the **Input** property after it has been received. It can also be used to react to error conditions. Table 15.2 lists the essential communication events.

Table 15.2   Communication events.

Constant	Value Of CommEvent	Description
comEvSend	1	There are fewer than **SThreshold** number of characters in the output buffer.
comEvReceive	2	Received **RThreshold** number of characters. This event is generated continuously until you use the **Input** property to remove the data from the input buffer.
comEvRing	6	Ring detected. Some UARTs (universal asynchronous receiver-transmitters) may not support this event.
comEvEOF	7	End Of File (ASCII character 26) character received.

The **Threshold** property specifies the number of characters in the output buffer that trigger the **CommEvent** procedure. The settings for this property follow:

- 0—**OnComm** is never triggered for data transmission.

- 1—**OnComm** is triggered when the output buffer is empty.

- n—**OnComm** is triggered when the number of unsent characters in the output buffer falls below n.

You can use the **OnComm** event to pace data transmission from your program to the **Output** property. When transmitting large quantities of data—for example, a text file—your program may write data to the Comm control's **Output** property faster than it can be sent, running the risk of an overflow error. You can eliminate this problem by using use the **comEvSend** event, which allows the program to send another block of data to the **Output** property only when the contents of the output buffer fall below a certain level.

The **RThreshold** property specifies how many characters must be received before triggering an **OnComm** event. If you want the program to respond each time a single character is received, set this property to one. If you set **RThreshold** to zero, **OnComm** will not be triggered, regardless of how many characters are received.

A Demonstration

To demonstrate the use of the Comm control, I have created a simple program that implements a dumb terminal. By definition, a *dumb terminal* does nothing more than send what you type to the serial port and display on screen any text received by the serial port. Text is displayed in a Text Box control. I could have used the **Print** method to display the text directly on a form, but the Text Box's built-in scrolling capabilities are useful when the text exceeds the form length. The form has only two controls: the Text Box and one MSComm control. Set the Text Box's **Multiline** property to True, and its **ScrollBars** property to Both. The form's objects and properties are given in Listing 15.1, and the operating program is shown in Figure 15.1.

Listing 15.1 Objects and properties in COMMDEMO.FRM.

```
Begin VB.Form Form1
    Caption        =    "Terminal"
    Begin VB.TextBox Text1
        MultiLine      =    -1  'True
        ScrollBars     =    3  'Both
    End
    Begin MSCommLib.MSComm MSComm1
    End
End
```

The code for this program is shown in Listing 15.2. In the **Form_Load** event procedure, we initialize the Comm control and open the port. I selected the communication parameters of 14000,E,7,1, because they are required by my CompuServe connection to test the program. You will need to set these parameters according to your own requirements. Note that I also set the **RThreshold** property to one to trigger the **OnComm** event each time a single character is received.

The Text Box control's **KeyPress** event procedure links the user's input to the Comm control. Rather than sending each individual character as it is typed, this procedure saves the input in a buffer and sends it all at once when the user presses the Enter key.

Received data is handled in the **OnComm** event procedure. After checking the **CommEvent** property to see that the event was indeed triggered by receipt of data, the code adds the received character to the end of the Text Box's **Text** property, then moves the insertion point to the end of the text.

Figure 15.1 Executing the "dumb terminal" program.

Listing 15.2   Code in COMMDEMO.FRM.

```
Option Explicit

Dim Buf1 As String

Private Sub Text1_KeyPress(KeyAscii As Integer)

' Add the key to the buffer.
Buf1 = Buf1 & Chr$(KeyAscii)

' If it was a carriage return, send the buffer contents
' to the Comm control and empty the buffer.
If KeyAscii = 13 Then
    MSComm1.Output = Buf1
    Buf1 = ""
End If

End Sub

Private Sub Form_Load()

' Initialize the Comm control.
MSComm1.CommPort = 1
MSComm1.Settings = "14000,E,7,1"
Debug.Print "----------------"


' Comm event will be triggered when a single character is received.
MSComm1.RThreshold = 1

' Open the port.
MSComm1.PortOpen = True

End Sub

Private Sub Form_Resize()

' Set Text Box to fill the form.
Text1.Width = Form1.ScaleWidth
Text1.Height = Form1.ScaleHeight
Text1.Left = 0
Text1.Top = 0

End Sub


Private Sub Form_Unload(Cancel As Integer)

' Close the port.
MSComm1.PortOpen = False
```

```
End Sub

Private Sub MSComm1_OnComm()

Dim s As String

' When a comm event occurs.

' Was it a "receive" event? If so, add the received character
' to the Text Box and set the insertion point at the end of
' the text. Other events are ignored.

Select Case MSComm1.CommEvent
    Case comEvReceive
        s = MSComm1.Input
        If Asc(s) = 13 Then s = vbCrLf
        Text1.Text = Text1.Text & s
        Text1.SelStart = Len(Text1.Text)
End Select

End Sub
```

If you use this program with a modem, you'll have to type the modem commands yourself (the commands are usually sent automatically by a communication program). Most modems adhere to the **AT** command set, originally developed by Hayes for its modems. The first command you should send is **ATZ**, which resets and initializes the modem. The model will respond OK. A few other commands are listed in Table 15.3; refer to your modem documentation for more information.

This very basic demonstration program is intended to show you only the fundamentals of using the Comm control. As it stands, the program includes no error handling and is vulnerable to many problems in use. Even with the Comm control, writing a full-featured and reliable serial communication program is a major task. Whenever I need anything but the most basic communication capabilities in a Visual Basic program, I always investigate the third-party market for a custom control rather than trying to do the job myself using the Comm control.

Table 15.3   Modem commands.

Command	Description
ATDT	Dial the following number using tone dialing. For example, ATDT5551212 would cause the modem to dial 555-1212.
ATE	Disable echoing of input. Use this command if the program is displaying everything you type twice.
ATH	Hang up the phone.

Chapter 16
Multimedia Magic

*Some say that
multimedia is the
wave of the future.
If this is true,
Visual Basic can
be your surfboard.*

Everyone seems to be going multimedia crazy. You can't open a daily newspaper without seeing ads for "multimedia PCs" on sale at the local lawn and garden store or gas station. An exaggeration perhaps, but you know what I mean. Lots of people have heard about multimedia, and more and more of them are expecting to see multimedia when they fire up their PCs.

What does this mean for you, Joe or Jane Programmer? When programming for fun, multimedia projects can be enjoyable and rewarding. If you program for a living, knowing multimedia is a necessity. You can bet your competition does. Whatever the reasons, you'll be pleasantly surprised at how easy multimedia programming is, because all of the essential capabilities are built into Visual Basic and Windows.

I won't pretend that this chapter provides complete coverage of Visual Basic's multimedia capabilities. The subject would require an entire book, and in fact, a very good book has been written by Anthony Potts, Chris D. Coppola, and Scott Jarol: *Visual Basic 5 Web & Multimedia Adventure Set*, published by The Coriolis Group. For an in-depth treatment, I suggest you turn to this book. My goal in this chapter is simply to show you how to perform the basic, common multimedia operations—namely, playing sound and video.

What Is Multimedia?

The meaning of the word *multimedia* is more elusive than it appears at first glance. *Media* is the plural of *medium*, a means or method of communication. Multimedia, then, literally means *more than one method of communication*. When your kid sister is screaming at you and whacking you on the head at the same time, that's multimedia.

Of course, this is a far cry from computer multimedia. When you experience a computer playing stereo sound through a pair of high-tech speakers while showing a video on screen, that's multimedia. But what about a hypertext presentation that combines text and pictures—is that multimedia? How about an animated icon? Determining the exact boundaries can be difficult, but it really doesn't matter. Whether you call it multimedia, interface enhancement, or chopped liver, the bottom line is still the same: You need to know how to program this stuff. Thanks to Windows and Visual Basic, the challenge has been greatly simplified.

The Multimedia PC Standard

While not all multimedia requires special hardware, much of it does. To reduce confusion and give developers a target platform, Microsoft developed the *Multimedia PC (MPC) standard*, a specification of the minimum hardware required for a computer to be considered MPC compatible:

- A 386SX or better microprocessor

- A minimum of 2MB of memory

- A VGA display system

- An MPC-compatible sound card supporting PCM playback of WAV files, MIDI (Musical Instrument Digital Interface) playback through a synthesizer, and an internal audio mixer

- A CD-ROM drive with a seek time under one second and a data transfer rate of at least 150K per second

By today's hardware standards, such a system seems almost quaint. In fact, you probably couldn't buy a system with exactly those specifications without heading for the flea market in Last Chance, Nev. With a CD-ROM built into almost every PC sold today, the only necessary addition is the sound card. If your system is not MPC ready, I recommend investigating the various available multimedia kits that include a sound card, speakers, CD-ROM drive, and software. This route is probably the easiest and most economical way to upgrade.

Note that the equipment on an MPC-compatible PC does not encompass all the possible multimedia hardware. Various kinds of specialized devices, such as video disk players and image scanners, are supported under Windows' multimedia capabilities. The MPC standard simply defines the minimum level of hardware that a developer can assume the end user will have.

The Windows Media Control Interface

Programs use the Windows *Media Control Interface* (MCI) to interact with multimedia hardware. Hardware can consist of any media devices that Windows supports: audio CD players, audio boards, MIDI sequencers, videodisc players, and videotape players and recorders. At the software end is a standard command syntax. Your program issues standard commands; the MCI, working with the specific drivers for the device in use, translates these commands to the exact signals required to carry out the requested action. Thus, the **Play** command starts playback, whether it's an audio CD, a MIDI file, or a video clip. Figure 16.1 illustrates the relationship between your program, the MCI, and multimedia devices. Table 16.1 lists the multimedia devices supported by Windows. New devices are added as they become popular, so this list may have already expanded by the time you read this.

Table 16.1   *Multimedia devices supported by Windows.*

Device ID	Description
AVIVideo	Digital video
CDAudio	Standard audio CD
DAT	Digital audio tape
DigitalVideo	Digital video
MMMovie	Multimedia movie
Other	Undefined device
Overlay	Analog video
Scanner	Image scanner
Sequencer	MIDI sequencer
VCR	Videocassette recorder
Videodisc	Videodisc player
WaveAudio	Digital audio

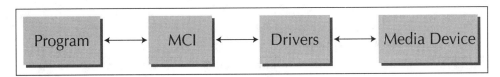

Figure 16.1   *The Media Control Interface mediates interactions between your program and multimedia hardware devices.*

Note that the term *device* does not refer to a discrete physical component, such as a sound card or a CD-ROM drive. It's more accurate to think of a device as one format of multimedia data that Windows is capable of playing. For example, CDAudio and WaveAudio are two distinct multimedia devices that use the computer's sound card to play digital music. They differ in the source of the digital data: for CDAudio, an audio CD in the CD-ROM drive; for WaveAudio, a file on disk. AVIVideo requires no special hardware to play digital video images on standard video display hardware (although a sound card, if present, will be used to play the accompanying soundtrack).

How Multimedia Sound Works

The two types of multimedia sound are digital and MIDI. With digital sound, the original audio waveform is sampled digitally, and the resulting digital samples, or numerical values, are saved. During playback, those digital values are retrieved and sent to a digital-to-analog converter (DAC) on the sound card, which converts them back into a reasonable approximation of the original waveform. The source of the digital data can be either a WAV file (*.WAV) on disk or a standard audio CD in the computer's CD-ROM drive.

Musical Instrument Digital Interface (MIDI) sound stores a series of commands. The commands specify the length, loudness, pitch, and other characteristics of each note. During playback, the commands are sent to the MIDI synthesizer on the sound card, which converts them into the corresponding sounds.

MCI Commands

A program controls multimedia devices by means of MCI commands, a remarkably simple set of commands applicable to all multimedia devices. Although some commands are specific for certain devices, the basic sequence of steps for using a multimedia device usually goes like this:

1. Open the device. For some devices, this step includes specifying the file where the data is stored—for example, a WAV file on disk. For other devices, such as playing audio from a CD or video from a videodisc, the data is part of the device, so there is no file to open.

2. Play the device (or, in some cases, record). This step may include pausing, seeking to a new location in the data, and so on.

3. Close the device.

Let's take a look at some simple MCI commands. To play a WAV file—perhaps CHIMES.WAV, which comes with Windows—here is the first command:

```
Open c:\media\chimes.wav type waveaudio alias chime
```

The **Open** command opens the desired WAV file, specifies its type (from Table 16.1), so Windows knows which driver to use, and assigns an *alias*—a name you can use in subsequent commands to refer to this device. Opening the device does not actually play the sound. The command for that is:

```
Play chime
```

You use the **Play** command with the alias assigned to the device. The sound will start playing, and control will pass back to the program. Although CHIMES.WAV is a short sound, you can play longer sounds that continue to play to the end while the program performs other tasks. When you finish with the device, you close it as follows:

```
Close chime
```

The **Close** command terminates play, so you have to delay its execution until the sound has completed playing. I'll show you how to do this later.

The basic MCI commands are listed in Table 16.2, although you will not be exploring them all here. My goal is to show you how to perform the most common multimedia tasks in your Visual Basic program. For more details about multimedia, refer to one of the books published on the topic.

Table 16.2   The basic MCI commands.

Command	Action
Capability	Requests information about a device's capabilities
Close	Closes a device
Info	Requests specific information about a device (such as its driver name)
Open	Opens and initializes a device
Pause	Suspends playback or recording
Play	Starts playback
Record	Begins recording
Resume	Resumes play or recording on a paused device
Save	Saves recorded data
Seek	Moves to a specific position on the media
Set	Changes a device's control settings
Status	Obtains device status information
Stop	Stops playback or recording

Note that you cannot simply type these commands into Basic code; you have to send them to the MCI. How? Examining the two available methods is the topic for the remainder of this chapter.

Sending MCI Commands With mciSendString

One way to send commands to the MCI is to use the function **mciSendString**. Not a part of Visual Basic, this function is part of the Windows Applications Programming Interface (API), the huge collection of functions that provides most of Windows' capabilities. When a Visual Basic program—or one written in any other language, for that matter—performs any operating system-related task, it is actually calling Windows API functions to do the job. When you open a file by writing code in Basic, Visual Basic translates it into the necessary Windows API call to perform the task. Not all API capabilities are included in Visual Basic; but fortunately, when you run into this situation, you can call the API function directly—which is exactly what you will do here.

Before a program can use a Windows API function, you must declare it. The declaration provides the program with certain information about the function, such as its name, the library it is in, and the number and types of its arguments. You can save time by copying API function declarations from the API Text Viewer application (typically installed along with Visual Basic) and pasting them into our code.

> ## TIP Using The API Text Viewer
>
> The API Text Viewer is part of the default Visual Basic installation. To run it, find the entry "API Text Viewer" on your Windows Start menu (its exact location on the menu depends on your Visual Basic installation. Select Open Text File from the File menu, and load WIN32API.TXT. Then in the API Type box select Constants (to view predefined Windows constants), Declares (to view Windows API function declarations), or Types (to view predefined Windows data types). Select an item in the Available Items list and click on Add to put it in the Selected Items list. Once you have all the desired items selected, click on the Copy button to copy the contents of the Selected Items box to the Clipboard. Switch to Visual Basic and paste the items into your code.

Here's the declaration for the **mciSendString** function:

```
Declare Function mciSendString Lib "winmm" Alias "mciSendStringA" _
    (ByVal lpstrCommand As String, ByVal lpstrReturnString As String, _
    ByVal uReturnLength As Long, ByVal hwndCallback As Long) As Long
```

This declaration tells you the following:

- The function is named **mciSendString**.

- It is located in the library named WINMM (a library is a disk file where Windows keeps its functions).

- Its alias (the name it goes under in the library) is mciSendStringA. While this alias is essential for the function declaration, it has no other relevance to your program.

- It takes four arguments—two **Strings** and two **Longs**.

- It returns a type **Long** value.

The declaration must be placed in one of two locations:

- For calling the function only from within one form module, place the declaration in the General Declarations section of the module's code. Remember to place the **Private** keyword at the beginning of the declaration, because **Public** declarations (the default) are not permitted in form modules.

- When calling the function from more than one module, place it in a Basic module that is part of the project.

Now let's look at the function's arguments. The first one, **lpstrCommand**, is a string containing the command that you want to send to the MCI (these are the commands shown previously). The second argument, **lpstrReturnString**, is used by the MCI to return a message to the calling program. Not all commands result in a return message. The third argument, **uReturnLength**, specifies the length of the returned string. The final argument is used to specify a callback function that is executed when the command has completed executing. The function returns zero if it is successful in carrying out the requested action, and a non-zero error code otherwise.

Callback functions are used by some Windows API functions when they need to interact with the calling program. When a program calls an API function that uses a callback, it passes the address of the callback function as an argument to the API function. Callback itself is a regular Visual Basic function that you write, limited only by the requirements of the API function. To get the address of a function, use the **AddressOf** operator. Thus, if your callback function for use with **mciSendString** is named **MyCallBack**, you would call the API function as follows:

```
retval = mciSendString(cmd, reply, 0, AddressOf(MyCallBack)
```

The multimedia tasks in this chapter are relatively simple, however, and do not require the use of a callback function. Later, I'll show you another way to detect when a command has completed. Now for a real example. Once you have declared the function, you play a MIDI file as follows:

```
cmd = "Open " & Chr$(34) & "C:\win95\media\canyon.mid" & Chr$(34) & _
    "type sequencer alias canyon"
retval = mciSendString(cmd, reply, 0, 0)
cmd = "play canyon"
retval = mciSendString(cmd, reply, 0, 0)
' In a real program we would have to wait
' for play to finish before closing the device.
cmd = "close canyon"
retval = mciSendString(cmd, reply, 0, 0)
```

Note how the file name itself is enclosed in double quotes by using **Chr$(34)**. If you executed this code as is—with the **Close** command sent immediately after the **Play** command—you would hear nothing. The device would be closed immediately. You need some way to pause until the playback is complete—whether sound or video. Two methods are available for doing this.

One method uses the **Wait** parameter to the **Play** command. **Wait** instructs the MCI not to accept any other commands, such as **Close**, until the current playback is complete:

```
cmd = "play canyon wait"
retval = mciSendString(cmd, reply, 0, 0)
cmd = "close canyon"
retval = mciSendString(cmd, reply, 0, 0)
```

With this code, the full CANYON.MID file will play. Because the program is frozen during playback, however, the user cannot continue with other tasks. Thus, **Wait** is a good solution for short sounds where a "frozen program" is not a problem. For longer playback, it clearly will not suffice. For this, you can use the **Status** command, which has the following syntax:

```
Status device parameter
```

The *device* argument specifies which device's status we are requesting; this is the name we assigned with the **Alias** keyword when we opened the device. The *parameter* argument specifies the actual status we are requesting. Table 16.3 lists the **Status** parameters commonly needed for sound and video devices.

Here is a method that uses the **Status** command to delay issuing the **Close** command until the music file is finished playing:

```
cmd = "Open " & Chr$(34) & "C:\win95\media\canyon.mid" & Chr$(34) & _
    "type sequencer alias canyon"
retval = mciSendString(cmd, reply, 0, 0)
cmd = "play canyon"
retval = mciSendString(cmd, reply, 0, 0)

' Wait for play to finish before closing.
cmd = "status canyon mode"
do
    retval = mciSendString(cmd, reply, 0, 0)
until reply <> "playing"

cmd = "close canyon"
retval = mciSendString(cmd, reply, 0, 0)
```

Did you notice a problem with this approach? The program is not technically frozen as the sound plays, but it is effectively frozen while it mindlessly executes a loop over and over. We'll see a way to use Visual Basic's Timer control to get around this problem later in the demonstration program. We'll also see how to use a callback function. First, let's look at some of the other MCI commands.

The Seek Command

The **Seek** command repositions the pointer in a device. The pointer indicates the current playing position. **Play** stops when we use **Seek**, and any subsequent **Play** command resumes playing from the new position. The syntax of this command is:

```
Seek to position
```

The most common use for **Seek** is to reset the file pointer to the beginning of the file, which is accomplished by using a value of zero for the *position* argument. If you want to seek to any location other than the beginning, you must specify the *position* argument in the device's current **TimeFormat** (discussed later in the chapter).

Table 16.3   Status parameters for sound and video devices.

Parameter	Meaning
length	Length of the file in frames (video) or samples (sound)
mode	Returns the device's current mode: "not ready", "paused", "playing", "seeking", or "stopped"
position	Current position in the file; sample for sound, frame for video
ready	Returns True if the device is ready
window handle	Returns the handle of the window being used for video playback

The Set Command

Set allows you to control certain aspects of playback, such as individual speakers for sound playback and display of video playback. The syntax is:

```
Set device setting
```

The *device* argument is the alias established for the device when it was opened. The *setting* argument is one of the following, which should be self-explanatory:

- Audio all on (or off)
- Audio left on (or off)
- Audio right on (or off)
- Video on (or off)

The Capability Command

Use the **Capability** command to determine if an opened device has a specified capability. Initiating this command sends a capability name as an argument:

```
Capability CapabilityName
```

In this case, the **mciSendString** function returns True in the **ReturnString** argument if the device has the capability, False if not. Note that these return values are the strings "True" and "False" and not the usual logical values. The most essential capabilities are listed here:

- Can eject
- Can save
- Can play
- Can stretch
- Can record
- Can reverse
- Has audio
- Has video
- Uses files
- Uses palettes

Dealing With Errors

Like all other aspects of programming, the MCI has the potential for errors. A CD not inserted in the drive, a corrupt AVI file, or a malfunctioning sound card are examples of the many situations that can conspire to interfere with smooth multimedia presentations. Errors of this nature are not trappable using Visual Basic's standard error-handling mechanisms (covered in Chapter 25). Even so, a well-designed program must detect multimedia errors and handle them gracefully, reporting needed corrective action to the user whenever possible. Fortunately, the MCI provides the necessary capabilities.

As you may recall, the return value of the **mciSendString** function is zero on success and a non-zero error code if an error occurred. Central to MCI error trapping, then, is checking the return value of **mciSendCommand** every time a command is issued. If the return value is zero, everything is fine. If not...well, to be honest, a numerical error code is not much help. Sure, you could whip out your reference books and look it up, but is there a better way?

Definitely. The better way is the **mciGetErrorString** function. Passing the numerical error code to this API function returns a string that describes the exact nature of the error. Because this is not a Visual Basic function, but rather a part of the Windows API, you must declare it as follows:

```
Declare Function mciGetErrorString Lib "winmm" Alias "mciGetErrorStringA" _
    (ByVal dwError As Long, ByVal lpstrBuffer As String, _
    ByVal uLength As Long) As Long
```

The **dwError** argument is the error code returned by **mciSendString**. The **lpstrBuffer** argument is a string variable where the descriptive error message will be placed. This should be a fixed-length string at least 255 characters long. The final argument, **uLength**, specifies the length of **lpstrBuffer**, in characters. Assuming that the variable **Cmd** contains an MCI command, the code to handle an MCI error would look like this:

```
Dim ErrorMessage As String * 255, ReturnString As String * 255

x = mciSendString(Cmd, ReturnString, 255, 0)
if x <> 0 then
    r = mciGetErrorString(x, ErrorMessage, 255)
    MsgBox(ErrorMessage)
End If
```

Demonstrating The MCI Commands

The project SOUND1 presents a relatively simple demonstration of the multimedia techniques discussed so far. The program displays a blank form with a single menu command, File Open. You can open a video file (*.AVI), a WAV file (*.WAV), or a MIDI sequencer file (*.MID). The program will play it through to the end and close the file. You can then open another file and play it. Despite the program's name, it will play video as well as sound files.

What's unusual about this program is the method used to determine when playback is complete. As mentioned earlier, a well-designed multimedia program will not "freeze" while a command is executing, so we need some way to detect when a command has been completed. One approach is using **mciSendCommand** to send the command

```
status alias mode
```

to the device. The return value argument to the **mciSendString** function will contain a string giving the device's current mode. While the device is playing, the return string will be "playing." By checking the device mode repeatedly, you know it's safe to close the device as soon as the returned value is not "playing." How can you do this?

The answer lies in Visual Basic's Timer control. Set the timer interval, start the timer, and it will repeatedly count down to zero, reset itself to the specified interval, then start counting down again. Each time the Timer counts to zero, its **Timer** event procedure is triggered. Code in this procedure can obtain the MCI device mode and close it once playback is completed.

To specify the Timer control's countdown interval, set its **Interval** property. The unit used is milliseconds, or thousandths of a second. Next, set its **Enabled** property to True to begin timing, and set **Enabled** to False to terminate timing. The Timer control is never visible on screen (except during program design); it just works in the background. You can have more than one Timer control on the same form.

Now let's get to work on the demonstration project. Start with a blank form and add one Timer control and one CommonDialog control, leaving the properties of both at their default settings. Create a File menu with two commands, Open and Exit. The form's objects and properties are given in Listing 16.1. Remember that this type of listing is not code you type in, but rather a shorthand way of listing the types and properties of the controls to be placed on the form.

Listing 16.1   Objects and properties in SOUND1.FRM.

```
Begin VB.Form Form1
   Caption      =   "MCI Demonstration"
   Begin VB.Timer Timer1
   End
   Begin MSComDlg.CommonDialog CommonDialog1
   End
   Begin VB.Menu mnuFile
      Caption     =   "&File"
```

```
        Begin VB.Menu mnuFileOpen
            Caption      =    "&Open"
            Shortcut     =    ^O
        End
        Begin VB.Menu mnuSeparator
            Caption      =    "-"
        End
        Begin VB.Menu mnuFileExit
            Caption      =    "E&xit"
        End
    End
End
```

The program code is presented in Listing 16.2. From what you have learned in the text and the comments in the code, you should be able to figure out how the code works. Remember that you must place the two API function declarations in the General Declarations section of the form's code. You can eliminate typing by copying the declarations from the API text viewer application provided with Visual Basic.

Listing 16.2   Code in SOUND1.FRM.

```
Option Explicit

Private Declare Function mciSendString Lib "winmm" Alias "mciSendStringA" _
    (ByVal lpstrCommand As String, ByVal lpstrReturnString As String, _
    ByVal uReturnLength As Long, ByVal hwndCallback As Long) As Long

Private Declare Function mciGetErrorString Lib "winmm" Alias _
    "mciGetErrorStringA" (ByVal dwError As Long, ByVal lpstrBuffer _
    As String, ByVal uLength As Long) As Long

' Constant for the MCI alias since we'll only
' have one device open at a time.

Const ALIAS = "MyDevice"


Private Sub Form_Load()

' Set up the Open dialog's filter.

CommonDialog1.Filter = _
    "WAVE (*.WAV)|*.wav|MIDI (*.MID)|*.mid|Video (*.AVI)|*.avi"

End Sub


Private Sub Form_Unload(Cancel As Integer)
```

```
Dim cmd As String, ret As String * 255, x As Long

' When the form unloads be sure the device is closed.

cmd = "close " & ALIAS
x = mciSendString(cmd, ret, 255, 0)

End Sub


Private Sub mnuFileExit_Click()

End

End Sub


Private Sub mnuFileOpen_Click()

Dim cmd As String, devicetype As String, ret As String * 255
Dim rv As Long, rv1 As Long

' Display the Open dialog.
CommonDialog1.ShowOpen

' Exit if user canceled.
If CommonDialog1.filename = "" Then Exit Sub

' Get the selected file name extension.
cmd = UCase$(Right$(CommonDialog1.filename, 3))

' Set the "type" argument depending on the
' extension of the file selected.

Select Case cmd
    Case "AVI"
        devicetype = "avivideo"
    Case "MID"
        devicetype = "sequencer"
    Case "WAV"
        devicetype = "waveaudio"
    Case Else
        MsgBox ("Invalid file format")
        Exit Sub
End Select

' Set up the MCI command and send it.
cmd = "open " & Chr$(34) & CommonDialog1.filename & Chr$(34) & _
    " type " & devicetype
cmd = cmd & " alias " & ALIAS
```

```
rv = mciSendString(cmd, ret, 255, 0)

' On error.
If rv <> 0 Then
    rv1 = mciGetErrorString(rv, ret, 255)
    MsgBox ("Error opening device: " & ret)
    Exit Sub
End If

' Send the "play" command.
cmd = "play " & ALIAS
rv = mciSendString(cmd, ret, 255, 0)

If rv <> 0 Then
    rv1 = mciGetErrorString(rv, ret, 255)
    MsgBox ("Error playing device: " & ret)
    Exit Sub
End If

' Play command successful. Enable the timer and set a 1000 msec interval.
' Disable the File menu.
Timer1.Interval = 1000
Timer1.Enabled = True
mnuFile.Enabled = False

End Sub


Private Sub Timer1_Timer()

Dim cmd As String, ret As String * 255, rv As Long

' Each time the timer counts down, check the MCI device to see if it
' is still playing.

' Set up the MCI command and send it.
cmd = "status " & ALIAS & " mode"
rv = mciSendString(cmd, ret, 255, 0)

' If the mode is not "playing" then we are done and can close the device,
' disable the timer, and enable the File menu.
If Left$(ret, 7) <> "playing" Then
    cmd = "close " & ALIAS
    rv = mciSendString(cmd, ret, 255, 0)
    Timer1.Enabled = False
    mnuFile.Enabled = True
End If

End Sub
```

Using The Visual Basic Multimedia Control

The second method for sending MCI commands is Visual Basic's Multimedia control. When displayed on a form, this control provides an array of buttons for controlling a multimedia device. The control is shown in Figure 16.2. The buttons are defined, from left to right, as Prev(ious), Next, Play, Pause, Back, Step, Stop, Record, and Eject.

The first step in using the Multimedia control is to set its **FileName** property or its **DeviceType** property. Set the **FileName** property when the data to be played is in a file that specifies the type of device to be opened—for example, WAV, MIDI, and AVIVideo files. Set the **DeviceType** property when the device does not use files—such as CD Audio—or with a compound device where the associated file's extension does not specify the type of device.

Next, open the device by setting the Multimedia control's **Command** property to **Open**. The control takes care of the details of sending the command to the MCI and obtaining the necessary information about the device. When it comes to actually manipulating the device, you have two choices:

- *Have the control visible on screen* (**Visible** property = True). When the user clicks on the buttons on the control, the appropriate commands are sent to the device.

- *Hide the control* (**Visible** property = False). To execute commands, place them in the control's **Command** property.

Of course, you can use these two methods in tandem. If the control is visible, you can still send commands by placing them in the **Command** property. Likewise, if the control is hidden, it can be made visible if needed.

Much of the appeal of the Multimedia control lies in simplifying tasks that would be more difficult to accomplish by directly accessing the MCI, as shown earlier in this chapter. The control has many properties that correspond to information about the open multimedia device, such as the information accessible with the **Capabilities** command. For example, simply read the Multimedia control's **CanEject** property to determine if the open device can eject its media, and read the **Mode** property to determine the current state of the device. Let's take a closer look at some of these properties (refer to Visual Basic Help for details on all Multimedia control properties).

Figure 16.2 *The Multimedia control.*

Multimedia Control Properties

The **Mode** property returns one of the following values (as a type **Long**), indicating the current mode of the open device as shown in Table 16.4.

The **CanEject, CanPlay, CanStep,** and **CanRecord** properties return True or False, depending on whether the open device has the indicated capability.

The **AutoEnable** property determines if the individual buttons on the Multimedia control are automatically enabled and disabled to reflect the capabilities of the open device (**AutoEnable** = True), or whether the program must enable and disable individual buttons by setting the corresponding **ButtonEnabled** property (**AutoEnable** = False), where **Button** is either Back, Eject, Next, Pause, Play, Prev, Record, Step, or Stop.

The **Enabled** property controls user access to the entire Multimedia control. If **Enabled** is set to False, the user cannot select any of the control's buttons.

The **Command** property mentioned earlier sends commands to an MCI device. Set the Multimedia control's **Command** property to a valid MCI command string, and the command is sent to the open MCI device associated with the control. The valid commands are **Open, Close, Play, Pause, Stop, Back, Step, Prev, Next, Seek, Record, Eject, Sound,** or **Save**. The command is executed immediately, and the error code is stored in the **Error** property.

The **TimeFormat** property sets the format that the device uses to measure time. Several different time formats are available; the Visual Basic Help system offers detailed information. Knowing the current time format is essential, because the **From, To, Length, TrackLength, Position, TrackPosition,** and **Start** properties all use the current time format. Each type of device has a default time format that can be changed if desired. Note, however, that certain devices do not support all the available time formats. If you attempt to set the **TimeFormat** property to an unsupported value, the setting is ignored and the old

Table 16.4   Mode property values.

Value	Constant	Meaning
524	mciNotOpen	Device is not open.
525	mciStop	Device is stopped.
526	mciPlay	Device is playing.
527	mciRecord	Device is recording.
528	mciSeek	Device is seeking.
529	mciPause	Device is paused.
530	mciReady	Device is ready.

Table 16.5 Default time format settings for common devices.

Constant	Value	Default	Description
mciFormatMilliseconds	0	WAV and MIDI	Time is expressed in milliseconds.
mciFormatMfs	2	CDAudio	Minutes, seconds, and frames are packed into a four-byte type **Long**. The least significant byte holds the minutes value, the next byte holds seconds, the next byte holds frames, and the most significant byte is not used.
mciFormatFrames	3	AVI (digital video)	Time is expressed in frames.

setting is retained. The default time format settings for the most common devices are shown in Table 16.5.

Upon examining Table 16.5, you may wonder why the time format used for CDAudio includes frames. If you insert an audio CD in your CD-ROM drive and open the device, the Multimedia control returns the **TimeFormat** value. I don't see what use the Frame value plays in this format, but we can't argue with Microsoft.

The **Orientation** property determines whether the Multimedia control is displayed horizontally (the default) or vertically. Set this property to the constant **mciOrientHorz** (value = 0) for a horizontal control, or to **mciOrientVert** (value = 1) for a vertical control.

The **Wait** property works just like the **Wait** argument in a command sent directly to the MCI. Set **Wait** to True to have execution return to your program only after the MCI has completed the current operation. If **Wait** is False (the default), execution returns immediately.

Multimedia Control Events

The Multimedia control supports only eight events. Two of these—**DragOver** and **DragDrop**—operate the same as events of the same name associated with many other Visual Basic controls. The other six events are unique to the Multimedia control. Some of these events enhance the usefulness of the Multimedia control, allowing us to do things that would not be possible by sending commands directly to the MCI.

Four of the events are related to the individual buttons on the control. Each of the buttons—Back, Eject, Next, Pause, Play, Prev, Record, Step, and Stop—has its own discrete event procedures. They are as follows:

The **ButtonClick** event occurs when the button is clicked. The default is for each button, when clicked, to send the corresponding command to the MCI. These commands are shown in Table 16.6.

You can specify additional code to be executed with (or instead of) the button's command when it is clicked on. The skeleton of each button click procedure looks like this:

```
Sub MMControl_ButtonClick (Cancel As Integer)

End Sub
```

MMControl is the name of the Multimedia control, and **Button** is the name of the button (Back, Eject, and so on). When the button is clicked, code placed in the event procedure is executed. If the **Cancel** argument is left at its default value of False, the button's command is sent to the MCI after the code in the procedure is executed. If **Cancel** is set to True, the command is not sent (but the code in the procedure is still executed). It's easy to see how flexible this arrangement can be: When a button is clicked on, you can execute your own code, the default command, or both.

The **ButtonGotFocus** event procedure executes when the button receives the focus, and the **ButtonLostFocus** procedure executes when the button loses the focus. No special features are attached to these event procedures.

The **ButtonCompleted** event is triggered when the MCI operation started by a Multimedia control button click is complete. For example, if the user clicks on the Play button, the **PlayCompleted** event procedure will be executed when the play is completed. The **ButtonCompleted** event procedure looks like this:

```
Sub MMControl_ButtonCompleted (Errorcode As Long)

End Sub
```

Table 16.6 MCI button commands.

Button	Command Sent To MCI
Back	MCI_STEP
Step	MCI_STEP
Play	MCI_PLAY
Pause	MCI_PAUSE
Prev	MCI_SEEK
Next	MCI_SEEK
Stop	MCI_STOP
Record	MCI_RECORD
Eject	MCI_SET with the MCI_SET_DOOR_OPEN parameter

The **Errorcode** argument will be zero if the operation completed without an error. It will be set to a non-zero value if the operation did not complete successfully. When an error is detected, you can use the **Error** and **ErrorMessage** properties (discussed soon) to determine the nature of the error.

The **Done** event procedure is executed when an MCI command finishes executing. This event procedure is not automatically executed, but rather, is controlled by the Multimedia control's **Notify** property. **Notify** is normally False, which means that the **Done** event will not be triggered. If you set **Notify** to True, however, the **Done** event will be triggered at the completion of the next MCI command executed. This is true both for MCI commands that result from clicking on one of the control buttons and for commands executed by means of the control's **Command** property.

The **Done** event procedure is passed a type **Integer** argument named **NotifyCode**. The value in this argument indicates the result of the MCI operation that just completed. This value is the same as that in the **NotifyValue** property, as shown in Table 16.7.

Remember that setting **Notify** to True affects only the next MCI command to be issued—not any subsequent commands or the command currently being executed (if any). You must set **Notify** to True before each and every MCI command for which you want the **Done** event procedure triggered.

Perhaps you have already seen how the **Done** event and the **ButtonCompleted** event make it possible for us to detect when the command has completed executing—something done with a callback function when sending commands directly to the MCI. By knowing when the play operation is complete, you can close the device or perform whatever other actions you need to take.

The **StatusUpdate** event occurs each time the Multimedia control checks the status of the device associated with it. The interval at which this checking occurs is specified by the **UpdateInterval** property. The default value of 1,000 milliseconds results in status checks every second. Code in the **StatusUpdate** event procedure can be used to provide the user with information about the current operation, obtained from Multimedia control properties, such as **Mode**, **Length**, and **Position**.

Table 16.7   Values for the Done event procedure.

Value	Constant	Result
1	mciSuccessful	Command completed successfully
2	mciSuperseded	Command was superseded by another command
4	mciAborted	Command was aborted by the user
8	mciFailure	Command failed

Handling Multimedia Control Errors

As mentioned earlier, using the Multimedia control has the potential for errors. A well-designed program must detect multimedia errors and handle them gracefully, reporting needed corrective action to the user when possible. Fortunately, the Multimedia control provides you with the necessary capabilities:

- Most important are the **Error** and **ErrorMessage** properties. The **Error** property contains the error code returned by the last MCI command, and the **ErrorMessage** property provides a string description of the error. When everything works okay, the error code is zero, and the string in **ErrorMessage** is "The specified command was carried out." You can check these properties in the **StatusUpdate** event procedure to keep a constant eye on the progress of the MCI command.

- The second tool for dealing with errors is the **NotifyCode** argument passed to the **Done** event procedure. If this argument is equal to **mciFailure** (value = 8), the command failed, and we can look in the **Error** and **ErrorMessage** properties for details.

- The third tool is the **ErrorCode** argument passed to the **ButtonCompleted** event procedures. If **ErrorCode** is not zero, an error occurred. Once again, check the **Error** and **ErrorMessage** properties for details on the error.

A Multimedia Control Demonstration

Now that we have explored the more important details of the Multimedia control, let's see just how easy it is to use. The project SOUND2 uses the Multimedia control to implement a simple media player. You can open a media file (MIDI, WAV, or AVI) or the CD Audio device (assuming an audio CD is in the drive). Then you can use the Multimedia control's buttons to play the device. There's no error handling in the program—a feature you might want to add. In fact, you could add any number of enhancements to the program. The Multimedia control has enough power to serve as the heart of a full-featured media player. A good project to tackle on your own would be modifying this program so that the Multimedia control is hidden, but still used as the program's interface to the MCI.

The program, shown operating in Figure 16.3, has a single form with two controls: Multimedia and CommonDialog. There's also a File menu with three commands: Open, Play CD, and Exit. The form's objects and properties are shown in Listing 16.3 and its code in Listing 16.4.

Figure 16.3 *The SOUND2 media player.*

Listing 16.3 Objects and properties in SOUND2.FRM.

```
Begin VB.Form Form1
    Caption         =   "Multimedia Player"
    Begin MSComDlg.CommonDialog CommonDialog1
    End
    Begin MCI.MMControl MMControl1
    End
    Begin VB.Menu mnuFile
        Caption         =   "&File"
        Begin VB.Menu mnuFileOpen
            Caption         =   "&Open"
        End
        Begin VB.Menu mnuFilePlayCD
            Caption         =   "&Play CD"
        End
        Begin VB.Menu mnuSeparator
            Caption         =   "-"
        End
        Begin VB.Menu mnuFileExit
            Caption         =   "E&xit"
        End
    End
End
```

Listing 16.4 Code in SOUND2.FRM.

```
Option Explicit

Const mciPause = 529
Dim DeviceOpen As Boolean

Private Sub Form_Load()

Dim x As Integer, y As Integer

' Initialize flag.
DeviceOpen = False

' Set form size and control position.
x = Form1.Width - Form1.ScaleWidth
y = Form1.Height - Form1.ScaleHeight

Form1.Width = MMControl1.Width + x
Form1.Height = MMControl1.Height + y

MMControl1.Left = 0
MMControl1.Top = 0

CommonDialog1.Filter = "Wave (*.WAV)|*.wav|MIDI (*.MID)|*.mid|Video
(*.AVI)|*.avi"
```

```
End Sub

Private Sub Form_Unload(Cancel As Integer)

' Close the device.

MMControl1.Command = "Close"

End Sub

Private Sub MMControl1_Done(NotifyCode As Integer)

' Enable the File menu.
mnuFile.Enabled = True

End Sub

Private Sub MMControl1_PlayClick(Cancel As Integer)

' Set Notify so the Done event will be triggered.
MMControl1.Notify = True
' Disable the menu while play is in progress.
mnuFile.Enabled = False

End Sub

Private Sub MMControl1_StopClick(Cancel As Integer)

' Enable the menu.
mnuFile.Enabled = True

End Sub

Private Sub mnuFileExit_Click()

End

End Sub

Private Sub mnuFileOpen_Click()

' If the device is open, close it.
If DeviceOpen Then
    MMControl1.Command = "Close"
    DeviceOpen = False
End If

' Show the Open dialog.
CommonDialog1.ShowOpen
```

```
' If user cancels, exit sub.
If CommonDialog1.FileName = "" Then Exit Sub

' Set MM control properties.
MMControl1.FileName = CommonDialog1.FileName
MMControl1.DeviceType = ""
MMControl1.Command = "Open"
DeviceOpen = True

End Sub

Private Sub mnyFilePlayCD_Click()

' Open the CD Audio device. The CD should already be
' inserted in the drive.
MMControl1.DeviceType = "CDAudio"
MMControl1.Command = "Open"
DeviceOpen = True

End Sub
```

PART 4

Programming For The Internet

Chapter 17

ActiveX Controls

With Visual Basic you can create your own ActiveX controls—software components you can use in program development and on the Web.

ActiveX is one of the most heavily hyped terms in history—and with the Microsoft juggernaut behind it, you can bet that is some serious hyping. Despite all the hoopla, ActiveX is indeed an important and powerful technology, and if you use or program for Windows, it is something you need to know about. You learned how to create one type of ActiveX component in Chapter 8. In this chapter, we will cover another type, the ActiveX control.

First, you should know that, popular perception to the contrary, ActiveX has nothing specifically to do with the Internet or the World Wide Web. It can be used on the Web (as I'll explain later in the chapter), but that is not the only thing—or even the most important thing—for which ActiveX is designed. Confused? There's good reason if you are. Let me explain.

For a number of years, Microsoft's technology for software components—sharing of capabilities between chunks of software—was called Object Linking and Embedding (OLE). When the Web began heating up a couple of years ago, the Java language was introduced and attracted a lot of attention because of its capability for creating applets that could be interactively downloaded from the Web. The enormous surge of interest in Java made it clear to Microsoft that it had better join the parade before it missed out on the next big thing.

The response from Microsoft was something called ActiveX. In its first incarnation, ActiveX referred to software components that were created using OLE technology and designed specifically for use over the Web. If you first heard about ActiveX at that time, you would naturally assume that ActiveX and the Web are closely linked. But, as we all know, things change.

I can't tell you why, but I do know that over the past year or so, the term *ActiveX* has slowly grown to encompass everything that used to fall under the term *OLE*. In other words, ActiveX no longer refers to Web-specific tools, but to a wide range of technologies for sharing software capabilities. You saw some uses of ActiveX in Chapter 8, where I developed an ActiveX server that exposed certain software objects for use by clients on the same system. That is just one of many ways that a Visual Basic programmer can use ActiveX technology.

ActiveX Controls

An ActiveX control is the same as a standard Visual Basic control in that it provides a prepackaged, reusable software component. Many of Visual Basic's intrinsic controls are, in fact, ActiveX controls (a few use the older technology called OCX controls). ActiveX controls usually provide some sort of visual interface element, but this is not a strict requirement.

An ActiveX control is unique in its ability to be contained within something else. A familiar example is a control contained within a Visual Basic form. ActiveX controls are not limited to Visual Basic, however. More and more Windows development tools support ActiveX; some well-known examples are Delphi, Visual C++, and PowerBuilder. Although these tools differ from Visual Basic in many respects, they share the ability to drop ActiveX controls onto a form, providing all of the control's functionality, with little or no programming.

Of course, as a programmer, you need to be able to create ActiveX controls, not just use them. Using ActiveX controls is not a major challenge: From the Visual Basic programmer's perspective, they closely resemble non-ActiveX controls. In both cases, the control appears in the Visual Basic toolbox; it has properties, methods, events, and so on. For example, the Check Box control is an "old-fashioned" OCX control, while the TreeView control is an ActiveX control. ActiveX controls do have capabilities not found in the older OCX controls, but these features are not immediately obvious.

Creating an ActiveX control is a relatively simple task in Visual Basic. For the most part, the procedure is the same as creating a standard Visual Basic executable. You start with a form, place controls on it (including other ActiveX controls), and then write code to define properties and methods and to deal with events. When you compile the project to an OCX file, Visual Basic takes care of all the details. And yes, ActiveX controls are saved in files with an .OCX extension, just as the older OCX controls. The Windows registry makes information about the capabilities of a given OCX file available to potential container programs.

An ActiveX control does not have to contain other controls. You can draw the control using Visual Basic's various graphics methods, such as **Line** and **Circle** (as covered in Chapter 12).

Creating An ActiveX Control

In this section, I will take you through the process of creating, testing, and using an ActiveX control. The control will be relatively simple, as my goal is to present the procedures that are specific for creating ActiveX controls. What goes *in* the control does not differ from "regular" Visual Basic programming. In other words, the functionality of an ActiveX control is created in essentially the same way as the functionality of a standard Visual Basic executable—you place controls on a form, write event procedures, manipulate properties, and so on. You'll also find some elements in common with creating other ActiveX objects (as you learned in Chapter 8), specifically the use of property procedures to define properties for your object (in this case, the control you are creating).

What will the demonstration control do? Its name, FancyCmdButton, describes it well. It will serve the same function as a regular Visual Basic Command Button, which the user can click on to trigger an action. It will have a slightly more appealing appearance: a colored background that changes to indicate that it has been clicked. Most ActiveX controls are significantly more complicated than this. However, our example is ideal for demonstrating the major parts of creating and testing an ActiveX control.

Many of the procedures involved in creating our ActiveX control could be performed using the Class Builder utility you learned about in Chapter 6. I am going to work through each step without using the utility, because it will be a better way for you to learn the nuts and bolts of creating an ActiveX control. Once you understand the procedure, then you can use the Class Builder utility for your future projects to save time and effort.

Start by firing up Visual Basic and selecting New Project from the File menu. Select ActiveX Control from the available project types. Visual Basic starts the new project and adds a UserControl designer to it. (A UserControl object is the foundation of all ActiveX controls you create in Visual Basic.) Your screen will look like Figure 17.1.

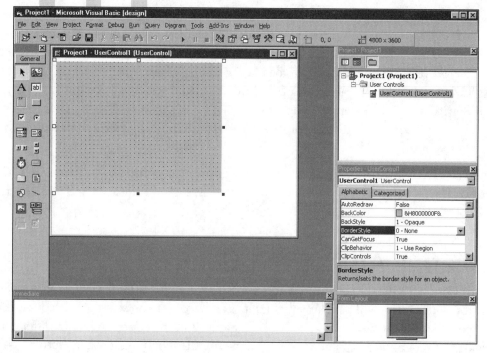

Figure 17.1 *The Visual Basic screen after starting a new ActiveX control project.*

You should note the following elements:

- The UserControl Designer window displays the default project name (Project1) and control name (UserControl1) in its title bar. This will change once we assign meaningful names to the project and control.

- The gray rectangle in the window represents the new control. It is similar to a standard Visual Basic form in some respects, but it does not have a border or title bar (although you can add a border).

- The Form Layout window does not show the control. The control's display position is determined by its container, not by any properties you set during design.

The next step is to set some of the project properties. Select Project1 Properties from the Project menu to display the Project Properties dialog box (shown in Figure 17.2). Display the General tab, make the following entries, then close the dialog box:

- *Project name*—AXCTRLDEMO is the name that will be assigned to the final compiled OCX file.

- *Project description*—Fancy Command Button is the description users will see when they use the OCX control in other projects.

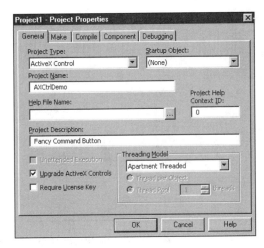

Figure 17.2 *The Project Properties dialog box.*

Next, you need to change the **Name** property of the control itself. Be sure that the control is selected in the Designer window, as indicated by handles around its periphery. In the Properties window, find the **Name** property and change it to FancyCmdButton. This name will now appear in the designer's title bar.

Now is a good time to save the project. Select Save Project from the File menu, saving both the control and the project under the default names that Visual Basic suggests: FANCYCMDBUTTON.CTL and AXCTRLDEMO.VBP.

Although the basic framework of the control is in place, it still doesn't do anything. To add functionality, start by placing a Shape control in the upper left corner of the control. Set its properties as shown in Table 17.1.

Next, add a Label control on top of the Shape control, setting its properties as shown in Table 17.2. Then, reduce the size of the UserControl. The exact size is not crucial—just keep it fairly small. At this stage, your screen will look like Figure 17.3.

Table 17.1 *Shape control property settings.*

Property Name	Setting
BorderStyle	0 — Transparent
FillColor	&H0000FF00& (or any light green)
FillStyle	0 — Solid
Shape	4 — Rounded Rectangle
Name	shpButton

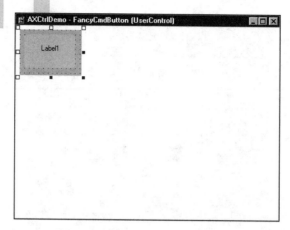

Figure 17.3 *The FancyCmdButton ActiveX control after adding Shape and Label controls.*

Table 17.2 Label control property settings.

Property Name	Setting
BackStyle	0 — Transparent
Name	lblButton
ForeColor	Black
Alignment	2 — Center

The FancyCmdButton control now has all of the subcomponents (other controls) it needs, but that's not enough, of course. What will it do? How will it appear? Now we need to add the code that will bring our ActiveX control to life.

Our first concern is its appearance. When displayed within a container, we want the Shape control to fill the entire area of the ActiveX control; we also want the Label to be the same width as the Shape control and to be centered vertically. The code to perform these actions should be placed within the UserControl's **Resize** event procedure. Display the Code Editing window in the usual manner, then select UserControl in the object list at the top of the window. Finally, select Resize in the Procedure list. Add the code in Listing 17.1 to this event procedure.

Listing 17.1 The UserControl's Resize event procedure.

```
Private Sub UserControl_Resize()

' Change the position and size of the Shape control
' to fill the FancyCmdButton control's entire area.
shpButton.Move 0, 0, ScaleWidth, ScaleHeight
' Make the Label control the same width as the Shape
```

```
' control and center it vertically.
lblButton.Move 0, (ScaleHeight - lblButton.Height) / 2, ScaleWidth

End Sub
```

Testing The ActiveX Control

The control is not finished, but it is ready to be tested. How do you test an ActiveX control that you are developing? An ActiveX control cannot run by itself; it needs a container. You have two choices:

- *You can use Microsoft Internet Explorer or another ActiveX-capable browser as the test container.* After all, one important use for ActiveX controls is on Web pages, so in some situations testing your control in a browser is perfectly appropriate. If you have not created a separate test project (as described later), and the ActiveX control project is the only one loaded into the Visual Basic environment, then "running" the project will start Internet Explorer and display an instance of the ActiveX control. The control must be compiled first, as described later in the section titled "Compiling the ActiveX Control." You can try out the control's capabilities, as well as modify the associated HTML file if you want to test the control in combination with some scripting language elements. These procedures are beyond the scope of this book, although I will touch on them later in the chapter when I cover using ActiveX controls on the Web.

- *You can create a separate Visual Basic project to test the control.* This is the preferred testing method, because it provides greater flexibility. Creating a test project is our next topic.

Creating The Test Project

To test an ActiveX control, you need a separate Visual Basic project with a form on which you can place an instance of the control. Rather than starting a separate copy of Visual Basic, you can use one of Visual Basic's handier features: You can define a *project group* that contains two or more independent projects. In this case, the ActiveX control will be one project, and the second project will be a standard Visual Basic executable to test the ActiveX control.

To create a project group, select Add Project... from the File menu, then select Standard EXE as the project type. You'll now have two designers open: one for the ActiveX control project and one for the Standard EXE project you just created. Both projects will be listed in the Project window, as shown in Figure 17.4. Next, save the project group by selecting Save Project Group from the File menu. Use the file names given here (the extensions are added automatically by Visual Basic):

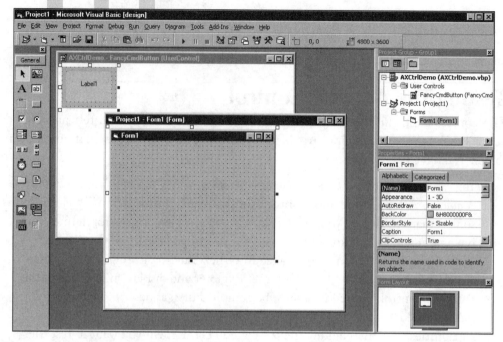

Figure 17.4 *A Visual Basic project group can contain two or more independent projects.*

- *Form*—TestAXCtl_Form1.frm

- *Project*—TextAXCtl.vbp

- *Project group*—TestAXCtl.vbg

Running The ActiveX Control At Design Time

You may think that the heading of this section makes no sense; didn't I just say that an ActiveX control cannot run by itself? Yes, but now I am using *run* in a different sense. An ActiveX control does not run in the same sense as a standard Visual Basic executable. When an ActiveX control "runs," it makes itself available only for insertion into other projects. This is exactly what we want: to run the ActiveX control, so it becomes available to insert onto the test project's form, while the test project remains in design mode. This is precisely what Visual Basic's project groups are intended for.

The way it works is simple. Begin by closing the ActiveX control's designer by clicking on the close button (the X) in its title bar. This puts the ActiveX control into run mode. The only sign of your ActiveX control now is the UserControl icon on the Toolbox (it is labeled in Figure 17.5). Next, make the test project's form active and double-click on the UserControl icon to place an instance of it on the form, as shown in Figure 17.5.

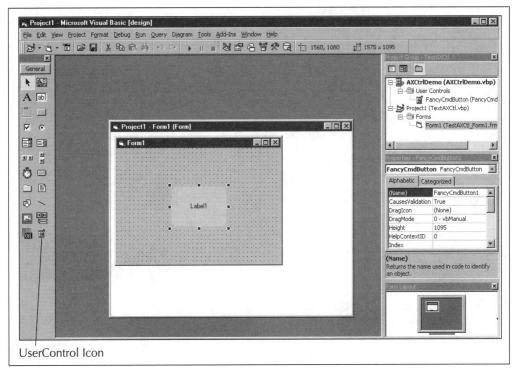

UserControl Icon

Figure 17.5   *The test project form after placing an instance of the UserControl on it.*

Look in the Properties window: The new control instance has been given a default name, FancyCmdButton1, and it has its own set of properties. Change the **Name** property to FCB1 (for the sake of brevity). To take the ActiveX control out of run mode and back into design mode, double-click on its name in the Project window. When the ActiveX control designer opens up again, you'll see that the instance of the control on the test project form becomes hatched, indicating that the control is no longer active. This is shown in Figure 17.6.

ActiveX Control Events

You'll discover one difference between ActiveX controls and standard executable programs: An ActiveX control has a defined behavior not only at execution (when it is executing within its container) but also at design time. To illustrate this, open the UserControl's **Resize** procedure and add the following line to the existing code:

```
Debug.Print "Resize event"
```

Close the ActiveX control designer to run the ActiveX control. On the test project form, change the size of the FancyCmdButton control. You'll see by the messages displayed in

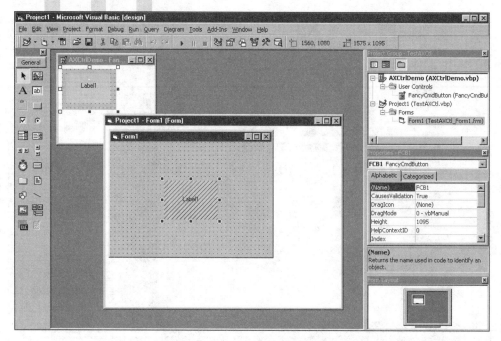

Figure 17.6 *When the ActiveX control is placed back in design mode, the instance on the test project form displays a hatch pattern.*

the Immediate window that its **Resize** event procedure fires each time you resize the control, even though the test project is still in design mode. If you add a second instance of the FancyCmdButton control to the form, you'll see that the **Resize** event fires then, too. Delete the second control—if you placed one—before continuing.

Now let's take a look at some of the other events that occur during the life of an ActiveX control. When working with these events, you must understand the ephemeral nature of an ActiveX control. You may think that once an ActiveX control is placed on a form, that's it; the control is created and continues to exist as a component of the form from then on. Things are not so simple.

When you place an ActiveX control on a Visual Basic form during program design, an instance of the control is created in memory. When you run the program, that instance is destroyed and a new runtime instance is created; it is this instance that will be in operation as the program executes. When you terminate the program to return to design mode, the runtime instance of the control is destroyed, and yet another instance is created and displayed on the form in the Visual Basic designer. As you can see, rather than having a single instance of the control remaining, three have actually been created and destroyed.

Here's another situation. Suppose you have designed an ActiveX control in Visual Basic and created a test form. When you close the ActiveX designer and place an instance of the control on the test form, you create an instance (as described in the previous paragraph). If you then reopen the ActiveX designer, so that the control on the test form is displayed with hatching, the control instance is destroyed. When you close the ActiveX designer, a new instance of the control is created (and the control on the test form is displayed without hatching).

If you place two or more instances of a control on a form, each instance undergoes its own creation-destruction-creation cycle.

It's pretty complicated, isn't it? You'll feel more comfortable with it after a while, particularly after I present some programming techniques later in this chapter that assist you in keeping track of the creation and destruction of control instances. For now, what you should remember is that an ActiveX control has certain events that are triggered in response to control creation and destruction. Some of these events have to do with the control's properties—a topic we'll be covering. For now, let's just look at the events without worrying about the details:

- *Initialize*—Occurs each and every time an instance of the control is created. It is always the first event that occurs for the control.

- *InitProperties*—Occurs only when the control is placed on a form—in other words, the first time an instance is created. You can use this event procedure to set a control's initial values.

- *ReadProperties*—Occurs the second and subsequent times an instance of a control is created. In other words, this event occurs every time a control instance is created *except* the first time (when **InitProperties** occurs instead).

- *Resize*—Occurs every time a control instance is created and every time its size is changed, either by the programmer in design mode or by code during program execution.

- *Paint*—Occurs whenever the control's container tells the control to redraw itself. If you are creating your control's visual appearance with drawing methods, the code should go in this event procedure.

- *WriteProperties*—Occurs during design time when an instance of the control is destroyed and at least one of its properties has been changed.

- *Terminate*—The last event to occur when a control instance is destroyed.

To get a handle on when these various control events occur, you can use the same technique that you used earlier for the **Resize** event procedure: Place a **Debug.Print** statement in each event procedure to print the appropriate message to the Immediate window. The code is shown in Listing 17.2. With this code in your ActiveX project, you can trace events as they occur during the lifetime of your ActiveX control.

Listing 17.2   Using the Debug.Print statement to track the occurrence of events.

```
Private Sub UserControl_Initialize()
    Debug.Print "Initialize event"
End Sub

Private Sub UserControl_InitProperties()
    Debug.Print "InitProperties event"
End Sub

Private Sub UserControl_Paint()
    Debug.Print "Paint event"
End Sub

Private Sub UserControl_ReadProperties(PropBag As PropertyBag)
    Debug.Print "ReadProperties event"
End Sub

Private Sub UserControl_Terminate()
    Debug.Print "Terminate event"
End Sub

Private Sub UserControl_WriteProperties(PropBag As PropertyBag)
    Debug.Print "WriteProperties event"
End Sub
```

Responding To Events

When dealing with ActiveX controls, you have to consider events occurring at three levels:

- The constituent controls used to create the ActiveX control, such as the Shape and Label controls in the demonstration project, may need to respond to events.

- The ActiveX control may need to respond internally to events, such as the user clicking on the control.

- The container object may need to respond to events that occur to the ActiveX control.

If you think about this for a moment, you can see that events may need to be "passed along" from one object to another. For example, if the user clicks on the Label control in the demonstration ActiveX control—and you want the container object to be able to respond—pass the event "up" to the container. This is accomplished using Visual Basic's **RaiseEvent** statement. The syntax is as follows:

```
RaiseEvent EventName [(ArgList)]
```

EventName is the name of the event to fire, and **ArgList** is an optional list of arguments. Before you can use **RaiseEvent**, you must declare an event procedure for the event you will raise. This declaration must be at the module level of the module in which the event will be raised; it takes the following form:

```
[Public] Event EventName [(ArgList)]
```

EventName and **ArgList** are, respectively, the name of the event and an optional argument list. Include the optional **Public** keyword if the event needs to be detected by another module; otherwise, it will be available only within the module where it is raised. When the event is raised, the argument list used in the **RaiseEvent** statement must match the list in the event procedure declaration.

What events are available? The usual repertoire of Visual Basic events is at your disposal, such as **Click** and **MouseDown**. Without **RaiseEvent**, the control would be able to use events internally, but if you want the container to be able to respond to events, you will have to raise them.

Before we write the event code for the FancyCmdButton control, let's think for a moment about what it needs to do:

- When the user presses the mouse button when the pointer is on the control, the control's background color should change.

- When the user releases the mouse button, the background color should change back, and a **Click** event should be raised, so the container object can respond to it.

For the first task, we will use the **MouseDown** event. But where will this event be detected? The ActiveX control consists of both a Label control and a Shape control, plus the underlying UserControl. Clearly, the Label control must respond to **MouseDown**. Shape controls do not detect mouse events, so mouse action on our Shape control will be automatically passed through to the underlying UserControl. Thus, the UserControl's **MouseDown** event procedure will also be used.

In figuring out how to handle the first task, we learn how to do the second, as well. We will use the **MouseUp** event procedure of the Label control and UserControl.

Start by opening the Code window for the FancyCmdButton control. Select General in the Object list and Declarations in the Procedure box, then add the code shown in Listing 17.3. This code declares a variable and a constant for manipulating the control's color and declares the **Click** event procedure, so that we can use the **RaiseEvent** statement.

Listing 17.3   Code in the General Declarations section of the ActiveX control module.

```
Option Explicit

' Variable for the old color.
Dim OldColor As Long

' Constant for the "clicked" color (this is red).
Const NEWCOLOR = &HFF&

' Declare a Public Click event procedure.
Public Event Click()
```

The next code must be added to the **MouseDown** and **MouseUp** event procedures of the Label and FancyCmdButton. In the Code Editing window, use the Object and Procedure lists to select these procedures, then add the code shown in Listing 17.4. This listing combines the code for the two **MouseDown** and two **MouseUp** event procedures.

Listing 17.4   The MouseDown and MouseUp event procedures for the FancyCmdButton and the Label control.

```
Private Sub lblButton_MouseDown(Button As Integer, Shift As Integer, X As
Single, Y As Single)

'Save the original fill color.
OldColor = shpButton.FillColor
' Change to the "clicked" fill color.
shpButton.FillColor = NEWCOLOR

End Sub

Private Sub lblButton_MouseUp(Button As Integer, Shift As Integer, X As
Single, Y As Single)

' Restore the original fill color.
shpButton.FillColor = OldColor
' Raise the click event.
RaiseEvent Click
```

```
End Sub

Private Sub UserControl_MouseDown(Button As Integer, Shift As Integer, X As
Single, Y As Single)

' Save the old fill color.
OldColor = shpButton.FillColor
' Change to the "clicked" fill color.
shpButton.FillColor = NEWCOLOR

End Sub

Private Sub UserControl_MouseUp(Button As Integer, Shift As Integer, X As
Single, Y As Single)

' Restore the original fill color.
shpButton.FillColor = OldColor

' Raise a Click event.
RaiseEvent Click

End Sub
```

This completes the code required to have our FancyCmdButton control respond to user clicks by changing its background color and raising a click for its container to respond to. The next task is to add the code to the test project, enabling it to respond to that event. Close the UserControl, and display the Code window for the test project form (TestAXCtl_Form1). Add the single line of code in Listing 17.5 to the form's **Click** event procedure.

Listing 17.5   *The container form's Click event procedure.*

```
Private Sub FCB1_Click()

MsgBox ("I've been clicked")

End Sub
```

The project is now ready to take for a spin. Be sure that the FancyCmdButton designer is closed, as indicated by the control on the test form displayed without hatch marks. Also, be sure that the test project is the startup project, as indicated by its name displayed in bold in the Project Explorer window. If it is not, right-click on the project name and select Set As Startup from the pop-up menu. Then, press F5 to run the test project. You'll see its form displayed, as shown in Figure 17.7. When you position the mouse pointer over the control and press the mouse button, you'll see the button's background color change to red. When you release the mouse button, the color changes back to green and a message appears indicating that the form has detected the click.

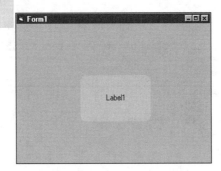

Figure 17.7 *Testing the FancyCmdButton control.*

ActiveX Testing Options

Even if you have created a test project for your ActiveX control, you have the option of testing the control in the Internet Explorer Web browser. If the test project is set as the startup project, the control will run in your test project. If you make the ActiveX control project the startup, then the control will run in Internet Explorer.

Before we continue adding to the demonstration control, think for a moment about what happens when you execute the test program and click on the FancyCmdButton control. The **MouseDown** and **MouseUp** events are detected by the ActiveX control itself, which responds by changing its background color. In addition, a **Click** event is raised, and that event is detected by the container—the test program. In response to that event, a message box is displayed.

Adding Properties To The Control

Properties are added to an ActiveX control in the same manner as for any other ActiveX object, as you learned in Chapter 6. To define a property, you create property procedures. The **Get** procedure makes the property available for reading, and the **Let** procedure is used to set the property value. To define a read-only property, you can create a **Get** procedure without a corresponding **Let**. (Please turn back to Chapters 7 and 8 if you need a refresher on property procedures.)

We will create a single property for the FancyCmdButton. It will be called **Caption**, and it will determine the text that is displayed on the control. Because the value will be stored in the Label control's **Caption** property, we do not need to declare a separate variable to hold it.

Here are the steps to follow:

1. Open the FancyCmdButton designer, and then open its Code window.

2. Select Add Procedure from the Tools menu to display the Insert Procedure dialog box.

3. Specify the procedure name **Caption**, and select the Property and Public options. Then click on OK.

4. Visual Basic will create skeletons of the **Let** and **Get** procedures for you, displaying them in the Code Editing window. Add the code shown in Listing 17.6. Be sure to change the type of the **Get** procedure from **Variant** to **String**. Make the same change for the type of the argument to the **Let** procedure. Remember that the **Get** procedure's return type must be the same as the type of the **Let** procedure's argument.

Listing 17.6   *Get and Let procedures for the Caption property.*

```
Public Property Get Caption() As String
    Caption = lblButton.Caption
End Property

Public Property Let Caption(ByVal vNewValue As String)
    lblButton.Caption = vNewValue
End Property
```

Once you have added this code, close the ActiveX designer to put the FancyButtonControl in run mode. Display the test form with the FancyCmdButton on it and click on the button to select it. Look in the Properties window (refer to Figure 17.8), and you'll see that the control's property list now includes a **Caption** property—the one you just defined—in addition to the UserControl's default properties. If you change this property during design, the text you specify will be displayed on the FancyCmdButton when the test project runs. You could also set the property in code. To try this out, place the following line of code in the test project's **Form_Load** procedure:

```
FCB1.Caption = "Click Me"
```

You'll see that the button displays "Click Me" when the program runs.

Figure 17.8   *ActiveX control properties that you define are listed in the Visual Basic Properties window along with the default properties.*

Adding A Property Page To The Control

You have already seen that the ActiveX control properties you define are automatically displayed in the Visual Basic Properties window. You also have the option of connecting a *property page* to the control. A property page is simply a different method of displaying and accessing the control's properties. Each property page you define will become a separate tab in the object's Properties dialog box. You must design the page, which is done in much the same way as designing a Visual Basic form. Visual Basic takes care of all the details of displaying the tabs, and managing the OK, Cancel, and Apply buttons.

Property pages are useful when several properties interact in a complex fashion. You can design the property page so that related properties are grouped together, making it easier for the user to set them properly. Property pages are useful for controls that you plan to distribute internationally, because the captions on the property page can easily be changed to suit different language requirements. Finally, property pages permit controls to be used with development tools that don't have Properties windows.

To add a property page to the FancyCmdButton, click on AXCtrlDemo in the Project window to make the control project current. Then, select Add Property Page from the Project menu. In the next dialog box, select the Property Page icon. (If you like, you can explore the other option—the Visual Basic Property Page wizard—on your own.) Visual Basic adds a property page to the project, as shown in Figure 17.9. The Property Page form

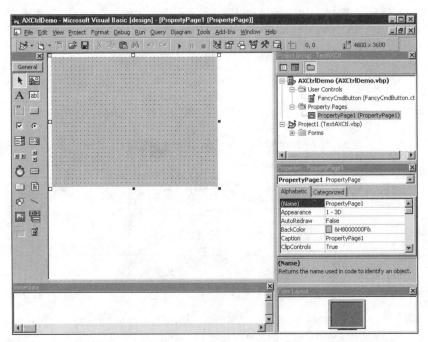

Figure 17.9 *After adding a property page, a blank property page is displayed.*

is displayed, and its properties are listed in the Properties window. Note that the Visual Basic title bar indicates that the Property Page designer is active by displaying [PropertyPage1 (PropertyPage)]. Note also that a Property Page entry has been added to the listing in the Project window.

In the Properties window, change the property page's **Name** property to FCBGeneral and the **Caption** property to General. The caption will be displayed as the tab title in the Properties dialog box; the name identifies it as the FancyCmdButton's General property tab. Select Save from the File menu and save the property page under the suggested name, which is the same as the **Name** property you just assigned (FCBGeneral). Visual Basic automatically adds the .PAG extension to property page files.

The next task is to design the property page itself, placing controls on it to permit the user to read and set the control's properties. Because the FancyCmdButton control has only a single property, **Caption**, this will be a quick task. Designing a property page is essentially the same as designing a regular Visual Basic form: drag and drop controls and so on.

Start by placing a Label control on the property page. Set the Label's **Caption** property to Caption. Place a Text Box control under the Label, and set its **Text** property to a blank string and its **Name** property to txtCaption. At this point, your property page will look like Figure 17.10.

The property page interacts with the control it is attached to by using events. Whenever a property page is opened, it receives a **SelectionChanged** event. It receives the same event if and when the user changes the controls that are selected on the current form (remember, the property page will be used when the user is designing a form and has placed one of your controls on it). Our task is complicated by the fact that the user can select more than one control—it is perfectly possible for a user to place two or more FancyCmdButton controls on a form and select all of them. Because a property page is modeless, the user can change the selected controls while the property page remains open.

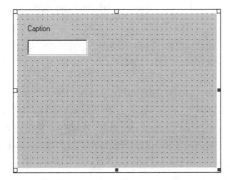

Figure 17.10   *The property page after placing its two controls.*

Basically, you have two options for dealing with multiple selected controls. The one you use will depend on the nature of the specific property. For some properties, such as **ForeColor**, it makes sense to permit the user to change the property setting for two or more controls at once. Note that I am using **ForeColor** as a generic example—it is not a property of our FancyCmdButton control. In contrast, other properties are not appropriate for such batch changes; if multiple controls are selected, you want to disable that property. The **Caption** property of our demonstration control falls into the latter category.

Dealing with the possibility of multiple selected controls is simplified by the **SelectedControls** collection, which provides a zero-based index list of the control(s) that are currently selected on the form. You can query this collection's **Count** property to see if more than one control is selected, then take the appropriate action. For the single property on the FancyCmdButton's property page, use the code shown in Listing 17.7. This code is placed in the property page's **SelectionChanged** event procedure.

Listing 17.7   The property page's SelectionChanged event procedure.

```
Private Sub PropertyPage_SelectionChanged()

' Enable the Text Box for the Caption
' property only if there is a single
' control selected.
If SelectedControls.Count = 1 Then
    txtCaption.Enabled = True
    ' Display the current property value on the property page.
    txtCaption.Text = SelectedControls(0).Caption
Else
    txtCaption.Enabled = False
End If

End Sub
```

The code we have written takes care of displaying the current property value on the property page when the page is opened. It also disables the Text Box on the property page if more than one FancyCmdButton control is selected. We still have to write the code that moves information in the other direction: from the property page to the control's actual properties. This code is divided into two parts.

First, every property page has a **Changed** property. You need to write code that sets this property to True if the user makes any changes to the properties listed on the page. When its **Changed** property is True, the property page automatically enables its Apply button, which the user clicks on to apply the new properties to the control. The ideal place to do this is in the Text Box's **Change** event procedure, which will be fired whenever the user changes the contents of the Text Box. To add this code, be sure that the property page is displayed (if not, double-click on FCBGeneral in the Project box). Then double-click on the single Text Box on the page to display the code for its **Change** event procedure and add the code shown in Listing 17.8.

Listing 17.8   The Change event procedure for the Text Box on the property page.

```
Private Sub txtCaption_Change()

    ' Set the property page's Changed
    ' property to True if the user
    ' changes the contents of the Text Box.
    Changed = True

End Sub
```

Second, to apply the change, use the property page's **ApplyChanges** event. This event is fired when the user clicks on either the OK or the Apply button in the Property Page dialog box. Your job is to place code in this event procedure that will copy property values from the controls on the property page to the actual control properties. The details of how this is handled will depend on the specifics of your control, its properties, and so on. The code is simple for the single property in the demonstration project, consisting of the single line shown in Listing 17.9.

```
Private Sub PropertyPage_ApplyChanges()

SelectedControls(0).Caption = txtCaption.Text

End Sub
```

If we had permitted simultaneous changes to multiple selected controls, we could have used the following code. (Caution! Don't use this code in the project.)

```
Private Sub PropertyPage_ApplyChanges()

' Declare a generic Object variable.
Dim objControl As Variant
' Loop through all selected controls.
For Each objControl In SelectedControls
  objControl.Caption = txtCaption.Text
Next

End Sub
```

While we have created the property page for the FancyCmdButton control, we have yet to connect it to the control. Here are the required steps:

1. Double-click on FancyCmdButton in the Project window to open the designer.

2. In the Property list, scroll down to the **PropertyPages** property. The current setting of this property will be (none).

3. Click on the button with the ellipsis (...) to display the Connect Property Pages dialog box (see Figure 17.11). The dialog lists the FCBGeneral page that we just designed, as well as three standard property pages that Visual Basic makes available to you.

4. Click on the FCBGeneral property page name to display a check mark in the box next to it, then click on OK.

Now that the property page is connected to the control, you can use it to set the control's properties—in this case, there is only one property. To try it out, you must first close the Property Page designer. Just like a control, a property page must be in run mode to be available to its connected control. Then, double-click on Form1 in the Project box to display the form for the test program. Right-click on the FancyCmdButton control on the form and select Properties from the pop-up menu. The property page we designed will be displayed, as shown in Figure 17.12.

Change the **Caption** property on the property page, then click on either OK or Apply. You'll see the new property reflected immediately on the control on the test form.

Compiling The ActiveX Control

As long as your ActiveX control is part of a Visual Basic project, it can be used within that project—but that's all. To make it available to other applications, you must compile it into an OCX file. In this section, I'll show you how to compile the demonstration ActiveX control that we created and how to use the compiled version in your project. To compile the ActiveX control, follow these steps:

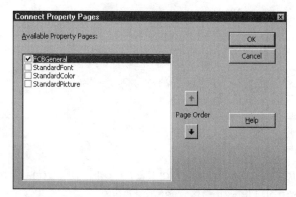

Figure 17.11   *Connecting a property page to the FancyCmdButton control.*

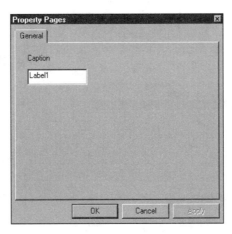

Figure 17.12 *Displaying the property page for the FancyCmdButton control.*

1. Be sure all parts of the project group are in design mode.

2. In the Project window, click on AXCtrlDemo to make it the active project.

3. Open the File menu and select Make AXCtrlDemo.OCX. Visual Basic displays the Make Project dialog box. If you want the OCX file in a different folder, select it here. You can accept the default name for the OCX file, which is the same as the project name (AXCtrlDemo). You can also assign a different name, such as FancyCmdButton, if you wish.

4. Click on OK. Visual Basic will compile the project. No message is displayed upon completion, but if you look in the specified folder, you will find the OCX file.

5. On the File menu, select Remove Project to remove the ActiveX control project from the project group. Visual Basic will display a warning message, because the control is referenced from another part of the project group—but that is okay.

Once you have compiled the ActiveX control into an OCX file and removed the ActiveX project from the project group, Visual Basic will automatically switch to using the compiled version in the test project. You'll see that the icon for the ActiveX control is still displayed in the Visual Basic Toolbox. You can add other instances of the control to the project's form, access its property page, and so on.

Using The ActiveX Control In Other Projects

When you start a new Visual Basic project, you will not automatically have access to the ActiveX controls you have created. To add them to the Toolbox, you must select Components from the Project menu to display the Components dialog box (see Figure 17.13). Place a check mark next to the control or controls you want available in your project

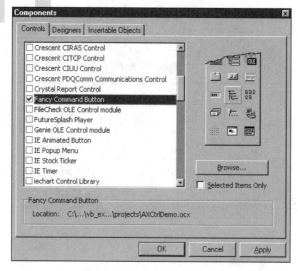

Figure 17.13   *Making an ActiveX control available in your project with the Components dialog box.*

(controls you created are listed by the name you assigned). In the case of the demonstration control, it will be listed as Fancy Command Button. At that point, the control will be available to your project, just as any other ActiveX control.

Distributing ActiveX Controls

If you have poured a lot of effort into designing an ActiveX control, you may want to distribute it to other users. Maybe you can even sell a few copies. Fortunately, the complexities of distribution are handled nicely by the Visual Basic Package and Deployment Wizard, covered in Chapter 26. Simply specify the ActiveX control project, and the wizard will walk you through the steps of creating the required distribution files/diskettes.

Using ActiveX Controls On The Web

Before beginning this subject, let me warn you that I will be providing only the most rudimentary coverage of using ActiveX controls on the Web. It's a complex topic—certainly not something that you should attempt unless you are quite familiar with various aspects of the Web and Web-site management. Even so, I want to cover the basics, so you will at least have a start. You'll need a little Internet knowledge to follow this section, however.

What exactly does it mean to "use" an ActiveX control on the Web? Remember that one of the important characteristics of an ActiveX control is its ability to be contained within something. In the section on testing your ActiveX control, you saw how you can use either a Visual Basic project or a Web browser to contain an ActiveX control. To use a Web browser, you must reference the control within a Hypertext Markup Language (HTML) document. When the HTML document is viewed within a Web browser, the ActiveX control and its functionality are part of the page. How is this done?

An HTML document contains not only the text to be displayed, but also a variety of HTML codes that control the text formatting, page layout, and other aspects of the page's appearance. To include an ActiveX control in an HTML document, the <OBJECT> code is used. Here's an example of the HTML code that would insert an AnimatedButton object on an HTML page:

```
<OBJECT ID="anbtn1" WIDTH=104 HEIGHT=60
 CLASSID="CLSID:0482B100-739C-11CF-A3A9-00A0C9034920">
    <PARAM NAME="_ExtentX" VALUE="2752">
    <PARAM NAME="_ExtentY" VALUE="1588">
    <PARAM NAME="defaultfrstart" VALUE="0">
    <PARAM NAME="defaultfrend" VALUE="-1">
    <PARAM NAME="mouseoverfrstart" VALUE="0">
    <PARAM NAME="mouseoverfrend" VALUE="-1">
    <PARAM NAME="focusfrstart" VALUE="0">
    <PARAM NAME="focusfrend" VALUE="-1">
    <PARAM NAME="downfrstart" VALUE="0">
    <PARAM NAME="downfrend" VALUE="-1">
</OBJECT>
```

Let's dissect this code to see what its components are:

- The first line specifies the object's ID, which is similar to an object's **Name** property. It also specifies the object's screen display size.

- The second line specifies the object's class identifier, a unique alphanumeric code that identifies the specific ActiveX control being referred to.

- The third through twelfth lines pass parameters to the object. Essentially, these are object property values that will be in effect when the object is first created as part of the page.

- The final line marks the end of the ActiveX object code.

How do you access the information required to place these codes in your HTML documents? Microsoft has provided a couple of handy tools for this purpose. One of them, the ActiveX Control Lister, or ACLIST, is provided on this book's CD-ROM. When it runs, it presents you with a list of all the available ActiveX controls. Double-click on a control name, and the relevant information is placed on the Clipboard, allowing you to paste it into your HTML document. The other Microsoft tool, called the ActiveX Control Pad, provides the same ability to paste ActiveX information into HTML documents, along with other HTML document creation capabilities. You can download this program from Microsoft's Web Site at **www.microsoft.com/workshop/author**.

For controls you have created, another method is available. When you test the control in a browser, as described earlier in this chapter, Visual Basic creates a small HTML file containing a reference to the control. The file is named *xxxx*.html, where *xxxx* is the control name. For example, here are the contents of FancyCmdButton.html, the test html file created for the ActiveX control developed in this chapter:

```
<HTML><BODY>
<OBJECT classid="clsid:B710E225-EA43-11D1-AF5F-00A024D13692">
</OBJECT>
</BODY></HTML>
```

By viewing this file, you can obtain the class ID for the control.

What happens when a Web browser loads an HTML document containing code meant to load an ActiveX object? First of all, it depends on the browser—not all browsers support ActiveX controls. At this writing, only Microsoft Internet Explorer version 3 and higher provides this support. I suspect that Netscape Navigator will soon follow.

In any event, when a browser that supports ActiveX controls encounters this code, it checks to see if the ActiveX control has been installed on the local system (identifying the control by means of the class ID in the code). If so, an instance of the control is created and loaded into the page, with the browser serving as container.

What if the ActiveX control has not been installed? Here's the beauty of using ActiveX on the Web. The browser will download the control from the Web site itself and install it on your system. Thus, the Web developer can use ActiveX controls on his or her Web pages without being concerned about whether or not the users have the controls installed. Once the control has been installed, that's it—there's no need to install it again. It will be available for any future use.

The ability to download and install ActiveX controls automatically from a remote site is indeed powerful. It opens several other concerns, however, including the process of installing controls on a Web site, so they are available for download. Security issues are also important. Visual Basic provides some sophisticated tools for distributing applications, and I will cover these in Chapter 26.

Chapter 18

Using The Internet Controls

Visual Basic supplies you with controls to perform the most commonly needed Internet tasks.

Once you become familiar with the Visual Basic way of programming, your first thought when faced with a particular programming task is to look for an existing component to do the job. What about writing Internet-capable programs? The same approach works here, too. Microsoft provides two components, the Internet Transfer control and the WebBrowser control, that encapsulate all of the Internet functionality most programmers will ever need. In this chapter, we will take a detailed look at the Internet Transfer control and a quick look at the WebBrowser control.

Unfortunately, these two controls are available only with the Professional and Enterprise editions of Visual Basic. As of this writing, Microsoft did not plan to include them with the Learning Edition. The WebBrowser control is also part of the installation of Microsoft Internet Explorer 4.x.

Internet programming with Visual Basic (or any other development tool, for that matter) can be divided into two areas:

- *Writing applications that use the Internet, but do not run on the Internet*—An example would be a word processing program that permits users to open and save documents on a remote Internet server.

- *Writing applications that actually run on the Internet*—An example would be a program that lets users access a catalog over the Internet and place orders.

The controls covered in this chapter are used to write the first type of application. Writing applications that run on the Internet is possible with the Professional and Enterprise editions of Visual Basic, but that topic is beyond the scope of this book.

The Internet Transfer Control

Microsoft has encapsulated a lot of commonly needed Internet functionality in the Internet Transfer control (ITC). Specifically, this control provides capabilities for Hypertext Transfer Protocol (HTTP) and File Transfer Protocol (FTP) transfers. You don't have the flexibility you would if you were programming directly, making the required Winsock and other calls, but for most programming needs, the Internet Transfer control provides all you need—and, it's a lot easier.

The Internet Transfer control is not a replacement for a Web browser. This control can be used to transfer information between client and server using HTTP or FTP protocols, but it does not display Web pages in their proper format (or in any format at all, for that matter), does not permit navigation of links, and so on. If you want to retrieve the text of a Web page for processing, this is the control to use. For example, you could use the Internet Transfer control as the basis for an automated Web search engine, downloading the contents of pages and looking for specified keywords. If you want to incorporate browsing capabilities into your Visual Basic application, use the WebBrowser control (covered later in this chapter).

> **TIP New And Improved**
>
> If you have tried to use earlier versions of the Internet Transfer control, you probably came away very frustrated. The first couple of releases of this control were buggy, and programmers found them difficult or impossible to use. I am happy to report that the current ITC is much improved and seems finally to have all of its bugs worked out.

The Internet Transfer control is an "invisible" control, much like Visual Basic's Timer control. It is not seen while the program is executing, but rather, exists behind the scenes doing its job.

Using The Internet Transfer Control For HTTP

HTTP is the foundation for the World Wide Web. Web pages are written in Hypertext Markup Language (HTML), and HTTP is the protocol by which Web pages are transferred from place to place. Every time someone logs onto a Web site, HTTP is at work. HTML files are standard text files that can be viewed and edited with any text editor. What makes them special is that they contain HTML codes that control the formatting and display of the contents in a Web browser.

Don't let the term *protocol* intimidate you. A protocol is nothing more than a set of rules about how some task is to be accomplished. HTTP is the universally accepted specification for transferring HTML documents over a network. The inner workings of HTTP are somewhat complex, but the ITC hides all the details from you.

HTTP is a relatively simple protocol, which is one factor that probably has contributed to its popularity and widespread adoption. It is a *stateless* protocol, meaning that no persistent connection is established between the client and the server. The client sends a request that is addressed to the server; when the server receives the request, it sends a response addressed to the client. A good analogy is the postal system, where you can send a letter and receive a reply without ever establishing a discrete connection between you and your correspondent. A telephone conversation is a good example of a protocol that is not stateless, because a discrete connection is established and maintained throughout the session.

The simplest way to use the Internet Transfer control is with the **OpenURL** method. Here's how it works (in this and other examples, we will assume the form includes an Internet Transfer control named Inet1):

```
Inet1.OpenURL(URLName, DataType)
```

URLName is the full URL that you want to open; it can be either an FTP or HTTP server (FTP is covered in more detail later in the chapter). The *DataType* argument specifies whether you are retrieving text or binary data. Possible values are **icString** (the default, value = 0) and **icByteArray** (value = 1). The method's return value is the complete data returned by the site. The data is returned *synchronously*, meaning that program execution pauses until the data has been retrieved. This is an important point, as we will see later.

The data returned by the **OpenURL** method should be put in a string variable or a byte array (or the equivalents), depending on the setting of the *DataType* argument. The following code retrieves the text contents of the default file at the indicated site (which happens to be my Web page) and displays it in a Text Box:

```
Text1.Text = Inet1.OpenURL("http://www.pgacon.com", icString)
```

If you want to retrieve a specific file, specify it in the URL:

```
Text1.Text = Inet1.OpenURL("http://www.pgacon.com/books.htm", icString)
```

While the **OpenURL** method is convenient and easy to use, I suggest you stay away from it. Why? There are two reasons:

- **OpenURL** operates synchronously, which means that code following the method call does not execute until the request is complete. Using the Internet Transfer control's other methods (which I will explain soon) provides *asynchronous* operation, in which your program can be doing other tasks while the Internet Transfer control executes the command. The control then notifies the program, by means of an event, when it is finished.

- Using methods other than **OpenURL** provides you with greater flexibility. You can, for example, retrieve just the header of a Web page instead of the entire page.

These other methods do not return the downloaded data in the same way that **OpenURL** does. Rather, the data is placed in the Internet Transfer control's internal buffer. Before getting to the details of the methods, we need to see how you retrieve data from this buffer. First, let's look at the Internet Transfer control's single event, which is essential for retrieving data from the buffer.

What State Am I In?

The Internet Transfer control's one event occurs whenever the state of the control changes, reflecting a change in the connection status of the control, the receipt of some data, or some other communication event that your program may need to know about (including, as we will see, errors). The associated event procedure has the following declaration:

```
Inet1_StateChanged(ByVal State As Integer)
```

State is a value identifying the new state of the control. The possible values, the defined constants, and their meanings are described in Table 18.1.

Using the **StateChanged** event is an essential part of using the Internet Transfer control's advanced methods—that is, methods other than **OpenURL**. We'll see how soon. You can also use this event to provide status messages to the user, giving information on what tasks the control is doing or has completed. Listing 18.1 shows the code to do this. In this example, I am using a Text Box control named txtStatus to display the status messages. You could just as well use various other methods, such as a status bar, to display the messages.

You should note that the control state identified by the number 11, **icError**, indicates that an error has occurred. But what error? Lots can go wrong when trying to transfer information over the Internet. Fortunately, the Internet Transfer control has two properties, **ResponseCode** and **ResponseInfo**, that provide a numerical code and a text description

Table 18.1   State values for the StateChanged event.

Constant	Value	Description
icNone	0	No state to report.
icResolvingHost	1	The control is looking up the IP address of the specified host computer.
icHostResolved	2	The control successfully found the IP address of the specified host computer.
icConnecting	3	The control is connecting to the host computer.
icConnected	4	The control successfully connected to the host computer.
icRequesting	5	The control is sending a request to the host computer.
icRequestSent	6	The control successfully sent the request.
icReceivingResponse	7	The control is receiving a response from the host computer.
icResponseReceived	8	The control successfully received a response from the host computer.
icDisconnecting	9	The control is disconnecting from the host computer.
icDisconnected	10	The control successfully disconnected from the host computer.
icError	11	An error occurred in communicating with the host computer.
icResponseCompleted	12	The request has completed, and all data has been received.

of the most recent error. You can see that the code in Listing 18.1 uses these properties to provide the user with a description of any error that occurs.

Listing 18.1   Using the StateChanged event to provide status messages to the user.

```
Private Sub Inet1_StateChanged(ByVal State As Integer)

Select Case State
    Case icResolvingHost ' 1
        txtStatus.Text = "Looking up IP address of host computer"
    Case icHostResolved  ' 2
        txtStatus.Text = "IP address found"
    Case icConnecting ' 3
        txtStatus.Text = "Connecting to host computer"
    Case icConnected ' 4
        txtStatus.Text = "Connected"
```

```
      Case icRequesting ' 5
         txtStatus.Text = "Sending a request to host computer"
      Case icRequestSent ' 6
         txtStatus.Text = "Request sent"
      Case icReceivingResponse ' 7
         txtStatus.Text = "Receiving a response from host computer"
      Case icResponseReceived ' 8
         txtStatus.Text = "Response received"
      Case icDisconnecting ' 9
         txtStatus.Text = "Disconnecting from host computer"
      Case icDisconnected ' 10
         txtStatus.Text = "Disconnected"
      Case icError ' 11
         txtStatus.Text = "Error " & Inet1.ResponseCode & _
            " " & Inet1.ResponseInfo
      Case icResponseCompleted ' 12
         txtStatus.Text = "Request completed - all data received"
End Select

End Sub
```

You should be aware that **StateChanged** events are generated by the **OpenURL** method, even though, given the fact that this method operates synchronously, the events are not really needed. Problems can arise in a program that uses **OpenURL**, as well as the other asynchronous methods, because the **StateChanged** event will be fired, and the associated code executed, at times when it is not needed and may, in fact, cause mischief. The solution I use for this potential problem is to maintain a global flag that indicates when **OpenURL** is active:

```
Dim UsingOpenURL As Boolean
...

UsingOpenURL = True
buf = Inet1.OpenURL(...)
UsingOpenURL = False
Then in the StateChanged event procedure:

Private Sub Inet1_StateChanged(ByVal State As Integer)

If UsingOpenURL Then Exit Sub
...

End Sub
```

Getting Chunks

Now let's get back to the problem of retrieving data from the control's buffer. This is done with the **GetChunk** method. The syntax is as follows:

```
Inet1.GetChunk( size [,DataType] )
```

The *size* argument specifies how many bytes of data to retrieve; it is a type **Long**. The optional *DataType* argument specifies whether the data is text or binary. You use the same values for this argument as with the **OpenURL** method: **icString** (the default, value = 0) and **icByteArray** (value = 1). If you try to retrieve more bytes of data than are present in the buffer, you'll simply get whatever is there. If you retrieve only part of the data in the buffer, the remainder of the data stays in the buffer ready to be retrieved with the next call to **GetChunk**.

Remember, however, that we are dealing here with asynchronous data retrieval. This means that when you execute one of the data retrieval methods that places data in the Internet Transfer control's buffer, program execution continues while the control waits for the data. How, then, do you know when the data has been received and is waiting in the buffer to be retrieved with **GetChunk**?

The answer lies in the **StateChanged** event. Two of the possible events, as described earlier, can signal the successful receipt of data: **icResponseReceived** (value = 8) and **icResponseCompleted** (value = 12). The technique is to place the calls to **GetChunk** in the **StateChanged** event procedure, executing them if, and only if, one of these states has occurred. To allow for the possibility that more than one call to **GetChunk** will be necessary to retrieve all the data in the buffer, we can use a loop. Listing 18.2 shows the code, which displays the full buffer contents in a Rich Text Box control named RTB1.

Listing 18.2   Using GetChunk in the StateChanged event procedure to retrieve data from the Internet Transfer Control buffer.

```
Private Sub Inet1_StateChanged(ByVal State As Integer)

Dim s1, s2

Select Case State
    ' Other cases not shown.
    Case icResponseCompleted
    s1 = ""
    s2 = ""
        Do
            s1 = Inet1.GetChunk(512, icString)
            s2 = s2 & s1
        Loop Until s1 = ""
        RTB1.Text = s2
End Select

End Sub
```

The **icResponseReceived** state does not always mean that there is data in the buffer. Some operations, such as handshaking with an FTP site, result in this state without any data being placed in the buffer. If you wait for **icResponseCompleted**, you can be sure that any and all data has been received.

The Execute Method

Perhaps the most important method you'll use with the Internet Transfer control is **Execute**. With this method, you can send a variety of commands to the remote computer. The syntax is:

```
Inet1.Execute (url, operation, data, requestHeaders)
```

The *url* argument specifies the remote computer that the command will be sent to. This argument is optional; if it is omitted, the URL specified in the control's **URL** property is used. The *operation* argument specifies the command to be sent, as explained later. The remaining two arguments are used only with certain commands.

The commands that you can send with the **Execute** method depend on the connection protocol—FTP or HTTP. For an HTTP connection, four commands are available:

- **GET**—Retrieves data from the server
- **HEAD**—Retrieves the header only from the server
- **POST**—Sends additional data required to complete a request
- **PUT**—Uploads a file to the server

Use of the **POST** and **PUT** commands is beyond the scope of this book. If you want to use these commands, you need to be fairly knowledgeable about the details of HTTP.

When using the **HEAD** command, you will receive the HTTP headers, which are intercepted by the control and do not appear in the buffer. The most common use for the **HEAD** command is to verify that a URL is functioning without the overhead of retrieving the entire content with **GET**. Simply execute **HEAD**, and if the operation succeeds (as indicated by the "Response Completed" value being detected in the **StateChanged** event procedure), you know the URL is functional.

The Internet Transfer control is most commonly used with **GET**. When using **Execute** with **GET**, the data returned by the server is placed in the Internet Transfer control's internal buffer. You retrieve the data using the **GetChunk** method, as explained earlier. Here are some examples of using **Execute** with **GET**.

To retrieve the entire default Microsoft home page:

```
Inet.Execute "http://www.microsoft.com" , "GET"
```

To retrieve the "books" page from my Web site:

```
Inet1.Execute "http://www.pgacon.com/books.htm", "GET"
```

You can use the **GET** command to submit data to Common Gateway Interface (CGI) scripts—for example, submitting queries to Web search engines. You need to know the proper syntax, of course. For example, the following command searches the Yahoo site for references to "bananas."

```
Inet1.Execute "http://search.yahoo.com/bin/search?p=banana" , "GET"
```

Types Of Errors

The many things that can go wrong when using the Internet Transfer control can be divided into two categories:

- *Certain situations generate an error in the control, resulting in the **StateChanged** event procedure being passed the **icError** value.* Examples include trying to connect to a nonexistent Web site, or if your connection to the Internet is not functioning properly.

- *Other situations may not generate an error in the control, even though something is not working properly.* For instance, if you request a nonexistent file from a functioning Web site, no error is generated; instead, the HTTP host returns an "Object Not Found" message. Even when a control error does not occur, your program needs to be on the alert for messages returned from the server indicating that something has gone wrong.

An HTTP Demonstration

The program presented in this section demonstrates using the Internet Transfer control for HTTP transfers. It is not intended to perform any task beyond helping you gain some familiarity with how the control works. The program is shown in Figure 18.1. The form contains a Rich Text Box control to display the information returned from the server, and a Text Box to display status messages as reported by the **StatusChanged** event procedure. Other elements include Text Boxes and Option Buttons to permit you to specify the URL and the command to be sent. Of course, an Internet Transfer control is on the form as well. I have enabled this program to use all four of the HTTP-related commands—**GET, HEAD, PUT**, and **POST**—so you can experiment with them. More details on the program's objects and properties are presented in Listing 18.3.

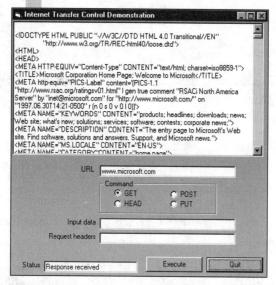

Figure 18.1 *The Internet Transfer control demonstration program.*

Get Connected

For this or any other Internet program to work, you must be connected to the Internet. If you connect via a local area network, then your connection should be ready to use at all times (assuming you have configured it properly). If you connect via a modem, you must use the Windows Dial Up Networking feature to connect to your Internet Service Provider.

Listing 18.3 *Objects and properties in ITC_DEMO.FRM.*

```
Begin VB.Form Form1
  Begin VB.TextBox txtHeaders
    Height        =    285
    Left          =    2280
    TabIndex      =    14
    Top           =    5280
    Width         =    3495
  End
  Begin VB.Frame Frame1
    Caption       =    "Command"
    Begin VB.OptionButton optPUT
      Caption     =    "Put"
    End
    Begin VB.OptionButton optHead
      Caption     =    "HEAD"
    End
    Begin VB.OptionButton optPost
      Caption     =    "POST"
```

```
      End
      Begin VB.OptionButton optGet
         Caption        =    "GET"
         Value          =    -1   'True
      End
   End
   Begin VB.TextBox txtInput
   End
   Begin VB.TextBox txtURL
   End
   Begin VB.CommandButton Command1
      Caption        =    "Quit"
      Index          =    1
   End
   Begin VB.CommandButton Command1
      Caption        =    "Execute"
      Index          =    0
   End
   Begin VB.TextBox txtStatus
   End
   Begin RichTextLib.RichTextBox RT1
   End
   Begin InetCtlsObjects.Inet Inet1
   End
   Begin VB.Label Label4
      Alignment      =    1    'Right Justify
      Caption        =    "Request headers"
   Begin VB.Label Label3
      Alignment      =    1    'Right Justify
      Caption        =    "Input data"
   End
   Begin VB.Label Label2
      Alignment      =    1    'Right Justify
      Caption        =    "URL"
   End
   Begin VB.Label Label1
      Alignment      =    1    'Right Justify
      Caption        =    "Status"
   End
End
```

The program's code is shown in Listing 18.4. When the user clicks on the Execute button, the program gathers the URL and command information from the various controls and uses the **Execute** method to send the resulting command to the specified URL. The response, if any, is displayed in the box. The current state of the Internet Transfer control is displayed in the Status box. If an error occurs, a dialog box pops up with information about the error.

Listing 18.4   Code in ITC_DEMO.FRM.

```vb
Option Explicit

Private Sub Command1_Click(Index As Integer)

Select Case Index
    Case 0  ' Execute
        Command1(0).Enabled = False
        Call Execute
    Case 1  ' Quit
        End
End Select

End Sub

Private Sub Form_Load()

Inet1.Protocol = icHTTP

End Sub

Private Sub Inet1_StateChanged(ByVal State As Integer)

Dim S1 As String, s2 As String

Select Case State
    Case icResolvingHost ' 1
        txtStatus.Text = "Looking up IP address of host computer"
    Case icHostResolved  ' 2
        txtStatus.Text = "IP address found"
    Case icConnecting ' 3
        txtStatus.Text = "Connecting to host computer"
    Case icConnected ' 4
        txtStatus.Text = "Connected"
    Case icRequesting ' 5
        txtStatus.Text = "Sending a request to host computer"
    Case icRequestSent ' 6
        txtStatus.Text = "Request sent"
    Case icReceivingResponse ' 7
        txtStatus.Text = "Receiving a response from host computer"
    Case icResponseReceived ' 8
        txtStatus.Text = "Response received"
    Case icDisconnecting ' 9
        txtStatus.Text = "Disconnecting from host computer"
    Case icDisconnected ' 10
        txtStatus.Text = "Disconnected"
    Case icError ' 11
        txtStatus.Text = "Error " & Inet1.ResponseCode & _
            " " & Inet1.ResponseInfo
        MsgBox (txtStatus.Text)
```

```
            Command1(0).Enabled = True
        Case icResponseCompleted ' 12
            txtStatus.Text = "Request completed - all data received"
            S1 = ""
            s2 = ""
            Do
                S1 = Inet1.GetChunk(512, icString)
                s2 = s2 & S1
            Loop Until S1 = ""
            RT1.Text = s2
            Command1(0).Enabled = True
    End Select

End Sub

Public Sub Execute()

Dim Operation As String

RT1.Text = ""
If optGet.Value Then Operation = "GET"
If optHead.Value Then Operation = "HEAD"
If optPost.Value Then Operation = "POST"
If optPut.Value Then Operation = "PUT"

If txtInput.Text <> "" And txtHeaders.Text <> "" Then
    Inet1.Execute txtURL.Text, Operation, _
        txtInput.Text, txtHeaders.Text
ElseIf txtInput.Text <> "" Then
    Inet1.Execute txtURL.Text, Operation, txtInput.Text
Else
    Inet1.Execute txtURL.Text, Operation
End If

End Sub
```

Using The Internet Transfer Control For FTP

FTP is similar to HTTP in that it is a protocol for transferring files between computers. It differs in not being a stateless protocol, because a control connection is maintained between client and server for the duration of an FTP session. It is also a lot more powerful than HTTP, with many more commands and security features.

FTP Logons

While HTTP servers require no logon, FTP servers do. Even if the server permits unrestricted access (called *anonymous logon*), your program must send a username and password. The username and password sent by the Internet Transfer control are determined by its **Username** and **Password** properties. The value of the **Username** property is sent to the remote server as the username for logon. If this property is blank (Null or ""), then "anonymous" is sent. The process is a bit more complicated with the **Password** property, as explained in Table 18.2.

There is one illegal combination: You cannot have a non-Null **Password** property combined with a Null **Username** property. Note that leaving both of these properties blank results in the standard anonymous FTP logon: a username of "anonymous" and a password consisting of your email address (as obtained from the system settings).

I have experienced a bug in the Internet Transfer control where it sometimes does not send "anonymous" as the username when the **Username** property is blank. Perhaps this problem will be fixed, but you can easily work around it by explicitly assigning the string "anonymous" to the **Username** property.

Using The OpenURL Method

The **OpenURL** method is the easiest way to perform some FTP tasks. To obtain the directory of an FTP site (the directory is an FTP site's "default" file):

```
Text1.Text = Inet1.OpenURL("ftp://ftp.microsoft.com", icString)
```

To download a file from an FTP site, you need to use binary mode, unless you are sure it is a text file (although binary mode works fine for text files, too):

```
Dim buf() as Byte
buf() = Inet1.OpenURL("ftp://ftp.microsoft.com/anyfile.exe" , _
    icByteData)
```

Then you can save the downloaded file to disk as follows:

```
Open "c:\programs\anyfile.exe" For Binary as #1
Put #1,, buf()
Close #1
```

Using The Execute Method

For most FTP commands, you must use the Internet Transfer control's **Execute** method. You saw this method used for HTTP transfers earlier in the chapter. With FTP, **Execute** is

Table 18.2   How the Internet Transfer control handles passwords.

Username Property	Password Property	Password Sent To Server
Null or ""	Null or ""	User's email address
Non-null string	Null or ""	""
Null	Non-null string	Error
Non-null string	Non-null string	Password property

considerably simpler, because it uses only two of the arguments. For FTP tasks, therefore, the syntax of **Execute** is:

```
Inet1.Execute (url, operation)
```

The *url* argument is the URL of the FTP site, including directory, if desired. *Operation* is a string containing the FTP command and any needed parameters. This is how FTP works: The command and any needed parameters are always together in a single string, separated by a single space. Use the **GetChunk** method to obtain data returned by the FTP server. I explained how to use **GetChunk** earlier in the chapter; the techniques are the same for FTP as for HTTP.

When working with FTP connections, keep these two points in mind:

- The commands you send are carried out by the remote FTP server. Although FTP syntax is fairly well standardized, some exceptions still exist out there on the Internet. If a command does not work, the problem may be at the other end.

- The commands you can use depend on your privileges on the remote server. With anonymous login, all you will be able to do in most cases is download files. Permission to upload files, create new directories, delete files, and so on must be granted by the server administrator. Table 18.3 summarizes the most commonly needed FTP commands.

Table 18.3   Commonly needed FTP commands.

Command	Description
CD *path*	Changes to the remote directory specified in *path*.
CDUP or CD..	Changes to parent directory.
CLOSE	Closes the current FTP connection.
DELETE *file1*	Deletes the remote file specified in *file1*.
DIR *file1* or **LS** *file1*	Searches the directory specified in *file1*. Wildcards are permitted using the remote host's syntax. If *file1* is not specified, returns a full listing of the current working file. **DIR** returns a more detailed listing than **LS**.
MKDIR *path*	Creates a remote directory as specified in *path*.
PUT *file1 file2* or **SEND** *file1 file2*	Copies local file (*file1*) to remote file (*file2*).
PWD	Returns the current directory name.
QUIT	Terminates the current user.
RECV *file1 file2* or **GET** *file1 file2*	Copies remote file (*file1*) to local file (*file2*).

(continued)

Table 18.3   Commonly needed FTP commands (continued).

Command	Description
RENAME *file1 file2*	Renames the remote file (*file1*) to the new name (*file2*).
RMDIR *path*	Removes the remote directory specified in *path*.
SIZE *file1*	Returns the size of the file or directory specified in *file1*.

An FTP Demonstration

Perhaps the best way to understand using the Internet Transfer control for FTP transfers is to see it in action. The program presented in this section, FTP_DEMO, provides fundamental FTP capabilities in a relatively simple program. You can log on to any FTP server, either as a registered user or as an anonymous guest, and view a listing of the default directory. You can change to different directories, and you can download and upload files depending on your permission level. The program is shown in Figure 18.2.

When programming the Internet Transfer control, you must pay strict attention to the **StillExecuting** property. Because the **Execute** method operates asynchronously, the control can still be busy executing the most recent **Execute** command, even though execution has returned to your program code. If your program tries to call **Execute** again, an error will occur. Therefore, you must check the status of the **StillExecuting** property and call **Execute** only when this property is False. You can see how I did this by looking at the listing for this program.

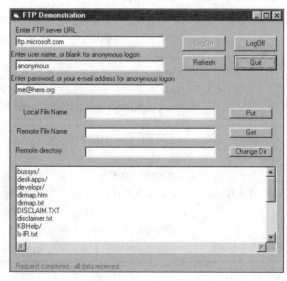

Figure 18.2   The FTP demonstration program.

I called the program FTP_DEMO. Its objects and properties are given in Listing 18.5, and its code in Listing 18.6. I am not going to walk you through all the steps of creating this program, because you should have no problem understanding how the code operates. Be aware that FTP_DEMO is a bare-bones program; although it has basic error-handling capabilities, it has no provisions for user errors, such as trying to **GET** a nonexistent file. Also, there are no warnings about overwriting existing files, so use caution.

Listing 18.5   *Objects and properties in FTP_DEMO.FRM.*

```
Begin VB.Form Form1
   Caption         =    "FTP Demonstration"
   StartUpPosition =    3  'Windows Default
   Begin VB.CommandButton Command2
      Caption      =    "Change Dir"
      Index        =    2
   End
   Begin VB.CommandButton Command2
      Caption      =    "Get"
      Index        =    1
   End
   Begin VB.CommandButton Command2
      Caption      =    "Put"
      Index        =    0
   End
   Begin VB.TextBox txtRemoteDir
   End
   Begin InetCtlsObjects.Inet Inet1
   End
   Begin VB.TextBox txtRemoteFileName
   End
   Begin VB.TextBox txtLocalFileName
   End
   Begin VB.CommandButton Command1
      Caption      =    "Quit"
      Index        =    3
   End
   Begin VB.CommandButton Command1
      Caption      =    "LogOff"
      Index        =    2
   End
   Begin VB.CommandButton Command1
      Caption      =    "Refresh"
      Index        =    1
   End
   Begin VB.CommandButton Command1
      Caption      =    "LogOn"
      Index        =    0
   End
```

```
     Begin VB.TextBox txtDirectory
        Locked          =    -1   'True
        MultiLine       =    -1   'True
        ScrollBars      =    3    'Both
     End
     Begin VB.TextBox txtPassword
     End
     Begin VB.TextBox txtUserName
     End
     Begin VB.TextBox txtURL
     End
     Begin VB.Label Label6
        Caption         =    "Remote directory"
     End
     Begin VB.Label Label5
        Caption         =    "Remote File Name"
     End
     Begin VB.Label Label4
        Caption         =    "Local File Name"
     End
     Begin VB.Label lblStatus
        ForeColor       =    &H000000FF&
     End
     Begin VB.Label Label3
        Caption         =    "Enter password, or your
                             e-mail address for anonymous logon"
     End
     Begin VB.Label Label2
        Caption         =    "Enter user name, or blank"
     End
     Begin VB.Label Label1
        Caption         =    "Enter FTP server URL"
     End
End
```

Listing 18.6   Code in FTP_DEMO.FRM.

```
Option Explicit

Private Sub Command1_Click(Index As Integer)

Select Case Index
    Case 0 ' Logon
        txtDirectory.Text = ""
        Call LogOnToHost
    Case 1 ' Refresh
        Call RefreshDir
    Case 2 ' LogOff
        txtDirectory.Text = ""
        Inet1.Cancel
```

```
                Call SetCmdButtons(False)
                lblStatus.Caption = "Logged Off"
        Case 3 ' End
                Inet1.Cancel
                End
End Select

End Sub

Private Sub Command2_Click(Index As Integer)

Select Case Index
        Case 0 ' put
                If txtLocalFileName.Text = "" Then
                        MsgBox ("Enter a file name to put.")
                        Exit Sub
                End If
                Call PutFile
        Case 1 ' get
                If txtRemoteFileName.Text = "" Then
                        MsgBox ("Enter a file name to get.")
                        Exit Sub
                End If
                Call GetFile
        Case 2 ' cd
                If txtRemoteDir.Text = "" Then
                        MsgBox ("Enter a directory name.")
                        Exit Sub
                End If
                Call ChangeDir
End Select

End Sub

Private Sub Form_Load()

Call SetCmdButtons(False)

End Sub

Private Sub Inet1_StateChanged(ByVal State As Integer)

Dim vtData As Variant
Dim strData As String

Select Case State
        Case icResolvingHost ' 1
                lblStatus.Caption = _
                        "Looking up IP address of host computer"
```

```
      Case icHostResolved  ' 2
          lblStatus.Caption = _
              "IP address found"
      Case icConnecting ' 3
          lblStatus.Caption = _
              "Connecting to host computer"
      Case icConnected ' 4
          lblStatus.Caption = "Connected"
      Case icRequesting ' 5
          lblStatus.Caption = _
              "Sending a request to host computer"
      Case icRequestSent ' 6
          lblStatus.Caption = "Request sent"
      Case icReceivingResponse ' 7
          lblStatus.Caption = _
              "Receiving a response from host computer"
      Case icResponseReceived ' 8
          lblStatus.Caption = "Response received"
      Case icDisconnecting ' 9
          lblStatus.Caption = _
              "Disconnecting from host computer"
      Case icDisconnected ' 10
          lblStatus.Caption = "Disconnected"
      Case icError ' 11
          lblStatus.Caption = "Error " _
              & Inet1.ResponseCode & _
              " " & Inet1.ResponseInfo
      Case icResponseCompleted ' 12
          lblStatus.Caption = _
              "Request completed - all data received"
          ' Get first chunk.
          Do While True
              vtData = Inet1.GetChunk(1024, icString)
              If Len(vtData) = 0 Then Exit Do
              DoEvents
              strData = strData & vtData
          Loop
          txtDirectory.Text = strData
End Select

End Sub

Public Sub LogOnToHost()

' Logs on to the specified FTP host and
' displays the directory.

On Error GoTo ErrorHandler
```

```
If txtURL = "" Or txtPassword = "" Then
    MsgBox ("You must specify a URL and Password")
    Exit Sub
End If

Command1(0).Enabled = False
Inet1.Protocol = icFTP
Inet1.URL = txtURL.Text
If txtUserName.Text = "" Then
    Inet1.UserName = "anonymous"
Else
    Inet1.UserName = txtUserName.Text
End If
Inet1.Password = txtPassword.Text
Inet1.Execute , "DIR"
Call SetCmdButtons(True)

Exit Sub

ErrorHandler:

If Err = 35754 Then
    MsgBox ("Unable to connect to remote host")
Else
    MsgBox (Err.Description)
End If
Call SetCmdButtons(False)
Inet1.Cancel

End Sub

Public Sub PutFile()

' Puts the local file specified in
' txtLocalFileName to the remote server.

Dim RemoteFileName As String, cmd As String

RemoteFileName = InputBox("Name for remote file?", _
    "Get", txtLocalFileName.Text)

cmd = "PUT " & RemoteFileName & " " _
    & txtLocalFileName.Text
If InetCtrlIsReady(True) Then
    Call SendCommand(cmd)
End If

Exit Sub

End Sub
```

```
Public Sub GetFile()

' Retrieves the file specified in txtRemoteFileName.
' Stores using user-specified local name.
Dim LocalFileName As String, cmd As String

On Error GoTo ErrorHandler

LocalFileName = InputBox("Name for local file?", _
    "Get", txtRemoteFileName.Text)

cmd = "GET " & txtRemoteFileName.Text & " " & _
    LocalFileName
If InetCtrlIsReady(True) Then
    Call SendCommand(cmd)
End If

Exit Sub

ErrorHandler:
MsgBox (Err.Description)

End Sub

Public Sub ChangeDir()

Dim cmd As String

' Changes to the remote directory specified
' in txtRemoteDir.Text then displays the
' directory.

cmd = "CD " & txtRemoteDir.Text
If InetCtrlIsReady(True) Then
    Call SendCommand(cmd)
    Do
        DoEvents
    Loop Until InetCtrlIsReady(False)
    txtDirectory.Text = ""
    Call SendCommand("DIR")
End If

End Sub

Public Sub SetCmdButtons(LoggedOn As Boolean)

Dim i As Integer

' Sets command button states for logged on
' or logged off situation.
```

```
   If LoggedOn Then
   ' Change command buttons for logged on state.
      Command1(0).Enabled = False ' Logon button
      Command1(1).Enabled = True ' Refresh button
      Command1(2).Enabled = True ' Logoff button
      For i = 0 To Command2.Count - 1
          Command2(i).Enabled = True
      Next
   Else
   ' Change command buttons for logged off state.
      Command1(0).Enabled = True   ' Logon
      Command1(1).Enabled = False ' Refresh button
      Command1(2).Enabled = False ' Logoff button
      For i = 0 To Command2.Count - 1
          Command2(i).Enabled = False
      Next
   End If

End Sub

Public Sub RefreshDir()

' Refreshes the remote directory listing.

If InetCtrlIsReady(True) Then
    txtDirectory.Text = ""
    Call SendCommand("DIR")
End If

End Sub

Public Sub SendCommand(cmd As String)

On Error GoTo ErrorHandler

Inet1.Execute , cmd
Exit Sub

ErrorHandler:

MsgBox (Err.Description)
Resume Next

End Sub

Public Function InetCtrlIsReady(ShowMessage As Boolean) _
    As Boolean

' Returns True if the Internet Transfer Control is
' ready to execute another command. Displays an
' error message if the control is busy and ShowMessage
```

```
' is True.

Dim buf As String

If Inet1.StillExecuting Then
    If ShowMessage Then
        buf = "The control has not "
        buf = buf & "completed executing" & vbCrLf
        buf = buf & "the last request. "
        buf = buf & "Please wait and try again."
        MsgBox (buf)
    End If
    InetCtrlIsReady = False
Else
    InetCtrlIsReady = True
End If

End Function
```

Internet Transfer Control Properties

I have mentioned some of the Internet Transfer control properties. You can get a lot of use out of the control without worrying about most of its properties. For special situations, however, you may need to change some of them from their default values. I have not listed the standard control properties, such as **Name** and **Index**, but only those specific to this control.

AccessType determines how the control accesses the Internet. The possible settings are:

- *icUseDefault (value = 0)*—The control uses the default access settings found in the registry to access the Internet. This is the default property setting.

- *icDirect (value = 1)*—The control has a direct connection to the Internet.

- *icNamedProxy (value = 2)*—The control uses the proxy server specified in the **Proxy** property.

Document specifies the name of the file that will be used with the **Execute** method if a document is not specified in the method's arguments. If this property is left blank, the server's default document is returned, or for write operations, an error occurs.

Password specifies the password used when the control is logging onto a remote server.

Protocol specifies the Internet protocol that will be used with the **Execute** method. The possible settings are shown in Table 18.4. The setting of this property interacts with the protocol, if any, included in the URL used with the **OpenURL** and **Execute** methods, and also with the **URL** property. If, for example, you call **Execute** and specify a URL, such as http://www.microsoft.com, then this property updates to reflect the HTTP protocol.

Table 18.4   Valid settings for the Internet Transfer control's Protocol property.

Constant	Value	Protocol
IcUnknown	0	Unknown.
IcDefault	1	Default protocol.
IcFTP	2	File Transfer Protocol.
IcReserved	3	Reserved for future use.
IcHTTP	4	Hypertext Transfer Protocol.
IcHTTPS	5	Secure HTTP.

Proxy specifies the name of the proxy server used to communicate with the Internet. This property is used only if the **AccessType** property is set to **icNamedProxy**.

RequestTimeout specifies the amount of time (in seconds) to wait for a response to a request before a time-out expires. If no response occurs within the specified time, and if the request was made with the **OpenURL** method (synchronous), an error is generated. If the request was made with the **Execute** method, the **StateChanged** event will occur with an error code. Set this property to zero to disable time-outs (the control will wait as long as needed).

ResponseCode returns the error code from when the **StateChanged** event occurs with the **icError** argument.

ResponseInfo provides a text description of the most recent error that occurred.

StillExecuting returns True if the control is busy; otherwise, False.

URL specifies the URL, including protocol, that is used by the **Execute** or **OpenURL** methods. If a URL is specified as a method argument, this property is updated to reflect that URL.

Username specifies the user name that will be sent as a logon to remote computers. If this property is blank, then "anonymous" is sent.

The WebBrowser Control

The WebBrowser control lets you drop a fully functional Web browser onto a Visual Basic form. It has all the capabilities required to view, navigate, and process HTML pages. In fact, it is the same ActiveX component used in Microsoft's Internet Explorer browser.

Perhaps referring to this control as a partially functional Web browser would be more accurate, because it does not have its own menus, toolbar, or other elements that you are used to seeing in a standalone browser application. These elements—or whatever user interface components your application needs—must be provided as part of the Visual Basic program.

Code in your program manipulates the WebBrowser control by means of its properties and methods. This enables the programmer to provide just the Web functionality that is desired. For example, you could write a browser that permits the user to access only pages on your company's own Web pages, preventing them from wasting time at other sites.

The WebBrowser control is fairly easy to use. Basic operation can be achieved with very few program statements. For example, to view a particular Web page, all that is required is to place a WebBrowser control on a form and then place the following line of code in the form's **Load** event procedure (assuming the control's name is WB1):

```
WB1.Navigate "www.wherever.com"
```

Figure 18.3 shows The Coriolis Group's Web page displayed in a WebBrowser control. Once a page is displayed, the user can access all of the navigation and other features provided as part of the page. Other capabilities—for example, a Back button—must be implemented by the programmer.

For details on the WebBrowser control's methods and properties, refer to the Visual Basic online Help system. Space limitations prevent me from giving it a full treatment. WebBrowser is a powerful component and should be all you ever need if you want to incorporate Web-browsing capabilities in your Visual Basic applications.

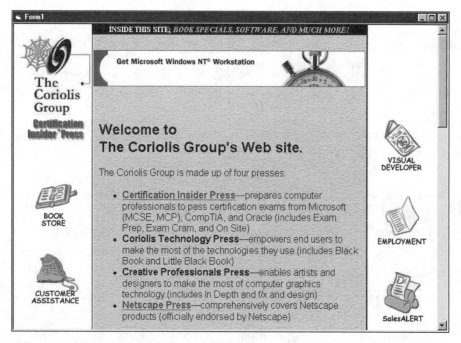

Figure 18.3 *Using the WebBrowser control to view Web pages.*

PART 5

Database Programming

Chapter 19

Database Basics

One of the most outstanding features of Visual Basic is the powerful assortment of database programming tools it provides. In this chapter, we'll start examining these tools.

If you surveyed all the computers in the world, what kind of program would be running most often? Not games, not word processors, but database programs. When a long distance company calls to pitch its service, the agent uses a database program. When someone sends an order for elk-lined pajamas to L.L. Bean, the order goes into a database program. When the clerk at the auto parts store checks to see whether they have a left-handed cam inverter for your 1971 Ford Falcon, he or she uses a database program. Wherever information needs to be managed, you usually find a database program at work.

A good percentage of those programs were created with Visual Basic. Recognizing that database programming is in great demand, Microsoft wisely included a slew of powerful database tools in Visual Basic. The Basic language itself has all the features you need to create a simple database program from scratch, as you'll see in the early part of this chapter. Visual Basic also includes some specialized database tools that permit you to create sophisticated user interfaces and access a variety of standard database file formats, all with relatively little programming.

We'll look at some of Visual Basic's database tools later in the chapter. First, we need to get some basics under our belt.

So, What's A Database?

A *database* is a collection of information, or data, arranged in a particular manner. The basic unit of information in a database is called a *record*. Each record in a database contains two or more *fields* that hold specific types of information. Perhaps the most common example of a database is an address list. Each entry in the database constitutes one record: an individual's name and address information. Each record in the database contains fields that hold separate items of information: first name, last name, address, city, and so on. These fields are the same for every record in the database, and they are assigned names identifying the data they contain.

A database is sometimes displayed in row and column format. Each row contains one record, and each column contains one field, as illustrated in Figure 19.1. In this case, a single record can be referred to as a *row*, and an individual field as a *column*. The entire collection of records is called a *table*. Some databases contain more than one table, with the records in each table having a different field structure. We will deal with multiple-table databases in later chapters; for now, we'll stick to single-table databases.

A database program is designed to let you work with the information in a database. Some capabilities are common to any database program—adding, finding, and deleting records, for example. Many other capabilities are customized to fit a specific program. In an address list database, for example, you may want the ability to print envelopes and sort the records by ZIP code. A graphics database might need the ability to input and store images from a scanner. The possibilities are endless. If you write database programs as part of your job, you never know what someone might ask you to do next. Here's one of the advantages of Visual Basic: As a full-featured programming language, it offers the flexibility to build many capabilities right into the database program. Thanks to its database tools, most of the fundamental database tasks are simple to accomplish.

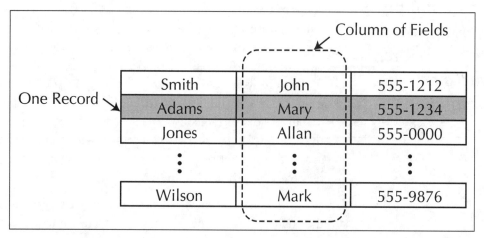

Figure 19.1   *A database table has one row per record and one column per field.*

Doing It From Scratch

Before Visual Basic had specialized database tools, programmers had no choice but to create all of the program's functionality by using Visual Basic's standard controls and the Basic language. Many database programs were created this way. This approach is still possible, but the practice of programming database applications "from scratch" is a lot less common. Still, you should know the process for a couple of reasons. For certain relatively simple database tasks, the old methods are more than adequate and provide a smaller, faster program that avoids the overhead associated with the specialized data access tools. Later in the chapter, when I cover the Jet database engine (one of Visual Basic's database tools), I'll explain some of the factors to consider when deciding upon the best approach. In addition, learning how to create a database program without using the specialized tools will teach you some valuable programming techniques.

The program we'll develop in this section is a bare-bones address list. It's not something you would actually use to keep track of names and addresses, because it's lacking a number of features that most people would consider essential. It demonstrates the fundamentals of roll-your-own database programming, however, as well as several other Visual Basic techniques. After you complete this project, you'll have a basic, but perfectly functional, program that you can enhance as needed.

Planning The Database

What features do we want in the address-list program? Most fundamental, of course, is keeping track of people's address information. The first step is to define a data structure to hold the required information, as shown here:

```
Type Address
    FName As String * 20
    LName As String * 20
    Address As String * 40
    City As String * 15
    State As String * 2
    Zip As String * 5
End Type
```

The user-defined **Address** type gives us a place to store address information while the program is running. It also defines the structure of the random access file used for disk storage of the database information. We reviewed the relationship between a user-defined type and random access files in Chapter 13; now, we'll see them in action.

The program should have the basic features of viewing records, adding new records, deleting records that are no longer needed, and editing existing records. We'll also add the

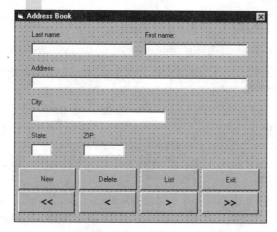

Figure 19.2 *The completed address database form.*

ability to display an alphabetical list of all records. A number of other features are possible, but let's stop here. We want the project to be manageable. Later, I'll describe some other features you might want to add.

Designing The Form

The address form needs one Text Box for each of the six pieces of information, or fields, that every address record will contain. Each Text Box also requires an identification label. Command Buttons arranged in two control arrays of four buttons each will permit the user to enter commands. Start a Standard EXE project and place these controls on the form. The completed form, which is saved as ADDRESS.FRM, is shown in Figure 19.2. The upper row of Command Buttons is assigned the **Name** property of **cmdAction**, with **Index** properties zero to three, from left to right. The lower set of Command Buttons is named **cmdMove** and has the same **Index** properties as **cmdAction**. The full description of this form's objects and properties is given in Listing 19.1. Save the project under the name ADDRESS.

Listing 19.1 *Objects and properties in ADDRESS.FRM.*

```
Begin VB.Form frmAddress
   BorderStyle   =   1  'Fixed Single
   Caption       =   "Address Book"
   MaxButton     =   0   'False
   MinButton     =   0   'False
   Begin VB.CommandButton cmdAction
      Caption        =   "List"
      Index          =   2
   End
   Begin VB.CommandButton cmdAction
```

```
          Caption          =    "Exit"
          Index            =    3
     End
     Begin VB.CommandButton cmdAction
          Caption          =    "Delete"
          Index            =    1
     End
     Begin VB.CommandButton cmdAction
          Caption          =    "New"
          Index            =    0
     End
     Begin VB.CommandButton cmdMove
          Caption          =    ">>"
          Index            =    3
     End
     Begin VB.CommandButton cmdMove
          Caption          =    ">"
          Index            =    2
     End
     Begin VB.CommandButton cmdMove
          Caption          =    "<"
          Index            =    1
     End
     Begin VB.CommandButton cmdMove
          Caption          =    "<<"
          Index            =    0
     End
     Begin VB.TextBox txtZip
     End
     Begin VB.TextBox txtState
     End
     Begin VB.TextBox txtCity
     End
     Begin VB.TextBox txtAddress
     End
     Begin VB.TextBox txtFName
     End
     Begin VB.TextBox txtLName
     End
     Begin VB.Label Label6
          Caption          =    "ZIP:"
     End
     Begin VB.Label Label5
          Caption          =    "State:"
     End
     Begin VB.Label Label4
          Caption          =    "City:"
     End
     Begin VB.Label Label3
          Caption          =    "Address:"
```

```
    End
    Begin VB.Label Label2
        Caption         =    "First name:"
    End
    Begin VB.Label Label1
        Caption         =    "Last name:"
    End
End
```

Adding A Basic Module

Rather than placing all of the program code in the form module, we will use a Basic module to hold the Type definition and the global variable declarations. A Basic module contains no visual elements—only code. Why bother with a separate module? Why not just place all the code in the form module?

The most important reason is that you can reuse Basic modules, which serve as software components. When writing procedures that have general utility, place them in a Basic module. To use those procedures in another Visual Basic project, simply add the Basic module to the project (using the Add File command on the Project menu).

A less important, although still valid, reason is that a Basic module is the best place to declare variables and define types that are global to two or more modules. This is what we will do in the current project.

Notice that the Basic module in this project contains no procedures, only variable declarations. Strictly speaking, we could have finished this project without a Basic module, but the preferred programming practice is to place global variable declarations in a Basic module rather than scattering them around the various form modules (we will be adding a second form to this project in a bit). Bottom line: You need to learn to use Basic modules, and now is as good a time as any.

To add a Basic module to the project, pull down the Project menu and select Add Module. A Code Editing window will open with a default name in its title bar. Enter the code shown in Listing 19.2. After you have finished entering the code, select Save from the File menu and assign the name ADDRESS.BAS to the code module file.

Listing 19.2   Code in ADDRESS.BAS.
```
Option Explicit

Type Address
    FName As String * 20
    LName As String * 20
    Address As String * 40
    City As String * 15
```

```
    State As String * 2
    Zip As String * 5
End Type

Public CR As Address
Public EnteringNew As Boolean
Public CurrentRecord As Integer
Public NumberOfRecords As Integer
Public OldRecord As Integer
Public FullFileName As String
Public FileNum As Integer
Public Const FILENAME = "ADDRESS.DAT"
```

Look at the code in Listing 19.2. First, the **Type** statement defines the user-defined data structure, **Address**. This structure contains six fixed-length string elements to hold the six fields of the address record. Next are declarations of the program's global variables. Note the use of the **Public** keyword in place of the usual **Dim** keyword. By using **Public**, you specify that the variable is global to all modules in the program, not just to the module where it is declared. If we had used **Dim** instead, the scope of these variables would be limited to the Basic module.

The first variable (**CR**) is an instance of the **Address** type. The program will use **CR** to hold the current record. Don't we need an array of type **Address** to hold the entire database? That's one solution, but I've used a different method. The database itself will remain stored on disk. Only the current record—the one being viewed, modified, or added—will be read into memory. Changes to the database will immediately and automatically be written to disk.

Note that we define a constant to hold the name of the database file. The program always works with the same database file, assuming that most people need only a single address list. We could modify the program to let the user specify the database file if that feature would be valuable. The Common Dialog control would simplify the task of opening and saving files, and you could add this feature to the program if desired.

The other variables should be self-explanatory. You'll see how they are applied in subsequent code listings.

Using Multiple Forms

In the address database's design specification, we said that the program should be able to list all entries in the database in alphabetical order. Rather than trying to squeeze this list onto our existing form, we'll use a separate form. The List Box control is ideal for displaying our list, because it has a **Sorted** property that causes items in the List Box to automatically sort alphabetically when it is set to True.

To add a second form to the project, select Add Form from the Project menu. A new, blank form will be displayed. Place a List Box control on the form; the size and position do not matter, because they will be set in code when the form is displayed. Set the List Box's **Sorted** property to True, and the form's **Caption** property to Address List. Select Save File from the File menu and save the form as FRMLIST.FRM. The form's objects and properties are given in Listing 19.3.

Listing 19.3   Objects and properties in FRMLIST.FRM.

```
Begin VB.Form frmList
    Caption         =   "Address List"
    Begin VB.ListBox List1
        Sorted          =   -1  'True
    End
End
```

When a project contains more than one form, how does it know where to start when the program executes? Every multiple-form project has a *startup form*, which is displayed first when the program begins execution. The display of other forms is then controlled by program code. By default, the first form you create in a project is the startup form. To change the startup form, select Properties from the Project menu, then click on the General tab in the displayed dialog box. Pull down the Startup Object list and select the desired startup form. We don't need to change the startup form for this project.

You can also specify that a Basic module be executed first when the program runs. To do this, select Sub Main from the Startup Object list and then put the code you want executed when the program starts in a procedure named **Main** in the Basic module. This technique is not commonly used, but it can be valuable when initialization code in the Basic module must be executed before any forms are loaded. Once the initialization is complete, code in the Basic module displays the program's first form.

Chameleon Command Buttons

Let's take a few minutes to think about the program's eight Command Buttons. Four of them navigate among the records: forward or back one record, and to the first or last record. What other commands might the user need to enter? An Exit button is necessary, of course, and a List button for displaying the alphabetical list. These two buttons will be available at all times. This brings our total, so far, up to six buttons, but there are still more commands to consider. The program will always be in one of two states: browsing and editing records, or entering a new record (indicated by the **EnteringNew** Boolean variable). If the user is entering a new record, Save and Cancel commands are needed. If the program is in the browsing state, New (to begin entering a new record) and Delete (to delete the current record) commands are needed. This adds up to four commands for only two remaining Command Buttons. Do we need to add two more buttons?

No. We can use a programming trick that allows a single Command Button to serve two or more purposes. By changing the button's **Caption** property, and by using a flag variable to determine what the program does when the button is clicked, two of the Command Buttons can serve double duty. Here's how it works:

- When the program starts, the buttons will display the New and Delete captions that we assigned during form design. The **EnteringNew** flag variable is set to False. The button's **Click** event procedure tests the value of **EnteringNew** and directs execution accordingly.

- If the user clicks on the New button, **EnteringNew** is set to True, and the button captions are changed to Save and Cancel. Code in the **Click** event procedure can now direct execution differently, because **EnteringNew** has a different value.

- When the user clicks on Save or Cancel, the process is reversed: **EnteringNew** is set to False again, and the button captions are set back to New and Delete.

Some of this action goes on in the **Click** event procedure for the array of Command Buttons. You'll find this code in Listing 19.4.

Listing 19.4   The Command Buttons' Click event procedure.

```
Private Sub cmdAction_Click(Index As Integer)

' For the control array of four "action" buttons.

Dim Reply As Integer

If EnteringNew Then      ' If we're entering a new record, the first two
    Select Case Index    ' buttons have different meanings.
        Case 0      ' Save.
            Call SaveCurrentRecord
            EnteringNew = False
            cmdAction(0).Caption = "New"
            cmdAction(1).Caption = "Delete"
        Case 1      ' Cancel.
            CurrentRecord = OldRecord
            EnteringNew = False
            cmdAction(0).Caption = "New"
            cmdAction(1).Caption = "Delete"
            Call DisplayRecord(CurrentRecord)
        Case 2      ' List.
            frmList.Show
        Case 3      ' Exit.
            Call ByeBye
    End Select
```

```
Else                    ' If we're not entering a record.
    Select Case Index
        Case 0      ' New.
            EnteringNew = True
            Call AddNewAddress
        Case 1      ' Delete.
            Reply = MsgBox("Delete this address?", vbYesNo + vbQuestion)
            If Reply = vbYes Then
                txtFName.Text = ""
                txtLName.Text = ""
                txtAddress.Text = ""
                txtCity.Text = ""
                txtState.Text = ""
                txtZip.Text = ""
                Call SaveCurrentRecord
            End If
        Case 2      ' List.
            frmList.Show
        Case 3      ' Exit.
            Call ByeBye
    End Select
End If

End Sub
```

Two items in Listing 19.4 require special mention:

- If the user selects the List button, this line of code is executed:

  ```
  frmList.Show
  ```

  The first part, frmList, is the name of the form where the records will be listed.
  The **Show** method does just what it implies: Shows the form. What happens next
  is determined by code in that form module, which we will deal with soon.

- If the Exit button is selected, the program calls the **ByeBye** procedure, closing the
  file and using the **Unload** statement to unload the program's forms (see Listing 19.5).

Listing 19.5   The ByeBye procedure ends the program.
```
Public Sub ByeBye()

' Close the data file and end the program.

Close #FileNum
Unload frmAddress
Unload frmList

End Sub
```

Table 19.1   Possible values for UnloadMode.

Constant	Value	Meaning
vbFormControlMenu	0	The user chose the Close command from the form's Control menu.
vbFormCode	1	The **Unload** statement is invoked from code.
vbAppWindows	2	The current Windows session is ending.
vbAppTaskManager	3	The Windows Task Manager is closing the application.
vbFormMDIForm	4	An MDI child form is closing, because the MDI form is closing.

Why not execute the **End** statement to end the program? We would like to let the user confirm, just in case the Exit button was clicked by accident. **End** does not permit this, because it terminates the program immediately. In contrast, unloading a form triggers its **QueryUnload** event procedure. Code in this procedure can query the user to confirm the desire to end the program. The skeleton of this procedure is shown here:

```
Private Sub Form_QueryUnload(Cancel As Integer, UnloadMode As Integer)

End Sub
```

The **UnloadMode** argument specifies how the **Unload** event was triggered. Table 19.1 shows the possible values.

In our case, the **UnloadMode** argument will have the value one. Because we don't really care why the form is being unloaded, however, we will just ignore this argument. The **Cancel** argument, on the other hand, is central to the purpose of this procedure. If code in the procedure sets **Cancel** to any nonzero value, the **Unload** event is canceled and the program does not terminate. If **Cancel** is left at its initial zero value, the program terminates. In our program, we'll display a message box with Yes and No buttons asking if the user really wants to exit, then set the value of **Cancel** accordingly. This procedure is shown in Listing 19.6.

Listing 19.6   The QueryUnload event procedure.

```
Private Sub Form_QueryUnload(Cancel As Integer, UnloadMode As Integer)

' If the user tries to exit, confirm.

Dim Reply As Integer

Reply = MsgBox("Exit - are you sure?", vbYesNo + vbQuestion)
```

```
If Reply = vbYes Then
    Call ByeBye
Else
    Cancel = True    ' Setting Cancel to a non-zero value
End If                ' cancels the exit.

End Sub
```

Initializing The Program

Program initialization steps are carried out in the **Form_Load** event procedure, shown in Listing 19.7. The first step is to generate the full path of the data file, using the **Path** property of the App object to obtain the program directory. We then add a backslash and the data file name, which is contained in the constant FILENAME. Next, the file is opened specifying RANDOM mode and a record length equal to the length of the user-defined type **Address**, obtained by passing an instance of type **Address** to the **Len** function. You can obtain the number of records in the file by dividing the file length by the record length.

If no records are in the file—in other words, if we are starting a new database—a message box asks whether the user wants to start entering addresses. If the reply is No, the program terminates. Otherwise, the **EnteringNew** flag is set, the form is displayed, and the **AddNewAddress** procedure is called to permit entry of the first record. If the file is not empty, the form and the first record's data are displayed.

Listing 19.7   The Form_Load event procedure.

```
Private Sub Form_Load()

Dim Reply As Integer

' Generate the full data file path and name.
' We store it in the application directory.
FullFileName = App.Path & "\" & FILENAME
FileNum = FreeFile

' Open the data file and calculate the number of records in it.
Open FullFileName For Random As #FileNum Len = Len(CR)
NumberOfRecords = (LOF(FileNum) / Len(CR))

' If the file is empty (just created).
If NumberOfRecords = 0 Then
    Reply = MsgBox("New file—start entering addresses?", vbYesNo, _
        "New file")
    If Reply = vbYes Then
        EnteringNew = True
        Form1.Show
```

```
        Call AddNewAddress
    Else
        Close (FileNum)
        End
    End If
Else        ' If the file is not empty, display the first record.
    CurrentRecord = 1
    EnteringNew = False
    Call DisplayRecord(CurrentRecord)
End If

End Sub
```

Adding an address involves calling the **AddNewAddress** procedure, which is shown in Listing 19.8. New records are always added at the end of the file. The procedure starts by incrementing the variable **NumberOfRecords** by one, then setting **CurrentRecord** to point at this new, blank record. The previous value of **CurrentRecord** is saved, so we can revert to it should the user cancel entry of the new address. The two Command Button captions are changed (as discussed earlier), the six Text Boxes are cleared, and the focus is set to the LastName Text Box in preparation for data entry.

Listing 19.8 *The AddNewAddress procedure.*

```
Public Sub AddNewAddress()

' Add a new address to the database.

' Add new record at the end of the file.
NumberOfRecords = NumberOfRecords + 1

' Remember the previous current record number.
OldRecord = CurrentRecord

' Set current record pointer to slot for new record.
CurrentRecord = NumberOfRecords

' Change captions on two of the command buttons.
cmdAction(0).Caption = "Save"
cmdAction(1).Caption = "Cancel"

' Erase contents of the text boxes.
txtFName.Text = ""
txtLName.Text = ""
txtAddress.Text = ""
txtCity.Text = ""
txtState.Text = ""
txtZip.Text = ""
```

```
' Set the focus to the Last Name text box.
txtLName.SetFocus

End Sub
```

After entering the address data in the Text Boxes, the user can click on Save, to save the new address, or Cancel, to delete. Clicking on Save calls the procedure **SaveCurrentRecord** to save the new record, then resets the Command Button captions and **EnteringNew** flag. The code for the **SaveCurrentRecord** procedure, shown in Listing 19.9, copies the data from the Text Boxes to the **CR** structure, then uses the **Put** statement to save **CR** to the file. Remember, the variable **CurrentRecord** has already been set to point at the new record at the end of the file.

Listing 19.9   The SaveCurrentRecord procedure.
```
Public Sub SaveCurrentRecord()

' Saves the current record.

CR.LName = txtLName.Text
CR.FName = txtFName.Text
CR.Address = txtAddress.Text
CR.City = txtCity.Text
CR.State = txtState.Text
CR.Zip = txtZip.Text

Put #FileNum, CurrentRecord, CR

End Sub
```

The **DisplayRecord** procedure handles displaying a record. Passed the desired record number as its one argument, this procedure reads the specified record from the file into the structure **CR**, then copies the individual fields from **CR** into the six Text Boxes on the form. This code is shown in Listing 19.10.

Listing 19.10   The DisplayRecord procedure.
```
Public Sub DisplayRecord(Record As Integer)

' Reads the specified record from the file and displays it.
Get #FileNum, Record, CR

txtLName.Text = CR.LName
txtFName.Text = CR.FName
txtAddress.Text = CR.Address
txtCity.Text = CR.City
txtState.Text = CR.State
```

```
txtZip.Text = CR.Zip

End Sub
```

The last procedure in the program's main form is concerned with navigating the address records in response to clicks of the lower set of Command Buttons. The **Click** event procedure for this control array is presented in Listing 19.11. The code should be easy to understand; it sets the **CurrentRecord** variable to point at the desired record, then calls **DisplayRecord** to load and display that record.

Listing 19.11   The Navigation Button's Click event procedure.

```
Private Sub cmdMove_Click(Index As Integer)

' For the control array of "movement" buttons.

' If we're entering a new record we don't want these
' buttons to work.
If EnteringNew Then Exit Sub

' Save the current record in case it has been edited.
Call SaveCurrentRecord

Select Case Index
    Case 0       ' First record.
        CurrentRecord = 1
    Case 1       ' Previous record.
        CurrentRecord = CurrentRecord - 1
        If CurrentRecord < 1 Then
            CurrentRecord = 1
            MsgBox ("Already at first record!")
        End If
    Case 2       ' Next record.
        CurrentRecord = CurrentRecord + 1
        If CurrentRecord > NumberOfRecords Then
            CurrentRecord = NumberOfRecords
            MsgBox ("Already at last record!")
        End If
    Case 3       ' Last record.
        CurrentRecord = NumberOfRecords
End Select

Call DisplayRecord(CurrentRecord)

End Sub
```

The List Form

We've already designed the form that will display the alphabetical list of addresses. What about its code? When the form is activated by the **Show** method, it is loaded and displayed just like a program's startup form at the beginning of program execution. We'll use its **Load** event procedure to perform the form's main task: reading all of the address records from the disk file and placing them in the List Box. This procedure will be executed when the **Show** method is used in the program's main form to display the list form. This simple code is shown in Listing 19.12. We set up a loop that will start at record one and progress to the last record. Each record is read into the **CR** structure; then the various parts of the address, starting with the last name, are concentrated into a temporary string variable before being loaded into the List Box with the **AddItem** method. Because we set the List Box's **Sorted** property to True, the List Box will automatically sort the items.

Listing 19.12   The List Form's Load event procedure.

```
Private Sub Form_Load()

Dim i As Integer, buf As String

' When the form loads, go through the entire database
' file reading each record and adding it to the list box.

For i = 1 To NumberOfRecords
    Get #FileNum, i, CR
    buf = RTrim$(CR.LName)
    buf = buf & ", " & RTrim$(CR.FName)
    buf = buf & "    " & RTrim$(CR.Address)
    buf = buf & ", " & RTrim$(CR.City)
    buf = buf & " " & RTrim$(CR.State)
    buf = buf & " " & RTrim$(CR.Zip)
    List1.AddItem buf
Next i

End Sub
```

The final item is the **Resize** event procedure shown in Listing 19.13. Code in this procedure sets the size of the List Box to fill the form, a familiar technique.

Listing 19.13   The List Form's Resize event procedure.

```
Private Sub Form_Resize()

' Make the list box the same size as the form.

List1.Left = 0
List1.TOP = 0
```

```
List1.Width = frmList.ScaleWidth
List1.Height = frmList.ScaleHeight

End Sub
```

Additional Features For The Address Database

Our address database works pretty well. We can enter new addresses, view and edit existing ones, and so on. After you use it for a short time, however, the shortcomings will become apparent. The most important feature it lacks, at least in my mind, is the ability to search for records based on a person's name. You certainly don't want to scroll through several hundred addresses just to find one. The ability to print envelopes would be nice, too, as would fields for additional information, such as phone numbers.

A more serious drawback is the way the program handles deleted records. When you delete a record, the program does not actually remove that record from the file. Rather, as was shown in Listing 19.4, it simply erases the contents of the record's fields. The blank record still takes up space in the file and will still display as we scroll through the database. There are several approaches we can take to solve this problem:

- *Add code that will skip over blank records during the scrolling process or when the records are listed.* The blank records will still take up disk space, but at least they won't be displayed.

- *Change the code.* Instead of always adding new records at the end of the file, it will look through the file for an empty record and place the new one there, moving to the end only if there are no empty spaces.

- *Compact the database file on a regular basis—for example, each time the program starts.* Compacting consists of going through the file looking for empty records and filling them, usually by moving data from the last record in the file to the blank record.

I leave these improvements to you, if you are interested. Remember, the purpose of this program is to show you how to create a database program without using Visual Basic's specialized database tools. This may be the "old" way of doing it, but remember that I am not using "old" in a pejorative sense. Just because it is the old way does not automatically make it inferior to the new way. Now that you know how it is handled, you can make up your own mind.

Using Visual Basic's Database Tools

If you do not want to program your database application from scratch, you can use Visual Basic's tools to simplify your task. In fact, Visual Basic's database toolbox contains an embarrassment of riches; sometimes, the problem faced by a new programmer is trying to figure out all of the ways that Visual Basic can do database programming. That, however, is a topic for Chapters 21 and 22. For the present, I want to show you the fundamentals of using the specialized database tools in a program. Once you have the basics under your belt, you will be ready to take on some more advanced database topics in later chapters.

The Jet database engine is your highly skilled database programming assistant. In this context, the term *engine* is not used to mean a source of power—as in an automobile engine—but rather a mechanism or device. The Jet database engine sits between your Visual Basic program and the database file that contains the records. The program pulls levers and pushes buttons on its side of the engine, and the gears, cams, and springs in the engine go to work and perform the requested action on the database. The result, if requested, pops out of a slot ready for program use.

Of course, "pulling levers and pushing buttons" means sending commands, but the basic idea is the same. We tell the engine *what* we want to accomplish, and the engine worries about *how* to do it. Part of the beauty of this system is the ability of the database engine to work with several different kinds of databases, including those shown here:

- Microsoft Access

- Microsoft Excel Worksheets

- Lotus 1-2-3 spreadsheets

- Paradox versions 3.x, 4.x, and 5.x

- dBASE III, IV, and 5

- Microsoft FoxPro, versions 2, 2.5, 2.6, 3, and DBC

- ODBC

In other words, we can write a Visual Basic program to manipulate data in any of these database formats. Of course, all types of databases use the same logical file-table-record-field format, but each type of database file uses its own proprietary method of storing the data and its related information. The Jet database engine translates your program's requests into the specific commands required by the database file format in use. The Jet database engine that Visual Basic uses is actually the same one used by Microsoft's Access database program.

A Visual Basic program can interact with a database on two levels:

- *The most common is to connect the Visual Basic program to an existing database.* The program can add, delete, print, and otherwise manipulate the data in the database, but it cannot change the structure of the database. In other words, it cannot create a new database, add or delete tables in an existing database, or change the field structure of records in a table.

- *The second level of access permits not only database manipulation, but database creation and modification as well.* Thus, the user of the Visual Basic program can create a database from scratch, specifying the tables and fields it is to contain.

The second level is considerably more complicated to program, and we will not pursue it further in this book. The first approach—where the database structure already exists and is fixed—is by far the most useful and the one you will encounter most often.

The database that our Visual Basic program will manipulate must already exist. It may be a client's database that contains thousands of records, or it might be a brand-new database created as part of the program development process. A new database can be empty—that is, contain no data—but its table and record structure must be defined.

How do you, the Visual Basic developer, create a database to be used by your program? You use a tool provided with Visual Basic, called the Visual Data Manager, or VisData. You start the Visual Data Manager from the Add-Ins menu. VisData's four main functions are to:

- Create a new database from scratch, defining its table and record structure.

- Open an existing database and examine its table and record structure.

- Open an existing database and add, delete, or edit records.

- Create indexes for a database.

Visual Data Manager is a programmer's tool that is part of Visual Basic. It is not something you distribute with your applications. I'll show you how to use VisData in Chapter 21.

The Database-Program Link

A complex chain of links exists between the database table and what the user sees and does in the program. The complexity lies in the details that go on behind the scenes. The parts handled by the programmer are actually relatively simple.

The first link, the one closest to the database, is the Jet database engine. The programmer rarely has to be concerned with the engine—it's just there, doing its job.

The next link is the Data control. This is a specialized control whose task is to serve as a link between your program and a database table. The Data control is placed on a form like any other control. It displays as a horizontal bar with arrows at either end, as shown in Figure 19.3. To use a data control, you must "attach" it to a database file and to a specific table within that file. Then the Data control will allow you to browse through the records in the table using its arrows and to manipulate the table data using its methods.

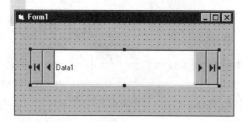

Figure 19.3 *A Data control.*

The third link in the chain between user and database is one or more *data-aware controls* (sometimes called *data-bound controls*). A data-aware control can be linked to either a specific Data control or a specific field in the table to which the Data control is linked. Once the link is in place, data is automatically transferred back and forth between the database table and the control. If you move to a certain record in the database, that record's data is displayed in the control. If you enter new data in the control, the new data is saved in the database. All this is handled automatically, with little or no need for programming. The links between a data aware control and a database table are diagrammed in Figure 19.4.

Several of Visual Basic's controls are data aware. The Check Box, Text Box, Label, Picture, Image, List Box, OLE, and Combo Box controls can be bound to a single field of a table linked to the Data control. The MaskedEdit and 3DCheckBox controls, available in the Professional Edition of Visual Basic, are also data aware. These controls deal with a single record at a time. The DataList, DataCombo, DataGrid, and MSHFlexGrid controls, which are also data aware, are used to display or manipulate several records at once.

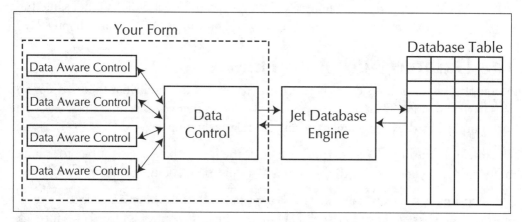

Figure 19.4 *The links between a data-aware control and a database table.*

Except for the last four controls, the data-aware controls do not have to be used in conjunction with a Data control. In other words, their data-awareness is an option.

Designing The Database

To demonstrate the Jet database engine and the associated controls, I wanted to design a database similar to the address list database that we created earlier in the chapter using traditional Basic programming methods. Rather than creating another address list, however, I thought we should try something different. Looking around my living room, I came up with the answer: my scattered collection of more than 1,000 LPs and CDs, in serious need of organization. A database to keep track of my recordings and their shelf locations would be a good start. While different in detail from the address database developed earlier, the musical recordings database will be similar enough in basic structure and functionality to provide a good comparison.

Using The Visual Data Manager To Create The Database

The first step is to create the blank database the program will use. This database will have the table and field structure required to keep track of the LPs and CDs. Then, once the database exists, we can write a Visual Basic program to access and manipulate it.

To begin, select Visual Data Manager from the Add-Ins menu. VisData will start and display a blank window. Select New from the File menu. The next menu lets you select the database format: You should select Microsoft Access, then Version 7 MDB from the next menu. Unless you have a specific reason to use a different database file format, I suggest you use this one for your new databases.

Next, the New Database dialog box is displayed. Select the folder where you want the database located. For our purposes, this should be the folder where the Visual Basic project will be placed. Type the database name "Music" in the File name box, and click on the Save button.

The Visual Data Manager will now display the Database window, with the single entry of Properties. Right-click on Properties and select New Table from the pop-up menu. VisData will display the Table Structure dialog box, which is shown in Figure 19.5.

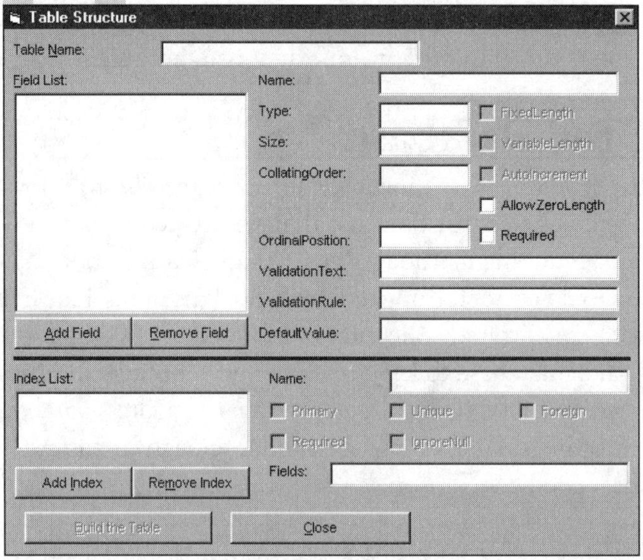

Figure 19.5 *The Table Structure dialog box.*

In the Table Name box at the top of the dialog box, type the table name. We'll call it "Recordings". Next, use this same dialog box to define the fields that will be in this table. Follow these steps for each field:

1. Click on the Add Field button to display the Add Field dialog box (Figure 19.6).

2. Type the field name in the Name box.

3. Pull down the Type list and select the data type of the field. You have all of Visual Basic's data types available, plus a couple of new ones (don't worry about these just yet).

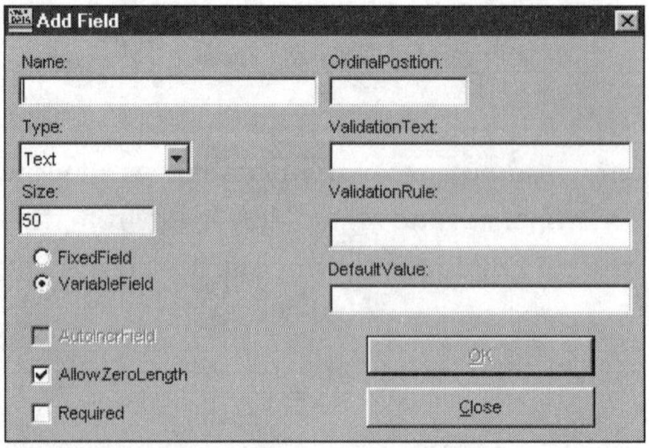

Figure 19.6 *The Add Field dialog box.*

4. If you are creating a field with the Text data type, specify the length of the field in the Size box (the maximum number of characters it can contain). A Size value will display for other data types, but this is for your information only; you can't change it.

5. Click on OK.

6. Repeat Steps 2 through 5 to define additional fields. When you have defined all of the fields in your database table, click on Close.

You'll notice that several other options are available in the Add Field dialog box. While you do not need them for this example, you need to know about a couple of them:

- *AutoIncrField*—Available only if the field is a type **Long**. When selected, the database engine will automatically fill the field with unique, sequential numbers for each record. This option is useful when you need a field that will uniquely identify each record.

- *AllowZeroLength*—For **Text** type fields only. If selected, a zero-length string is considered a valid entry for the field.

- *Required*—For all field types. If selected, the database engine will not allow the field to be left empty (null).

When you close the Add Field dialog box, the fields you defined will be listed in the Field List section of the Table Structure dialog box. To delete a field, click on it and select Delete. To change a field definition, you must first delete it, then use the Add Field command to redefine it.

For our musical recordings database, we will need the fields whose names and lengths are shown in Table 19.2. These are all Text fields. When you are finished, the Table Structure dialog box will resemble Figure 19.7.

Table 19.2 Text fields.

Field	Length
Composer/Group	40
Title	40
Media	4
Publisher	12
Location	6
Notes	50

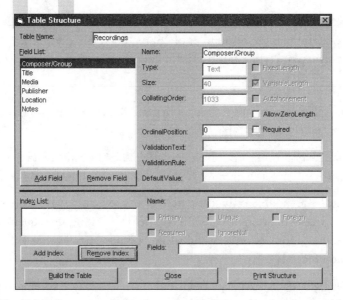

Figure 19.7   *The Table Structure dialog box after defining the database table's fields.*

The next step is to define an index for our table. This task is handled in the lower part of the Table Structure dialog box. A table does not have to have an index, but the advantages include faster queries and automatic sorting of records. Each index is linked to one field in the table, used for sorting the table (based on the data in that field) and for speeding queries on that field. While a table can have more than one index, we will create only one, linked to the Title field. Because we want the database sorted on this field, and because the database's search capabilities will be limited to the Title field, this index will suit our needs perfectly.

To create the Title index, click on the Add Index button in the Table Structure dialog box to display the Add Index to Recordings dialog box, shown in Figure 19.8. Enter the index name—in this case, ByTitle—in the Name box, then click on the name of the field you want the index based on in the Available Fields list. This adds it to the Indexed Fields box. We'll be using the Title field, of course. Turn the Primary and Unique options off, then click on OK. We could add another index at this point, but we are finished; click on Close to return to the Table Structure dialog box.

We could add more fields to the index definition. In the case of identical data in the first field, the data in these additional fields would be used to determine the index order. We need only the one field, however.

We are now finished defining the structure of the database table. Click on the Build the Table button, and VisData will generate the blank database based on the table specifications you entered. When it is complete, you will find a file named MUSIC.MDB located

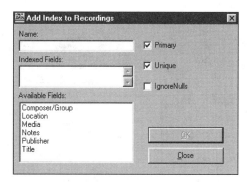

Figure 19.8   *Adding an index to the table.*

in the Visual Basic project directory. This is the database table that the database program will use. It contains no data yet, but it does have the table structure that we just defined.

> ### Modifying Database Tables
>
> We can use the Visual Data Manager to open an existing database and change the field structure of a table. Most of these changes—modifying the data type of a field or changing its length—will result in data loss. This is one reason to plan carefully before designing the database tables and entering data. When changing the table structure becomes a necessity, you are almost always better off creating a brand-new table with the desired structure and then writing a Visual Basic program to transfer existing data from the old table to the new one. Doing this is easier than it might seem. Simply place two Data controls on a form, one linked to each table, and each with the required number of Text Box controls linked to it. Use the techniques covered later in this chapter to read each record from the old table into one set of Text Boxes, transfer it to the other set, and then save it in the new table.

We have only one more step before closing the Visual Data Manager. While we have defined the structure of our database table, it is empty—that is, it contains no data. This is okay, because you can place code in your Visual Basic program that will deal with an empty database table. We can skip adding this special code to our program, however, if we add at least a single record to the database table using Visual Data Manager. Real data is fine, although we can add a dummy record and instruct our users to delete it when they enter real data.

To add a record to the table we just defined, right-click on the Recordings table name in the Database window and select Open. The dialog box shown in Figure 19.9 will open, providing a Text Box for each of the fields in the table, plus a variety of Command Buttons. Click on the Add record button, then type the dummy record's data into the fields in the dialog box. Enter anything you want, such as strings of Xs. Click on the Update but-

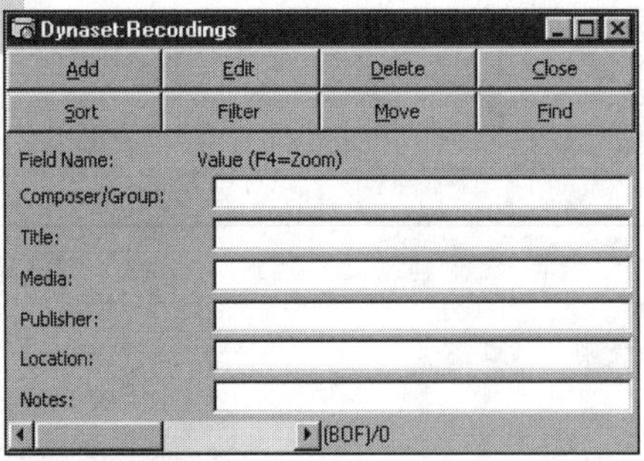

Figure 19.9 *Entering a "dummy" record in the Recordings table.*

ton, followed by the Close button. The table now has one record in it, and you can close the Visual Data Manager (select File | Exit) and return to Visual Basic.

Designing The Database Program's Main Form

The program's main form needs Text Box controls to display the database fields. It also requires labels to identify those Text Boxes; Command Buttons to carry out the various program actions; and a Data control to interface with the database. The form is shown in Figure 19.10, and its objects and properties are presented in Listing 19.14. Rather than guiding you through every step of creating this form, I'll refer you to the figure and the listing, which provide all the necessary information. I will point out that the Command Buttons are in a control array, so it's important to match the **Caption** and **Index** properties as indicated.

Listing 19.14   Objects and properties in MUSIC.FRM.

```
Begin VB.Form Form1
    Caption         =    "Music Database"
    Begin VB.CommandButton Command1
        Caption         =    "E&xit"
        Index           =    4
    End
    Begin VB.CommandButton Command1
        Caption         =    "&List"
        Index           =    3
    End
    Begin VB.CommandButton Command1
        Caption         =    "&Find a Record"
        Index           =    2
    End
    Begin VB.CommandButton Command1
        Caption         =    "&Delete Current Record"
        Index           =    1
    End
```

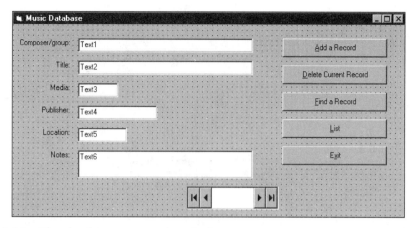

Figure 19.10   *The database program's main form.*

```
Begin VB.CommandButton Command1
   Caption              =   "&Add a Record"
   Index                =   0
End
Begin VB.TextBox txtNotes
   DataField            =    "Notes"
   DataSource           =    "Data1"
End
Begin VB.TextBox txtLocation
   DataField            =   "Location"
   DataSource           =   "Data1"
End
Begin VB.TextBox txtPublisher
   DataField            =   "Publisher"
   DataSource           =   "Data1"
End
Begin VB.TextBox txtMedia
   DataField            =   "Media"
   DataSource           =   "Data1"
End
Begin VB.TextBox txtTitle
   DataField            =   "Title"
   DataSource           =   "Data1"
End
Begin VB.TextBox txtComposer
   DataField            =   "Composer/Group"
   DataSource           =   "Data1"
End
Begin VB.Data Data1
   Connect              =   "Access"
   Exclusive            =   0    'False
   Options              =   0
   RecordsetType        =   1    'Dynaset
```

```
   End
   Begin VB.Label Label6
      Alignment              =    1  'Right Justify
      Caption                =    "Notes:"
   End
   Begin VB.Label Label5
      Alignment              =    1  'Right Justify
      Caption                =    "Location:"
   End
   Begin VB.Label Label4
      Alignment              =    1  'Right Justify
      Caption                =    "Publisher:"
   End
   Begin VB.Label Label3
      Alignment              =    1  'Right Justify
      Caption                =    "Media:"
   End
   Begin VB.Label Label2
      Alignment              =    1  'Right Justify
      Caption                =    "Title:"
   End
   Begin VB.Label Label1
      Alignment              =    1  'Right Justify
      Caption                =    "Composer/group:"
   End
End
```

Binding Controls To The Data Table

Once the form has been designed, you need to bind the controls to the data. This requires two steps:

1. Bind the Data control to a specific database file and to a specific table within that file.

2. Bind each data-aware control to the Data control and a specific field in the table to which the Data control is bound.

As you might expect, you do this with the control properties. For the Data control, set its **DatabaseName** property to the database you just created, MUSIC.MDB, and set its **RecordSource** property to **Recordings**. (Because a database can have more than one table, you must specify the exact table to which the Data control is linked.) Also, set the Data control's **RecordsetType** property to **1 -Dynaset** (more on Recordsets and Dynasets soon). For each of the six Text Box controls, set the **DataSource** property to **Data1**, pointing at the Data control. Then, set the **DataField** property of each control to the name of its associated field: Composer/Group for the first Text Box, Title for the second, and so on.

Although the program is not complete, we can run it and see the power of data-aware controls in action. The "dummy" record we entered in the database from the Visual Data Manager will be displayed in the Text Box controls. Had we entered multiple records, we would be able to move among them by clicking on the arrows on the Data control—all this without a single line of code. We do, however, need some code—although surprisingly little—to complete the database program's functionality.

Adding The Remaining Code

The code for the array of Command Buttons is remarkably simple, largely because of the power of the database engine. This code is shown in Listing 19.15. To add a new record, you just call the **AddNew** method of the Recordset object associated with the Data control. Other than the convenient touch of setting the focus to the first Text Box, that's all there is to it. The **AddNew** method takes care of clearing the Text Boxes in preparation for entry of new data, as well as saving the new data once it has been entered. Compare this with the code for adding a new record in this chapter's first program—what a difference.

Deleting a record is equally easy. Executing the Recordset object's **Delete** method is all that is required. Follow this with the **MoveNext** method, which displays the next record, so the form's Text Boxes do not remain blank.

Finding a particular record requires a call to the **FindRecord** procedure, which we'll create soon. Likewise, for listing all records, you rely on the **Show** method to display a separate form.

Listing 19.15   *The Command Button Click event code.*

```
Private Sub Command1_Click(Index As Integer)

Select Case Index
    Case 0      ' Add
        txtComposer.SetFocus
        Data1.Recordset.AddNew
    Case 1      ' Delete
        Data1.Recordset.Delete
        Data1.Recordset.MoveNext
    Case 2      ' Find
        Call FindRecord
    Case 3      ' List
        1stForm.Show
    Case 4      ' Exit
        End
End Select

End Sub
```

Recordsets

A Recordset is a type of Visual Basic object that acts as an abstract representation of an actual database table on disk. Your program accesses and manipulates the data in the table by means of the Recordset object, which has its own properties and methods. When a form containing a Data control is loaded, and if that Data control is validly linked to a table in a database, a Recordset object is automatically created and available for use by means of the Data control's **Recordset** property. A Recordset can also be created in code—independent of a Data control—but we will not explore this technique in this chapter. For a complete look at the many properties and methods of the Recordset object, refer to the Visual Basic Help system.

The Recordset object is not only powerful, it is also complex. To complicate matters, you can choose from three types of Recordsets: Table, Dynaset, and Snapshot. Each uses basically the same commands, but they interact differently with their underlying table (called the *base* table) or tables. The Recordset types provide the following:

- A *Snapshot type of Recordset provides a static, read-only copy of the base table.* The records in the base table cannot be deleted or modified (although new records can be inserted). Changes to the base table—in a multiuser environment, for example, when another user adds data to the table—are not reflected in the Snapshot. Technically speaking, a Snapshot-type Recordset contains the results of an SQL query operation on the base table. In other words, the Snapshot contains selected records from the base table. When attached to a Data control, a Snapshot's initial condition is to contain all the records from the base table—in other words, the results of a "select all records" query. Snapshot-type Recordsets are intended for situations where your program will be reading but not modifying the table data, such as in report generation.

- A *Dynaset-type Recordset provides dynamic access to a table's records.* Records can be added, deleted, and edited. Also, changes to the table made by others are reflected in the Dynaset. Otherwise, a Dynaset is very much like a Snapshot type.

- A *Table-type Recordset provides the most direct access to all of the base table's records.* No SQL query is implicit in a Table type, so it always includes all of the table's records. This type of Recordset provides quick access to all of the table's records, but extracting particular sets of records can require some complicated programming.

Of course, my descriptions of the three types of Recordsets are rather oversimplified. Other differences exist among them that only come into play in the most complicated and demanding types of database applications, where tables contain hundreds of thousands of records. With a few exceptions, such as the Snapshot-type Recordset's inability to update records in the base table, the three types have the same capabilities. The main difference among them is in database performance (speed). Further discussion in this area is beyond the scope of an introductory book, but the amount of published information is abundant if you are interested. I will just leave you with this bit of advice: When in doubt, use a Dynaset.

SQL
SQL stands for *Structured Query Language*, an industry-standard database manipulation language originally developed by IBM. You can use SQL for many tasks, such as selecting a subset of records from a table. I will have more to say about SQL in Chapter 20.

Finding A Record

Finding a particular record in the database table is also simplified by the Recordset object's methods. Our database program will be limited to searching the Title field, but the same methods apply to searches, or *queries*, on other fields. While a **Recordset** method performs the actual search, some additional programming is required to prepare for the search and respond to its result. This step is accomplished in the **FindRecord** procedure, which is shown in Listing 19.16.

Listing 19.16   The FindRecord procedure.

```
Public Sub FindRecord()

Dim Template As String
Dim Previous As String

Template = InputBox("Find what?", "Find a Title")

' If user selects Cancel a blank string is returned.
If Template = "" Then Exit Sub

' Save the current position.
Previous = Data1.Recordset.Bookmark

' Set up the search template and use the FindFirst
' method to perform the search.
Template = "[Title]= " & Chr$(34) & Template & Chr$(34)
Data1.Recordset.FindFirst Template

' If no match, return to original record and
' display a message.
If Data1.Recordset.NoMatch Then
    Data1.Recordset.Bookmark = Previous
    MsgBox ("No match found")
End If

End Sub
```

The procedure first uses the **InputBox** function to ask the user what to search for. **InputBox** displays a dialog box with a prompt, a Text Box where the user types a response, and OK and Cancel buttons. If the user selects OK, the string entered in the Text Box is returned by the function. If the user selects Cancel, an empty string is returned, in which case the user exits the procedure.

The next step is incorporating the desired search template into a command string that can be passed to the Recordset object's **FindFirst** method. This string consists of the name of the field you are querying (in brackets), followed by an equal sign and the string for which you are searching (in single or double quotes). For example, to find records where the Title field contains "Rubber Soul" (the title of a Beatles album, for those of you too young to know), you would use this command string:

```
[Title] = "Rubber Soul"
```

While either single or double quotes will work to enclose the search string, I prefer using double quotes. This permits the search string itself to contain a single quote, letting us search for other Beatles titles, such as "Hard Day's Night." Because you cannot enter a double quote directly into a Basic string, use the **Chr$** function to return the double quote character, passing the argument of **34** (the ASCII code for the double quote). You can see how this is accomplished in the listing.

The **FindRecord** procedure uses the Recordset object's **Bookmark** property to keep track of the record that is current before the search is performed. This step is necessary: If the **FindFirst** method finds no match, it makes the first record in the table current. If you want the record that was displayed when the search was initiated to remain displayed should the search fail, you must make a note of it and explicitly return there. The **Bookmark** property returns a string value that identifies the current record. Understanding the nature of this string is not necessary. Just save it. If the search fails, assign it back to the Recordset's **Bookmark** property to make that record current again.

How do you know if the search has failed? Because the Recordset object's **NoMatch** property is False unless a search has failed, we can determine the search outcome by testing this property. If the search is successful, the matching record automatically becomes current and is displayed in the bound controls. The **FindFirst** method looks for the first record that exactly matches the search template. The **FindLast** method finds the last matching record, in effect searching from the end of the table. If you have used **FindFirst** to locate the first match, you can use the **FindNext** method one or more times to locate subsequent matching records.

Fine-Tuning The Search

What if you don't want the search restricted to exact matches? For example, if you enter the search string "Hard", you would like the search to locate titles, such as *A Hard Day's Night* and *Hard Times*. To accomplish this, you must use the **Like** keyword in the command string you pass to the **FindFirst** or **FindNext** methods. You can use the * wildcard to represent any string of zero or more characters. For example, the command string

```
[Title] Like "*Hard*"
```

will find any record whose Title field contains the word "Hard". The **Like** keyword is a SQL keyword, and the Jet database engine understands SQL. In other words, you can pass SQL statements to the **FindNext** method and to related Recordset object methods. SQL is a complex and powerful database language that I will not attempt to cover in this book. If you want to learn more about SQL, you can look at the Visual Basic Help system or refer to one of the many books published on the topic.

Listing All Records

As with the earlier address-list database program, we would like the capability to display an alphabetical list of all the records in the database. As before, we'll use a separate form with a List Box control, adding a Command Button to close the list window. As an added feature, we'll include code that will display the program's main form, the entire record for a title when the user clicks on that title in the list.

To create the form, select Form from the Insert menu. Set the form's **Name** property to lstForm, and its **Caption** property to List All Recordings. Save the form with the name FRMLIST2. Add a List Box and a Command Button control. Set the Command Button's **Caption** property to &Close, making sure that the List Box's **Sort** property is set to True. Don't worry about the size and position of these controls, as they will be set in code. Listing 19.17 shows the objects and properties for this form.

Listing 19.17   Objects and properties in FRMLIST2.FRM.

```
Begin VB.Form lstForm
    Caption      =   "List All Recordings"
    Begin VB.CommandButton cmdClose
        Caption      =   "&Close"
    End
    Begin VB.ListBox List1
    End
End
```

The code in FRMLIST2.FRM contains only four event procedures. The **Click** procedure for the Command Button is simple, using only the **Unload** statement to unload the form and return the focus to the program's main form.

The **Form_Load** procedure is somewhat more complex. Here you need to extract the Title field data from all of the records in the Recordings table and load them into the List Box (which automatically sorts them). Start by saving the current record's bookmark, so you can return to it when you are finished:

```
Bookmark = Form1.Data1.Recordset.Bookmark
```

Next, we want to move to the first record in the Recordset, then loop one at a time through all of them. To do this, you need to know how many records exist. You can obtain this information from the Recordset object's **RecordCount** property. Before you read this property, however, you must move to the end of the Recordset with the **MoveLast** method. Why? A Dynaset-type Recordset does not necessarily read all of the table's records into memory at once; until it has actually read the entire table, it will not have an accurate record count. Therefore, you need to force a read to the end of the table with the **MoveLast** method. Now the **RecordCount** property will contain an accurate count of the records. After storing that value, you can use **MoveFirst** to move to the first record:

```
Form1.Data1.Recordset.MoveLast
NumRecs = Form1.Data1.Recordset.RecordCount
Form1.Data1.Recordset.MoveFirst
```

You are now ready to load the List Box. Using the **Clear** method first—to be sure the List Box is empty—you loop through the table, reading the Title field from each record and loading it into the List Box with the **AddItem** method. Finally, you return to the original record that was saved:

```
List1.Clear

For i = 0 To NumRecs - 1
    x = Form1.Data1.Recordset.Fields("Title").Value
    If IsNull(x) Then x = ""
    Form1.Data1.Recordset.MoveNext
    List1.AddItem x
Next i

Form1.Data1.Recordset.Bookmark = Bookmark
```

Note the complex line of code that actually retrieves the Title data from the current record and stores it in the string variable x. It may be easier to read this line from right to left:

"The Value of the Field named Title in the Recordset that is associated with the Data control named Data1 on the form named Form1."

TIP   Control Names And Forms

Note the syntax you use to refer to a control on another form. A control name by itself automatically refers to the current form—that is, the form whose module contains the code. To refer to a control on a different form, precede the control name with the form name and a period. If the form referred to has not yet been loaded, it will be loaded (but not displayed).

How do you go about displaying a record on the main form when the user clicks on its title in the list? My approach is to use the **FindFirst** method to search for the record. Because the title was retrieved directly from the database table, you know a match will occur when we search for that title. You should place the required code in the List Box's **Click** event procedure. When the user selects an item in a List Box—either by clicking the mouse or using the keyboard—the **Click** event is generated. Obviously, the program will permit either mouse or keyboard input. The numerical position of the selected item in the list is returned by the **ListIndex** property. To get the item itself, we use the **ListIndex** property as the index to the List Box's **List** property. The following code places the title from the List Box in a query string:

```
Template = "[Title] = " & Chr$(34) & List1.List(List1.ListIndex) & Chr$(34)
Form1.Data1.Recordset.FindFirst Template
```

Finally, you must code the form's **Resize** event procedure, which sets the List Box and Command Button sizes to fill the form. We have already reviewed this procedure, so I won't go into detail. The complete code for FRMLIST2.FRM is presented in Listing 19.18.

Listing 19.18   Code in FRMLIST2.FRM.

```
Option Explicit

Private Sub cmdClose_Click()

Unload lstForm

End Sub

Private Sub Form_Load()

Dim x As Variant, NumRecs As Integer
Dim i As Integer, Bookmark As String
```

```
Bookmark = Form1.Data1.Recordset.Bookmark
Form1.Data1.Recordset.MoveLast
NumRecs = Form1.Data1.Recordset.RecordCount
Form1.Data1.Recordset.MoveFirst

List1.Clear

For i = 0 To NumRecs - 1
    x = Form1.Data1.Recordset.Fields("Title").VALUE
    If IsNull(x) Then x = ""
    Form1.Data1.Recordset.MoveNext
    List1.AddItem x
Next i

Form1.Data1.Recordset.Bookmark = Bookmark

End Sub

Private Sub Form_Resize()

List1.Left = 0
List1.TOP = 0
List1.Width = lstForm.ScaleWidth
List1.Height = lstForm.ScaleHeight * 0.9
cmdClose.TOP = List1.Height + 1
cmdClose.Left = 0
cmdClose.Width = lstForm.ScaleWidth
cmdClose.Height = lstForm.ScaleHeight * 0.1

End Sub


Private Sub List1_Click()

Dim Template As String

' Set up the template and perform the search. Since
' we know that there must be a matching title we do not
' have to provide for the possibility of no match.

' We use Chr$(34) to enclose the search template in double
' quotes. This permits the template to contain single quotes, which
' is not possible if the template itself is enclosed in double quotes.

Template = "[Title] = " & Chr$(34) & List1.List(List1.ListIndex) & Chr$(34)
Form1.Data1.Recordset.FindFirst Template

End Sub
```

This completes our musical recordings database program. It provides all the functionality of the address list program, but with fewer lines of code. The executing program, with both forms displayed, is shown in Figure 19.11. The ease with which we created this program reflects the power of Visual Basic's Data control and the data-aware controls that can be linked to it. Even so, several features that would be desirable in even a simple database program are missing. No error trapping exists, which is perhaps the most serious omission. Error trapping permits a program to deal gracefully with errors, such as a corrupt database file, disk problems, and the like. Likewise, we have no data validation, ensuring that the user does not enter invalid data—for example, a title that is longer than the maximum 40 characters permitted by the table definition. We will delve into these and other important database topics in the following chapters.

Of course, this is a simple database program that requires none of the sophisticated and complex features of many commercial applications. Visual Basic's database tools provide for these as well, and we'll see in the next several chapters how to approach the design of a database program with a variety of features that would be required in a real-world project you might create for a paying client.

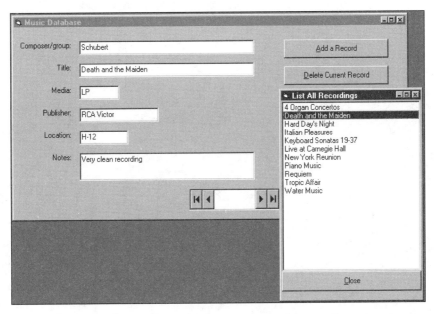

Figure 19.11   *The musical recordings database program in operation.*

Chapter 20

Alphabet Soup: ODBC, ADO, And More

Trying to understand Visual Basic's database terminology can be frustrating. Here's a crash course on what all of those acronyms stand for.

From the very beginning, Microsoft has viewed database development as one of Visual Basic's main uses. Over the years, newer and better database tools have been added to Visual Basic to ensure that programmers always have the latest technology at their fingertips. As new tools have been added, however, older tools haven't been discarded, but instead they've been kept as part of Visual Basic to ensure backward-compatibility with older programs. Consequently, Visual Basic's database toolbox can be rather confusing to a new programmer who is trying to figure out which tool to use for a specific job and how the various tools relate to each other. As they say in baseball, "You can't tell the players apart without a scorecard." This chapter is your scorecard for the Visual Basic database game.

Why does Visual Basic have so many players? The main reason is that database technology is constantly evolving. As new data access models are introduced, the older models cannot simply be dropped, because they are needed to support older applications that were written using these technologies.

Some Terminology

Undoubtedly, experienced database programmers throw around a lot of weird terms. Before continuing with this chapter, you need to know a few of these terms:

- *Back end*—This part of a database application maintains the data and performs the actual database functions. (Sometimes called *server*.) This part exchanges commands and data with the *client*, the part of the database system that the user interacts with.

- *Client*—The part of a database application the user interacts with. (Also called the *front end*.) The client's job is to handle the display and entry of data. This part generally does not perform any actual database functions, which are the job of the server, or *back end*.

- *Cursor*—A temporary, read-only table that holds the results of a *query*.

- *Data source*—Unfortunately, this term has two meanings that are only partially related. Generally, a data source is the ultimate origin of the data—the name of the file(s) in which the data is located and, when needed, the name of the computer where the files are located. In Visual Basic, *data source* also refers to the object that provides the data to your program. For example, an ADO Data control can serve as a program's data source.

- *Front end*—See *client*

- *Query*—A set of instructions for retrieving, modifying, inserting, or deleting data in a database.

- *Server*—See *back end*. Also refers to a remote computer where the database's back end is located.

Structured Query Language

Structured Query Language is almost always referred to as SQL (pronounced "S-Q-L," not "sequel," as it is more commonly but incorrectly pronounced). SQL is designed specifically for accessing and manipulating databases, and it has become the *de facto* standard for database programming. I am not aware of any relational database back end that doesn't support SQL (although they often support other proprietary languages, as well).

SQL originated in 1974 at an IBM research lab as the *Structured English Query Language*, or SEQUEL. Since then, the language has evolved into today's SQL. Unfortunately, the plural—SQLs—should probably be used, because no single accepted SQL standard exists. Not only do several SQL "standards" exist, but many vendors have added product-specific extensions (extra features) to SQL for their database programs. Access SQL, supported by the Access database engine, is a good example. While the bulk of the language is common to all the different implementations, differences do exist.

Unlike Basic and most other programming languages, SQL is a *nonprocedural* language, which means that SQL contains no statements or constructs to control the sequence, or order, of program execution. Thus, SQL does not have the equivalent of Basic's **If...Then...Else** or **Select Case** statements, nor does SQL support named procedures. SQL statements are limited to expressing *what* you want to do; the program that carries out the SQL instructions interprets the statement and returns the result.

Before going any further, take a look at a couple of example SQL statements, to get familiar with its structure. These examples work with a table named Clients that has fields named FirstName, LastName, Address, City, State, ZIP, and Telephone. To obtain a list of all the records for individuals in New York, the following SQL statement is used:

```
SELECT * FROM Client WHERE State = 'NY'
```

Can you see why SQL is described as "English-like"? The meaning of this command is clear: Select all fields from the table named Clients where the State field contains NY. What if you don't need all the fields in the result? The following SQL statement displays only the FirstName, LastName, and Telephone fields from those records where the State field contains NY:

```
SELECT FirstName, LastName, Telephone FROM Client WHERE State = 'NY'
```

The following statement goes one step further and sorts the result list by LastName:

```
SELECT FirstName, LastName, Telephone FROM Client WHERE State = 'NY' _
   ORDER BY LastName
```

Remember, SQL is not a Visual Basic technology per se, but rather a universal (or nearly universal) database language that Visual Basic supports. The database project in the next few chapters demonstrates how to perform a variety of database manipulations by using SQL. This project doesn't attempt to cover the entire SQL language—that topic is large enough for its own book. Generally, trying to learn a great deal of SQL right off the bat isn't a good idea. Start by working through the next few chapters. Then, when venturing out on your own database projects, you can turn to an SQL reference, as needed, to accomplish specific tasks.

OLE DB

OLE DB is a set of Component Object Model (COM) interfaces that provide program-mers with access to a variety of information sources. The goal of OLE DB is to provide *universal* data access—access that can deal with any type of data, regardless of its format, and that is not restricted to certain data sources. The OLE DB interfaces support the data management capabilities of each type of data source. OLE DB is not accessed directly from Visual Basic, but instead is accessed indirectly via ActiveX Data Objects (ADO).

ADO

ActiveX Data Objects provide Visual Basic programmers with an application-level inter-face to OLE DB. You rarely, if ever, need to worry about OLE DB—it's just there doing its job—so you can think of ADO as an interface directly to the data source. ADO is new in this release of Visual Basic and is considered by Microsoft to be its "premier" data access technology. If you have used earlier versions of Visual Basic for database programming, you may be familiar with the older technologies: *Remote Data Objects* (RDO) and *Data Access Objects* (DAO). These technologies are still supported by Visual Basic. In fact, the Data control, used in the sample application developed in Chapter 19, makes use of these older technologies. However, for new projects, you should use ADO. Two ways exist to use ADO: directly in code or indirectly via the ADO Data Control.

Accessing ADO In Code

The ADO model contains seven classes. As with any other object-oriented model, to use the ADO classes, you first must create instances of them (objects) and then work with those objects' methods and properties. For example, two of the objects in ADO are Connection and Command. To use these objects, you must first create instances of them, as follows:

```
Dim con As New ADODB.Connection
Dim cmd As New ADODB.Command
```

Then, you associate the Connection object with a specific data source:

```
con.ConnectionString = "YourConnectionString"
con.ConnectionTimeout = 30
con.Open
```

Next, specify a command and associate it with the Connection object:

```
cmd.Name = "YourCommand"
cmd.ActiveConnection = con
```

A lot more details are involved, of course, but this should give you the general idea. Direct manipulation of ADO is done in code, without any visual controls directly involved in the process.

ADO Data Control

The other way to access objects in ADO is to use the ADO Data Control. This control is conceptually identical to the intrinsic Data Control that is used in Chapter 19. When placed on a form, the ADO Data Control looks like Figure 20.1. It is linked to a data source and to one or more data-aware controls. The ADO Data Control lets the user move from record to record in the database, and the data is automatically displayed in the data-aware controls. Changes to the data are automatically written to the data source. More details for the ADO Data Control are provided in the database project that is developed in later chapters.

ODBC

Open Database Connectivity (ODBC) provides an Applications Programming Interface (API) that contains procedures for performing various data-manipulation tasks. A program calls these API procedures, as needed, and the ODBC Driver Manager passes the calls to the appropriate driver. *Appropriate* means the driver that is designed for the particular data source that is in use. This is where the *open* part of the ODBC name comes from. Any data source publisher can write an ODBC driver for its own data format.

ODBC is generally considered obsolete. The only reason to use ODBC in a new database project is if you need to access a data source that is in an obscure format, unsupported by ADO, for which an ODBC driver exists. Even in this situation, you probably are better off opting to use DAO, because it supports ODBC databases.

DAO

Data Access Objects (DAO) is similar to ODBC in that it provides an API that your program can call to perform data-manipulation tasks. DAO differs from ODBC in that it uses the Microsoft Jet Database Engine rather than a driver provided by the data source publisher. DAO is optimized to work with data source files in the MDB format (the same

Figure 20.1   *The ADO Data Control.*

format used by the Microsoft Access database program). However, DAO also supports ODBC databases, as well as data sources in a variety of formats, including Paradox, FoxPro, dBase, Excel, and Lotus 1-2-3.

RDO

The *Remote Data Objects* (RDO) programming model was developed specifically to deal with the special requirements of accessing the data source via a network, referred to as *remote data access*. RDO works by adding a layer on top of ODBC to handle the special needs of remote access, such as establishing connections and creating results sets. In some situations, RDO works with DAO to perform the required tasks. RDO can be implemented totally in code or via the RemoteData control.

Implementing RDO in a Visual Basic application is very similar to using DAO. In fact, a Visual Basic application that uses the Data control and DAO can easily be converted to use the RemoteData control and RDO. The few differences arise primarily because RDO is designed for use only with strictly relational databases. RDO relies on the data source to process queries because RDO has no query processor of its own.

The Bottom Line

You probably aren't too interested in memorizing the details of every database technology that Visual Basic supports. My bet is that you are more concerned with writing programs and want to know which database technology you should use. Fortunately, the answer is simple: Use ADO. This is not just my opinion, it is Microsoft's opinion as well. Using ADO makes sense, of course, because ADO is the latest database technology and as such, it improves on and simplifies capabilities of the earlier technologies. Even so, you should know at least a little bit about the other database programming techniques, particularly if you are a professional programmer. You never know when a paying client will ask you to modify an existing Visual Basic database program that was written before ADO came on the scene.

Chapter 21

Database Programming: Tools And Design

So, you want to play with the database big shots? Visual Basic is the key, but picking up some basics about database design and programming tools first, will give you a big boost. Then, you can start designing your own database application.

Database programming is unlike any other kind of programming that you've ever used. Sure, a simple database such as the one that you tackled in Chapter 19 can be slapped together pretty easily with a little common sense and a few fundamental programming skills. But quite honestly, that's kid stuff. The database applications that paying customers want are many times more complex—and correspondingly more difficult to program.

Visual Basic simplifies many aspects of database programming, but it doesn't remove the need for skill and care on the programmer's part. You need to know some fundamentals of database design and understand the tools that Visual Basic offers for database development. You will use some of these tools in the relational database that you develop in the next few chapters, but many other Visual Basic tools are available that you won't need to use in that project. This chapter offers a quick lesson in database programming fundamentals and a brief overview of some of the more important components of the Visual Basic database toolbox.

Some More Terminology

When you do serious database development, you work almost exclusively with *relational* databases. But to work with relational databases, you first must know exactly what a relational database is and be familiar with the specialized terminology that is thrown around by database developers.

Relational Databases

With rare exceptions, all modern database development involves *relational* databases, rather than *flat file* databases, such as the one that you developed in Chapter 19. A flat file database contains only a single table—thus, it is two-dimensional, or *flat*. One dimension is represented by the *fields*, or *columns*, and the other dimension is represented by the *records*, or *rows*. Flat file databases are perfectly suitable for tasks such as address lists, but as users' demands grow more complex, the flat file structure soon reveals its weaknesses.

The contrast between flat file and relational databases can be shown best through an example. For this example, I'll use a database that is intended to keep track of inventory for an electronics store. Each record in the database table contains the following fields, which are necessary to hold the information about a single stock item:

- Stock Number
- Description
- Type
- Wholesale Cost
- Retail Price
- Quantity On Hand
- Manufacturer Name
- Manufacturer Order Number
- Manufacturer Street Address
- Manufacturer City
- Manufacturer State
- Manufacturer ZIP
- Manufacturer Telephone

This list may seem adequate at first glance, but imagine what happens if the store has many stock items from one manufacturer. For each stock item, the manufacturer's name, address, and other information have to be entered, even though this data is the same in each case. This approach is highly inefficient, not only because it wastes operator time and increases the chance of errors, but also because it consumes valuable disk space by storing all the duplicate information. The solution? A *relational* database. Instead of a single table that contains all the necessary information, the relational database contains multiple tables, with the information spread among them. For this example, the relational database structure might consist of two tables, as follows:

The Stock Items table:

- Stock Number
- Description
- Type
- Wholesale Cost
- Retail Price
- Quantity On Hand
- Manufacturer Name

The Manufacturers table:

- Manufacturer Name
- Manufacturer Street Address
- Manufacturer City
- Manufacturer State
- Manufacturer ZIP
- Manufacturer Telephone

The information is not duplicated unnecessarily within this structure. One record exists in the Manufacturers table for each manufacturer, and one record exists in the Stock Item table for each stock item. The two tables are linked by the one field they have in common, Manufacturer Name. A relational database manager—the application program—has the capability to relate or *join* the tables in various ways, as required by the user. For example, in this application, the user probably wants (among other things) the following:

- An automatic prompt for the manufacturer's address information (if the manufacturer isn't already entered in the Manufacturers table) when a new entry is created in the Stock Items table.

- The capability to print out or display the manufacturer's address for a particular stock item.

- The capability to list all stock items that come from a specific manufacturer.

With two or more tables, the database is no longer flat—the multiple tables add a third dimension. The tables are designed to hold all the needed information. The relational database program can *relate* information in one table to information in other tables in a variety of ways, such as those just listed. The term *relational* derives from this capability.

Tables Are Tables

An individual table in a relational database is really no different than a table in a flat file database. Each column, or field, holds an individual piece of information, while each record, or row, holds all the information about an individual item. Note that in almost all cases, each table in a database represents something that exists in the real world—people, invoices, parts, orders, and so on.

Database programming uses some additional terminology. A table is sometimes referred to as an *entity* or an *entity class*. Rows (records) are sometimes called *tuples* or *entity occurrences*. Columns (fields) may be called *attribute classes*. An attribute class or field represents the most granular level of data—the smallest unit of information. The intersection of a row and column—a single field in a specific record—is an *attribute*. An attribute represents one unit of information about a real-world object, such as a specific individual's last name or a specific company's ZIP code.

Tables in a relational database have one requirement that is not necessary for flat file databases. Each table must have a *primary key*, a field that uniquely identifies each record in the table. In other words, the data in the primary key field must be unique for each record in the table. In the example database, Stock Number is the primary key field for the Stock Items table, and Manufacturer Name is the primary key field for the Manufacturers table. Most relational database applications support *compound* primary keys, which are primary keys that consist of data from more than one field. Compound primary keys can be used when the combined data from two or more fields uniquely identifies each record, as opposed to data from a single field.

You must be alert for situations in which the data being placed in the table does not include a primary key. In a table that contains name and address information, for example, you can't be sure that the first name, last name, or even telephone number won't be duplicated between two or more records. Granted, duplication in some situations is extremely unlikely. For example, if Social Security Number is one of the table's fields, it may be used as the primary key—because it is unique for each individual. Lacking such a unique field, however, you can create your own primary key by adding a field to the table that will contain data that you know is unique, such as a sequential number that is incremented for each new record that is added. Note that the primary key field doesn't have to contain meaningful data (although this is preferred)—just *unique* data.

A *foreign key* is a field whose data serves to link the records in the table with the primary key in another table. The data in a foreign key field doesn't have to be unique for each record—in fact, it rarely is unique. In the Stock Items table, Manufacturer Name is the foreign key. The Manufacturers table doesn't have a foreign key.

Tables are sometimes referred to as primary and dependent. A *dependent* table is one in which the records depend on information in another table for completion. The records in a *primary* table have no such dependency, being complete in and of themselves. In the example, the Stock Items table is dependent, requiring information from the Manufacturers table to provide complete data for one stock item. The Manufacturers table is a primary table, because it doesn't depend on another table to provide complete information about a manufacturer (address, telephone, and so on). Generally, primary tables are created to avoid duplicate information being placed in another table.

Sorting Records

In a relational database, the records in each table do not exist in any meaningful order. In most cases, the physical order of records in the disk file is the order in which the records are entered—which rarely, if ever, has any meaning. Of course, the structure of the disk files is something that you should never have to be concerned about. Any decent relational database application should completely isolate the user from any worries about disk files, file structure, and the like.

Does this mean that you can't sort the records in your tables? Of course not—sorting is an important aspect of using databases. Rather than physically sorting the records, however, a database application uses *logical* sorting, based on *indexes*.

Used in this context, *index* doesn't mean the same thing as the index in the back of a book, although the meaning is similar, because a database index also indicates where to find things. Each index is based on one or more fields in the table. The index itself is sorted based on the data in that field, and each entry in the index contains a *pointer* that specifies the physical location of the corresponding record in the table. This format is illustrated in Figure 21.1.

When you want records to be sorted based on a particular field, simply tell the database program to use the index that is based on that field. During display, printing, and so on, the table records appear in the order specified by the index. You can quickly change to

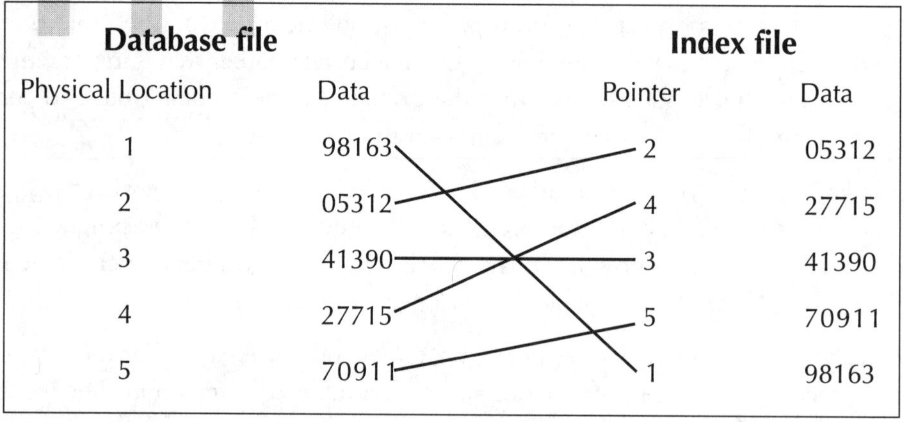

Database file		Index file	
Physical Location	Data	Pointer	Data
1	98163	2	05312
2	05312	4	27715
3	41390	3	41390
4	27715	5	70911
5	70911	1	98163

Figure 21.1 *Each index entry contains a pointer to the location of its corresponding record.*

another sort order—ordering by name rather than ZIP code, for example—by using another index.

In addition to sorting the records in a table, an index greatly speeds up searches, or *queries*, based on the data in the indexed field. If you are searching for data in a nonindexed field, the database application must look through all the records, one at a time, for a match. If the field has been indexed, however, a *binary search algorithm* can be used, which greatly increases the speed of the process. Here's how a binary search works:

1. It locates and reviews whichever record falls in the middle of the index.

2. Is this record a match? If so, it is finished. If not, it continues with Step 3.

3. Is the item that you are searching for "less than" the data in the current record? If yes, the matching record (if any) must be in the first half of the index. If not, the matching record must be in the second half of the index.

4. It discards the half of the index in which the match is *not* located, and returns to Step 1, repeating the process until it finds the record.

While you are designing a database, the following question usually arises: By which field or fields should a table be indexed? Although you increase your options by having more indexes, you also slow down performance, because all the indexes must be updated whenever new records are entered. A table should be indexed based on its primary key field, which some database applications do automatically. A table should also be indexed based on any foreign indexes that it may contain. Other indexes depend on the details of the application, and are usually restricted to fields that are used as the basis for queries.

Joins

Extracting information from database tables is one of the most common tasks that database users need to perform. When this operation involves two or more tables, it is called a *multitable select*—or, more commonly, a *join*. Three possible types of join exist to join two tables:

- *One-to-one join*—Occurs when only one record in a dependent table relates to a record in a primary table. One-to-one relationships are rare in relational databases. When two tables stand in a one-to-one relationship, combining their fields into a single table usually is a better solution. The fact that a one-to-one relationship exists indicates that no data would be duplicated if the tables were combined.

- *One-to-many join*—Occurs when multiple records in the dependent table relate to a single record in the primary table. This join is the most common and most useful type of join that is used in relational database programs. In the electronics store example, a many-to-one relationship exists between the Stock Items table and the Manufacturers table—multiple stock items exist for each manufacturer.

- *Many-to-many join*—Occurs when multiple records in the dependent database relate to multiple records in the primary table. For example, if each stock item may be obtained from several manufacturers, and each manufacturer makes several stock items, you have a many-to-many join. Obviously, this kind of join can't be based on a primary key field in either table. Strictly speaking, a many-to-many join is not a true join, because it requires an intervening table (the *relation table*) to hold the values of the foreign keys, and relational database theory only defines joins between two tables. The relation table stands in a one-to-many relationship with each of the other tables.

Database Front End Applications

When you work with Visual Basic to create a database application, you're actually generating a database *front end*, which is an application that can be used to view and manipulate data in a database. The *back end* is the set of related database tables—and in some cases, the database engine that serves as the interface between the front end and the tables. The terms *client* and *server* are sometimes used instead of front end and back end.

Why bother with this separation between the front and back ends of a database? Why not just combine all database functionality into a single application? The answers to these questions is clear if you consider how most organizations use a database. An organization's various databases cover a wide range of information—personnel records, salary information, sales data, inventory information, and so on. The various users within the organization, however, need to access selected subsets of this information in specific ways. The personnel department, for example, requires access to the personnel data and needs to look at information such as Social Security contributions and medical insurance payments. The shipping department has no use for personnel information (and may even be denied access to it), but shipping does need to view sales and inventory data.

If the front and back ends of the database were combined in a single application, a single application would have to cover the needs of all potential users. It would be unavoidably large, complex, and cumbersome—not to mention difficult to customize for new or changed needs of a specific group of users. Additionally, and perhaps even more importantly, maintaining database integrity and validity would become a nightmare.

The front end/back end approach avoids most of these problems. Each group of users can be given its own specialized software that is designed to do just what the group needs it to do, and nothing more. With a single program—the back end's database engine—coordinating all access to the actual database files, matters of integrity and validity can be dealt with more easily, and controlling access to different parts of the database becomes feasible.

Database front ends fall into two categories:

- *Decision-support applications*—Enable users to view and query information in the database, but do not permit them to add or modify information.

- *Transaction-processing applications*—Include the capability to add, delete, and edit data in the database.

Decision-support applications, which vary widely in scope, are the most common type of database front end. This type of program can be extremely specialized and limited—for example, an application that displays only client and sales information can be designed for sales personnel. These programs can also be extremely flexible, as in complex management-information systems (MIS) that provide summary data on all information in a company's database. Decision-support applications generally have read-only access to the database files—that is, they can read the data but can't change it.

Two approaches, often combined, can be taken toward the design of decision-support applications. Users can be given one or more fixed, nonmodifiable ways of examining the data, or they can be given the capability to design custom queries and reports. The former method has the advantage of requiring less training of the final users, but productivity suffers if the program's predefined capabilities aren't closely matched to the users' needs.

Transaction-processing applications provide the capability to add new data to a database and to edit or delete existing data. Because a transaction-processing application can change the actual table data, some additional programming considerations come into play.

The application has the responsibility of preserving the integrity, or accuracy, of the data in the tables.

Many databases are *client/server* databases. The terms *client* and *server* are being used somewhat differently here than they were earlier in the chapter, although it is still related to the concept of front end and back end. A client/server database refers to a *multiuser* database, to which multiple front ends are connected from different computers scattered around an organization. The client computers are connected via a network to the server computer on which the database back end is located. Multiuser client/server databases present some special problems, which are dealt with in Chapter 24.

Should Visual Basic Be Your Database Development Tool?

Before moving to the main subject of how to use Visual Basic to create relational database front-end applications, an important question must be addressed: Should you use Visual Basic at all? I know this may sound like heresy coming from an avowed Visual Basic fan, but I would be remiss in my duties if I skipped this issue. The simple fact is that Visual Basic is *not* the preferred choice in all circumstances. This statement is not a slur on Visual Basic—no other tool brings such a combination of ease of use and power to database development—but to expect any one tool, no matter how terrific, to be the best choice for all jobs is unrealistic. This section briefly looks at some of the factors to consider when deciding whether to use Visual Basic.

Programmer, Know Thyself

One of the most important factors when deciding on a database-development tool is to assess your own experience and knowledge. Obviously, you are interested in Visual Basic or you wouldn't be reading this book. But are you a complete novice at Basic, or do you have many years of Basic programming experience (with, for example, Quick Basic) and are new only to the "Visual" part? Perhaps you are an expert in xBase programming (the language used by the dBase family of database products and several clones, such as FoxPro) and are investigating Visual Basic as an alternate tool. If you currently have a programming project that is a "rush" job, with strict deadlines, you may be wise to go with the development tool that you know best and leave Visual Basic on the shelf until next time. If your timetable is more relaxed, however, that project may be a good opportunity to hone your Visual Basic skills while working on a real-world project.

Is It A Legacy Database?

If you are being asked to write new front-end applications for an existing, or *legacy*, database, the nature of the existing database may place restrictions on your choice of development tools. Clearly, the existing data has to be retained, so the new application must be able to access it. Many old database systems run on mainframes or minicomputers and use obscure or antiquated database file formats. If you are completely revamping the entire system, you may be able to convert existing data files to a different format. If parts of the existing system will remain in use, you can't modify the data file format. Instead, you have to select a development tool that supports that format. The next chapter provides information about the database formats supported by Visual Basic.

The Visual Basic Fan Club

As you can see, a few issues might steer you away from using Visual Basic for a specific database-application development project. In the absence of such particular issues, however, the selection of a development tool is still an important decision. I can't claim to be completely objective, primarily because I have more extensive knowledge of Visual Basic than any other database development tool. That aside, here are some of the reasons why I think that Visual Basic leads the pack in Windows database development:

- *Cost*—You can distribute as many copies of a Visual Basic application as you like, without paying royalties. Many other development tools require payment of a license fee for each distributed copy of the final application. Furthermore, Visual Basic's purchase price is considerably lower than many other database-development tools.

- *Flexibility*—As a full-featured programming language, Visual Basic provides much more flexibility than development tools that are designed solely for database development.

- *Software components*—Visual Basic's support for ActiveX controls means that you have dozens of functional modules that you can drop into your application, providing sophisticated capabilities with little programming effort.

- *OLE and OLE Automation*—With full support for OLE and OLE Automation (which was covered in an earlier chapter), a Visual Basic application has the capability to interact and integrate with other OLE applications.

- *Visual Basic for Applications*—Microsoft is actively pushing Visual Basic for Applications (VBA) as the common control and macro language for all Windows applications. VBA has a great deal in common with Visual Basic, and programmers who learn to use Visual Basic will have a leg up on using VBA to integrate their applications with other Windows programs.

For More Information

Visual Basic database programming is a large and complex subject. The next few chapters provide a good start, but not much more. When you're finished with this book, you should have a firm grasp of the techniques needed to create a single-user, relational-database front end for both a decision-support application and a transaction-processing application. Using Visual Basic for professional database development, however, requires some real, in-depth understanding. Several books cover Visual Basic database programming exclusively, going into much more detail than I can here. If you finish this book and discover that your Visual Basic database programming needs are more demanding, I suggest that you read one of the more-specialized Visual Basic programming books.

The next section covers the database development tools that Visual Basic provides. As the previous chapter discusses, Visual Basic offers several different database technologies. The discussion in this chapter is limited to ActiveX Data Objects, or ADO, the newest and most powerful database tool in the Visual Basic arsenal.

The Data Object Model

Microsoft and Visual Basic approach databases based on something I call—for lack of an official name—the *data object model*. Why that name? Because, to a large extent, all the components that make up a database are objects. And what is an object? It's a type of software component, just like the software components that you use daily in Visual Basic. Objects contain variables (properties) and subprograms (methods), and data objects sometimes contain members that are also objects. At times, objects are referred to as *interfaces*, because the object's properties and methods provide an interface between the outside world (the program that is using the object) and its inner workings.

The ADO model is the specific data object model addressed here. This model contains the following seven objects:

- *Connection object*—Represents the link between the datasource in use and the ADO objects.

- *Command object*—Represents a query or statement that is sent to the datasource for processing.

- *Recordset object*—Represents a set of data records that is returned by the datasource in response to a query.

- *Field object*—Represents a single column of data within a Recordset object.

- *Error object*—Contains information about error conditions reported by the datasource.

- *Parameter object*—Represents a single piece of information, or parameter, associated with a Command object.

- *Property object*—Represents a property of an ADO object.

The objects in the ADO model are organized as follows, and as diagrammed in Figure 21.2:

- Each Connection object contains an **Errors** collection, which in turn contains zero, one, or more Error object(s) representing errors (if any) that have been reported.

- Each Command object contains a **Parameters** collection, which contains as many Parameter objects as are required for the current command.

- Each Recordset object contains a **Fields** collection, which contains one Field object for each column in the record set.

- Each of the six object types mentioned in the preceding three bullets contains a **Properties** collection, which contains the required number of Property objects.

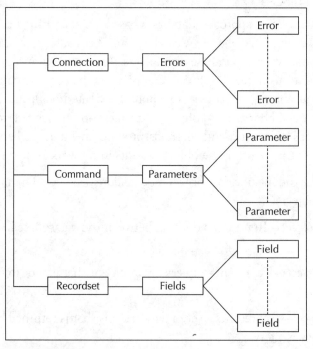

Figure 21.2 *The ADO object model. This figure omits the Properties collection and the Property objects that are common to all the ADO interfaces.*

In broad outline, a typical ADO session proceeds as follows:

1. Create the Connection object. This includes setting properties appropriate for the desired datasource. For example, the **ConnectionString** property must include information such as the datasource name, user identification, password, and cursor location.

2. Open the connection. Use the Connection object's **Open** method to create the actual link to the datasource.

3. Create the Command object. Set its properties and Parameter objects to create the query or statement that you want to submit to the datasource.

4. Associate the Command object with the Connection object. This has the effect of submitting the query or statement to the datasource.

5. Use the results set. The results of the query are returned in a Recordset object.

6. Terminate the connection to the datasource.

Using The ADO Data Control

While the ADO data model is relatively simple and easy to use, the programmer's task is made even easier by the ADO Data control. You had a brief look at this control in Chapter 20. Placed on a form, the ADO Data control serves as the datasource—the link between your program and the ADO interfaces. You program an ADO Data control by setting its properties and calling its methods. The control then takes care of the details of creating the required ADO interfaces. By binding other Visual Basic controls, such as Text Boxes, to the ADO Data control, the information is automatically transferred between the database and your program's visual display. The ADO Data control works very much like the Data control used in Chapter 19's Music database program, but the ADO Data control uses the newer ADO data model rather than the older DAO model.

Accessing Databases Without The ADO Data Control

In spite of the ADO Data control's convenience, it does have limitations. For one, only a subset of Visual Basic controls can be bound to the ADO Data control. For another, use of Recordset objects is not as flexible when an ADO Data control is used. Chapter 20 presents some examples of accessing a database without using an ADO Data control. But even with its fairly minor limitations, using the ADO Data control undoubtedly simplifies your programming tasks. I make use of the ADO Data control whenever possible. After all, one of the main reasons I use Visual Basic is to take advantage of the many software components that it offers. If I wanted to do everything myself, I would program in C++.

Creating Databases At Runtime

So far, you have dealt only with situations where the database already exists on disk, having been initially created using the Visual Data Manager. An existing database created by any other method—with the Access or Paradox database programs, for example—is handled the same way. But what if the database doesn't exist? Can you create one from scratch using Visual Basic? The answer is "yes, but...."

Why the qualification? Indeed, you can create new databases in Visual Basic code, by defining the table and record structure, and then adding new data. In that sense, you can use Visual Basic to write a program that permits users to define their own databases from scratch, rather than limiting them to databases that already exist. Here comes the catch: I generally don't recommend the approach just mentioned, because creating a database from scratch requires a lot of complicated and difficult programming. Not only do you have to accept user specifications regarding table structure, field names, data types, and the like—and convert this information into the necessary commands to create the database—but you also have to provide the capability to design forms and reports, if the data is to be of any value to the user.

While this type of program can and has been written successfully in Visual Basic, writing such a program is not for the faint-hearted. Even if you find a custom control that provides much of the required functionality, the project is still daunting, with a lot of potential pitfalls. A much better approach is to use a dedicated database front-end generator, such as Visual Data Manager, Access, or Paradox, which have built-in functionality for creating new databases and designing forms. If you decide to take this approach and avoid Visual Basic altogether, your job as a programmer is to use the application's internal programming language (Access Basic for Access, PAL for Paradox) to create the customized interfaces and queries that the client requires. Alternatively, after the database has been created, you can combine a commercial program (Access or Paradox) for database design and creation with a custom Visual Basic program for decision support and transaction processing.

Data-Aware Controls

Although data-aware controls were introduced earlier in the book, now is the time to look at the full complement. Data-aware controls work in conjunction with an ADO Data control. A data-aware control can be *bound* to a specific field in the data table for which an ADO Data control is serving as datasource. This binding is accomplished with the control's **DataSource** property (set to the name of the ADO Data control) and its **DataField** property (set to the name of the desired field in the data table). Ten data-aware controls are provided with the Professional Edition of Visual Basic. The following is a brief review of Visual Basic's data-aware controls, each of which can be bound to a single field in a data table:

- *Label*—Used for static display of text data. The user cannot edit or otherwise modify data that is displayed in a Label control.

- *Text Box*—Used for dynamic display of text data. The user can edit or enter data in a Text Box control.

- *Check Box*—Used for dynamic display of Boolean (Yes/No, True/False) data.

- *Combo Box*—The Text Box portion of the Combo Box displays the data in the linked field. The List Box portion contains items that have been added specifically with the **AddItem** method. If the user selects an item from the list, that item replaces the original field data. A Combo Box can be used for data entry/editing when the user must select from a predefined list of possibilities.

- *List Box*—Similar to a Combo Box.

- *Picture Box*—Can display a graphical image from a bitmap, icon, or metafile that is stored in a linked image/binary data field.

- *Image*—Similar to a Picture Box, but uses fewer resources and offers less capability.

- *OLE*—Serves as a container for an OLE object and can be bound to a data table.

- *MaskedEdit*—Similar to a Text Box, but permits the definition of masks that control data input.

- *RichTextBox*—Similar to a Text Box control, but provides additional formatting capabilities.

As useful as these controls are, they are all limited to displaying data from *one* field in *one* record at a time. This is simply too limited for certain applications. Three custom data-aware controls can provide additional capabilities: DataGrid, DataList, and DataCombo.

The DataGrid Control

The DataGrid control provides a *grid*, or *matrix*, of cells. Each column in the grid displays data from one field in the linked data table, and each row displays data from one record. A DataGrid control is shown in Figure 21.3, displaying data from the Music database developed in an earlier chapter.

By default, a DataGrid control displays all the table's fields and records, with vertical and/or horizontal scrollbars if the data is too wide or too tall to display completely. The user can move from cell to cell, viewing and editing data. The bottom row on the control, marked by an asterisk in the left column, can be used to enter new data (this is

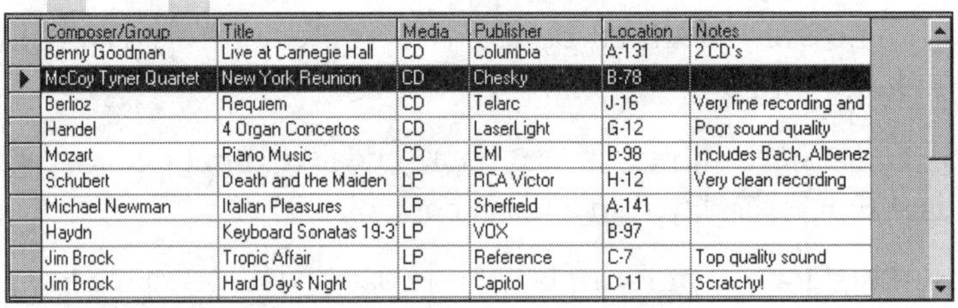

Composer/Group	Title	Media	Publisher	Location	Notes
Benny Goodman	Live at Carnegie Hall	CD	Columbia	A-131	2 CD's
McCoy Tyner Quartet	New York Reunion	CD	Chesky	B-78	
Berlioz	Requiem	CD	Telarc	J-16	Very fine recording and
Handel	4 Organ Concertos	CD	LaserLight	G-12	Poor sound quality
Mozart	Piano Music	CD	EMI	B-98	Includes Bach, Albenez
Schubert	Death and the Maiden	LP	RCA Victor	H-12	Very clean recording
Michael Newman	Italian Pleasures	LP	Sheffield	A-141	
Haydn	Keyboard Sonatas 19-3	LP	VOX	B-97	
Jim Brock	Tropic Affair	LP	Reference	C-7	Top quality sound
Jim Brock	Hard Day's Night	LP	Capitol	D-11	Scratchy!

Figure 21.3 *The DataGrid control.*

not shown in Figure 21.3). Column widths can be changed, fonts can be specified, and many other aspects of the control's appearance and behavior can be manipulated via control properties.

The DataGrid control consists of a **Columns** collection, with one Column object for each column (field) in the control. A DataGrid control can contain a maximum of 32,767 columns; the number of rows is limited only by system resources. Each column is a partially independent object with its own properties. Thus, some properties belong to the DataGrid control itself and affect operation and appearance of the entire control, but each column also has its own set of properties. Each Column object has its own caption (header), font, and so on. The **Columns** collection has properties that relate to all columns, such as **Count**, which returns the number of columns in the control.

The DataGrid control's features are covered further in the upcoming demonstration program. Refer to the Visual Basic Help system for complete details on its properties, methods, and events.

The DataList And DataCombo Controls

The DataList and DataCombo controls are similar to the regular Combo Box and List Box controls: all four controls provide a list of items from which the user can choose; the difference lies in data binding ability. The DataList and DataCombo controls display a list of items, and the DataCombo adds a TextBox that displays the currently selected item, and permits entry/editing by the user. These controls differ from the standard Combo Box and List Box controls, however, because they are data-aware and can be automatically loaded with values from a datasource.

The DataList and DataCombo controls can be extremely useful, to speed the task of data entry and to reduce the chance of errors. For example, when a new Invoice record is entered, the Customer and each Item likely come from existing tables in the database. Rather than require the operator to manually enter the customer name or the item's stock number, you can display a DataList control for each field in the data table, showing all the currently available values for that entry. The following demonstration project shows how these controls are used in this manner.

Designing The Database Application

In the remainder of this chapter and in the next two chapters, I walk you through all the steps of planning and programming a relational database application by using Visual Basic's ADO model. Before writing a single line of code, however, some planning is in order. How careful and thorough you are during the planning stages has a major impact on your speed and efficiency in completing the project—not to mention the quality of the finished product. The remainder of this chapter covers some general considerations related to database design, walking you through the first steps of designing the demonstration database program. The discussion is limited to designing a new database from scratch, whereby no existing tables or applications are considered. If your own project involves a legacy database, the design process is different. Although you probably won't have the option of changing the table structure, the other considerations still apply.

Fundamental Design Considerations

Database design remains as much an art as a science. While some rules and guidelines apply, no well-defined design method regularly produces properly designed databases. The knowledge and skill of the programmer come into play in ways that can almost be called intuition. Ask an experienced database programmer why he or she designed a table in a certain way, and you may hear an answer like, "I don't know—it just seemed the obvious way to do it."

The demonstration database covered here is a fairly simple project, and the reasons behind design decisions will most likely be clear to you. With more complex projects—and some databases involve dozens of tables—the table design may be much less obvious. And although alternative designs might work, they will not work as well as the optimal design.

The Design Process

Laying out a fixed sequence of steps to design a database is impossible. It's a fluid process, with lots of interaction between the various stages. You often have to go back and change something that was decided earlier, such as a table structure or a key field, because of unforeseen problems that arise. Of course, minimizing those setbacks is important—every time you have to change something, you waste time and effort. By paying attention to the basic principles discussed in this chapter, as well as by gaining progressively more experience, you can minimize mistakes—but don't count on ever being able to eliminate mistakes entirely.

Here, then, are the most important steps to follow in designing a Visual Basic database application. Remember that this sequence is not fixed, although following a similar order generally is the best approach. In spite of any other variations, the first step should always be to gather information.

Gathering Information

In many respects, gathering information is the most important step in database design. No matter how skilled you are as a programmer, you can't create an application for a certain task unless you know exactly what that task is. Generally, the database will have a formal specification, whether provided by the client or noted as a result of conversations with the client. This specification will include information such as lists of the items (entities) that need to be tracked, the individual pieces of information about each item (attributes) that must be recorded, and the types of forms and reports that must be generated. While this information is essential, don't stop there. Ask for all the paper data forms that are currently in use. Find out which data-related tasks are performed frequently and which ones are rarely, if ever, necessary. When replacing a legacy system, talk to the operators to discover what they like and don't like about the current software. The more information at your command, the easier your job will be.

Designing The Tables

After you have all the necessary information, designing the database tables is usually the next step. Because the tables are the foundation of the database, this order makes perfect sense. Table design is a paper-and-pencil process, because visual representations of tables and the relationships between them can be a big help in the design process. Perhaps the most fundamental rule is to create tables that are based on important entities in the assortment of data that the database will contain—people, orders, invoices, and so on. Be sure that the data type of each field is appropriate for the data that it will hold, and that the length of text fields is matched to the information that will be placed in them. When the data lends itself to being divided into tables in two or more ways, make a decision based on how the data will be used and on the availability of keys and links.

Plan The Links

Sketch out the links between tables. To be useful, every table in a relational database must be linked to at least one other table. In most cases, links should be of the one-to-many (1:M) variety. A table structure with 1:1 links usually benefits from redesign, while many:many (M:M) links require special treatment.

Decide On Primary Keys, Foreign Keys, And Indexes

Every table should have a primary key, even if it is a surrogate key that you generate. Every table on the "many" side of a 1:M link also needs a foreign key, usually the same data item as the primary key in the table to which it is linked. Choose the fields that will be used for indexes. Each table should be indexed based on its primary key field, and also based on any fields that will be used regularly to search or sort the table records.

Sketch Out The Forms

After the tables have been designed, you can start sketching the Visual Basic forms that the program will use. Form design is based on the table structure, and also depends heavily on how the users need to view and edit the information. You should test your preliminary form designs, if possible, by incorporating them into a dummy program and allowing the people who will be using the database to try them. Form designs are easier to change now than at a later stage of program development. After completing this stage of design, you should have a preliminary idea of how many forms the program will have, and which controls each form needs.

Plan The Flow Of Execution

After you have a clear idea of the program's forms, you should think about program execution. What will the user see when the program starts? How will the user select program functions—menus, toolbars, or command buttons? How do the forms relate to each other? For example, can the user move from a data entry form to a query form directly, or must the user first close the data entry form and return to the opening screen? The users' needs should also influence this stage of design. Will a single operator be responsible for taking orders and entering inventory, frequently switching from one task to the other? Or will these two tasks be performed by different operators, with no need to quickly switch between them?

Gotchas

Rarely has a programmer completed a database design project without looking back and wishing that he or she had done something differently. Personally, I've never discovered any sure guarantees to avoid this. However, you can lessen the number and severity of these hindsight problems by keeping in mind a relatively small number of database design boo-boos. Here's a list of database design dos and don'ts:

Keep Your Data Atomic

No, that doesn't mean your database should be radioactive! Data that is *atomic* can't be broken down any further into smaller chunks of data—at least not meaningful chunks. This relates to the field structure of your tables. An Address table with a single Name field that holds each person's full name doesn't have atomic data, because it can be further subdivided into first name and last name. Problems would arise later with this table when you need to perform manipulations based on only part of the field data, such as sorting the records by last name. Writing code to extract the last name from each Name field is unnecessarily cumbersome. The best approach is to separate your data into the smallest meaningful pieces—at the beginning: combining data is always easier than extracting or separating it.

Of course, this rule must be applied in combination with some common sense. If you need to break peoples' names into First Name and Last Name fields, shouldn't you have a separate field for Middle Initial? The answer is no, because the isolated middle initial is not meaningful in any sense—to my knowledge, no one has ever wanted to sort a database by middle initials. The standard practice is to include the middle initial in the First Name field.

Use A Primary Key Field

Although this has been mentioned before, it bears repeating: Every table should have a primary key, a field whose data uniquely identifies each record. For many tables, this isn't a problem—one of the required data fields provides a primary key. Other tables, usually the "many" tables in a one-to-many relationship, do not have a field whose data uniquely identifies each record. You then have two methods for creating a primary key.

Most databases have the capability to use *compound* keys, whereby the data in two or more fields combine to provide a unique identifier. For example, in a database of musical recordings, combining the Performer field with the Title field could provide a unique value for each record. This method has two advantages: no extraneous field additions to the table are necessary to provide a primary key, and the primary key consists of meaningful data. A possible disadvantage is that the resulting keys may be rather long, such as "The Chicago Symphony Orchestra—Beethoven's Sixth Symphony." Any processing that uses such a lengthy key will be correspondingly slow.

The second approach is to create a new field whose sole purpose is to hold an arbitrary key generated by the application, such as a sequential number or a letter-number combination. This is sometimes called a *surrogate* key. The disadvantage of this approach is that you have to add meaningless data to the table—data that takes up space but has no purpose other than to serve as the primary key. On the other hand, such keys are likely to be concise, which speeds processing. One compromise is to generate a unique value for the primary key field that combines part of the record's "real" data with a generated number. Using the musical recordings database as an example, you could create a unique key field that consists of the first five letters of the Title field, followed by a sequential number—such as Beeth001.

Avoid Bad Keys

No precise definition of a "bad" primary key exists, but you do have some definite guidelines to follow. Avoid using a big field—one that contains a sizable chunk of data—because the processing overhead required to maintain and use such a key slows down the application. This is particularly true when the primary key is used to index the table, which is a common practice. Don't use a field in which data is likely to change, such as telephone numbers. When a primary key's data changes, all associated indexes must be updated. Even more problematic, the data in all linked foreign keys must be updated, as well.

The data in the primary key *must* be unique for each record. Even if the data ostensibly *should* be unique—such as Social Security Number—nothing guarantees that a typing error during data entry won't result in a duplicate number. Most database applications give you the option of designating a field as a primary key, and then it checks each new entry against existing entries to ensure that no duplicates exist. This doesn't solve the problem of typographical errors, of course, but at least it guarantees that the primary key field remains unique.

Use Descriptive Table And Field Names

This one might seem like a no-brainer, but you would be surprised at how many people ignore it. Assign names to your tables and fields that describe the data they contain. Some tradeoffs do exist between clarity and brevity, but the names should be such that anyone who has some familiarity with the database data will be able to tell from the field and table names exactly what is being stored where. For a field that will hold Part Number, for example, PN is too cryptic, while Part Number is probably unnecessarily long. PartNo would be a good compromise.

Do Not Use Duplicate Field Names

With one exception, you should never use the same field name in different tables in the same database. Doing so is just asking for confusion. For example, a database might contain a Suppliers table and a Customers table, each of which has a field for a telephone number. You shouldn't call that field TelNo in both tables, even though doing so might seem perfectly logical. Instead, create two field names, such as CustTelNo and SuppTelNo. Not only does this avoid the possible confusion of duplicate field names, but it also follows the previous suggestion to use descriptive field names.

The one exception to this rule is the case of foreign key fields, which can have the same field name as the field they link to in the related table.

Be Aware Of International Issues

Many databases need to accommodate international information that is expressed or formatted differently than it is in the United States, such as addresses, currencies, and phone numbers. Even if a database is intended for use only with domestic data, including the required flexibility for international use may be a good idea. Windows itself provides some features to help you deal with different number and time formats and other related issues. Look in Windows Help under Regional Settings.

The Job

In this and the next few chapters, you are going to develop a complete relational database system for an imaginary client. You'll start from scratch with the client's requests and specifications, and then work though all the design and development stages until you have a complete, tested, and functioning product. Approaching the task in this way should be much more informative (and interesting) than if I simply presented the finished program to you and tried to explain how it works.

Before describing the project, I want to mention a dilemma that I face as a computer book author. When I create a demonstration program, I have to find a good balance between two extremes. On one hand, I could create a complete program that has all the details, capabilities, and safety features that are needed for use in a real-world setting, with no further additions required. On the other hand, I could create a program that contains only the bare essentials needed to illustrate the principles and techniques being discussed— with no concern for how this knowledge is applied in a real, functioning program.

In the first approach, the programming techniques that I am trying to communicate may be obscured by details that, while necessary to the final program, are irrelevant to the topic under discussion. The second approach is flawed by the fact that the reader learns the techniques in isolation and never sees how they are integrated into a complete program. My approach is to try to walk a middle line between these two extremes. In the database project that you are going to develop, you will receive enough real-world detail to understand how things are handled, but not so much detail that the main topic— relational database design—is obscured. As you examine the project, you may see several places where the program is lacking a feature that would be necessary for a real, commercial application. Don't fret—I'm aware of them, too.

The Client

Your imaginary client is the GrapeVine Distributing Company, a firm that distributes wine to local restaurants, liquor stores, and hotels. An old, family-run firm, it has been using an antiquated paper-based system to keep track of customers, inventories, and invoices. While old wine may be good, GrapeVine realizes that old business methods are not. It wants to computerize its system, and you are the lucky programmer selected for the job. The basic specifications of the project have already been sketched out by the client:

- The business needs to keep a customer list, including company name, address, and phone number, as well as the name of the wine buyer. This list will be used to generate shipping labels and invoices, and for promotional mailings and similar tasks.

- The business also needs to keep track of inventory. For each wine, the firm needs to record a description, its type, vintage year, the quantity on hand, and the wine's quality rating, as assigned by a popular wine magazine. Furthermore, the business needs to record the wine's cost (the price it pays), its wholesale price (what the business charges its customers), and the suggested retail price.

- Finally, the business needs a method to enter and keep track of orders. Some orders come by mail, others over the phone. In some cases, the customers know exactly what they want; other times, they ask the firm to suggest something: "I want a French or Czechoslovakian red that I can sell for under $15.00."

You now have sufficient information to start designing the database. The first step is to design the tables.

Designing The Tables

The preferred database design is one in which tables represent actual objects, at least as closely as possible. With this in mind, you can quickly see that the client's database naturally divides itself into three tables: one for customers, one for wines, and one for invoices. Each is a physical object that exists in the real world, and each is a unit of information that is of interest to the client. Starting with the customers table (which is cleverly called "Customers"), you can plan for the following fields:

Field Name	*Description*
CompanyName	Name of customer firm
Address	Customer's street address
City	Customer's city
State	Customer's state
ZIP	Customer's ZIP code
Contact	Name of contact person
Phone	Contact's phone number

At first glance, this table looks adequate, but two potential problems already exist. First, by placing the contact person's entire name in one field, isn't this table violating the principle of atomicity that was covered earlier? Strictly speaking...yes, it is. Should the contact person's name be split into FirstName and LastName fields? In this case, that isn't necessary. The function of this table is such that the contact name is not a central piece of information—the business never sorts the table records by contact name—so placing the entire name in one field doesn't cause any problems.

The second problem with this table design is—you got it—no primary key field. You can't be sure that any of these fields, even CompanyName, will always be unique for each record. Even if you felt sure that CompanyName would always be unique, an existing company can sometimes change its name. As explained earlier, you shouldn't select any field as a primary key if its data is subject to change. Therefore, you need to add a surrogate key field, named CustID (for Customer Identification) in this example, to hold a unique identifier for each customer. This unique identifier will be generated later.

The following are the preliminary specifications for the table that will hold information about the wines:

Field Name	Description
StockNo	Stock number
Description	Description from wine's label
Country	Country of origin
Year	Vintage year
Rating	Wine's rating
OurCost	What we pay per unit
WholesaleCost	What we charge per unit
RetailPrice	Suggested retail price per unit
QOH	Quantity on hand

This table, too, may seem adequate at first glance, but then you begin thinking about some conversations that you overheard down at the GrapeVine offices. Things like "Hey Charlie, the Downtown Hotel wants a case of fancy white Burgundy for the mayor's reception. Got any ideas?" or "The fraternity guys want a case of the cheapest red we've got—what shall we send them?" It seems that some characteristics of wines don't fit into this preliminary table design. A quick phone call to the folks at GrapeVine confirms your suspicions. Every wine has a color—red, white, or rose—as well as a type that specifies its region of origin and/or the grape varieties used in making it. This can be important information in making a sale, so it should be included in the database. Therefore, you need to add two more fields—Color and Type—to the Wines table.

The last table you need to design is the Invoices table. Each Invoice record has a unique invoice number, the order date, the customer's purchase-order number, and the customer identification number. In addition, you need to make room for the items that are ordered— for each item, the stock number and the quantity. But wait—how many items should you allow on each invoice? Some invoices may include only a couple of items, while others will have dozens. How can you handle this? You have just run into....

The Problem Of Repeating Fields

Many database designs run into the problem of repeating fields. To illustrate exactly what this means, consider the Invoices table that you are creating to hold information about invoices. A basic table design might look something like the following:

Field Name	*Description*
CustID	Customer identification number
Date	Date of invoice
InvNo	Invoice number (primary key field)
CustPO	Customer's purchase order number
StockNo	Stock number for the item ordered
Quantity	Quantity ordered

However, this permits only one type of item to be recorded per invoice record. Thus, some more fields need to be added to the table:

CustID
Date
InvNo
CustPO
StockNo1
Quantity1
StockNo2
Quantity2
StockNo3
Quantity3

Now you have what are called *repeating fields*—the StockNo and Quantity fields repeat, to permit entry of more than one item. In certain situations, where you know that the number of items—or whatever it might be that is being repeated—will be strictly limited to a small number, this type of table structure may be satisfactory. Generally, however, it should be avoided. No matter how many times you repeat the field or fields, the chance always exists that you won't repeat it enough times to hold some records. And for most records, the majority of the repeated fields go unfilled, thus wasting disk space. Remember that all fields in a database table—even empty ones—take up space.

The solution is to split the data into two tables. One table holds the information that is unique to each invoice. The other table holds the individual line items. This relationship is illustrated in Figure 21.4.

The link between these two tables is provided by the InvNo (Invoice Number) field. InvNo is the primary key for the Invoices table and a foreign key for the Items table.

You may have noticed that the Items table doesn't have a primary key. InvNo, StockNo, and Quantity will not be unique for each record in the table. In terms of the information that this table needs to hold, a primary key field isn't necessary. In terms of database design, however, providing every table with a primary key is a good idea. If no meaningful data is available to serve as a primary key, you can add an additional field to the table

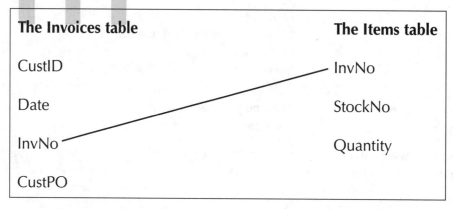

The Invoices table

CustID

Date

InvNo

CustPO

The Items table

InvNo

StockNo

Quantity

Figure 21.4 *The relationship between the Invoices table and the Items table that solves the problem of repeating fields.*

structure and have the database program generate unique sequential numbers to serve as the primary key.

Your table definitions are complete—at least for now. Figure 21.5 shows the table structure, the primary keys in each table, and the links between them.

Carefully examine this database design. No problems are apparent. No data is duplicated. Each table has a primary key field, and each table is linked to at least one other table. Take a look at the type of links you have:

Link	Type
CUSTOMERS:INVOICES	1:M
WINES:ITEMS	1:M
INVOICES:ITEMS	1:M

No 1:1 links exist that might suggest a need to redesign the table. Nor do any M:M (many to many) links exist that require special treatment. You can safely conclude that you have a good database table design. If you're lucky, this design will remain unchanged throughout the remainder of the project.

Creating The Database

Now that you have your table design, you can use Visual Data Manager to create the database and its tables. You also need to place some data in the tables; otherwise, you have nothing to use when testing forms and other parts of the program. Ideally, this should be real data provided by your client. If that is not available, you can create "dummy" data and delete it from the database later.

It's time to use Visual Data Manager (VisData) to create the database and its tables. The basics of using VisData are covered in Chapter 19, so please refer to that section if your

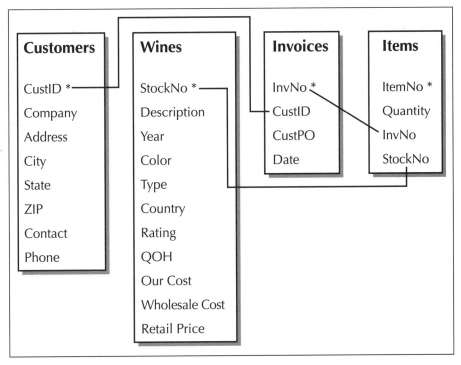

Figure 21.5   *The table structure for the GRAPEVINE database (an asterisk marks primary key fields; lines indicate links).*

memory needs jogging. Create a database named GRAPEVINE (using Microsoft Access version 7), with the following four tables, labeled here for identification as Tables 21.1 through Table 21.4.

You may have some questions about the data type that I selected for some of these fields. You may even believe that a different data type would be more appropriate in some cases. Let me explain:

- *ZIP in the CUSTOMERS table*—Since ZIP code is a number, why not use a numeric data type? Some ZIP codes begin with zero; if the data type were numeric, you would have to write special code to display or print the leading zero. By using a text field, you avoid this problem.

- *Phone in the CUSTOMERS table*—Why not use a length-10 text field, since a phone number contains only 10 digits (including area code)? The separators could be added later when the number is displayed. This argument is valid, but this involves only two extra characters, or bytes, per phone number for the separators (the dashes in a phone number, such as 919-555-1212). By storing the phone number fully formatted, you save programming hassles at the cost of taking up a trivial amount of extra space.

Table 21.1   The CUSTOMERS table.

Field Name	DataType, Length
CustID	Long Integer (turn on AutoIncrField option)
Company	text, 24
Address	text, 30
City	text, 15
State	text, 2
ZIP	text, 5
Contact	text, 24
Phone	text, 12

Table 21.2   The WINES table.

Field Name	Data Type, Length
StockNo	text, 10
Description	text, 40
Year	text, 4
Color	text, 5
Type	text, 15
Country	text, 15
Rating	Integer
QOH	Integer
OurCost	Currency
WholesaleCost	Currency
RetailPrice	Currency

Table 21.3   The INVOICES table.

Field Name	Data Type, Length
InvNo	Long Integer (turn on AutoIncrField option)
CustID	text, 8
CustPO	text, 12
Date	Date/Time

Table 21.4   The ITEMS table.

Field Name	Data Type, Length
ItemNo	Long Integer (turn on AutoIncrField option)
Quantity	Integer
InvNo	Long
StockNo	text, 10

- *InvNo in the* INVOICES *table*—Why not make this a text field, so that the invoice identifiers can include letters as well as numbers? You have no reason to do this, beyond meeting client desires, such as wanting to continue with the existing system that uses an alphanumeric code for invoices. Using a numeric variable type makes generating sequential, unique values for this field easy. Because your client has no special needs in this area, go with the numbers.

- *ItemNo in the* ITEMS *table*—The reasoning explained in the previous paragraph applies here, as well.

After the table definitions are complete, you can close the Visual Data Manager. You're not finished with the Visual Data Manager, by any means. You still need to enter the initial data in the tables. Additionally, you will discover that VisData provides many other tools for defining various characteristics of the tables. For example, is a field allowed to be blank, or must some data be entered in it? Subjects such as this are covered in later chapters.

Chapter 22

Forms And Fields, Fields And Forms

To avoid certain pesky problems, you can use field properties to match the tables to the data. You also need to design forms for viewing and manipulating the data.

In modern databases, a field is not just a simple container into which you can toss a chunk of data. Fields have numerous properties that you can set so that the characteristics of the field match the needs of the database. This is an important part of database programming, because improperly set field properties can lead to a lot of problems down the road. After covering fields, this chapter moves on to a very important—and I think fun—part of the project: designing the forms.

Field Properties

Each field in a table definition has a set of properties. Three of these properties were used to design the structure of the database tables in Chapter 21: the **Name** property, specifying the field name; the **Type** property, specifying its data type; and (for Text fields only) the **Size** property, specifying the field size or maximum number of characters the field can hold. Fields have several other properties, and using them judiciously is an important part of database design. This section first looks at these properties, and then shows you how to set them for the demonstration project.

Validation Properties

The term *validation* refers to the process of ensuring that the data entered in a field meets certain criteria. Some validation rules are quite simple, such as requiring that the field contain some data and not be left empty. Other validation rules can be much more involved, such as requiring that the entry in a Part Number field consists of two letters, followed by a four-digit number. An Access database (the format you are using for the GrapeVine project that was started in the previous chapter) provides several properties that determine if and how a field's data is validated:

- **ValidationRule**—An SQL statement used to validate the data that is entered into a field. When the SQL statement is applied to the data in the field, it must evaluate to True; otherwise, an error message is displayed (see the **ValidationText** property). The **ValidationRule** property takes the form of an SQL **WHERE** clause minus the **WHERE** keyword.

- **ValidationText**—The error text that is displayed when the conditions specified by the **ValidationRule** property are not met.

- **ValidateOnSet**—If this property is True, the validation rule (if any) associated with the field is applied as soon as the field's value is set or changed. If set to False, validation occurs only when the entire record is updated (along with validation for other fields).

- **Required**—This property determines whether the field can contain a Null value. Null is a special Visual Basic value that is used to indicate missing or unknown data, and it is designated by the **Null** keyword. A Null value in a field is not the same as a blank field, a zero-length string, or a zero value. Some fields, particularly those defined as the primary key, cannot contain Null values.

- **AllowZeroLength**—This property specifies whether a zero-length string ("") is permitted in a type Text or Memo field.

Using these validation properties is one approach to performing validation checks on data. Sometimes, however, using the **Validate** event is preferable. This event is covered later in the chapter.

Other Field Properties

You should also know about several miscellaneous field properties:

- **OrdinalPosition**—This property specifies the relative position of the field in the table, with zero being the first position. When fields are displayed—for example, in a DataGrid control—the default display order is determined by the ordinal positions of the fields, which are determined by the order in which they were added to the table during database design.

- **DefaultValue**—A string or a Basic expression that evaluates to the appropriate data type for the field. When a record is created, this value is automatically entered in the field, and can be changed by the user, if desired.

- **CollatingOrder**—This property specifies the order used when sorting records that are based on text data in the field. This property is an integer value that indicates the language rules to be used for sorting. The default is **dbSortGeneral** (value = 1033), which uses the general sort order appropriate for English, French, German, Portuguese, Italian, and Modern Spanish. Specialized collating orders are available for Dutch, Greek, Hebrew, and several other languages (see Visual Basic Help for details).

- **DataUpdatable**—This property specifies whether the data in the field can be changed.

Setting Field Properties For The Demonstration Database

Now that you know what the various field properties do, you can set them for the GRAPE-VINE database. The procedure for setting field properties is as follows:

1. In Visual Basic, select Visual Data Manager from the Add-Ins menu.

2. In VisData, use the File Open command to open the GRAPEVINE.MDB database.

3. The Database Window displays the names of the four tables that you previously created: Customers, Wines, Items, and Invoices. Click on the plus sign (+) next to the name of the table with the field properties you want to edit.

4. Under the table name, you should see a Fields heading. Click on the plus sign next to the heading to view a list of the table's fields, as shown for the Customers table in Figure 22.1.

5. Click on a field name, or the plus sign next to it, to open a list of its properties. Figure 22.2 shows the properties of the CustID field in the Customers table (before editing the properties).

6. Double-click on a property name to open a dialog box where you can edit the property setting. If you try to edit a read-only property, a message to that effect is displayed.

7. Click on OK when you finish editing the property, to close the dialog box. Click on Cancel to retain the original property setting.

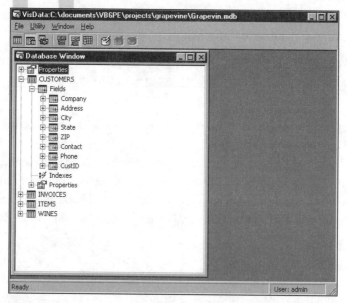

Figure 22.1 *The fields in the Customers table.*

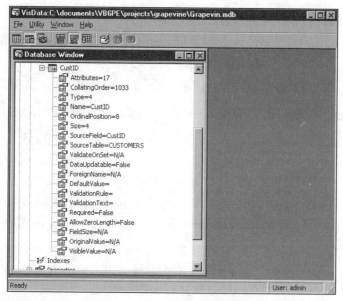

Figure 22.2 *The properties of the CustID field in the Customers table.*

8. Repeat Steps 6 and 7 to edit other properties of this field.

9. Repeat Steps 5 through 8 to edit the properties of other fields in the current table, as needed.

10. Repeat Steps 3 through 9 to edit the properties of fields in another table.

11. As you work, click on the minus sign next to an expanded heading to collapse it and hide the subheadings.

12. When finished, select Exit from the File menu to close VisData and return to Visual Basic.

Finding Your Way Around VisData

The Database Window in VisData is arranged hierarchically. The most basic display consists of the database's table names plus an entry called Properties, under which you find the properties that apply to the database as a whole. Click on the plus sign next to a table name to see three headings—one each for Fields, Indexes, and Properties. At this level, the Properties heading contains those properties that apply to the specific table. Open the Fields heading for a list of the table's fields, and then open an individual field for a list of its field-specific properties. Double-click on a property name to edit the property.

For your database, only relatively minor changes to the default property settings are required. All of your data validation will be done in code, so you don't need any entries to the **ValidationRule** or **ValidationText** properties. The required property changes are listed in the following section. Using the procedures just explained, make the following changes:

- *In the CUSTOMERS table*—CustID, Company, Address, City, State, and ZIP are all required fields, so **Required** should be True. Because you can't be sure each firm has a specific contact person and phone number, these fields may be left blank, with the property setting of **Required** = False.

- *In the WINES table*—All fields in this table are required entries except for RetailPrice. **Required** should be True for all fields except RetailPrice, where **Required** = False.

- *In the INVOICES table*—The InvNo field properties do not need to be changed. For the other three fields in this table, set **Required** to True.

- *In the ITEMS table*—The ItemNo field properties do not need to be changed. The other three fields in this table are required, so set **Required** to True.

That's it—all field properties are set as needed. You can now turn your attention to the database's indexes.

Defining Indexes

Along with setting field properties, the Visual Data Manager also defines indexes in a database. To review briefly, an *index* is a logical sorting, or ordering, of the records in a table, based on the data contained in one or more fields. To define an index for a table, start the Visual Data Manager and open the database file (if necessary). Then:

1. In the Database Window, right-click on the table name and select Design from the pop-up menu. This opens the Table Structure dialog box.

2. Click on the Add Index button to open the Add Index dialog box, shown in Figure 22.3.

3. Type a descriptive index name in the Name box.

4. In the Available Fields list, click on the name of the field or fields upon which this index will be based.

5. Turn the Primary, Unique, and IgnoreNulls options on or off, as needed.

6. Click on OK to define the index; click on Close after you have defined all needed indexes for this table.

The indexes to define for the GRAPEVINE database are shown in Table 22.1. For the database you are developing, use the techniques just described to define the indexes in Table 22.1.

Tradeoffs In Using Indexes

Selection and design of indexes is a subjective process to some extent. Defining an index on a field is not necessary for sorting the records based on that field or searching for data in that field. However, having an index certainly speeds up these operations. Of course, overhead is involved in every index. Each time the user adds a new record or edits an existing record, all the table's indexes are automatically updated by the database engine. This updating takes time. While the time may not be noticeable initially when the database is small, time can become a problem later when the database has grown to thousands of records.

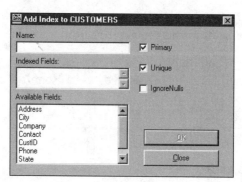

Figure 22.3   *The Add Index dialog box.*

Table 22.1   GRAPEVINE database indexes and attributes.

Table	Index Name	Field	Primary	Unique
CUSTOMERS	CustID	CustID	y	y
	Company	Company	n	n
WINES	StockNo	StockNo	y	y
	Type	Type	n	n
	RetailPrice	RetailPrice	n	n
INVOICES	InvNo	InvNo	y	y
	CustID	CustID	n	y
ITEMS	ItemNo	ItemNo	y	y
	StockNo	StockNo	n	n
	InvNo	InvNo	n	n

TIP   Maintaining Record Integrity

What is *referential integrity*? To answer this question, think for a moment about the purpose of a relationship between a dependent and a primary table. In a record in the dependent table, the value of the foreign key indicates or "points" to a record in the primary table that contains related information. For example, in the Invoices table of the GRAPEVINE) database, the value in the CustID field matches a single record in the Customers table. As a result, each Invoice record is linked to the required customer information. When referential integrity is enforced, the database engine checks to see whether the primary table contains a matching record whenever a record in the dependent table is entered or edited. If referential integrity is enforced for the Customers:Invoices relationship, the database engine checks for a matching record in the Customers table each time the user enters or edits a record in the Invoices table.

For the current demonstration, you don't need to enforce referential integrity. As you'll see later, the way you enter data into the foreign key fields ensures the existence of a matching primary key.

The Validate Event

A vital part of any well designed database program is validating the data being entered. By preventing the entry of invalid data, you can save a lot of headaches down the road. Certain kinds of validation can be accomplished by using the field object's validation properties, as discussed earlier in the chapter. Considering the limitations of these properties, I have found the **Validate** event to be much more useful. This event applies to a wide variety of controls—anything that you would possibly use for data entry/editing in a database project. The **Validate** event works in tandem with the **Causes Validation** property. If the focus is moved from one control to another, the first control's **Validate** event is fired if the second control's **Causes Validation** property is True.

Here's an example. You have a data entry form with a Text Box that is bound to an ADO Data control. The form also has an OK Command Button to confirm data entry, and a Help Command Button to display help information. Set the **Causes Validation** property to True for the OK button and to False for the Help button. If the user enters or edits data in the Text Box and then clicks on the OK button, the Text Box's **Validate** event is fired, and code in the event procedure can be used to validate the data. In contrast, if the user clicks on the Help button, the **Validate** event is not fired.

The **Validate** event procedure has the following structure:

```
Private Sub object_Validate(KeepFocus As Boolean)
...
End Sub
```

Code in the procedure can set *KeepFocus* to True to cause the control to keep the focus after the event procedure executes. Leaving *KeepFocus* at the default value of False permits the focus to move away from the control. Here's an example **Validate** procedure that ensures that the data entered in the Text Box is a number:

```
Private Sub Text1_Validate(KeepFocus As Boolean)

If Not IsNumeric(Text1.Text) Then
    KeepFocus = True
    MsgBox "You must enter a number here."
End If

End Sub
```

What sort of things do you look for when validating data? It depends on the specific situation, of course, but several general criteria are often used:

- *Is a number within a certain range?* For example, a Quantity on Hand field may be zero or positive, but never negative.

- *Is a text entry the proper length or within the acceptable length range?* For example, a ZIP code (entered as text) must be 5 characters long (or 10 characters for "ZIP + 4").

- *Does a text entry fit the required format?* Your firm's Stock Numbers may all follow the format XXXNNNN, where X is a letter and N is a number; any other format of entry should be rejected.

- *Is a Date entry within the allowable time span?* For example, if an employee's birth date is entered as May 4, 1852, you can be reasonably sure a mistake was made.

The Basic language provides a full range of tools for validating data. Use of the **Variant** data type in data-validation routines is recommended. The automatic "awareness" of data type that **Variant** variables provide can eliminate some tedious coding, particularly when converting strings to numbers and numbers to strings. Functions such as **IsNumeric** and **IsDate** make certain types of validation trivial, while Visual Basic's various string functions, such as **Len** and **Instr**, can be used to validate string data.

Fundamental Program Structure

Before starting on a project of this complexity, you should always consider the various options that Visual Basic provides for the overall program structure and appearance. You know that the program requires several "forms" to display the database data in various ways and to permit entry and editing of data (why forms is in quotes will become clear). The user also needs a way to move between forms, selecting the task to be performed. First, look at the available options for displaying program elements:

- *Use the multiple document interface (MDI) architecture.* In an MDI program, one "master" form (the MDI form) serves as a *parent* or container for all other forms, or *child* forms. Any number of child forms can exist; and while multiple child forms can be displayed at one time, only one can be active. Display of child forms is limited to the internal area of the parent form: If the parent form does not occupy the full screen, the child forms cannot be moved outside of it. Each child form can have its own menu; when the form is active, this menu is displayed on the menu bar of the parent form. If you have used a Windows word processor, such as Microsoft Word, you have seen an MDI program in action.

- *Use a collection of non-MDI forms.* This configuration also uses multiple forms, but with no parent and no children. Each form is an independent entity that displays its own menu and can be moved and sized independently of the other forms.

- *Use a single form with multiple Picture Box forms.* Remember that a Picture Box control can be used as a container for other controls. In this design, the program consists of a single Visual Basic form with several Picture Box controls on it. Each Picture Box contains the controls required for a particular program function—one for entry of records in the Customers table, another for creating new Invoice records, and so on. Code in the program determines which of the Picture Box controls is visible and active at a given time, permitting the display of multiple "forms" on a single form.

Several options are also available for user control of the program. Of course, you can use these different control methods in combination with each other, but for the sake of simplicity, your demonstration project is limited to only one method. In a real, commercial application, you'll probably want to use two—for example, a Toolbar plus menus. Here are the main ways that you can design a program to accept commands from the user:

- Create a menu system containing the commands
- Display Command Buttons for the commands
- Design a Toolbar with buttons for the commands

For the purposes of the demonstration program, I decided to use an MDI interface with a Toolbar. Some other choices might have worked equally well, but this approach gives you the opportunity to learn how to implement an MDI interface and a Toolbar—two important Visual Basic tools.

Preliminary Form Design

Rather than trying to tackle the entire project at once, you start by designing and coding the simpler forms, and creating the MDI interface. For both the Customers table and the Wines table, you need a form that permits entering new records, editing existing records, and deleting existing records. These forms should be fairly straightforward, requiring a Text Box and identifying Label for each field, and a group of Command Buttons for the various actions. You'll also want a way to list all the records in the table on a single form, with the option of sorting the list based on different fields. In this situation, the DataGrid custom control comes in handy. But first you need the parent MDI form and its Toolbar.

Creating The MDI Form And Toolbar

Creating the MDI form first is not necessary—but it isn't a bad idea, either. Start a new standard EXE project and select Add MDI Form from the Project menu. Change the form's **Caption** property to "Grapevine Wine Distributors". You can leave the form's **Name** property at the default value of MDIForm1, but when you save it, use the name GRAPEVINE.FRM (Use GRAPEVINE as the project name, too). Click-and-drag the Toolbar icon in the Toolbox to place a Toolbar on the form. Remember, if the Toolbar icon is not displayed in the Toolbox, you must use the Project, Components command to load it. The Toolbar is part of the set referred to as the Windows Common Controls. When you select this item in the Components dialog box, several controls, including the Toolbar, will be added to the Visual Basic toolbox.

Working With The Toolbar Control

The Toolbar starts out empty, with no buttons. You have the option of using text or images on the Toolbar buttons. For images, bind the Toolbar to an ImageList control, which manages the images (icons or bitmaps) that are displayed on the Toolbar buttons. For the present project, just use text buttons. I presented information on using the ImageList control in Chapter 7.

Before you start to work on the Toolbar buttons, set the **Align** property of the Toolbar to Top, causing the Toolbar to position itself automatically at the top of the container form, filling it from side to side. This property must be set in the regular Visual Basic properties window—not in the Toolbar's pop-up property sheet, which you use next.

The Toolbar is an object with its own properties, and it contains several Button objects with their own properties. When a Toolbar control is selected on the Visual Basic design screen, the Properties window displays the Toolbar's properties, which control variables such as the button size and font. To access **Button** properties and add or delete buttons, you need to display the Toolbar's property sheet by right-clicking on the control and selecting Properties from the menu that is displayed. The Toolbar Control properties page—another name for dialog box—is shown in Figure 22.4.

This dialog box has the following three tabs from which to choose settings:

- *General*—Toolbar properties (a subset of those available in the Visual Basic Properties window)

- *Buttons*—Button properties, adding and deleting buttons

- *Picture*—Displaying images on buttons

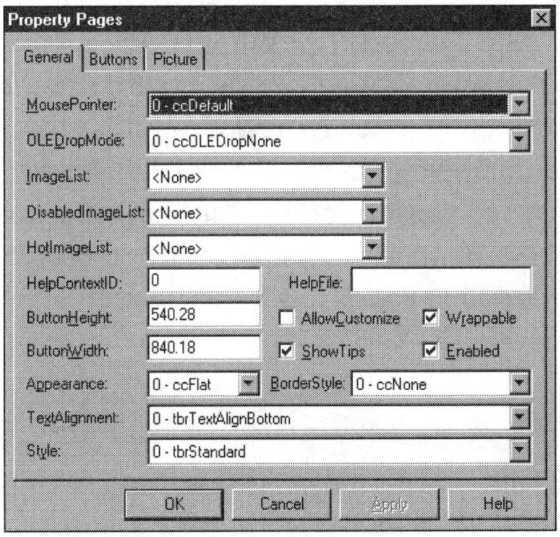

Figure 22.4 *The Toolbar Control's Property Pages dialog box.*

You will use the General and Buttons tabs for your project. Here are descriptions of the properties on the General tab; the settings needed for the current project are in parentheses:

- **AllowCustomize**—Permits the user to customize the Toolbar at runtime (off). Customization involves double-clicking on the Toolbar to display the Customize Toolbar dialog box, which permits you to add and remove buttons and change their order.

- **ShowTips**—Displays a ToolTip (programmer defined) if the mouse cursor rests on the button briefly (on).

- **Enabled**—Same as for other Visual Basic controls—activates or deactivates the Toolbar (on).

- **Wrappable**—Indicates whether the Toolbar buttons wrap to multiple rows, if needed, when the container window is resized (on).

- **MousePointer**—Displays when the pointer is over the Toolbar (ccDefault).

- **ImageList**—When displaying images on the buttons, the ImageList controls where the images are stored (none).

- **ButtonHeight** and **ButtonWidth**—Show the size of the buttons, expressed in the ScaleMode units of the Toolbar's container. The **ButtonWidth** property is automatically adjusted to match the longest label (**Caption** property) on a button (default settings).

Before you get to the details of adding buttons to the Toolbar, you need to understand the relationship between a Toolbar control and its buttons. As mentioned previously, each button is represented by a Button object, and all the Button objects on a Toolbar are represented by the **Buttons** collection. The **Buttons** collection is a standard Collection object, which you have met several times already. Briefly, the **Buttons** collection is a 1-based group of indexed Button objects (1-based means that the first button has index 1 rather than 0, which is more common in some other parts of Visual Basic). In code, therefore, you can access individual buttons and the **Buttons** collection by using standard Visual Basic collection syntax. If your Toolbar is named Toolbar1, for example, you can create a type **Button** variable that points to a specific button in one of several ways. First, declare the variable:

```
Dim btnX As Button
```

Then, retrieve a specific button by its index number:

```
Set btnX = Toolbar1.Buttons(2)      'Second button on Toolbar
```

You can also reference a button by a unique key (such as the Button object's **Key** property):

```
Set btnX = Toolbar1.Buttons("second") ' If Key = "second"
```

You can also use the **Item** method:

```
Set btnX = Toolbar1.Buttons.Item(2)
```

After you retrieve the desired button, you can set its properties; for example:

```
btnX.Caption = "Close"
btnX.Enabled = False
```

The Toolbar control provides a great deal of flexibility, including the ability to add and remove buttons at runtime. (Refer to the Visual Basic Help system for more details.) Note that Toolbar buttons can be used in two basic ways. One way is to initiate a process, similar to a Command Button control; the Save Project and Open Project buttons on the Toolbar in the Visual Basic development environment operate in this fashion. The second way is to turn on and off options, like the Lock Controls button on the Toolbar in the Visual Basic development environment. You determine how a Button operates by manipulating its properties.

Back to the project: After setting the Toolbar control's **General** properties, as previously described, click on the Buttons tab, shown in Figure 22.5. You will add three buttons to the Toolbar, for now. Here are the basic steps to follow for each button:

1. Click on Insert Button and a new button is inserted to the right of the current button (as indicated in the Index box). If no buttons exist, the new button becomes the first

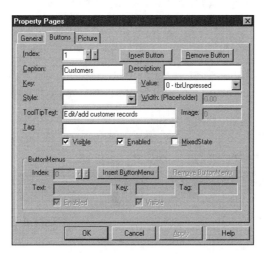

Figure 22.5   *The Buttons tab on the Toolbar control's Property Pages dialog box.*

button at the left of the Toolbar. If necessary, use the left and right arrow buttons to make the appropriate button current, before clicking on the Insert button.

2. Type the button's caption in the Caption box.

3. Repeat Steps 1 and 2 for additional buttons, and then click on OK.

While these are the minimum steps required to add a button to a Toolbar, the Button object offers several other useful properties:

- **Caption**—The text displayed on the button.

- **Description**—The button description displayed at runtime in the Customize Toolbar dialog box.

- **Key**—A unique string that identifies the button.

- **Value**—Whether the button is pressed (Value = 1) or unpressed (Value = 0).

- **Style**—The button's style (see Table 22.2).

- **PlaceholderWidth**—The width of a button if its **Style** is set to PlaceHolder.

- **Tag**—This property is not used by Visual Basic. It serves as a location for extra data (in string format) that your program can use in any manner that it requires (same as the **Tag** property of other controls).

- **ToolTipText**—The text that is displayed next to the mouse cursor when it is placed on a button briefly (but only if the Toolbar's **ShowTips** property is True).

- **Image**—The index of the button's image in the associated ImageList control.

- **Visible**—Indicates whether the button is visible. If a button's **Visible** property is False, buttons to the right move over to fill in the space where the button would be displayed if **Visible** = True.

- **Enabled**—Indicates whether the button is active (can be clicked).

- **MixedState**—Controls whether the button is displayed in the mixed state (grayed out). A mixed-state button can still be active (Enabled).

Now, what about this **Style** property? A Button object can have one of six different styles. Clearly, some Button properties are not relevant for certain styles. The available styles, the defined constants available for setting them, and their descriptions are given in Table 22.2.

Table 22.2   Available styles for a Button object.

Constant	Value	Description
tbrDefault	0	(Default) Button. The button is a regular push button.
tbrCheck	1	Check. The button is a check button, which can be checked or unchecked.
tbrButtonGroup	2	ButtonGroup. All buttons with this style constitute a group. One, and only one, button in a group can be depressed at a given time; clicking on one button automatically "unclicks" the one that was depressed previously. A Toolbar can have only one group.
tbrSeparator	3	Separator. The button functions as a separator with a fixed width of eight pixels.
tbrPlaceholder	4	Placeholder. The button appears and functions like a separator but has a settable width. A "button" with this style can be used to place another control on a Toolbar. For example, to place a drop-down Text Box on a Toolbar, add a Button with the PlaceHolder style and adjust its width to the desired size. Then, place a Combo Box of the same width on the placeholder button.
tbrDropDown	5	Dropdown. Shows an arrow next to the button that, when clicked on, displays a programmer-defined drop-down menu of command choices.

Adding Buttons To The Toolbar

That was a long detour to cover the details of the Toolbar control. Getting back on track, it's time to create the three buttons for the Toolbar on your MDI form. Using the techniques explained earlier, add three buttons—leaving all of their properties at the default setting, except as shown in Table 22.3.

After adding these buttons, close the Toolbar's property sheet. Your MDI form should resemble Figure 22.6.

Table 22.3   Nondefault properties for the three Toolbar buttons.

Index	Caption	ToolTipText
1	Customers	Edit/add customers
2	Wines	Edit/add wines
3	Exit	Exit program

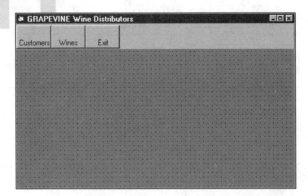

Figure 22.6 *The MDI form and Toolbar after adding the first three Toolbar buttons.*

As you might guess, responding to Toolbar button clicks is accomplished in an event procedure. The Toolbar object has a **ButtonClick** event procedure that is called when any of the control's buttons are clicked on. This procedure is passed a type **Button** argument that specifies which button was clicked on. You can query the **Button** argument's properties to identify the button, and you can use any of the properties that are unique to each button, such as **Index** or **Caption**. To add code to this event procedure, right-click on the Toolbar and select View Code from the pop-up menu. A Code Editing window opens; if necessary, select ButtonClick from the Procedure list at the top of the window.

The code for this procedure is shown in Listing 22.1. Notice that you respond to clicks of the "Customers" and "Wines" buttons by displaying the appropriate form. These forms haven't been designed yet, but you can reference them in code, as long as you don't try to execute the code (which would cause an error message, of course). Clicking on the Exit button displays a message box first, confirming that the user wants to exit, and then uses End to terminate the program.

Listing 22.1   The Toolbar control's ButtonClick event procedure.

```
Private Sub Toolbar1_ButtonClick(ByVal Button As Button)

Dim Reply As Integer

Select Case Button.Caption
    Case "Customers"
        frmCustomers.Show
    Case "Wines"
        frmWines.Show
    Case "Exit"
        Reply = MsgBox("Quit program - are you sure?", _
            vbYesNo + vbQuestion, "Quit?")
```

```
        If Reply = vbYes Then End
End Select

End Sub
```

One last thing before you leave the MDI form: place the following line of code in the General section of the form's code:

```
Public EnteringRecord As Boolean
```

Then, put this line in the **Form_Load** event procedure:

```
EnteringRecord = False
```

These lines declare the flag variable and initialize it to the proper value when the program loads.

Designing The Customers Form

The next task is to design the form to display customer information. To add a new form to the project, select Form from the Insert menu. This form will have the **Name** property "frmCustomers" and will be saved with the file name CUSTOMERS.FRM. You need to add the following items to this form:

- A control array of eight Text Box controls, one for each field in the Customers table.

- A control array of eight Label controls, one to identify each Text Box. The Label controls don't have to be in a control array, but using cut-and-paste is easier than dragging each individual control when placing several controls of the same type.

- A control array of four Command Buttons.

- One ADO Data control.

When you place the Text Box controls on the form, add them in the order that a user would want to move between them—that is, in the same order as the fields are arranged in the database table. By adding the controls in this order, the tab order will be arranged similarly, and the user can Tab and Shift+Tab between Text Boxes in the most efficient order. Although you can change tab order later, after adding the controls, adding them in the correct order now saves time. The completed form is shown in Figure 22.7.

Before you set other object properties, you first need to set the ADO Data control's properties, to connect it to the Customers table in the GRAPEVINE database. The **ConnectionString** property is set first. Select the ADO Data control, select the

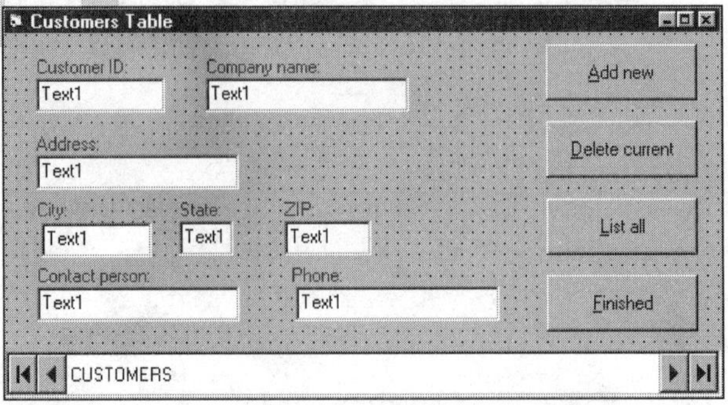

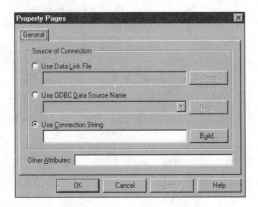

Figure 22.7 *The completed Customers form.*

ConnectionString property in the Properties window, and then click on the button with the three dots. Visual Basic displays the General tab of the control's Property Pages dialog box, as shown in Figure 22.8.

Three ways exist to specify the connection between the control and a database. You will use a Connection String. Select the option for Connection String and then click on the Build button. After you are familiar with database programming, you may be able to write the connection string from scratch, but for now, let Visual Basic help you. The Data Link Properties dialog box is displayed.

This dialog box has several tabs on it; the Connection tab is shown in Figure 22.9. Here's what you need to do:

1. On the Provider tab, select Microsoft Jet 3.51 OLE DB Provider.

2. On the Advanced tab, select the ReadWrite option and deselect all others.

3. On the Connection tab, click on the button with the three dots and then locate and select the GRAPEVINE.MDB database file. Then, click on the Test Connection button to verify that the connection to the database is working.

Figure 22.8 *The ADO Data control's Property Pages dialog box.*

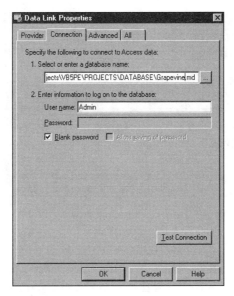

Figure 22.9   *The Data Link Properties dialog box.*

When finished, click on OK. The connection string is entered into the Property Page. Click on OK again to accept this as the ADO Data control's **ConnectionString** property.

The next property of the ADO Data control that you need to set is **RecordSource**. This property is the statement, usually expressed in SQL, that specifies which records are to be returned by the control. The specification includes both the table name and a criterion for records to be returned from that table. The statement you use is the following:

```
select * from customers
```

This is a very simple SQL statement that says, when translated into English, "select all records from the customers table." To enter this property, display the property page for the **RecordSource** property (Figure 22.10) and select 1 - adCmdText as the command type. Then, enter the preceding SQL statement in the Command text (SQL) box, and click on OK.

Finally, set the ADO Data control's **Caption** property to "Customers" and its **Align** property to vbAlignBottom. This last property causes the control to align itself automatically at the bottom of whatever form it is on. Now you can set the properties of the other controls on the Customers form. Generally, the properties are left at their default settings. Here are the most important changes you need to make:

1. Set the **TabStop** property of the first Text Box (the one for the CustID field) to False and the **Locked** property to True. Because the attribute of this field was set to

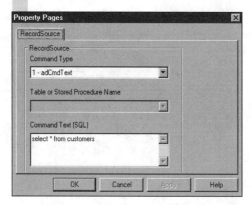

Figure 22.10   *Setting the RecordSource property of the ADO Data Control.*

AutoIncrField during database design, the database engine automatically generates unique values for this field. The user doesn't need access to this Text Box. Note that setting **Locked** to True prevents the user from editing the Text Box, but does not prevent you from changing it in code.

2. For each Text Box, set the **DataSource** property to ADODC1 (the default name of the ADO Data control) and the **DataField** property to the appropriate field. Note that the **DataField** property offers you a drop-down list of all the fields in the Customers table. If you had not connected the ADO Data control to the data source first, this list would not be available.

3. Set the form's **BorderStyle** property to Fixed Single, so that the user can't change its size at runtime.

4. Be sure that the **Index** properties of the Command Buttons match their captions, as follows: Add New (0), Delete Current (1), List All (2), Finished (3).

Save the form as CUSTOMER.FRM, and assign a **Name** property of "frmCustomers". Be sure to set the form's **MDIChild** property to True, to make it a child of the MDI form that you created earlier, and change the **Caption** property to "Customers Table".

Designing The Wines Form

Conceptually, the Wines Form is quite similar to the Customers form that you just created. However, for the Wines form, you will implement one new technique: you will use a Combo Box in place of a Text Box for data entry for some of the fields. You can consider a Combo Box as a combination of a Text Box and List Box; users can either type data into the Text Box part of the control or select from the drop-down list of items. A Combo Box is appropriate when the data entry into a particular field (either usually or always) consists of an item from a predefined list. This is the case for the Color and Type fields in the Wines table. Note that using a Combo Box does not force a selection from the list—users can always type something else—but using a Combo Box does make the entry of list items faster and error-free.

Select Insert Form to add a new form to the project. The form's **Name** property should be set to "frmWines", and it should be saved under the name WINES.FRM. This form will contain the following controls:

- A control array of nine Text Box controls, one for each field in the Customers table except for the Color and Type fields

- Two Combo Box controls for the Color and Type fields

- A control array of 11 Label controls, one to identify each Text Box and Combo Box

- A control array of four Command Buttons

- One ADO Data control

After placing the controls, the form should look like Figure 22.11.

Here are the most important changes you need to make to the form and control properties:

1. Add the individual Text Box controls in the proper order, so that the resulting tab order is correct. You can always modify the **TabIndex** properties later, if necessary. Be sure to include the Combo Box controls in the desired position in the tab order.

2. For the ADO Data control, follow the techniques previously described for the Customers form to connect it to the GRAPEVINE database and to set the **RecordSource** to select all records from the Wines table (SQL statement = "select * from wines"). Set the **Caption** property to "Wines" and the **Align** property to vbAlignBottom.

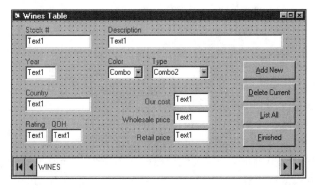

Figure 22.11   *The Wines form.*

3. For each Text Box and Combo Box, set the **DataSource** property to ADODC1 and the **DataField** property to the appropriate field. Set the **Name** property of the two Combo Boxes to "ComboType" and "ComboColor".

4. Set the form's **BorderStyle** property to Fixed Single, its **Caption** property to "Wines Table", and its **MDIChild** property to True.

5. Make sure that the **Index** properties of the Command Buttons match their captions, as follows: Add New (0), Delete Current (1), List All (2), Finished (3).

Designing The List Form

Part of your design plan is to have the ability to list all the records in both the Wines and the Customers table. You included a List All button on both the Customers and Wines forms, but how can you implement a list of all records? The DataGrid control provides the ideal solution—it is designed for just this kind of task. You will create a single form for listing records, and then specify which table's records are to be displayed in code before the form is displayed.

Add a new form to the project. Set its **Name** property to "frmList" and save it as LIST1.FRM. Add one DataGrid control, one ADO Data control, and one Command Button control to the form. Set the DataGrid's **DataSource** property to ADODC1 and its **Align** property to Top. The ADO Data control's **ConnectString** should be set to the GRAPEVINE.MDB database, as you have done for the other ADO Data controls. The ADO Data control's **RecordSource** property, however, doesn't need to be set at this time, because it will be set in code. You should make the ADO Data control's **Visible** property False, however, because you won't need this control to be visible on the form. Change the Command Button's **Caption** property to &Finished.

Writing The Code

Now that you have designed the project's first three forms, you can turn your attention to writing the code that gives these forms their functionality. Of course, these three forms are only part of what the project requires—so why not design the remaining forms before starting on Basic code? This is one approach, but my own experience has proven that working on the project one section at a time—both forms and code—gives better results. This way, you have part of the program working properly before moving on to the next part. You can expect to have to make changes later. You already have enough forms designed to provide part of the program's functionality, such as entering, editing, and listing records in the Customers and Wines table. Making sure that this much is working before you move on to the next challenge is a good idea.

The Basic Module

Complex projects such as this one almost always require a Basic module for declaration of global variables and similar tasks. To add a Basic module, select Add Module from the Project menu. Type the following code:

```
' True when entering a record, False otherwise.

Global EnteringRecord As Boolean
```

Save the module under the name GRAPEVINE (Visual Basic adds the .BAS extension).

Coding The Customers Form

The initial approach to coding this form is to provide its basic functions, but not necessarily everything that you eventually want it to include. You'll write code to permit users to enter, edit, delete, and list records, and leave the code writing for data validation until later.

In the Customers form, you again use the "chameleon Command Button" technique covered earlier in the book, permitting the four Command Buttons to do the work of six. When the user views or edits records in the default state, the global variable EnteringRecords is False and the first two Command Buttons have the captions "Add New" and "Delete Current". When the user clicks on the Add New button, EnteringRecords is toggled to True, the Add New button's caption is changed to Save, and the Delete Current button's caption is changed to Cancel. When the user clicks on Save or Cancel after entering the new record, the process is reversed. While the user is entering a new record, you also want the List and Finished Command Buttons and the Data control to be disabled.

As for the database itself, the commands are fairly simple and consist of methods belonging to the RecordSet object. The RecordSet object is associated with the ADO Data control and is automatically created when the control connected to a data source and a query is run. Here are the methods you'll use:

- **AddNew**—Clears the bound controls in preparation for entry of new data
- **Update**—After an **AddNew**, copies the data entered in the bound controls into a new record in the table
- **Delete**—Deletes the current record from the table
- **CancelUpdate**—After an **AddNew**, cancels the add record operation
- **Refresh**—Updates the RecordSet to reflect any changes that have occurred
- **MoveNext**—Moves to the next record

- **MoveLast**—Moves to the last record

- **Requery**—Repeats the active query and refreshes displayed data

As for the List All command, the capabilities of the DataGrid control make it simple to code. You only have to set the properties of the ADO Data control to which the DataGrid is bound so they point at the same database and table as the Customer form's ADO Data control. Then, refresh the ADO Data control, and use the **Show** method to display the form. Here's the code:

```
frmList.Adodc1.ConnectionString = Adodc1.ConnectionString
frmList.Adodc1.RecordSource = Adodc1.RecordSource
frmList.Caption = "Customers Table"
frmList.Adodc1.Refresh
frmList.Show
```

The full **Command1_Click** event procedure for the Customers form is shown in Listing 22.2.

Listing 22.2   The Command1_Click event procedure in CUSTOMER.FRM.

```
Private Sub Command1_Click(Index As Integer)

Dim Reply As Integer

Select Case Index
    Case 0        ' Add New or Save.
        If EnteringRecord Then        ' Save command.
            ' Save the new record.
            Adodc1.Recordset.Update
            EnteringRecord = False
            ' Change command buttons.
            Command1(0).Caption = "&Add New"
            Command1(1).Caption = "&Delete Current"
            ' Enable the data control.
            Adodc1.Enabled = True
            Adodc1.Recordset.Requery
            Adodc1.Recordset.MoveLast
            ' Enable List and Finished buttons.
            Command1(2).Enabled = True
            Command1(3).Enabled = True
        Else                          ' Add New command.
            EnteringRecord = True
            ' Put focus in first text box. This is actually the
            ' second TextBox as the first one (CustID) is locked.
            Text1(1).SetFocus
            ' Disable List and Finished buttons.
            Command1(2).Enabled = False
```

```
            Command1(3).Enabled = False
            ' Change command buttons.
            Command1(0).Caption = "&Save"
            Command1(1).Caption = "&Cancel"
            ' Disable the data control.
            Adodc1.Enabled = False
            ' Add a new record.
            Adodc1.Recordset.AddNew
        End If
    Case 1      ' Delete current or Cancel.
        If EnteringRecord Then       ' Cancel command.
            Reply = MsgBox("Discard current entry?", vbYesNo + vbQuestion, _
            "Cancel Entry")
            If Reply = vbNo Then Exit Sub
            Adodc1.Recordset.CancelUpdate
            Adodc1.Refresh
            EnteringRecord = False
            'Change button captions.
            Command1(0).Caption = "&Add New"
            Command1(1).Caption = "&Delete Current"
            ' Enable List and Finished buttons.
            Command1(2).Enabled = True
            Command1(3).Enabled = True
            ' Enable ADO Data control.
            Adodc1.Enabled = True
        Else                            ' Delete Current command.
            Reply = MsgBox("Delete this record?", vbYesNo + _
                vbQuestion, "Cancel Entry")
            If Reply = vbNo Then Exit Sub
            Adodc1.Recordset.Delete
            Adodc1.Recordset.MoveNext
        End If
    Case 2      ' List all.
        frmList.Adodc1.ConnectionString = Adodc1.ConnectionString
        frmList.Adodc1.RecordSource = Adodc1.RecordSource
        frmList.Caption = "Customers Table"
        frmList.Adodc1.Refresh
        frmList.Show
    Case 3      ' Finished.
        Hide
End Select

End Sub
```

Coding The Wines Form

The code for the Wines form is a bit more complicated. As for handling the Command Buttons, follow the exact same procedure as you did for the Customers form, including the use of chameleon Command Buttons. The code for this event procedure is shown in Listing 22.3.

Listing 22.3   The Command1_Click event procedure in WINES.FRM.

```
Private Sub Command1_Click(Index As Integer)

Dim Reply As Integer

Select Case Index
    Case 0        ' Add New or Save.
        If EnteringRecord Then       ' Save command.
            ' Save the new record.
            Adodc1.Recordset.Update
            EnteringRecord = False
            ' Relock the StockNo TextBox.
            Text1(0).Locked = True
            ' Change command buttons.
            Command1(0).Caption = "&Add New"
            Command1(1).Caption = "&Delete Current"
            ' Enable the ADO Data control.
            Adodc1.Enabled = True
            Adodc1.Recordset.Requery
            Adodc1.Recordset.MoveLast
            ' Enable List and Finished buttons.
            Command1(2).Enabled = True
            Command1(3).Enabled = True
        Else                         ' Add New command.
            EnteringRecord = True
            ' Unlock the StockNo Text Box.
            Text1(0).Locked = False
            ' Put focus in first text box.
            Text1(0).SetFocus
            ' Disable List and Finished buttons.
            Command1(2).Enabled = False
            Command1(3).Enabled = False
            ' Change command buttons.
            Command1(0).Caption = "&Save"
            Command1(1).Caption = "&Cancel"
            ' Disable the data control.
            Adodc1.Enabled = False
            ' Add a new record.
            Adodc1.Refresh
            Adodc1.Recordset.AddNew
        End If
    Case 1        ' Delete current or Cancel.
        If EnteringRecord Then        ' Cancel command.
            Reply = MsgBox("Discard current entry?", vbYesNo + vbQuestion, _
            "Cancel Entry")
```

```
            If Reply = vbNo Then Exit Sub
            Adodc1.Recordset.CancelUpdate
            Adodc1.Refresh
            Adodc1.Enabled = True
            ' Relock the StockNo TextBox.
            Text1(0).Locked = True
            EnteringRecord = False
            ' Enable List and Finished buttons.
            Command1(2).Enabled = True
            Command1(3).Enabled = True
            Command1(0).Caption = "&Add New"
            Command1(1).Caption = "&Delete Current"
        Else                        ' Delete Current command.
            Reply = MsgBox("Delete this record?", vbYesNo + vbQuestion, _
            "Cancel Entry")
            If Reply = vbNo Then Exit Sub
            Adodc1.Recordset.Delete
            Adodc1.Recordset.MoveNext
        End If
    Case 2      ' List all.
        frmList.Caption = "Wines Table"
        frmList.Adodc1.ConnectionString = frmWines.Adodc1.ConnectionString
        frmList.Adodc1.RecordSource = frmWines.Adodc1.RecordSource
        frmList.Adodc1.Refresh
        frmList.Show
    Case 3      ' Finished.
        Hide
End Select

End Sub
```

The Wines form is different, because the Combo Box controls that are used for entry of the Color and Type data must be loaded with the appropriate choices, in order for those choices to be available when the user displays the form. Place this code in the **Form_Load** event procedure, as shown in Listing 22.4. Another method is to load each Combo Box from a text file that is kept in the same directory as the database, or from a dedicated table within the database itself. In fact, this method is preferable for a commercial program, because this method permits changes to the Color and Type lists without modifying the source code and recompiling the program—editing the text file is all that is needed.

Listing 22.4   The Form_Load event procedure in WINES.FRM.

```
Private Sub Form_Load()

' Load the Combo boxes.

ComboColor.AddItem "red"
ComboColor.AddItem "white"
```

```
ComboColor.AddItem "rose"
ComboColor.AddItem "dessert"
ComboColor.AddItem "sparkling"

ComboType.AddItem "Chardonnay"
ComboType.AddItem "Pinot noir"
ComboType.AddItem "Burgundy"
ComboType.AddItem "Pinot blanc"
ComboType.AddItem "Barolo"
ComboType.AddItem "Barbaresco"
ComboType.AddItem "Cabernet"
ComboType.AddItem "Semillion"
ComboType.AddItem "Bordeaux"
ComboType.AddItem "Chateauneuf de Pape"
ComboType.AddItem "White zinfandel"
ComboType.AddItem "Champagne"
Adodc1.Refresh

End Sub
```

Coding The List Form

Coding the List form is very simple, because most of the form's work is already handled by the DataGrid control—all that functionality is built right in, so you don't have to do a thing. (Aren't software components great?) However, you do need to add a little code. In the **Form_Resize** event procedure, you need to adjust the control sizes; this code is shown in Listing 22.5. Note that you are concerned only with the height of the DataGrid control; when you set its **Align** property to vbAlignTop, it is automatically positioned at the top of the form and is sized to match the form's width.

Listing 22.5   The Form_Resize event procedure in LIST1.FRM.

```
Private Sub Form_Resize()

' Set size and position of controls.

DataGrid1.Height = ScaleHeight - Command1.Height
Command1.Top = ScaleHeight - Command1.Height
Command1.Left = 0
Command1.Width = ScaleWidth

End Sub
```

The only other code required for the List form is to place the single line of code

```
Hide
```

in the Command Button's **Click** event procedure. By hiding the List form, you automatically return to the form that called it—the Customers form or the Wines form—which had remained inactive in the background while the List form was displayed.

What Now?

The answer to that one is easy: Try it out. Now you have a partially functional database front end to take on a trial run. Watch for error messages; if any appear, check your code to be sure that you entered everything properly. Currently, the program gives you the capability to add new records to the Customers and Wines tables, edit and delete existing records, and view a list of all records in either table. Note that changes to the table data made in List view are saved, providing another way for the user to edit table data.

You're off to a good start. But clearly, you have a long road ahead before you have a fully functional program.

Chapter 23

Wrapping It Up: Validation Code And The Invoices Form

The final steps in our database project are to write data validation code and to design the form for creating invoices.

A well-written program does everything it can to prevent errors. Certain types of errors are impossible to prevent—you can't control when a disk drive is going to crash, for example. Other errors can be avoided, particularly errors in data entry. Knowing something about the data that belongs in a particular field allows you to verify that new or edited data meets the required criteria. You start this chapter by writing validation code to handle this data-verification task, and then you begin creating a more complicated form for the database program: the Invoice Entry form. You then will have a functional—though admittedly barebones—relational database.

Validation Code

You can take any one of several approaches to validating data in a database front end. In some cases, only one of these approaches will work, while at other times, you can use whichever approach you prefer. Remember, the important thing is not *how* you validate the data, but that you *do* validate the data.

Blocking Keystrokes

One validation method simply prevents the entry of inappropriate keystrokes into a Text Box, thus preventing the entry of invalid data in the first place. For example, in a ZIP code field, you know that only the 10 numerical digits are permitted (plus a hyphen if 9-digit ZIP codes are allowed). You can use the Text Box's **KeyPress** event procedure to filter keystrokes. This procedure receives a type **Integer** argument named **KeyAscii**, which contains the numerical code of the key that was pressed. Code in the procedure can examine this value and determine whether it is one of the allowed keys. If it is not permitted, setting the **KeyAscii** argument to zero cancels the keystroke, preventing it from reaching the underlying control. For example, the following code permits entry of the digits zero through nine only, beeping if any other key is pressed. In all cases, you must pass through the Backspace character (**KeyAscii** value of eight), or else users will not be able to use the Backspace key to erase characters. Here's the code:

```
Private Sub Text1_KeyPress(KeyAscii As Integer)

If KeyAscii = 8 Then Exit Sub

If KeyAscii < 48 Or KeyAscii > 57 Then
    Beep
    KeyAscii = 0
End If

End Sub
```

ANSI Codes

Keyboard and other characters are represented internally by ANSI codes (also known as ASCII codes), with numeric values in the range of 0 through 255, representing each character. The **KeyPress** event procedure receives as its argument the ANSI code of the pressed key, so your code must either use these codes for its comparisons or use the **Chr$** function to convert the code into its corresponding character. Thus, this line of code

```
If KeyAscii = 76
```

and this line

```
If Chr$(KeyAscii) = "L"
```

both test for the uppercase "L" character. See the Character Set topic in Visual Basic Help for a listing of all characters and their ANSI codes.

Using Control Events

Another approach to validating data is to use the Text Box's events to run validation code. One event that can be used for this purpose is **LostFocus**. Put code in this event procedure both to examine the data in the control when the user moves the focus away and to verify that the code meets the criteria. Using a ZIP code field as an example again, you could verify that exactly five characters were entered, as follows:

```
Private Sub Text1_LostFocus()

If Len(Text1.Text) <> 5 Then
    MsgBox ("This field must contain 5 characters")
    Text1.SetFocus
End If

End Sub
```

If a number of characters other than five is entered, a message box is displayed, and then the focus is set back to the Text Box to permit the user to edit it. Another event that can be used to validate data is **Validate**. It is a bit more flexible than **LostFocus**, because you have some control over when the **Validate** event occurs. A control's **Validate** event is fired when the control loses the focus, but only if the focus moves to a control whose **CausesValidation** property is set to True. Thus, on a data entry form with several Text Box controls, you could place validation code in each individual Text Box's **Validate** event procedure, and then set **CausesValidation** to True for the form's OK button and False for the Help button. The validation code is executed when the user clicks on OK, but not when the user clicks on Help. The **Validate** event procedure is passed a single argument called **KeepFocus**. Setting **KeepFocus** to True or False determines whether the control keeps the focus. Here is an example of code that is used to verify that the value entered in a Text Box is between 10 and 20:

```
Private Sub Text1_Validate(KeepFocus As Boolean)

If Val(Text2.Text) < 10 Or Val(Text2.Text) > 20 Then
    KeepFocus = True
    MsgBox "Please enter a number between 10 and 20"
End If

End Sub
```

Using Database Engine Errors

Another validation method is to use the database engine's validation capabilities. Based on the properties you set for each field, as well as the indexes and keys defined, the database engine triggers an error that your program can trap. For example, if you define an index on a particular field and check the Unique option, the database engine checks to see whether a newly entered or edited value in the field is, in fact, unique (not duplicated in any other record in the table). If a duplicate is found, error number -2147467259 is generated. Your program can trap the error and respond accordingly.

TIP ADO Error Numbers

The error number -2147467259 is admittedly rather cumbersome. At the time I am writing this, Visual Basic is not quite ready for release, and one of the things still missing is a set of defined constants for ADO-related errors. By the time you are working with the release version of Visual Basic 6, I expect the set of defined constants will have been added. Check the online help and the Constants section of the API text viewer.

Validating Data In The GrapeVine Database

Now that you know the different approaches to data validation, turn your attention back to the GRAPEVINE database. This section doesn't include every bit of data validation that the database could possibly use; instead, it limits validation to a few essential areas. Most importantly, this section demonstrates the various validation methods I have explained.

Validating Data In The Wines Form

In the Wines form, you are going to validate the StockNo field to ensure that a duplicate stock number is not entered. Because you defined this field as being unique, the database engine actually performs the validation for you and reports an error if a duplicate number is entered. Your job, therefore, is not to validate the data per se, but to detect a "duplicate stock number" error and handle it in a manner that permits the user to change the data as needed.

The error-handling code needs to go in the **Command1_Click** event procedure, because that is where the ADO Data control's **Update** method is called. You wrote most of the **Command1_Click** event procedure in the previous chapter, so you just need to add to it. At the beginning of the procedure, before the Select Case Index statement, add the following line of code:

```
On Error GoTo Errorhandler
```

Then, at the end of the procedure, just before the **End Sub** statement, add the following:

```
Exit Sub

Errorhandler:

If Err.Number = -2147467259 Then
    MsgBox ("Duplicate stock number not permitted")
    Text1(0).SetFocus
Else
    MsgBox ("Error " & Err.Number & ": " & Err.Description)
End If
```

Note that the error-handling code deals specifically with the "duplicate stock number" error and simply reports any other errors that occur. If you find that the Wines form tends to generate other ADO errors, you can modify the error-handling code to deal with them also.

In the Wines form, you also want to verify that the entry in each of the price fields contains only numbers and, optionally, a decimal point. For this validation task, use the Text Box control's **KeyPress** event, to ensure that only the desired characters—in this case, numbers and the period or decimal point—can be entered in the Wines form's three price fields. The **KeyPress** event procedure for the WINES.FRM Text1 control is shown in Listing 23.1.

Listing 23.1   *The Text1_KeyPress event procedure in WINES.FRM.*

```
Private Sub Text1_KeyPress(Index As Integer, KeyAscii As Integer)

' Filter only for the 3 price fields, which have indexes 6, 7, and 8.

If Index < 6 Or Index > 8 Then Exit Sub

' 46 = period, 8 = Backspace
If (KeyAscii < 48 Or KeyAscii > 57) And KeyAscii <> 46 _
   And KeyAscii <> 8 Then
    Beep
    KeyAscii = 0
End If

End Sub
```

Validating Data In The Customers Form

For the Customers table, the following two verifications are most crucial:

- That the ZIP code field contains 5 characters

- That the Company, Address, City, and State fields all contain data

First tackle the ZIP code field. You'll use the **LostFocus** event, which is triggered whenever the control loses the focus. During data entry or editing, the control loses focus when the user tabs to the next Text Box. It also occurs if the focus is on the ZIP code field when one of the Command Buttons is clicked on. Listing 23.2 shows the code to place in the **Text1_LostFocus** event procedure. Because this is a control array, it is necessary to identify the ZIP code field by the **Index** property.

Listing 23.2   The LostFocus event procedure for the Text Box array in CUSTOMER.FRM.

```
Private Sub Text1_LostFocus(Index As Integer)

' Verify that entry in ZIP field has 5 characters. The index
' of that TextBox is 5.

If Index = 5 Then
    If Len(Text1(5).Text) <> 5 Then
        MsgBox ("ZIP code must have 5 characters")
        Text1(5).SetFocus
    End If
End If

End Sub
```

For the next validation task, you'll use the **Validate** event. You want this event to fire during data entry whenever the focus moves from one of the Text Boxes to another control, *except* if the user clicks on the Cancel button. Therefore, the first step is to set the **CausesValidation** property of the Cancel button (**Index** 1 in the control array) to False, leaving this property at its default value of True for all the other controls on the form. Next, place the code from Listing 23.3 in the **Validate** event procedure for Text1. Here's how it works:

1. Verify that the focus has left one of the Text Boxes that you are interested in (Company, Address, City, or State), which have **Index** properties of one through four. If not, exit the sub procedure.

2. See whether the Text Box is empty. If not, the validation has succeeded, so exit the sub procedure.

3. Construct an error message that is appropriate for the specific Text Box that is being tested.

4. Display the message and set **KeepFocus** to True.

Listing 23.3   Using the Validate event to verify data.

```
Private Sub Text1_Validate(Index As Integer, _
    KeepFocus As Boolean)

'Validate that the Company, Address,
' City, and State boxes are not empty.

Dim msg As String

If Index < 1 Or Index > 4 Then Exit Sub
If Len(Text1(Index).Text) > 0 Then Exit Sub
msg = ""
Select Case Index
    Case 1:
        msg = "company"
    Case 2:
        msg = "address"
    Case 3:
        msg = "city"
    Case 4:
        msg = "state"
End Select

If msg <> "" Then
    KeepFocus = True
    MsgBox ("The " & msg & " field may not be left blank.")
End If

End Sub
```

After entering the validation code presented in the previous sections, you can run the program again. The functionality of the program will not appear to be different than before, *unless* you try to enter invalid data that is caught by one of the validation methods that you have added. I'm sure that you can think of other aspects of data entry that would benefit from validation. Now that you know the validation methods available, try writing the code yourself.

Entering Orders

The last steps in your database development project involve entering orders and generating invoices. After all, that's the main job of this database: to permit the entry of order information. Take a moment to think about what the user of the program needs to do for each order:

- *Specify the customer who is placing the order.* To minimize the chance for errors, you'll design the program so that the customer is selected from a list of names that is already in the Customers table. If it's a new customer, the customer data has to be entered using the Customers form, before the order can be entered.

- *Enter the customer's purchase order (PO) number.* Because you have no way of knowing the customer's PO number ahead of time to generate it in code, this item of information has to be entered manually at the time of the customer's order.

- *Enter the order date.* You can let the computer enter the order date, retrieving the date from its clock and entering it in the proper database field.

- *Select one or more wines.* For each wine, the quantity being ordered must be specified, too. Again, simplify the operator's task and minimize errors by requiring that each wine be selected from a list of wines that is already entered in the Wines table.

You can already see, perhaps, that the preceding tasks are the most complex part of the project. All four database tables are involved: the Customers and Wines tables, to permit selection; the Invoices table, to add a new invoice record; and the Items table, to add one or more new records. Juggling all of these tables and keeping everything straight is not a trivial task, but as we design this form you'll see that Visual Basic provides many tools that greatly simplify the challenge.

The Invoices Form

The Invoices form will contain the following visible objects:

- A list of customers from which the user can select, implemented by using the DataList control.

- A Text Box for entry of the customer's Purchase Order number.

- A Text Box where the date is automatically entered by code.

- A Text Box where the selected customer's identification (the value of the CustID field in the Customers table) is entered. You find out soon how to do this automatically by using the DataList control.

- A list of the wines ordered, implemented as a DataGrid control.

- Three command buttons.

Some hidden controls are also required:

- *Two ADO Data controls*—One each for the Customers and Items tables. You access the Invoices table without an ADO Data control.

- *Several Text Box controls*—These serve for data transfer and temporary storage.

Before you start, take a look at how the DataList control works—you'll be using two of them in this part of the project.

The DataList Control

The DataList control is similar to a regular List Box control in that it displays a list of items from which the user can select. However, the DataList control can be bound to an ADO Data control so that it automatically displays the contents of a specified field in the Recordset associated with the bound ADO Data control. Two control properties determine what the DataList control displays:

- *RowSource*—The name of the ADO Data control.

- *ListField*—The name of the field to display in the list. Must be a valid field in the Recordset of the ADO Data control specified by the **RowSource** property.

So far, so good. But wait, there's more. The DataList control has **BoundColumn** and **BoundText** properties that really make it useful. The **BoundColumn** property specifies a field in the bound Recordset—a different field than is specified by the **ListField** property. When the users select an item in the DataList control, they are effectively selecting a record in the associated Recordset. The **BoundText** property then makes available the value of the corresponding field—the field specified by the **BoundColumn** property—in the selected record.

This is somewhat confusing, so take a look at a specific example. When a user of your program creates an invoice, the user needs to be able to select from a list of customers. To fulfill this need, you'll add an ADO Data control linked to the Customers table, and then bind a DataList control to that ADO Data control. You will set the **ListField** property to Company and the **BoundColumn** property to CustID. The DataList control will display a list of names of all companies in the Customers table. When the user selects a name by clicking on it, the selected customer's CustID becomes available in the DataList control's **BoundText** property.

Starting The Form

With the database project loaded, use the Insert Form command to add a new form to the project. Change its **BorderStyle** property to Fixed Single and its **Caption** property to New Order. Add a control array of three Command Buttons and set their **Caption** properties as follows:

Index 0:	&Save
Index 1:	&Add Wine
Index 2:	&Cancel

Next, add an ADO Data control and set its properties as follows:

Name:	AdodcCustomers
Caption:	Customers
Visible:	False
RecordSource:	Select * from Customers order by Company

A slightly more complex SQL statement is used for the **RecordSource** property, to select all records from the Customers table and sort them by the Company field. Use the procedures that you learned in the previous chapter to set the control's **ConnectionString** property to point to the GRAPEVINE database. Note that the **Caption** property is a convenience that enables you to distinguish this ADO Data control from the other controls that you will be adding. (At design time only, of course—the control isn't visible while the program is running.)

Next, add a DataList control. Remember, you may need to use the Project, Components command to add this custom control to your Toolbox. Set its properties as follows:

Name:	DataListCustomers
RowSource:	AdodcCustomers
ListField:	Company
BoundColumn:	CustID

To see how the DataList control works, you are going to print the value of its **BoundText** property whenever the user selects an item from the list. The place for this is in the DataListCustomers control's **Click** event procedure. Add the code as follows:

```
Private Sub DataListCustomers_Click()

Debug.Print DataListCustomers.BoundText

End Sub
```

The Invoices form also needs two Text Box controls, for the customer's PO number and for the date:

For the PO number Text Box, set its properties as follows:

      Name: txtCustPO

      Caption: CustPO

For the date Text Box, set its properties as follows:

      Name: txtDate

      Caption: Date

Finally, you need to add a button to the main form's Toolbar to display the Invoices form. Add a button to the Toolbar with the caption "Orders" and then add code to the Toolbar's **ButtonClick** event procedure, as shown in Listing 23.4. The new code is the **Case "Orders"** statement and the lines following it.

Listing 23.4 *Modified ButtonClick event procedure for the Toolbar.*

```
Private Sub Toolbar1_ButtonClick(ByVal Button As Button)

Dim Reply As Integer

Select Case Button.Caption
    Case "Customers"
        frmCustomers.Show
    Case "Wines"
        frmWines.Show
    Case "Orders"
        frmInvoice.txtCustPO.Text = ""
        frmInvoice.txtDate = ""
        frmInvoice.Command1(0).Enabled = False
        frmInvoice.Command1(1).Enabled = False
        frmInvoice.Show
    Case "Exit"
        Reply = MsgBox("Quit program - are you sure?", _
                vbYesNo + vbQuestion, "Quit?")
        If Reply = vbYes Then End
End Select

End Sub
```

Only a few lines of code are executed when the user clicks on the Orders button. The first code line clears the txtCustPO and txtDate Text Boxes. The captions that you placed in those Text Boxes were intended only to help identify the controls during program design, and are not needed during program execution. Two of the Command Buttons are disabled, and then the final line displays the Invoices form that you just designed.

You have plenty more to add to this form, but you've gone far enough at this point to test the form to see how the DataList control works. Start the program and click on the Orders button on the Toolbar. The form that you just created appears, and a list of customers is displayed in the DataList control. Click on a company name, and its CustID is displayed in the Immediate Window. This is how you obtain the CustID for the Invoices record; remember that CustID is the field that links the Customers and the Invoices tables.

Connecting To The Items Table

The form needs a connection to the Items table, of course, and you use another ADO Data control for this purpose. Add the ADO Data control and set its properties as follows:

Name:	AdodcItems
Caption:	Items
Visible:	False
RecordSource:	Select * from Items

Again, set the control's **ConnectionString** property to point to the GRAPEVINE database. Now you need three Text Box controls to be bound to the fields in the Items table (the fourth field, ItemNo, is automatically generated by the database engine, because it was defined as an AutoIncrement field). Add the following Text Box controls to the form:

For the Quantity field:

Name:	txtQuantity
DataSource:	AdodcItems
DataField:	Quantity
Visible:	False

For the InvNo field:

Name:	txtInvNumber
DataSource:	AdodcItems
DataField:	InvNo
Visible:	False

For the StockNo field:

Name:	txtStockNo
DataSource:	AdodcItems

DataField:	StockNo
Visible:	False

The **Visible** property for all of these Text Boxes is set to False, because the user doesn't need to see them—they are used only as temporary storage locations for data that is being put in the Items table. You will soon see how this is done.

One more thing related to the Items table needs to be discussed. When the user starts a new invoice and begins selecting wines, you want to display a list of the wines (items) that have already been selected. The ideal control for this purpose is the DataGrid control. Add a DataGrid control to the Invoices form, along the bottom edge, and set its properties as follows:

Name:	DataGridItems
Align:	2 - vbAlignBottom
DataSource:	AdodcItems
Caption:	Items Selected

At this stage your Invoices form will look like Figure 23.1.

The next task is to create the form that will allow the user to select wines to add to an invoice.

The Select Wine Form

After the Invoices form is displayed and the user has started a new invoice by selecting a customer, you need a way to select the individual wines that make up the order. For each wine, you need the quantity and the stock number to insert into the Items table. (The

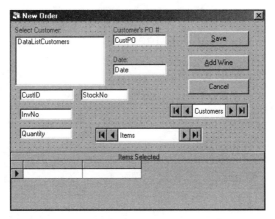

Figure 23.1   *The Invoices form during program design.*

other two fields in this table are the item number (ItemNo), which is automatically generated by the database engine, and the invoice number (InvNo), which is obtained from the
Invoices table.) To select a wine, use the same technique that you used earlier: allow the
user to select from a list. You'll again use the DataList control, to display the Description
field from the Wines table and provide the Stock Number of the selected wine.

Use the Insert Form command to add a new form to the project. Set the form's **Caption**
property to Select Wine and its name to frmSelectWine. The **BorderStyle** property should
be Fixed Single. Then, add the following controls to the form and set their properties
as indicated:

ADO Data control:

ConnectionString:	(to GRAPEVINE as before)
Name:	AdodcWines
RecordSource:	Select * from wines order by description
Visible:	False
Caption:	Wines

DataList control:

Name:	DataList1
ListField:	Description
BoundColumn:	StockNo
RowSource:	AdodcWines

Text Box:

Name:	txtQuantity
Text:	(blank string)

Command Button (in a control array):

Index:	0
Caption:	&OK

Command Button (in a control array):

Index:	1
Caption:	&Cancel

For the DataList control, you set the **ListField** property to Description, so that the control displays the wine descriptions. You also set the **BoundColumn** property to StockNo, so that the **BoundText** property returns the StockNo value for the selected wine. Finally, you need to add two label controls to identify the DataList control and the Text Box. When you finish designing this form, it should look something like Figure 23.2.

The only initialization step required for this form is to set the value in the Quantity Text Box; this is done in the form's **Load** event procedure. You use a default value of 12, because that is the most commonly ordered quantity of wine. As a convenience, when the user selects a wine by clicking on it in the DataList control, you will move the focus to the txtQuantity box. These procedures are shown in Listing 23.5.

Listing 23.5   The Select Wine form's Load and DataList1_Click event procedures.

```
Private Sub Form_Load()

txtQuantity.Text = 12

End Sub

Private Sub DataList1_Click()

txtQuantity.SetFocus

End Sub
```

Finally, this form needs a procedure for the Command Buttons. If the user selects the Cancel button, code sets the value in the Quantity Text Box to zero. This signals the calling function that the user canceled (as you'll see later). If the user selects a wine and then clicks on OK, several steps must be performed:

1. Verify that a wine has been selected and a quantity entered.

2. Copy the quantity value from the txtQuantity box on the Select Wine form to the txtQuantity Text Box on the Invoices form.

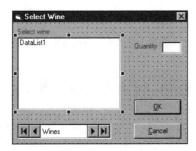

Figure 23.2   *The Select Wine form.*

3. Copy the StockNo value from the DataList control's **BoundText** property to the txtStockNo Text Box on the Invoices form.

4. Enable the Save button on the Invoices form. This button was previously disabled because, before any wines were selected, you had nothing to save.

5. Hide the Select Wine form.

The code for the Select Wine form's Command Button's **Click** event procedure is presented in Listing 23.6.

Listing 23.6   The Click event procedure for the Select Wine form's Command Buttons.

```
Private Sub Command1_Click(Index As Integer)

Select Case Index
    Case 0       ' OK
        ' Be sure data has been entered.
        If DataListWines.BoundText = "" Or txtQuantity.Text = "" Then
            MsgBox ("You must select a wine and specify a quantity.")
            txtQuantity.SetFocus
            Exit Sub
        End If
        ' Copy the data for the selected wine to
        ' the Invoices form.
        frmInvoice.txtStockNo.Text = DataListWines.BoundText
        frmInvoice.txtQuantity.Text = txtQuantity.Text
        ' Enable the "Save" button on the Invoices form.
        frmInvoice.Command1(0).Enabled = True
        ' Hide the SelectWine form.
        Hide
    Case 1       ' Cancel, as indicated by this Text Box being 0.
        frmInvoice.txtQuantity.Text = ""
        Hide
End Select
```

Connecting To The Invoices Table

Because the main purpose of this form is to enter orders or invoices, it must be connected to the Invoices table in your database, which is your next step. To illustrate how to access a database without the ADO Data control, you will use ADO objects and code only for this task.

You need to do two things with the Invoices table. First, when a user starts a new invoice, you need to add a new record to the table representing the new invoice. In addition, you need to get the InvNo value that is assigned to this record automatically by the database engine. This value is needed for new records in the Items table, to associate each item (wine) with the corresponding invoice. Second, you need to consider what happens if the user cancels the entry of a new invoice. Good database design requires that the associated record in the Invoices table be deleted.

I wrote a single function to perform both of these tasks. Called CreateNewInvoice, it takes a single argument named **Delete**. If **Delete** is zero, the function adds a new record to the Invoices table, using values for CustID, CustPO, and Date that are obtained from the Invoices form. The InvNo value of the newly added record is then saved in the global variable InvoiceNumber, so that it is available to the code that adds new records to the Items table. If passed a non-zero value as its argument, the function deletes the record in the Invoices table that has that InvNo value.

First, put the global variable declaration in the General section of the Invoice form's code:

```
Dim InvoiceNumber
```

Next, add the **CreateNewInvoice** procedure, as shown in Listing 23.7. Here is a description of how the code works:

1. Create new Connection and Recordset objects.

2. Set up error handling. Error-handling code does nothing more than display error information.

3. Build the connection string for the Connection object. If you are unsure of the details of what goes in this string, see the tip "Connection String Blues."

Connection String Blues

Until you become familiar with connection string syntax, constructing a valid connection string can be a daunting prospect. Fortunately, Visual Basic can help you construct a valid connection string to use with a Connection object. Place a temporary ADO Data control on a form and double-click on its Connection String property in the Properties window to open the object's property page. Select the Use Connection String option and click on the Build button to display the Data Link Properties dialog box. Make entries here to specify the details of the data connection that you want to establish, then close both the Data Link and Property Page dialog boxes. The ADO Data control will now have the desired connection string in its **ConnectionString** property. Copy it from there to your code, then delete the ADO Data control.

4. Set other Connection object properties as needed, and then call the **Open** method to set up the connection to the database.

Then, if you are creating a new record (**Delete = 0**):

5. Open the Recordset, associating it with the previously opened Connection object and populating it with all records from the Invoices table.

6. Execute the Recordset object's **AddNew** method, to create a new record.

7. Place new data in the record's fields. Note that the ! operator is used to indicate a specific record in a specific Recordset.

8. Retrieve the new record's automatically generated InvNo value and store it in the global variable InvoiceNumber.

Or, if you are deleting a record (**Delete > 0**):

5. Set up a command string to delete records where the InvNo field has the value specified in the **Delete** argument.

6. Execute the Recordset object's **Open** method with this command, to perform the deletion.

7. Set the global variable InvoiceNumber to zero.

Whether deleting or adding a record, the final step is to set both the Connection and Recordset object variables to Nothing, because you are done using them. This is automatically done at the end of the procedure when the variables go out of scope, but explicitly destroying them in code is good practice, to ensure that unneeded instances are not left.

Listing 23.7   The CreateNewInvoice procedure.

```
Public Sub CreateNewInvoice(Delete As Variant)

' If Delete = 0 then creates a new record
' in the Invoices table.
' If Delete > 0 then deletes the record in
' the Invoices table where InvNo = Delete.

Dim strConnect As String, cmd As String
Dim cnInv As New ADODB.Connection
Dim rsInv As New ADODB.Recordset

On Error GoTo ADOError

strConnect = "Provider=Microsoft.Jet.OLEDB.3.51;"
strConnect = strConnect & "Persist Security Info=False;"
' Be sure to edit the next line to point
' at your database file.
strConnect = strConnect & _
    "Data Source=C:\documents\vb6pe\projects\grapevine\Grapevine.mdb"

cnInv.ConnectionString = strConnect
cnInv.ConnectionTimeout = 10
cnInv.CursorLocation = adUseNone
cnInv.Open
```

```
If Delete = 0 Then
    rsInv.Open "select * from invoices", _
        cnInv, adOpenDynamic, adLockOptimistic, adCmdText
    rsInv.AddNew
    rsInv!CustPO = txtCustPO.Text
    rsInv!Date = txtDate.Text
    rsInv!CustID = DataListCustomers.BoundText
    rsInv.Update
    ' Store invoice number.
    InvoiceNumber = rsInv!InvNo
Else
    ' Delete the newly added record.
    cmd = "delete * from invoices where InvNo = " & Delete
    rsInv.Open cmd, cnInv, adOpenDynamic, adLockOptimistic, adCmdText
    InvoiceNumber = 0
End If

Set rsInv = Nothing
Set cnInv = Nothing

Exit Sub

ADOError:

MsgBox ("Create invoice: " & Err.Description)
InvoiceNumber = 0

End Sub
```

Completing The Invoices Form

Now that the Select Wine form is complete, and you have written the code to connect to the Invoices table, you can place the finishing touches on the Invoices form. First, briefly review the procedures that are involved in creating a new invoice:

1. User clicks on the Orders button on the main form's Toolbar to display the Invoices form.

2. User selects a customer and enters the customer PO number.

3. User clicks on the Add Wine button. If necessary, a new record is added to the Invoices table. The Select Wine form is displayed.

4. User selects a wine and enters a quantity, and then clicks on OK. Information about the selected wine is copied back to the Invoices form, and the item is displayed in the DataGrid control. The new record is added to the Items table. If the user cancels the item, the update of the Items table is aborted. The Select Wines form is hidden.

5. Repeat Steps 3 and 4 to add additional wines to the invoice.

6. If the user clicks Save on the Invoices form, the form is hidden (all new data has already been saved). If the user cancels the entire invoice, the new record in the Invoices table is deleted. All associated records in the Items table should be deleted as well.

You have already written the code to perform most of these tasks, but you still need to write the code for the Command Buttons on the Invoices form. It is this code that ties everything together. The **Click** event procedure is presented in Listing 23.8.

Listing 23.8 *Command Button Click event procedure for the Invoices form.*

```
Private Sub Command1_Click(Index As Integer)

Select Case Index
    Case 0        ' Save invoice button.
        ' Hide the grid then hide the form.
        DataGridItems.Visible = False
        InvoiceNumber = 0
        Hide
    Case 1        ' Add wine to invoice button.
        If txtCustPO.Text = "" Then
            MsgBox ("Customer PO required.")
            txtCustPO.SetFocus
            Exit Sub
        End If
        ' Create a new Item.
        AdodcItems.Recordset.AddNew
        ' If a new invoice has not been created, then
        ' create a new record in the Invoices table.
        If InvoiceNumber = 0 Then CreateNewInvoice (0)
        ' Put the invoice number in the text box that
        ' is bound to that field in the Items table.
        txtInvNumber.Text = InvoiceNumber
        ' Call AddWine function, which returns True if the user
        ' selects a wine, False if they Cancel.
        If AddWine() Then    ' If a wine was selected
            ' Update the table and refresh it to include
            ' only items that are part of the current invoice.
            AdodcItems.Recordset.Update
            AdodcItems.RecordSource = _
                "Select * from Items where InvNo = " _
                & txtInvNumber.Text
            AdodcItems.Refresh
            ' Make the DataGrid visible and refresh it.
            DataGridItems.Visible = True
            DataGridItems.Refresh
        Else  ' If the user canceled entry of a wine,
            ' cancel the new record. It is necessary
            ' to temporarily disconnect the DataGrid
            ' from the ADO Data control to prevent an error.
```

```
              Set DataGridItems.DataSource = Nothing
              AdodcItems.Recordset.CancelUpdate
              Set DataGridItems.DataSource = AdodcItems
          End
      Case 2      ' Cancel new invoice.
          ' If the user cancels the entire invoice.
          If InvoiceNumber <> 0 Then
              InvoiceNumber = 0
              ' Delete new records from the Items table.
              AdodcItems.Recordset.Filter = adFilterFetchedRecords
              AdodcItems.Recordset.Delete adAffectGroup
              DataGridItems.Visible = False
              ' Delete new record from the Invoices table.
              CreateNewInvoice (InvoiceNumber)
          End If
          Hide
End Select

End Sub
```

The final procedure that you need is the **AddWine** function, which links code in the Invoices form to the Select Wine form. This function, shown in Listing 23.9, is called by code in the **Command1_Click** event procedure when the user clicks the Add Wine button. It displays the Select Wine form by executing its **Show** method. The form is displayed modally by passing the argument 1 to the **Show** method, which means that the user cannot interact with any other forms until this form is explicitly removed by code. Remember, in the Select Wine form, the txtQuantity Text Box is set to zero if the user selects Cancel. Otherwise, it is a non-zero value. The value of this Text Box is used by code in **AddWine** to determine whether the function should return True or False. This return value is then used by code in **Command1_Click**, as was shown in Listing 23.8, to determine whether the user entered a valid wine or canceled the operation.

Listing 23.9   *The AddWine function.*

```
Public Function AddWine() As Boolean

' Show the wine selection form.
frmSelectWine.Show 1

' If the user selected cancel it is indicated
' by a blank in the txtQuantity box.
If txtQuantity.Text <> "" Then
    AddWine = True
Else
    AddWine = False
End If

End Function
```

Trying It Out

Believe it or not, your database program is finished—at least as complete as you are going to make it! You can try it out and see how all the features work together by using the sample GRAPEVINE.MDB database on the CD, which has a small amount of data already entered. Figure 23.3 shows the program while a new wine is being added to an invoice.

I will be the first to admit that this program needs a great deal more refinement before it is even close to being ready for release to a paying customer. At the very least, you would need to add such features as the ability to print invoices and shipping labels, update the Quantity on Hand field in the Wines table when an order is filled, permit viewing a list of all invoices—the list could go on and on. The program also needs work in the area of error trapping, a topic that is covered in Chapter 25.

To bring the project to a stage where the program is ready for commercial release would require a lot more work—and a lot more pages in this book. Don't worry, I'm going to stop here. My goal is to teach you the fundamentals of Visual Basic database programming, and I think—or at least hope—that I've accomplished that goal. One thing is certain: You'll discover a world of riches within Visual Basic's database capabilities as you explore database programming in greater depth.

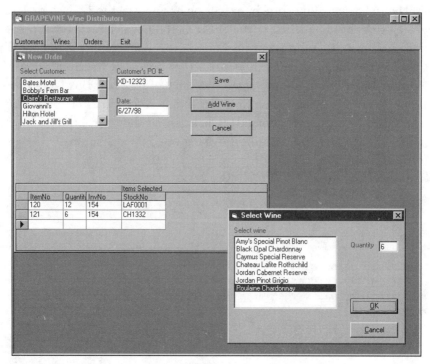

Figure 23.3 *Adding a wine to an invoice.*

Chapter 24

Client/Server Programming

Client/server computing is a powerful tool that is applicable to many data-processing needs.

Finding a personal computer that exists in isolation, without being part of a network, is becoming more and more difficult. Networked computers are the norm, particularly in the workplace. Why are networks becoming so prevalent? The main reason is the need to share information. Whether it is a product catalog, technical-specification summary, or accounting data, most of the information that businesses and organizations deal with is used by more than one person. Networks have the potential to provide other benefits, as well. Modern networks use an approach called *client/server architecture*, and Visual Basic provides the tools that developers need to use this technology. This chapter covers the basics of client/server computing, as implemented in Visual Basic.

Client/server programming is an enormously complex topic, so please do not expect more than a brief introduction in this chapter. My goal is merely to acquaint you with the capabilities of this approach and introduce you to some of the tools that Visual Basic provides to implement client/server applications. Be aware that most of the tools required to implement client/server applications are available only with the Enterprise Edition of Visual Basic.

Some Background

Back in the old days, 20 and 30 years ago, computers were large, expensive devices that required a lot of care and attention. Each person who needed computer power couldn't possibly have his or her own computer. The solution was to keep the computer, or *main-frame*, at a centralized location and provide each user with a terminal (screen and key-board) that was connected to the mainframe. The terminals were referred to as *dumb* terminals, because they possessed no data-processing power of their own—they served merely to accept keystrokes and send them to the mainframe, and to receive data from the mainframe and display it. Both the data and the application logic (programs) were located on the mainframe.

This approach, sometimes called a *centralized architecture*, worked well enough in many cases, but it had the disadvantage of all the application logic being located on the central mainframe, which meant that one computer had to perform all data-processing tasks. No matter how powerful the machine, it could still get bogged down with multiple requests, resulting in a slow response time from the user's perspective.

The introduction of personal computers (PCs) didn't remove the need to share informa-tion. The first solution to sharing data was jokingly called "sneaker-net," because you would copy the needed information to a diskette then run down the hall to give it to whoever needed it. A more realistic way to share data was the *file server architecture*, in which each user had his or her own computer, or *workstation*, connected to a shared file server via the network. The file server itself was a "personal" computer, typically with beefed up memory and a large hard disk. The data that needed to be shared was located on the file server, while the application logic, or programs, were located on the individual workstations. When a user needed some shared information, a request was sent to the file server, which opened the relevant file and transferred the file over the network to the user's workstation, where all data processing was performed. The file server also permitted users to share physical resources, such as printers and modems.

The file server architecture worked perfectly well, but it had some negative points that were almost the reverse of the problems with the centralized architecture discussed earlier. Because all processing was performed on the workstations, each individual workstation had to be powerful enough—processor speed, memory, and so forth—to perform all the computing tasks required by the user. While an individual PC may not cost too much, providing dozens of users with state-of-the-art machines can make a significant dent in anyone's budget.

Multiuser Database Considerations

Visual Basic is commonly used to create database implementations that are designed to run in a file server environment. When a database is designed for simultaneous use by multiple users, the transaction-processing front ends must be concerned with the *concurrency* and the *consistency* of the database tables. Concurrency problems can arise if two or more users attempt to update the same record simultaneously. The outcome of the simultaneous update requests may not be predictable—one update or the other may prevail. Consistency problems may occur when one user updates a set of records, and another user attempts to view those records while that transaction is in progress. The data the second user sees may be incorrect, reflecting only part of the update transaction.

The solution to both concurrency and consistency problems involves *locking* the record during an update, thus preventing any other user from accessing the record until the update is completed. Concurrency problems are prevented, because one update is forced to wait until the other update is completed, ensuring that both updates are reflected in the record. Consistency problems are avoided, because the second user can't access and view the records until the first user's update transaction is completed.

Advances in programming and hardware technology led to the development of the client/server architecture. In this architecture, the strong points of the centralized and file server architectures are combined, while avoiding the weak points of both. Two separate application programs, one running on the server computer and the other on the client computer, cooperate to perform the required task. Data-processing chores are split between two machines, enabling more efficient allocation of computing resources. Data transfer across the network is minimized, also. A couple examples of the client/server architecture are presented next.

Shared hardware resources, such as printers, are an important part of the client/server architecture. When a client needs to print a document, the application on the client computer (a word processor, for example) sends the document across the network to the server computer. On the server computer, a separate program, called the *Print Manager*, accepts the document, places it in the print queue, monitors the progress of printing, and notifies the client computer when the printing job is complete.

The preceding example is accurate, but somewhat trivial. A much more important use of the client/server architecture is in a database management system (DBMS). The next example illustrates the contrast between the operation of a file server architecture and a client/server architecture.

Imagine a centralized database of inventory information for an automobile parts manufacturer. Suppose that an employee needs to obtain the current price for a particular part, identified by part number. On a system that uses the file server architecture, here's what happens:

1. The user types the request into the client computer, and the client computer sends the request across the network to the file server.

2. The file server opens the database file and sends the entire file across the network to the client computer.

3. The program on the client computer searches through the entire database, looking for the requested part number. After completing the search, the program displays the price information to the user.

On a system that uses a client/server architecture, the sequence of events is a bit different:

1. The user types the request into the client computer, and the client computer sends the request across the network to the file server.

2. A program on the server opens the database, searches for the requested part number, and extracts the price information.

3. The price information is returned over the network to the client computer, which then displays the information to the user.

The client/server architecture drastically decreases network traffic and improves response time, compared to the file server architecture. In addition, security matters are simplified, because the database file is never transported off the server computer.

Two-Tier Vs. Three-Tier Client Server

Almost as soon as the client/server architecture was put into use, its own limitations became apparent. As initially envisioned, the client/server architecture splits the application logic between two machines—the client and the server—and hence is referred to as the *two-tier client/server model*. The following are two of the more important problems of the client/server architecture:

- *Lack of scalability*—The division of the application logic between the client and server machines was an important advance, but all the processing still had to be performed on one machine or the other. As an organization expanded and its data-processing requirements increased, a corresponding increase in the power and processing speed of the client/server system wasn't possible—other than to replace the client and/or server computers with more powerful units.

- *Difficulty of implementing business rules*—Almost without exception, every database management system requires the implementation of a fairly complex set of business rules. In a two-tier system, the only option was to implement the business rules either on the client computers or as part of the database back end on the server computer. Thus, the programmer's task was made even more difficult, because of this inability to centralize business rules and separate them from other aspects of data processing.

TIP   What Are Business Rules?

A *business rule* is a requirement or specification that is placed on data processing by the policies of a specific company, and doesn't relate directly to the data itself. For example, the company may require that orders for computer software over $500 be approved by a supervisor. Another business rule might forbid orders to be processed from any customer who has an account past due for more than 90 days. Because such rules change frequently and require consistency across the entire database management system, their implementation needs to be centralized and kept independent from other aspects of data processing.

The development of the three-tier model was one solution to these and other problems inherent in the two-tier client/server model. Actually, referring to it as a *three-tier model* is somewhat inaccurate, because, theoretically, no limit exists to the number of tiers, or *layers*, that can be used in a client/server architecture. Even so, of the various possible multiple-tier models the three-tier model is the most commonly used.

All multiple-tier models depend on the capability to build partitioned applications. In a *partitioned application*, the code is broken into logical and semi-independent units that work together to perform a specific task. Dividing application logic strictly into "client side" and "server side" categories is no longer necessary. These units of code can be deployed on any computer on the network, which has numerous advantages, most notably the following:

- Logically separate parts of the application can be broken into separate code components, and no longer have to be shoehorned into either the client or the server application logic. Specifically, relating this to the discussion earlier, the code that implements your business rules can be made separate and independent from other parts of the application. As a result, this code can be shared among applications and is much easier to maintain and update.

- A scalable network is much easier to establish. As processing needs grow, additional computers can be added to the network, and one or more of the partitioned code components can be installed on the added computers. A common implementation is to install a *business server* between the client workstations and the data server. The code components that implement the business rules execute on the business server, which results in this processing load being removed from the data server and workstation computers. The business server is "between" the client workstations and data server in a logical sense of the term, not in the way the computers are physically wired.

> ### Servers And Servers
>
> If you're new to client/server computer systems—and maybe even if you're not—the use of the term *server* can be confusing. *Server* is used to mean a variety of things, depending on the context. When referring to hardware, a server is any computer that provides file, printer, or other services to remote users. However, software can also be called a server—for example, SQL Server is a program that accepts and processes SQL commands. An ActiveX component that is exposed for use by others is also occasionally referred to as a server. (Chapter 8 explains how to create ActiveX servers.) Just pay attention to the context in which *server* is used and you shouldn't have any difficulty.

COM And DCOM

You met COM, or the *Component Object Model*, earlier in this book. To recap, COM is a specification for component software that stipulates how such components are assembled and how they communicate with each other. ActiveX—a central part of Visual Basic and Windows programming—is one implementation of COM. Because the basis of client/ server computing involves partitioning applications into independent units, client/server computing and COM are related. COM, and specifically ActiveX, serves an integral role in using Visual Basic to create client/server applications.

As an example—using the previous business rules problem—you can use ActiveX and a three-tier client/server architecture to write an ActiveX component that contains the code to implement the rule stating "purchases over $500 must be approved by supervisor." All database transactions involving orders are routed to this ActiveX component, which then does the following:

1. Checks to see whether the order is over $500.

2. If the order is over $500, checks to see whether the "approved by" field is filled in.

3. Verifies that the person named in the "approved by" field is at the supervisor level.

4. If the order is okay, passes the order to the data server for processing. Otherwise, returns the response "supervisor approval needed" to the client.

Because this ActiveX "rules" component can run on any computer on the network, not just the client or server machines, processing can be spread out in the most efficient manner, to provide a quick response.

Distributed Component Object Model (DCOM) is a protocol that permits applications to make remote, object-oriented procedure calls. (DCOM used to be called *Network OLE*.) In other words, a component that supports DCOM can communicate with other components by using a variety of network protocols, including the Hypertext Transport Protocol (HTTP), the protocol used on the Internet. With DCOM, the software components that make up a business application can be distributed across a local network, intranets, or the entire Internet. A business rule component, for example, could be maintained at a central location and accessed across the Internet by client/server applications at various remote offices. Updates and revisions to the business rules would be applied instantly to all relevant transactions throughout the enterprise.

In-Process And Out-Of-Process Servers

A server, or software component, can run either in-process or out-of-process. An *in-process server* runs in the same process space as the client application that is calling the server, while an *out-of-process server* runs in a different process space than the client application. An in-process server must be running on the same machine as the client, while an out-of-process server can be running on a remote computer. ActiveX Dynamic Link Libraries (DLLs) are in-process servers, while ActiveX EXEs are out-of-process servers.

The code that a client uses to access a server is the same in either case, but communication between the client and the server is always faster for an in-process server, even compared to an out-of-process server on the same machine. To implement an in-process DLL server, however, the component has to be installed on every client machine. A trick around this limitation is to set up the DLL so that it is *parented* by an EXE. Because an in-process server runs in the same process space as the client application, if the in-process server crashes, the client application crashes with it. An out-of-process server is not crash-proof, but if it crashes, it doesn't affect the client application. Table 24.1 presents some of the factors that you should consider when you select how to implement and deploy an ActiveX component.

Tools For Client/Server Programming

Microsoft provides a variety of tools to assist you in client/server development. Some of these tools are part of Visual Basic, while others are independent utilities. This section briefly describes the more important of these tools.

Table 24.1   The pros and cons of ActiveX server types.

Component Type	Pros	Cons
DLL (in process)	Quickest loading and execution	Local deployment required; no crash protection
EXE (local)	Good crash protection	Somewhat slower loading and execution
EXE (remote)	Remote execution, good crash protection	Much slower execution; affected by network traffic

Client Registration Utility

For a client to make use of a server, the server must be registered on the client system. The registration process inserts information about the server into the Windows 95/98/NT registry. This registration can be accomplished in several ways:

- EXE servers register themselves automatically when executed.

- Using Visual Basic to compile a DLL or EXE server automatically registers the server.

- The Package and Deployment Wizard can create a setup program for the server that installs and registers the component.

Servers can also be registered from the command line by using the Client Registration Utility. To register a component using this utility, the server must be compiled with the Remote Server Files option turned on. This option is found on the Component tab of the Project Properties dialog box. When this option is enabled, Visual Basic creates a VBR file, which contains the registration information for the component. You then run CLIREG32.EXE from the command line, passing the name of the VBR file as its parameter. This utility provides options for remote registration, user authentication, and so on.

Remote Automation Connection Manager

If your application's software components are going to be scattered across the network, an obvious problem is how a particular client application is going to know where its various components are located. Solving that problem is the job of the *Remote Automation Connection Manager* (RACM), which supplies a user-friendly interface with which you can tell your system where to find a particular component. This program (RACMGR32.EXE) is located in the System folder (Windows 95/98) or in the System32 folder (Windows NT). The RACM displays a list of all available component classes, as shown in Figure 24.1. The right side of the dialog box is used to specify the details of how a client application can make contact with the remote component. This information includes the network address

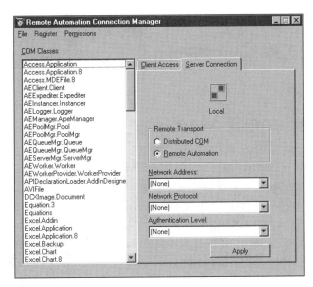

Figure 24.1   *Defining a remote automation connection in the Remote Automation Connection Manager.*

of the remote computer where a component is located, the network protocol to be used for communication, and if required, the level of authentication to be used. Additional security options are set on the Client Access tab of the RACM.

Behind the scenes of the RACM, the component's address in the registry is being changed between local and remote. When a specific component is specified as remote, the local symbol at the top of the RACM dialog box changes to a remote symbol (two connected boxes). You can quickly switch a specific component between local and remote, and back again, by selecting the appropriate command from the Register menu. Be aware, however that the RACM does not test the validity of the remote connection that you specify.

Perhaps the best way to think about the RACM is as a type of telephone directory. When you want to talk to someone, you don't really care where they are located, as long as you have the proper phone number to reach them. When you use the RACM to specify a component's remote location, you essentially are changing its "phone number" in the registry.

Automation Manager

For a component to be available remotely, the computer on which it is located must be running the Automation Manager. This program, located in the System directory as AUTMGR32.EXE, runs in the background and intercepts client requests that come over the network. As Figure 24.2 shows, the Automation Manager's window displays the number of current connections and the number of objects currently connected to.

Figure 24.2   *The Automation Manager.*

Visual Component Manager

Undeniably, you cannot benefit from a software component if you don't know that it exists. This problem is particularly acute in larger organizations where several, or even dozens, of people may be involved in writing applications for the enterprise. Joe Schmoe down the hall may already have written just the component that you need for your project—but how are you supposed to know about it? For component reuse to become reality, individual programmers need information not only about which components are available, but how each component can be used, as well. The Visual Component Manager, shown in Figure 24.3, performs this job. You start the Visual Component Manager (VCM) from Visual Basic's View menu.

Using the Visual Component Manager involves three parts. First, a component must be *published*, so that information about it is included in the VCM database. To publish a component, load the project files into Visual Basic and select Publish from the Tools menu. The Tools menu presents the following two options:

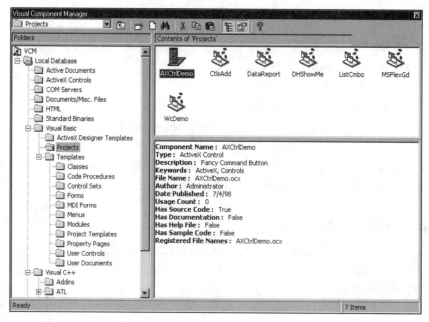

Figure 24.3   *The Visual Component Manager.*

- *Source Files*—Select this option if you want to publish the project source code files, making them available to other developers who may want to examine your code and perhaps make modifications to suit their exact needs.

- *Build Outputs*—Select this option if you want to compile and publish the component's executable files, making the component itself available to other developers who want to use it in their projects.

Note that you can publish a component both as source files and as build outputs. Whichever publishing option you select, the Publishing Wizard walks you through the steps that are required in the publishing process, such as entering a description and selecting keywords for the component. Other ways to commence the publishing process are to right-click in the VCM dialog box and select New from the shortcut menu, or to select the component in Windows Explorer and drag it to a folder in the VCM.

The second part of using Visual Component Manager is to find components. If a programmer needs a component for a specific task, the programmer can open the VCM and search to see whether a suitable component has been published. The VCM provides a flexible keyword and search mechanism. Components can be located by their name, type, description, keywords, and annotations. You don't even need to know a component's name to find it. Of course, the usefulness of the VCM's search capabilities is completely dependent on the care that is used when components are published. If a component is published with too little descriptive detail, or with inappropriate keywords, then finding it in the VCM database will be difficult or impossible for other programmers.

After a component is located, the final part of the VCM is to add the component to your Visual Basic project. This is probably the simplest part of using Visual Component Manager—simply right-click on the component in the VCM and select Add To Project from the shortcut menu. If the component requires COM registration, the VCM automatically performs this task.

Summing Up

This has been an extremely superficial introduction to client/server programming. It is a very complex subject, and I can't do more than scratch the surface within a single chapter. At least you now have some idea of the techniques and capabilities of this powerful tool, and are equipped to seek out additional information if you ever need to use client/server programming. Numerous books are available that are devoted entirely to this subject.

PART 6
Final Touches

Chapter 25
Error Handling

This is one of the shortest chapters in the book, and you may think it's one of the least interesting. In truth, it may be the most important.

Writing error-handling code is undoubtedly the least interesting part of programming. The code doesn't do anything exciting or flashy—no multimedia extravaganzas, no lightning-fast math calculations, no clever user interfaces—but the fact remains that a program without well-designed and carefully implemented error-handling code is almost guaranteed to have its users clamoring for the programmer's blood, your blood. Pay attention to this chapter, and you may live to a ripe old age.

What Errors Need Handling?

Computer programs are rife with possibilities for errors. In fact, several different categories of errors can occur. *Syntax errors* happen when you make a mistake writing the program: using an undeclared variable (only when using **Option Explicit**, of course, which you always should do), passing the wrong number and/or type of arguments to a function, or misspelling a function name. Pesky as these types of errors are, they are rarely serious problems. Visual Basic catches them as soon as you try to run the program in the Visual

Basic development environment. Depending on the specific error, Visual Basic will highlight the offending line of code or display a dialog box with a description of the error. In the latter case, click on the Debug button to go to the line of code where the error occurred. These built-in capabilities make finding and fixing syntax errors easy; they almost never survive in a program to cause problems for the end user.

Other types of errors, however, are not dealt with so easily. They usually don't make themselves known during program development when you can easily fix them. Rather, they wait until the program is in the hands of the end user. Why are these errors so tough to handle? Because they usually depend on factors that are out of your control. Here are a few examples:

- The program prompts the user to enter a number, but he or she enters a string instead.

- The program tries to read from a file that has been deleted.

- The user enters data that results in an attempt to divide by zero.

- The program tries to write data to drive A: with no diskette inserted in the drive.

- The program tries to access a network file when the user does not have sufficient access rights.

The list could go on and on. Literally hundreds of these runtime errors are possible, and no programmer—regardless of how clever—can guarantee that none of them will occur. The programmer's job is to provide error-handling code in the program, ensuring that any errors that do crop up will not have serious consequences for the user. This task is done using Visual Basic's error-trapping capabilities.

What happens if you don't trap errors? If the program is running in the Visual Basic development environment, most errors result in the display of a dialog box describing the error, as shown in Figure 25.1. The dialog box displays the error number and a brief description of the error. The program at this point is suspended. If you click on the End button in the dialog box, the program terminates. If you click on Debug, the program remains suspended and the cursor is positioned on the line of code that caused the error. You can edit the code to try to eliminate the error, then press F5 to continue the program execution where it stopped. (Certain types of changes to the code do not permit continuing program execution; they require the program to be restarted. Visual Basic informs you when this is the case.)

If you are running the Visual Basic program as a standalone EXE file, untrapped errors are also reported by a dialog box giving the error number and a brief description. Of course, you don't have the option to edit the code to correct the error. Because end users will be

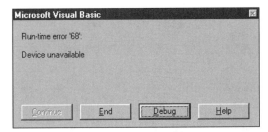

Figure 25.1   *Untrapped errors are reported in Visual Basic by a dialog box.*

executing your program as a standalone, whenever an untrapped error occurs, they are faced with a terse message and a nonfunctional program. Proper error trapping will let you avoid this situation.

Trapping Errors

Trapping errors is similar in some respects to handling events. If you think of an error as an event, and error-handling code as an event procedure, you'll have a good start toward understanding how Visual Basic deals with errors. The difference is that an error does not trigger a discrete event procedure. Rather, you use the **On Error** statement to specify the exact code location where execution is supposed to pass when an error occurs. Here's an example. The statement

```
On Error Goto ErrorHandler
```

tells Visual Basic that when an error occurs, execution passes to the line of code identified by the label ErrorHandler. Labels that identify locations in code consist of a name followed by a colon, as shown in these three examples:

```
ErrorHandler:
IfError:
OJSimpson:
```

The rules for line labels are the same as for Basic variable names—the only difference is the colon at the end. Each procedure's error-handling code is traditionally placed at the end of the procedure, between the last "regular" statement in the procedure and the **End Sub** or **End Function** statement at the end. You must place an **Exit Sub** or **Exit Function** statement just before the label identifying the error-handling code to prevent execution from falling into the error-handling code. Here are the basics:

```
Sub MySub()

On Error Goto Errorhandler

' Procedure statements go here.
```

```
Exit Sub

Errorhandler:

' Error handling code goes here.

End Sub
```

The line label identifying the error-handling code must be in the same procedure as the **On Error Goto** statement that specifies it. This means that error-handling code is local to procedures (both event and general procedures). You might think that this is a bad idea; wouldn't it be better to have a single comprehensive error handler that deals with errors occurring in all parts of the program? Not really. Because each procedure tends to deal with one discrete aspect of the program (at least if you're programming properly), the type of errors it could possibly generate will be limited. For instance, a Text Box's **Change** event procedure may need to deal with improper data entry, but it will never be faced with a disk access or printer error. Therefore, each procedure's error-handling code can be relatively simple and concise—dealing only with that procedure's potential errors. In addition, by including error-handling code in procedures, each procedure becomes an independent entity that is not dependent on code elsewhere in the program.

There are two variants of the **On Error** statement. The statement

```
On Error Goto 0
```

causes error trapping to be disabled; the program will respond to errors in the default manner by displaying the terse dialog box described previously. The statement

```
On Error Resume Next
```

instructs the program to ignore the error temporarily and to continue executing with the statement immediately following the one that caused the error. This does not mean that you are ignoring the error (a bad idea, to be sure), but that you are deferring handling of the error for the moment. This technique is used in situations where the information needed to diagnose the error accurately is not immediately available.

Now you know how to trap errors by directing program execution to a special section of code when an error occurs. Several burning questions remain to be answered: for example, how do you know *which* error has occurred, and what can you do about it? I'll deal with these questions soon; first, let's look at a sample procedure that contains error-trapping code, just to give you a feel for how it works. This sample procedure is presented in Listing 25.1. The comments in the code explain how it works. This procedure contains no real code, just the error-trapping statements and comments.

Listing 25.1   *How error trapping works.*

```
Private Sub MyDemoProcedure()

' At this point in the code, before any On Error has been executed,
' errors will be reported by a dialog box in the default fashion.

On Error Go To ErrorHandler:

' In this section of code, when an error occurs, execution will
' pass to the location identified by the ErrorHandler label.

On Error Goto 0

' In this section of code, error trapping is disabled. Errors
' will be reported to the user in the default dialog box format.

On Error Resume Next

' In this section of code, error trapping is deferred.

On Error Go To ErrorHandler:

' In this section, error trapping is again directed to the code
' following the ErrorHandler label.

Exit Sub

' The Exit Sub is required so execution does not fall into the
' following error handling code.

ErrorHandler:

' The error handling code is placed here.

End Sub
```

The Resume Statement

The **Resume** statement is used within error-handling code to instruct the program where to continue execution after the error has been handled. **Resume** can be used only within error-handling code; otherwise, an error occurs. There are several variants of **Resume**. When used by itself, it means "try again to execute the statement that caused the error." This is appropriate in situations where the cause of the error has been fixed. In other circumstances, however, this is not possible. If you want execution to continue somewhere other than the statement that caused the error, you have the following two choices:

- **Resume Next** continues execution immediately after the statement that caused the error.

- **Resume** *label* continues execution with the program line identified by *label*. The line identified by *label* must be in the same procedure as the **Resume** statement (the same procedure where the error occurred).

I will provide more information later on deciding which of the **Resume** statements you should use.

The ERR Object

Much of Visual Basic's ability to deal with errors comes from the ERR object. Each Visual Basic program automatically has a single ERR object associated with it. ERR has global scope, meaning it can be accessed from anywhere in a program. At any moment, ERR contains (in its properties) information about the most recent error that has occurred. The properties you'll need most often are these:

- *Number*—A type **Long** value identifying the specific error that occurred.

- *Description*—A brief text description of the error.

- *Source*—A string identifying the name of the object or application that generated the error.

The first two properties of the ERR object provide the same numerical code and text description displayed in the error dialog box when an untrapped error occurs. As such, they do not provide a great deal of information. The value of these properties lies in giving your program access to this information in code, enabling it to determine which error occurred and then to take appropriate action. The **Source** property is not much use in a self-contained application, because it will return only the name of the Visual Basic project. It is more useful when using external objects, as covered later in the chapter.

Let's look at an example. If a program uses a diskette drive, a common potential error that should be trapped is the absence of a diskette in the drive. Attempting to open a file under these conditions results in error number 71. The error-handling code would look something like Listing 25.2.

Listing 25.2   *Using the ERR object's Number property to identify the error.*

```
Private Sub SaveData()

Dim f As Long

On Error GoTo FileError
```

```
f = FreeFile

Open "a:\junk.dat" For Binary As #f

' Code to write data goes here.

Close #f

Exit Sub

FileError:

If Err.Number = 71 Then
    MsgBox ("Please insert a diskette in drive A:, then click OK")
    Resume
End If

End Sub
```

If there is no diskette in drive A: when this procedure executes, attempting to execute the **Open** statement will cause error number 71 to occur. Execution will pass to the FileError label, and the ERR object's **Number** property will be tested against the value 71. Because it matches, the program will display a message box prompting the user to insert a diskette. When the user closes the message box, the **Resume** statement will cause execution to continue with the statement that caused the error—in this case, the **Open** statement. Because a diskette is now in the drive, the statement will execute with no error.

Although the code in Listing 25.2 works, you would not want to place it in a real program. Suppose the user does not have a diskette handy. The program should offer the option of canceling the disk write operation. Listing 25.3 shows an improvement on the previous example, providing the user with the option of inserting a diskette and continuing, or canceling.

Listing 25.3   *Improved error-handling code offers the user a choice.*

```
Private Sub SaveData()

Dim f As Long, Reply As Integer
Dim msg As String

On Error GoTo FileError

f = FreeFile

Open "a:\junk.dat" For Binary As #f

' Data writing code goes here.
```

```
Close #f

Exit Sub

FileError:

If Err.Number = 71 Then
    msg = "Please insert a diskette in drive A:, then click Retry."
    msg = msg & VbCRLF
    msg = msg & "Or click Cancel to try again later."
    Reply = MsgBox(msg, vbRetryCancel, "Disk error")
    If Reply = vbRetry Then
        Resume
    ElseIf Reply = vbCancel Then
        Resume Finish
    End If

    ' Other error handling code goes here.

Finish:

End If

End Sub
```

Now when error number 71 is trapped, a message box is displayed offering users the choice of inserting a disk immediately or canceling the save operation and trying again later (a desirable option for some situations—if the user happens to be out of diskettes and must go fetch one, for example). If the user selects Retry, the **Resume** statement is used to re-execute the **Open** statement. If the user selects Cancel, the **Resume** *label* is used to direct execution out of the procedure.

While improved over the original, this error-handling code is still incomplete. If a different error occurred, execution would still pass to FileError. The **If** condition would not be True, however, so the associated statements would not be executed. Instead, execution would leave the procedure, and the error would be left hanging.

Does this mean the error-handling code in each procedure must explicitly deal with every single possible error? No, that would be impractical. I'll show you how to create a more generic error handler later in the chapter.

Sometimes, error-handling code will test the value of **ERR.Number** as soon as the error is trapped (as in the previous example). At other times, the numerical error value will not be tested immediately. When this happens, you retrieve the value of **ERR.Number** and save it in a regular variable. Why? Remember that the ERR object contains information about the single most recent error. If a second error occurs between the time of the first error and retrieving the value of **ERR.Number**, you receive the numerical code for the second error; information about the first error is lost.

As you might well imagine, Visual Basic has a whole slew of trappable errors. How do you find out about them? Activate the Visual Basic Help system and search for "trappable errors" to receive a list of error message categories, such as OLE Automation Messages and Miscellaneous Messages. Select the desired category for a list of related errors and their numerical codes. Select an individual error message to view more details on the causes and possible remedies (if any) for the error condition.

> ### TIP Message Boxes And Line Breaks
>
> Sometimes, the message you want to display in a message box is too long to fit on one line. To break a long message into two or more lines, place **vbCRLF** in the message at the desired break points. This is a defined constant for the newline character. If you place two of these characters, one after the other, you'll skip two lines.

Using On Error Resume Next

As I have already mentioned, executing the **On Error Resume Next** statement is necessary when you want to defer error trapping. If this statement is in effect when an error occurs, execution continues with the statement immediately following the one that caused the error. This type of deferred error trapping is most useful when our program is accessing objects—such as OLE automation objects—because it permits you unambiguously to identify the object that caused the error. The basic sequence of code is as follows:

1. Execute **On Error Resume Next**.

2. Access or manipulate the OLE automation object.

3. Immediately test **Err.Number** to see if an error has occurred; if so, handle it.

Listing 25.4 illustrates this technique. The code attempts to use the **GetObject** function to access a nonexistent object. This causes error 432, defined as "File name or class name not found during OLE Automation operation." The **If** statement tests for this value in **Err.Number**, and if it is found, displays a dialog box with a message including the name and source of the error. The error source is obtained from the ERR object's **Source** property, which contains the name of the object or application that caused the most recent error. In this example, it will return the name of the Visual Basic project. In other cases, such as passing a nonsupported command to an existing OLE Automation object, the object name will be returned.

Finally, the **Clear** method is executed to clear all of the ERR object's properties. This ensures that the old information from this error will not "hang around" and be misinterpreted later. The **Clear** method is invoked automatically whenever an **On Error**, **Resume**, **Exit Sub**, or **Exit Function** statement is executed.

Listing 25.4   Demonstrating deferred error handling when accessing objects.

```
Private Sub AccessObject()

Dim MyObj As Object
Dim msg As String

On Error Resume Next    ' Defer error trapping.
' Try to start a non-existent object.
MyObj = GetObject("MyWord.Basic")

' Test for error 432
If Err.Number = 432 Then    ' OLE Automation error.

    ' Tell user what happened.
    msg = "An error occurred attempting to open the OLE object!"
    msg = msg & VbCRLF
    msg = msg & "Error source: " & Err.Source
    msg = msg & VbCRLF & "Error number: " & Err.Number
    MsgBox (msg)
    ' Clear the Err object properties.
    Err.Clear
End If

End Sub
```

Raising Errors

When working on your project's error-handling code, mimicking the occurrence of certain runtime errors is often useful, so you can see exactly how your error-handling routines work. You can mimic errors in code using the ERR object's **Raise** method. The syntax is as follows:

```
Err.Raise number, source, description, helpfile, helpcontext
```

The only required argument is *number*, which is a **Long** integer that identifies the error. To mimic a specific Visual Basic error, use the number associated with the error, as indicated in the Help information. The other arguments are optional:

- *source*—String expression naming the object or application that generated the error. When setting this property for an object, use the form project.class. If *source* is not specified, the programmatic ID of the current Visual Basic project is used.

- *description*—String expression describing the error. If unspecified, the value in *number* is examined. If it can be mapped to a Visual Basic runtime error code, the string that would be returned by the **Error** function is used as *description*. If no Visual Basic error corresponds to *number*, the "Application-defined or object-defined error" message is used.

- *helpfile*—The fully qualified path to the Microsoft Windows Help file in which help on this error can be found. If unspecified, Visual Basic uses the fully qualified drive, path, and file name of the Visual Basic Help file.

- *helpcontext*—The context ID identifying a topic within *helpfile* that provides help for the error. If omitted, the Visual Basic Help file context ID for the error corresponding to the **Number** property is used, if it exists.

The following line of code, for example, will simulate a "Disk not ready" error:

```
Err.Raise 71
```

Where Is The Error Statement?

Earlier versions of Visual Basic used the **Error** statement to simulate runtime errors. **Error** is still supported, but only for purposes of backward compatibility. You should always use the **Raise** method in new code to simulate errors.

User-Defined Errors

In addition to dealing with runtime errors, you can use Visual Basic's error-handling capabilities to define your own errors. Two approaches are possible: raising errors that you define and returning errors from functions.

Raising Your Own Errors

The first approach is to assign an unused error number to an occurrence that you want to treat as an error. When the error condition occurs (as determined by your code), you use the **Raise** method to trigger the error and Visual Basic's usual error-handling methods (**OnError Goto**, and **Resume**) to deal with it. Thus, a procedure could contain one error handler that deals with both "regular" system errors—such as disk drives not being ready—as well as your user-defined errors.

Let's try an example. Create a new project with a single form, placing the code in Listing 25.5 in the form's **Click** event procedure. When you run the project and click on the form, you will be prompted to enter a name—any name, except "Bill". If you follow instructions and enter, say, "Gladys", you will be rewarded with a "Thank You" message. If you enter "Bill", however, the **If** statement uses the **Raise** method to trigger an error with the **Number** 1234 and the **Description** "Not Bill, dummy!" The **On Error Goto** statement specifies that execution was to pass to the location identified by the label ErrorHandler. Code in the error handler checks to see if the error was the user-defined error identified by the **Number** property 1234. If so, the code displays a message consisting of the error's **Description** property.

Listing 25.5   *Using the Raise method to generate user-defined errors.*

```
Private Sub Form_Click()

Dim buf As String

On Error GoTo ErrorHandler

GetData:

buf = InputBox("Enter any name except 'Bill'.")
If buf = "Bill" Then Err.Raise 1234, , "Not Bill, dummy!"

MsgBox ("Thank you")

Exit Sub

ErrorHandler:

If Err = 1234 Then
    MsgBox (Err.Description)
    Resume GetData
End If

End Sub
```

Error numbers from 0 to 1000 are reserved for use by Visual Basic (although not all of them are actually used). In regular code—code that is not in a class module—you can use any number between 1001 and 65535. When raising an error in a class module, you must add your error code number to the **vbObjectError** constant. For example, if the previous code were in a class module, you would write the following:

```
If buf = "Bill" Then Err.Raise vbObjectError + 1234, , "Not Bill, dummy!"
```

Returning Errors From Functions

The second approach to user-defined errors allows you to return an error value from a function. By returning an error value rather than the normal return value, you can signal the calling code that an error has occurred within the function. But how do you distinguish an error value from a nonerror value?

The technique makes use of the flexibility of the **Variant** data type. Recall from Chapter 4 that a **Variant** can hold a variety of subtypes of data—one of which is **Error**. To convert a "regular" number into a type **Error**, you use the **CVErr** function. Thus, if **X** and **Y** are both type **Variant** variables, the code

```
X = 1234
Y = CVErr(1234)
```

results in X containing a subtype **Integer** and Y containing a subtype **Error**. Both have the same numerical value, but the subtype is different. You can tell if a **Variant** contains an **Error** subtype with the **IsError** function. When passed a type **Variant**, this function returns True if the subtype is **Error**; otherwise, it returns False.

Listing 25.6 shows an example of using this type of user-defined error. Two procedures are included here: one is a general function; the other is the **Click** event procedure for the project's form. When you run the project (assuming you know enough by now to create a new project and add these procedures on your own), click on the form, and the program will prompt you for a number. Your entry is passed to the **SquareRoot** function, and the following steps occur:

1. **IsNumeric** (one of Visual Basic's built-in functions) tests whether the value you entered is a number. If it is not, then **CVErr** is used to pass back a type **Error** with the value 1002 as the function's return value.

2. If the value is a number, check to see that it is not negative. (You may recall from high school algebra that negative numbers do not have square roots.) If the value is negative, then **CVErr** is used to pass back a type **Error** with the value 1001 as the function's return value.

3. If the value passes these tests, it must be a non-negative number. You can take its square root and return the answer as a regular number.

It is now up to the calling program to test the value returned by the **SquareRoot** function to determine if an error has occurred. This is done in two stages. First, the **IsError** function is used to determine if the return value is type **Error**. If it is not, the function returns a valid answer, and you can display it. If an **Error** is returned, the next step is testing the value that was returned to determine which type of error occurred. Note that you use the **CInt** function to convert the type **Error** value into a plain type **Integer** before comparing it with the constants 1001 and 1002. You could also have written the following, and it would work just as well:

```
If answer = CVErr(1002) Then
```

Listing 25.6   *Returning a type Error from a function.*

```
Public Function SquareRoot(X As Variant)

If Not IsNumeric(X) Then
    SquareRoot = CVErr(1001)
ElseIf X < 0 Then
    SquareRoot = CVErr(1002)
Else
    SquareRoot = X ^ 0.5
End If

End Function

Private Sub Form_Click()

Dim num As Variant, answer As Variant

num = CVar(InputBox("Enter number for square root:"))
answer = SquareRoot(num)
If IsError(answer) Then
    If CInt(answer) = 1002 Then
        MsgBox ("Positive numbers only, please!")
        Exit Sub
    End If
    If CInt(answer) = 1001 Then
        MsgBox ("That's not a number!")
        Exit Sub
    End If
End If

MsgBox ("The square root of " & num & " is " & answer)

End Sub
```

General Error-Handling Code

As I mentioned earlier, explicitly testing for every individual error that might conceivably occur in each procedure is not practical. Does this mean you can just ignore other errors? Not necessarily. You may not be able to explicitly handle an unexpected error, but at least you can inform the users of the nature of the error, so they can report it to you, permitting you to fix the problem in the code. The goal is to provide information about the nature of the error and where it occurred—both in terms of which form and which procedure it is in. You can obtain the name of the form from the property **Screen.ActiveForm.Name**. As for determining the procedure, declare a string variable and load it with the procedure name. An example is shown in Listing 25.7.

Listing 25.7   Code for reporting information on untrapped errors.

```
Dim ProcName As String
ProcName = "Form_DblClick"

On Error GoTo ErrorHandler

' Other code here

ErrorHandler:

msg = "An untrapped error has occurred. Please make a " & VbCRLF
msg = msg & "note of the following information." & VbCRLF & VbCRLF
msg = msg & "Error number: " & Err.Number & VbCRLF
msg = msg & "Description: " & Err.Description & VbCRLF
msg = msg & "Location: " & Screen.ActiveForm.Name & VbCRLF
msg = msg & "Procedure: " & ProcName
MsgBox (msg)
```

Perhaps more than any other aspect of a Visual Basic Program, the burden for well-designed error handling rests on the programmer. There are no clever controls that you can "drop in" to do the job for you. The errors that need to be addressed and the way they are handled will depend to a large degree on the specifics of your program. It's tempting to skimp on error handling or to leave it for the end of the project. Wrong! Keep error handling in mind from the start, building it right into your program—not tacking it on at the end. You'll save time and grief in the long run. Trust me on this—I know from experience.

Chapter 26

Debugging And Distributing Your Applications

Writing a Visual Basic program is not enough. You must also debug it so it works properly, and you must distribute it to your end users.

To my mind, writing a Visual Basic program is the fun part. Okay, it may not always be fun, but there's always the challenge of making the computer do just what you want it to do. Software development means more than just writing a program, however. Once the program is nearing its final form, you need to be sure it is free of bugs. Then, of course, you must tackle the job of actually distributing the program to the end users. Debugging and distributing may not be as much fun as writing the program, but they are necessary tasks.

Finding And Fixing Program Bugs

The time has come for us to take on program bugs—what they are and what you can do about them. Bugs are one of the two main types of problems your programs can experience. (The other—runtime errors—was covered in Chapter 25.)

What's A Bug?

A *bug* is a code error that prevents your program from operating correctly. We're not talking about an error that prevents the program from executing or that can be caught by Visual Basic's error-trapping mechanisms. Rather, a bug is a logical mistake in the program's source code that causes the program to behave incorrectly. Here are some examples of the kinds of problems bugs can cause:

- A financial program that calculates and displays incorrect loan payments

- A graphics program that applies improper colors to images

- Any program that does not respond properly to user commands

These are just a few examples; there are plenty more, and I can guarantee that you will run into some of them. Dealing with bugs is a two-part process that begins with avoiding them in the first place. No, it isn't feasible to avoid all bugs in all programs (at least I haven't been able to), but you can greatly decrease their frequency with good programming practice. (As you have probably noticed by now, teaching and encouraging good programming practices are among the major goals of this book.)

Here are some of the most essential guidelines to follow when it comes to avoiding program bugs:

- *Always use **Option Explicit**, so variable declaration is required*. This prevents the pernicious "misspelled variable name" error that is perhaps the most common cause of bugs in Visual Basic.

- *Divide your code into relatively small, manageable procedures*. Large, complex procedures are more prone to bugs, and more difficult to debug, than short, simple ones.

- *Use global and public variables sparingly*. Stick with local variables within procedures as much as possible, resorting to global and public variables only when unavoidable.

- *Use the proper data type for your program's data*. Using type **Integer** for certain calculations can result in rounding errors, which can cause bugs.

Regardless of how carefully you work, some bugs are likely to crop up in your programs—particularly as you move into more complex projects. Almost all bugs can be traced to a program variable taking on an improper value or to program execution taking an unexpected path (or a combination of both). Visual Basic provides debugging tools that help track down both kinds of problems.

Using The Debug.Print Statement

With the **Debug.Print** method, you can display information about program status during execution. The information is displayed in the Immediate window, which opens automatically when you execute a program within the Visual Basic environment. To use **Debug.Print**, include the statement in your code, followed by a list of one or more program variables or string constants that you want to display. For example, the statement

```
Debug.Print X, Y
```

will display the values of the variables X and Y in the Immediate window. Likewise, executing the statement

```
Debug.Print "Entering Calculate procedure"
```

will display the indicated text. Each **Debug.Print** statement outputs on a new line in the Immediate window. If you execute **Debug.Print** with no arguments, it outputs a blank line. You can display the value of any program variables or object properties with **Debug.Print**. You can also use it to evaluate and display the result of any Basic expression.

The beauty of the **Debug.Print** statement is that it is ignored when you create an executable version of your project. It is operative only when a program is executed within the Visual Basic development environment, and it has no effect on the size or execution of the final program. Thus, you can use it freely during program development.

Setting Breakpoints

A *breakpoint* causes program execution to pause when it reaches a specified line of code. You can set breakpoints on one or more lines of code in your program. When execution reaches a breakpoint, the program pauses and the line of code is highlighted in the Code Editing window. While execution is paused, you can take several actions to help locate a program bug. I will describe these options soon.

 Breaking Program Execution

When you set a breakpoint in a line of code, execution pauses just *before* the statement on that line is executed. The statement where the breakpoint is located will be the first one executed when you continue execution.

To set a breakpoint, move the editing cursor to the line of code where you want execution to pause. Press F9 or select Toggle Breakpoint from the Debug menu. This displays a line that a breakpoint has been set on, with a different-colored background and a dot in the left margin. Press F9 or select Toggle Breakpoint again to remove the breakpoint from a line of code. You can set as many breakpoints as you need.

To clear all breakpoints, press Ctrl+Shift+F9 or select Clear All Breakpoints from the Debug menu. Note that you can't undo this command; your breakpoints are lost and can only be reset manually, one at a time.

Another way to break program execution is based on the value of program variables rather than on specific code location. This technique will be covered in the next section.

When a breakpoint is encountered, a Visual Basic program enters *break mode*. You can enter break mode manually while the program is executing by selecting Break from the Run menu or clicking on the Break button on the toolbar. Entering break mode manually is useful when you realize you should have, but did not, set a breakpoint at a particular location in the code. If a Basic statement was executing at the moment, execution will pause at that statement. Quite often, however, no Basic statement will be executing; the program will be waiting for an event to occur. In this case, you cannot say "where" in your code execution halted, because the next Basic statement to be executed usually depends on the event that is received.

While your program is paused at a breakpoint, you have the following execution commands available to you. They are located on the Run menu, represented by toolbar buttons:

- *Continue*—Resumes program execution with the next statement.
- *End*—Terminates program execution.
- *Restart*—Restarts the program. Selecting Restart has the same effect as selecting End followed by Run.

While a program is paused, you can track down bugs in a number of different ways. These are covered in the following sections.

Using Watch Expressions

A *watch expression* is a Basic expression whose value is monitored, or watched, during program debugging. A watch expression can be any Basic expression—a program variable, an object property, a function call, or a combination of these elements. You can use any of Visual Basic's mathematical and logical operators, as well as its built-in functions, to create a watch expression. As mentioned earlier, a prime cause of program bugs is a program variable or property taking on an inappropriate value. By setting a watch, you can keep an eye on the value of the variable or property to see if and when it changes.

You can use a watch expression in several ways:

- You can monitor its value. Visual Basic will display the expression value in the Watches window, which opens automatically when you define a watch expression. The displayed value is updated whenever the program enters break mode.

- You can specify that the program pause (enter break mode) whenever the value of the expression changes.

- You can specify that the program enter break mode whenever the value of the expression becomes True.

To set a watch expression, select Add Watch from the Debug menu. Visual Basic will open the Add Watch dialog box, which is shown in Figure 26.1. If the editing cursor is on the name of a variable or property at the time you display the dialog box, the variable or property name will automatically be entered in the Expression box in the Add Watch dialog box (as is Total in the figure). Also, if you first select a Basic code expression, then the selected code will be entered here.

Next, you will need to enter or edit the desired watch expression in the Expression box— unless, of course, the desired expression was entered automatically. Finally, select the desired type of watch in the Watch Type section of the dialog box, then click on OK. (The Context setting in the Add Watch dialog box will be explained later.)

When you add a watch—no matter what type it is—it will be displayed in the Watches window, as shown in Figure 26.2. Each watch expression is displayed on its own line. The icon at the left end of the line identifies the type of watch (watch, break when changes, or break when True). When you first add items to the Watches window (also shown in Figure 26.2), the Value column displays <Out of context>, and the Type column displays Empty. These will change when the program executes.

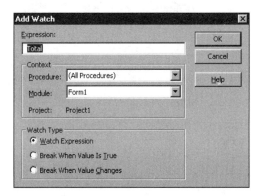

Figure 26.1 *The Add Watch dialog box.*

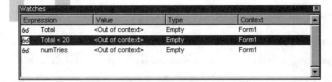

Figure 26.2 *The Watches window after adding several watches, but before executing the program.*

Let's look at some watch expression examples. Table 26.1 lists the purpose, type, and expression for a variety of debugging situations.

When you execute a program where watches are set, every time the program breaks, the information displayed in the Watches window is updated. This occurs regardless of whether the break was caused by a breakpoint set on a line of code or by a Break When Value Changes or Break When Value Is True watch expression. Then, the Watches window displays the following:

- *Value*—The current value of the expression or <Out of context> (I will explain this soon).

- *Type*—The data type of the expression—**Single, Double, Integer**, etc.

Working In The Watches Window

While the program is in break mode, you can do several things in the Watches window to assist your debugging. Right-click on any watch expression to display the shortcut menu shown in Figure 26.3. Your choices are:

Table 26.1 *Sample watch expressions.*

Purpose	Type Of Watch	Watch Expression
To monitor the value stored in the string variable **Name**	Watch Expression	Name
To monitor the length of the text stored in **Name**	Watch Expression	**Len(Name)** Note: **Len** is one of Visual Basic's built-in functions
To break when X is less than 0	Break when Value is True	X < 0
To break when the **Text** property of the Text Box named Data1 changes	Break when Value Changes	Data1.Text
To break when the Text Box named Data1 is blank	Break When Value is True	Data1.Text = "" or **Len(Data1.Text) = 0**

- *Edit Watch*—Opens the Edit Watch dialog box to make changes to the specified watch expression.

- *Add*—Opens the Add Watch dialog box to add a new watch expression to the Watches window.

- *Delete*—Deletes the selected watch expression.

- *Continue*—Continues program execution (equivalent to pressing F5 or clicking on the Continue button on the toolbar).

- *End*—Ends program execution (equivalent to clicking on the End button on the toolbar).

You can also modify the value of variables in the Watches window. Click on any watch expression once to highlight it, then click on the value displayed in the Value column. You can now edit the displayed value. When you move off the line by clicking on another expression or pressing the up or down arrow key, the variable takes on the value you entered. This value will remain in effect when you continue program execution. You'll find this technique useful for testing the effects that different variable values will have on the program execution.

Context And Watch Expressions

I have mentioned the term *context* a couple of times in relation to watch expressions. Context is closely related to the concept of variable scope that I covered in Chapter 5. To jog your memory, *scope* refers to the parts of a Visual Basic project in which a particular variable is visible or accessible. Likewise, the *context* of a watch expression determines the parts of the project where the expression is evaluated. Any watch expression's context has three parts:

Figure 26.3   *Right-clicking on a watch expression displays this shortcut menu.*

- *Procedure*—Which procedure or procedures is the expression evaluated in? The default is the procedure that the variable is declared in (for local variables) or all procedures (for global variables).

- *Module*—Which of the project modules will the expression be evaluated in? The default is the module where the term resides. In a multiple-module project, you can extend the context of a watch expression to all modules.

- *Project*—The current project. This setting cannot be changed.

Generally, you should leave the context settings at their default values for any watch expression. Extending an expression's context beyond the default setting will slow program execution and should be done only when you have a specific reason to do so. When the program is in break mode and a watch expression displays <Out of context> in the Watches window, it simply means that the current break location is outside that expression's context. This is rarely a problem; in parts of the program where a variable or property is out of context, it should not be contributing to any bugs.

Quick Watches

If you want to take a quick look at the value of a variable or expression, you can use a *quick watch*. While your program is in break mode, position the editing cursor on the variable or property name you are interested in or highlight the expression you want to evaluate. Then press Shift+F9 or select Quick Watch from the Debug menu. The Quick Watch dialog box is displayed, as shown in Figure 26.4. The parts of this dialog box are as follows:

- *Context*—The current context (that is, the project, module, and procedure where execution is paused)

- *Expression*—The selected variable or property name or expression

- *Value*—The current value of the expression or <Out of context>, if appropriate

While the Quick Watch dialog box is displayed, click on the Add button to add the expression to the Watches window. Click on Cancel to close the dialog box.

Figure 26.4   *The Quick Watch dialog box.*

Checking Values

In break mode, you can rest the mouse cursor on a variable or property name in the Code Editing window to see a small, pop-up window with the current value displayed.

Using The Immediate Window

The Immediate window is automatically displayed in the Visual Basic environment when you run a program. It does not display anything at first, and in fact, it will remain blank if you do not use it. It is called the Immediate window, because any code you type into it is executed immediately. You can use the Immediate window whether or not a program is executing. To display it when no program is executing, select Immediate Window from the View menu or press Ctrl+G.

When a program is not executing, the primary use for the Immediate window is to evaluate Basic expressions. If you type a line of Basic code in the Immediate window (or copy and paste it from the Code Editing window) and then press Enter, the code is executed immediately. Typically, you will use the **Print** statement to evaluate the value of expressions. Thus, if you enter

```
print cos(.5)
```

and press Enter, Visual Basic will display 0.877582561890373 in the Immediate window.

The Immediate window is much more useful in break mode, when program execution is paused. Then, you can view and change the value of any variables and properties that are available within the current context. For example, if execution is paused within a procedure that declares a variable named **Total**, then executing

```
Print Total
```

in the Immediate window will display the current value of the variable. Executing

```
Total = 10
```

will change the value of **Total** to 10. You are probably thinking you can accomplish these same tasks—viewing and changing a variable or property's value—from the Watches window, and you are correct. The Immediate window, however, provides additional flexibility, permitting you to perform these tasks without cluttering the Watches window with too many expressions.

Controlling Execution During Debugging

The Debug menu has several commands that give you some control over the path of program execution. Two of these commands are used in break mode and are related to the next statement to be executed when execution resumes (by selecting Continue):

- *Show Next Statement*—Moves the editing cursor to the next statement that will be executed when execution is continued. By default, this is the statement where the breakpoint is set.

- *Set Next Statement*—Instructs Visual Basic that the next statement to be executed is the one containing the editing cursor.

Why would you want to change the next statement? When the program is paused in break mode, you can use this command to move the next statement "back," so that one or more statements immediately before the break location will be executed again. You can also move it ahead, so that one or more statements immediately following the break location will be skipped. Combined with changing variable values (using the Watches and Immediate windows, as described earlier), this technique can be powerful in helping you locate the program locations where bugs occur.

The Run to Cursor command on the Debug menu can be useful in a similar manner. Selecting this command while in break mode causes execution to continue up to the line of code where the cursor is located. Execution will stop at any breakpoints encountered along the way, however.

Single Stepping Your Program

When debugging a program, you'll find it useful at times to step through the program one line at a time. No, you do not have to set a breakpoint on every single line of code. Instead, use the Step commands from the Debug menu. These commands are listed in Table 26.2.

You can see that Step Into and Step Over have the same effect if the next statement is *not* a procedure call.

Distributing Your Program

If the Visual Basic program you are writing is for your own use only, simply make an EXE file and place the executable in the appropriate folder on your hard disk. For most programs, however, you will need some way to distribute them to other users—from a few colleagues in your department to millions of customers worldwide. Fortunately, Visual Basic provides tools to simplify this task.

Preparing a Visual Basic program for distribution consists of two parts: You must create the setup program that the end user runs to install your program; you must package the pro-

Table 26.2   Visual Basic's Step commands.

Command	When Program Has Not Yet Started	When Program Is Paused At A Breakpoint	Shortcut Key
Step Into	Executes the first statement. If the first statement is a procedure call, pauses at the first statement in the procedure.	Executes the next statement. If the next statement is a procedure call, pauses at the first statement in the procedure.	F8
Step Over	Executes the first statement. If the first statement is a procedure call, executes all statements in the procedure, and pauses at the first statement following the procedure.	Executes the next statement. If the next statement is a procedure call, executes all statements in the procedure and pauses at the first statement following the procedure.	Shift+F8
Step Out	Not available.	If execution is paused in a procedure, executes the remainder of the procedure and pauses at the first statement following the procedure.	Ctrl+Shift+F8

gram and its setup files so they can be placed on diskettes, a CD-ROM, or the Internet. The setup program is normally created automatically for you, but you have the option of customizing it. Packaging of the program files is accomplished by the Package and Deployment Wizard.

Creating The Setup Program

As with most Windows programs, a Visual Basic program is installed by running SETUP.EXE. When you create a distribution package for a Visual Basic program, SETUP.EXE is automatically included as part of the package. This program has basically only one function: to execute the program SETUP1.EXE. This may seem like a strange way to do things, but there is a reason behind it. While SETUP is fixed and cannot be changed, you can customize SETUP1 to meet the specific setup requirements of your program. In fact, SETUP1 is itself a Visual Basic program, located in the folder \VB98\ WIZARDS\PDWIZARD\SETUP1.

Here's how it works: When you run the Package and Deployment Wizard (covered later in the chapter), it includes SETUP1.EXE, which will be included in your program's distribution package. If you have customized and compiled SETUP1, your changes will be included; otherwise, the default version is used.

When would you need to customize SETUP1? To be honest, almost never. I have written and distributed quite a few Visual Basic programs, and I have not needed to do so even once. The possibility does exist, however. For example, you might want to give your users the option of either installing a large Help file to their hard disk or running it from the distribution CD-ROM. The basic procedure for customizing SETUP1 is as follows:

1. Open the SETUP1 project.

2. Create one or more new forms to display information and collect user responses about the available installation options.

3. Select the form frmSetup1 and display the code in the **Form_Load** procedure.

4. Locate the call to the procedure **ShowBeginForm**. Immediately after this call, add code to display your option dialog boxes. For simple options, you may be able to use the **MsgBox** function to input Yes/No answers.

5. Add code to the **Form_Load** procedure as required by your installation options. You will find comments interspersed in the source code explaining what exactly needs to be added.

6. Compile the SETUP1 project to create SETUP1.EXE.

7. Run the Package and Deployment Wizard to create a distribution package for your program.

8. Locate the SETUP.LST file that was created by the wizard. This file contains information about the files and icons that are part of the program installation. Use any text editor, such as WordPad, to make necessary additions and changes to this file.

You'll find more detailed information on editing SETUP.LST and other aspects of customizing the setup program in the online Visual Basic Help system. It is not a difficult process, and as I have mentioned, it is something you will rarely need to do. Remember, whether or not you customize your setup, be sure to test it thoroughly before distributing it.

The Package And Deployment Wizard

The Package and Deployment Wizard (or PD Wizard) is on the same level as sliced bread and indoor plumbing in terms of being a great thing. Assembling all the files needed to distribute your Visual Basic application and packaging them for distribution would be a miserable task without this tool. You can run the PD Wizard either as an add-in in Visual Basic or as a standalone. To run it as an add-in, use the Add-In Manager (select Add-In Manager from the Add-Ins menu in Visual Basic) to load the PD Wizard. Load the project you want to package/distribute into Visual Basic, then run the PD Wizard from the Add-Ins menu. To run it as a standalone, execute the file PDCMDLN.EXE. In either case, when the program starts, you'll see the opening screen shown in Figure 26.5.

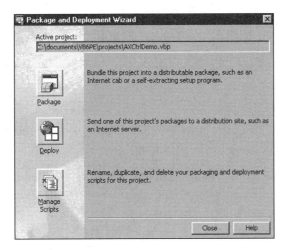

Figure 26.5   *The PD Wizard's opening screen.*

As the name suggests, the PD Wizard has two functions:

- *Packaging your program*—Determining which files are needed and combining them and the setup program into a compressed form. Packaging can also include the process of copying distribution files to diskettes.

- *Deploying this package*—Moving it to a network or Internet site where people can access it.

These two functions are accessed via the corresponding buttons on the PD Wizard's opening screen. The third button, Manage Scripts, is used to work with scripts that let you automate some of the PD Wizard's functions for repetitive tasks. I will not be dealing with script management in this book.

Packaging Your Application

You have several distribution options when packaging your application:

- Distributing the program on multiple diskettes, splitting files that are too large to fit onto a single diskette.

- Placing the distribution files in a hard-disk directory for distribution over a network or mastering onto CD-ROM.

- Distributing your application across the Internet using the automatic code download capability of Microsoft Internet Explorer.

To start creating your distribution package, load the desired project. Recompiling your project to an EXE (or whatever the target is) is a good idea, because the PD Wizard requires up-to-date files before it can do its job. If the wizard detects out-of-date or unsaved files, it will prompt you to correct the situation before continuing.

Next, start the PD Wizard and click on the Package button. You'll be offered a choice of package types. The types available will depend on the type of project:

- *Standard Setup Package*—The correct choice for EXE projects and any other type of project that will be installed with a setup program and distributed on disks or on a local network.

- *Internet Package*—Available only for ActiveX projects. It creates a package that will be installed by downloading from an Internet site.

On the next screen, shown in Figure 26.6, you select a folder where the PD Wizard will place the setup package. Placing each package in its own folder is advisable to avoid confusion. Click on the Network button to select a folder on the network (assuming, of course, that you are connected to one). Click on the New Folder button to create a new folder with a name different from the one suggested by the PD Wizard.

The next screen (Figure 26.7) lists all of the files the PD Wizard will include in your setup package. To add files, click on the Add button. Files you might need to add include a README.ME file, help files, licensing information, and the like. You should never need to add an actual program component, because the PD Wizard will have already included all required items. You can also remove a file from the distribution package by clearing the checkbox next to its name in the list. I strongly suggest that you never do this, because the files included in the list are required for your application to install and run correctly.

The next screen lets you select whether your package will be compressed into a single cab file (a cab file, short for cabinet, is a type of compressed file used by Microsoft for program distribution) or into multiple cabs. If you select multiple cabs, you can also select the maximum size for each file to match the distribution media. For example, select 1.44MB if your program will be distributed on standard high-density diskettes.

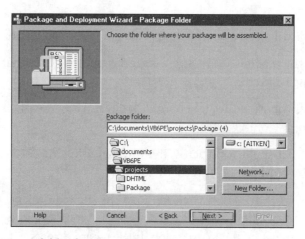

Figure 26.6 *Selecting a folder for the setup package.*

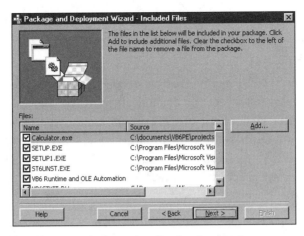

Figure 26.7   *Selecting files to include in the distribution package.*

The next few screens let you select options, such as the name your program will be assigned when it is installed and the location of the program on the user's Start menu. You can make your selections, using the PD Wizard prompts to help you if needed. When asked whether to designate shared files, accept the default settings, unless you have a specific reason to change them. The final screen lets you enter a name for the setup script. All the choices you made will be saved in this script. Then, the next time you run the wizard to package this application, you can reload the script to save time.

The last step is to click on Finish. The PD Wizard will create the distribution files in the specified folder and display a summary report. All you need to do is copy the resulting files (SETUP.EXE, one or more cab files, and SETUP.LST) to the distribution disks, and you are ready to start distributing your program. If you will be distributing the program via the Internet or a network, you'll use the deployment part of the wizard next to deploy the files.

Deploying Your Application

If your package will not be distributed on disks, the next step is to deploy it—copy it to a Web server or folder. The first option is most useful, as the PD Wizard will actually log onto the desired Web site and upload files. Deploying to a folder is useful only if your computer is itself the Web server or if you want to upload the files manually at a later time.

To deploy a package, start the PD Wizard and click on the Deploy button. On the first screen, you can either load a deployment script or select (none) if you are starting a new deployment. Next, select the package to deploy and choose between Web publishing and folder deployment. For folder deployment, the only remaining task is to select the destination folder. Web publishing has a few more steps on subsequent PD Wizard screens:

1. *Select the files to deploy.* You should not remove any of the automatically selected files unless you are sure of what you are doing. Add files, such as READ.ME documents, as needed.

2. *Specify the destination URL and publishing protocol (Figure 26.8).* The URL is, of course, the destination for the package (for example, http://www.yoursite.com/). For the protocol, select either HTTP Post or FTP, depending on what the destination server supports. The end result is the same in either case. Select the Unpack and Install Server-Side cab only if necessary—for example, if deploying a DHTML application. Note that the protocol specified in the URL (HTTP:// or FTP://) must match the publishing protocol selected.

3. *Next you will be asked whether to save the URL and publishing protocol in the registry as a Web Publishing Site.* Select Yes, then specify a name for this site.

4. *Enter a name for the deployment script.* All of the information you entered will be saved and can be recalled again if you need to redeploy the same package.

5. *Click on Finish.* The PD Wizard will begin the deployment procedure. You may be asked for a logon and password, depending on the security measures in effect at the destination site. When the process is complete, the wizard will display a report detailing which files were uploaded, any errors that were encountered, and so on.

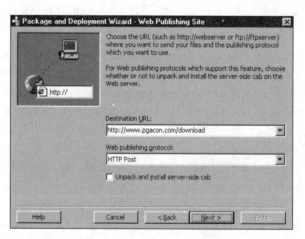

Figure 26.8 *Specifying the destination URL and protocol for Web publishing.*

A Word Of Warning

Deploying your Visual Basic applications on the Web can be a tricky business. Part of the problem comes from the fact that you are usually dealing with a remote computer that is not under your control. More difficulties arise from the lack of universally accepted standards. If you are deploying to a server that is running Windows NT and Microsoft's Web server software, the job is a lot more likely to go smoothly than if you are deploying to a server running Sun Unix and the Netscape Web server. If you run into problems, the best approach is to find out as much as you can about the destination server and whether it supports the operations you are attempting. A chat with the Webmaster is usually helpful, too.

Chapter 27

Using The Windows API

Your Visual Basic programs can access all the power of Windows by calling procedures in the Windows API.

In working with Visual Basic, you've seen how it has a number of built-in procedures that perform such commonly needed tasks as string manipulation, graphics, and mathematical calculations. In a similar fashion, the Windows operating system has a large collection of built-in procedures. These procedures are part of the Windows Applications Programming Interface, or API. By calling these API procedures directly from your Visual Basic program, you can provide additional functionality with relatively little programming effort. In this chapter, I'll show you how to use API calls in your Visual Basic programs as well as a sophisticated API technique called callbacks.

What Is The Windows API?

The Windows API is a huge collection of procedures that can be called by any program running under Windows. In fact, the API is behind a great deal of what every Windows program offers. Displaying screen windows, using the printer, displaying text, using menus—these are all handled by the API. You cannot overestimate the importance of the API. From a programmer's perspective, Windows *is* the API.

When you write a Visual Basic program, you are accessing the API indirectly. You create your program by placing controls, setting properties, executing methods, and so on. When the program runs, Visual Basic translates your instructions into calls to the appropriate API procedures, which perform much of the actual job of the program. You can also call API procedures directly, a task similar to calling a regular Basic procedure.

Why call the API directly? As powerful as Visual Basic is, it does not provide access to all of the capabilities of the Windows API. If you know what's available in the API—and how to reach it—you'll have that many more tools available when creating a Visual Basic program.

The API procedures are located in files called *dynamic link libraries*, or DLLs. DLL files are installed on your disk when you install Windows. They are loaded into memory whenever a Windows application calls them. Many applications install their own DLL files, but we are interested only in those that are part of the Windows 95 operating system. There is only a single copy of each API procedure, which is shared by all programs that need it. This is called *dynamic linking*—hence, the name *dynamic link library*.

The Windows API contains a huge number of procedures capable of performing just about any task you can imagine—and probably a lot that you can't. You'll find procedures for window management, file manipulation, printer control, menus and dialog boxes, memory management, graphics drawing, multimedia, string manipulation...well, you get the idea. Reference material on the API runs to multivolume sets with more than 1,000 pages. Within the context of this book, providing information on even a small fraction of the available API procedures would be impossible. Instead, my goal in this chapter is to show you the general methods for calling API procedures from your Visual Basic programs. For information on specific procedures, I suggest you turn to one of the numerous API reference books.

Accessing The Windows API

As mentioned earlier, calling an API procedure from a Visual Basic program is similar to calling a general Basic function or procedure. If the API procedure is a function—that is, if it returns a value to the calling program—you use the function name on the right side of an assignment statement, assigning its return value to a variable of the appropriate type. For an API procedure that does not return a value, you use the **Call** statement. As with any procedure, you must pass it the correct number and types of arguments.

Let's look at a simple example. If **MyAPISub** is an API procedure, and **MyAPIFunc** is an API function that returns an integer, you would call them as shown here (ignoring arguments for now):

```
Call MyAPISub()
RetVal = MyAPIFunc()
```

Before you can call an API procedure, it must be declared in the program using the **Declare** statement. The **Declare** statement informs Visual Basic about the name of the procedure, as well as the number and types of arguments it takes. The **Declare** statement takes one of the following forms, depending on whether the API procedure returns a value to the calling program or not:

```
Declare Sub APIProcName Lib DLLname [([argumentlist])]
```

```
Declare Function APIProcName Lib DLLname [([argumentlist])] [As type]
```

APIProcName is the name of the API procedure, and *DLLname* is a string literal specifying the name of the DLL file that contains the procedure. The *type* at the end of the function declaration declares the data type of the value returned by a function; *argumentlist* is a list of variables representing arguments passed to the function or procedure when it is called. Most arguments to API procedures must be passed with the **ByVal** keyword. The argument list has the following syntax:

```
ByVal argname1 [As type] [,ByVal argname2 [As type]]...
```

For the statement to work, the components of the **Declare** statement must be specified exactly. If the **Declare** statement contains an error, the call to the API procedure generates a "Reference to undefined function or array" error message when you run the program. The **Declare** statements required by many API procedures are rather long and involved. Here's an example:

```
Declare Function SendDlgItemMessage Lib "user32" Alias _
    "SendDlgItemMessageA" (ByVal hDlg As Long, ByVal nIDDlgItem As Long, _
    ByVal wMsg As Long, ByVal wParam As Long, lParam As Any) As Long
```

For now, don't worry about the **Alias** keyword—which I'll explain later—or what the API procedure does. I'm just using this as an example of a real API procedure declaration. I'm glad to report that you will rarely, if ever, need to type them into your programs. Visual Basic includes a program called the API Text Viewer that provides a complete listing of **Declare** statements for all of the API functions. You can simply copy one or more **Declare** statements to the Clipboard and paste them into your program. The API Text Viewer also provides information on defined Windows constants and types. You can start the API Text Viewer by clicking on its icon in the Visual Basic program group that was created when Visual Basic was installed. Please refer to your Visual Basic documentation for information on how to use the viewer.

Declare statements should usually be placed in the general declarations section of the module that calls the procedures. See the following section on the **Private** and **Public** keywords for more information on the location of **Declare** statements.

TIP DLL Procedure Names Are Case-Sensitive

In Windows 95, DLL procedure names should carry a warning label that reads, "Case-sensitive area—enter with care." All it takes to get a runtime error is one letter typed in the wrong case. There's no alternative but to be extremely careful when typing procedure names.

The Alias, Private, And Public Keywords

These three keywords are optional components of a **Declare** statement. The **Alias** keyword lets you define an alternate name, or *alias*, for the DLL procedure. This allows you to use a different name to call the procedure—a name other than the one it is assigned in the DLL. For example, the statement

```
Declare Function APIProc1 Lib "MyDLL" Alias "APIProc2" () as Long
```

declares that the DLL named MyDLL contains a procedure named **APIProc2**, which we will call **APIProc1** in the program.

Why are aliases necessary? The most common reason is that some DLL procedures have the same name as a Visual Basic reserved word. In this situation, trying to use the DLL procedure under its "real" name can cause confusion and errors. By assigning an alias, you can use both the DLL procedure and the reserved word without conflict. Other uses of **Alias** are internal to the API and are not related to Visual Basic itself. **Declare** statements that you copy from the API Text Viewer already contain the required aliases. The only time you'll need to add one yourself is when a DLL function name conflicts with a Basic function or procedure that you defined in your program.

Using the **Public** and **Private** keywords allows you to control where in your program an API declaration is effective. This determines which of the program's modules can use the declared procedure. If a procedure is declared **Public**, you can use it in all of the program's modules. **Public** is the default, so including the keyword in the **Declare** statement is optional. A procedure declared **Private** can be used only by code in the module that contains the **Declare** statement. The **Public** or **Private** keyword goes at the beginning of the **Declare** statement:

```
Public Declare Sub APIProc1
Private Declare Function APIProc2
```

Within a form module, only **Private** procedure declarations are allowed, meaning that you can place **Public** declarations only in code modules. The primary use for making a procedure declaration **Private** occurs when you are writing a form module that you intend to use in other programs as a software component. A software component needs to be completely portable. This means that any API procedures it uses must be declared within the module, requiring the **Private** keyword. This ensures that the module is completely self-contained.

Declaring API Functions As Procedures

Most of the procedures in the API are functions—in other words, they return a value to the calling program. While your program will often need the return value, this will not always be the case. When an API function's return value is not needed, you can declare and use the API procedure as one that does not return a value, simplifying its use in the program. For example, the **SetTextAlign** API procedure specifies the alignment of text that is printed on the screen. It is a function with the following declaration:

```
Declare Function SetTextAlign Lib "gdi32" (ByVal hDC As Long, _
    ByVal wFlags As Long) As Long
```

A Visual Basic program would call it this way:

```
RetVal = SetTextAlign(...)
```

The value this API function returns is the previous text alignment setting. This value is not much use to most programs. To use **SetTextAlign** as a procedure, you would declare it as

```
Declare Sub SetTextAlign Lib "GDI" (ByVal hDC As Long, ByVal wFlags _
    As Long)
```

and call it using the **Call** statement:

```
Call SetTextAlign(...)
```

You cannot define an API procedure as both a function and a procedure in the same program with the same name. If you want to use an API procedure both ways, you can declare it with an **Alias** name:

```
Declare Sub SetTextAlign Lib "GDI" (...)
Declare Function SetTextAlignFunction Lib "GDI" Alias _
    "SetTextAlign" (...) As Long
```

You can then call it using whichever declaration fits the situation at hand:

```
Call SetTextAlign (...)
```

or

```
RetVl = SetTextAlignFunction (...)
```

A Windows API Demonstration

The program I will develop in this section not only shows you a real example of using an API procedure, but it also does something useful. When you use Visual Basic's **Print** method to display text on a form or a Picture Box, the position of the text is determined by the object's **CurrentX** and **CurrentY** properties, which give the horizontal and vertical positions of the current position where the text will appear. The text is always left-aligned with respect to this position. Visual Basic itself provides no other alignment options.

You can, however, use a Windows API call to obtain different types of text alignment—both vertical and horizontal. This is accomplished with the **SetTextAlign** procedure. Its declaration is:

```
Declare Sub SetTextAlign Lib "gdi32" (ByVal hDC As Long, ByVal wFlags _
    As Long)
```

The argument **hDC** specifies the **hDC** property of the object you are printing to, and the argument **wFlags** contains the flags specifying the desired text alignment. These flags specify the text justification with respect to the object's current position. You can specify both vertical and horizontal justification. The possible values for horizontal alignment are defined by the following Windows global constants:

- **TA_CENTER**—Centers the text at the current position
- **TA_LEFT**—Positions the left edge of the text at the current position (the default)
- **TA_RIGHT**—Positions the right edge of the text at the current position

You can also specify vertical alignment. To understand vertical alignment, consider the total vertical extent that characters can span, using these terms:

- **BOTTOM**—The lowest any character extends, such as the descenders on g and y
- **TOP**—The highest any character extends, such as tall uppercase letters or diacritical marks, such as Ä and é
- **BASELINE**—The bottom of characters that don't have descenders, such as a and c

The vertical alignment options are defined using the following terms:

- **TA_BASELINE**—Font baseline aligned with the current position
- **TA_BOTTOM**—Font bottom aligned with the current position
- **TA_TOP**—Font top aligned with the current position (the default)

Because the available text alignment settings operate with respect to the object's current position, the **SetTextAlign** procedure does not align text with respect to the edges of the print area, as a word processing program does. If you want to specify alignment with respect to the object edges, you must do some fiddling in code. For example, to right-align text in a Picture Box so that the right edge of the text lines up with the right edge of the Picture Box, set the Picture Box's **CurrentX** property to the right edge (obtained from the **ScaleWidth** property), then use the **SetTextAlign** procedure to set right alignment before displaying the text with the **Print** method. Similarly, to center text in a Picture Box, first set **CurrentX** to the center of the box (ScaleWidth/2) and then use **SetTextAlign** to specify center alignment.

Now let's move on to the demonstration program. This program displays text in a Picture Box. First, vertical and horizontal lines are drawn to mark the center of the box. Two sets of option buttons allow you to select both vertical and horizontal text alignment. All alignment is with respect to the box's center, marked by the two lines.

Start a new standard EXE project. On the form, add a Picture Box, a Command Button, and two Frame controls. On each of the Frame controls, create a control array of three Option Buttons. The program is shown executing in Figure 27.1.

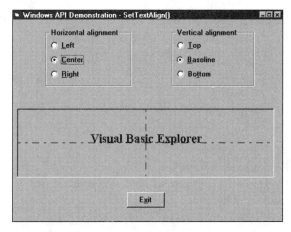

Figure 27.1 *Using a Windows API procedure to align text.*

The object properties are shown in Listing 27.1; the form's code is shown in Listing 27.2.

Listing 27.1   Objects and properties in ALIGNTXT.FRM.

```
Begin VB.Form frmTxtAlign
   BorderStyle   =   1  'Fixed Single
   Caption       =   "Windows API Demonstration - SetTextAlign()"
   Begin VB.CommandButton cmdExit
      Caption      =   "E&xit"
   End
   Begin VB.PictureBox Picture1
      DrawStyle    =   3  'Dash-Dot
      BeginProperty Font
         name      =   "Times New Roman"
         size      =   15.75
      EndProperty
   End
   Begin VB.Frame Frame2
      Caption      =   "Horizontal alignment"
      Begin VB.OptionButton HorizAlign
         Caption   =   "&Left"
         Index     =   0
      End
      Begin VB.OptionButton HorizAlign
         Caption   =   "&Center"
         Index     =   1
      End
      Begin VB.OptionButton HorizAlign
         Caption   =   "&Right"
         Index     =   2
      End
   End
   Begin VB.Frame Frame1
      Caption      =   "Vertical alignment"
      Begin VB.OptionButton VertAlign
         Caption   =   "&Top"
         Index     =   0
      End
      Begin VB.OptionButton VertAlign
         Caption   =   "&Baseline"
         Index     =   1
      End
      Begin VB.OptionButton VertAlign
         Caption   =   "Bo&ttom"
         Index     =   2
      End
   End
End
```

Listing 27.2   Code in ALIGNTXT.FRM.

```
Option Explicit

Const TA_LEFT = 0
Const TA_RIGHT = 2
Const TA_CENTER = 6
Const TA_TOP = 0
Const TA_BOTTOM = 8
Const TA_BASELINE = 24

Const MESSAGE = "Visual Basic Blue Book"

Private Declare Sub SetTextAlign Lib "gdi32" (ByVal hDC As Long, _
    ByVal wFlags As Long)


Private Sub cmdExit_Click()

End

End Sub


Private Sub Form_Load()

+' Set default option button.

HorizAlign(0).VALUE = True
VertAlign(0).VALUE = True

End Sub


Private Sub HorizAlign_Click(Index As Integer)

' If the alignment option has been changed,
' repaint the Picture Box.

Picture1_Paint

End Sub


Private Sub Picture1_Paint()

Dim wFlags As Long

' Clear the picture box.
Picture1.Cls
```

```
' Draw centered vertical and horizontal lines.
Picture1.Line (0, Picture1.ScaleHeight / 2)-Step(Picture1.ScaleWidth, 0)
Picture1.Line (Picture1.ScaleWidth / 2, 0)-Step(0, Picture1.ScaleHeight)

' Place the current position at the intersection of the lines.
Picture1.CurrentY = Picture1.ScaleHeight / 2
Picture1.CurrentX = Picture1.ScaleWidth / 2

' Set wFlags to reflect the alignment options selected.
If HorizAlign(0).VALUE Then wFlags = TA_LEFT
If HorizAlign(1).VALUE Then wFlags = TA_CENTER
If HorizAlign(2).VALUE Then wFlags = TA_RIGHT

If VertAlign(0).VALUE Then wFlags = wFlags Or TA_TOP
If VertAlign(1).VALUE Then wFlags = wFlags Or TA_BASELINE
If VertAlign(2).VALUE Then wFlags = wFlags Or TA_BOTTOM

' Set the new alignment.
Call SetTextAlign(Picture1.hDC, wFlags)

' Display the text.
Picture1.Print MESSAGE

End Sub

Private Sub VertAlign_Click(Index As Integer)

' If the alignment option has been changed,
' repaint the picture box.

Picture1_Paint

End Sub
```

Note how we draw the lines in the box. First, the Picture Box's **DrawStyle** property is set to 3-Dash-Dot, giving us lines with a dot-dash pattern. Then, in code, we use the **Line** method to draw the lines, obtaining the needed coordinates from the control's **ScaleHeight** and **ScaleWidth** properties:

```
Picture1.Line (0, Picture1.ScaleHeight / 2)-Step(Picture1.ScaleWidth, 0)
Picture1.Line (Picture1.ScaleWidth / 2, 0)-Step(0, Picture1.ScaleHeight)
```

When you use this method to set text alignment, be aware that the alignment you set with **SetTextAlign** is guaranteed to be in effect for only a single **Print** method. Suppose, for example, you change text alignment and then execute these statements:

```
PictureBox.Print "text1"
PictureBox.Print "text2"
```

The specified alignment may not be used for the second message. You must call **SetTextAlign** before each and every **Print** method. Because Visual Basic treats multiple arguments to a **Print** method as two distinct **Print** methods, the following still may not work:

```
PictureBox.Print "text1";"text2"
```

Avoid the potential problem by concatenating the strings before executing **Print**:

```
PictureBox.Print "text1" & "text2"
```

Using Callbacks

A few of the Windows API functions use *callbacks*. A callback is used when the API function requires some assistance from your program. You write a function in your Visual Basic program, called, appropriately enough, a *callback function*, that performs the actions required by the API function. Your program calls the API function, which, in turn, calls the callback function as needed. These are the four steps for using a callback:

1. The program calls the API function.

2. The API function performs some processing and then calls the callback function.

3. The callback function performs its task and returns execution to the API function.

4. The API function returns execution to your Visual Basic program. In some cases, execution passes back and forth multiple times between the API function and the callback function before the API function terminates. The process is outlined in Figure 27.2.

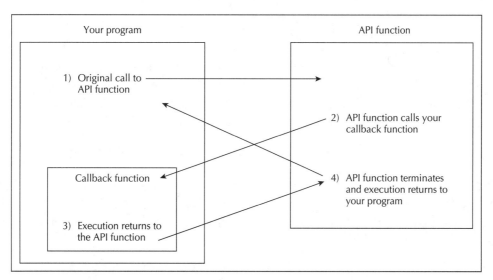

Figure 27.2   *Operation of an API function that uses a callback.*

How does the API function know about the callback function? You tell it, that's how. One of the arguments that your program must pass to the API function is the address of the callback function. This is sometimes called a *function pointer*, as you will know if you've worked with C or C++. The API function uses this address to call the callback function when it needs to. You use the **AddressOf** operator to provide the address of a function defined in your Visual Basic program.

For example, **EnumWindows** is one of the API functions that requires a callback. Its purpose is to loop through all of the top-level windows on the screen, permitting you to obtain information about, or perform some action with, some or all of the windows. Its prototype in a Visual Basic program is:

```
Declare Function EnumWindows lib "user32" _
    (ByVal lpEnumFunc as Long, _
     ByVal lParam as Long ) As Long
```

In this declaration, **lpEnumFunc** is the address of your program's callback function (which I'll explain soon), and **lParam** is a parameter that the API function passes to the callback function when it is called. Note that this is a common feature of API functions that use callbacks—you can pass a parameter to the API function to be passed to the callback function. How this parameter is used (if at all) depends on the needs of the API function and how you write the callback function.

The return value of **EnumWindows** is True if the function was successful, and False otherwise. If the callback procedure in your Visual Basic program was named **EnumWinCallBack**, you would call the API function as follows:

```
retval = EnumWindows(AddressOf EnumWinCallBack, 0)
```

The callback function must have the proper signature—that is, its parameters and return value must meet the specifications of the API function it is used with. If you think about it for a moment, this makes perfect sense. The callback procedure is going to be called by the API procedure, which is going to pass certain arguments and expect a certain return value. For **EnumWindows**, the callback procedure header is:

```
Function ProcName(hWnd as Long, lParam As Long) As Long
```

You can see that when the API procedure **EnumWindows** calls the callback procedure, it will pass two type **Long** parameters and expect a type **Long** return value. If the signature of the callback procedure does not exactly match what the API procedure expects, you can find yourself in big trouble.

Here's a brief review of how callbacks work (I know I am repeating some information, but it is important for you to grasp this concept):

1. Your Visual Basic program calls the API procedure.

2. The API procedure performs some processing, then calls the callback procedure in your Visual Basic program.

3. The callback procedure performs the required tasks, then terminates. Execution returns to the API procedure.

4. The API procedure performs additional processing, if required, which may include additional calls to the callback procedure. Note that execution always passes from the callback procedure to the API procedure; execution never passes from the callback procedure directly back to the Visual Basic program.

5. The API procedure terminates, and execution returns to your Visual Basic program.

You must observe several rules and cautions when using callbacks. First of all, both the callback procedure and the call to the API procedure must be placed in a Basic module. They cannot be part of a form or class module. The Basic module must be part of the same project, as well. Also, you can use **AddressOf** only with user-defined functions—not with external functions declared with the **Declare** statement or with functions referenced from type libraries.

There are also some caveats regarding errors. Because the caller of a callback is not within your program, you must be sure that an error in the callback procedure is not propagated back to the caller. You can accomplish this by placing the **On Error Resume Next** statement at the beginning of the callback procedure.

Working with callback functions can be tricky, because you lose the stability of the Visual Basic development environment any time you call a DLL. When working with callbacks, you will find that it is especially easy to cause the application to crash, so save frequently and keep backups. Areas that require special attention when working with callbacks include the following:

- *Your application can fire a callback function while in break mode.* The code will be executed, but any breaks or steps will be ignored. You cannot do a reset in break mode when a callback function is on the stack.

- *The callback function may be treated by Windows as relocatable code.* If you delete a callback function while in break mode, Windows may loose track of its location in memory. This is particularly likely if you delete a callback function in break mode and then retype it. The bottom line? Don't delete callback functions in break mode.

- *Pay strict attention to the callback function's signature.* If you pass a callback function that takes a different number of arguments than the caller expects, your application may fail.

- *You can use **AddressOf** only to pass a function pointer to a DLL procedure, and not from one part of a Visual Basic program to another.*

A Callback Demonstration

One of the important uses for callbacks is for API functions that provide certain kinds of system information. Often, you cannot know the amount of information ahead of time.

A good example is windows. As I mentioned earlier, the API procedure **EnumWindows** provides information on the top-level screen windows. Because you cannot know ahead of time how many windows there are, dealing with the information can be difficult. Instead, the API function uses a callback and works by iterating through all the windows. For each window, **EnumWindows** calls the callback function, passing information about the single window that was just processed. Code in the callback function does whatever is necessary with the information, displaying it in a List Box, for example. The process repeats until all the windows have been processed. On each iteration, **EnumWindows** calls your callback function and passes it the handle (hWnd) of an active top-level window. It loops through all of the active windows, calling the callback for each one, and returns to the calling Visual Basic program once it has processed all of the windows. This iterative process is illustrated in Figure 27.3.

Your program can do a lot with this information, but I'll keep it simple for the demonstration. Given an hWnd, you can use the API functions **GetWindowsText** and **GetClassName** to retrieve the window's title-bar text and the name of its underlying class. A third func-

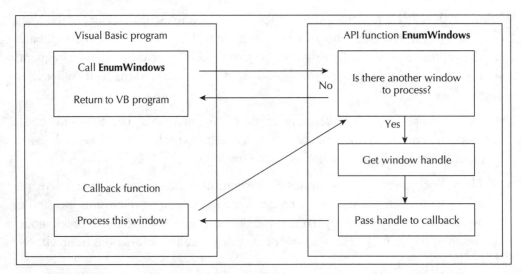

Figure 27.3   *How **EnumWindows** uses a callback to provide information about all windows.*

tion, **GetWindowTextLength**, retrieves the length of the text in the window's title bar and permits us to skip over windows with no titles, where the text length is zero.

To create the demonstration program, place a List Box control on a form. Assign the name frmCallback to the form and the name lstWindows to the List Box. Place the following single line of code in the form's **Load** event procedure:

```
Call GetWindows
```

Next, use the Add Module command on the Project menu to add a Basic module to the project. Add the code in Listing 27.3 to the module. When you run the program, the List Box is filled with the titles and class names of all current top-level windows (those that have some title text, that is).

One fine point bears mentioning. Notice how the strings **buf1** and **buf2** are loaded with spaces before being passed to the API functions **GetWindowsText** and **GetClassName**. To be honest, I'm not sure why this is, but I am sure that without this step—if you declare the string, but don't initialize it—the API call will crash.

Listing 27.3   Code in ENUM_WIN.BAS.

```
Option Explicit

Declare Function GetWindowTextLength Lib _
    "user32" Alias "GetWindowTextLengthA" _
    (ByVal hWnd As Long) As Long

Declare Function GetWindowText Lib _
    "user32" Alias "GetWindowTextA" _
    (ByVal hWnd As Long, ByVal lpString As _
    String, ByVal cch As Long) As Long

Declare Function GetClassName Lib _
    "user32" Alias "GetClassNameA" _
    (ByVal hWnd As Long, ByVal lpClassName _
    As String, ByVal nMaxCount As Long) As Long

Declare Function EnumWindows Lib "user32" _
    (ByVal lpEnumFunc As Long, ByVal lParam As Long) _
    As Long

Function EnumWinCB(ByVal hWnda As Long, _
    lParam As Long) As Long

Dim buf1 As String, buf2 As String, buf3 As String
Dim length As Long
```

```
On Error Resume Next

' Pad the strings with spaces.
buf1 = Space(255)
buf2 = Space(255)

' Get the length of the window text.
length = GetWindowTextLength(hWnda)

' Retrieve information about this window only if
' the text is not empty.
If length > 0 Then
    ' Get the window's title.
    GetWindowText hWnda, buf1, 254
    ' Get the associated class name.
    GetClassName hWnda, buf2, 254
    ' Concatenate the information.
    buf3 = Left$(buf1, length) & ": " & buf2
    ' Stuff it in the list box.
    frmCallback.lstWindows.AddItem buf3
End If

' Return True so EnumWindows() will continue.
EnumWinCB = 1

End Function

Public Sub GetWindows()

Dim retval As Long

retval = EnumWindows(AddressOf EnumWinCB, 0)

If Not retval Then
    MsgBox ("Error enumerating windows.")
    End
End If

End Sub
```

Index

Symbols

& (ampersand)
  access key specifier, 53
  long type declaration character, 67
  string concatenation operator, 81
* (asterisk)
  multiplication operator, 59, 80
  wildcard character, 370
@ (at sign)
  currency type declaration character, 67
\ (backslash)
  integer division, 80
^ (caret)
  exponentiation operator, 80
, (comma)
  field delimiter, 351
  location of **Print #** statement, 353–355
" (double quotation mark)
  field delimiter, 351
E+ characters, format specifier, 111
= (equal sign)
  assignment operator, 58
  "equal to" comparison operator, 83
! (exclamation point)
  single type declaration character, 67

> "greater than" comparison operator, 83
>= "greater than or equal to" comparison
  operator, 83
< "less than" comparison operator, 83
<= "less than or equal to" comparison operator, 83
- (minus sign)
  subtraction operator, 80
<> "not equal to" comparison operator, 83
% (percent sign)
  integer type declaration character, 67
+ (plus sign)
  addition operator, 80
  string concatenation operator, Basic, 81
(pound sign)
  double type declaration character, 67
  format specifier, 111
? (question mark)
  wildcard character, 370
; (semicolon)
  location of **Print #** statement, 353–355
  Print method modifier, 335
/ (slash)
  division operator, 80
_ (space+underscore)
  line continuation character, 85
0 (zero character)
  format specifier, 111

A

F

P

Q

R

X

What's On The CD-ROM

The companion CD-ROM for *Visual Basic 6 Programming Blue Book* contains source code for the book's projects—including GRAPEVINE, the main database project—as well as shareware, freeware, and demo programs to help you master Visual Basic 6 for your Windows and Internet programming needs:

- *CoffeeCup HTML Editor++ 98*—A Hypertext Markup Language editor with 10 built-in Java scripts and more than 100 animated GIFs (unlimited shareware version).

- *CoffeeCup ImageMapper++*—A fully functional image mapper (unlimited shareware version).

- *Site Sweeper*—Provides an automatic, comprehensive analysis of your Web site, from broken links and incorrect image references to complete information about all the files on your site (trial version).

- *QuickSite*—QuickSite wizards walk you through Web site creation and management tasks to help you produce a well-organized site (trial version).

- *SQL Station*—SQL Station Coder, a component of SQL Station, is a development environment for database server-side objects and code, such as stored procedures, triggers, functions, tables and indexes (trial version).

- *Setup Factory*—A visual install builder.

- *AutoPlay Menu Studio*—A development tool for creating AutoPlay menus.

- *VBAdvantage*—A powerful Visual Basic development utility that enhances the VB design time environment.

- *Olectra Resizer*—A design-time ActiveX control for Visual Basic that adds intelligent resizing and layout management to forms without any programming.

- *Q-Diagnostic*—Allows you to monitor and analyze your database (trial edition).

See the readme file for, descriptions, copyrights, installation instructions, limitations, and other important information.

Requirements:

- Minimum of a 486 or equivalent processor
- 16MB of RAM is suggested
- Windows 95, 98, or NT
- Visual Basic 6